Revenue Statistics

1965-2014

SPECIAL FEATURE: THE IMPACT OF THE MOVE TO THE 2008 SYSTEM OF NATIONAL ACCOUNTS (SNA) ON THE MEASUREMENT OF TAX TO GROSS DOMESTIC PRODUCT (GDP) RATIOS

Statistiques des recettes publiques

1965-2014

ÉTUDE SPÉCIALE : EFFETS DE L'ADOPTION DU SYSTÈME DES COMPTES NATIONAUX (SCN) DE 2008 SUR LE CALCUL DES RATIOS RECETTES FISCALES-PRODUIT INTÉRIEUR BRUT (PIB)

OECD

BETTER POLICIES FOR BETTER LIVES

This work is published on the responsibility of the Secretary-General of the OECD. The opinions expressed and arguments employed herein do not necessarily reflect the official views of the Organisation or of the governments of its member countries.

Cet ouvrage est publié sous la responsabilité du Secrétaire général de l'OCDE. Les opinions et les interprétations exprimées ne reflètent pas nécessairement les vues de l'OCDE ou des gouvernements de ses pays membres.

This document and any map included herein are without prejudice to the status of or sovereignty over any territory, to the delimitation of international frontiers and boundaries and to the name of any territory, city or area.

Ce document et toute carte qu'il peut comprendre ne préjugent en rien du statut de tout territoire, de la souveraineté s'exerçant sur ce dernier, du tracé des frontières et limites internationales, et du nom de tout territoire, ville ou région.

Please cite this publication as:
OECD (2015), *Revenue Statistics 2015*, OECD Publishing.
http://dx.doi.org/10.1787/10.1787/

Merci de citer cet ouvrage comme suit :
OCDE (2015), *Statistiques des recettes publiques 2015*, Éditions OCDE.
http://dx.doi.org/10.1787/10.1787/

ISBN 978-92-64-24518-9 (print/*imprimé*)
ISBN 978-92-64-24519-8 (PDF)

Annual/*Annuel* : Revenue Statistics/Statistiques des recettes publiques
ISSN 1560-3660 (print/*imprimé*)
ISSN 1996-3726 (online/*en ligne*)

The statistical data for Israel are supplied by and under the responsibility of the relevant Israeli authorities. The use of such data by the OECD is without prejudice to the status of the Golan Heights, East Jerusalem and Israeli settlements in the West Bank under the terms of international law.

Les données statistiques concernant Israël sont fournies par et sous la responsabilité des autorités israéliennes compétentes. L'utilisation de ces données par l'OCDE est sans préjudice du statut des hauteurs du Golan, de Jérusalem-Est et des colonies de peuplement israéliennes en Cisjordanie aux termes du droit international.

Corrigenda to OECD publications may be found on line at: *www.oecd.org/publishing/corrigenda*.
Les corrigenda des publications de l'OCDE sont disponibles sur : *www.oecd.org/editions/corrigenda*.

Foreword

This annual publication provides information on tax levels and tax structures in OECD countries. It was prepared under the auspices of the Working Party on Tax Policy Analysis and Tax Statistics of the Committee on Fiscal Affairs and is published under the responsibility of the Secretary-General of the OECD.

Avant-propos

Cette publication annuelle fournit des informations sur les niveaux d'imposition et la structure de la fiscalité dans les pays de l'OCDE. Elle a été préparée sous les auspices du Groupe de travail sur l'analyse des politiques et des statistiques fiscales du Comité des affaires fiscales; elle est publiée sous la responsabilité du Secrétaire général de l'OCDE.

Table of contents

Table des matières

List of tables/Liste des tableaux

Part I/Partie I

Tax revenue trends, 1965-2014/Tendances des recettes fiscales, 1965-2014

Part II/Partie II

Tax levels and tax structures, 1965-2014/Niveaux et structures des impôts, 1965-2014

Part III/Partie III

Country tables, 1965-2013/Tableaux par pays, 1965-2013

Part IV/Partie IV

Tax revenues by sub-sectors of general government
Recettes fiscales par sous-secteur d'administration

List of charts/Liste des graphiques

Part I/Partie I

Tax revenue trends, 1965-2014/Tendances des recettes fiscales, 1965-2014

Part II/Partie II

Tax levels and tax structures, 1965-2013/Niveaux et structures des impôts, 1965-2013

Part IV/Partie IV

Tax revenues by subsectors of general government, 2013
Recettes fiscales par sous-secteurs d'administration, 2013

Executive summary

The tax burden continued to rise in OECD countries in 2014, increasing by 0.2 percentage points to an average of 34.4% of gross domestic product (GDP). This increase continues the recent upward trend as the OECD average tax burden has increased in every year since 2009 when the ratio was 32.7%. The 2014 figure is the highest ever recorded OECD average tax to GDP ratio since the OECD began measuring the tax burden in 1965. The tax burden is measured by taking the total tax revenues received as a percentage of GDP.

The increase in tax ratios between 2009 and 2014 is due to a combination of factors. The largest contributors have been increases in revenue from taxes on consumption and taxes on personal incomes and profits, which combine to account for around two thirds of the increase. Revenues from social security contributions and property taxes account for the majority of the remainder. Discretionary tax changes have played an important role, as many countries have either raised tax rates and/or broadened tax bases. In addition, personal income tax systems tend to be progressive. As incomes grow, taxpayers pay a higher percentage of their incomes in tax. This in turn means that governments collect higher revenues as a proportion of GDP in periods of income growth.

The term "taxes" in this publication refers to compulsory, unrequited payments to general government. Taxes are "unrequited" in the sense that the benefits provided by governments to taxpayers are not normally allocated in proportion to their payments, as outlined in the Interpretative Guide to the Revenue Statistics in Annex A of this report. The OECD methodology classifies a tax according to its base: income, profits and capital gains; payroll; property; goods and services; and other taxes. Compulsory social security contributions paid to general government are also treated as taxes, and are classified under a separate heading. Detailed information on the tax concept, the classification of taxes and the accrual basis of reporting is set out in the Interpretative Guide.

The report also analyses the share of tax revenue attributed to the various levels of government; federal or central; state (regional); local and social security funds. This year's edition also includes a special chapter on the impact of the move to the 2008 System of National Accounts (SNA) on the measurement of tax to GDP ratios.

Key findings

Tax burdens continued to rise in 2014

- The average tax burden in OECD countries increased by 0.2 percentage points to 34.4% in 2014. This followed a rise of 1.5 percentage points between 2009 and 2013, reversing the decline from 34.1% to 32.7% between 2007 and 2009. The 2014 figure is the highest ever recorded OECD average tax to GDP ratio since the OECD began measuring the tax burden in 1965.
- The ratio of tax revenues to GDP rose in 16 of the 30 OECD countries for which 2014 data are available compared with 2013, and fell in 14. Between 2009 and 2014, there were increases for 22 of these countries, a decline in seven, with one unchanged.
- About 80% of the increase in revenue between 2013 and 2014 is the result of rising revenues from a combination of consumption taxes and taxes on personal income and profits. This combination also accounts for two thirds of the rise in revenues between 2009 and 2014.
- The largest tax ratio increases between 2013 and 2014 were in Denmark (3.3 percentage points) and Iceland (2.8 percentage points). Other countries with substantial rises were Greece (1.5 percentage points), Estonia (1.1 percentage points) and New Zealand (1.0 percentage point).
- The largest falls were in Norway (1.4 percentage points) and Czech Republic (0.8 percentage points). Luxembourg and Turkey showed falls of 0.6 percentage points.
- Underlying the OECD average, individual countries show widely differing trends. For example, Spain recorded a fall of 3.3 percentage points between 2007 and 2014, while Greece recorded an increase of 4.7 percentage points.
- Historically, tax-to-GDP ratios increased through the 1990s, to a peak OECD average of 34.2% in 2000. They fell back slightly between 2001 and 2004, but then rose again between 2005 and 2007 to an average of 34.1% before falling back sharply during the crisis.
- Denmark has the highest tax-to-GDP ratio among OECD countries (50.9% in 2014), followed by France (45.2%) and Belgium (44.7%).
- Mexico (19.5% in 2014) and Chile (19.8%) have the lowest tax-to-GDP ratios among OECD countries. They are followed by Korea, which has the third lowest ratio among OECD countries at 24.6%, and the United States at 26.0%.
- Compared with 2007 (pre-recession) tax to GDP ratios, the ratio in 2014 was still down by 3 percentage points or more in three countries – Israel, Norway and Spain. The biggest fall has been in Spain - from 36.5% in 2007 to 33.2% of GDP in 2014 (3.3 percentage points).
- The tax burden in Greece increased from 31.2% to 35.9% between 2007 and 2014. Two other countries; Denmark and Turkey showed increases of more than 4 percentage points over the same period.
- Data for 2013, the latest year for which a breakdown of revenues by category of tax is available for all OECD countries, show that revenues from personal and corporate income taxes are now recovering following the sharp falls of 2008 and 2009. However, the share of these taxes in total revenues remains at 33.7%, somewhat below their 36.0% share in 2007. On the other hand, the share of social security contributions has increased by 1.6 percentage points to an average of 26.1% of total revenue.
- In 2013, an average of 24% of revenues is attributed to sub-central levels of government in Federal countries in the OECD - about two thirds of this is attributed to State and one third to local governments. The same applies to Spain that is classified as a regional country in the publication. In the 25 unitary countries about 12% of revenues are attributed to local governments.

Résumé

En 2014, la pression fiscale dans les pays de l'OCDE a continué d'augmenter de 0.2 points de pourcentage pour atteindre 34.4 % du produit intérieur brut (PIB) en moyenne. Cette augmentation est dans la continuité de l'évolution de la pression fiscale dans la moyenne des pays de l'OCDE qui augmente tous les ans depuis 2009 où le ratio était de 32.7 %. Le chiffre de 2014 est le plus élevé obtenu depuis que l'OCDE a commencé à mesurer la pression fiscale en 1965. La pression fiscale correspond au montant total des recettes fiscales recouvrées, exprimé en pourcentage du PIB.

La progression de la charge fiscale entre 2009 et 2014 s'explique par plusieurs facteurs. Deux tiers de cette progression viennent de l'augmentation des recettes de l'impôt sur la consommation et de l'impôt sur le revenu et les bénéfices. Les recettes des cotisations de sécurité sociale et des impôts sur le patrimoine sont majoritairement à l'origine du reste de l'évolution des ratios d'imposition. Les modifications discrétionnaires de la fiscalité ont joué un rôle important, de nombreux pays ayant relevé les taux et/ou élargi les bases d'imposition. De plus, l'imposition des revenus des personnes physiques tend à être progressive. Quand les salaires augmentent, les contribuables versent en impôts une part plus importante de leurs revenus. Ceci implique qu'en période de croissance des revenus, les gouvernements collectent une part plus élevée des recettes publiques en proportion du PIB.

Le terme « impôt » se réfère aux versements obligatoires sans contrepartie aux administrations publiques. Dans le Guide d'interprétation des statistiques des recettes publiques figurant à l'annexe A de cette publication, les impôts sont « sans contrepartie » car les prestations fournies par les administrations aux contribuables ne sont pas normalement proportionnelles à leurs paiements. Dans la classification de l'OCDE, les impôts sont ventilés en fonction de l'assiette : revenu, bénéfices et gains en capital; salaires; patrimoine; biens et services et autres impôts. Les cotisations obligatoires de sécurité sociale versées aux administrations publiques sont aussi traitées comme des impôts et classées dans une rubrique spécifique. Des informations plus détaillées sur la notion d'impôt, la classification des impôts et l'enregistrement sur la base des droits constatés figurent dans le Guide d'interprétation.

Ce rapport propose également une analyse de la part des recettes fiscales allouée aux différents niveaux d'administration : État fédéral ou administration centrale, administration d'un État fédéré (ou d'une région), administrations locales et caisses de sécurité sociale.

Cette édition contient aussi un chapitre spécial concernant les effets de l'adoption du Système des Comptes Nationaux (SCN) de 2008 sur le calcul des ratios recettes fiscales-produit intérieur brut.

Principales conclusions

La pression fiscale a continué d'augmenter en 2014

- En 2014, la pression fiscale moyenne dans les pays de l'OCDE a augmenté de 0.2 points de pourcentage pour atteindre 34.4 %. Ceci fait suite à une hausse de 1.5 points de pourcentage entre 2009 et 2013 renversant la baisse de 34.1 % à 32.7 % entre 2007 et 2009. Le chiffre de 2014 est le plus élevé depuis que l'OCDE a commencé à mesurer la pression fiscale en 1965.
- Dans 16 pays des 30 pays de l'OCDE pour lesquels on dispose de données concernant 2014, on constate une hausse des recettes fiscales rapportées au PIB par rapport à 2013 et une évolution inverse dans 14 pays. Entre 2009 et 2014, il y a eu une augmentation des ratios pour 22 pays, une diminution des ratios pour sept pays et un ratio inchangé dans un pays.
- Environ 80 % de l'augmentation des recettes entre 2013 et 2014 résulte des recettes tirées des impôts sur la consommation et de l'impôt sur le revenu et les bénéfices. Ces deux composantes représentent également deux tiers de l'augmentation entre 2009 et 2014.
- Les hausses les plus fortes de la pression fiscale entre 2013 et 2014 ont eu lieu au Danemark (3.3 points de pourcentage) et en Islande (2.8 points). La charge fiscale est aussi plus importante en Grèce (1.5 points), en Estonie (1.1 point) et en Nouvelle-Zélande (1.0 point).
- Les baisses les plus marquées sont en Norvège (1.4 points de pourcentage) et en République tchèque (0.8 points). Le Luxembourg et la Turquie ont eu une baisse de 0.6 points.
- Les pays intégrés dans la moyenne OCDE se caractérisent par des tendances très différentes. Par exemple, l'Espagne a eu une baisse de 3.3 points de pourcentage entre 2007 et 2014 alors que la Grèce a eu une augmentation de 4.7 points de pourcentage.
- Les rapports impôt/PIB ont progressé pendant les années 90, jusqu'à culminer à 34.2 % (moyenne de l'OCDE) en 2000. Un léger repli a eu lieu entre 2001 et 2004, suivi d'un rebond entre 2005 et 2007 (34.1 % en moyenne), précédant une forte baisse pendant la crise.
- De tous les pays de l'OCDE, le Danemark est celui qui affiche le rapport impôt/PIB le plus élevé (50.9 % en 2014), suivi de la France (45.2 %) et de la Belgique (44.7 %).
- Le Mexique (19.5 % en 2014) et le Chili (19.8 %) sont en revanche les pays de l'OCDE enregistrant les rapports impôt/PIB les plus bas, suivis de la Corée, arrivant en troisième position, avec un taux de 24.6 %, et des États-Unis, affichant un chiffre de 26.0 %.
- Les chiffres de 2014 sont encore inférieurs de plus de 3 points de pourcentage à ceux de 2007 (avant la récession) dans trois pays : l'Espagne, Israël et la Norvège. En Espagne, le ratio est passé de 36.5 % en 2007 à 33.2 % en 2014 (3.3 points de pourcentage).
- Entre 2007 et 2014, la pression fiscale en Grèce a été portée de 31.2 % à 35.9 %. Le Danemark et la Turquie ont vu la charge fiscale croître de plus de 4 points de pourcentage.
- Les données de 2013, dernière année pour laquelle on dispose d'une ventilation des recettes par catégorie d'impôt pour tous les pays de l'OCDE, montrent que les recettes des impôts sur les revenus et sur les bénéfices se redressent après avoir fortement baissé en 2008 et 2009. La part de ces impôts dans le total des recettes (33.7 %) demeure légèrement inférieure à ce qu'elle était en 2007 (36.0 %). La part des cotisations de sécurité sociale s'est accrue d'1.6 point de pourcentage pour atteindre en moyenne 26.1 % des recettes totales.
- En 2013, dans les pays fédéraux de l'OCDE, 24 % des recettes sont attribuées aux niveaux infranationaux d'administration, dont deux tiers reviennent aux administrations d'un état et un tiers aux administrations locales. Ceci s'applique également à l'Espagne qui est définie comme un pays régional dans cette publication. Dans les 25 pays unitaires, environ 12 % des recettes sont attribuées aux administrations locales.

Introduction

The purpose of this annual publication is to provide internationally comparative data on tax levels and tax structures in member countries of the OECD. The taxes imposed in each country are presented in a standardised framework based upon the OECD classification of taxes and its Interpretative guide as contained in Annex A to this Report.

Starting in 2004, the data for recent years in this publication are mainly reported on an accrual basis, rather than the cash basis that has been used in previous editions. The reasons for this change were discussed in Special Feature S.2 of the 2003 edition. Details of the practical implementation of this change were given in Special Feature S.1 of the 2004 edition.

The criteria followed for the grouping of taxes are not affected by this change to accrual reporting and are primarily the basis on which a tax is charged and secondly whether households or other entities pay the tax. Borderline classification cases, where definitional issues and other difficulties arise, are noted in the Interpretative guide. Footnotes which accompany the country tables in Part III record where countries deviate from the guidelines.

The data for the Report has, for the most part, been provided by Delegates to Working Party No. 2 on Tax Policy Analysis and Tax Statistics of the Committee on Fiscal Affairs. The OECD acknowledges the co-operation of the International Monetary Fund, whose classification of tax revenues – although in a number of respects less detailed – is in many respects similar to that of the OECD.[1] The most important of the other classifications currently in use is the System of National Accounts (henceforth referred to as SNA) and the European System of Integrated Economic Accounts of EU member states (henceforth referred to as ESA), which is primarily an elaboration of SNA, though differing from it in certain respects. Subject to a few exceptions, SNA/ESA figures can be reconciled with the figures in the present Report, since SNA criteria and definitions have been adopted unless the contrary is specifically indicated.

The material is organised in four parts. Part I summarises tax trends of the past 50 years focusing in turn on tax levels (section I.A), tax structures (section I.B) and taxes by level of government (section I.C). Section I.D discusses the impact of GDP revisions. This year's issue also carries a special feature on "The impact of the move to the 2008 system of national accounts (SNA) on the measurement of tax to gross domestic product (GDP) ratios". Part II contains a set of comparative statistical tables for years 1965-2013 (section II.A) and a series of comparative graphs which show the differences between countries as regards tax levels and tax structures (section II.B). Estimates of 2014 tax revenues are presented in section II.C for all countries for which such data are available. Part III provides statistical tables with a detailed breakdown of tax revenues by country for years between 1965 and 2013 (section III.A).[2] A second series of tables shows how countries finance their social benefits (section III.B), followed by a series of tables detailing taxes and social security contributions paid by general government (section III.C). Part IV attributes tax revenues to general government by the following sub-sectors: central, state; local and social security funds.

Notes

1. See IMF, *Government Finance Statistics Manual 2014* (Washington, DC, International Monetary Fund, 2014).
2. Because of space limitations data are shown for selected years between 1965 and 2013. Data for years not shown are available online.

Introduction

Le but de cette publication annuelle est de présenter des données permettant d'effectuer des comparaisons internationales sur les niveaux d'imposition et la structure de la fiscalité dans les différents pays membres de l'OCDE. Les impôts perçus dans chaque pays sont présentés sous une forme normalisée selon le modèle de classification des impôts de l'OCDE et son guide d'interprétation qui figure à l'Annexe A de ce rapport.

À partir de l'année 2004, les données de cette publication concernant les années récentes sont surtout enregistrées sur la base des droits constatés et non plus sur la base des décaissements qui était utilisée pour les éditions précédentes. Les motifs de ce changement ont été examinés dans l'Étude spéciale S.2 de l'édition de 2003. On trouvera des précisions sur l'application pratique de ce changement dans l'Étude spéciale S.1 de l'édition 2004.

Les critères retenus pour la classification des impôts ne sont pas affectés par cette adoption de l'enregistrement sur la base des droits constatés et sont constitués essentiellement par l'assiette de l'impôt et en second lieu par la question de savoir si les ménages ou autres entités paient l'impôt. Les cas particuliers de la classification, dans lesquels des questions de définition ainsi que d'autres problèmes se posent, sont mentionnés dans le Guide d'interprétation. Les notes de bas de page qui accompagnent les tableaux par pays de la Partie III enregistrent les cas dans lesquels les pays s'écartent des principes directeurs.

Les données utilisées ont été fournies pour la plupart par les Délégués du Groupe de travail n°2 du Comité des affaires fiscales sur l'analyse des politiques et les statistiques fiscales. L'OCDE remercie de sa coopération le Fonds monétaire international dont la classification des recettes publiques – bien qu'elle soit, à certains égards, moins détaillée – est à bien des égards semblable à celle de l'OCDE[1]. Parmi les autres classifications actuellement utilisées, les plus importantes sont le Système de comptabilité nationale (appelé ci-après SCN) et le Système européen de comptes économiques intégrés des États membres de l'Union européenne (appelé ci-après SEC) qui constitue essentiellement un approfondissement du SCN bien qu'il en diffère à certains égards. Sous réserve de quelques exceptions mineures, les chiffres du SCN ou du SEC peuvent être rattachés directement à ceux de la présente étude car les critères et définitions du SCN ont été adoptées sauf mention contraire expresse.

Cette publication comprend quatre parties. La Partie I indique succinctement l'évolution de la fiscalité au cours des 50 dernières années en mettant l'accent successivement sur les niveaux d'imposition (section I.A), sur les structures fiscales (section I.B) et sur la répartition des impôts par niveau d'administration (section I.C). La section 1.D discute l'impact de la révision des données du PIB. La publication de cette année comporte également une étude spéciale sur le « Effets de l'adoption du système des comptes nationaux (SCN) de 2008 sur le calcul des ratios recettes fiscales-produit intérieur brut (PIB) ». La Partie II contient une série de tableaux statistiques comparatifs pour les années 1965-2013 (section II.A) et une série de graphiques comparatifs qui indiquent les différences entre les pays quant au niveau d'imposition et aux structures fiscales (section II.B). Des estimations des recettes fiscales pour 2014 sont présentées à la section II.C pour tous les pays dans lesquels de telles données sont disponibles. La troisième partie contient des tableaux statistiques comportant une ventilation détaillée des recettes fiscales par pays pour les années comprises entre 1965 et 2013 (section III.A)[2] et elle indique en outre comment les pays financent leurs régimes de prestations sociales (section III.B) ainsi que les cotisations sociales versées par les administrations (section III.C). La Partie IV ventile les recettes publiques entre les sous-secteurs ci-après : administration fédérale ou centrale, administration des États, administrations locales et de sécurité sociale.

Notes

1. Voir, FMI, *Government Finance Statistics Manual* 2014 (Washington, DC, Fonds Monétaire International 2014).
2. En raison du manque de place, les données indiquées concernent une sélection d'années entre 1965 et 2013. Les données portant sur les autres années sont disponibles en ligne.

PART I

Tax revenue trends, 1965-2014

PARTIE I

Tendances des recettes fiscales, 1965-2014

Revenue Statistics 1965-2014
Statistiques des recettes publiques 1965-2014

PART I

Tax revenue trends, 1965-2014

Introduction

This annual Report presents detailed internationally comparable data on tax revenues of OECD countries for all levels of government. The latest edition provides outturn (i.e. final) data on tax revenues in 1965-2014. In addition, provisional estimates of tax revenues in 2014 are included for almost all OECD countries.

In this Report, taxes are defined as compulsory, unrequited payments to general government. Taxes are unrequited in the sense that benefits provided by government are not normally in proportion to their payments.

In the OECD classification, taxes are classified by the base of the tax:

- Income and profits (heading 1000)
- Payroll and workforce (heading 3000)
- Property (heading 4000)
- Goods and services (heading 5000)
- Other (heading 6000)
- Compulsory social security contributions paid to general government are treated as taxes (heading 2000)

Much greater detail on the tax concept, the classification of taxes and the accrual basis of reporting is set out in the OECD Interpretative Guide at Annex A of this Report.

All of the averages presented in this Report are unweighted.

A. Tax Ratios

a. Provisional data on tax ratios for 2014

New OECD data in the annual *Revenue Statistics* publication show that tax revenues as a percentage of GDP continue to recover gradually from the falls in almost all countries in 2008 and 2009 that stemmed from the financial and economic crisis. The average tax to GDP ratio in OECD countries was 34.4 %[1] in 2014 compared with 34.2 % in 2013 and 33.8 % in 2012. The 2014 figure is the highest recorded OECD average tax to GDP ratio since records began in 1965 (Table A, Table 2).

- Denmark had the highest tax to GDP ratio in 2014 (50.9 %) and Mexico the lowest (19.5 %).
- Of the 30 countries for which data for 2014 are available the ratio of tax revenues to GDP compared to 2013 rose in 16 and fell in 14.
- Between 2013 and 2014, the largest tax ratio increases were in Denmark (3.3 percentage points explained by an increase in taxes on income and profits as a percentage of GDP) and in Iceland (2.8 due to higher revenues from taxes on goods and services and taxes on income and profits). Other countries with substantial rises in their tax to GDP ratio between 2013 and 2014 were Greece (1.5 percentage points), Estonia (1.1) and New Zealand (1.0).

Table A. **Total tax revenue as % of GDP**

	1965	1975	1985	1995	2000	2007	2009	2011	2013	2014 provisional
Australia	20.6	25.4	27.8	28.2	30.4	29.7	25.8	26.3	27.5	n.a.
Austria	33.6	36.4	40.5	41.1	42.1	40.5	41.0	41.0	42.5	43.0
Belgium	30.6	38.8	43.5	42.6	43.6	42.6	42.1	43.0	44.7	44.7
Canada	25.3	31.5	31.9	34.9	34.9	32.3	31.4	30.2	30.5	30.8
Chile	..	..	..	18.4	18.8	22.8	17.2	21.2	20.0	19.8
Czech Republic	..	..	..	34.9	32.5	34.3	32.4	33.4	34.3	33.5
Denmark [1]	29.1	37.0	43.9	46.5	46.9	46.4	45.2	45.4	47.6	50.9
Estonia	..	..	..	36.2	31.0	31.1	34.9	31.9	31.8	32.9
Finland	30.0	36.1	39.1	44.5	45.8	41.5	40.9	42.0	43.7	43.9
France [1]	33.6	34.9	41.9	41.9	43.1	42.4	41.3	42.9	45.0	45.2
Germany [2]	31.6	34.3	36.1	36.2	36.2	34.9	36.1	35.7	36.5	36.1
Greece [1]	17.1	18.6	24.5	27.7	33.2	31.2	30.8	33.5	34.4	35.9
Hungary	..	..	..	41.0	38.7	39.6	39.0	36.5	38.4	38.5
Iceland	25.5	29.2	27.4	30.4	36.2	38.7	32.0	34.4	35.9	38.7
Ireland	24.5	27.9	33.7	31.8	30.9	30.4	27.6	27.4	29.0	29.9
Israel [3]	..	..	..	35.5	34.9	34.3	29.7	30.8	30.6	31.1
Italy	24.7	24.5	32.5	38.6	40.6	41.7	42.1	41.9	43.9	43.6
Japan	17.8	20.4	26.7	26.4	26.6	28.5	27.0	28.6	30.3	n.a.
Korea	..	14.9	15.8	19.1	21.5	24.8	23.8	24.2	24.3	24.6
Luxembourg	26.4	31.1	37.4	35.2	37.1	36.6	39.0	37.9	38.4	37.8
Mexico	..	..	15.2	14.9	16.5	17.6	17.2	19.5	19.7	19.5 [4]
Netherlands	30.9	38.2	39.8	38.9	36.8	36.1	35.4	35.9	36.7	n.a.
New Zealand	23.2	27.5	29.5	35.6	32.5	34.0	30.5	30.9	31.4	32.4
Norway	29.4	38.8	41.9	40.0	41.9	42.1	41.2	42.0	40.5	39.1
Poland	..	..	..	37.7	33.1	34.8	31.5	32.0	31.9	n.a.
Portugal	15.7	18.9	24.1	29.4	31.2	32.0	30.0	32.5	34.5	34.4
Slovak Republic	..	..	..	39.6	33.6	29.2	28.9	28.7	30.4	31.0
Slovenia	..	..	..	38.4	36.6	37.1	36.2	36.5	36.8	36.6
Spain [1]	14.3	18.0	26.8	31.3	33.4	36.5	29.8	31.3	32.7	33.2
Sweden	31.4	38.9	44.8	45.6	49.0	45.0	44.1	42.5	42.8	42.7
Switzerland	16.6	22.5	23.9	25.5	27.6	26.1	27.1	27.0	26.9	26.6
Turkey	10.6	12.0	11.5	16.8	24.2	24.1	24.6	27.8	29.3	28.7
United Kingdom	29.3	34.2	35.1	31.9	34.7	34.1	32.3	33.6	32.9	32.6
United States	23.5	24.6	24.6	26.4	28.2	26.7	23.0	23.6	25.4	26.0
Unweighted average:										
OECD Total	**24.8**	**28.6**	**31.5**	**33.6**	**34.2**	**34.1**	**32.7**	**33.3**	**34.2**	**34.4** [5]

n.a indicates not available.

1. The total tax revenues have been reduced by the amount of any capital transfer that represents uncollected taxes.
2. Unified Germany beginning in 1991.
3. The data for Israel are supplied by and under the responsibility of the relevant Israeli authorities. The use of such data by the OECD is without prejudice to the status of the Golan Heights, East Jerusalem and Israeli settlements in the West Bank under the terms of international law.
4. Secretariat estimate, including expected revenues collected by state and local governments.
5. Calculated by applying the unweighted average percentage change for 2014 in the 30 countries providing data for that year to the overall average tax to GDP ratio in 2013.

StatLink http://dx.doi.org/10.1787/888933276519

- The largest falls in the tax ratio between 2013 and 2014 were in Norway (1.4 percentage points due to a decline in taxes on income and profits) and Czech Republic (0.8 due to a decline in taxes on goods and services). Luxembourg showed a fall of 0.6 percentage points.
- Compared with 2007 (pre-recession) tax to GDP ratios, the ratio in 2014 was still down by more than 3 percentage points in three countries (Israel, Norway and Spain). The biggest fall has been in Spain, from 36.5 % in 2007 to 33.2 % of GDP in 2014.

- The tax burden in Greece increased from 31.2 % to 35.9 % between 2007 and 2014. Two other countries (Denmark and Turkey) showed increases of 4 percentage points or more over the same period.

b. Final data on tax ratios for 2013

The latest year for which tax to GDP ratios are based on final revenue data and available for all OECD countries is 2013 (Chart A). These data show that tax ratios vary considerably across countries.

- In 2013, Denmark had the highest tax to GDP ratio (47.6 %), followed by France, Belgium and Italy.
- In contrast, eight countries – Australia, Chile, Ireland, Korea, Mexico, Switzerland, Turkey and the United States – had tax ratios of below 30 %.
- Mexico had the lowest ratio at 19.7 % followed by Chile at 20.0 %.
- The tax ratio in the OECD area as a whole (un-weighted average) rose by 0.9 percentage points from 2011 to 34.2 % in 2013 (see Table A).
- Relative to 2011, overall tax ratios rose in 27 OECD member countries and fell in 7.
- The largest increases in the ratio were in Denmark (2.2 percentage points), France (2.1), Italy and Portugal (2.0).
- Six other countries – Belgium, Finland, Hungary, Japan, Slovak Republic and the United States – saw increases between 1.7 and 1.9 percentage points from 2011 to 2013.
- The largest reductions were in Norway (1.5 percentage points) and Chile (1.2).

The key changes in the tax to GDP ratio of the main tax headings between 2011 and 2013 were as follows:

- Revenues from taxes on income (personal and corporate income taxes together) as a percentage of GDP increased from 11.1 % in 2011 to 11.5 % in 2013 on average. The largest increases were in Denmark and Portugal (1.9 percentage points). Norway and Chile reported the largest falls in this ratio (by 1.8 and 1.6 percentage points of GDP respectively) (Table B).
- There were increases in the corresponding ratios for:
  - Social security contributions from 8.9 to 9.1 % (Table 13).
  - Property taxes from 1.8 to 1.9 % (Table 21).
  - Taxes on goods and services from 10.8 to 11.0 % (Table 23).
- The ratio was unchanged for payroll taxes at 0.4 % of GDP in both years (Table 19).

Aggregate tax ratios often figure prominently in policy debates and they are sometimes linked directly to the economic performance of nations. A special feature included in section S.2 of the 1999 edition of this Report explained why figures on tax revenues measured as a percentage of GDP should generally be interpreted with caution. More specifically, the revised guidelines set out in the 2008 System of National Accounts (SNA) that have been used to estimate the value of GDP for 31 of the 34 OECD countries, have resulting in higher GDP levels. As a consequence, the revised tax ratios reported in this publication are lower than tax to GDP ratios before these revisions. To limit any distortionary impact over the reporting period, the present edition of the Report employs revised GDP estimates for 1965 and later years in those cases where OECD countries have not reported revised GDP figures. The scale of the GDP revisions is considered in greater detail in the "Methodology issues" section below.

Table B. Taxes on income and profits as % of GDP

	1965	1975	1985	1995	2000	2007	2009	2011	2013	2014 provisional
Australia	10.5	14.2	15.2	15.6	17.7	17.7	14.4	15.5	15.7	n.a.
Austria	8.6	9.5	10.7	10.8	12.0	12.2	11.5	11.7	12.3	12.7
Belgium	8.5	15.3	17.6	16.3	16.9	15.3	14.3	14.9	15.9	16.1
Canada	9.7	14.9	14.1	16.2	17.5	15.8	14.9	14.3	14.5	14.7
Chile	..	..	..	4.6	4.4	10.4	5.4	8.5	6.9	6.5
Czech Republic	..	..	..	8.7	7.4	8.5	6.9	6.8	7.1	7.1
Denmark [1]	13.6	21.8	25.7	29.3	28.8	27.9	27.7	27.9	29.8	33.2
Estonia	..	..	..	10.9	7.7	7.4	7.4	6.4	7.2	7.6
Finland	12.4	15.6	16.0	16.1	19.7	16.3	14.6	14.9	15.2	15.3
France [1]	5.3	5.5	6.7	6.8	10.7	10.1	8.6	9.8	10.9	10.5
Germany [2]	10.7	11.8	12.6	11.0	10.9	10.9	10.4	10.5	11.3	11.0
Greece [1]	1.6	2.5	4.3	6.2	8.9	7.3	7.5	7.1	7.6	8.7
Hungary	..	..	..	8.6	9.4	10.0	9.6	6.3	6.8	6.5
Iceland	5.5	6.7	6.2	10.4	14.4	17.6	15.1	15.7	16.8	18.0
Ireland	6.3	8.4	11.6	12.8	13.5	12.5	10.7	10.7	11.7	12.1
Israel	..	..	..	12.5	13.9	12.6	9.0	9.3	9.7	9.7
Italy	4.4	5.3	12.0	13.6	13.5	14.1	13.7	13.4	14.5	14.2
Japan	7.8	9.1	12.2	10.1	9.3	10.4	8.0	8.6	9.8	9.8
Korea	..	3.6	4.2	5.8	6.2	7.9	6.8	7.3	7.1	7.2
Luxembourg	9.5	13.4	16.1	13.8	13.4	12.7	13.8	13.5	13.5	13.1
Mexico	..	..	3.4	3.7	4.5	4.9	4.9	5.3	6.0	5.8
Netherlands	11.0	13.3	10.5	10.3	9.3	10.2	10.0	9.6	9.1	n.a.
New Zealand	14.1	18.3	20.5	21.8	19.5	21.4	17.3	16.6	17.4	18.0
Norway	12.8	13.4	16.6	14.1	18.8	20.2	18.9	20.5	18.7	16.9
Poland	..	..	..	10.9	6.7	7.9	6.8	6.4	6.2	n.a.
Portugal	3.9	3.3	6.2	7.9	9.2	9.0	8.4	9.3	11.2	10.7
Slovak Republic	..	..	..	10.1	6.9	6.1	5.5	5.5	6.0	6.3
Slovenia	..	..	..	6.4	6.8	8.7	7.5	7.2	6.4	6.5
Spain [1]	3.5	4.0	6.7	9.1	9.5	12.3	8.9	9.1	9.6	9.6
Sweden	17.2	19.6	18.9	17.9	20.0	17.4	15.5	14.8	14.8	14.8
Switzerland	6.8	10.7	11.0	11.1	12.2	12.1	12.7	12.5	12.4	12.3
Turkey	3.1	5.1	4.3	4.8	7.1	5.7	5.9	5.8	5.9	6.1
United Kingdom	10.8	15.3	13.6	11.8	13.5	13.4	12.4	12.3	11.7	11.4
United States	11.3	11.3	11.2	12.0	14.1	12.9	9.2	10.7	12.0	12.5
Unweighted average:										
OECD Total	**8.7**	**10.9**	**11.8**	**11.5**	**12.2**	**12.3**	**11.0**	**11.1**	**11.5**	**11.7** [3]

n.a. indicates not available.

1. The total tax revenues have been reduced by the amount of any capital transfer that represents uncollected taxes.
2. Unified Germany beginning in 1991.
3. Calculated by applying the unweighted average percentage change for 2014 in the 30 countries providing data for that year to the overall average tax to GDP ratio in 2013.

StatLink http://dx.doi.org/10.1787/888933276522

c. *Tax ratios changes between 1965 and 2013*

The evolution of the changes in tax ratios between 1965 and 2013 is as follows:

- The average tax to GDP ratio in the OECD area increased from 24.8 % to 34.2 % (9.4 percentage points) between 1965 and 2013 (Table 2).
- The historical development of tax ratios for individual OECD countries varies greatly, as shown in Charts B, C, D and E. Each chart relates national changes in the tax ratio to the OECD average, for the periods 1965-75, 1975-85, 1985-95 and 1995-2013, respectively. Despite the increase, on average across the OECD countries total tax revenues as a percentage of GDP have fallen in some countries.

- Between 1965 and 1975, the tax burden in the OECD area increased by 3.8 percentage points (Chart B). Until the first oil shock (1973 to 1974), strong, almost uninterrupted income growth enabled tax levels to rise in all OECD countries. In part, tax levels rose automatically through the effect of fiscal drag on personal income tax schedules.
- Between 1975 and 1985, the tax burden in the OECD area increased by 2.9 percentage points (Chart C). After the mid-1970s, the combination of slower real income growth and higher levels of unemployment apparently limited the revenue raising capacity of governments. But during and after the deep recession following the second oil shock (1980), countries in Europe saw tax levels rise further, to finance higher spending on social security and rein in budget deficits.
- Between 1985 and 1995, the tax burden in the OECD area increased by a further 2.1 percentage points (Chart D). After the mid-1980s, most OECD countries substantially reduced the statutory rates of their personal and corporate income tax, but the negative revenue impact of widespread tax reforms was often offset by reducing or abolishing tax reliefs.
- Between 1995 and 2000 the average OECD tax to GDP ratio rose to 34.2%, its highest recorded level at that time. It fell back slightly between 2001 and 2004, but then rose again between 2005 and 2007 before falling back following the crisis. Taking these changes together the average tax level in the OECD area increased by 0.6 percentage points between 1995 and 2013 (Chart E).
- Such averages for the OECD area as a whole conceal the great variety in national tax burdens. In 1965, measures of tax to GDP ratios in OECD countries ranged from 10.6 % in Turkey to 33.6 % in France. By 2013 the corresponding range was from 19.7 % in Mexico to 47.6 % in Denmark. The trend towards higher tax levels over this period reflects the need to finance sizeable increase of public sector outlays in almost all OECD countries.

B. Tax structures

Tax structures are measured by the share of major taxes in total tax revenue. While, on average, tax levels have generally been rising, the share of main taxes in total revenues – the tax structure or tax "mix" – has been remarkably stable over time. Nevertheless, several trends have emerged up to 2013 (the latest year for which data is available for all 34 OECD countries) (Table C).

Taxes on income and profits

- On average, OECD countries collected 33.7 % of their tax revenues through taxes on income and profits (personal and corporate income taxes taken together) (Table 8). Taxes on personal and corporate incomes remain the most important source of revenues used to finance public spending in fifteen OECD countries, and in nine of them – Australia, Canada, Denmark, Iceland, Ireland, New Zealand, Norway, Switzerland and the United States – the share of income taxes in the tax mix exceeds 40 % – (Table 6).
- Revenues from personal income taxes are 25 % of total taxes on average in 2013 compared with around 30 % in the 1980s (Table 10). About two percentage points of this reduction can be attributed to the impact on the average of a number of relatively new entrants to the OECD from Eastern Europe for which tax revenue data is only available from the 1990s onwards. These countries tend to have relatively low personal income tax revenues and high revenues from social security contributions, but this impact is observed on the post 1990 data only.

Table C. **Tax structures in the OECD-area**

	1965	1975	1985	1995	2005	2010	2013
Personal income tax	26	30	30	26	24	24	25
Corporate income tax	9	8	8	8	10	8	8
Social security contributions[1]	18	22	22	25	25	26	26
(employee)	*(6)*	*(7)*	*(7)*	*(9)*	*(9)*	*(9)*	*(10)*
(employer)	*(10)*	*(14)*	*(13)*	*(14)*	*(14)*	*(15)*	*(15)*
Payroll taxes	1	1	1	1	1	1	1
Property taxes	8	6	5	5	6	5	6
General consumption taxes	12	13	16	19	20	20	20
Specific consumption taxes	24	18	16	13	11	11	10
Other taxes [2]	2	2	2	3	3	3	3
Total	**100**	**100**	**100**	**100**	**100**	**100**	**100**

Note: Percentage share of major tax categories in total tax revenue. Data are included from 1965 onwards for Australia, Austria, Belgium, Canada, Denmark, Finland, France, Germany, Greece, Iceland, Ireland, Italy, Japan, Luxembourg, the Netherlands, New Zealand, Norway, Portugal, Spain, Sweden, Switzerland, Turkey, United Kingdom and United States; from 1972 for Korea; from 1980 for Mexico; from 1990 for Chile; from 1991 for Hungary and Poland; from 1993 for the Czech Republic and from 1995 for Estonia, Israel, the Slovak Republic and Slovenia.

1. Including social security contributions paid by the self-employed and benefit recipients (heading 2300) that are not shown in the breakdown.
2. Including certain taxes on goods and services (heading 5200) and stamp taxes.

Source: OECD (2015), "Revenue Statistics: Comparative tables", OECD Tax Statistics Database, DOI: *http://dx.doi.org/10.1787/data-00262-en.*

StatLink http://dx.doi.org/10.1787/888933276537

- The variation in the share of the personal income tax between countries is considerable. In 2013, it ranged from a low of 10% and 11 % in the Slovak Republic and the Czech Republic respectively to 39 % in Australia and 55% in Denmark (Table 10).
- The sharp fall in the share of revenues from corporate income taxes in total taxation in 2008 and 2009 did not continue into 2011 and 2012, but the share of these taxes in total revenues remains, at 9 % in 2012, below its 11 % share in 2007 (Table 12).
- The share of the corporate income tax in total tax revenues shows a considerable spread, from 3-4 % (Greece, Hungary and Slovenia) to 18 % (Australia) and 22 % (Norway). Apart from the spread in statutory rates of the corporate income tax, these differences are at least partly explained by institutional factors or the exploitation of mineral deposits, for example:
  - the degree to which firms in a country are incorporated,
  - taxation of oil revenues,
  - the erosion of the corporate income tax base, for example as a consequence of generous depreciation schemes and,
  - other instruments to postpone the taxation of earned profits.

Social security contributions

- Social security contributions as a share of total tax revenues were 26% in 2013. They were highest in the Czech Republic and the Slovak Republic (43-44 %). In contrast, Australia and New Zealand do not have social security contributions (Table 14). OECD countries also show a wide variety in the relative proportions of social security contributions paid by employees and employers – (Tables 16 and 18).

Property taxes

- Between 1965 and 2013, the share of taxes on property fell from 8 % to 6 % of total tax revenues on average.
- In relative terms, property taxes have a share exceeding 10 % of total tax revenue – in four countries (Canada, Korea, the United Kingdom and the United States) (Table 22).

Consumption taxes

- The share of taxes on consumption (general consumption taxes plus specific consumption taxes) fell from 36 % to 31 % between 1965 and 2013 (Table 26).
- During this period, the composition of taxes on goods and services has fundamentally changed. A fast-growing revenue source has been general consumption taxes, especially the value-added tax (VAT) which is now found in thirty-three of the thirty-four OECD countries.
- General consumption taxes presently produce 20 % of total tax revenue, compared with only 12 % in the mid-1960s (Table 28).
- In fact, the substantially increased importance of the value-added tax has served to counteract the diminishing share of specific consumption taxes, such as excises and custom duties.
  - Between 1965 and 2013 the share of specific taxes on consumption (mostly on tobacco, alcoholic drinks and fuels, including some newly introduced environment-related taxes) was more than halved.
  - Rates of taxes on imported goods were considerably reduced everywhere, reflecting a global trend to remove trade barriers.
  - Nevertheless, countries such as Mexico (around 32 %) and Turkey (around 22 %) still collect a relatively large part of their tax revenues by way of taxes on specific goods and services (Table 30).

C. Taxes by level of government

Table D shows the relative share of tax revenues attributed to the various sub-sectors of general government and how it has changed between 1975 and 2013.

Federal and Regional countries

- In 2013, the share of central government receipts in the eight federal OECD countries varied from 31 % in Germany to 80 % in Australia and Mexico.
- In 2013, the share of the states varied from 2 % in Austria, 3 % in Mexico and 6 % in Belgium to 40 % in Canada. The share of local government varied from 1 % in Mexico to 15 % in Switzerland and the United States.
- Between 1975 and 2013 the share of federal government revenues declined by about eight percentage points in Belgium and less rapidly in Canada, Germany and the United States.
- The share of federal government revenues increased in Austria and Switzerland by 15 and five percentage points respectively. There was little change in Australia and Mexico.
- Of the seven federal countries with social security funds the share increased in five, the exceptions being Canada and Mexico where it slightly declined.

Table D. Attribution of tax revenues to sub-sectors of general government as % of total tax revenue

	Supranational			Central government			State or Regional government			Local government			Social Security Funds		
	1975	1995	2013	1975	1995	2013	1975	1995	2013	1975	1995	2013	1975	1995	2013
Federal countries															
Australia	..	..	..	80.1	77.5	80.8	15.7	19.0	15.8	4.2	3.4	3.4	0.0	0.0	0.0
Austria	..	0.0	0.3	51.7	64.8	66.5	10.6	1.8	1.6	12.4	4.1	3.2	25.3	29.3	28.4
Belgium	1.4	1.0	0.7	65.3	60.2	57.1	..	1.8	5.5	4.4	4.8	4.7	28.8	32.1	32.0
Canada	..	..	..	47.6	39.1	41.6	32.5	37.1	39.6	9.9	9.8	9.3	10.0	14.0	9.4
Germany	1.2	0.6	0.4	33.5	31.4	31.4	22.3	21.6	21.9	9.0	7.4	8.2	34.0	39.0	38.1
Mexico	..	..	..	..	80.1	80.1	..	2.1	3.1	..	1.1	1.2	..	16.6	15.5
Switzerland	..	..	..	30.7	31.4	35.2	27.0	23.8	24.6	20.3	17.6	15.2	22.0	27.3	25.1
United States	..	..	..	45.4	41.3	41.2	19.5	20.1	20.2	14.7	13.4	14.5	20.5	25.2	24.2
Unweighted average	1.3	0.6	0.5	50.6	53.2	54.2	21.3	15.9	16.5	10.7	7.7	7.5	20.1	22.9	21.6
Regional country															
Spain[1]	..	0.5	0.4	48.2	50.4	42.1	..	4.8	13.7	4.3	8.5	9.9	47.5	35.8	34.0
Unitary countries															
Chile	..	..	..	..	89.9	87.0	..	..	..	..	6.5	7.3	..	3.6	5.7
Czech Republic	..	..	0.4	..	57.7	55.2	..	..	..	..	0.9	1.3	..	41.4	43.2
Denmark	1.1	0.5	0.3	68.9	68.2	73.3	..	..	..	30.0	31.3	26.3	0.1	0.0	0.1
Estonia	..	..	0.5	..	72.1	69.5	..	..	..	..	13.1	13.3	..	14.8	16.7
Finland	..	0.4	0.2	56.0	46.6	47.6	..	..	..	23.5	22.3	23.4	20.4	30.8	28.9
France	0.7	0.4	0.2	51.2	42.3	33.6	..	..	..	7.6	11.0	12.9	40.6	46.3	53.3
Greece	..	0.6	0.2	67.1	66.8	63.6	..	..	..	3.4	0.9	5.6	29.5	31.7	30.5
Hungary	..	..	0.2	..	63.8	60.5	..	..	..	..	2.5	5.9	..	33.6	33.3
Iceland	..	..	..	81.3	79.2	73.4	..	..	..	18.7	20.8	26.6	0.0	0.0	0.0
Ireland	2.3	1.5	0.5	77.4	83.1	82.0	..	..	..	7.3	2.7	3.1	13.1	12.7	14.4
Israel	..	..	..	..	80.0	76.1	..	..	..	..	5.9	7.3	..	14.1	16.6
Italy	..	0.4	0.3	53.2	62.7	53.8	..	..	..	0.9	5.4	16.2	45.9	31.5	29.8
Japan	..	..	..	45.4	41.2	35.0	..	..	..	25.6	25.3	24.2	29.0	33.5	40.9
Korea	..	..	..	89.0	69.2	58.1	..	..	..	10.1	18.7	15.5	0.9	12.1	26.4
Luxembourg	0.8	0.4	0.1	63.6	67.1	68.4	..	..	..	6.7	6.4	3.5	29.0	26.1	28.0
Netherlands	1.5	1.2	1.0	58.9	54.1	54.4	..	..	..	1.2	2.7	3.7	38.4	42.0	40.8
New Zealand	..	..	..	92.3	94.7	93.3	..	..	..	7.7	5.3	6.7	0.0	0.0	0.0
Norway	..	..	..	50.6	58.4	86.9	..	..	..	22.4	19.6	13.1	27.0	22.0	0.0
Poland	..	..	0.3	..	61.9	48.2	..	..	..	..	8.3	12.9	..	29.8	38.6
Portugal	..	1.3	0.7	65.4	71.9	67.6	..	..	..	0.0	5.4	7.0	34.6	21.4	24.7
Slovak Republic	..	..	0.5	..	62.5	53.6	..	..	..	..	1.3	2.9	..	36.2	43.1
Slovenia	..	..	0.4	..	51.8	49.1	..	..	..	..	6.3	10.8	..	41.9	39.7
Sweden	..	0.4	0.3	51.3	46.9	49.9	..	..	..	29.2	30.9	36.9	19.5	21.8	12.8
Turkey	..	..	..	..	75.1	63.8	..	..	..	..	12.8	8.8	..	12.1	27.4
United Kingdom	1.0	1.0	0.5	70.5	77.5	75.8	..	..	..	11.1	3.7	4.9	17.5	17.8	18.8
Unweighted average	1.2	0.7	0.4	65.1	65.8	63.2	..	..	..	12.8	10.8	12.0	21.6	23.1	24.6

1. Spain is constitutionally a non-federal country with a highly decentralised political structure.

StatLink http://dx.doi.org/10.1787/888933276542

- Spain is now classified as a regional rather than a unitary country because of its highly decentralised political structure. In 2013 the share of central government receipts was 42 % compared with 14 % for the regional government. Between 1975 and 2013, the share of local government receipts increased from 4 % to 10 % and the share of social security funds declined from 48 % to 34 %.

Unitary countries

- In unitary OECD countries, the share of central government receipts in 2013 varied from 34 % in France and 35 % in Japan to 93 % in New Zealand.
- The local government share varied from 1 % in the Czech Republic to 37 % in Sweden.
- Between 1975 and 2013 there have been shifts to local government of 5 percentage points or more in six countries – France, Iceland, Italy, Korea, Portugal and Sweden and smaller increase in the Netherlands. Shifts of 5 percentage points or more in the other direction occurred in two countries – Norway and the United Kingdom.
- Between 1975 and 2013, there were increases in the share of social security funds of 7 or more percentage points in four countries – Finland, France, Japan and Korea and corresponding decreases in three others – Italy, Norway and Portugal. In two other countries – Poland and Turkey – the data showed an increase of 7 percentage points or more between 1995 and 2013.
- The guidelines for attributing these revenue shares to the different levels of government are based on the final version of the 2008 System of National Accounts. These guidelines are discussed in the special feature S.1 in the 2011 edition of OECD Revenue Statistics.

EU member states in the OECD

- The "supranational" column of Table D reports taxes collected on behalf of the European Union (EU) by the twenty-one EU member states that are members of the OECD. For years prior 1998, custom duties collected on behalf of the EU by national tax administrations of the EU member states are included under heading 5123. From 1998 onwards, these custom duties are shown as a "memorandum" item since they represent a tax imposed by the EU and collected by national administrations. However they continue to be part of the aggregate revenue figures which represent all taxes imposed within the territory of EU member states. This approach ensures consistency of the time series, and ensures that the tax to GDP ratio measures are immune to changes in the relative share of customs duties in (1) the composition of EU financing resources and (2) national tax mixes of EU member states. The amounts of customs duties concerned are shown in Table E.

D. The impact of GDP revisions on reported tax levels

The tax ratios shown in this Report express aggregate tax revenues as a percentage of GDP. It is important to recognise that the value of this ratio depends on its denominator (GDP) as well as its numerator (tax revenue), and that the denominator is subject to historical revision.

The numerator (tax revenue)

- For the numerator, the OECD Secretariat uses revenue figures that are submitted annually by correspondents from national Ministries of Finance, Tax Administrations or National Statistics Offices. Although provisional figures for most countries become available with a lag of about six months, finalised data become available with a lag of around one and a half years. Final revenue data for 2013 were received during the period May-August 2015.
- In thirty OECD countries the reporting year coincides with the calendar year. In four countries – Australia, Canada, Japan and New Zealand – have different reporting years. Reporting year 2013 includes Q2/2013-Q1/2014 (Canada, Japan) and Q3/2013-Q2/2014 (Australia, New Zealand) respectively (Q = quarter).

Table E. **Customs duties collected on behalf of the European Union**

In millions of national currency

	2000	2005	2008	2009	2011	2012	2013	2014[2]
Austria[1]	356	325	371	320	378	344	328	368
Belgium[1]	960	1 208	1 420	1 147	1 316	1 284	1 230	1 307
Czech Republic	..	5 586	6 323	5 548	6 961	6 172	5 544	6 968
Denmark	2 325	2 833	3 106	2 647	3 177	2 962	2 926	3 001
Estonia[1]	..	22	33	20	29	29	29	30
Finland[1]	129	148	205	152	189	184	166	170
France[1]	1 513	1 583	1 615	1 461	1 866	1 883	1 842	1 827
Germany[1]	3 394	3 433	4 036	3 778	4 556	4 417	4 251	4 608
Greece[1]	210	262	305	252	186	162	148	165
Hungary	..	26 572	26 689	25 657	27 462	27 206	26 337	31 947
Ireland[1]	208	226	245	208	240	242	247	275
Italy[1]	1 536	1 785	2 200	2 008	2 319	2 077	1 890	2 022
Luxembourg[1]	27	21	18	13	17	15	15	19
Netherlands[1]	1 310	1 265	1 788	1 518	1 997	2 159	2 210	2 258
Poland	..	1 098	1 572	1 308	1 447	1 611	1 613	n.a.
Portugal[1]	204	145	177	154	168	155	144	147
Slovak Republic[1]	..	75	156	111	157	129	115	127
Slovenia[1]	..	34	76	57	62	54	52	52
Spain[1]	970	1 436	1 578	1 328	1 554	1 436	1 316	1 512
Sweden	3 450	4 327	5 212	4 764	5 399	4 995	4 976	5 737
United Kingdom	1 800	1 908	2 297	2 435	2 925	2 885	2 914	2 949

n.a. indicates not available.

1. For euro area countries, the figures are in euros for all years.
2. Estimates.

StatLink http://dx.doi.org/10.1787/888933276557

The denominator (GDP)

- For the denominator, the GDP figures used for this Report are the most recently available on 1 September 2015. By that time, the 2013 and 2014 GDP figures were available for all OECD countries.
- Using these GDP figures ensures a maximum of consistency and international comparability for the reported tax to GDP ratios.
- The GDP figures are based on the OECD Annual National Accounts (ANA-SNA) for the thirty OECD countries where the reporting year is the actual calendar year.
- Where the reporting year differs from the calendar year, the annual GDP estimates are obtained by aggregating quarterly GDP estimates provided by the OECD Statistics Directorate for those quarters corresponding to each country's fiscal (tax) year. For example, in the case of Canada Q2/2013-Q1/2014

Revisions to the numerator and denominator

Both the numerator (tax revenues) and the denominator (the GDP figure) are subject to revisions, as more accurate estimates of the amounts involved become available. Such revisions will directly impact on published tax ratios.

- If the tax figure is revised upward and the GDP figure remains unchanged, the tax ratio will increase.
- If the GDP figure is revised downward, the tax ratio will also go up, even though aggregate tax revenues have not increased.

- Conversely, a higher GDP estimate implies a lower tax ratio, even if the amount collected in taxes has not changed.
- Revenue data, especially for recent years, can be subject to infrequent and usually minor revisions. GDP figures are revised and updated more frequently, though not necessarily for all countries at the same time, reflecting better data sources and improved estimation procedures. Generally these revisions have a rather limited impact on tax ratios.
- Occasionally, however, GDP figures may change in a more fundamental way when internationally agreed guidelines to measure the value of GDP are changed. The latest such change relates to the System of National Accounts 2008 (2008 SNA) which has now largely replaced its predecessor, the System of National Accounts 1993 (1993 SNA). An earlier version of the System of National Accounts was set up in 1968.
- The twenty-one OECD countries that are member states of the EU have to adhere to the European System of Integrated Economic Accounts (ESA) for computing their GDP figures. The ESA is primarily an elaboration of SNA, though differing from it in several minor aspects which are not pertinent to this Report. Following the 2008 revision to the System of National Accounts, the 1995 ESA was replaced by the 2010 ESA.
- So far, the 2008 SNA applies to the GDP figures presented in this publication for 31 countries. The exceptions are Chile, Japan, and Turkey which will follow over the next few months. The GDP figures for these thirty one countries are, with the exception of odd figures in particular years, higher following the application of the new SNA because of both methodological changes and the impact of improved data sources.
- The tax revenue figures reported in *Revenue Statistics* have hardly been affected by the changes to the definitions and standards in the SNA/ESA but in some countries there have been some adjustments as the opportunity has been taken to improve data sources and methodologies for compiling the national accounts figures (including tax revenues). However these changes have been generally relatively smaller than the changes to the GDP figures and tax ratios have generally fallen for those countries that have implemented the revised statistical framework. These issues are discussed in more detail in the special feature S.1. to this report.
- One particular problem raised by the 2008 SNA/2010 ESA revisions is that countries have varied in the period for which they have revised their GDP figures. To limit this distortionary impact, the OECD Statistics Directorate/Centre for Tax Policy and Administration have estimated revised GDP estimates for 1965 and later years in those cases where OECD countries have not reported revised GDP figures.

Note

1. Calculated by applying the unweighted average percentage change for 2014 in the 30 countries providing data for that year to the overall average tax to GDP ratio in 2013.

Chart A. **Total tax revenue as % of GDP, 2013**
Graphique A. **Total des recettes fiscales en pourcentage du PIB, 2013**

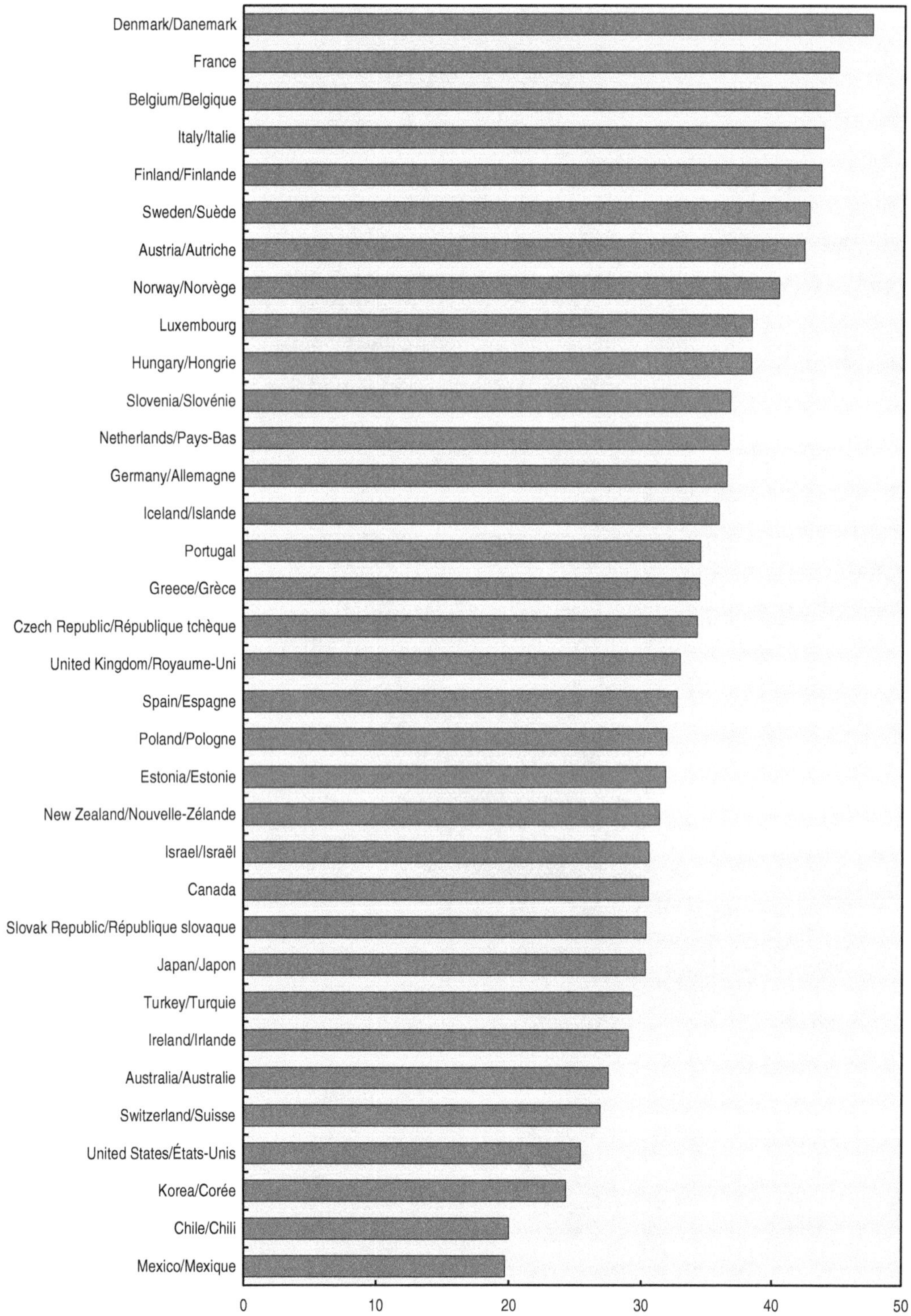

Note: Countries have been ranked by their total tax revenue to GDP ratios./Les pays sont classés en fonction du total des recettes fiscales par rapport au PIB.
Source: Table 1./Tableau 1.

StatLink http://dx.doi.org/10.1787/888933276303

Chart B. **Changes in tax to GDP ratio (in % points)**
Graphique B. **Variations du niveau d'imposition (en points de %) 1965-75**

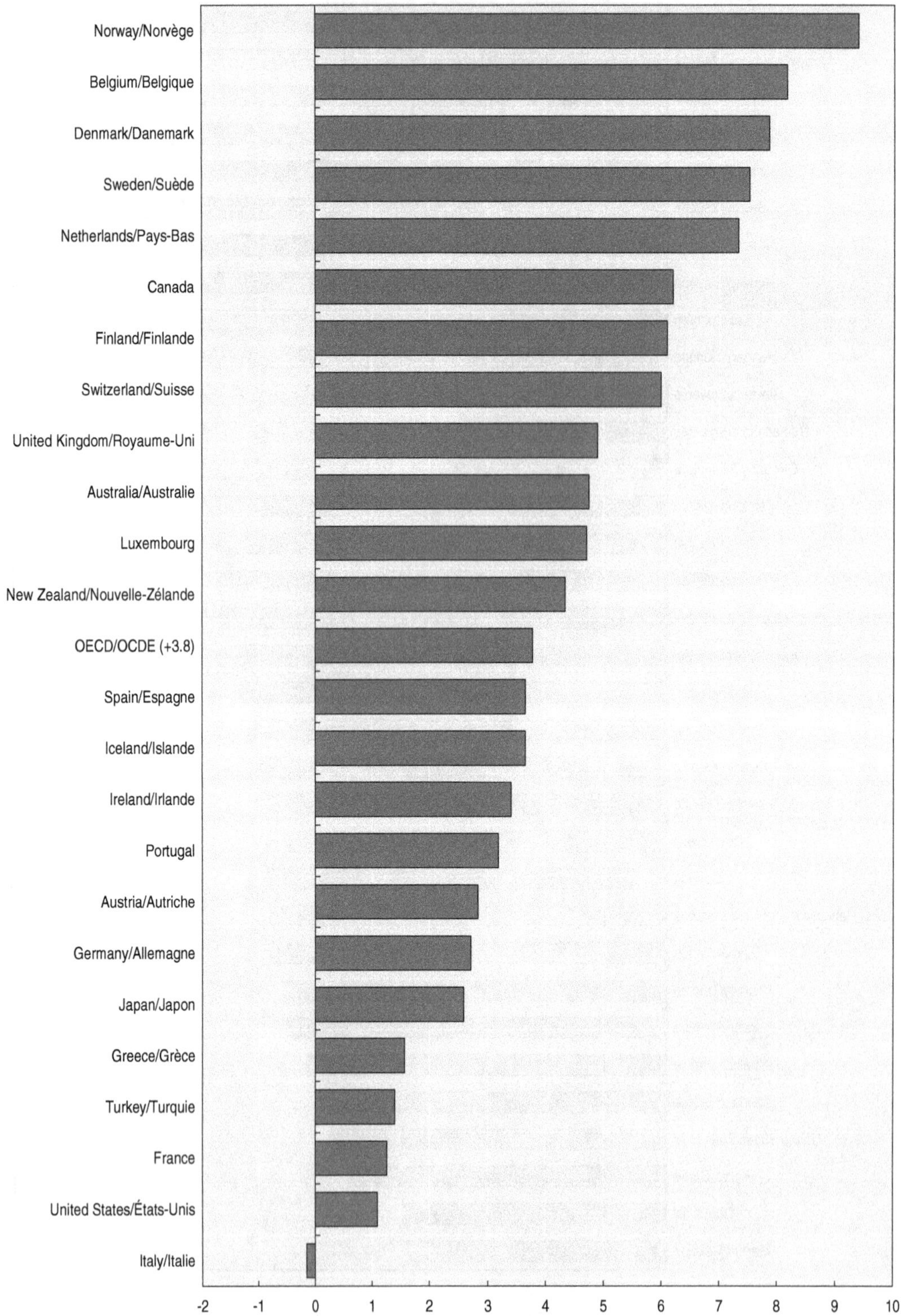

Source: Table 2./Tableau 2.

StatLink http://dx.doi.org/10.1787/888933276318

Chart C. **Changes in tax to GDP ratio (in % points)**
Graphique C. **Variations du niveau d'imposition (en points de %) 1975-85**

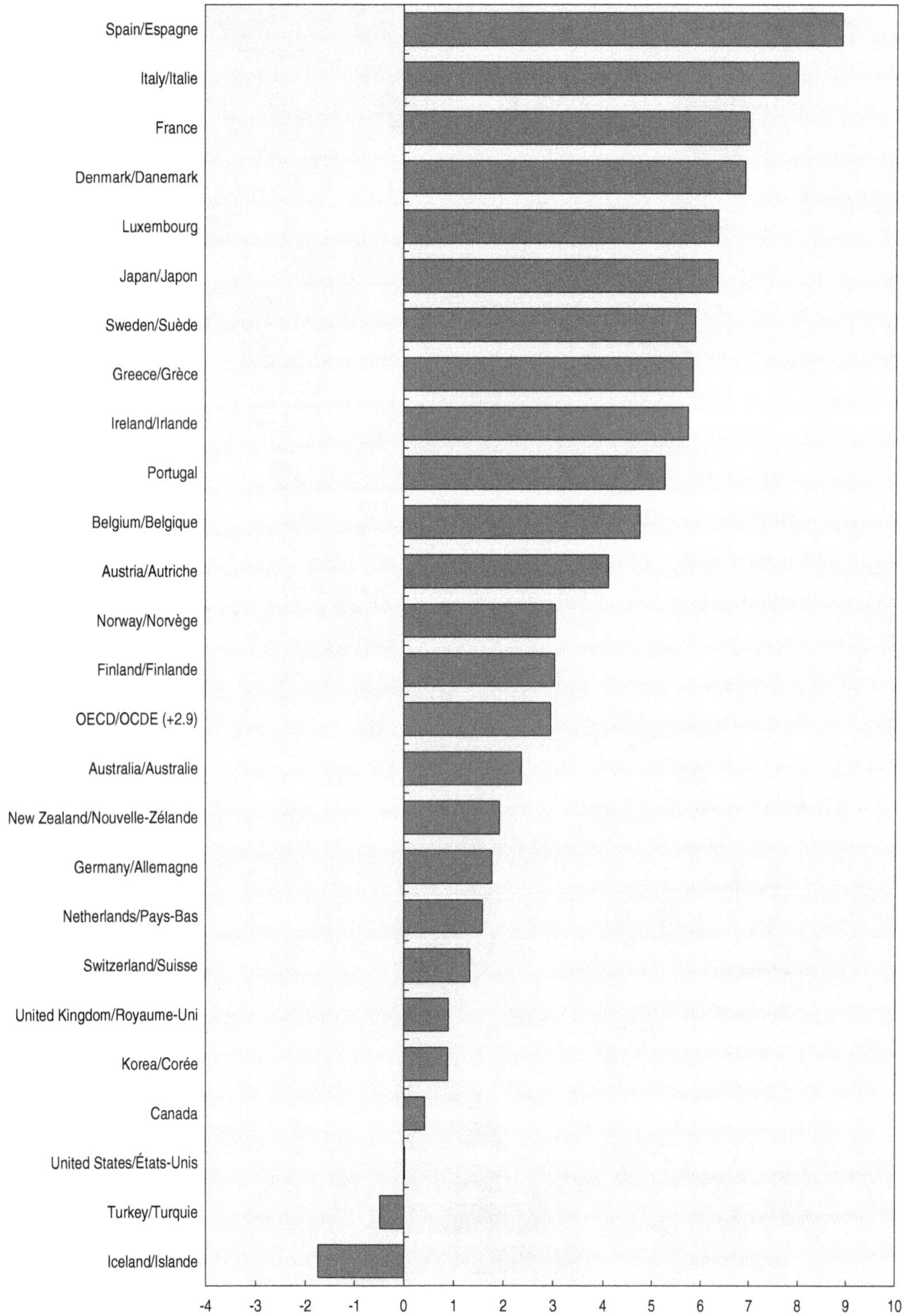

Source: Table 2./Tableau 2.

StatLink http://dx.doi.org/10.1787/888933276325

Chart D. **Changes in tax to GDP ratio (in % points)**
Graphique D. **Variations du niveau d'imposition (en points de %) 1985-95**

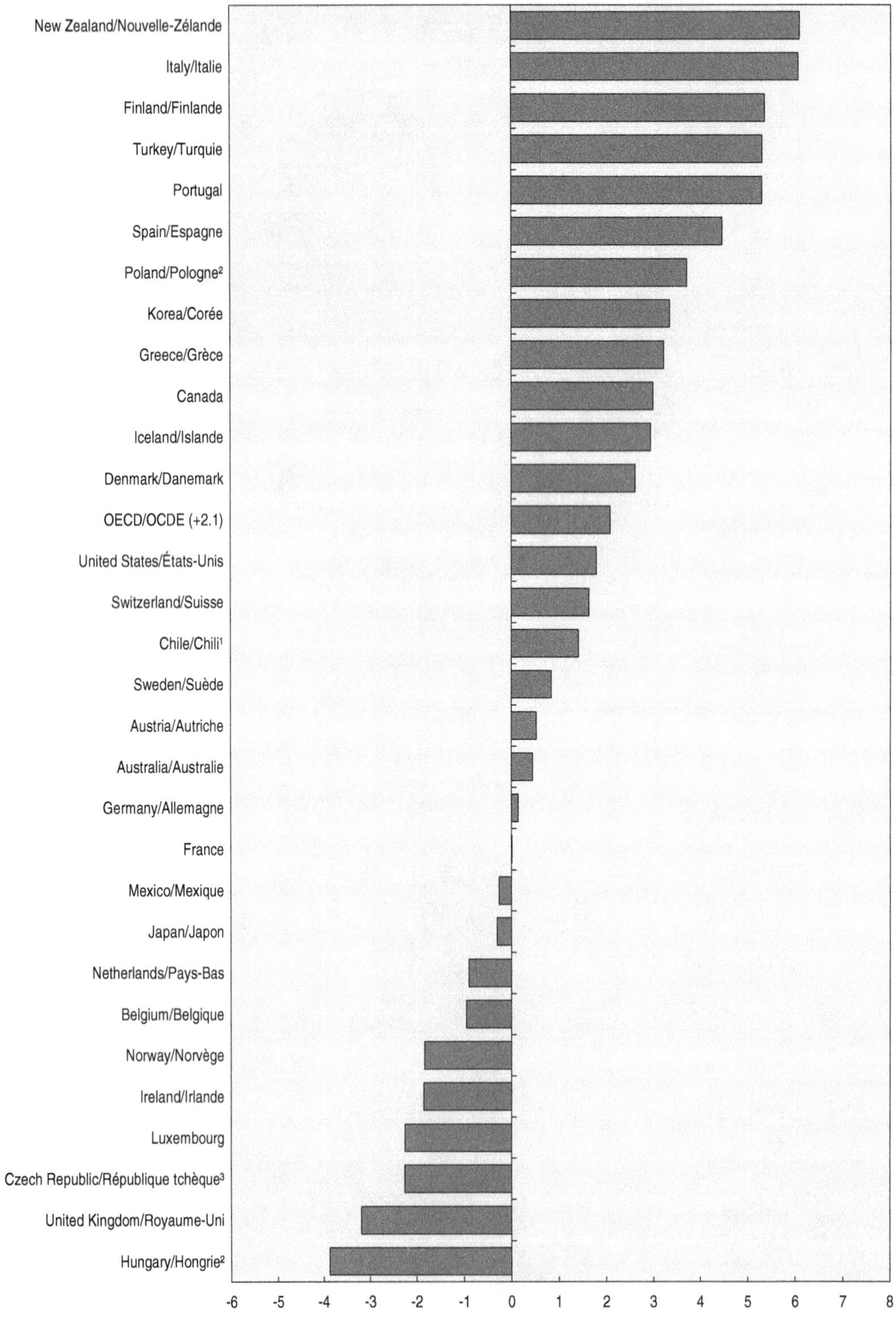

1. 1990-95.
2. 1991-95.
3. 1993-95.

Source: Table 2./Tableau 2.

StatLink http://dx.doi.org/10.1787/888933276336

Chart E. **Changes in tax to GDP ratio (in % points)**
Graphique E. **Variations du niveau d'imposition (en points de %)**
1995-2013

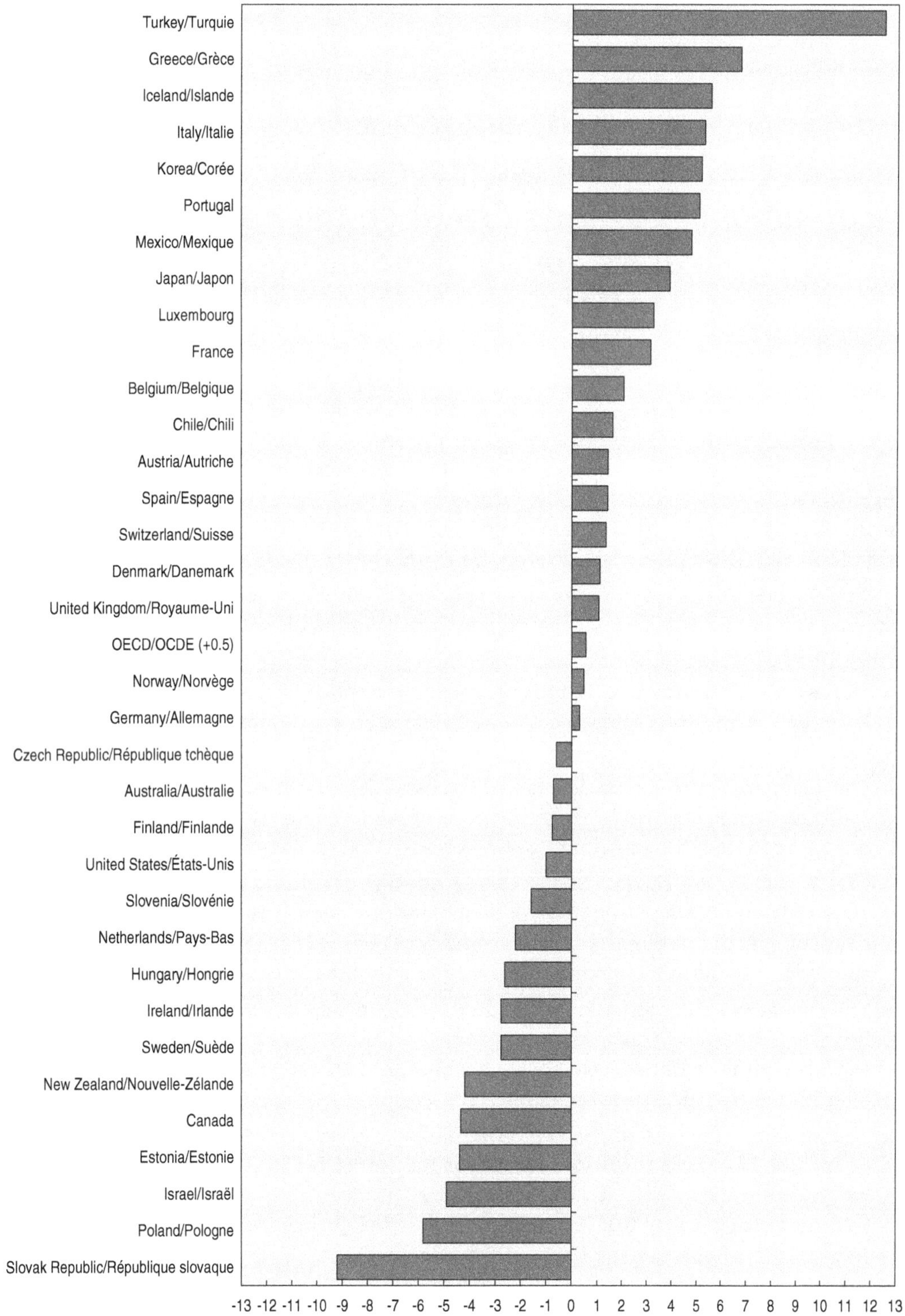

Source: Table 2./Tableau 2.

StatLink http://dx.doi.org/10.1787/888933276349

Special feature
S.1. The impact of the move to the 2008 system of national accounts (SNA) on the measurement of tax to gross domestic product (GDP) ratios

In 2009, the United Nations Statistical Commission endorsed a revised set of international standards for the compilation of national accounts known as the SNA 2008 to replace the previous 1993 version. This was followed by a revision of the European equivalent of the SNA, the European System of National Accounts (ESA) 2010. The latter standards are, with a few exceptions fully compatible with the SNA 2008.

This Special Feature examines the impact of countries adopting a revised set of standards from the SNA 2008 on their reported GDP and tax levels. Some of the patterns observed are:

- The average OECD tax to GDP ratio[1] following the move to the SNA 2008/ESA 2010 is lower by around 1 percentage point and the difference is steady over the 2000 to 2013 period.
- The adoption of new standards has had a substantial impact on observed GDP levels in OECD countries with an average increase of 3.8%. There was significant variation between countries ranging from 7.8% in Korea to 0.2% in Luxembourg.
- Of the average increase of 3.8%, 3.1% is attributed to the change in international standards and 0. 7% to a statistical benchmark revision (enhanced data sources or country specific national accounts methodologies). The change in international standards was the more important factor in 25 out of the 31 countries.
- The changes to the international standards in the new SNA/ ESA have had little or no impact on the levels of tax revenues published in the *OECD Revenue Statistics* publication. However, some countries have shown changes to their tax revenue figures due to the effect of the statistical benchmark revisions.
- The impact of changes on the tax to GDP ratios also varies widely across the member countries. The largest revision occurs for the Netherlands (-2.8 percentage points) whereas the ratio in Luxembourg increased by 0.9 percentage points. For the majority of countries the change in GDP levels as opposed to the changes in the tax revenue figures had the larger impact on the tax to GDP measures.

1. Introduction

In 2009, the United Nations Statistical Commission endorsed a revised set of international standards for the compilation of national accounts known as the SNA 2008 to replace the previous 1993 version. This was followed by a revision of the European equivalent of the SNA, the ESA 2010. The latter standards are, with a few exceptions fully compatible with the SNA 2008.

The actual timing of the implementation of the new standards varies depending on individual country circumstances. At the time of the compilation of the tax to GDP ratio data published in *OECD Revenue Statistics* 2014, 29 out of 34 OECD countries had adopted the new methodology with the following timing:

- 2009 – Australia
- 2012 – Canada
- 2013 – Israel, Mexico and the United States
- 2014 – Austria, Belgium, Czech Republic, Denmark, Estonia, Finland, France, Germany, Greece, Hungary, Iceland, Ireland, Italy, Korea, Luxembourg, the Netherlands, Poland, Portugal, Slovak Republic, Slovenia, Spain, Sweden, Switzerland and the United Kingdom.

Of the remaining five countries, New Zealand and Norway implemented the revised standards later in 2014. Turkey is set to follow in 2015 with Chile and Japan in 2016.

These developments have directly impacted on both the measurement of GDP and as a result the levels of tax to GDP ratios reported in the *OECD Revenue Statistics* database. The Special Feature considers:

- The range of changes in the levels of GDP and the ratios of tax to GDP observed in OECD countries that have moved to either SNA 2008 or ESA 2010.
- The underlying reasons for these changes.
- The relationship between the changes to the levels of GDP and the resulting changes to the tax to GDP ratio measures.

Some indication of the impact of the new SNA can be identified by considering Figure S1 which compares the trend from the year 2000 onwards in the OECD average tax to GDP ratio reported in the 2014 edition of the *Revenue Statistics* with the corresponding trend reported in the 2013 edition. This comparison is essentially illustrative because it only captures the impact on the figures of the 26 countries. These are the 24 countries that moved to new standards in 2014 plus Israel and Mexico. The impact of the changes in the figures for the 3 other countries switching to the new standards prior to 2014 (Australia, Canada and the United States) is incorporated in both sets of figures. However, the following conclusions can be drawn:

- The average tax to GDP ratios reported in the 2014 edition are lower than before by around 1 percentage point. This reflects the fact that GDP levels have increased in all years between 2000 and 2012 for the vast majority of countries that have implemented the new standards.

Figure S1. **Comparison of the average OECD total tax revenue as a percentage of GDP for the years 2000 to 2012 in the Revenue Statistics 2013 edition (RS13) and Revenue Statistics 2014 edition (RS14)**

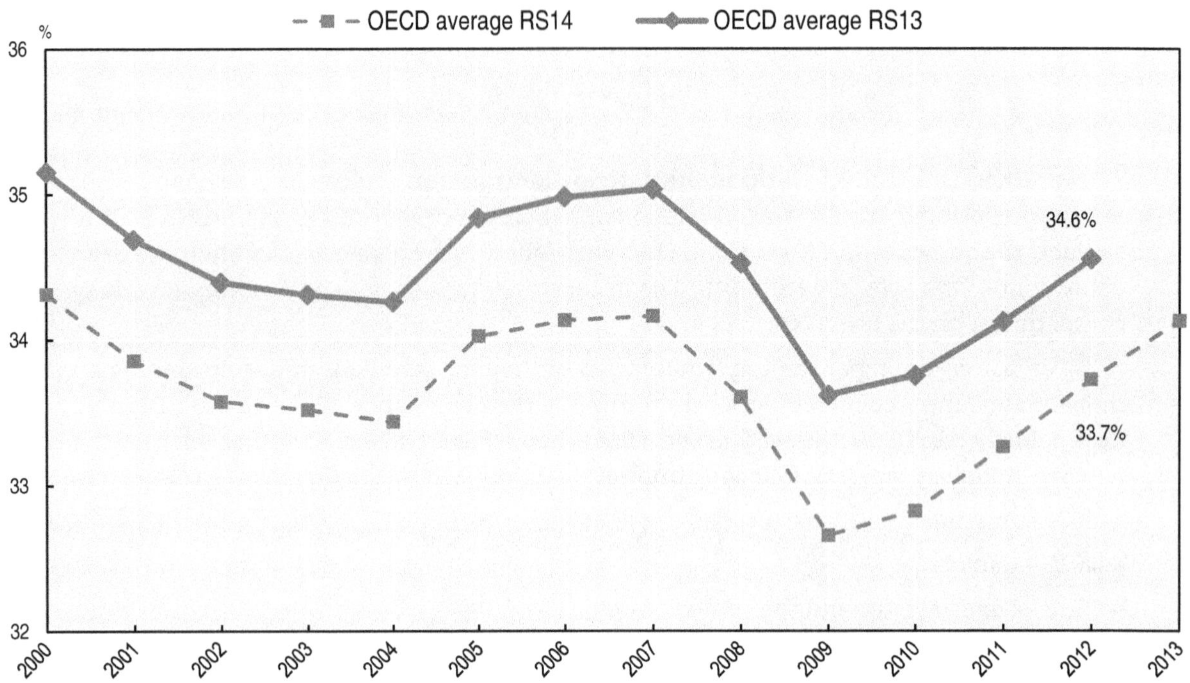

StatLink http://dx.doi.org/10.1787/888933276353

- The trend of the OECD average tax to GDP ratio in the 2014 *Revenue Statistics* publication follows very closely that contained in the 2013 edition but at a lower level.
- The dates of the all-time peak tax to GDP ratio figure and the most recent low point were not affected by the changes. In the both 2013 and 2014 editions, the OECD average tax to GDP ratio reached its peak level in the year 2000 at 35.2% (2013 edition) and 34.3% (2014 edition). The corresponding measures for the most recent low point in 2009 were 33.6% (2013 edition) and 32.7% (2014 edition).

2. The range of changes in GDP levels in individual OECD countries

The OECD Statistics Directorate has carried out a survey of OECD countries to identify both the size of the change in GDP levels arising from the adoption of the new standards and the underlying reasons. A report on this work is contained in an *OECD Statistics Brief* (February 2015 – No. 20) titled "New Standards for compiling national accounts: what's the impact on GDP and other macro-economic indicators?" written by Peter van de Ven.

In addition to the 29 countries that had switched to SNA 2008/ESA 2010 by the time of *OECD Revenue Statistics* 2014, this survey also covered New Zealand and Norway which made the change later in the year. For most of the countries this analysis focused on year 2010, though there were some exceptions that are listed in the footnotes to Figures S2/S3 and Table S1.

Figure S2 shows how the impact on GDP levels from the move to SNA 2008/ESA 2010 varied between the individual countries:

- The changes ranged from an increase of 7.8% in Korea to 0.2% in Luxembourg.

Figure S2. **Increases in GDP in 2010 for OECD countries as they moved to the new systems of national accounts**

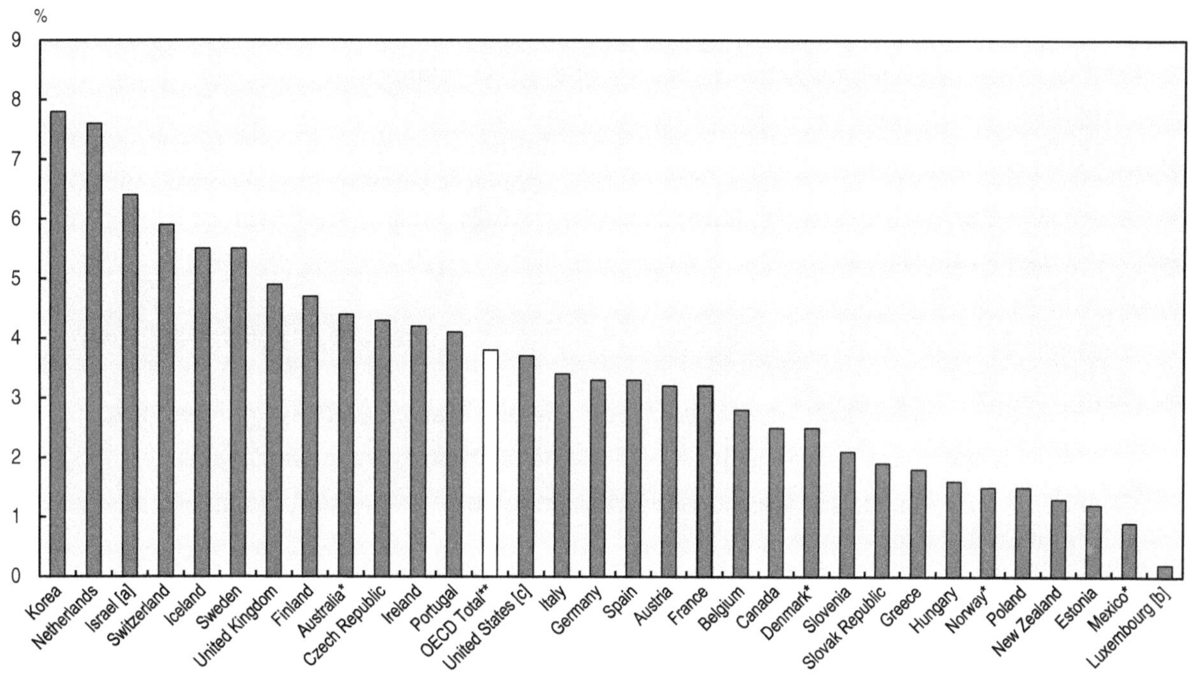

* Data for Australia: 2007; Denmark: 2008; Mexico: 2008; and Norway: 2011.

a) Capitalisation of military expenditures has not been implemented yet.

b) Almost all military equipment was capitalised under ESA95, since it can also be used for civilian purposes.

c) Military expenditures had already been capitalised in the National Income and Product Accounts (NIPAs). An estimation of impact on GDP is 0.5.

** OECD Total corresponds to those countries with available data.

StatLink http://dx.doi.org/10.1787/888933276367

- Other countries with increases of over 5% were the Netherlands (7.6%), Israel (6.4%), Switzerland (5.9%) and Sweden (5.5%).
- Other countries with increases of below 2% were Mexico (0.9%), Estonia (1.2%), New Zealand (1.3%), Norway and Poland (both 1.5%).
- The OECD average increase in GDP was 3.8%.

3. The main reasons for the revision of the GDP figures

The changes in international standards associated with new SNA/ESA were the major factor in the increases to GDP described in section 2 above but not the only one. At the same time, many countries used this opportunity to review and improve their data sources and methodologies for compiling national accounts indicators (including GDP) – referred to as the statistical benchmark revision. This is further explained by the following paragraph contained in *OECD Statistics Brief* No. 20 also referred to in section 2 above.

The primary goal of national accounts is the compilation of macro-economic aggregates that are consistent over time. For this reason, national accounts typically try to avoid the regular introduction of changes in standards, data sources and methodologies that would affect over-time consistency. Newly developed source data and latest available methodologies are only introduced when compiling a new benchmark estimate. Past time series are then back casted to arrive at a new consistent set of data. Most countries have used the opportunity of the changeover in standards to also introduce a new statistical benchmark estimate, i.e. to introduce new sources and methods. In some countries this actually has a larger impact than the changes in international standards. Furthermore, a distinct issue regarding the implementation of the SNA relates to the inclusion of illegal activities. Both the SNA 1993 and the SNA 2008 argue that illegal activities should be included. In practice however many countries did not explicitly include estimates for these activities, although part of the related transactions may have been included implicitly. The decision, at the European level, to fully include these activities in the national accounts estimates has raised some eyebrows in the media, the public and the economic research alike.

The main changes in the international standards that impacted on the measurement of GDP can be summarised as follows:

- Enlarging the capital base to include expenditure on Research and Development (R&D).
- Enlarging the capital base to include expenditure on military weapons systems.
- Other changes relating to the recording of pension entitlements and the measurement of financial services.

The main changes relating to the statistical benchmark revision can be summarised as:

- New or improved data sources.
- The inclusion of illegal activities.[2]
- Other including revisions to estimating methodologies.

Table S1 presents the overall impact of the benchmark revision on GDP levels by type of revision. Figure S3 presents a corresponding graphical representation comparing the relative impacts of the changeover of standards and the statistical benchmark revision to the total increase. The main conclusions of these figures are as follows:

- The OECD average increase in GDP was 3.8%. Of this, 3.1% related to the change in international standards and 0.7% to the statistical benchmark revision.
- The most important contributing factor related to the inclusion of expenditure on R&D in the capital base which caused an average increase of 2.2%.
- The inclusion of expenditure on military weapons systems in the capital base and the adoption of new and improved data sources contributed increases of 0.3% respectively.
- The change in international standards had a larger contribution to the increase in GDP than the statistical benchmark revision in 25 out of the 31 countries. The statistical benchmark revision was higher most notably in Iceland, Israel, and the Netherlands and to a lesser extent in Italy, Spain and United Kingdom.

4. The relationship between the changes to the levels of GDP and the resulting changes to the tax to GDP ratio measures in OECD *Revenue Statistics*.

a. Changes to the tax to GDP ratio measures

The range of changes to the GDP levels in OECD countries resulting from the benchmark revision is described in Sections 2 and 3 above. The changes to the GDP levels in turn impacted on the associated tax to GDP ratios. The latter were also dependent on the changes to the levels of tax revenues observed in the same year.

Table S1. **The overall impact of the benchmark revision on GDP-levels, by type of revision, year 2010**

	Overall impact								
			Change over of standards				Statistical Benchmark revision		
			R&D	Military weapons systems	Other		New/improved sources	Illegal activities	Other
Australia*	**4.4**	**3.9**	1.4	0.3	2.2	**0.5**	n.a	n.a	n.a.
Austria	**3.2**	**3.8**	2.3	0.0	1.4	**-0.6**	1.1	0.0	-1.7
Belgium	**2.8**	**2.5**	2.4	0.0	0.1	**0.3**	-0.3	0.4	0.2
Canada	**2.5**	**1.7**	1.2	0.1	0.4	**0.8**	n.a	n.a	n.a.
Chile	-	-	-	-	-	-	-	-	-
Czech Republic	**4.3**	**3.1**	1.2	0.1	1.7	**1.2**	1.1	0.0	0.1
Denmark*	**2.5**	**2.7**	2.6	0.1	0.0	**-0.2**	-0.6	0.2	0.2
Estonia	**1.2**	**1.4**	0.9	0.4	0.0	**-0.2**	-0.2	0.0	0.0
Finland	**4.7**	**4.2**	4.0	0.2	0.0	**0.5**	0.5	0.0	0.0
France	**3.2**	**2.4**	2.2	0.2	0.0	**0.8**	0.8	0.0	0.0
Germany	**3.3**	**2.7**	2.3	0.1	0.3	**0.6**	0.2	0.1	0.3
Greece	**1.8**	**1.3**	0.6	0.6	0.2	**0.6**	-0.1	0.0	0.6
Hungary	**1.6**	**1.6**	1.2	n.a.	n.a	**0.0**	-0.1	0.0	0.1
Iceland	**5.5**	**1.4**	1.4	0.0	0.0	**4.1**	3.6	0.5	0.0
Ireland	**4.2**	**3.6**	3.5	0.0	0.1	**0.6**	0.0	0.6	0.0
Israel[a]	**6.4**	**2.3**	2.2	0.0	0.1	**4.1**	3.2	0.0	0.9
Italy	**3.4**	**1.5**	1.3	0.2	0.0	**1.9**	0.4	1.0	0.5
Japan	-	-	-	-	-	-	-	-	-
Korea	**7.8**	**5.1**	3.6	0.3	1.2	**2.7**	n.a	n.a	n.a.
Luxembourg[b]	**0.2**	**1.6**	0.5	0.0	1.2	**-1.4**	0.0	0.2	-1.7
Mexico*	**0.9**	**1.5**	1.4	0.0	0.0	**-0.6**	0.0	0.0	-0.6
Netherlands	**7.6**	**1.7**	1.8	n.a.	n.a	**5.9**	4.6	0.4	0.9
New Zealand	**1.3**	**1.3**	1.1	0.1	0.1	**0.0**	0.0	0.0	0.0
Norway*	**1.5**	**1.6**	1.4	0.2	0.0	**-0.1**	n.a.	n.a.	n.a.
Poland	**1.5**	**1.2**	0.5	0.2	n.a.	**0.2**	n.a.	0.7	n.a.
Portugal	**4.1**	**2.1**	1.3	0.1	0.8	**2.0**	1.4	0.4	0.3
Slovak Republic	**1.9**	**1.8**	0.6	0.1	1.1	**0.1**	0.2	0.0	-0.1
Slovenia	**2.1**	**2.0**	1.9	0.1	0.0	**0.1**	0.3	0.0	-0.2
Spain	**3.3**	**1.6**	1.2	0.2	0.2	**1.7**	0.0	0.9	0.8
Sweden	**5.5**	**4.4**	4.0	0.4	0.0	**1.1**	1.1	0.0	0.0
Switzerland	**5.9**	**3.5**	n.a	n.a.	n.a.	**2.3**	n.a.	n.a.	n.a.
Turkey	-	-	-	-	-	-	-	-	-
United Kingdom	**4.9**	**2.3**	1.6	0.2	0.4	**2.6**	2.0	0.6	0.0
United States[c]	**3.7**	**4.0**	2.5	0.5	0.9	**-0.3**	-0.4	0.0	0.1
OECD Total**	**3.8**	**3.1**	2.2	0.3	0.6	**0.7**	0.3	0.2	0.1

* Data for Australia: 2007; Denmark: 2008; Mexico: 2008; and Norway: 2011.

** OECD Total corresponds to those countries with available data.

a) Capitalisation of military expenditures has not been implemented yet.

b) Almost all military equipment was capitalised under ESA95, since it can also be used for civilian purposes.

c) Military expenditures had already been capitalised in the National Income and Product Accounts (NIPAs). An estimation of impact on GDP is 0.5.

StatLink http://dx.doi.org/10.1787/888933276615

In fact, the changes to the international standards in the new SNA/ESA have had little or no impact on the levels of tax revenues published in the *OECD Revenue Statistics* publication. In drawing this conclusion, it should be borne in mind that:

- The changes to the SNA/ESA accounting standards for payable tax credits have not been reflected in the *OECD Interpretative Guide*. The same is true for the new ESA accounting standards on the VAT own resources.

Figure S3. **The impact of the changeover of standards and of the statistical benchmark revision on GDP-levels, year 2010**

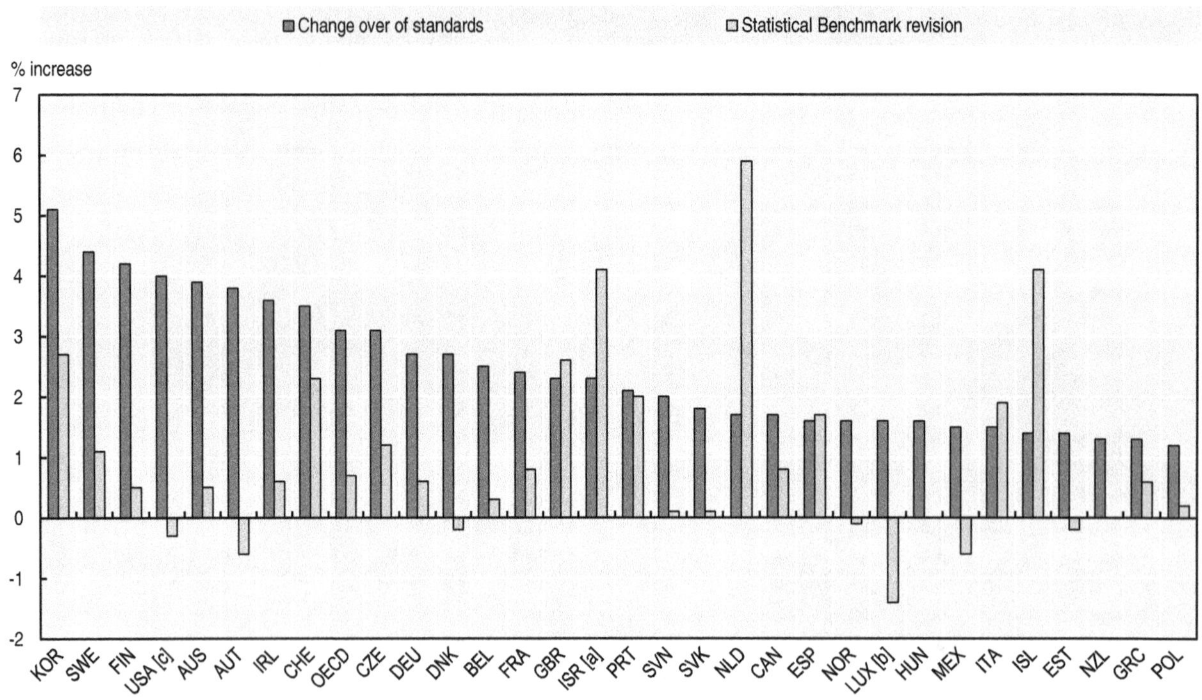

* Data for Australia: 2007; Denmark: 2008; Mexico: 2008; and Norway: 2011.

** OECD Total corresponds to those countries with available data.

a) Capitalisation of military expenditures has not been implemented yet.

b) Almost all military equipment was capitalised under ESA95, since it can also be used for civilian purposes.

c) Military expenditures had already been capitalised in the National Income and Product Accounts (NIPAs). An estimation of impact on GDP is 0.5.

StatLink http://dx.doi.org/10.1787/888933276374

- The *Revenue Statistics* has previously anticipated, since the 2012 edition, the new SNA/ESA to classify the new bank levies and financial stability schemes as taxes.

However, at the same time, some countries have shown some changes to their tax revenue figures due to the effect of the statistical benchmark revisions. The percentage changes to the 2010 tax revenue figures can be summarised as follows:

- The largest percentage increases were in Ireland (5.7%) and Greece (3.1%). Portugal (1.9%), the Slovak Republic (1.5%) and Luxembourg (1.0%) were the other countries with increases of 1% or more.
- The largest declines were in Spain (-4.9%) and Denmark (-2.4%). Slovenia (-1.1%), and the United States (-1.0%) were the other countries with increases of 1% or more.
- There were 12 countries where the changes in tax revenues were either nil or less than 0.1%.

The corresponding range of changes in the tax to GDP ratio in OECD countries resulting from the benchmark revision are shown in Figure S4. These figures are based on the following comparisons:

- Australia – The 2008 and 2009 editions for the year 2007.
- Canada and the United States – The 2012 and 2013 editions for the year 2010.
- The Czech Republic, Finland, France, Iceland, Mexico and Switzerland – The 2013 and 2014 editions for the year 2010.

Figure S4. **Change in the tax to GDP ratios for OECD countries that have moved to SNA 2008/ESA 2010, year 2010**

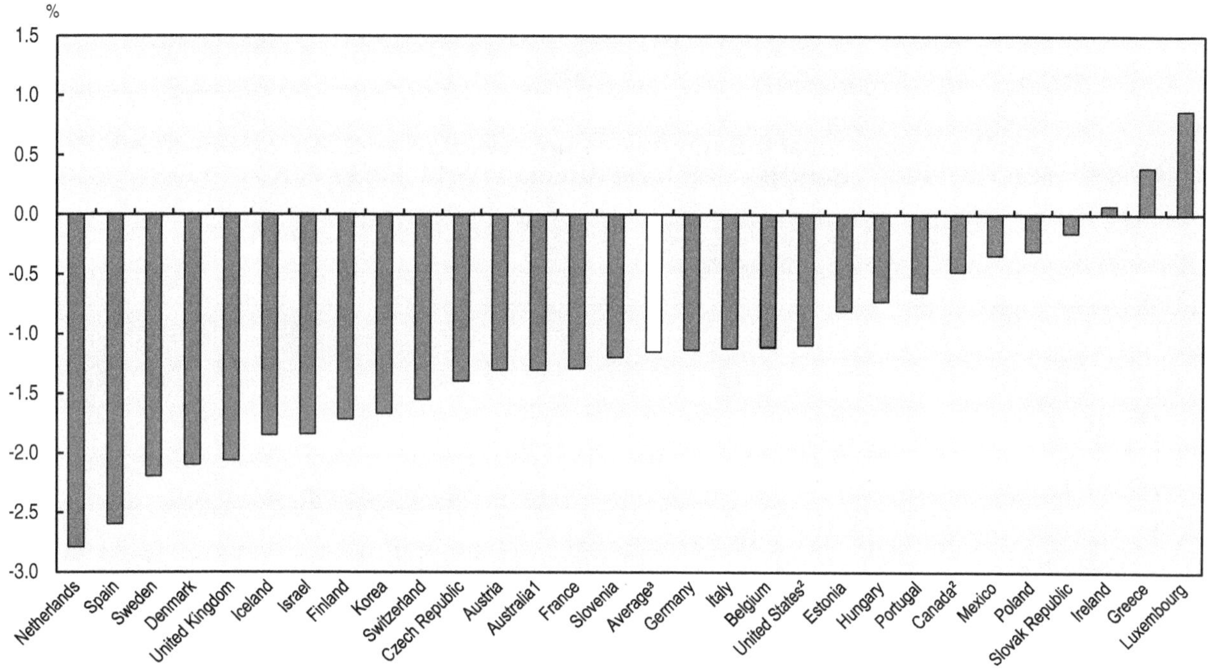

Note: Year 2007 for Australia which moved to SNA 2008 in 2009. Canada moved to SNA 2008 in 2012 and the USA in 2013. Comparisons are made on the year 2010 for both countries.

StatLink http://dx.doi.org/10.1787/888933276382

- The remainder of the 29 countries listed in section 1 – The 2013 and 2014 editions for the year 2010. For these countries, the SNA based changes to the tax revenue figures shown for 2010 in the 2015 edition were also taken into account.

It should be noted that the underlying change in the GDP figures in the relevant edition of *OECD Revenue Statistics* is different for some countries compared with that shown in Figure S2. This is because in some cases there were subsequent adjustments to the GDP figures after they were compiled for the relevant *Revenue Statistics* publication but before the benchmark revisions took place. This is clearly the case for Luxembourg where the change in the GDP figure published in the 2014 edition of *OECD Revenue Statistics* compared with the 2013 edition is actually negative leading to a positive change in the tax to GDP ratio.

The main conclusions from Figure S4 are as follows:

- Of the 29 countries that moved to the new standards when the figures for the 2014 edition of *OECD Revenues Statistics* had been compiled, all except three; Greece, Luxembourg and Ireland experienced a decline in the tax to GDP ratio subsequent to the change being made.
- The changes ranged from a decline of 2.8 percentage points in the Netherlands to an increase of 0.9 percentage points in Luxembourg. Denmark, Spain, Sweden and the United Kingdom were the only other countries with a decline of more than two percentage points.
- The average among the 29 countries was a decline of 1.2 percentage points.

b. The relative impacts of changes to tax revenues and changes to GDP on the tax to GDP ratio measures

Figure S5 illustrates the relative contributions of the changes to tax revenue and changes to GDP on the change in tax to GDP ratio measures. The 29 countries are shown in decreasing order of change in the tax to GDP ratio.

Figure S5. **The relative impacts of the changes to tax revenues and GDP on the change in tax to GDP ratios for OECD countries that have moved to SNA 2008 / ESA 2010, year 2010**

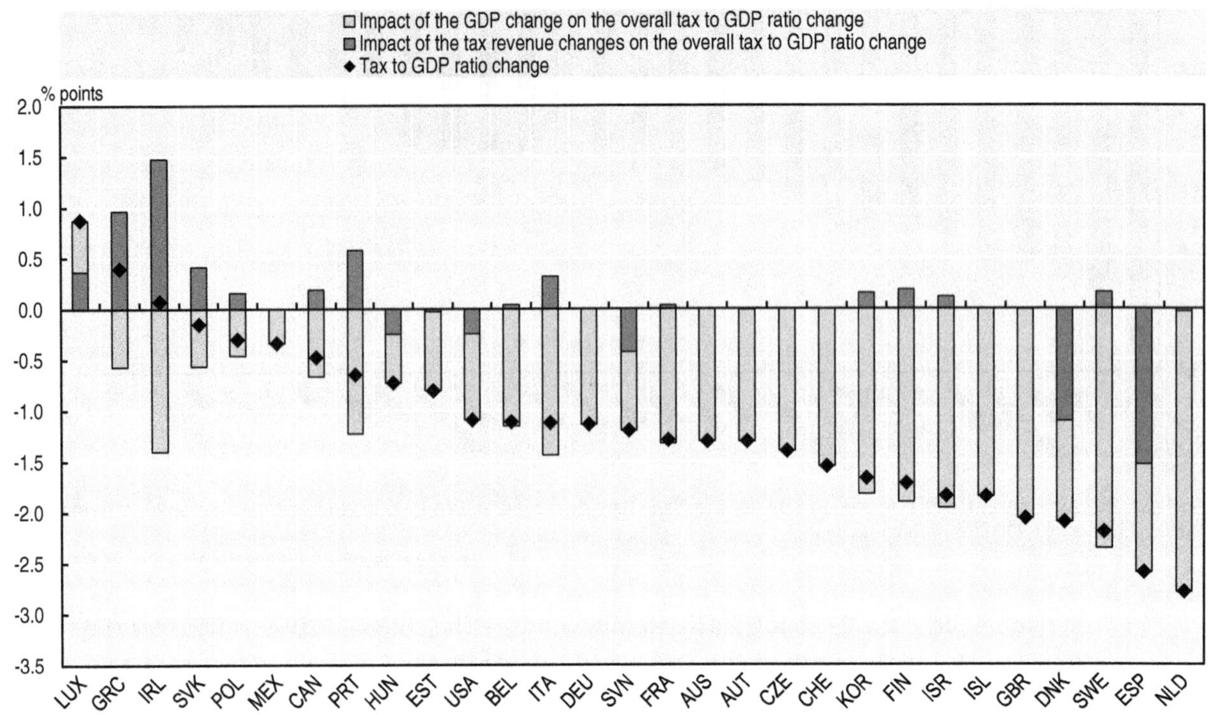

Note: Year 2007 for Australia which moved to SNA 2008 in 2009. Canada moved to SNA 2007 in 2012 and the USA in 2013. Comparisons are made on the year 2010 for both countries.

StatLink http://dx.doi.org/10.1787/888933276396

- Luxembourg is the only country with a positive change in the level of GDP. In contrast the impact of the benchmark review on tax revenues is a mixture of positive in some countries, negative in others and with a nil or negligible effect in around 40% of the countries.
- In some countries the direction of change in tax revenues adds to the direction of change in the GDP. In other countries the two work in opposite directions. However in the majority of countries the impact of the change in GDP makes a significantly larger contribution to the change in the tax to GDP ratio figure than the change in tax revenues.
- There are four countries that are major exceptions to the conclusion of the second bullet. In both Greece and Ireland, at the top end of the distribution, the contribution of the higher tax revenues more than offsets the contribution of the higher GDP as the two impact in opposite directions on the tax to GDP ratio. In contrast at the lower end of the distribution, in Denmark and Spain, the contribution of lower tax revenues is greater than the impact of higher GDP levels as the two work in the same direction to reduce the tax to GDP ratio.

The above changes have implications for ranking list of OECD countries in terms of decreasing order of tax to GDP ratio. However a precise assessment of these changes is prevented by the following factors:

- In some cases, it is not straightforward to disentangle revisions due to the methodological changes from corrections to data sources and other modifications. Moreover the analyses here necessarily focus only on one year – 2010 – and the results could be slightly different for other years.
- At the time of publication of *OECD Revenue Statistics 2014*, 5 out of 34 countries had not switched to SNA 2008.
- The other countries have made the transition to the new standards over a period of years, the first being Australia in the 2009 edition.
- Other factors have impacted on the ranking list over the period of transition.

Some observations on the ranking list in the year 2010 can be made as follows:

- Denmark, despite one of the largest falls in tax to GDP ratio resulting both from lower tax revenues and higher GDP, remains with the highest tax to GDP ratio in the OECD. Mexico continues to have the lowest.
- There has also been little impact on the ranking orders at the upper and lower ends of the distribution.
- In the middle of the distribution, Spain fell by 6 places due to a combination of lower tax revenues and higher GDP. Four other countries had moves of three places; Greece and Luxembourg moved upwards with Israel and the Netherlands moving in the opposite directions.
- Any changes in the ranking order for the other countries were for two places or less.

Notes

1. In this paper, the average OECD tax to GDP ratio refers to the unweighted average of the results for the 34 OECD countries. This measure assumes that each country has an equal weight in the calculation.
2. The arrangement at the European level to extend GDP figures to cover illegal activities focussed on prostitution, the production and trafficking of drugs and alcohol and tobacco smuggling.

Revenue Statistics 1965-2014
Statistiques des recettes publiques 1965-2014

PARTIE I

Tendances des recettes fiscales, 1965-2014

Introduction

Les *Statistiques des recettes publiques* sont une publication annuelle qui présente des données détaillées permettant de comparer, à l'échelle internationale, les recettes fiscales perçues par tous les niveaux d'administration dans les pays de l'OCDE. La dernière édition fournit des informations sur les recettes fiscales au cours de la période 1965-2013. En outre, des estimations provisoires relatives aux recettes fiscales pour l'année 2014 sont indiquées pour la plupart des pays de l'OCDE.

Dans ce rapport, les impôts désignent les versements obligatoires sans contrepartie aux administrations publiques. Les impôts sont sans contrepartie en ce sens que les prestations fournies par les administrations ne sont pas normalement proportionnelles à leurs paiements.

Dans la classification de l'OCDE, les impôts sont ventilés en fonction de leur base :

- revenus et bénéfices (rubrique 1000)
- salaire et main-d'œuvre (rubrique 3000)
- patrimoine (rubrique 4000)
- biens et services (rubrique 5000)
- autres impôts (rubrique 6000)
- Les cotisations obligatoires de sécurité sociale versées aux administrations publiques sont traitées comme des impôts (rubrique 2000)

On trouvera des précisions sur la notion d'impôt, la classification des impôts et l'enregistrement sur la base des droits constatés dans le Guide d'interprétation de l'OCDE qui figure à l'annexe A du présent rapport.

Les moyennes présentées dans ce rapport ne sont pas pondérées.

A. Niveau d'imposition

a. Données provisoires relatives aux ratios fiscaux pour 2013

Les nouvelles données de l'OCDE qui figurent dans la publication annuelle *Statistiques des recettes publiques* montrent que les recettes fiscales exprimées en pourcentage du PIB continuent de se rétablir progressivement, après les baisses enregistrées dans pratiquement tous les pays en 2008 et 2009 sous l'effet de la crise économique et financière. Le ratio moyen des recettes fiscales rapportées au PIB dans les pays de l'OCDE était de 34.4 %[1] en 2014, contre 34.2 % en 2013 et 33.8 % en 2012. Le chiffre de 2014 est le plus élevé obtenu depuis le début de l'enregistrement des données en 1965. (Tableau A, Tableau 2).

- En 2014, le Danemark enregistrait le ratio le plus élevé (50.9 %) et le Mexique celui le plus faible (19.5 %).
- Sur les 30 pays pour lesquels on dispose de données se rapportant à 2014, le ratio des recettes fiscales au PIB a augmenté depuis 2013 dans 16 pays et diminué dans 14 pays.

Tableau A. **Total des recettes fiscales en % du PIB**

	1965	1975	1985	1995	2000	2007	2009	2011	2013	2014 provisoire
Australie	20.6	25.4	27.8	28.2	30.4	29.7	25.8	26.3	27.5	n.d.
Autriche	33.6	36.4	40.5	41.1	42.1	40.5	41.0	41.0	42.5	43.0
Belgique	30.6	38.8	43.5	42.6	43.6	42.6	42.1	43.0	44.7	44.7
Canada	25.3	31.5	31.9	34.9	34.9	32.3	31.4	30.2	30.5	30.8
Chili	..	..	..	18.4	18.8	22.8	17.2	21.2	20.0	19.8
République tchèque	..	..	..	34.9	32.5	34.3	32.4	33.4	34.3	33.5
Danemark[1]	29.1	37.0	43.9	46.5	46.9	46.4	45.2	45.4	47.6	50.9
Estonie	..	..	..	36.2	31.0	31.1	34.9	31.9	31.8	32.9
Finlande	30.0	36.1	39.1	44.5	45.8	41.5	40.9	42.0	43.7	43.9
France[1]	33.6	34.9	41.9	41.9	43.1	42.4	41.3	42.9	45.0	45.2
Allemagne[2]	31.6	34.3	36.1	36.2	36.2	34.9	36.1	35.7	36.5	36.1
Grèce	17.1	18.6	24.5	27.7	33.2	31.2	30.8	33.5	34.4	35.9
Hongrie	..	..	..	41.0	38.7	39.6	39.0	36.5	38.4	38.5
Islande	25.5	29.2	27.4	30.4	36.2	38.7	32.0	34.4	35.9	38.7
Irlande	24.5	27.9	33.7	31.8	30.9	30.4	27.6	27.4	29.0	29.9
Israel[3]	..	..	..	35.5	34.9	34.3	29.7	30.8	30.6	31.1
Italie	24.7	24.5	32.5	38.6	40.6	41.7	42.1	41.9	43.9	43.6
Japon	17.8	20.4	26.7	26.4	26.6	28.5	27.0	28.6	30.3	n.d.
Corée	..	14.9	15.8	19.1	21.5	24.8	23.8	24.2	24.3	24.6
Luxembourg	26.4	31.1	37.4	35.2	37.1	36.6	39.0	37.9	38.4	37.8
Mexique	..	..	15.2	14.9	16.5	17.6	17.2	19.5	19.7	19.5[4]
Pays-Bas	30.9	38.2	39.8	38.9	36.8	36.1	35.4	35.9	36.7	n.d.
Nouvelle-Zélande	23.2	27.5	29.5	35.6	32.5	34.0	30.5	30.9	31.4	32.4
Norvège	29.4	38.8	41.9	40.0	41.9	42.1	41.2	42.0	40.5	39.1
Pologne	..	..	..	37.7	33.1	34.8	31.5	32.0	31.9	n.d.
Portugal	15.7	18.9	24.1	29.4	31.2	32.0	30.0	32.5	34.5	34.4
République slovaque	..	..	..	39.6	33.6	29.2	28.9	28.7	30.4	31.0
Slovénie	..	..	..	38.4	36.6	37.1	36.2	36.5	36.8	36.6
Espagne[1]	14.3	18.0	26.8	31.3	33.4	36.5	29.8	31.3	32.7	33.2
Suède	31.4	38.9	44.8	45.6	49.0	45.0	44.1	42.5	42.8	42.7
Suisse	16.6	22.5	23.9	25.5	27.6	26.1	27.1	27.0	26.9	26.6
Turquie	10.6	12.0	11.5	16.8	24.2	24.1	24.6	27.8	29.3	28.7
Royaume-Uni	29.3	34.2	35.1	31.9	34.7	34.1	32.3	33.6	32.9	32.6
États-Unis	23.5	24.6	24.6	26.4	28.2	26.7	23.0	23.6	25.4	26.0
Moyenne non pondérée										
OCDE Total	**24.8**	**28.6**	**31.5**	**33.6**	**34.2**	**34.1**	**32.7**	**33.3**	**34.2**	**34.4**[5]

n.d. signifie non disponible.

1. Le total des recettes fiscales a été diminué du montant de tout transfert en capital représentant les recettes non collectées.
2. Allemagne unifiée à partir de 1991.
3. Les données statistiques concernant Israël sont fournies par et sous la responsabilité des autorités israéliennes compétentes. L'utilisation de ces données par l'OCDE est sans préjudice du statut des hauteurs du Golan, de Jérusalem Est et des colonies de peuplement israéliennes en Cisjordanie aux termes du droit international.
4. Estimation du Secrétariat, incluant les recettes escomptées collectées par les administrations d'État et locales.
5. Calculé en appliquant le pourcentage moyen non pondéré de variation pour 2014 dans les 30 pays qui ont communiqué des données pour cette année au ratio moyen global impôts/PIB en 2013.

StatLink http://dx.doi.org/10.1787/888933276565

- Entre 2013 et 2014, les hausses les plus prononcées du ratio ont été constatées au Danemark (3.3 points de pourcentage, en raison de la hausse des impôts sur le revenu en pourcentage du PIB) et en Islande (2.8 points, principalement causée par la hausse des recettes provenant des impôts sur les biens et services et l'augmentation des impôts sur le revenu). Les autres pays dont le ratio impôts/PIB a connu une augmentation substantielle entre 2013 et 2014 sont la Grèce (1.5 points), l'Estonie (1.1 points) et la Nouvelle-Zélande (1.0 points).

Tableau B. **Impôts sur le revenu et les bénéfices en % du PIB**

	1965	1975	1985	1995	2000	2007	2009	2011	2013	2014 provisional
Australie	10.5	14.2	15.2	15.6	17.7	17.7	14.4	15.5	15.7	n.d.
Autriche	8.6	9.5	10.7	10.8	12.0	12.2	11.5	11.7	12.3	12.7
Belgique	8.5	15.3	17.6	16.3	16.9	15.3	14.3	14.9	15.9	16.1
Canada	9.7	14.9	14.1	16.2	17.5	15.8	14.9	14.3	14.5	14.7
Chili	..	..	..	4.6	4.4	10.4	5.4	8.5	6.9	6.5
République tchèque	..	..	..	8.7	7.4	8.5	6.9	6.8	7.1	7.1
Danemark[1]	13.6	21.8	25.7	29.3	28.8	27.9	27.7	27.9	29.8	33.2
Estonie	..	..	..	10.9	7.7	7.4	7.4	6.4	7.2	7.6
Finlande	12.4	15.6	16.0	16.1	19.7	16.3	14.6	14.9	15.2	15.3
France[1]	5.3	5.5	6.7	6.8	10.7	10.1	8.6	9.8	10.9	10.5
Allemagne[2]	10.7	11.8	12.6	11.0	10.9	10.9	10.4	10.5	11.3	11.0
Grèce[1]	1.6	2.5	4.3	6.2	8.9	7.3	7.5	7.1	7.6	8.7
Hongrie	..	..	..	8.6	9.4	10.0	9.6	6.3	6.8	6.5
Islande	5.5	6.7	6.2	10.4	14.4	17.6	15.1	15.7	16.8	18.0
Irlande	6.3	8.4	11.6	12.8	13.5	12.5	10.7	10.7	11.7	12.1
Israel	..	..	..	12.5	13.9	12.6	9.0	9.3	9.7	9.7
Italie	4.4	5.3	12.0	13.6	13.5	14.1	13.7	13.4	14.5	14.2
Japon	7.8	9.1	12.2	10.1	9.3	10.4	8.0	8.6	9.8	9.8
Corée	..	3.6	4.2	5.8	6.2	7.9	6.8	7.3	7.1	7.2
Luxembourg	9.5	13.4	16.1	13.8	13.4	12.7	13.8	13.5	13.5	13.1
Mexique	..	..	3.4	3.7	4.5	4.9	4.9	5.3	6.0	5.8
Pays-Bas	11.0	13.3	10.5	10.3	9.3	10.2	10.0	9.6	9.1	n.d.
Nouvelle-Zélande	14.1	18.3	20.5	21.8	19.5	21.4	17.3	16.6	17.4	18.0
Norvège	12.8	13.4	16.6	14.1	18.8	20.2	18.9	20.5	18.7	16.9
Pologne	..	..	..	10.9	6.7	7.9	6.8	6.4	6.2	n.d.
Portugal	3.9	3.3	6.2	7.9	9.2	9.0	8.4	9.3	11.2	10.7
République slovaque	..	..	..	10.1	6.9	6.1	5.5	5.5	6.0	6.3
Slovénie	..	..	..	6.4	6.8	8.7	7.5	7.2	6.4	6.5
Espagne[1]	3.5	4.0	6.7	9.1	9.5	12.3	8.9	9.1	9.6	9.6
Suède	17.2	19.6	18.9	17.9	20.0	17.4	15.5	14.8	14.8	14.8
Suisse	6.8	10.7	11.0	11.1	12.2	12.1	12.7	12.5	12.4	12.3
Turquie	3.1	5.1	4.3	4.8	7.1	5.7	5.9	5.8	5.9	6.1
Royaume-Uni	10.8	15.3	13.6	11.8	13.5	13.4	12.4	12.3	11.7	11.4
États-Unis	11.3	11.3	11.2	12.0	14.1	12.9	9.2	10.7	12.0	12.5
Moyenne non pondérée										
OCDE Total	**8.7**	**10.9**	**11.8**	**11.5**	**12.2**	**12.3**	**11.0**	**11.1**	**11.5**	**11.7**[3]

n.d. signifie non disponible.

1. Le total des recettes fiscales a été diminué du montant de tout transfert en capital représentant les recettes non collectées.
2. Allemagne unifiée à partir de 1991.
3. Calculé en appliquant le pourcentage moyen non pondéré de variation pour 2014 dans les 30 pays qui ont communiqué des données pour cette année au ratio moyen global impôts/PIB en 2013.

StatLink http://dx.doi.org/10.1787/888933276573

- Entre 2013 et 2014, les diminutions les plus importantes du ratio concernent la Norvège (1.4 points de pourcentage à cause de la baisse des impôts sur le revenu et les bénéfices) et la République tchèque (0.8 points en raison de la baisse des impôts sur les biens et services). Le Luxembourg a vu son ratio décliner de 0.6 points de pourcentage.
- Le ratio fiscal en 2014 était encore inférieur de plus de 3 points de pourcentage à son niveau de 2007 (avant la récession) dans trois pays : Espagne, Israël et Norvège. La baisse la plus forte s'est produite en Espagne, où le ratio est passé de 36.5 % du PIB en 2007 à 33.2 % en 2014.

- La charge fiscale en Grèce a augmenté de 31.2 % à 35.9 % entre 2007 et 2014. Deux autres pays – Danemark et Turquie – ont enregistré des hausses de 4points de pourcentage, voire plus, au cours de la même période.

b. Données définitives relatives aux ratios fiscaux pour 2013

La dernière année pour laquelle on dispose de ratios des recettes fiscales rapportées au PIB fondés sur des recettes fiscales définitives pour tous les pays de l'OCDE est 2013 (graphique A). Les chiffres montrent que ces ratios diffèrent fortement selon les pays.

- En 2013, le Danemark avait le ratio des recettes fiscales rapportées au PIB le plus élevé (47.6 %), suivi par la France, la Belgique et l'Italie.
- Au contraire, huit pays – l'Australie, le Chili, la Corée, les États-Unis, l'Irlande, le Mexique, la Suisse et la Turquie – enregistraient des niveaux d'imposition inférieurs à 30 %.
- Le Mexique avait le ratio le plus faible (19.7 %), suivi du Chili (20.0 %).

Depuis 2011, le ratio des recettes fiscales rapportées au PIB dans la zone OCDE (moyenne non pondérée) a augmenté de 0.9 points pour atteindre 34.2 % en 2013 (voir le Tableau A).

- Par rapport à 2011, la charge fiscale a augmenté dans 27 pays membres de l'OCDE et a diminué dans 7 pays.
- Les augmentations les plus importantes ont été constatées au Danemark (2.2 points de pourcentage), en France (2.1 points), en Italie et au Portugal (2.0 points).
- Six autres pays – Belgique, États-Unis, Finlande, Hongrie, Japon et République slovaque – ont enregistré des augmentations comprises entre 1.7 et 1.9 points de pourcentage entre 2011 et 2013.
- Les diminutions les plus marquées ont été constatées en Norvège (1.5 points de pourcentage) et au Chili (1.2 points).

Les principaux changements affectant le ratio des recettes fiscales rapportées au PIB pour les grandes rubriques d'impôt entre 2011 et 2013 sont les suivants :

- Les recettes des impôts sur le revenu des personnes physiques et sur les bénéfices des sociétés exprimées en pourcentage du PIB ont en moyenne augmenté de 11.1 % en 2011 à 11.5 % en 2013. Les augmentations les plus importantes ont eu lieu au Danemark et au Portugal (1.9 points). La Norvège et le Chili ont enregistré la diminution la plus forte de ce taux, respectivement de 1.8 et 1.6 points de PIB (Tableau B).
- Il y a eu des augmentations du ratio des recettes fiscales rapportées au PIB pour les catégories suivantes :
  - Cotisations de sécurité sociale: augmentation de 8.9% à 9.1 % (Tableau 13).
  - Impôts sur le patrimoine: augmentation de 1.8% à 1.9 % (Tableau 21).
  - Impôts sur les biens et services: augmentation de 10.8 % à 11.0 % (Tableau 23).
- Le ratio est resté inchangé pour les impôts sur les salaires à 0.4 % du PIB en 2011 et 2013 (Tableau 19).

Les niveaux globaux d'imposition tiennent souvent une place essentielle dans les débats politiques et sont parfois directement associés à l'efficacité économique des nations. Une Étude spéciale qui figurait dans la section S.2 de l'édition 1999 de ce rapport expliquait pourquoi les chiffres relatifs aux niveaux d'imposition doivent être interprétés avec prudence. Plus précisément, les directives révisées énoncées dans le Système des comptes nationaux (SCN) de 2008 qui sont utilisées pour estimer le PIB de 31 des 34 pays membres de l'OCDE ont eu pour effet d'accroître son niveau. En conséquence, les ratios impôts/PIB révisés présentés dans cette publication sont systématiquement inférieurs aux ratios rapportés avant ces changements. Afin de limiter cet effet de distorsion pour la période concernée, on a utilisé dans la présente édition du rapport des estimations du PIB révisé pour 1965 et les années suivantes quand les pays de l'OCDE n'ont pas fourni de chiffres révisés du PIB. La section « Questions méthodologiques » ci-dessous examine plus en détail l'ampleur des révisions du PIB.

c. *Variations de la pression fiscale entre 1965 et 2013*

L'évolution des coefficients de pression fiscale entre 1965 et 2013 est la suivante :

- Le coefficient moyen dans la zone OCDE a augmenté de 24.8 % à 34.2 % (9.4 points) entre 1965 et 2013 (Tableau 2).
- L'évolution historique des ratios d'imposition dans les différents pays de l'OCDE varie fortement, comme le montrent les graphiques B, C, D et E. Chaque graphique rapproche les évolutions observées dans les différents pays du niveau d'imposition moyen de la zone OCDE respectivement pour les périodes 1965-75, 1975-85, 1985-95 et 1995-2013. Bien que les recettes fiscales totales exprimées en pourcentage du PIB aient augmenté en moyenne dans les pays de l'OCDE, le ratio d'imposition a baissé dans certains pays.
- Entre 1965 et 1975, la charge fiscale dans la zone OCDE a augmenté de 3.8 points (graphique B). Jusqu'au premier choc pétrolier (1973-74), une croissance des revenus forte et presque ininterrompue a permis aux niveaux d'imposition d'augmenter dans tous les pays de l'OCDE. Les niveaux d'imposition ont augmenté automatiquement sous l'effet de la progressivité des barèmes de l'impôt sur le revenu des personnes physiques.
- Entre 1975 et 1985, la charge fiscale dans la zone OCDE a augmenté de 2.9 points (graphique C). Après le milieu des années 70, le ralentissement de la croissance des revenus réels, combiné à l'augmentation du chômage, ont limité la capacité des pouvoirs publics à prélever des recettes. Cependant, à partir de la profonde récession qui a suivi le second choc pétrolier (1980), les pays européens ont été amenés à augmenter leurs impôts pour financer la hausse des dépenses de sécurité sociale et s'efforcer de maîtriser les déficits budgétaires.
- Entre 1985 et 1995, la charge fiscale dans la zone OCDE a de nouveau augmenté de 2.1 points (graphique D). Après le milieu des années 80, la plupart des pays de l'OCDE ont sensiblement réduit les taux de leurs impôts sur le revenu des personnes physiques et sur les bénéfices des sociétés, mais l'incidence sur les recettes publiques des vastes réformes fiscales qui ont été engagées est restée limitée dans la mesure où, en même temps, la base de ces impôts était élargie par une réduction ou une suppression des déductions fiscales.
- Entre 1995 et 2000, le taux moyen d'imposition dans la zone OCDE a atteint 34.2 %, soit le niveau le plus élevé enregistré à cette époque. Il s'est ensuite légèrement replié entre 2001 et 2004, avant de repartir à la hausse entre 2005 et 2007, puis de retomber sous l'effet de la crise. En résumé, la charge fiscale moyenne dans la zone OCDE a augmenté de 0.1 point entre 1995 et 2012 (graphique E).
- Ces moyennes concernant l'ensemble de la zone OCDE dissimulent la grande variété des charges fiscales nationales. En 1965, les niveaux d'imposition étaient compris entre 10.6 % en Turquie et 33.6 % en France. En 2013, ces niveaux oscillaient entre 19.7 % au

Mexique et 47.6 % au Danemark. La tendance continue à l'augmentation des niveaux d'imposition reflète le besoin de financer la hausse marquée des dépenses du secteur public dans presque tous les pays de l'OCDE.

B. Structures fiscales

Les structures fiscales sont mesurées par la part des principaux impôts dans les recettes fiscales totales. Si, en moyenne, les niveaux d'imposition ont généralement augmenté, la part des principaux impôts dans les recettes totales – la structure fiscale ou le « dosage » des impôts – a fait preuve d'une stabilité remarquable dans le temps. Néanmoins, plusieurs tendances se manifestent jusqu'en 2013 (dernière année pour laquelle on dispose de données concernant les 34 pays de l'OCDE) (Tableau C).

Tableau C. **Structure fiscale dans la zone OCDE**

	1965	1975	1985	1995	2005	2010	2013
Impôts sur le revenu des personnes physiques	26	30	30	26	24	24	25
Impôts sur les bénéfices des sociétés	9	8	8	8	10	8	8
Cotisation de sécurité sociale [1]	18	22	22	25	25	26	26
(employé)	*(6)*	*(7)*	*(7)*	*(9)*	*(9)*	*(9)*	*(10)*
(employeur)	*(10)*	*(14)*	*(13)*	*(14)*	*(14)*	*(15)*	*(15)*
Impôts sur les salaires et la main d'oeuvre	1	1	1	1	1	1	1
Impôts sur le patrimoine	8	6	5	5	6	5	6
Impôts généraux sur la consommation	12	13	16	19	20	20	20
Impôts sur des biens et services déterminés	24	18	16	13	11	11	10
Autres [2]	2	2	2	3	3	3	3
Total	**100**	**100**	**100**	**100**	**100**	**100**	**100**

Note : Part des principales catégories d'impôts dans les recettes fiscales totales (en pourcentage). Les données sont incluses depuis 1965 pour l'Australie, l'Autriche, la Belgique, le Canada, le Danemark, la Finlande, la France, l'Allemagne, la Grèce, l'Islande, l'Irlande, l'Italie, le Japon, le Luxembourg, les Pays-Bas, la Nouvelle-Zélande, la Norvège, le Portugal, l'Espagne, la Suède, la Suisse, la Turquie, le Royaume-Uni et les États-Unis. Les données sont incluses depuis 1972 pour la Corée, depuis 1980 pour le Mexique, depuis 1990 pour le Chili, depuis 1991 pour la Hongrie et la Pologne, depuis 1993 pour la République tchèque, depuis 1995 pour l'Estonie, Israël, la République slovaque et la Slovénie.

1. Y compris les cotisations de sécurité sociale versées par les travailleurs indépendants et les bénéficiaires (rubrique 2300) qui n'apparaissent pas dans la ventilation entre salariés et employeurs.
2. Y compris certaines taxes sur les biens et services (rubrique 5200) et droits de timbre.

Source : OCDE (2015), « Recettes fiscales : Tableaux comparatifs », *Base de données des Statistiques fiscales de l'OCDE*, DOI: *http://dx.doi.org/10.1787/data-00262-fr*.

StatLink http://dx.doi.org/10.1787/888933276582

Impôts sur le revenu et les bénéfices

- En moyenne, les pays de l'OCDE collectent 33.7% de leurs recettes fiscales via les impôts sur le revenu et les bénéfices (somme des impôts sur le revenu des personnes physiques et sur les bénéfices des sociétés, Tableau 8). Ces impôts restent la principale source de recettes utilisées pour financer les dépenses publiques dans quinze des pays de l'OCDE, tandis que dans neuf d'entre eux – Australie, Canada, Danemark, États-Unis, Irlande, Islande, Norvège, Nouvelle-Zélande et Suisse – leur part dans le total des impôts excède 40 % (Tableau 6).
- En 2013, les recettes issues de l'impôt sur le revenu des personnes physiques représentent en moyenne 25 % du total des recettes, contre 30 % environ au cours des années 80 (Tableau 10). Dans cette baisse, deux points environ peuvent être attribués à l'inclusion dans la zone OCDE de pays d'Europe de l'Est pour lesquels les données relatives aux recettes fiscales ne sont disponibles qu'à partir des années 90. Dans ces

pays, les recettes générées par l'impôt sur le revenu sont relativement faibles, alors que celles liées aux cotisations de sécurité sociale sont plus élevées, mais l'effet de l'inclusion de ces pays concerne seulement les données postérieures à l'année 1990.

- Les différences observées entre les pays sont considérables pour ce qui est de l'importance de l'impôt sur le revenu des personnes physiques. En 2013, la part de cet impôt allait d'un minimum de 10% à 11 % respectivement en République tchèque et en République slovaque, à 39 % en Australie et 55 % au Danemark (Tableau 10).
- La forte baisse de la part des recettes tirées des impôts sur les bénéfices des sociétés dans le total des recettes fiscales constatée en 2008 et 2009 ne s'est pas poursuivie en 2011 et 2012, mais la part de ces impôts dans le total des prélèvements en 2012, soit 9 %, reste inférieure à leur niveau de 2007, lorsqu'elle s'établissait à 11 % (Tableau 12).
- La part des impôts sur les bénéfices des sociétés dans les recettes fiscales totales affiche une dispersion considérable, de 3-4 % (Grèce, Hongrie et Slovénie) à 18 % (Australie) et 22 % (Norvège). Hormis la dispersion des taux légaux d'imposition des sociétés, ces différences sont au moins partiellement imputables à des facteurs institutionnels ou à l'exploitation des gisements de minerai, par exemple :
  - la proportion des entreprises constituées sous forme de sociétés,
  - la taxation des recettes pétrolières,
  - l'érosion de la base d'imposition des sociétés consécutive, par exemple, à des méthodes généreuses de calcul de l'amortissement,
  - d'autres instruments permettant de différer l'imposition des bénéfices.

Cotisations de sécurité sociale

- En 2013, les cotisations de sécurité sociale représentaient 26 % du total des recettes fiscales. Elles étaient les plus élevées en République tchèque et en République slovaque (43-44 %). En revanche, l'Australie et la Nouvelle-Zélande ne collectent pas de cotisations de sécurité sociale (Tableau 14). On observe par ailleurs de grandes différences entre les pays de l'OCDE pour ce qui est des parts relatives des cotisations de sécurité sociale versées par les salariés et par les employeurs (voir les Tableaux 16 et 18).

Impôts sur le patrimoine

- Entre 1965 et 2013, la part des impôts sur le patrimoine a été ramenée en moyenne de 8 % à 6 % du total des recettes fiscales.
- En termes relatifs, la part des impôts sur le patrimoine est supérieure à 10 % du total des recettes fiscales dans quatre pays : Canada, Corée, États-Unis et Royaume-Uni (Tableau 22).

Impôts sur la consommation

- La part des impôts sur la consommation (impôts généraux sur la consommation plus impôts spécifiques sur la consommation) a diminué de 36 % à 31 % entre 1965 et 2013 (Tableau 26).
- Pendant cette période, la composition des taxes sur les biens et services s'est profondément modifié. Les impôts généraux sur la consommation ont vu leur importance en tant que source de recettes s'affirmer rapidement, notamment pour la taxe sur la valeur ajoutée (TVA) qui est désormais appliquée dans 33 des 34 pays de l'OCDE.

- Les impôts généraux sur la consommation représentent actuellement 20 % des recettes fiscales totales, contre seulement 12 % au milieu des années 60 (Tableau 28).
- En fait, la montée en puissance de la taxe sur la valeur ajoutée a contribué à compenser la diminution de la part des impôts spécifiques sur la consommation, tels que les droits d'accise et les droits de douane.
  - Entre 1965 et 2013, la part des impôts spécifiques sur la consommation (surtout sur le tabac, les boissons alcoolisées et le carburant, y compris certaines taxes environnementales récemment instaurées) a été réduite de plus de la moitié.
  - Les taux des impôts sur les produits importés ont fortement baissé dans tous les pays, ce qui s'explique par la tendance générale à la suppression des obstacles aux échanges.
  - Néanmoins, le Mexique (environ 32 %) et la Turquie (environ 22 %) collectent encore une part relativement importante de leurs recettes fiscales totales sous forme de taxes sur des biens et services spécifiques (Tableau 30).

C. Répartition des impôts par niveaux d'administration

Le Tableau Dindique la part relative des recettes fiscales attribuées aux différents sous-secteurs des administrations publiques et son évolution au cours de la période 1975-2013.

Pays fédéraux et régionaux

- En 2013, dans les huit pays fédéraux de l'OCDE, la part des recettes de l'administration centrale variait de 31 % en Allemagne à 80 % en Australie et au Mexique.
- En 2013, la part des collectivités régionales ou provinciales s'échelonnait entre 2 % en Autriche, 3 % au Mexique, 6 % en Belgique et 40 % au Canada. La part des collectivités locales était comprise entre 1 % au Mexique et 15 % en Suisse et aux États-Unis.
- Entre 1975 et 2013, la part des recettes de l'administration fédérale a reculé d'environ huit points de pourcentage en Belgique, tandis qu'elle a décliné moins rapidement en Allemagne, au Canada et aux États-Unis.
- La part des recettes de l'administration fédérale a augmenté en Autriche et en Suisse respectivement de 15 et 5 points. Il y a eu peu de changement en Australie et au Mexique.
- La part des caisses de sécurité sociale a augmenté dans cinq des sept pays fédéraux, à l'exception du Canada et du Mexique où elle a légèrement diminué.
- L'Espagne est maintenant classée dans la catégorie « pays régional » plutôt que dans celle des « pays unitaires » à cause de sa structure politique fortement décentralisée. En 2013, la part des recettes de l'administration centrale était de 42 %, contre 14 % pour les collectivités régionales. Entre 1975 et 2013, la part des recettes des collectivités locales a augmenté de 4 % à 10 % et la part des caisses de sécurité sociale a baissé de 48 % à 34 %.

Pays unitaires

- Dans les pays unitaires de l'OCDE, la part des recettes de l'administration centrale en 2013 se situait entre 34 % en France et 35% au Japon, et 93 % en Nouvelle-Zélande.
- La part des collectivités locales variait de 1 % en République tchèque à 37 % en Suède.
- Entre 1975 et 2013, les transferts aux collectivités locales ont augmenté de 5 points ou plus dans six pays – Corée, France, Islande, Italie, Portugal et Suède, mais ont moins

Tableau D. **Répartition des recettes fiscales entre les sous-secteurs de l'Administration en % du total des recettes fiscales**

	Supranationale			Administration centrale			Administration d'un Etat/Régions			Administrations locales			Administrations de sécurité sociale		
	1975	1995	2013	1975	1995	2013	1975	1995	2013	1975	1995	2013	1975	1995	2013
Pays fédéraux															
Australie	..	..	..	80.1	77.5	80.8	15.7	19.0	15.8	4.2	3.4	3.4	0.0	0.0	0.0
Autriche	..	0.0	0.3	51.7	64.8	66.5	10.6	1.8	1.6	12.4	4.1	3.2	25.3	29.3	28.4
Belgique	1.4	1.0	0.7	65.3	60.2	57.1	..	1.8	5.5	4.4	4.8	4.7	28.8	32.1	32.0
Canada	..	..	..	47.6	39.1	41.6	32.5	37.1	39.6	9.9	9.8	9.3	10.0	14.0	9.4
Allemagne	1.2	0.6	0.4	33.5	31.4	31.4	22.3	21.6	21.9	9.0	7.4	8.2	34.0	39.0	38.1
Mexique	..	..	..	..	80.1	80.1	..	2.1	3.1	..	1.1	1.2	..	16.6	15.5
Suisse	..	..	..	30.7	31.4	35.2	27.0	23.8	24.6	20.3	17.6	15.2	22.0	27.3	25.1
Etats-Unis	..	..	..	45.4	41.3	41.2	19.5	20.1	20.2	14.7	13.4	14.5	20.5	25.2	24.2
Moyenne non pondérée	1.3	0.6	0.5	50.6	53.2	54.2	21.3	15.9	16.5	10.7	7.7	7.5	20.1	22.9	21.6
Pays régional															
Espagne[1]	..	0.5	0.4	48.2	50.4	42.1	..	4.8	13.7	4.3	8.5	9.9	47.5	35.8	34.0
Pays unitaires															
Chili	..	..	..	..	89.9	87.0	..	..	..	..	6.5	7.3	..	3.6	5.7
République tchèque	..	..	0.4	..	57.7	55.2	..	..	..	..	0.9	1.3	..	41.4	43.2
Danemark	1.1	0.5	0.3	68.9	68.2	73.3	..	..	..	30.0	31.3	26.3	0.1	0.0	0.1
Finlande	..	..	0.5	..	72.1	69.5	..	..	..	..	13.1	13.3	..	14.8	16.7
Estonie	..	0.4	0.2	56.0	46.6	47.6	..	..	..	23.5	22.3	23.4	20.4	30.8	28.9
France	0.7	0.4	0.2	51.2	42.3	33.6	..	..	..	7.6	11.0	12.9	40.6	46.3	53.3
Grèce	..	0.6	0.2	67.1	66.8	63.6	..	..	..	3.4	0.9	5.6	29.5	31.7	30.5
Hongrie	..	..	0.2	..	63.8	60.5	..	..	..	..	2.5	5.9	..	33.6	33.3
Islande	..	..	..	81.3	79.2	73.4	..	..	..	18.7	20.8	26.6	0.0	0.0	0.0
Irlande	2.3	1.5	0.5	77.4	83.1	82.0	..	..	..	7.3	2.7	3.1	13.1	12.7	14.4
Israel	..	..	..	..	80.0	76.1	..	..	..	..	5.9	7.3	..	14.1	16.6
Italie	..	0.4	0.3	53.2	62.7	53.8	..	..	..	0.9	5.4	16.2	45.9	31.5	29.8
Japon	..	..	..	45.4	41.2	35.0	..	..	..	25.6	25.3	24.2	29.0	33.5	40.9
Corée	..	..	..	89.0	69.2	58.1	..	..	..	10.1	18.7	15.5	0.9	12.1	26.4
Luxembourg	0.8	0.4	0.1	63.6	67.1	68.4	..	..	..	6.7	6.4	3.5	29.0	26.1	28.0
Pays-Bas	1.5	1.2	1.0	58.9	54.1	54.4	..	..	..	1.2	2.7	3.7	38.4	42.0	40.8
Nouvelle-Zélande	..	..	..	92.3	94.7	93.3	..	..	..	7.7	5.3	6.7	0.0	0.0	0.0
Norvège	..	..	..	50.6	58.4	86.9	..	..	..	22.4	19.6	13.1	27.0	22.0	0.0
Pologne	..	..	0.3	..	61.9	48.2	..	..	..	..	8.3	12.9	..	29.8	38.6
Portugal	..	1.3	0.7	65.4	71.9	67.6	..	..	..	0.0	5.4	7.0	34.6	21.4	24.7
République slovaque	..	..	0.5	..	62.5	53.6	..	..	..	..	1.3	2.9	..	36.2	43.1
Slovénie	..	..	0.4	..	51.8	49.1	..	..	..	..	6.3	10.8	..	41.9	39.7
Suède	..	0.4	0.3	51.3	46.9	49.9	..	..	..	29.2	30.9	36.9	19.5	21.8	12.8
Turquie	..	..	..	..	75.1	63.8	..	..	..	..	12.8	8.8	..	12.1	27.4
Royaume-Uni	1.0	1.0	0.5	70.5	77.5	75.8	..	..	..	11.1	3.7	4.9	17.5	17.8	18.8
Moyenne non pondérée	1.2	0.7	0.4	65.1	65.8	63.2	..	..	..	12.8	10.8	12.0	21.6	23.1	24.6

1. L'Espagne est constitutionnellement un pays non fédéral mais avec une structure politique très décentralisée.

StatLink http://dx.doi.org/10.1787/888933276590

progressé aux Pays-Bas. Une diminution des transferts de 5 points ou plus s'est produite dans deux pays – Norvège et Royaume-Uni.

- Entre 1975 et 2013, la part des caisses de sécurité sociale a progressé de 7 points ou plus dans quatre pays – Corée, Finlande, France et Japon –, tandis qu'elle enregistrait des baisses du même ordre de grandeur dans trois pays – Italie, Norvège et Portugal. Entre 1995 et 2013, cette part a augmenté de 7 points ou plus dans deux autres pays (Pologne et Turquie).

- Les directives suivies pour attribuer ces parts des recettes aux différents niveaux d'administration s'appuient sur la version finale du Système des comptes nationaux de 2008. Ces directives sont examinées dans l'Étude spéciale S.1 de l'édition 2011 des Statistiques des recettes publiques de l'OCDE.

États membres de l'UE dans l'OCDE

- Dans le tableau D, la colonne « supranationale » donne le montant des impôts collectés pour le compte de l'Union européenne par les 21 États membres de l'UE qui sont membres de l'OCDE. Pour les années antérieures à 1998, les droits de douane collectés pour le compte de l'Union européenne par les administrations fiscales des États membres de l'UE figurent dans la rubrique 5123. À partir de 1998, ces droits de douane sont indiqués en tant que poste « pour mémoire » car ils sont en fait imposés par l'Union européenne et collectés pour son compte par les administrations fiscales nationales. Toutefois, ils continuent de faire partie du total des recettes fiscales collectées dans les États membres de l'UE. Cette approche permet d'assurer la cohérence des séries chronologiques et évite que les ratios des recettes fiscales aux PIB subissent les effets des changements de la part relative des droits de douane dans 1) la composition des ressources de financement de l'UE et 2) la composition des différents impôts des États membres de l'UE. Le Tableau E résume les montants de ces droits de douane.

Tableau E. **Droits de douanes collectés pour le compte de l'Union européenne**

En millions de monnaie nationale

	2000	2005	2008	2009	2011	2012	2013	2014[2]
Autriche[1]	356	325	371	320	378	344	328	368
Belgique[1]	960	1 208	1 420	1 147	1 316	1 284	1 230	1 307
République tchèque	..	5 586	6 323	5 548	6 961	6 172	5 544	6 968
Danemark	2 325	2 833	3 106	2 647	3 177	2 962	2 926	3 001
Estonie[1]	..	22	33	20	29	29	29	30
Finlande[1]	129	148	205	152	189	184	166	170
France[1]	1 513	1 583	1 615	1 461	1 866	1 883	1 842	1 827
Allemagne[1]	3 394	3 433	4 036	3 778	4 556	4 417	4 251	4 608
Grèce[1]	210	262	305	252	186	162	148	165
Hongrie	..	26 572	26 689	25 657	27 462	27 206	26 337	31 947
Irlande[1]	208	226	245	208	240	242	247	275
Italie[1]	1 536	1 785	2 200	2 008	2 319	2 077	1 890	2 022
Luxembourg[1]	27	21	18	13	17	15	15	19
Pays-Bas[1]	1 310	1 265	1 788	1 518	1 997	2 159	2 210	2 258
Pologne	..	1 098	1 572	1 308	1 447	1 611	1 613	n.d.
Portugal[1]	204	145	177	154	168	155	144	147
République slovaque[1]	..	75	156	111	157	129	115	127
Slovénie[1]	..	34	76	57	62	54	52	52
Espagne[1]	970	1 436	1 578	1 328	1 554	1 436	1 316	1 512
Suède	3 450	4 327	5 212	4 764	5 399	4 995	4 976	5 737
Royaume-Uni	1 800	1 908	2 297	2 435	2 925	2 885	2 914	2 949

n.d. signifie non disponible.

1. Pour les pays de la zone euro, les montants sont exprimés en euros pour toutes les années.
2. Estimations.

StatLink http://dx.doi.org/10.1787/888933276609

D. Impact de la révision des données du PIB sur les niveaux d'imposition déclarés

Les coefficients de pression fiscale qui figurent dans ce rapport expriment les recettes fiscales globales en pourcentage du PIB. Il est important de tenir compte du fait que la valeur de ce ratio dépend de son dénominateur (PIB) et de son numérateur (recettes fiscales), le dénominateur étant sujet à des révisions historiques.

Le numérateur (recettes fiscales)

- En ce qui concerne le numérateur, le Secrétariat de l'OCDE utilise pour ce rapport les données relatives aux recettes fiscales qui lui sont fournies annuellement par les correspondants des ministères des Finances, des administrations fiscales nationales ou des services nationaux de statistiques. Bien que pour la plupart des pays, des chiffres provisoires soient disponibles avec un décalage d'environ six mois, les données finalisées le sont dans un délai d'environ dix-huit mois. Ainsi, les données définitives pour 2013 ont été reçues entre mai et août 2015.
- Dans trente pays de l'OCDE, l'année fiscale coïncide avec l'année civile. Elle en diffère dans quatre pays : Australie, Canada, Japon et Nouvelle-Zélande. Les déclarations pour l'année 2013 couvrent respectivement T2/2013-T1/2014 (Canada, Japon) et T3/2013-T2/2014 (Australie, Nouvelle-Zélande) (T = trimestre).

Le dénominateur (PIB)

- En ce qui concerne le dénominateur, ce rapport utilise les chiffres du PIB les plus récents dont on disposait au 1 septembre 2015. À cette date, les chiffres du PIB pour 2013 et 2014 étaient disponibles pour tous les pays de l'OCDE.
- L'utilisation de ces PIB harmonisés assure un maximum de cohérence et de comparabilité internationale aux ratios impôts/PIB.
- Les chiffres du PIB proviennent des Comptes nationaux annuels des pays membres de l'OCDE (CNA-SCN) pour les trente pays où l'année fiscale coïncide avec l'année civile.
- Lorsque l'année fiscale diffère de l'année civile, les estimations annuelles du PIB sont obtenues par l'agrégation des données fournies par la Direction des statistiques de l'OCDE pour les trimestres correspondants aux années fiscales de chacun des pays. Par exemple, dans le cas du Canada : T2/2013-T1/2014.

Révisions du numérateur et du dénominateur

Le numérateur (recettes fiscales) et le dénominateur du ratio (PIB) sont tous deux sujets à révision lorsque des données plus récentes sont disponibles. Une telle révision influe directement sur les coefficients de pression fiscale publiés.

- Si les recettes fiscales sont révisées à la hausse alors que le PIB demeure inchangé, le coefficient augmente.
- Si le montant du PIB est révisé à la baisse, le coefficient augmente aussi même si les recettes fiscales n'ont pas augmenté.
- À l'inverse, un PIB plus élevé entraîne un coefficient plus faible même si le montant des impôts collectés n'a pas varié.
- Pour les années les plus récentes en particulier, les montants des recettes ont pu faire l'objet de révisions peu fréquentes et de faible ampleur. Les données concernant le PIB

sont révisées et mises à jour plus fréquemment, mais pas nécessairement pour tous les pays en même temps, reflétant l'utilisation de sources et de procédures d'estimation plus fiables. En général, ces révisions ont une incidence assez limitée sur les ratios impôts/PIB.

- Toutefois, les chiffres du PIB peuvent parfois changer de façon plus fondamentale lorsque sont introduites au plan international de nouvelles procédures de calcul du PIB. Le changement le plus récent est la mise en œuvre du Système de comptabilité nationale de 2008 (SCN 2008) qui a maintenant largement remplacé son prédécesseur, le Système de comptabilité nationale de 1993 (SCN 1993). Une version plus ancienne du Système de comptabilité nationale a été mise en place en 1968.
- Les 21 pays de l'OCDE qui sont membres de l'UE sont tenus de se conformer au Système européen de comptes économiques intégrés (SEC) pour le calcul de leur PIB. Le SEC constitue essentiellement un approfondissement du SCN, bien qu'il en diffère sur certains points mineurs sans importance pour ce rapport. À la suite de la révision du SCN en 2008, le SEC de 1995 a été remplacé par le SEC de 2010.
- Jusqu'à présent, les chiffres du PIB présentés dans cette publication se fondent sur le SCN 2008 pour 31 pays. Les exceptions sont le Chili, le Japon, et la Turquie qui suivront lors des prochains mois. À l'exception de quelques chiffres concernant certaines années, les montants du PIB pour ces trente et un pays sont plus élevés suite à l'application du nouveau SCN. Ceci s'explique par les changements méthodologiques et aussi par l'amélioration des sources des données.
- Les chiffres des recettes fiscales publiés dans les *Statistiques des recettes publiques* ont été peu affectés par les changements de définitions et de normes intervenus dans le SCN/SEC. Néanmoins, il y a eu des ajustements dans certains pays qui ont saisi l'occasion d'améliorer les sources des données et les méthodologies de compilation des chiffres de comptabilité nationale (incluant les recettes fiscales). Ces changements dans les recettes fiscales ont le plus souvent été moins marqués que ceux associés aux chiffres du PIB et les ratios ont en règle générale diminué pour les pays qui ont appliqué le système révisé. Ces questions sont discutées plus en détail dans l'étude spéciale S.1. figurant dans ce rapport.
- Un problème particulier soulevé par la révision des systèmes SCN 2008/SEC 2010 est que la période couverte par les révisions du PIB varie selon les pays. Afin de limiter cet effet de distorsion, la Direction des statistiques de l'OCDE et le Centre de politique et d'administration fiscales ont calculé des estimations du PIB révisées pour 1965 et les années suivantes quand les pays de l'OCDE n'ont pas fourni de chiffres révisés du PIB.

Note

1. Calculé en appliquant le pourcentage moyen non pondéré de variation pour 2014 dans les 30 pays qui ont communiqué des données pour cette année au ratio moyen global impôts/PIB en 2013.

Étude spéciale S.1. Effets de l'adoption du système des Comptes nationaux (SCN) de 2008 sur le calcul des ratios impôts-produit intérieur brut (PIB)

Résumé

En 2009, la Commission de statistique des Nations Unies a adopté un ensemble révisé de normes internationales pour l'établissement des comptes nationaux, baptisé SCN 2008, qui a remplacé la précédente version, SCN 1993. Peu après, la révision de l'équivalent européen du SCN a conduit à la définition du système européen de comptes nationaux (SEC) 2010. Les normes SEC 2010 sont compatibles avec le SCN 2008, à de rares exceptions près.

Cette Étude spéciale analyse les effets de l'adoption des nouvelles normes SCN 2008 sur les données relatives au PIB et aux niveaux d'imposition des pays concernés. Les principales observations sont les suivantes :

- *L'adoption des normes SCN 2008/SEC 2010 a entraîné une baisse d'environ un point de pourcentage du ratio moyen recettes fiscales-PIB dans la zone OCDE*[1]*, un écart resté stable entre 2000 et 2013.*
- *L'adoption des nouvelles normes a donné lieu à une variation marquée du PIB dans les pays de l'OCDE, avec une révision à la hausse moyenne de 3.8 %. L'ampleur de cette révision a différé sensiblement selon les pays, s'échelonnant entre 7.8 % pour la Corée et 0.2 % pour le Luxembourg.*
- *La révision à la hausse moyenne de 3.8 % s'explique comme suit : 3.1 % découlent du passage aux nouvelles normes internationales, et 0.7 % d'une remise à niveau des données statistiques de référence (améliorations des sources de données ou des méthodologies de comptabilité à l'échelon national). Les modifications apportées aux normes internationales sont le principal facteur explicatif dans 25 des 31 pays concernés.*
- *L'évolution des normes internationales découlant du nouveau référentiel SCN/SEC a eu des effets limités, voire nuls, sur les données relatives aux recettes fiscales présentées dans les Statistiques des recettes publiques de l'OCDE. Dans certains pays, toutefois, le niveau des recettes fiscales a été modifié sous l'effet de la remise à niveau des données statistiques de référence.*
- *Les effets de ces changements sur les ratios recettes fiscales-PIB sont eux aussi très différents d'un pays membre à l'autre. La révision la plus importante est observée aux Pays-Bas (-2.8 points de pourcentage), alors que le ratio a été revu à la hausse de 0.9 point de pourcentage au Luxembourg. Dans la plupart des pays, la révision du niveau du PIB a eu plus d'impact sur le ratio recettes fiscales-PIB que la variation des données relatives aux recettes fiscales.*

1. Introduction

En 2009, la Commission de statistique des Nations Unies a adopté un ensemble révisé de normes internationales pour l'établissement des comptes nationaux, baptisé SCN 2008, qui a remplacé la précédente version, SCN 1993. Peu après, l'équivalent européen du SCN a été également modifié, ce qui a conduit à la mise en place du SEC 2010. Les normes SEC 2010 sont compatibles avec le SCN 2008 à de rares exceptions près.

Le calendrier de mise en œuvre effective des nouvelles normes dépend du contexte propre à chaque pays. À la date de la compilation des données permettant de calculer les ratios recettes fiscales-PIB publiés dans les *Statistiques des recettes publiques* de l'OCDE, 29 des 34 pays membres de l'OCDE avaient adopté la nouvelle méthodologie, selon la chronologie suivante :

- 2009 – Australie
- 2012 – Canada
- 2013 – États-Unis, Israël et Mexique
- 2014 – Allemagne, Autriche, Belgique, Corée, Danemark, Espagne, Estonie, Finlande, France, Grèce, Hongrie, Irlande, Islande, Italie, Luxembourg, Pays-Bas, Pologne, Portugal, République slovaque, République tchèque, Royaume-Uni, Slovénie, Suède et Suisse.

Parmi les cinq pays restants, la Nouvelle-Zélande et la Norvège ont adopté les normes révisées fin 2014, la Turquie prévoit une mise en œuvre des normes en 2015, le Chili et le Japon en 2016.

Cette situation a eu des conséquences directes sur la mesure du PIB et, partant, sur les ratios recettes fiscales-PIB figurant dans les bases de données des *Statistiques des recettes publiques* de l'OCDE. Cette Étude spéciale examine :

- L'ampleur des variations observées dans le niveau du PIB et des ratios recettes fiscales-PIB des pays de l'OCDE qui ont mis en œuvre le SCN 2008 ou le SEC 2010.
- Les causes sous-jacentes de ces variations.
- Les relations entre les changements constatés dans les données du PIB et ceux qui en découlent dans le ratio recettes fiscales-PIB

Les effets de l'adoption du nouveau SCN sont illustrés par le graphique S1 qui compare les deux séries correspondant au ratio moyen recettes fiscales-PIB dans les pays de l'OCDE, depuis 2000, figurant respectivement dans les éditions de 2013 et de 2014 des *Statistiques des recettes publiques* de l'OCDE. Cette comparaison est proposée uniquement à titre d'exemple car elle rend en compte des effets observés sur les statistiques dans 26 pays seulement, à savoir les 24 pays qui avaient adopté les nouvelles normes en 2014, plus Israël et le Mexique. Les deux séries de données prennent en compte les incidences de ces nouvelles normes dans trois autres pays qui les ont adoptées avant 2014 (l'Australie, le Canada et les États-Unis). Cela étant, cette comparaison permet d'établir les conclusions suivantes :

Graphique S1. **Recettes fiscales totales moyennes dans l'OCDE, en pourcentage du PIB, période 2000-12 : comparaison entre les éditions des *Statistiques des recettes publiques* de 2013 (SRP13) et de 2014 (SRP14)**

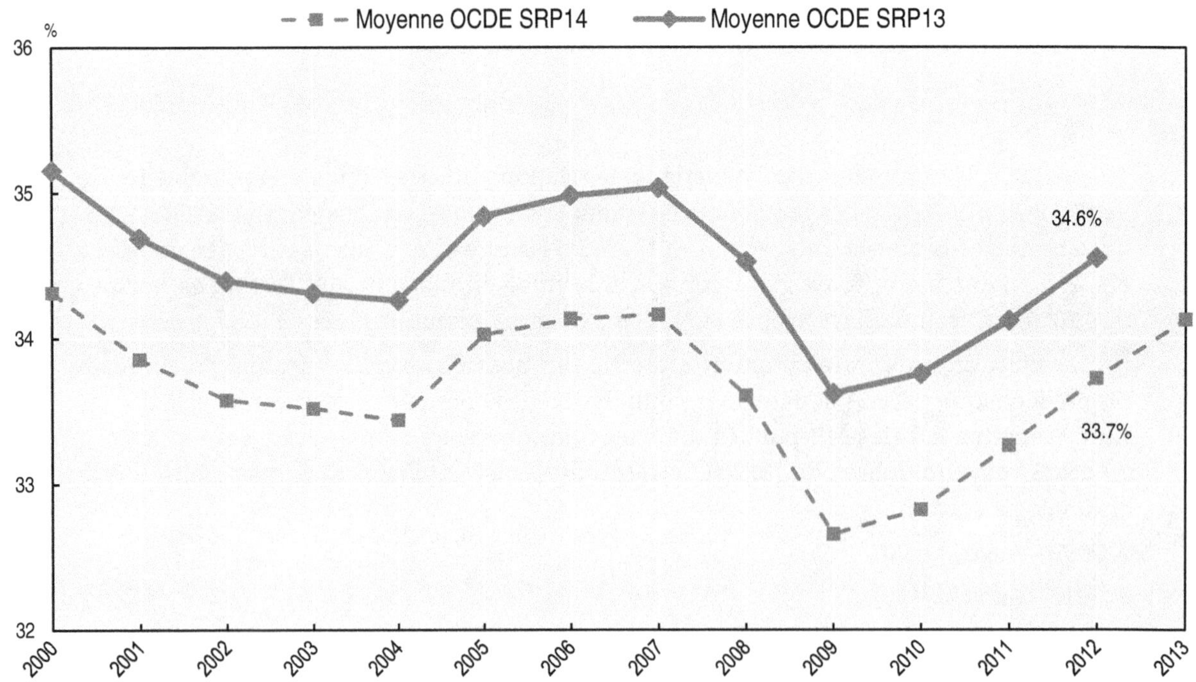

StatLink http://dx.doi.org/10.1787/888933276408

- Les ratios moyens recettes fiscales-PIB figurant dans l'édition de 2014 sont inférieurs d'environ un point de pourcentage des valeurs antérieures. Cela découle du fait que, dans la grande majorité des cas, les pays qui ont adopté les nouvelles normes ont constaté une augmentation du niveau de leur PIB sur toute la période 2000-12.
- L'évolution du ratio moyen recettes fiscales-PIB dans les pays de l'OCDE telle que figurant dans l'édition de 2014 des *Statistiques des recettes publiques* suit de très près celle de la même série présentée dans l'édition de 2013 de cette publication.
- Le changement n'a pas d'incidence sur la date du plus haut niveau historique et du plus bas niveau récemment enregistré par le ratio. Dans l'édition de 2013 comme dans celle de 2014, le plus haut niveau du ratio moyen recettes fiscales-PIB dans les pays de l'OCDE est atteint en 2000 avec 35.2 % (édition de 2013) et 34.3 % (édition de 2014). Le plus bas niveau des dernières années est, dans les deux cas, relevé en 2009 avec 33.6 % (édition de 2013) et 32.7 % (édition de 2014).

2. Ampleur des changements constatés dans les niveaux du PIB dans les différents pays de l'OCDE

La Direction des statistiques de l'OCDE a mené une étude dans les pays de l'OCDE pour mesurer l'ampleur des changements dans le niveau du PIB à la suite de l'adoption des nouvelles normes et en identifier les causes sous-jacentes. Le rapport correspondant à cette étude a été établi par Peter van de Ven, dans un numéro des *Cahiers statistiques de l'OCDE* (février 2015 – n° 20) disponible en anglais : « New standards for compiling national accounts: what's the impact on GDP and other macro-economic indicators ? »

Graphique S2. **Révision à la hausse du PIB constatée en 2010 par les pays de l'OCDE suite à l'adoption des nouvelles normes de comptabilité nationale**

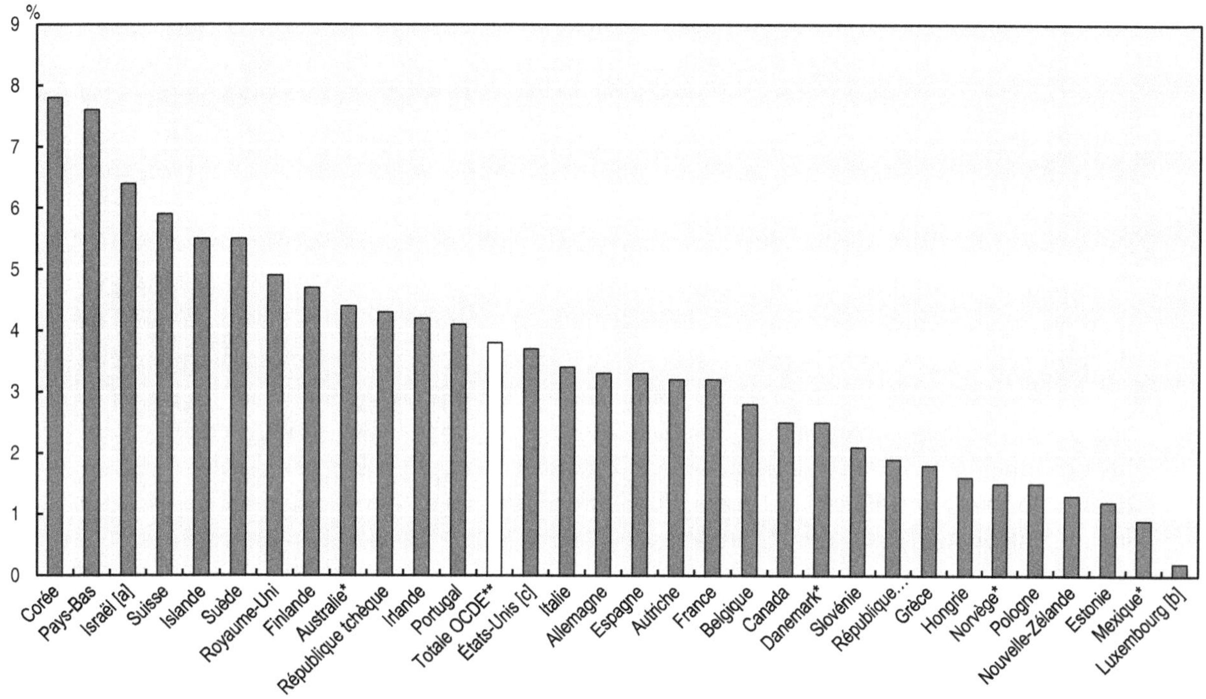

* Données pour l'Australie : 2007 ; Danemark : 2008 ; Mexique : 2008 ; et Norvège : 2011.

** Le Total OCDE correspond aux pays pour lesquels des données sont disponibles.

a) La capitalisation des dépenses militaires n'est pas encore appliquée.

b) La capitalisation de la quasi-totalité des équipements militaires avait été effectuée en vertu des normes SEC 95, ces équipements pouvant être aussi utilisés à des fins civiles.

c) La capitalisation des dépenses militaires avait déjà été effectuée dans les comptes nationaux des revenus et des produits (NIPA). Les effets sur le PIB ont été estimés à 0.5 point de pourcentage.

StatLink http://dx.doi.org/10.1787/888933276412

Outre les 29 pays qui avaient basculé vers SCN 2008/SEC 2010 à la date de l'édition de 2014 des *Statistiques des recettes publiques* de l'OCDE, l'étude a également couvert la Nouvelle-Zélande et la Norvège qui ont mis en œuvre les nouvelles normes par la suite en 2014. L'analyse a porté sur l'année 2010 pour la plupart des pays, les quelques exceptions étant citées dans les notes relatives aux graphiques S2/S3 et au tableau S1.

Le graphique S2 montre que les effets sur le PIB du passage aux normes SCN 2008/ SEC 2010 ont été différents selon les pays :

- Les variations se sont échelonnées entre une hausse de 7.8 % pour la Corée et de 0.2 % pour le Luxembourg.
- Parmi les pays ayant enregistré une hausse supérieure à 5 % figurent également les PaysBas (7.6 %), Israël (6.4 %), la Suisse (5.9 %) et la Suède (5.5 %).
- Ailleurs, la hausse constatée n'a pas dépassé 2 %, comme au Mexique (0.9%), en Estonie (1.2 %), en Nouvelle-Zélande (1.3 %), en Norvège et en Pologne (1.5 % dans les deux cas).
- La hausse moyenne observée dans la zone OCDE s'est établie à 3.8 %.

3. Principaux facteurs de la révision des données du PIB

Les changements introduits dans les normes internationales par le nouveau système SCN/SEC constituent le principal facteur explicatif des hausses du PIB décrites dans la section 2 ci-dessus, mais pas le seul. De nombreux pays ont décidé, à l'occasion du changement de normes, de conduire une démarche de révision et d'amélioration des sources des données et des méthodologies employées pour établir les indicateurs de la comptabilité nationale (dont le PIB) – démarche appelée ici révision des données statistiques de référence. Cette démarche est présentée plus en détail dans le paragraphe suivant, extrait du n° 20 des *Cahiers statistiques de l'OCDE* également cité dans la section 2.

Le principal objectif des comptes nationaux est la constitution d'agrégats macroéconomiques qui soient cohérents sur de longues périodes. De ce fait, les systèmes de comptabilité nationale cherchent généralement à limiter la fréquence des changements apportés aux normes, aux sources de données ou aux méthodologies afin de préserver la cohérence des indicateurs dans le temps. Les sources de données et les méthodologies les plus récentes sont adoptées exclusivement lorsque le pays procède à une remise à niveau de ses données de référence. Une extrapolation rétrospective est alors appliquée aux valeurs historiques des séries chronologiques de manière à disposer d'un nouvel ensemble de données cohérentes. La plupart des pays ont estimé que le passage aux nouvelles normes offrait l'opportunité d'une remise à niveau de leurs données statistiques de référence, c'est-à-dire, de la mobilisation de nouvelles sources et méthodes. De fait, dans certains pays, les effets de cette remise à niveau ont été plus importants que ceux liés au changement de normes. Une autre problématique entourant la mise en œuvre du SCN est celle de l'inclusion des activités illégales. Le SCN 2008, tout comme le SCN 1993, prévoit une prise en compte des activités illégales. Dans la pratique, toutefois, de nombreux pays n'ont pas inclus d'estimation de ces activités, même si une part des transactions liées à celles-ci a pu être comptabilisée de manière implicite. La décision prise à l'échelle européenne d'inclure pleinement ces activités dans les comptes nationaux a été accueillie avec circonspection par les médias et le grand public comme par les spécialistes de la recherche économique.

Les principales modifications des normes internationales ayant eu des effets sur le calcul du PIB peuvent être décrites à grands traits comme suit :

- Une définition élargie de la formation de capital fixe qui recouvre les dépenses de recherche-développement (R-D).
- Une définition élargie de la formation de capital fixe qui recouvre les dépenses en biens d'équipement militaires.
- Divers changements dans la comptabilisation des droits à pension et la valorisation des services financiers.

Les principaux changements relatifs à la révision des données statistiques de référence sont les suivants :

- Sources de données nouvelles ou améliorées.
- Inclusion des activités illégales[2]
- Autres changements, notamment des révisions des méthodologies d'estimation.

Le tableau S1 décrit l'effet total de la révision des données statistiques de référence sur les données du PIB par type de modification apportée. Le graphique S3 présente la comparaison des effets respectifs de l'adoption des nouvelles normes et de la remise à

Tableau S1. **Effet total de la révision des statistiques de référence sur les données du PIB, par type de modification apportée, pour l'année 2010**

	Effet total								
			Adoption des nouvelles normes				Révision des statistiques de référence		
			R-D	Équipements militaires	Autres		Sources nouvelles ou améliorées	Activités illégales	Autres
Australie*	**4.4**	**3.9**	1.4	0.3	2.2	**0.5**	n.a.	n.a.	n.a.
Autriche	**3.2**	**3.8**	2.3	0.0	1.4	**-0.6**	1.1	0.0	-1.7
Belgique	**2.8**	**2.5**	2.4	0.0	0.1	**0.3**	-0.3	0.4	0.2
Canada	**2.5**	**1.7**	1.2	0.1	0.4	**0.8**	n.a.	n.a.	n.a.
Chili	-	-	-	-	-	-	-	-	-
République tchèque	**4.3**	**3.1**	1.2	0.1	1.7	**1.2**	1.1	0.0	0.1
Danemark*	**2.5**	**2.7**	2.6	0.1	0.0	**-0.2**	-0.6	0.2	0.2
Estonie	**1.2**	**1.4**	0.9	0.4	0.0	**-0.2**	-0.2	0.0	0.0
Finlande	**4.7**	**4.2**	4.0	0.2	0.0	**0.5**	0.5	0.0	0.0
France	**3.2**	**2.4**	2.2	0.2	0.0	**0.8**	0.8	0.0	0.0
Allemagne	**3.3**	**2.7**	2.3	0.1	0.3	**0.6**	0.2	0.1	0.3
Grèce	**1.8**	**1.3**	0.6	0.6	0.2	**0.6**	-0.1	0.0	0.6
Hongrie	**1.6**	**1.6**	1.2	n.a.	n.a.	**0.0**	-0.1	0.0	0.1
Islande	**5.5**	**1.4**	1.4	0.0	0.0	**4.1**	3.6	0.5	0.0
Irlande	**4.2**	**3.6**	3.5	0.0	0.1	**0.6**	0.0	0.6	0.0
Israël[a]	**6.4**	**2.3**	2.2	0.0	0.1	**4.1**	3.2	0.0	0.9
Italie	**3.4**	**1.5**	1.3	0.2	0.0	**1.9**	0.4	1.0	0.5
Japon	-	-	-	-	-	-	-	-	-
Corée	**7.8**	**5.1**	3.6	0.3	1.2	**2.7**	n.a.	n.a.	n.a.
Luxembourg[b]	**0.2**	**1.6**	0.5	0.0	1.2	**-1.4**	0.0	0.2	-1.7
Mexique*	**0.9**	**1.5**	1.4	0.0	0.0	**-0.6**	0.0	0.0	-0.6
Pays-Bas	**7.6**	**1.7**	1.8	n.a.	n.a.	**5.9**	4.6	0.4	0.9
Nouvelle-Zélande	**1.3**	**1.3**	1.1	0.1	0.1	**0.0**	0.0	0.0	0.0
Norvège*	**1.5**	**1.6**	1.4	0.2	0.0	**-0.1**	n.a.	n.a.	n.a.
Pologne	**1.5**	**1.2**	0.5	0.2	n.a.	**0.2**	n.a.	0.7	n.a.
Portugal	**4.1**	**2.1**	1.3	0.1	0.8	**2.0**	1.4	0.4	0.3
République slovaque	**1.9**	**1.8**	0.6	0.1	1.1	**0.1**	0.2	0.0	-0.1
Slovénie	**2.1**	**2.0**	1.9	0.1	0.0	**0.1**	0.3	0.0	-0.2
Espagne	**3.3**	**1.6**	1.2	0.2	0.2	**1.7**	0.0	0.9	0.8
Suède	**5.5**	**4.4**	4.0	0.4	0.0	**1.1**	1.1	0.0	0.0
Suisse	**5.9**	**3.5**	n.a.	n.a.	n.a.	**2.3**	n.a.	n.a.	n.a.
Turquie	-	-	-	-	-	-	-	-	-
Royaume-Uni	**4.9**	**2.3**	1.6	0.2	0.4	**2.6**	2.0	0.6	0.0
États-Unis[c]	**3.7**	**4.0**	2.5	0.5	0.9	**-0.3**	-0.4	0.0	0.1
Totale OCDE**	**3.8**	**3.1**	2.2	0.3	0.6	**0.7**	0.3	0.2	0.1

* Données pour l'Australie : 2007 ; Danemark : 2008 ; Mexique : 2008; et Norvège : 2011.

** Le Total OCDE correspond aux pays pour lesquels des données sont disponibles.

a) La capitalisation des dépenses militaires n'est pas encore appliquée.

b) La capitalisation de la quasi-totalité des équipements militaires avait été effectuée en vertu des normes SEC 95, ces équipements pouvant être aussi utilisés à des fins civiles.

c) La capitalisation des dépenses militaires avait déjà été effectuée dans les comptes nationaux des revenus et des produits (NIPA). Les effets sur le PIB ont été estimés à 0.5 point de pourcentage.

StatLink http://dx.doi.org/10.1787/888933276628

niveau des données statistiques de référence dans l'effet total observé. Les principales conclusions qui en ressortent sont les suivantes :

- Le PIB a été revu à la hausse de 3.8 % en moyenne dans l'OCDE, dont 3.1 % sous l'effet du passage aux nouvelles normes internationales, et 0.7 % en raison d'une remise à niveau des données statistiques de référence.

Graphique S3. **Effets de l'adoption des nouvelles normes et de la remise à niveau des données statistiques de référence sur les données du PIB, pour l'année 2010**

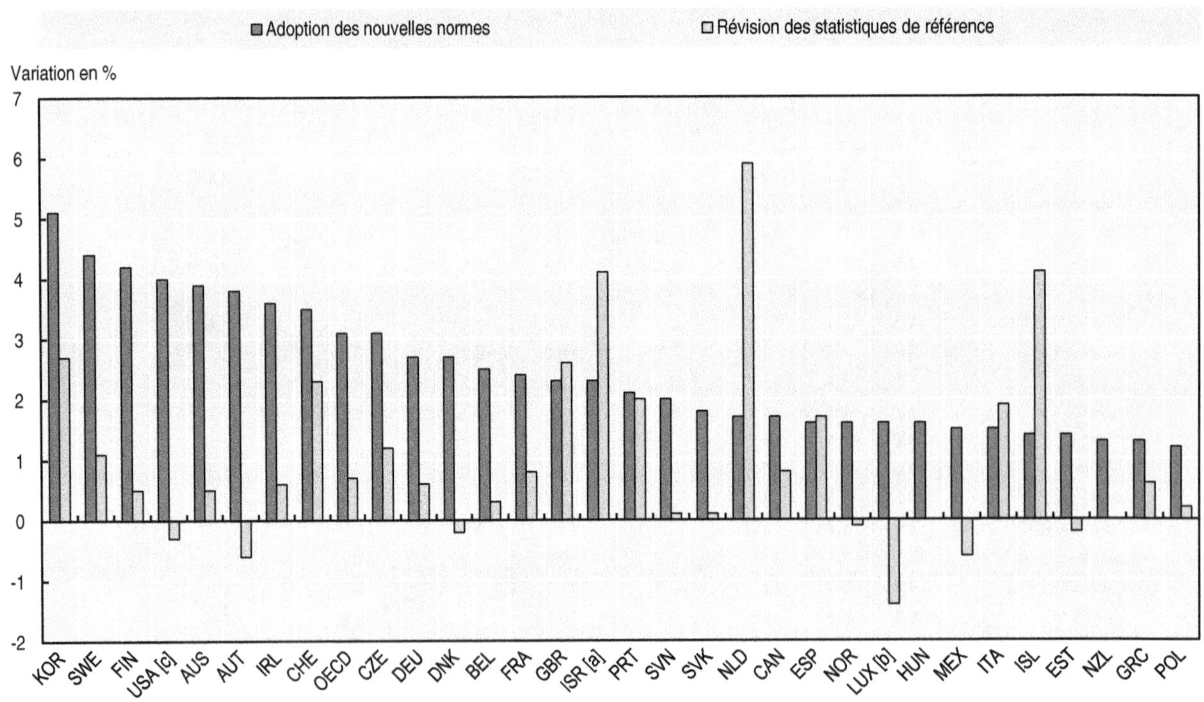

* Données pour l'Australie : 2007 ; Danemark : 2008 ; Mexique : 2008 ; et Norvège : 2011.

** Le Total OCDE correspond aux pays pour lesquels des données sont disponibles.

a) La capitalisation des dépenses militaires n'est pas encore appliquée.

b) La capitalisation de la quasi-totalité des équipements militaires avait été effectuée en vertu des normes SEC 95, ces équipements pouvant être aussi utilisés à des fins civiles.

c) La capitalisation des dépenses militaires avait déjà été effectuée dans les comptes nationaux des revenus et des produits (NIPA). Les effets sur le PIB ont été estimés à 0.5 point de pourcentage.

StatLink http://dx.doi.org/10.1787/888933276424

- Le principal facteur explicatif est la capitalisation des dépenses de R-D, qui a conduit à une révision à la hausse de 2.2 % en moyenne.
- La capitalisation des dépenses en biens d'équipement militaires et la mobilisation de sources de données nouvelles ou améliorées ont entraîné une révision à la hausse de 0.3 % chacune.
- Dans 25 des 31 pays concernés, la mise en œuvre des nouvelles normes a eu plus d'effet sur la révision à la hausse du PIB que la remise à niveau des données statistiques de référence. Les effets de la révision des données statistiques de référence ont été plus élevés en Islande, en Israël et aux Pays-Bas et, dans une moindre mesure, en Espagne, en Italie et au Royaume-Uni.

4. Relations entre le relèvement du niveau du PIB et les effets sur les ratios recettes publiques-PIB publiés dans les *Statistiques des recettes publiques* de l'OCDE

a. Variation des ratios recettes publiques-PIB

L'ampleur des changements dans les niveaux du PIB dans les pays de l'OCDE découlant de la remise à niveau des statistiques de référence fait l'objet des sections 2 et 3 ci-dessus. Les modifications apportées aux niveaux du PIB ont eu, à leur tour, des effets sur les ratios recettes fiscales-PIB. Ces ratios ont aussi varié en fonction de l'évolution des niveaux des recettes fiscales au cours de la même année.

De fait, les changements apportés aux normes internationales par le nouveau référentiel SCN/SEC ont eu des effets limités, voire nuls, sur les données relatives aux recettes fiscales figurant dans les *Statistiques des recettes publiques* de l'OCDE. En tirant cette conclusion, il convient de garder à l'esprit que :

- Les modifications apportées aux normes comptables du SCN/SEC concernant les crédits d'impôts récupérables n'ont pas été transposées dans le *Guide d'interprétation de l'OCDE*. Il en va de même pour les nouvelles normes comptables du SEC relatives aux ressources propres TVA.
- Les *Statistiques des recettes publiques* ont anticipé depuis l'édition 2012 le nouveau SCN/SEC en classant comme taxes les prélèvements sur les banques et les redevances de stabilité financière.

Cependant, certains pays ont enregistré des variations dans la valeur de leurs recettes fiscales à la suite d'une révision de leurs données statistiques de référence. Les variations constatées dans les données des recettes fiscales pour l'année 2010 peuvent être résumées comme suit :

- Les hausses les plus importantes, exprimées en pourcentage, ont été relevées en Irlande (5.7 %) et en Grèce (3.1 %). Le Portugal (1.9 %), la République slovaque (1.5 %) et le Luxembourg (1.0 %) ont tous trois enregistré une révision à la hausse de 1 % ou plus.
- Les baisses les plus marquées ont été constatées en Espagne (-4.9 %) et au Danemark (-2.4 %). La Suède (-1.1 %) et les États-Unis (-1.0 %) sont les deux seuls pays qui ont enregistré un recul égal ou supérieur à 1 %.
- Dans 12 autres pays, les variations ont été négligeables ou nulles.

Le graphique S4 présente les variations des ratios recettes fiscales-PIB constatées dans les pays de l'OCDE sous l'effet de la remise à niveau des statistiques de référence. Ces données ont été obtenues à partir des comparaisons suivantes :

- Australie : éditions de 2008 et de 2009 pour l'année 2007.
- Canada et États-Unis : éditions de 2012 et de 2013 pour l'année 2010.
- Finlande, France, Islande, Mexique, République tchèque et Suisse : éditions de 2013 et de 2014 pour l'année 2010.
- Pour le reste des 29 pays de la liste présentée dans la section 1 : éditions de 2013 et de 2014 pour l'année 2010. Pour ces pays, ont été pris en compte les changements liés au SCN apportés aux données des recettes fiscales pour l'année 2010 figurant dans l'édition de 2015.

Il convient de souligner que l'impact sous-jacent sur les données du PIB dans l'édition concernée des *Statistiques des recettes publiques* de l'OCDE diffère dans certains cas des variations présentées dans le graphique S2. En effet, dans certains cas, des ajustements ont été apportés aux données du PIB après la date de leur compilation aux fins à l'édition concernée des *Statistiques des recettes publiques* de l'OCDE, mais avant la remise à niveau des statistiques de référence. C'est clairement le cas du Luxembourg, pour lequel les données du PIB ont été revues à la baisse entre les éditions de 2013 et de 2014 des *Statistiques des recettes publiques* de l'OCDE, ce qui a entraîné un relèvement du ratio recettes fiscales-PIB.

Graphique S4. **Variation des ratios recettes fiscales-PIB observées dans les pays de l'OCDE qui ont mis en œuvre le SCN 2008 ou le SEC 2010 pour l'année 2010**

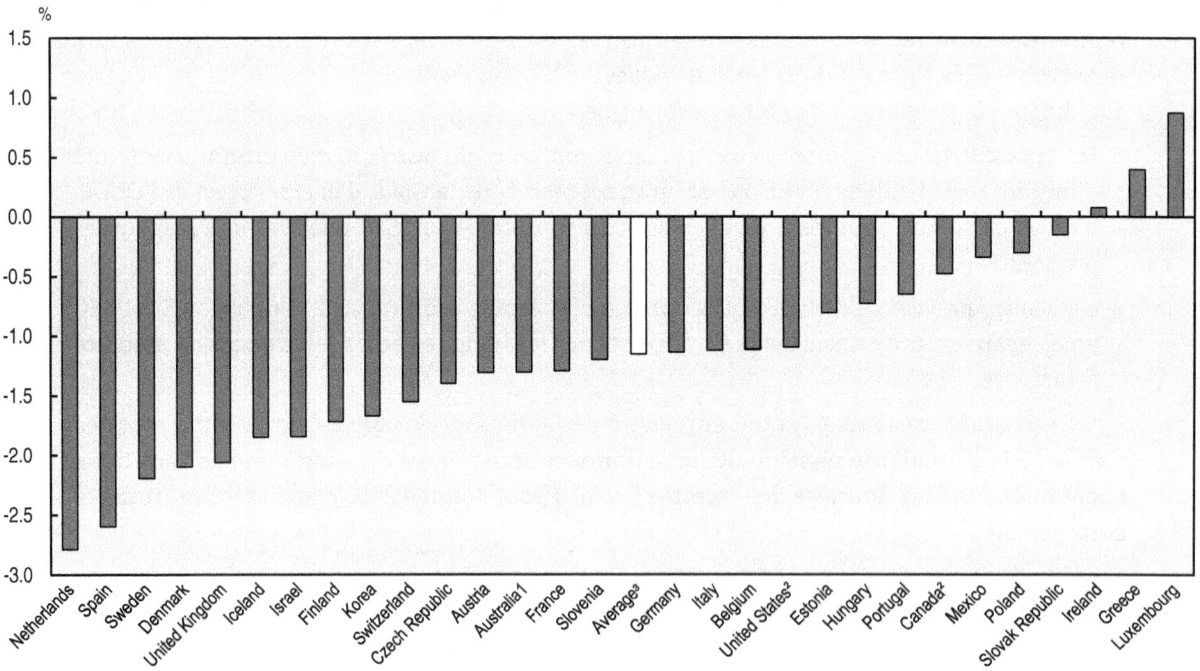

Note : Année 2007 pour l'Australie qui a adopté le SCN 2008 en 2009. Le Canada et les États-Unis ont adopté le SCN 2008 respectivement en 2012 et 2013. Pour ces deux pays, les comparaisons ont été établies pour l'année 2010.

StatLink http://dx.doi.org/10.1787/888933276439

Les principales conclusions qui ressortent du graphique S4 sont les suivantes :

- Des 29 pays qui avaient adopté les nouvelles normes lorsque les données ont été compilées aux fins de l'édition de 2014 des *Statistiques des recettes publiques*, tous, hormis trois d'entre eux : la Grèce, le Luxembourg et l'Irlande, avaient enregistré une baisse du ratio recettes fiscales-PIB dans l'édition des *Statistiques des recettes publiques* qui a suivi la mise en œuvre des changements.
- Les variations se sont échelonnées entre une baisse de 2.8 points de pourcentage aux Pays-Bas et une hausse de 0.9 point au Luxembourg. Le Danemark, l'Espagne, le Royaume-Uni et la Suède étaient les seuls pays ayant enregistré un recul du ratio supérieur à 2 points de pourcentage.
- En moyenne dans les 29 pays concernés, le ratio a baissé de 1.2 point de pourcentage.

b. Effets respectifs des variations des données relatives au PIB et aux recettes fiscales sur les ratios recettes fiscales-PIB

Le graphique 5 décrit les effets respectifs des changements dans les données relatives au PIB et aux recettes fiscales sur la variation des ratios recettes fiscales-PIB. Les 29 pays sont représentés selon l'ordre décroissant de la variation enregistrée par le ratio recettes fiscales-PIB.

- Le Luxembourg est le seul pays dans lequel le niveau du PIB a eu un effet positif. À l'inverse, la révision des statistiques de référence a fait évoluer les données relatives aux recettes fiscales à la hausse dans certains pays, à la baisse dans d'autres, les variations étant d'une ampleur négligeable ou nulle dans 40 % des cas environ.

Graphique S5. **Effets respectifs des variations des données relatives au PIB et aux recettes fiscales sur la variation des ratios recettes fiscales-PIB dans les pays de l'OCDE ayant adopté le SCN 2008 ou le SEC 2010, pour l'année 2010**[1, 2]

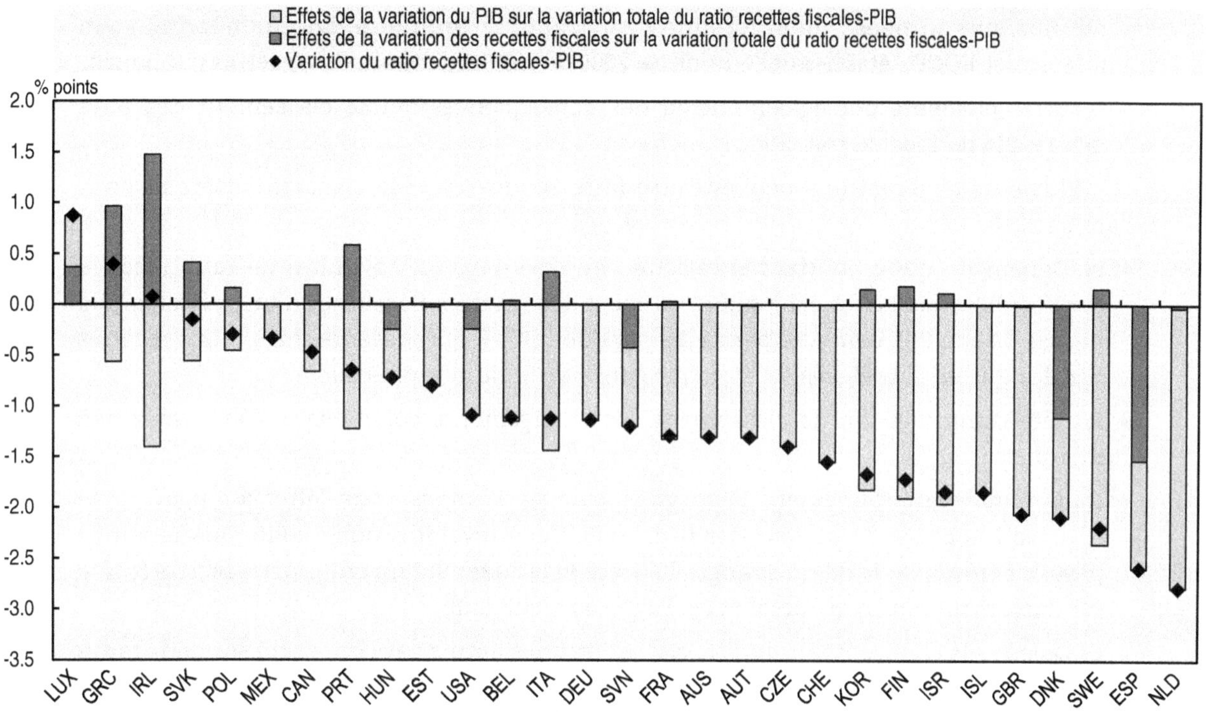

Note : Année 2007 pour l'Australie qui a adopté le SCN 2008 en 2009. Le Canada et les États-Unis ont adopté le SCN 2007 respectivement en 2012 et 2013. Pour ces deux pays, les comparaisons ont été établies pour l'année 2010.

StatLink http://dx.doi.org/10.1787/888933276445

- Dans certains pays, l'évolution des recettes fiscales a renforcé les effets de la variation du PIB, tandis que dans d'autres pays, l'évolution des deux variables a eu tendance à annuler les effets des changements constatés. Cela étant, dans la plupart des pays, la révision du niveau du PIB a eu sensiblement plus d'impact sur le ratio recettes fiscales-PIB que la variation des données relatives aux recettes fiscales.
- Quatre pays constituent une exception remarquable à la conclusion générale ci-dessus. En Grèce comme en Irlande, qui figurent en début de distribution, la hausse des données des recettes publiques l'a emporté sur celle du PIB, tirant à la hausse le ratio recettes fiscales-PIB, sachant qu'une hausse du numérateur et du dénominateur agissent en sens contraire sur l'évolution d'un ratio. À l'inverse, à la fin de la distribution, le Danemark et l'Espagne ont vu leur ratio reculer davantage sous l'effet de la baisse des recettes fiscales que du fait d'une revalorisation du PIB, sachant qu'une baisse du numérateur et une hausse du dénominateur agissent dans le même sens sur la baisse d'un ratio.

Les changements décrits ci-dessus ont des conséquences sur l'ordre de classement des pays de l'OCDE en termes de niveau du ratio recettes fiscales-PIB. Toutefois, plusieurs facteurs font obstacle à une analyse précise de ces changements :

- Dans certains cas, il n'est pas facile de distinguer les révisions dues aux changements de méthodologie des corrections apportées aux sources de données et des autres types de modifications. De plus, l'analyse se focalise uniquement sur une année – 2010 – et les résultats pourraient être légèrement différents pour d'autres années.

- À la date de la publication de l'édition de 2014 des *Statistiques des recettes publiques* de l'OCDE, 5 des 34 pays membres de l'OCDE n'avaient pas adopté le SCN 2008.
- Quant aux pays qui ont mis en œuvre les nouvelles normes, ils l'ont fait sur une période de plusieurs années : ainsi lorsque l'Australie, la première, adoptait le nouveau référentiel, l'OCDE établissait l'édition de 2009 de ses Statistiques des recettes publiques.
- D'autres éléments ont également eu des conséquences sur le classement des pays pendant la période de transition.

Plusieurs observations peuvent être faites concernant le classement établi pour l'année 2010 :

- Le Danemark, qui a pourtant enregistré l'une des plus fortes chutes du ratio recettes fiscales-PIB, sous l'effet conjugué d'un recul des recettes fiscales et d'une révision à la hausse de son PIB, demeure parmi les pays de l'OCDE qui présentent les ratios recettes fiscales-PIB les plus élevés. Le Mexique conserve le ratio le plus faible.
- En tête comme en fin de classement, les changements constatés ont été assez peu marqués.
- Dans le milieu du classement, l'Espagne reculé de six rangs, sous l'effet conjugué d'une révision à la baisse de ses recettes fiscales et d'une revalorisation du PIB. Quatre autres pays ont été déplacés de trois rangs : la Grèce et le Luxembourg ont progressé vers la tête du classement tandis qu'Israël et les Pays-Bas reculaient.
- Les éventuels changements dans le classement des autres pays ont porté sur deux rangs au plus.

Notes

1. Dans ce document, le ratio moyen recettes fiscales-PIB pour la zone OCDE désigne la moyenne non pondérée des résultats pour les 34 pays de l'OCDE. Cet indicateur suppose que chaque pays fait l'objet d'une pondération identique dans les calculs.
2. La décision au niveau de l'Union Européenne d'inclure les activités illégales dans les chiffres du PIB s'est focalisée sur la prostitution, la production et le trafic de drogues et d'alcools et la contrebande de tabac.

PART II

Tax levels and tax structures, 1965-2014

PARTIE II

Niveaux et structures des impôts, 1965-2014

PART II/ PARTIE II

A. Comparative tables, 1965-2013

In all of the following tables the symbol (..) indicates not available/or not applicable. The main series in this volume cover the years 1965 to 2013. Figures referring to 1966-79, 1981-89, 1991-99, 2001-06 and 2010 have been omitted because of lack of space. A complete series is, however, available on line. Data for 1955 and 1960 (for nineteen OECD countries) are provided in part V of the 1998 edition of this Report.

The Gross Domestic Product (GDP) figures are based on the 2008 System of National Accounts (SNA) for all OECD countries except Chile, Japan and Turkey.

A. Tableaux comparatifs, 1965-2013

Dans tous les tableaux suivants, le symbole (..) signifie que l'information n'est pas disponible ou qu'elle n'est pas significative. La principale série chronologique des statistiques de recettes fiscales couvre les années 1965 à 2013. Les chiffres de 1966-79, 1981-89, 1991-99, 2001-06 et 2010 ont été omis pour des raisons d'espace. Une série complète est, cependant, disponible en ligne. La partie V dans l'édition 1998 de ce Rapport fournit des données pour les années 1955 et 1960 (pour dix-neuf pays de l'OCDE).

Les chiffres du Produit Intérieur Brut (PIB) se fondent sur le Système de comptabilité nationale de 2008 (SCN 2008) pour tous les pays membres de l'OCDE à l'exception du Chili, du Japon et de la Turquie.

Treatment of capital transfers. Footnote 1 in tables 1 to 35 refers to the treatment of the capital transfers that some countries make to account for taxes that have been assessed but not collected. The capital transfer has been subtracted from the total tax revenue and this reduction has been allocated between tax headings in proportion to their tax revenues.

This applies to the following countries:

- Denmark from 1971.
- France from 1992.
- Greece for 1999 and 2000.
- Spain from 2000.

Traitements des transferts en capital. La note de bas de page n° 1 des tableaux 1 à 35 se réfère au traitement des transferts en capital que certains pays effectuent pour tenir compte des impôts qui ont été évalués mais non recouvrés. Le transfert en capital a été soustrait des recettes fiscales totales et cette réduction a été répartie entre les différentes rubriques en pourcentage de leurs recettes.

C'est le cas pour les pays suivants :

- Danemark à partir de 1971.
- France à partir de 1992.
- Grèce pour 1999 et 2000.
- Espagne à partir de 2000.

Table 1. **Total tax revenue as % of gross domestic product at market prices, 2013**
Tableau 1. **Total des recettes fiscales en % du produit intérieur brut aux prix du marché, 2013**

	Total Tax Revenue / Total des recettes fiscales	Excluding social security / Sécurité sociale non comprise
Australia / Australie	27.5	27.5
Austria / Autriche	42.5	27.9
Belgium / Belgique	44.7	30.5
Canada	30.5	25.7
Chile / Chili	20.0	18.5
Czech Republic / République tchèque	34.3	19.5
Denmark / Danemark[1]	47.6	47.5
Estonia / Estonie	31.8	20.8
Finland / Finlande	43.7	31.1
France[1]	45.0	28.3
Germany / Allemagne[2]	36.5	22.6
Greece / Grèce	34.4	23.7
Hungary / Hongrie	38.4	25.9
Iceland / Islande	35.9	32.2
Ireland / Irlande	29.0	23.9
Israel / Israël	30.6	25.5
Italy / Italie	43.9	30.8
Japan / Japon	30.3	17.9
Korea / Corée	24.3	17.9
Luxembourg	38.4	27.3
Mexico / Mexique	19.7	16.6
Netherlands / Pays-Bas	36.7	21.7
New Zealand / Nouvelle-Zélande	31.4	31.4
Norway / Norvège	40.5	31.0
Poland / Pologne	31.9	19.6
Portugal	34.5	25.6
Slovak Republic / République slovaque	30.4	17.1
Slovenia / Slovénie	36.8	22.0
Spain / Espagne[1]	32.7	21.4
Sweden / Suède	42.8	32.9
Switzerland / Suisse	26.9	20.1
Turkey / Turquie	29.3	21.2
United Kingdom / Royaume-Uni	32.9	26.7
United States / États-Unis	25.4	19.3
Unweighted average / Moyenne non pondérée		
OECD Average / Moyenne OCDE	**34.2**	**25.1**

1. The total tax revenue has been reduced by the amount of any capital transfer that represents uncollected taxes. The capital transfer has been allocated between tax headings in proportion to the reported tax revenue.
2. From 1991 the figures relate to the united Germany.
1. Le total des recettes fiscales a été diminué du montant de tout transfert en capital représentant les impôts non perçus. Le transfert en capital a été réparti entre les différentes rubriques en proportion des recettes fiscales.
2. Depuis 1991, les chiffres se rapportent à l'Allemagne unifiée.

StatLink http://dx.doi.org/10.1787/888933276631

Table 2. **Total tax revenue as % of GDP, 1965-1974**
Tableau 2. **Total des recettes fiscales en % du PIB, 1965-1974**

	1965	1966	1967	1968	1969	1970	1971	1972	1973	1974
Australia / Australie	20.6	19.9	20.4	20.4	20.7	21.1	21.9	21.4	22.5	24.7
Austria / Autriche	33.6	34.3	34.2	34.2	34.7	33.7	34.3	34.8	34.9	35.9
Belgium / Belgique	30.6	32.7	33.4	34.2	34.4	33.3	34.4	34.3	35.4	36.3
Canada	25.3	26.3	27.3	28.1	30.3	30.3	29.9	30.3	29.9	32.2
Chile / Chili	..	..	..	..	..	..	..	..	..	..
Czech Republic / République tchèque	..	..	..	..	..	..	..	..	..	..
Denmark / Danemark[1]	29.1	29.9	30.4	33.2	32.9	37.3	40.0	39.5	38.9	40.7
Estonia / Estonie	..	..	..	..	..	..	..	..	..	..
Finland / Finlande	30.0	31.2	32.0	32.4	31.0	31.2	32.8	33.2	34.0	33.3
France[1]	33.6	33.4	33.7	33.8	34.4	33.6	33.1	33.5	33.5	33.6
Germany / Allemagne[2]	31.6	32.2	32.2	32.2	33.9	31.5	32.0	33.5	35.0	34.9
Greece / Grèce[1]	17.1	18.3	19.2	19.9	19.6	19.1	19.0	18.9	17.3	18.2
Hungary / Hongrie	..	..	..	..	..	..	..	..	..	..
Iceland / Islande	25.5	..	..	..	..	26.7	..	..	..	..
Ireland / Irlande	24.5	26.5	27.0	27.4	28.1	27.6	28.6	27.4	27.6	28.0
Israel / Israël	..	..	..	..	..	..	..	..	..	..
Italy / Italie	24.7	24.5	25.3	26.1	25.5	24.8	25.5	25.4	23.1	24.2
Japan / Japon	17.8	17.2	17.7	17.9	18.3	19.2	19.5	20.1	21.8	22.3
Korea / Corée	..	..	..	..	..	..	..	12.4	12.0	13.1
Luxembourg	26.4	26.1	26.7	25.9	26.0	22.3	24.4	24.8	25.2	26.0
Mexico / Mexique	..	..	..	..	..	..	..	..	..	..
Netherlands / Pays-Bas	30.9	32.2	33.1	33.8	32.6	33.4	34.8	35.9	36.9	37.3
New Zealand / Nouvelle-Zélande	23.2	23.9	25.9	22.5	23.5	25.1	24.1	25.6	26.3	29.4
Norway / Norvège	29.4	30.6	32.4	33.3	34.6	34.3	36.7	38.6	39.0	38.6
Poland / Pologne	..	..	..	..	..	..	..	..	..	..
Portugal	15.7	16.1	16.7	16.8	17.4	17.6	17.3	17.1	16.7	17.1
Slovak Republic / République slovaque	..	..	..	..	..	..	..	..	..	..
Slovenia / Slovénie	..	..	..	..	..	..	..	..	..	..
Spain / Espagne[1]	14.3	13.3	16.5	15.6	16.0	15.5	15.8	16.6	17.2	16.6
Sweden / Suède	31.4	32.1	32.9	34.8	35.7	35.7	36.4	37.6	36.9	38.0
Switzerland / Suisse	16.6	17.2	17.2	18.0	18.9	18.2	17.9	18.3	20.2	20.9
Turkey / Turquie	10.6	10.7	11.4	11.3	12.2	8.6	12.2	11.1	11.6	10.5
United Kingdom / Royaume-Uni	29.3	30.0	31.8	33.0	34.7	35.0	33.1	31.6	29.7	32.8
United States / États-Unis	23.5	23.8	24.8	24.3	26.6	25.7	23.9	24.4	24.4	25.2
Unweighted average / Moyenne non pondérée										
OECD Average / Moyenne OCDE	**24.8**	**25.3**	**26.2**	**26.5**	**27.0**	**26.7**	**27.3**	**26.9**	**27.1**	**27.9**

1. The total tax revenue has been reduced by the amount of any capital transfer that represents uncollected taxes. The capital transfer has been allocated between tax headings in proportion to the reported tax revenue.
2. From 1991 the figures relate to the united Germany.

1. Le total des recettes fiscales a été diminué du montant de tout transfert en capital représentant les impôts non perçus. Le transfert en capital a été réparti entre les différentes rubriques en proportion des recettes fiscales.
2. Depuis 1991, les chiffres se rapportent à l'Allemagne unifiée.

StatLink http://dx.doi.org/10.1787/888933276645

Table 2. **Total tax revenue as % of GDP, 1975-1984** *(cont.)*
Tableau 2. **Total des recettes fiscales en % du PIB, 1975-1984** *(suite)*

	1975	1976	1977	1978	1979	1980	1981	1982	1983	1984
Australia / Australie	25.4	25.6	25.4	24.5	25.2	26.2	26.4	26.9	26.1	27.7
Austria / Autriche	36.4	36.3	36.6	38.8	38.2	38.7	39.7	38.5	38.2	39.9
Belgium / Belgique	38.8	39.0	40.9	41.5	42.2	40.6	40.8	42.0	42.7	43.5
Canada	31.5	31.0	30.2	29.9	29.6	30.5	32.7	32.5	31.9	32.0
Chile / Chili	..	..	..	..	..	..	..	..	..	..
Czech Republic / République tchèque	..	..	..	..	..	..	..	..	..	..
Denmark / Danemark[1]	37.0	37.9	38.3	39.5	40.5	41.3	41.0	39.9	41.5	42.6
Estonia / Estonie	..	..	..	..	..	..	..	..	..	..
Finland / Finlande	36.1	39.6	39.8	36.5	35.1	35.3	37.3	36.4	36.1	37.6
France[1]	34.9	36.7	36.7	36.7	38.1	39.4	39.5	40.3	40.7	41.8
Germany / Allemagne[2]	34.3	35.3	36.7	36.7	36.4	36.4	35.9	35.5	35.6	35.7
Greece / Grèce[1]	18.6	20.3	20.5	20.5	21.3	20.7	20.8	23.5	23.9	24.5
Hungary / Hongrie	..	..	..	..	..	..	..	..	..	..
Iceland / Islande	29.2	..	..	..	..	28.8	29.9	30.2	27.6	28.8
Ireland / Irlande	27.9	31.0	29.5	27.9	27.6	30.1	31.2	32.6	33.9	34.7
Israel / Israël	..	..	..	..	..	..	..	..	..	..
Italy / Italie	24.5	25.4	25.9	26.1	25.3	28.7	29.8	31.9	33.8	33.0
Japan / Japon	20.4	21.2	21.7	23.4	23.8	24.8	25.4	25.9	26.3	26.5
Korea / Corée	14.9	16.2	16.2	16.6	16.9	16.9	16.8	17.0	17.2	16.2
Luxembourg	31.1	31.2	34.6	35.2	33.0	33.8	34.7	35.9	37.8	36.4
Mexico / Mexique	..	..	..	..	..	14.5	14.1	14.4	16.0	15.6
Netherlands / Pays-Bas	38.2	38.1	38.9	39.6	40.0	40.3	39.4	40.1	41.2	39.5
New Zealand / Nouvelle-Zélande	27.5	28.2	31.3	29.1	29.8	29.6	31.1	31.8	29.8	29.0
Norway / Norvège	38.8	40.2	41.0	40.4	40.3	41.9	43.4	42.6	41.3	40.5
Poland / Pologne	..	..	..	..	..	..	..	..	..	..
Portugal	18.9	20.5	20.9	20.2	19.9	21.9	23.1	23.7	25.1	24.6
Slovak Republic / République slovaque	..	..	..	..	..	..	..	..	..	..
Slovenia / Slovénie	..	..	..	..	..	..	..	..	..	..
Spain / Espagne[1]	18.0	17.9	19.7	20.9	21.4	22.0	23.2	23.5	25.4	25.7
Sweden / Suède	38.9	42.7	44.7	45.1	43.9	43.7	45.0	44.0	44.7	44.3
Switzerland / Suisse	22.5	23.8	24.0	23.9	23.5	23.3	23.4	23.7	24.2	27.5
Turkey / Turquie	12.0	11.7	12.5	12.3	11.8	13.4	14.2	13.7	12.8	10.7
United Kingdom / Royaume-Uni	34.2	34.0	33.4	31.6	30.7	33.4	34.5	36.7	35.1	35.2
United States / États-Unis	24.6	24.0	25.2	25.0	25.2	25.5	25.9	26.0	24.0	24.1
Unweighted average / Moyenne non pondérée										
OECD Average / Moyenne OCDE	**28.6**	**29.5**	**30.2**	**30.1**	**30.0**	**30.1**	**30.7**	**31.1**	**31.3**	**31.4**

1. The total tax revenue has been reduced by the amount of any capital transfer that represents uncollected taxes. The capital transfer has been allocated between tax headings in proportion to the reported tax revenue.
2. From 1991 the figures relate to the united Germany.
1. Le total des recettes fiscales a été diminué du montant de tout transfert en capital représentant les impôts non perçus. Le transfert en capital a été réparti entre les différentes rubriques en proportion des recettes fiscales.
2. Depuis 1991, les chiffres se rapportent à l'Allemagne unifiée.

StatLink http://dx.doi.org/10.1787/888933276645

Table 2. **Total tax revenue as % of GDP, 1985-1994** *(cont.)*
Tableau 2. **Total des recettes fiscales en % du PIB, 1985-1994** *(suite)*

	1985	1986	1987	1988	1989	1990	1991	1992	1993	1994
Australia / Australie	27.8	28.5	28.6	28.3	28.0	28.1	26.6	26.1	26.5	27.4
Austria / Autriche	40.5	40.4	40.1	40.1	39.0	39.4	39.8	41.4	41.8	41.5
Belgium / Belgique	43.5	43.3	43.9	42.6	40.8	41.2	41.5	41.0	42.5	42.8
Canada	31.9	32.7	33.6	33.2	34.3	35.3	35.8	35.3	34.7	34.5
Chile / Chili	..	..	..	..	..	17.0	17.9	18.5	18.7	18.5
Czech Republic / République tchèque	..	..	..	..	..	..	..	..	37.1	35.8
Denmark / Danemark[1]	43.9	46.0	46.6	47.1	46.0	44.4	43.9	44.2	45.5	46.5
Estonia / Estonie	..	..	..	..	..	..	..	..	..	..
Finland / Finlande	39.1	40.3	38.7	42.0	41.5	42.9	44.4	44.0	43.5	45.5
France[1]	41.9	41.5	42.1	41.2	41.0	41.0	41.3	40.9	42.1	42.2
Germany / Allemagne[2]	36.1	35.8	36.3	36.0	36.2	34.8	35.0	35.9	35.8	36.2
Greece / Grèce[1]	24.5	25.7	26.1	23.6	22.9	25.1	25.2	26.0	26.5	26.7
Hungary / Hongrie	..	..	..	..	..	..	44.9	44.6	45.5	43.0
Iceland / Islande	27.4	27.6	28.0	30.5	30.6	30.1	30.5	31.3	30.3	29.8
Ireland / Irlande	33.7	34.4	34.6	35.7	32.5	32.4	33.0	33.3	33.3	34.4
Israel / Israël	..	..	..	..	..	..	..	..	..	..
Italy / Italie	32.5	34.0	34.1	34.6	35.6	36.4	36.8	39.0	40.6	38.7
Japan / Japon	26.7	27.7	28.6	29.0	29.3	28.5	28.2	26.7	26.8	25.8
Korea / Corée	15.8	15.4	15.7	15.6	16.3	18.8	18.5	18.4	18.8	18.9
Luxembourg	37.4	35.5	35.7	34.4	33.6	33.8	31.9	32.7	34.6	34.9
Mexico / Mexique	15.2	14.5	15.4	14.9	15.4	15.5	15.5	15.8	15.8	15.4
Netherlands / Pays-Bas	39.8	40.4	42.7	42.6	40.2	40.2	42.3	41.9	42.1	40.2
New Zealand / Nouvelle-Zélande	29.5	31.3	34.5	33.5	36.8	36.2	34.3	34.8	34.9	35.4
Norway / Norvège	41.9	43.6	41.9	41.4	39.7	40.2	40.4	39.5	38.7	40.0
Poland / Pologne	..	..	..	..	..	..	34.0	36.2	39.2	36.4
Portugal	24.1	25.5	24.0	25.6	26.3	26.5	27.5	29.5	28.0	28.8
Slovak Republic / République slovaque	..	..	..	..	..	..	..	..	..	..
Slovenia / Slovénie	..	..	..	..	..	..	..	..	..	..
Spain / Espagne[1]	26.8	28.2	30.0	30.1	31.8	31.6	31.9	32.9	32.0	32.0
Sweden / Suède	44.8	47.0	49.5	48.8	49.3	49.5	47.5	45.0	44.4	44.6
Switzerland / Suisse	23.9	24.8	24.6	24.8	24.1	23.6	23.5	23.9	24.5	24.9
Turkey / Turquie	11.5	13.0	14.0	13.2	13.9	14.9	15.6	16.7	16.9	16.5
United Kingdom / Royaume-Uni	35.1	35.5	34.0	33.8	33.0	32.9	31.7	30.9	29.9	30.6
United States / États-Unis	24.6	24.6	25.6	25.4	25.6	25.9	25.8	25.6	25.8	26.2
Unweighted average / Moyenne non pondérée										
OECD Average / Moyenne OCDE	**31.5**	**32.2**	**32.6**	**32.6**	**32.5**	**32.1**	**32.6**	**32.8**	**33.2**	**33.1**

1. The total tax revenue has been reduced by the amount of any capital transfer that represents uncollected taxes. The capital transfer has been allocated between tax headings in proportion to the reported tax revenue.
2. From 1991 the figures relate to the united Germany.
1. Le total des recettes fiscales a été diminué du montant de tout transfert en capital représentant les impôts non perçus. Le transfert en capital a été réparti entre les différentes rubriques en proportion des recettes fiscales.
2. Depuis 1991, les chiffres se rapportent à l'Allemagne unifiée.

StatLink http://dx.doi.org/10.1787/888933276645

Table 2. **Total tax revenue as % of GDP, 1995-2004** *(cont.)*
Tableau 2. **Total des recettes fiscales en % du PIB, 1995-2004** *(suite)*

	1995	1996	1997	1998	1999	2000	2001	2002	2003	2004
Australia / Australie	28.2	28.9	28.6	29.4	29.8	30.4	28.9	29.8	29.9	30.3
Austria / Autriche	41.1	42.4	43.2	43.3	42.9	42.1	43.7	42.5	42.3	41.8
Belgium / Belgique	42.6	43.0	43.5	44.1	43.9	43.6	43.5	43.6	43.1	43.2
Canada	34.9	35.1	35.9	35.9	35.7	34.9	34.3	32.8	32.7	32.5
Chile / Chili	18.4	19.6	19.1	18.8	18.1	18.8	19.0	19.0	18.7	19.1
Czech Republic / République tchèque	34.9	33.4	33.7	32.5	33.4	32.5	32.6	33.5	34.4	34.7
Denmark / Danemark[1]	46.5	46.7	46.7	47.3	47.9	46.9	45.9	45.4	45.6	46.4
Estonia / Estonie	36.2	34.2	34.2	34.0	32.5	31.0	30.3	31.1	30.8	31.1
Finland / Finlande	44.5	45.7	45.0	44.8	44.3	45.8	43.2	43.3	42.4	41.8
France[1]	41.9	43.0	43.3	43.1	43.9	43.1	42.7	42.1	42.0	42.2
Germany / Allemagne[2]	36.2	35.6	35.2	35.5	36.2	36.2	35.0	34.4	34.6	33.9
Greece / Grèce[1]	27.7	34.1	28.8	30.6	31.3	33.2	32.0	32.5	31.0	30.0
Hungary / Hongrie	41.0	39.6	37.9	37.6	38.4	38.7	37.8	37.4	37.4	37.2
Iceland / Islande	30.4	31.5	31.4	33.7	36.0	36.2	34.4	34.3	35.6	36.6
Ireland / Irlande	31.8	32.0	31.4	30.9	30.9	30.9	28.8	27.4	28.3	29.1
Israel / Israël	35.5	34.8	35.6	34.4	34.3	34.9	34.9	34.2	33.5	33.5
Italy / Italie	38.6	40.2	41.7	40.0	40.9	40.6	40.3	39.7	40.1	39.3
Japan / Japon	26.4	26.4	26.8	26.4	25.9	26.6	26.8	25.8	25.3	26.1
Korea / Corée	19.1	19.8	19.4	19.4	19.7	21.5	21.8	22.0	22.7	22.0
Luxembourg	35.2	35.6	37.3	37.4	36.4	37.1	38.1	38.0	38.1	37.0
Mexico / Mexique	14.9	15.0	15.6	14.8	15.5	16.5	16.8	16.2	17.1	16.8
Netherlands / Pays-Bas	38.9	38.3	38.3	36.3	37.2	36.8	35.7	35.2	34.6	34.8
New Zealand / Nouvelle-Zélande	35.6	33.7	33.9	32.3	32.3	32.5	31.9	33.2	33.1	34.1
Norway / Norvège	40.0	40.0	40.7	41.6	41.9	41.9	42.1	42.3	41.6	42.3
Poland / Pologne	37.7	36.8	36.3	35.5	35.2	33.1	33.0	33.2	32.6	32.2
Portugal	29.4	30.1	30.0	30.3	31.1	31.2	30.9	31.4	31.5	30.3
Slovak Republic / République slovaque	39.6	38.6	36.5	36.1	34.8	33.6	32.7	32.7	32.4	31.4
Slovenia / Slovénie	38.4	37.2	36.1	36.9	37.3	36.6	36.8	37.2	37.3	37.4
Spain / Espagne[1]	31.3	31.0	32.0	32.4	33.3	33.4	33.0	33.4	33.3	34.3
Sweden / Suède	45.6	47.4	48.3	48.4	48.8	49.0	46.8	45.2	45.5	45.6
Switzerland / Suisse	25.5	26.0	25.4	26.3	26.5	27.6	27.0	27.5	26.8	26.5
Turkey / Turquie	16.8	18.9	20.7	21.1	23.1	24.2	26.1	24.6	25.9	24.1
United Kingdom / Royaume-Uni	31.9	31.7	32.3	33.8	34.5	34.7	34.7	33.3	32.9	33.4
United States / États-Unis	26.4	26.9	27.3	27.7	27.8	28.2	27.1	24.9	24.4	24.6
Unweighted average / Moyenne non pondérée										
OECD Average / Moyenne OCDE	**33.6**	**33.9**	**33.9**	**33.9**	**34.2**	**34.2**	**33.8**	**33.5**	**33.5**	**33.4**

1. The total tax revenue has been reduced by the amount of any capital transfer that represents uncollected taxes. The capital transfer has been allocated between tax headings in proportion to the reported tax revenue.
2. From 1991 the figures relate to the united Germany.
1. Le total des recettes fiscales a été diminué du montant de tout transfert en capital représentant les impôts non perçus. Le transfert en capital a été réparti entre les différentes rubriques en proportion des recettes fiscales.
2. Depuis 1991, les chiffres se rapportent à l'Allemagne unifiée.

StatLink http://dx.doi.org/10.1787/888933276645

Table 2. **Total tax revenue as % of GDP, 2005-2013** *(cont.)*
Tableau 2. **Total des recettes fiscales en % du PIB, 2005-2013** *(suite)*

	2005	2006	2007	2008	2009	2010	2011	2012	2013
Australia / Australie	29.9	29.5	29.7	27.0	25.8	25.6	26.3	27.3	27.5
Austria / Autriche	40.9	40.4	40.5	41.4	41.0	40.8	41.0	41.7	42.5
Belgium / Belgique	43.1	42.8	42.6	43.0	42.1	42.4	43.0	44.0	44.7
Canada	32.3	32.6	32.3	31.5	31.4	30.4	30.2	30.7	30.5
Chile / Chili	20.7	22.0	22.8	21.4	17.2	19.5	21.2	21.5	20.0
Czech Republic / République tchèque	34.5	34.1	34.3	33.5	32.4	32.5	33.4	33.8	34.3
Denmark / Danemark[1]	48.0	46.4	46.4	44.9	45.2	45.3	45.4	46.4	47.6
Estonia / Estonie	29.9	30.4	31.1	31.3	34.9	33.2	31.9	32.1	31.8
Finland / Finlande	42.1	42.2	41.5	41.2	40.9	40.8	42.0	42.7	43.7
France[1]	42.8	43.1	42.4	42.2	41.3	41.6	42.9	44.1	45.0
Germany / Allemagne[2]	33.9	34.5	34.9	35.4	36.1	35.0	35.7	36.4	36.5
Greece / Grèce[1]	31.2	30.3	31.2	31.0	30.8	32.0	33.5	34.5	34.4
Hungary / Hongrie	36.8	36.7	39.6	39.5	39.0	37.3	36.5	38.6	38.4
Iceland / Islande	39.4	40.4	38.7	35.1	32.0	33.3	34.4	35.2	35.9
Ireland / Irlande	29.2	31.0	30.4	28.6	27.6	27.5	27.4	27.9	29.0
Israel / Israël	33.8	34.4	34.3	31.9	29.7	30.4	30.8	29.7	30.6
Italy / Italie	39.1	40.6	41.7	41.6	42.1	41.8	41.9	43.9	43.9
Japan / Japon	27.3	28.1	28.5	28.5	27.0	27.6	28.6	29.4	30.3
Korea / Corée	22.5	23.6	24.8	24.6	23.8	23.4	24.2	24.8	24.3
Luxembourg	38.3	36.3	36.6	37.2	39.0	38.1	37.9	38.8	38.4
Mexico / Mexique	17.7	17.9	17.6	20.7	17.2	18.5	19.5	19.5	19.7
Netherlands / Pays-Bas	36.1	36.4	36.1	36.5	35.4	36.2	35.9	36.1	36.7
New Zealand / Nouvelle-Zélande	36.0	35.4	34.0	33.3	30.5	30.6	30.9	32.4	31.4
Norway / Norvège	42.6	42.8	42.1	41.5	41.2	41.9	42.0	41.5	40.5
Poland / Pologne	33.3	33.9	34.8	34.5	31.5	31.4	32.0	32.3	31.9
Portugal	30.9	31.5	32.0	31.9	30.0	30.6	32.5	32.0	34.5
Slovak Republic / République slovaque	31.2	29.3	29.2	29.1	28.9	28.1	28.7	28.5	30.4
Slovenia / Slovénie	38.0	37.6	37.1	36.4	36.2	36.9	36.5	36.8	36.8
Spain / Espagne[1]	35.3	36.1	36.5	32.3	29.8	29.9	31.3	32.1	32.7
Sweden / Suède	46.6	46.0	45.0	44.0	44.1	43.2	42.5	42.6	42.8
Switzerland / Suisse	26.5	26.4	26.1	26.7	27.1	26.5	27.0	26.9	26.9
Turkey / Turquie	24.3	24.5	24.1	24.2	24.6	26.2	27.8	27.6	29.3
United Kingdom / Royaume-Uni	33.8	34.4	34.1	34.0	32.3	32.8	33.6	33.0	32.9
United States / États-Unis	25.9	26.6	26.7	25.2	23.0	23.2	23.6	24.1	25.4
Unweighted average / Moyenne non pondérée									
OECD Average / Moyenne OCDE	**33.9**	**34.1**	**34.1**	**33.6**	**32.7**	**32.8**	**33.3**	**33.8**	**34.2**

1. The total tax revenue has been reduced by the amount of any capital transfer that represents uncollected taxes. The capital transfer has been allocated between tax headings in proportion to the reported tax revenue.
2. From 1991 the figures relate to the united Germany.
1. Le total des recettes fiscales a été diminué du montant de tout transfert en capital représentant les impôts non perçus. Le transfert en capital a été réparti entre les différentes rubriques en proportion des recettes fiscales.
2. Depuis 1991, les chiffres se rapportent à l'Allemagne unifiée.

StatLink http://dx.doi.org/10.1787/888933276645

Table 3. **Total tax revenue (excluding social security) as % of GDP**
Tableau 3. **Total des recettes fiscales (sécurité sociale non comprise) en % du PIB**

	1965	1980	1990	2000	2007	2008	2009	2011	2012	2013
Australia / Australie	20.6	26.2	28.1	30.4	29.7	27.0	25.8	26.3	27.3	27.5
Austria / Autriche	25.2	26.7	26.4	27.8	26.9	27.6	26.7	26.9	27.5	27.9
Belgium / Belgique	21.0	28.9	27.5	30.2	29.5	29.5	28.2	29.1	29.9	30.5
Canada	23.9	27.3	31.0	30.2	27.6	26.9	26.5	25.6	26.0	25.7
Chile / Chili	..	..	15.4	17.4	21.5	20.0	15.8	19.9	20.1	18.5
Czech Republic / République tchèque	..	..	..	18.1	19.3	18.7	18.1	18.7	19.1	19.5
Denmark / Danemark[1]	28.2	41.1	44.4	46.2	46.3	44.8	45.1	45.3	46.3	47.5
Estonia / Estonie	..	..	..	20.0	20.7	19.9	22.0	20.1	20.7	20.8
Finland / Finlande	28.0	27.1	31.9	34.3	30.0	29.7	28.8	30.0	30.0	31.1
France[1]	22.1	22.6	22.9	27.5	26.7	26.4	25.1	26.6	27.6	28.3
Germany / Allemagne[2]	23.1	23.9	21.8	22.1	22.1	22.5	22.2	21.9	22.5	22.6
Greece / Grèce[1]	11.7	13.9	17.5	23.2	20.5	20.2	20.5	22.8	23.7	23.7
Hungary / Hongrie	..	..	..	27.3	26.7	26.7	26.8	24.1	26.0	25.9
Iceland / Islande	23.4	28.2	29.2	33.4	35.8	32.4	29.1	30.5	31.5	32.2
Ireland / Irlande	22.9	25.8	27.8	27.3	26.3	24.1	22.4	22.1	23.0	23.9
Israel / Israël	..	..	..	29.8	29.1	26.7	24.6	25.6	24.6	25.5
Italy / Italie	16.2	17.8	24.4	29.0	29.2	28.8	28.9	29.0	30.8	30.8
Japan / Japon	13.9	17.5	21.0	17.3	18.1	17.4	15.9	16.7	17.2	17.9
Korea / Corée	..	16.8	16.9	17.9	19.6	19.3	18.2	18.4	18.7	17.9
Luxembourg	17.8	24.1	24.7	27.5	26.5	26.6	27.4	26.8	27.5	27.3
Mexico / Mexique	..	12.4	13.4	13.8	14.9	18.1	14.3	16.7	16.6	16.6
Netherlands / Pays-Bas	21.4	24.9	25.2	22.5	23.5	23.0	22.6	22.1	21.4	21.7
New Zealand / Nouvelle-Zélande	23.2	29.6	36.2	32.5	34.0	33.3	30.5	30.9	32.4	31.4
Norway / Norvège	25.9	33.1	29.7	33.1	33.4	32.8	31.6	32.8	32.2	31.0
Poland / Pologne	..	..	..	20.0	22.8	23.1	20.3	20.7	20.1	19.6
Portugal	12.3	15.4	19.3	23.3	23.9	23.5	21.5	23.6	23.3	25.6
Slovak Republic / République slovaque	..	..	..	19.7	17.8	17.5	16.6	16.6	16.1	17.1
Slovenia / Slovénie	..	..	..	22.7	23.6	22.6	21.6	21.8	21.9	22.0
Spain / Espagne[1]	10.3	11.3	20.4	21.8	24.7	20.5	18.1	19.6	20.7	21.4
Sweden / Suède	27.6	31.2	36.0	36.1	33.2	33.0	33.2	32.6	32.4	32.9
Switzerland / Suisse	14.1	17.9	18.0	20.9	20.0	20.5	20.6	20.4	20.2	20.1
Turkey / Turquie	9.9	11.5	12.0	19.6	18.9	18.2	18.6	20.1	20.1	21.2
United Kingdom / Royaume-Uni	24.8	27.8	27.3	28.8	27.8	27.5	25.9	27.3	26.7	26.7
United States / États-Unis	20.4	19.9	19.3	21.5	20.4	18.9	16.7	18.1	18.6	19.3
Unweighted average / Moyenne non pondérée										
OECD Average / Moyenne OCDE	**20.3**	**23.2**	**24.7**	**25.7**	**25.6**	**24.9**	**23.8**	**24.4**	**24.8**	**25.1**

1. The total tax revenue has been reduced by the amount of any capital transfer that represents uncollected taxes. The capital transfer has been allocated between tax headings in proportion to the reported tax revenue.
2. From 1991 the figures relate to the united Germany.
1. Le total des recettes fiscales a été diminué du montant de tout transfert en capital représentant les impôts non perçus. Le transfert en capital a été réparti entre les différentes rubriques en proportion des recettes fiscales.
2. Depuis 1991, les chiffres se rapportent à l'Allemagne unifiée.

StatLink http://dx.doi.org/10.1787/888933276658

Table 4. **Total tax revenue as % of GDP – Three year moving average**
Tableau 4. **Total des recettes fiscales en % du PIB – Moyenne mobile sur trois ans**

	1966	1975	1985	1990	1995	2000	2003	2006	2009	2012
Australia / Australie	20.3	25.2	28.0	27.6	28.2	29.7	30.0	29.7	26.1	27.0
Austria / Autriche	34.0	36.2	40.3	39.4	41.7	42.9	42.2	40.6	41.1	41.7
Belgium / Belgique	32.2	38.0	43.4	41.2	42.8	43.6	43.3	42.8	42.5	43.9
Canada	26.3	31.5	32.2	35.1	34.9	35.0	32.6	32.4	31.1	30.5
Chile / Chili	..	..	..	..	18.8	18.6	18.9	21.8	19.4	20.9
Czech Republic / République tchèque	..	..	..	..	34.7	32.8	34.2	34.3	32.8	33.8
Denmark / Danemark[1]	29.8	38.9	44.5	45.0	46.8	47.0	45.9	47.1	45.3	46.7
Estonia / Estonie	..	..	..	..	..	31.2	31.0	30.5	33.1	31.9
Finland / Finlande	31.1	36.3	39.0	43.0	45.2	44.4	42.5	41.9	41.0	42.8
France[1]	33.6	35.1	41.7	41.1	42.7	43.5	42.3	42.9	42.0	44.3
Germany / Allemagne[2]	32.0	34.8	35.9	35.3	36.0	35.8	34.3	34.4	35.5	36.2
Greece / Grèce[1]	18.2	19.0	24.9	24.4	29.5	32.2	31.2	30.9	31.3	34.2
Hungary / Hongrie	..	..	..	..	41.2	38.3	37.3	37.7	38.6	37.8
Iceland / Islande	25.5	29.2	28.0	30.4	30.5	35.6	35.5	39.5	33.5	35.2
Ireland / Irlande	26.0	29.0	34.2	32.7	32.7	30.2	28.3	30.2	27.9	28.1
Israel / Israël	..	..	..	..	..	34.7	33.7	34.2	30.7	30.4
Italy / Italie	24.8	24.7	33.2	36.2	39.2	40.6	39.7	40.5	41.8	43.2
Japan / Japon	17.6	21.3	27.0	28.7	26.2	26.5	25.7	28.0	27.7	29.4
Korea / Corée	..	14.7	15.8	17.9	19.3	21.0	22.2	23.6	23.9	24.4
Luxembourg	26.4	29.4	36.4	33.1	35.2	37.2	37.7	37.0	38.1	38.4
Mexico / Mexique	..	..	15.1	15.5	15.1	16.3	16.7	17.7	18.8	19.6
Netherlands / Pays-Bas	32.1	37.9	39.9	40.9	39.2	36.6	34.9	36.2	36.0	36.2
New Zealand / Nouvelle-Zélande	24.3	28.4	29.9	35.8	34.9	32.3	33.5	35.1	31.4	31.5
Norway / Norvège	30.8	39.2	42.0	40.1	40.0	41.9	42.1	42.5	41.5	41.4
Poland / Pologne	..	..	..	..	37.0	33.8	32.7	34.0	32.5	32.1
Portugal	16.2	18.8	24.7	26.8	29.4	31.1	31.0	31.5	30.8	33.0
Slovak Republic / République slovaque	..	..	..	..	..	33.7	32.2	29.9	28.7	29.2
Slovenia / Slovénie	..	..	..	..	..	36.9	37.3	37.6	36.5	36.7
Spain / Espagne[1]	14.7	17.5	26.9	31.8	31.4	33.6	34.1	36.4	31.4	32.8
Sweden / Suède	32.1	39.9	45.4	48.8	45.9	48.2	45.4	45.8	43.8	42.6
Switzerland / Suisse	17.0	22.4	25.4	23.8	25.5	27.0	26.9	26.3	26.8	26.9
Turkey / Turquie	10.9	11.4	11.7	14.8	17.4	24.5	24.9	24.3	25.0	28.2
United Kingdom / Royaume-Uni	30.4	33.6	35.3	32.5	31.4	34.6	33.2	34.1	33.0	33.2
United States / États-Unis	24.0	24.6	24.4	25.8	26.5	27.7	24.6	26.4	23.8	24.3
Unweighted average / Moyenne non pondérée										
OECD Average / Moyenne OCDE	**25.4**	**28.7**	**31.7**	**32.4**	**33.6**	**34.1**	**33.5**	**34.1**	**33.0**	**33.8**

1. The total tax revenue has been reduced by the amount of any capital transfer that represents uncollected taxes. The capital transfer has been allocated between tax headings in proportion to the reported tax revenue.
2. From 1991 the figures relate to the united Germany.
1. Le total des recettes fiscales a été diminué du montant de tout transfert en capital représentant les impôts non perçus. Le transfert en capital a été réparti entre les différentes rubriques en proportion des recettes fiscales.
2. Depuis 1991, les chiffres se rapportent à l'Allemagne unifiée.

StatLink http://dx.doi.org/10.1787/888933276668

Table 5. **Tax revenue of main headings as % of GDP, 2013**
Tableau 5. **Recettes fiscales sous les principales rubriques en % du PIB, 2013**

	1000 Income & profits / Revenu & bénéfices	2000 Social security / Sécurité sociale	3000 Payroll / Salaires	4000 Property / Patrimoine	5000 Goods and services / Biens & services	6000 Others / Autres	EU Custom Duties / UE droits de douane
Australia / Australie	15.7	0.0	1.4	2.6	7.8	0.0	..
Austria / Autriche	12.3	14.6	2.9	0.7	11.7	0.2	0.1
Belgium / Belgique	15.9	14.2	0.0	3.5	10.8	0.0	0.3
Canada	14.5	4.8	0.6	3.2	7.4	0.0	..
Chile / Chili	6.9	1.4	0.0	0.8	10.8	0.0	..
Czech Republic / République tchèque	7.1	14.8	0.0	0.5	11.7	0.0	0.1
Denmark / Danemark[1]	29.8	0.1	0.3	1.8	15.4	0.0	0.2
Estonia / Estonie	7.2	11.1	0.0	0.3	13.0	0.0	0.2
Finland / Finlande	15.2	12.6	0.0	1.3	14.5	0.0	0.1
France[1]	10.9	16.7	1.6	3.8	10.8	1.1	0.1
Germany / Allemagne[2]	11.3	13.9	0.0	0.9	10.2	0.0	0.2
Greece / Grèce	7.6	10.7	0.0	2.6	13.5	0.0	0.1
Hungary / Hongrie	6.8	12.5	0.6	1.3	16.9	0.3	0.1
Iceland / Islande	16.8	3.7	0.3	2.5	12.0	0.6	..
Ireland / Irlande	11.7	5.2	0.2	2.1	9.7	0.0	0.1
Israel / Israël	9.7	5.1	1.2	2.7	11.9	0.0	..
Italy / Italie	14.5	13.1	0.0	2.7	11.5	2.0	0.1
Japan / Japon	9.8	12.4	0.0	2.7	5.3	0.1	..
Korea / Corée	7.1	6.4	0.1	2.5	7.5	0.7	..
Luxembourg	13.5	11.1	0.0	2.8	10.9	0.0	0.0
Mexico / Mexique	6.0	3.1	0.3	0.3	9.8	0.3	..
Netherlands / Pays-Bas	9.1	15.0	0.0	1.2	10.9	0.2	0.3
New Zealand / Nouvelle-Zélande	17.4	0.0	0.0	1.9	12.0	0.0	..
Norway / Norvège	18.7	9.5	0.0	1.2	11.1	0.0	..
Poland / Pologne	6.2	12.3	0.2	1.4	11.5	0.2	0.1
Portugal	11.2	8.9	0.0	1.1	12.9	0.3	0.1
Slovak Republic / République slovaque	6.0	13.3	0.0	0.4	10.4	0.0	0.2
Slovenia / Slovénie	6.4	14.8	0.1	0.6	14.7	0.0	0.1
Spain / Espagne[1]	9.6	11.3	0.0	2.2	9.2	0.3	0.1
Sweden / Suède	14.8	10.0	4.6	1.1	12.2	0.0	0.1
Switzerland / Suisse	12.4	6.7	0.0	1.8	6.0	0.0	..
Turkey / Turquie	5.9	8.0	0.0	1.4	13.5	0.5	..
United Kingdom / Royaume-Uni	11.7	6.2	0.0	4.0	10.8	0.0	0.2
United States / États-Unis	12.0	6.1	0.0	2.9	4.4	0.0	..
Unweighted average / Moyenne non pondérée							
OECD Average / Moyenne OCDE	**11.5**	**9.1**	**0.4**	**1.9**	**11.0**	**0.2**	**0.1**

1. The total tax revenue has been reduced by the amount of any capital transfer that represents uncollected taxes. The capital transfer has been allocated between tax headings in proportion to the reported tax revenue.
2. From 1991 the figures relate to the united Germany.
1. Le total des recettes fiscales a été diminué du montant de tout transfert en capital représentant les impôts non perçus. Le transfert en capital a été réparti entre les différentes rubriques en proportion des recettes fiscales.
2. Depuis 1991, les chiffres se rapportent à l'Allemagne unifiée.

StatLink *http://dx.doi.org/10.1787/888933276677*

Table 6. **Tax revenue of main headings as % of total taxation, 2013**
Tableau 6. **Recettes fiscales sous les principales rubriques en % du total des recettes fiscales, 2013**

	1000 Income & profits / Revenu & bénéfices	2000 Social security / Sécurité sociale	3000 Payroll / Salaires	4000 Property / Patrimoine	5000 Goods and services / Biens & services	6000 Others / Autres	EU Custom Duties / UE droits de douane
Australia / Australie	57.1	0.0	5.1	9.4	28.4	0.0	..
Austria / Autriche	29.0	34.3	6.9	1.7	27.5	0.4	0.2
Belgium / Belgique	35.6	31.7	0.0	7.8	24.2	0.0	0.7
Canada	47.5	15.8	2.1	10.4	24.2	0.0	..
Chile / Chili	34.8	7.2	0.0	4.1	54.0	-0.1	..
Czech Republic / République tchèque	20.8	43.2	0.0	1.4	34.3	0.0	0.4
Denmark / Danemark[1]	62.6	0.2	0.7	3.9	32.3	0.0	0.3
Estonia / Estonie	22.7	34.8	0.0	1.0	41.0	0.0	0.5
Finland / Finlande	34.7	28.9	0.0	2.9	33.2	0.1	0.2
France[1]	24.2	37.2	3.5	8.4	24.1	2.4	0.2
Germany / Allemagne[2]	31.0	38.1	0.0	2.5	28.0	0.0	0.4
Greece / Grèce	22.0	31.1	0.0	7.6	39.1	0.0	0.2
Hungary / Hongrie	17.7	32.6	1.5	3.4	44.0	0.7	0.2
Iceland / Islande	46.7	10.3	1.0	6.9	33.5	1.6	..
Ireland / Irlande	40.4	17.8	0.6	7.1	33.6	0.0	0.5
Israel / Israël	31.7	16.6	3.9	8.8	39.0	0.0	..
Italy / Italie	33.1	29.8	0.0	6.2	26.1	4.5	0.3
Japan / Japon	32.5	40.9	0.0	8.8	17.6	0.3	..
Korea / Corée	29.3	26.4	0.3	10.3	30.7	3.0	..
Luxembourg	35.3	28.8	0.0	7.3	28.4	0.1	0.1
Mexico / Mexique	30.2	15.5	1.7	1.5	49.8	1.3	..
Netherlands / Pays-Bas	24.7	40.8	0.0	3.4	29.6	0.5	0.9
New Zealand / Nouvelle-Zélande	55.5	0.0	0.0	6.1	38.4	0.0	..
Norway / Norvège	46.2	23.5	0.0	3.0	27.4	0.0	..
Poland / Pologne	19.5	38.6	0.8	4.4	35.9	0.6	0.3
Portugal	32.4	25.9	0.0	3.3	37.3	0.9	0.2
Slovak Republic / République slovaque	19.9	43.8	0.0	1.5	34.4	0.0	0.5
Slovenia / Slovénie	17.5	40.1	0.2	1.7	40.1	0.0	0.4
Spain / Espagne[1]	29.4	34.5	0.0	6.7	28.1	0.9	0.4
Sweden / Suède	34.5	23.3	10.6	2.5	28.6	0.1	0.3
Switzerland / Suisse	46.0	25.1	0.0	6.7	22.2	0.0	..
Turkey / Turquie	20.2	27.4	0.0	4.6	46.1	1.6	..
United Kingdom / Royaume-Uni	35.4	18.8	0.0	12.3	32.9	0.0	0.5
United States / États-Unis	47.2	24.2	0.0	11.3	17.4	0.0	..
Unweighted average / Moyenne non pondérée							
OECD Average / Moyenne OCDE	**33.7**	**26.1**	**1.1**	**5.6**	**32.7**	**0.6**	**0.4**

1. The total tax revenue has been reduced by the amount of any capital transfer that represents uncollected taxes. The capital transfer has been allocated between tax headings in proportion to the reported tax revenue.
2. From 1991 the figures relate to the united Germany.
1. Le total des recettes fiscales a été diminué du montant de tout transfert en capital représentant les impôts non perçus. Le transfert en capital a été réparti entre les différentes rubriques en proportion des recettes fiscales.
2. Depuis 1991, les chiffres se rapportent à l'Allemagne unifiée.

StatLink http://dx.doi.org/10.1787/888933276681

Table 7. **Taxes on income and profits (1000) as % of GDP**
Tableau 7. **Impôts sur le revenu et les bénéfices (1000) en % du PIB**

	1965	1980	1990	2000	2007	2008	2009	2011	2012	2013
Australia / Australie	10.5	14.7	16.0	17.7	17.7	16.0	14.4	15.5	15.9	15.7
Austria / Autriche	8.6	10.3	10.1	12.0	12.2	12.8	11.5	11.7	12.0	12.3
Belgium / Belgique	8.5	16.7	15.2	16.9	15.3	15.5	14.3	14.9	15.3	15.9
Canada	9.7	14.2	17.2	17.5	15.8	15.5	14.9	14.3	14.6	14.5
Chile / Chili	..	..	3.9	4.4	10.4	8.0	5.4	8.5	8.4	6.9
Czech Republic / République tchèque	..	..	..	7.4	8.5	7.6	6.9	6.8	6.9	7.1
Denmark / Danemark[1]	13.6	22.9	27.2	28.8	27.9	27.3	27.7	27.9	28.8	29.8
Estonia / Estonie	..	..	..	7.7	7.4	7.7	7.4	6.4	6.7	7.2
Finland / Finlande	12.4	13.8	16.8	19.7	16.3	16.0	14.6	14.9	14.6	15.2
France[1]	5.3	6.6	6.6	10.7	10.1	10.2	8.6	9.8	10.4	10.9
Germany / Allemagne[2]	10.7	12.8	11.3	10.9	10.9	11.3	10.4	10.5	11.1	11.3
Greece / Grèce[1]	1.6	4.0	5.0	8.9	7.3	7.2	7.5	7.1	8.3	7.6
Hungary / Hongrie	..	..	..	9.4	10.0	10.3	9.6	6.3	7.0	6.8
Iceland / Islande	5.5	7.4	8.9	14.4	17.6	17.0	15.1	15.7	15.9	16.8
Ireland / Irlande	6.3	11.0	12.3	13.5	12.5	11.3	10.7	10.7	11.4	11.7
Israel / Israël	..	..	..	13.9	12.6	10.6	9.0	9.3	9.1	9.7
Italy / Italie	4.4	8.9	13.3	13.5	14.1	14.3	13.7	13.4	14.3	14.5
Japan / Japon	7.8	11.4	14.3	9.3	10.4	9.6	8.0	8.6	9.1	9.8
Korea / Corée	..	4.3	6.2	6.2	7.9	7.6	6.8	7.3	7.4	7.1
Luxembourg	9.5	14.6	13.3	13.4	12.7	13.4	13.8	13.5	13.7	13.5
Mexico / Mexique	..	4.3	4.2	4.5	4.9	5.1	4.9	5.3	5.1	6.0
Netherlands / Pays-Bas	11.0	13.2	13.0	9.3	10.2	9.9	10.0	9.6	9.1	9.1
New Zealand / Nouvelle-Zélande	14.1	20.7	21.6	19.5	21.4	20.1	17.3	16.6	18.0	17.4
Norway / Norvège	12.8	17.5	14.2	18.8	20.2	20.9	18.9	20.5	20.1	18.7
Poland / Pologne	..	..	..	6.7	7.9	8.0	6.8	6.4	6.6	6.2
Portugal	3.9	4.3	6.8	9.2	9.0	9.1	8.4	9.3	8.9	11.2
Slovak Republic / République slovaque	..	..	..	6.9	6.1	6.4	5.5	5.5	5.5	6.0
Slovenia / Slovénie	..	..	..	6.8	8.7	8.2	7.5	7.2	6.9	6.4
Spain / Espagne[1]	3.5	5.7	9.7	9.5	12.3	9.9	8.9	9.1	9.7	9.6
Sweden / Suède	17.2	19.0	20.6	20.0	17.4	15.9	15.5	14.8	14.5	14.8
Switzerland / Suisse	6.8	10.6	11.2	12.2	12.1	12.6	12.7	12.5	12.3	12.4
Turkey / Turquie	3.1	6.9	5.0	7.1	5.7	5.8	5.9	5.8	6.0	5.9
United Kingdom / Royaume-Uni	10.8	12.6	12.9	13.5	13.4	13.6	12.4	12.3	11.8	11.7
United States / États-Unis	11.3	12.7	11.7	14.1	12.9	11.4	9.2	10.7	11.3	12.0
Unweighted average / Moyenne non pondérée										
OECD Average / Moyenne OCDE	**8.7**	**11.6**	**12.2**	**12.2**	**12.3**	**11.9**	**11.0**	**11.1**	**11.4**	**11.5**

1. The total tax revenue has been reduced by the amount of any capital transfer that represents uncollected taxes. The capital transfer has been allocated between tax headings in proportion to the reported tax revenue.
2. From 1991 the figures relate to the united Germany.
1. Le total des recettes fiscales a été diminué du montant de tout transfert en capital représentant les impôts non perçus. Le transfert en capital a été réparti entre les différentes rubriques en proportion des recettes fiscales.
2. Depuis 1991, les chiffres se rapportent à l'Allemagne unifiée.

StatLink http://dx.doi.org/10.1787/888933276692

Table 8. **Taxes on income and profits (1000) as % of total taxation**
Tableau 8. **Impôts sur le revenu et les bénéfices (1000) en % du total des recettes fiscales**

	1965	1980	1990	2000	2007	2008	2009	2011	2012	2013
Australia / Australie	50.7	56.1	57.1	58.0	59.6	59.1	55.9	59.1	58.1	57.1
Austria / Autriche	25.5	26.7	25.5	28.5	30.0	30.8	28.0	28.5	28.8	29.0
Belgium / Belgique	27.6	41.1	36.9	38.7	35.9	36.1	34.0	34.8	34.7	35.6
Canada	38.6	46.6	48.6	50.1	49.0	49.1	47.4	47.2	47.4	47.5
Chile / Chili	..	..	23.2	23.3	45.7	37.5	31.1	40.1	39.0	34.8
Czech Republic / République tchèque	..	..	..	22.8	24.8	22.7	21.2	20.3	20.5	20.8
Denmark / Danemark[1]	46.6	55.5	61.2	61.4	60.1	60.8	61.3	61.4	62.0	62.6
Estonia / Estonie	..	..	..	24.9	23.7	24.7	21.2	20.0	20.9	22.7
Finland / Finlande	41.4	39.1	39.2	43.1	39.2	38.9	35.8	35.4	34.2	34.7
France[1]	15.9	16.8	16.1	24.9	23.9	24.1	20.7	22.7	23.7	24.2
Germany / Allemagne[2]	33.8	35.1	32.4	30.1	31.2	31.8	28.9	29.5	30.4	31.0
Greece / Grèce[1]	9.1	19.4	19.9	26.8	23.3	23.3	24.2	21.2	23.9	22.0
Hungary / Hongrie	..	..	..	24.3	25.2	26.0	24.5	17.2	18.1	17.7
Iceland / Islande	21.4	25.6	29.7	39.9	45.4	48.5	47.3	45.5	45.2	46.7
Ireland / Irlande	25.7	36.5	38.0	43.6	40.9	39.6	38.8	39.2	40.7	40.4
Israel / Israël	..	..	..	39.8	36.7	33.3	30.2	30.2	30.8	31.7
Italy / Italie	17.8	31.2	36.5	33.2	33.7	34.3	32.5	31.9	32.6	33.1
Japan / Japon	43.9	46.1	50.2	34.8	36.4	33.6	29.5	30.2	31.1	32.5
Korea / Corée	..	25.5	32.8	28.8	31.8	31.0	28.5	30.1	29.9	29.3
Luxembourg	35.9	43.2	39.4	36.1	34.6	36.0	35.3	35.6	35.3	35.3
Mexico / Mexique	..	29.8	27.1	27.3	27.7	24.8	28.6	27.3	26.3	30.2
Netherlands / Pays-Bas	35.8	32.9	32.3	25.3	28.2	27.2	28.1	26.9	25.3	24.7
New Zealand / Nouvelle-Zélande	60.5	69.8	59.6	60.0	62.9	60.3	56.9	53.7	55.4	55.5
Norway / Norvège	43.4	41.8	35.2	45.0	47.9	50.4	45.9	48.7	48.3	46.2
Poland / Pologne	..	..	..	20.3	22.7	23.3	21.6	20.0	20.4	19.5
Portugal	24.6	19.7	25.7	29.6	28.1	28.5	28.0	28.5	27.8	32.4
Slovak Republic / République slovaque	..	..	..	20.5	20.9	22.1	19.1	19.1	19.5	19.9
Slovenia / Slovénie	..	..	..	18.5	23.3	22.6	20.8	19.8	18.8	17.5
Spain / Espagne[1]	24.5	26.0	30.6	28.4	33.6	30.7	30.0	29.1	30.0	29.4
Sweden / Suède	54.9	43.5	41.6	40.8	38.7	36.2	35.2	34.8	34.1	34.5
Switzerland / Suisse	41.1	45.3	47.2	44.2	46.4	47.2	46.9	46.4	45.6	46.0
Turkey / Turquie	29.6	51.8	33.5	29.5	23.7	23.9	24.1	21.0	21.8	20.2
United Kingdom / Royaume-Uni	37.0	37.8	39.3	39.1	39.4	40.0	38.5	36.7	35.6	35.4
United States / États-Unis	48.1	49.8	45.1	50.1	48.2	45.2	40.2	45.4	46.9	47.2
Unweighted average / Moyenne non pondérée										
OECD Average / Moyenne OCDE	**34.7**	**38.2**	**37.2**	**35.1**	**36.0**	**35.4**	**33.5**	**33.5**	**33.6**	**33.7**

1. The total tax revenue has been reduced by the amount of any capital transfer that represents uncollected taxes. The capital transfer has been allocated between tax headings in proportion to the reported tax revenue.
2. From 1991 the figures relate to the united Germany.
1. Le total des recettes fiscales a été diminué du montant de tout transfert en capital représentant les impôts non perçus. Le transfert en capital a été réparti entre les différentes rubriques en proportion des recettes fiscales.
2. Depuis 1991, les chiffres se rapportent à l'Allemagne unifiée.

StatLink http://dx.doi.org/10.1787/888933276700

Table 9. **Taxes on personal income (1100) as % of GDP**
Tableau 9. **Impôts sur le revenu des personnes physiques (1100) en % du PIB**

	1965	1980	1990	2000	2007	2008	2009	2011	2012	2013
Australia / Australie	7.1	11.5	12.1	11.5	10.9	10.1	9.6	10.3	10.7	10.8
Austria / Autriche	6.7	9.0	8.3	9.3	9.1	9.6	9.1	9.2	9.6	9.7
Belgium / Belgique	6.3	14.8	13.2	13.7	11.9	12.3	12.0	12.1	12.3	12.8
Canada	5.7	10.4	14.4	12.9	12.0	11.7	11.2	10.8	11.1	11.2
Chile / Chili	..	..	..	..	..	..	..	..	..	..
Czech Republic / République tchèque	..	..	..	4.2	4.0	3.5	3.5	3.5	3.6	3.7
Denmark / Danemark[1]	12.3	21.6	24.0	24.7	24.5	24.2	25.3	23.6	23.8	26.1
Estonia / Estonie	..	..	..	6.8	5.8	6.1	5.6	5.2	5.3	5.5
Finland / Finlande	10.0	12.6	14.9	14.0	12.5	12.7	12.7	12.3	12.5	12.8
France[1]	3.6	4.6	4.4	7.8	7.2	7.3	7.1	7.3	8.0	8.4
Germany / Allemagne[2]	8.2	10.8	9.6	9.2	8.7	9.4	9.1	8.8	9.3	9.5
Greece / Grèce[1]	1.2	3.1	3.5	4.8	4.6	4.7	4.9	4.8	7.0	6.1
Hungary / Hongrie	..	..	..	7.2	7.2	7.7	7.4	5.1	5.7	5.4
Iceland / Islande	5.0	6.7	8.1	12.6	13.1	12.6	12.1	13.0	13.2	13.8
Ireland / Irlande	4.1	9.6	10.7	9.9	9.2	8.6	8.4	8.5	9.1	9.3
Israel / Israël	..	..	..	10.2	7.8	7.0	5.9	5.6	5.4	5.5
Italy / Italie	2.7	6.6	9.6	10.1	10.7	11.2	11.2	11.1	11.7	11.7
Japan / Japon	3.9	6.0	7.9	5.6	5.6	5.7	5.4	5.3	5.5	5.8
Korea / Corée	..	1.9	3.8	3.1	4.1	3.7	3.4	3.5	3.7	3.7
Luxembourg	6.6	9.1	8.0	6.8	7.3	8.1	8.0	8.4	8.5	8.8
Mexico / Mexique	..	..	..	..	..	..	..	..	..	..
Netherlands / Pays-Bas	8.6	10.6	9.9	5.6	7.2	7.0	8.1	7.7	7.3	7.2
New Zealand / Nouvelle-Zélande	9.1	18.3	17.4	14.0	14.3	13.5	12.5	11.4	12.2	11.9
Norway / Norvège	11.7	11.9	10.5	10.1	9.4	8.9	9.9	9.7	9.7	9.9
Poland / Pologne	..	..	..	4.3	5.2	5.3	4.6	4.4	4.5	4.5
Portugal	..	..	4.2	5.5	5.4	5.4	5.6	6.0	5.9	7.8
Slovak Republic / République slovaque	..	..	..	3.3	2.9	3.1	2.8	2.9	2.9	2.9
Slovenia / Slovénie	..	..	..	5.5	5.5	5.7	5.7	5.6	5.7	5.2
Spain / Espagne[1]	2.0	4.5	6.9	6.2	7.4	6.9	6.5	7.1	7.3	7.3
Sweden / Suède	15.3	18.0	19.1	16.3	13.9	13.1	12.7	11.7	11.9	12.2
Switzerland / Suisse	5.5	9.1	7.8	8.2	8.3	8.3	8.7	8.5	8.5	8.5
Turkey / Turquie	2.6	5.8	4.0	5.4	4.1	4.0	4.0	3.8	4.0	4.1
United Kingdom / Royaume-Uni	9.7	9.8	9.7	10.2	10.2	10.2	9.8	9.4	9.1	9.1
United States / États-Unis	7.4	10.0	9.7	11.9	10.2	9.7	7.8	8.9	9.2	9.8
Unweighted average / Moyenne non pondérée										
OECD Average / Moyenne OCDE	**6.7**	**9.8**	**10.1**	**9.1**	**8.8**	**8.7**	**8.5**	**8.3**	**8.6**	**8.8**

1. The total tax revenue has been reduced by the amount of any capital transfer that represents uncollected taxes. The capital transfer has been allocated between tax headings in proportion to the reported tax revenue.
2. From 1991 the figures relate to the united Germany.

1. Le total des recettes fiscales a été diminué du montant de tout transfert en capital représentant les impôts non perçus. Le transfert en capital a été réparti entre les différentes rubriques en proportion des recettes fiscales.
2. Depuis 1991, les chiffres se rapportent à l'Allemagne unifiée.

StatLink http://dx.doi.org/10.1787/888933276715

Table 10. **Taxes on personal income (1100) as % of total taxation**
Tableau 10. **Impôts sur le revenu des personnes physiques (1100) en % du total des recettes fiscales**

	1965	1980	1990	2000	2007	2008	2009	2011	2012	2013
Australia / Australie	34.4	44.0	43.0	37.8	36.6	37.5	37.4	39.4	39.2	39.2
Austria / Autriche	20.0	23.2	21.0	22.2	22.5	23.2	22.3	22.5	22.9	22.9
Belgium / Belgique	20.5	36.4	32.0	31.4	27.9	28.5	28.5	28.2	27.9	28.6
Canada	22.6	34.1	40.8	36.8	37.1	37.1	35.7	35.8	36.2	36.6
Chile / Chili	..	..	..	..	..	..	..	..	..	..
Czech Republic / République tchèque	..	..	..	12.9	11.7	10.6	10.7	10.6	10.6	10.7
Denmark / Danemark[1]	42.1	52.3	54.0	52.7	52.8	53.9	56.0	52.0	51.4	54.8
Estonia / Estonie	..	..	..	22.1	18.5	19.5	16.0	16.2	16.5	17.3
Finland / Finlande	33.3	35.7	34.7	30.6	30.2	30.8	31.1	29.2	29.3	29.3
France[1]	10.6	11.6	10.7	18.0	17.1	17.4	17.3	17.0	18.0	18.6
Germany / Allemagne[2]	26.0	29.6	27.6	25.3	25.0	26.5	25.2	24.7	25.7	26.1
Greece / Grèce[1]	6.8	14.9	14.1	14.5	14.9	15.1	15.8	14.4	20.2	17.6
Hungary / Hongrie	..	..	..	18.6	18.2	19.4	18.9	13.9	14.7	14.1
Iceland / Islande	19.5	23.1	26.9	34.8	33.9	36.0	37.9	37.6	37.4	38.3
Ireland / Irlande	16.7	32.0	33.1	31.9	30.3	30.1	30.5	31.1	32.4	31.9
Israel / Israël	..	..	..	29.2	22.7	21.8	19.8	18.2	18.2	18.0
Italy / Italie	10.9	23.1	26.3	24.8	25.6	26.8	26.7	26.6	26.7	26.6
Japan / Japon	21.7	24.3	27.8	21.1	19.6	19.9	20.0	18.4	18.6	19.2
Korea / Corée	..	11.5	20.0	14.6	16.7	15.0	14.1	14.7	15.0	15.3
Luxembourg	24.9	27.0	23.6	18.3	19.9	21.7	20.6	22.2	21.9	22.8
Mexico / Mexique	..	..	..	..	..	..	..	..	..	..
Netherlands / Pays-Bas	27.7	26.3	24.7	15.2	19.9	19.1	22.8	21.5	20.2	19.5
New Zealand / Nouvelle-Zélande	39.4	61.6	48.0	43.1	42.1	40.7	41.1	37.0	37.7	38.0
Norway / Norvège	39.6	28.5	26.2	24.1	22.2	21.5	24.1	23.1	23.4	24.5
Poland / Pologne	..	..	..	13.1	14.9	15.5	14.5	13.7	13.9	14.0
Portugal	..	..	15.9	17.5	16.8	17.1	18.5	18.5	18.3	22.6
Slovak Republic / République slovaque	..	..	..	9.9	9.9	10.6	9.7	9.9	10.3	9.6
Slovenia / Slovénie	..	..	..	15.0	14.7	15.8	15.8	15.3	15.4	14.2
Spain / Espagne[1]	14.3	20.4	21.7	18.7	20.2	21.4	21.7	22.7	22.7	22.4
Sweden / Suède	48.7	41.0	38.5	33.2	30.9	29.8	28.8	27.5	28.0	28.4
Switzerland / Suisse	33.4	38.9	32.9	29.7	31.9	31.1	32.0	31.3	31.7	31.5
Turkey / Turquie	24.8	43.5	26.8	22.2	17.0	16.5	16.4	13.5	14.4	13.9
United Kingdom / Royaume-Uni	33.1	29.4	29.4	29.3	30.0	30.0	30.4	28.1	27.5	27.7
United States / États-Unis	31.7	39.1	37.6	42.1	38.2	38.5	34.2	37.9	38.3	38.7
Unweighted average / Moyenne non pondérée										
OECD Average / Moyenne OCDE	**26.2**	**31.3**	**29.5**	**25.3**	**24.7**	**24.9**	**24.8**	**24.1**	**24.5**	**24.8**

1. The total tax revenue has been reduced by the amount of any capital transfer that represents uncollected taxes. The capital transfer has been allocated between tax headings in proportion to the reported tax revenue.
2. From 1991 the figures relate to the united Germany.

1. Le total des recettes fiscales a été diminué du montant de tout transfert en capital représentant les impôts non perçus. Le transfert en capital a été réparti entre les différentes rubriques en proportion des recettes fiscales.
2. Depuis 1991, les chiffres se rapportent à l'Allemagne unifiée.

StatLink http://dx.doi.org/10.1787/888933276727

Table 11. **Taxes on corporate income (1200) as % of GDP**
Tableau 11. **Impôts sur les bénéfices des sociétés (1200) en % du PIB**

	1965	1980	1990	2000	2007	2008	2009	2011	2012	2013
Australia / Australie	3.4	3.2	4.0	6.2	6.8	5.8	4.8	5.2	5.2	4.9
Austria / Autriche	1.8	1.4	1.4	2.0	2.3	2.4	1.6	2.0	2.0	2.2
Belgium / Belgique	1.9	1.9	2.0	3.1	3.4	3.3	2.3	2.8	3.0	3.1
Canada	3.8	3.5	2.5	4.3	3.4	3.3	3.3	3.1	3.1	3.0
Chile / Chili	..	..	..	..	..	..	..	..	..	..
Czech Republic / République tchèque	..	..	..	3.2	4.5	4.1	3.4	3.2	3.3	3.4
Denmark / Danemark[1]	1.3	1.4	1.7	3.2	3.1	2.6	1.9	2.2	2.6	2.7
Estonia / Estonie	..	..	..	0.9	1.6	1.6	1.8	1.2	1.4	1.7
Finland / Finlande	2.4	1.2	1.9	5.7	3.7	3.3	1.9	2.6	2.1	2.4
France[1]	1.8	2.0	2.2	3.0	2.9	2.8	1.4	2.5	2.5	2.5
Germany / Allemagne[2]	2.5	2.0	1.7	1.8	2.2	1.9	1.3	1.7	1.7	1.8
Greece / Grèce[1]	0.3	0.8	1.4	4.0	2.5	2.4	2.5	2.2	1.2	1.3
Hungary / Hongrie	..	..	..	2.2	2.8	2.6	2.2	1.2	1.3	1.4
Iceland / Islande	0.5	0.7	0.8	1.2	2.4	1.8	1.7	1.7	1.9	2.2
Ireland / Irlande	2.2	1.4	1.6	3.6	3.3	2.7	2.3	2.2	2.3	2.4
Israel / Israël	..	..	..	3.4	4.2	3.2	2.5	3.0	2.7	3.5
Italy / Italie	1.7	2.2	3.7	2.8	3.7	3.6	3.0	2.6	2.9	3.2
Japan / Japon	3.9	5.4	6.4	3.7	4.8	3.9	2.6	3.4	3.7	4.0
Korea / Corée	..	1.9	2.4	3.0	3.7	3.9	3.4	3.7	3.7	3.4
Luxembourg	2.9	5.5	5.4	6.6	5.4	5.3	5.7	5.1	5.2	4.8
Mexico / Mexique	..	..	..	..	..	..	..	..	..	..
Netherlands / Pays-Bas	2.5	2.7	3.0	3.7	3.0	2.9	1.9	1.9	1.8	1.9
New Zealand / Nouvelle-Zélande	4.8	2.3	2.3	4.0	4.8	4.4	3.4	4.0	4.6	4.4
Norway / Norvège	1.1	5.6	3.6	8.8	10.8	12.0	9.0	10.8	10.3	8.8
Poland / Pologne	..	..	..	2.4	2.7	2.7	2.3	2.0	2.1	1.8
Portugal	..	..	2.1	3.8	3.6	3.6	2.8	3.3	2.9	3.4
Slovak Republic / République slovaque	..	..	..	2.6	2.9	3.1	2.5	2.4	2.4	2.9
Slovenia / Slovénie	..	..	..	1.1	3.2	2.5	1.8	1.7	1.2	1.2
Spain / Espagne[1]	1.3	1.1	2.8	3.0	4.5	2.7	2.1	1.7	2.0	2.0
Sweden / Suède	1.9	1.1	1.5	3.7	3.5	2.8	2.8	3.1	2.6	2.6
Switzerland / Suisse	1.3	1.5	1.7	2.4	2.8	3.0	2.8	2.8	2.8	2.8
Turkey / Turquie	0.5	0.6	1.0	1.8	1.6	1.8	1.9	2.1	2.0	1.9
United Kingdom / Royaume-Uni	1.3	2.8	3.3	3.4	3.2	3.4	2.6	2.9	2.7	2.5
United States / États-Unis	3.9	2.7	2.0	2.2	2.7	1.7	1.4	1.8	2.1	2.2
Unweighted average / Moyenne non pondérée										
OECD Average / Moyenne OCDE	**2.1**	**2.3**	**2.5**	**3.3**	**3.6**	**3.3**	**2.7**	**2.9**	**2.9**	**2.9**

1. The total tax revenue has been reduced by the amount of any capital transfer that represents uncollected taxes. The capital transfer has been allocated between tax headings in proportion to the reported tax revenue.
2. From 1991 the figures relate to the united Germany.

1. Le total des recettes fiscales a été diminué du montant de tout transfert en capital représentant les impôts non perçus. Le transfert en capital a été réparti entre les différentes rubriques en proportion des recettes fiscales.
2. Depuis 1991, les chiffres se rapportent à l'Allemagne unifiée.

StatLink http://dx.doi.org/10.1787/888933276737

Table 12. **Taxes on corporate income (1200) as % of total taxation**
Tableau 12. **Impôts sur les bénéfices des sociétés (1200) en % du total des recettes fiscales**

	1965	1980	1990	2000	2007	2008	2009	2011	2012	2013
Australia / Australie	16.3	12.2	14.1	20.2	23.0	21.6	18.5	19.7	18.9	18.0
Austria / Autriche	5.4	3.5	3.6	4.6	5.8	5.8	4.0	4.9	4.8	5.1
Belgium / Belgique	6.2	4.7	4.8	7.2	8.0	7.6	5.5	6.5	6.8	6.9
Canada	14.9	11.6	7.0	12.2	10.6	10.4	10.5	10.3	10.1	9.7
Chile / Chili	..	..	..	..	..	..	..	..	..	..
Czech Republic / République tchèque	..	..	..	9.9	13.1	12.1	10.5	9.7	9.9	10.1
Denmark / Danemark[1]	4.6	3.3	3.8	6.8	6.8	5.7	4.2	4.8	5.6	5.6
Estonia / Estonie	..	..	..	2.9	5.2	5.1	5.2	3.8	4.5	5.5
Finland / Finlande	8.1	3.4	4.5	12.5	9.0	8.1	4.7	6.2	4.9	5.4
France[1]	5.3	5.1	5.3	6.9	6.8	6.7	3.5	5.7	5.6	5.7
Germany / Allemagne[2]	7.8	5.5	4.8	4.8	6.2	5.3	3.7	4.7	4.7	4.9
Greece / Grèce[1]	1.8	3.8	5.5	12.0	7.9	7.8	8.1	6.6	3.4	3.9
Hungary / Hongrie	..	..	..	5.7	7.0	6.6	5.7	3.3	3.3	3.6
Iceland / Islande	1.8	2.5	2.8	3.3	6.1	5.2	5.2	5.0	5.4	6.0
Ireland / Irlande	9.1	4.5	4.9	11.7	10.7	9.5	8.4	8.0	8.2	8.4
Israel / Israël	..	..	..	9.6	12.1	10.1	8.6	9.7	9.2	11.4
Italy / Italie	6.9	7.8	10.0	6.9	8.8	8.6	7.0	6.2	6.7	7.2
Japan / Japon	22.2	21.8	22.4	13.8	16.8	13.7	9.6	11.8	12.5	13.2
Korea / Corée	..	11.0	12.8	14.1	15.1	15.9	14.4	15.4	14.9	14.0
Luxembourg	11.0	16.2	15.8	17.8	14.7	14.3	14.7	13.4	13.4	12.4
Mexico / Mexique	..	..	..	..	..	..	..	..	..	..
Netherlands / Pays-Bas	8.1	6.6	7.5	10.1	8.4	8.1	5.3	5.4	5.1	5.2
New Zealand / Nouvelle-Zélande	20.7	7.8	6.5	12.4	14.2	13.1	11.0	12.9	14.1	14.1
Norway / Norvège	3.8	13.3	9.0	20.9	25.7	29.0	21.8	25.6	24.9	21.7
Poland / Pologne	..	..	..	7.2	7.8	7.8	7.2	6.4	6.5	5.5
Portugal	..	..	8.0	12.1	11.3	11.4	9.5	10.0	9.1	9.9
Slovak Republic / République slovaque	..	..	..	7.7	10.0	10.5	8.6	8.4	8.4	9.5
Slovenia / Slovénie	..	..	..	3.1	8.6	6.8	5.0	4.5	3.4	3.3
Spain / Espagne[1]	9.2	5.1	8.8	8.9	12.4	8.4	7.2	5.5	6.4	6.2
Sweden / Suède	6.1	2.5	3.1	7.5	7.8	6.4	6.4	7.3	6.0	6.2
Switzerland / Suisse	7.7	6.4	7.1	8.8	10.8	11.1	10.5	10.5	10.4	10.5
Turkey / Turquie	4.8	4.1	6.7	7.3	6.8	7.3	7.7	7.5	7.4	6.3
United Kingdom / Royaume-Uni	4.4	8.4	9.9	9.7	9.5	10.0	8.1	8.6	8.1	7.7
United States / États-Unis	16.4	10.8	7.5	7.9	10.0	6.7	6.0	7.5	8.6	8.5
Unweighted average / Moyenne non pondérée										
OECD Average / Moyenne OCDE	**8.8**	**7.6**	**7.9**	**9.6**	**10.5**	**9.9**	**8.3**	**8.6**	**8.5**	**8.5**

1. The total tax revenue has been reduced by the amount of any capital transfer that represents uncollected taxes. The capital transfer has been allocated between tax headings in proportion to the reported tax revenue.
2. From 1991 the figures relate to the united Germany.

1. Le total des recettes fiscales a été diminué du montant de tout transfert en capital représentant les impôts non perçus. Le transfert en capital a été réparti entre les différentes rubriques en proportion des recettes fiscales.
2. Depuis 1991, les chiffres se rapportent à l'Allemagne unifiée.

StatLink *http://dx.doi.org/10.1787/888933276740*

Table 13. **Social security contributions (2000) as % of GDP**
Tableau 13. **Cotisations de sécurité sociale (2000) en % du PIB**

	1965	1980	1990	2000	2007	2008	2009	2011	2012	2013
Australia / Australie	0.0	0.0	0.0	0.0	0.0	0.0	0.0	0.0	0.0	0.0
Austria / Autriche	8.4	12.0	12.9	14.4	13.7	13.8	14.2	14.1	14.2	14.6
Belgium / Belgique	9.6	11.7	13.7	13.4	13.1	13.5	14.0	13.8	14.1	14.2
Canada	1.4	3.2	4.3	4.8	4.6	4.6	4.8	4.6	4.8	4.8
Chile / Chili	..	..	1.5	1.4	1.3	1.4	1.4	1.3	1.4	1.4
Czech Republic / République tchèque	..	..	..	14.4	15.0	14.8	14.2	14.6	14.8	14.8
Denmark / Danemark[1]	1.0	0.2	0.0	0.6	0.1	0.1	0.1	0.1	0.1	0.1
Estonia / Estonie	..	..	..	10.9	10.4	11.5	12.9	11.8	11.3	11.1
Finland / Finlande	2.1	8.2	11.0	11.6	11.5	11.5	12.2	12.1	12.6	12.6
France[1]	11.5	16.8	18.1	15.5	15.7	15.7	16.3	16.2	16.5	16.7
Germany / Allemagne[2]	8.5	12.5	13.0	14.1	12.8	12.9	13.9	13.8	13.9	13.9
Greece / Grèce[1]	5.4	6.8	7.6	10.1	10.7	10.7	10.3	10.8	10.8	10.7
Hungary / Hongrie	..	..	..	11.3	12.9	12.8	12.2	12.4	12.5	12.5
Iceland / Islande	2.1	0.6	0.9	2.8	2.9	2.7	2.9	3.9	3.6	3.7
Ireland / Irlande	1.6	4.3	4.6	3.7	4.1	4.5	5.2	5.3	4.9	5.2
Israel / Israël	..	..	..	5.1	5.2	5.3	5.1	5.3	5.1	5.1
Italy / Italie	8.4	10.9	12.0	11.6	12.5	12.8	13.2	12.9	13.1	13.1
Japan / Japon	3.9	7.2	7.5	9.4	10.4	11.1	11.0	11.9	12.2	12.4
Korea / Corée	..	0.2	1.9	3.6	5.1	5.4	5.6	5.8	6.1	6.4
Luxembourg	8.5	9.7	9.1	9.5	10.1	10.5	11.6	11.0	11.3	11.1
Mexico / Mexique	..	2.0	2.1	2.7	2.7	2.6	2.9	2.8	2.9	3.1
Netherlands / Pays-Bas	9.5	15.3	15.0	14.4	12.6	13.5	12.8	13.8	14.7	15.0
New Zealand / Nouvelle-Zélande	0.0	0.0	0.0	0.0	0.0	0.0	0.0	0.0	0.0	0.0
Norway / Norvège	3.5	8.9	10.6	8.8	8.8	8.6	9.6	9.3	9.3	9.5
Poland / Pologne	..	..	..	13.0	11.9	11.4	11.3	11.3	12.2	12.3
Portugal	3.4	6.5	7.2	7.9	8.1	8.4	8.5	8.9	8.7	8.9
Slovak Republic / République slovaque	..	..	..	14.0	11.4	11.6	12.3	12.1	12.3	13.3
Slovenia / Slovénie	..	..	..	13.9	13.4	13.8	14.6	14.7	14.9	14.8
Spain / Espagne[1]	4.0	10.7	11.2	11.6	11.8	11.8	11.8	11.7	11.5	11.3
Sweden / Suède	3.8	12.6	13.5	12.9	11.8	11.0	10.9	9.9	10.2	10.0
Switzerland / Suisse	2.5	5.5	5.6	6.8	6.1	6.2	6.5	6.6	6.7	6.7
Turkey / Turquie	0.6	1.9	2.9	4.5	5.2	6.1	6.0	7.8	7.5	8.0
United Kingdom / Royaume-Uni	4.5	5.6	5.6	5.9	6.3	6.5	6.4	6.3	6.3	6.2
United States / États-Unis	3.1	5.6	6.6	6.6	6.3	6.3	6.3	5.5	5.5	6.1
Unweighted average / Moyenne non pondérée										
OECD Average / Moyenne OCDE	**4.5**	**6.9**	**7.4**	**8.6**	**8.5**	**8.6**	**8.9**	**8.9**	**9.0**	**9.1**

1. The total tax revenue has been reduced by the amount of any capital transfer that represents uncollected taxes. The capital transfer has been allocated between tax headings in proportion to the reported tax revenue.
2. From 1991 the figures relate to the united Germany.
1. Le total des recettes fiscales a été diminué du montant de tout transfert en capital représentant les impôts non perçus. Le transfert en capital a été réparti entre les différentes rubriques en proportion des recettes fiscales.
2. Depuis 1991, les chiffres se rapportent à l'Allemagne unifiée.

StatLink http://dx.doi.org/10.1787/888933276759

Table 14. **Social security contributions (2000) as % of total taxation**
Tableau 14. **Cotisations de sécurité sociale (2000) en % du total des recettes fiscales**

	1965	1980	1990	2000	2007	2008	2009	2011	2012	2013
Australia / Australie	0.0	0.0	0.0	0.0	0.0	0.0	0.0	0.0	0.0	0.0
Austria / Autriche	24.9	30.9	32.9	34.1	33.7	33.3	34.8	34.3	34.1	34.3
Belgium / Belgique	31.4	28.8	33.2	30.7	30.8	31.4	33.2	32.2	32.0	31.7
Canada	5.6	10.5	12.1	13.6	14.4	14.7	15.4	15.2	15.5	15.8
Chile / Chili	..	..	9.0	7.3	5.6	6.4	8.3	6.3	6.5	7.2
Czech Republic / République tchèque	..	..	..	44.3	43.6	44.2	44.0	43.9	43.6	43.2
Denmark / Danemark[1]	3.3	0.4	0.0	1.4	0.2	0.1	0.1	0.2	0.2	0.2
Estonia / Estonie	..	..	..	35.3	33.3	36.6	36.9	37.0	35.3	34.8
Finland / Finlande	6.8	23.3	25.6	25.2	27.6	28.0	29.8	28.7	29.6	28.9
France[1]	34.2	42.7	44.1	36.0	37.1	37.3	39.4	37.9	37.4	37.2
Germany / Allemagne[2]	26.8	34.3	37.5	39.0	36.6	36.4	38.6	38.6	38.3	38.1
Greece / Grèce[1]	31.6	32.9	30.2	30.3	34.4	34.7	33.4	32.2	31.3	31.1
Hungary / Hongrie	..	..	..	29.3	32.7	32.4	31.3	34.0	32.5	32.6
Iceland / Islande	8.1	2.2	3.1	7.7	7.4	7.7	9.0	11.4	10.4	10.3
Ireland / Irlande	6.5	14.3	14.1	11.8	13.6	15.6	18.9	19.2	17.6	17.8
Israel / Israël	..	..	..	14.7	15.2	16.5	17.1	17.1	17.1	16.6
Italy / Italie	34.2	38.0	32.9	28.5	29.9	30.9	31.4	30.8	29.8	29.8
Japan / Japon	21.8	29.1	26.4	35.2	36.5	38.8	41.0	41.5	41.6	40.9
Korea / Corée	..	1.1	10.1	16.7	20.7	21.8	23.4	24.0	24.7	26.4
Luxembourg	32.3	28.7	27.0	25.7	27.5	28.4	29.8	29.1	29.1	28.8
Mexico / Mexique	..	14.1	13.4	16.5	15.3	12.7	16.7	14.5	14.9	15.5
Netherlands / Pays-Bas	30.8	38.1	37.4	39.1	34.9	37.0	36.2	38.4	40.8	40.8
New Zealand / Nouvelle-Zélande	0.0	0.0	0.0	0.0	0.0	0.0	0.0	0.0	0.0	0.0
Norway / Norvège	11.9	21.1	26.3	20.9	20.8	20.8	23.3	22.0	22.5	23.5
Poland / Pologne	..	..	..	39.4	34.3	33.1	35.7	35.4	37.7	38.6
Portugal	21.8	29.5	27.2	25.4	25.4	26.2	28.4	27.4	27.1	25.9
Slovak Republic / République slovaque	..	..	..	41.5	39.2	39.9	42.7	42.1	43.4	43.8
Slovenia / Slovénie	..	..	..	38.0	36.3	37.8	40.3	40.2	40.4	40.1
Spain / Espagne[1]	28.3	48.6	35.4	34.8	32.3	36.6	39.5	37.5	35.7	34.5
Sweden / Suède	12.1	28.8	27.2	26.3	26.2	25.0	24.6	23.3	24.0	23.3
Switzerland / Suisse	14.9	23.4	23.6	24.5	23.5	23.1	23.9	24.5	24.9	25.1
Turkey / Turquie	5.9	14.0	19.7	18.7	21.7	25.0	24.5	27.9	27.2	27.4
United Kingdom / Royaume-Uni	15.4	16.7	17.0	17.0	18.5	19.1	19.7	18.7	19.1	18.8
United States / États-Unis	13.3	21.9	25.6	23.6	23.5	25.1	27.3	23.2	22.7	24.2
Unweighted average / Moyenne non pondérée										
OECD Average / Moyenne OCDE	**17.6**	**22.1**	**21.9**	**24.5**	**24.5**	**25.2**	**26.4**	**26.1**	**26.1**	**26.1**

1. The total tax revenue has been reduced by the amount of any capital transfer that represents uncollected taxes. The capital transfer has been allocated between tax headings in proportion to the reported tax revenue.
2. From 1991 the figures relate to the united Germany.

1. Le total des recettes fiscales a été diminué du montant de tout transfert en capital représentant les impôts non perçus. Le transfert en capital a été réparti entre les différentes rubriques en proportion des recettes fiscales.
2. Depuis 1991, les chiffres se rapportent à l'Allemagne unifiée.

StatLink http://dx.doi.org/10.1787/888933276768

Table 15. **Employees' social security contributions (2100) as % of GDP**
Tableau 15. **Cotisations de sécurité sociale à la charge des salariés (2100) en % du PIB**

	1965	1980	1990	2000	2007	2008	2009	2011	2012	2013
Australia / Australie	0.0	0.0	0.0	0.0	0.0	0.0	0.0	0.0	0.0	0.0
Austria / Autriche	3.7	4.9	5.5	5.9	5.6	5.6	5.8	5.7	5.7	5.9
Belgium / Belgique	2.7	3.4	4.2	4.2	4.0	4.1	4.2	4.1	4.2	4.2
Canada	0.5	1.1	1.5	1.9	1.8	1.9	1.9	1.8	1.9	1.9
Chile / Chili	..	..	1.5	1.3	1.2	1.3	1.4	1.3	1.4	1.4
Czech Republic / République tchèque	..	..	..	3.3	3.3	3.3	2.9	3.0	3.0	3.0
Denmark / Danemark[1]	0.8	0.0	0.0	0.6	0.1	0.1	0.1	0.1	0.1	0.0
Estonia / Estonie	..	..	..	0.0	0.2	0.2	0.5	0.8	0.8	0.6
Finland / Finlande	0.0	1.2	1.3	2.1	2.2	2.1	2.3	2.6	2.9	2.9
France[1]	2.2	4.4	5.4	3.9	3.9	3.9	4.0	3.9	4.0	4.1
Germany / Allemagne[2]	3.7	5.6	5.6	6.2	5.6	5.6	6.1	6.1	6.2	6.2
Greece / Grèce[1]	2.2	3.0	3.8	4.0	4.0	4.0	4.1	4.3	4.3	4.4
Hungary / Hongrie	..	..	..	2.1	3.4	3.3	3.2	4.7	5.1	5.3
Iceland / Islande	0.0	0.0	0.1	..	..	..	..	..	..	..
Ireland / Irlande	0.8	1.4	1.5	0.9	1.0	1.1	1.9	1.9	1.8	1.9
Israel / Israël	..	..	..	3.3	3.5	3.6	3.5	3.6	3.4	3.3
Italy / Italie	..	2.0	2.3	2.2	2.2	2.4	2.4	2.3	2.3	2.4
Japan / Japon	1.3	2.5	3.0	3.9	4.3	4.8	4.7	5.2	5.3	5.4
Korea / Corée	..	0.0	0.7	1.4	2.1	2.2	2.2	2.4	2.6	2.7
Luxembourg	3.1	3.8	3.5	4.2	4.6	4.8	5.3	5.0	5.1	5.0
Mexico / Mexique	..	..	..	..	..	..	..	..	..	..
Netherlands / Pays-Bas	4.7	6.3	9.3	7.2	5.7	6.2	5.5	6.0	6.4	6.6
New Zealand / Nouvelle-Zélande	0.0	0.0	0.0	0.0	0.0	0.0	0.0	0.0	0.0	0.0
Norway / Norvège	0.0	2.1	3.4	3.0	2.9	2.9	3.2	3.1	3.1	3.7
Poland / Pologne	..	..	..	5.5	4.7	4.4	4.2	4.5	4.8	4.9
Portugal	1.3	2.5	2.6	3.3	3.6	3.8	3.8	3.8	3.7	3.8
Slovak Republic / République slovaque	..	..	..	2.9	2.7	2.8	3.0	2.9	3.0	3.0
Slovenia / Slovénie	..	..	..	7.7	7.1	7.3	7.6	7.5	7.5	7.4
Spain / Espagne[1]	0.9	2.4	1.8	1.9	1.9	1.9	1.8	1.9	1.8	1.8
Sweden / Suède	0.6	0.0	0.1	2.7	2.5	2.5	2.6	2.6	2.6	2.7
Switzerland / Suisse	1.1	2.4	2.5	3.1	2.8	2.9	3.0	3.1	3.1	3.1
Turkey / Turquie	0.3	0.7	1.1	1.6	2.1	2.0	2.2	2.8	2.9	3.2
United Kingdom / Royaume-Uni	2.1	2.2	2.2	2.4	2.5	2.5	2.5	2.5	2.5	2.4
United States / États-Unis	1.2	2.3	2.9	3.0	2.8	2.8	2.8	2.0	2.0	2.7
Unweighted average / Moyenne non pondérée										
OECD Average / Moyenne OCDE	**1.4**	**2.2**	**2.5**	**3.0**	**2.9**	**3.0**	**3.1**	**3.2**	**3.2**	**3.3**

1. The total tax revenue has been reduced by the amount of any capital transfer that represents uncollected taxes. The capital transfer has been allocated between tax headings in proportion to the reported tax revenue.
2. From 1991 the figures relate to the united Germany.

1. Le total des recettes fiscales a été diminué du montant de tout transfert en capital représentant les impôts non perçus. Le transfert en capital a été réparti entre les différentes rubriques en proportion des recettes fiscales.
2. Depuis 1991, les chiffres se rapportent à l'Allemagne unifiée.

StatLink http://dx.doi.org/10.1787/888933276772

Table 16. **Employees' social security contributions (2100) as % of total taxation**
Tableau 16. **Cotisations de sécurité sociale à la charge des salariés (2100) en % du total des recettes fiscales**

	1965	1980	1990	2000	2007	2008	2009	2011	2012	2013
Australia / Australie	0.0	0.0	0.0	0.0	0.0	0.0	0.0	0.0	0.0	0.0
Austria / Autriche	11.1	12.7	13.9	13.9	13.7	13.6	14.1	13.9	13.7	13.8
Belgium / Belgique	8.9	8.4	10.2	9.7	9.4	9.4	9.9	9.6	9.5	9.3
Canada	2.1	3.7	4.4	5.5	5.7	5.9	6.2	6.1	6.2	6.3
Chile / Chili	..	..	8.7	7.0	5.3	6.1	7.9	6.1	6.3	7.0
Czech Republic / République tchèque	..	..	..	10.0	9.7	9.9	8.8	9.0	8.9	8.8
Denmark / Danemark[1]	2.7	0.0	0.0	1.3	0.1	0.1	0.1	0.1	0.1	0.1
Estonia / Estonie	..	..	..	0.0	0.5	0.6	1.5	2.4	2.4	1.8
Finland / Finlande	0.0	3.3	2.9	4.7	5.2	5.1	5.6	6.2	6.7	6.6
France[1]	6.6	11.1	13.2	9.0	9.3	9.2	9.6	9.1	9.0	9.2
Germany / Allemagne[2]	11.8	15.3	16.2	17.2	16.1	15.9	17.0	17.1	17.0	16.9
Greece / Grèce[1]	13.0	14.5	15.1	11.9	13.0	13.1	13.4	12.8	12.5	12.6
Hungary / Hongrie	..	..	..	5.4	8.6	8.4	8.3	12.9	13.2	13.7
Iceland / Islande	0.0	0.0	0.3	..	..	..	..	..	..	..
Ireland / Irlande	3.2	4.7	4.6	2.8	3.2	3.8	6.9	7.0	6.5	6.5
Israel / Israël	..	..	..	9.6	10.3	11.3	11.7	11.5	11.5	11.0
Italy / Italie	..	6.9	6.3	5.4	5.3	5.7	5.7	5.5	5.2	5.6
Japan / Japon	7.2	10.2	10.6	14.5	15.0	16.7	17.6	18.0	18.0	17.7
Korea / Corée	..	0.0	3.9	6.3	8.4	8.9	9.4	9.9	10.5	11.1
Luxembourg	11.9	11.3	10.4	11.4	12.5	13.0	13.6	13.3	13.3	13.1
Mexico / Mexique	..	..	..	..	..	..	..	..	..	..
Netherlands / Pays-Bas	15.3	15.7	23.1	19.5	15.7	16.9	15.4	16.7	17.7	18.1
New Zealand / Nouvelle-Zélande	0.0	0.0	0.0	0.0	0.0	0.0	0.0	0.0	0.0	0.0
Norway / Norvège	0.0	5.0	8.4	7.2	6.9	6.9	7.8	7.5	7.6	9.3
Poland / Pologne	..	..	..	16.6	13.6	12.7	13.3	14.0	14.9	15.3
Portugal	8.5	11.3	9.9	10.7	11.3	11.8	12.7	11.6	11.5	11.0
Slovak Republic / République slovaque	..	..	..	8.5	9.3	9.6	10.2	10.0	10.4	10.0
Slovenia / Slovénie	..	..	..	20.9	19.1	19.9	20.9	20.6	20.3	20.1
Spain / Espagne[1]	6.5	10.8	5.8	5.6	5.2	5.8	6.2	5.9	5.6	5.4
Sweden / Suède	1.9	0.1	0.1	5.4	5.5	5.7	6.0	6.0	6.2	6.2
Switzerland / Suisse	6.4	10.4	10.7	11.3	10.8	10.7	11.1	11.4	11.6	11.7
Turkey / Turquie	2.6	5.1	7.4	6.7	8.8	8.4	9.0	10.0	10.4	10.9
United Kingdom / Royaume-Uni	7.0	6.4	6.6	6.8	7.2	7.4	7.8	7.4	7.5	7.4
United States / États-Unis	5.1	9.2	11.2	10.6	10.4	11.2	12.1	8.6	8.4	10.7
Unweighted average / Moyenne non pondérée										
OECD Average / Moyenne OCDE	**5.7**	**7.0**	**7.8**	**8.6**	**8.6**	**8.9**	**9.4**	**9.4**	**9.5**	**9.6**

1. The total tax revenue has been reduced by the amount of any capital transfer that represents uncollected taxes. The capital transfer has been allocated between tax headings in proportion to the reported tax revenue.
2. From 1991 the figures relate to the united Germany.
1. Le total des recettes fiscales a été diminué du montant de tout transfert en capital représentant les impôts non perçus. Le transfert en capital a été réparti entre les différentes rubriques en proportion des recettes fiscales.
2. Depuis 1991, les chiffres se rapportent à l'Allemagne unifiée.

StatLink http://dx.doi.org/10.1787/888933276787

Table 17. **Employers' social security contributions (2200) as % of GDP**
Tableau 17. **Cotisations de sécurité sociale à la charge des employeurs (2200) en % du PIB**

	1965	1980	1990	2000	2007	2008	2009	2011	2012	2013
Australia / Australie	0.0	0.0	0.0	0.0	0.0	0.0	0.0	0.0	0.0	0.0
Austria / Autriche	3.9	5.9	6.4	6.9	6.4	6.5	6.6	6.6	6.7	6.8
Belgium / Belgique	6.3	7.4	8.6	8.0	8.0	8.2	8.5	8.5	8.6	8.7
Canada	0.9	2.0	2.7	2.7	2.6	2.6	2.7	2.6	2.7	2.7
Chile / Chili	..	..	0.1	0.1	0.1	0.1	0.1	0.0	0.0	0.0
Czech Republic / République tchèque	..	..	..	9.3	9.4	9.3	8.8	9.3	9.3	9.4
Denmark / Danemark[1]	0.2	0.2	0.0	0.0	0.0	0.0	0.0	0.1	0.0	0.0
Estonia / Estonie	..	..	..	10.7	10.1	11.1	12.2	10.9	10.5	10.4
Finland / Finlande	2.0	6.6	8.9	8.5	8.4	8.6	9.0	8.6	8.8	8.8
France[1]	8.5	11.2	11.2	10.7	10.7	10.7	11.0	11.1	11.2	11.3
Germany / Allemagne[2]	4.6	6.7	6.6	7.0	6.1	6.1	6.5	6.4	6.5	6.5
Greece / Grèce[1]	2.1	3.0	3.8	4.7	4.9	5.0	4.7	4.8	4.8	4.6
Hungary / Hongrie	..	..	..	9.1	9.3	9.3	8.7	7.5	7.4	7.2
Iceland / Islande	2.1	0.6	0.9	..	..	..	..	..	..	..
Ireland / Irlande	0.8	2.8	2.9	2.6	2.9	3.2	3.2	3.1	2.9	3.0
Israel / Israël	..	..	..	1.5	1.4	1.3	1.3	1.4	1.3	1.4
Italy / Italie	..	8.1	8.6	8.1	8.6	8.8	9.1	8.9	8.9	8.8
Japan / Japon	1.7	3.7	3.6	4.4	4.7	5.0	5.0	5.4	5.5	5.6
Korea / Corée	..	0.2	0.9	1.5	2.3	2.4	2.5	2.6	2.7	2.9
Luxembourg	4.9	5.3	4.5	4.2	4.3	4.5	5.0	4.8	4.8	4.7
Mexico / Mexique	..	..	..	..	..	..	..	..	..	..
Netherlands / Pays-Bas	3.9	7.2	3.0	4.2	4.2	4.5	4.6	4.7	5.1	4.9
New Zealand / Nouvelle-Zélande	0.0	0.0	0.0	0.0	0.0	0.0	0.0	0.0	0.0	0.0
Norway / Norvège	3.0	6.4	6.7	5.3	5.4	5.2	5.8	5.6	5.7	5.8
Poland / Pologne	..	..	..	5.8	4.8	4.7	4.7	4.7	4.9	5.2
Portugal	2.1	3.9	4.3	4.6	4.5	4.6	4.7	5.1	5.0	5.1
Slovak Republic / République slovaque	..	..	..	9.0	6.1	6.5	6.7	6.5	6.7	7.5
Slovenia / Slovénie	..	..	..	5.3	5.2	5.4	5.6	5.6	5.7	5.7
Spain / Espagne[1]	3.1	8.3	8.0	8.4	8.6	8.5	8.2	8.2	7.9	7.8
Sweden / Suède	2.8	12.1	12.9	10.0	9.1	8.3	8.1	7.2	7.4	7.2
Switzerland / Suisse	1.1	2.5	2.5	3.1	2.8	2.9	3.0	3.1	3.1	3.1
Turkey / Turquie	0.3	1.1	1.6	2.2	2.4	3.0	3.3	4.1	4.1	4.5
United Kingdom / Royaume-Uni	2.2	3.4	3.2	3.3	3.6	3.8	3.7	3.6	3.7	3.6
United States / États-Unis	1.8	3.0	3.4	3.3	3.2	3.2	3.1	3.1	3.1	3.1
Unweighted average / Moyenne non pondérée										
OECD Average / Moyenne OCDE	**2.5**	**4.5**	**4.4**	**5.1**	**5.0**	**5.1**	**5.2**	**5.1**	**5.2**	**5.2**

1. The total tax revenue has been reduced by the amount of any capital transfer that represents uncollected taxes. The capital transfer has been allocated between tax headings in proportion to the reported tax revenue.
2. From 1991 the figures relate to the united Germany.
1. Le total des recettes fiscales a été diminué du montant de tout transfert en capital représentant les impôts non perçus. Le transfert en capital a été réparti entre les différentes rubriques en proportion des recettes fiscales.
2. Depuis 1991, les chiffres se rapportent à l'Allemagne unifiée.

StatLink http://dx.doi.org/10.1787/888933276790

Table 18. **Employers' social security contributions (2200) as % of total taxation**
Tableau 18. **Cotisations de sécurité sociale à la charge des employeurs (2200) en % du total des recettes fiscales**

	1965	1980	1990	2000	2007	2008	2009	2011	2012	2013
Australia / Australie	0.0	0.0	0.0	0.0	0.0	0.0	0.0	0.0	0.0	0.0
Austria / Autriche	11.6	15.3	16.2	16.4	15.9	15.7	16.2	16.1	16.0	16.0
Belgium / Belgique	20.6	18.1	20.9	18.3	18.8	19.1	20.2	19.7	19.6	19.5
Canada	3.5	6.6	7.6	7.8	8.2	8.3	8.7	8.7	8.8	8.9
Chile / Chili	..	..	0.3	0.3	0.2	0.3	0.4	0.2	0.2	0.2
Czech Republic / République tchèque	..	..	..	28.5	27.4	27.9	27.2	27.8	27.6	27.4
Denmark / Danemark[1]	0.6	0.4	0.0	0.0	0.0	0.0	0.0	0.1	0.1	0.1
Estonia / Estonie	..	..	..	34.7	32.4	35.5	34.8	34.2	32.6	32.7
Finland / Finlande	6.8	18.7	20.8	18.5	20.3	20.9	21.9	20.5	20.7	20.2
France[1]	25.3	28.4	27.2	24.8	25.2	25.4	26.7	25.9	25.4	25.1
Germany / Allemagne[2]	14.4	18.4	19.1	19.2	17.4	17.1	18.1	18.0	17.9	17.9
Greece / Grèce[1]	12.2	14.4	15.1	14.1	15.9	16.3	15.1	14.2	13.8	13.5
Hungary / Hongrie	..	..	..	23.6	23.6	23.4	22.3	20.6	19.1	18.6
Iceland / Islande	8.1	2.2	2.9	..	..	..	..	..	..	..
Ireland / Irlande	3.3	9.4	8.9	8.4	9.7	11.0	11.4	11.5	10.4	10.5
Israel / Israël	..	..	..	4.4	4.0	4.2	4.3	4.5	4.5	4.7
Italy / Italie	..	28.4	23.6	19.9	20.5	21.2	21.6	21.2	20.2	20.1
Japan / Japon	9.5	14.8	12.7	16.4	16.6	17.7	18.5	19.0	18.9	18.6
Korea / Corée	..	1.1	4.5	6.9	9.1	9.6	10.6	10.7	10.8	12.0
Luxembourg	18.6	15.8	13.2	11.2	11.8	12.1	12.8	12.5	12.4	12.2
Mexico / Mexique	..	..	..	..	..	..	..	..	..	..
Netherlands / Pays-Bas	12.6	17.8	7.5	11.3	11.7	12.2	13.0	13.1	14.0	13.4
New Zealand / Nouvelle-Zélande	0.0	0.0	0.0	0.0	0.0	0.0	0.0	0.0	0.0	0.0
Norway / Norvège	10.2	15.3	16.6	12.5	12.7	12.7	14.2	13.3	13.6	14.2
Poland / Pologne	..	..	..	17.5	13.9	13.5	14.8	14.5	15.3	16.3
Portugal	13.2	17.7	16.3	14.7	14.1	14.5	15.7	15.7	15.6	14.9
Slovak Republic / République slovaque	..	..	..	26.8	21.0	22.3	23.0	22.8	23.4	24.6
Slovenia / Slovénie	..	..	..	14.6	14.2	14.8	15.5	15.3	15.5	15.4
Spain / Espagne[1]	21.7	37.8	25.5	25.1	23.5	26.4	27.6	26.3	24.7	23.9
Sweden / Suède	8.9	27.6	26.0	20.4	20.2	18.8	18.3	16.9	17.4	16.8
Switzerland / Suisse	6.6	10.6	10.7	11.3	10.8	10.7	11.1	11.4	11.6	11.7
Turkey / Turquie	3.3	8.1	11.0	9.0	10.1	12.5	13.4	14.7	14.9	15.5
United Kingdom / Royaume-Uni	7.6	10.1	9.9	9.6	10.7	11.1	11.4	10.8	11.1	11.0
United States / États-Unis	7.6	11.9	13.2	11.8	11.8	12.6	13.6	13.3	13.0	12.2
Unweighted average / Moyenne non pondérée										
OECD Average / Moyenne OCDE	**9.8**	**14.0**	**12.7**	**14.3**	**14.1**	**14.6**	**15.1**	**14.8**	**14.7**	**14.6**

1. The total tax revenue has been reduced by the amount of any capital transfer that represents uncollected taxes. The capital transfer has been allocated between tax headings in proportion to the reported tax revenue.
2. From 1991 the figures relate to the united Germany.

1. Le total des recettes fiscales a été diminué du montant de tout transfert en capital représentant les impôts non perçus. Le transfert en capital a été réparti entre les différentes rubriques en proportion des recettes fiscales.
2. Depuis 1991, les chiffres se rapportent à l'Allemagne unifiée.

StatLink http://dx.doi.org/10.1787/888933276807

Table 19. **Taxes on payroll and workforce (3000) as % of GDP**
Tableau 19. **Impôts sur les salaires ou la main-d'œuvre (3000) en % du PIB**

	1965	1980	1990	2000	2007	2008	2009	2011	2012	2013
Australia / Australie	0.6	1.3	1.7	1.4	1.4	1.4	1.3	1.4	1.4	1.4
Austria / Autriche	2.6	2.7	2.4	2.7	2.6	2.7	2.8	2.8	2.9	2.9
Belgium / Belgique	0.0	0.0	0.0	0.0	0.0	0.0	0.0	0.0	0.0	0.0
Canada	0.0	0.0	0.8	0.7	0.6	0.6	0.7	0.6	0.6	0.6
Chile / Chili	..	..	0.0	0.0	0.0	0.0	0.0	0.0	0.0	0.0
Czech Republic / République tchèque	..	..	..	0.0	0.0	0.0	0.0	0.0	0.0	0.0
Denmark / Danemark[1]	0.0	0.0	0.3	0.2	0.2	0.2	0.2	0.3	0.3	0.3
Estonia / Estonie	..	..	..	0.0	0.0	0.0	0.0	0.0	0.0	0.0
Finland / Finlande	1.5	0.1	0.0	0.0	0.0	0.0	0.0	0.0	0.0	0.0
France[1]	1.6	0.9	0.8	1.0	1.2	1.2	1.3	1.3	1.4	1.6
Germany / Allemagne[2]	0.2	0.1	0.0	0.0	0.0	0.0	0.0	0.0	0.0	0.0
Greece / Grèce[1]	0.1	0.4	0.2	0.0	0.0	0.0	0.0	0.0	0.0	0.0
Hungary / Hongrie	..	..	..	1.4	0.6	0.6	0.6	0.5	0.5	0.6
Iceland / Islande	0.2	1.1	1.1	0.0	0.1	0.1	0.2	0.2	0.3	0.3
Ireland / Irlande	0.0	0.1	0.4	0.0	0.2	0.2	0.2	0.2	0.2	0.2
Israel / Israël	..	..	..	1.3	1.4	1.2	1.2	1.2	1.2	1.2
Italy / Italie	0.0	0.2	0.1	0.0	0.0	0.0	0.0	0.0	0.0	0.0
Japan / Japon	0.0	0.0	0.0	0.0	0.0	0.0	0.0	0.0	0.0	0.0
Korea / Corée	..	0.1	0.1	0.0	0.1	0.1	0.1	0.1	0.1	0.1
Luxembourg	0.2	0.2	0.0	0.0	0.0	0.0	0.0	0.0	0.0	0.0
Mexico / Mexique	..	0.2	0.2	0.2	0.2	0.3	0.3	0.3	0.3	0.3
Netherlands / Pays-Bas	0.0	0.0	0.0	0.0	0.0	0.0	0.0	0.0	0.0	0.0
New Zealand / Nouvelle-Zélande	0.0	0.0	0.0	0.0	0.0	0.0	0.0	0.0	0.0	0.0
Norway / Norvège	0.0	0.0	0.0	0.0	0.0	0.0	0.0	0.0	0.0	0.0
Poland / Pologne	..	..	..	0.2	0.3	0.3	0.3	0.3	0.3	0.2
Portugal	0.1	0.6	0.0	0.0	0.0	0.0	0.0	0.0	0.0	0.0
Slovak Republic / République slovaque	..	..	..	0.0	0.0	0.0	0.0	0.0	0.0	0.0
Slovenia / Slovénie	..	..	..	1.5	1.2	0.7	0.1	0.1	0.1	0.1
Spain / Espagne[1]	0.0	0.0	0.0	0.0	0.0	0.0	0.0	0.0	0.0	0.0
Sweden / Suède	0.0	1.1	1.2	2.1	2.5	3.7	3.7	4.2	4.4	4.6
Switzerland / Suisse	0.0	0.0	0.0	0.0	0.0	0.0	0.0	0.0	0.0	0.0
Turkey / Turquie	0.0	0.0	0.0	0.0	0.0	0.0	0.0	0.0	0.0	0.0
United Kingdom / Royaume-Uni	0.0	1.4	0.0	0.0	0.0	0.0	0.0	0.0	0.0	0.0
United States / États-Unis	0.0	0.0	0.0	0.0	0.0	0.0	0.0	0.0	0.0	0.0
Unweighted average / Moyenne non pondérée										
OECD Average / Moyenne OCDE	**0.3**	**0.4**	**0.3**	**0.4**	**0.4**	**0.4**	**0.4**	**0.4**	**0.4**	**0.4**

1. The total tax revenue has been reduced by the amount of any capital transfer that represents uncollected taxes. The capital transfer has been allocated between tax headings in proportion to the reported tax revenue.
2. From 1991 the figures relate to the united Germany.
1. Le total des recettes fiscales a été diminué du montant de tout transfert en capital représentant les impôts non perçus. Le transfert en capital a été réparti entre les différentes rubriques en proportion des recettes fiscales.
2. Depuis 1991, les chiffres se rapportent à l'Allemagne unifiée.

StatLink *http://dx.doi.org/10.1787/888933276819*

Table 20. **Taxes on payroll and workforce (3000) as % of total taxation**
Tableau 20. **Impôts sur les salaires ou la main-d'œuvre (3000) en % du total des recettes fiscales**

	1965	1980	1990	2000	2007	2008	2009	2011	2012	2013
Australia / Australie	3.1	5.0	6.1	4.5	4.7	5.1	5.2	5.2	5.2	5.1
Austria / Autriche	7.6	7.0	6.0	6.4	6.3	6.6	6.9	6.9	6.9	6.9
Belgium / Belgique	0.0	0.0	0.0	0.0	0.0	0.0	0.0	0.0	0.0	0.0
Canada	0.0	0.0	2.3	2.1	2.0	2.0	2.1	2.1	2.1	2.1
Chile / Chili	..	..	0.0	0.0	0.0	0.0	0.0	0.0	0.0	0.0
Czech Republic / République tchèque	..	..	..	0.0	0.0	0.0	0.0	0.0	0.0	0.0
Denmark / Danemark[1]	0.0	0.0	0.7	0.4	0.5	0.5	0.5	0.6	0.6	0.7
Estonia / Estonie	..	..	..	0.0	0.0	0.0	0.0	0.0	0.0	0.0
Finland / Finlande	5.2	0.2	0.0	0.0	0.0	0.0	0.0	0.0	0.0	0.0
France[1]	4.6	2.2	1.9	2.3	2.8	2.9	3.2	3.1	3.2	3.5
Germany / Allemagne[2]	0.6	0.2	0.0	0.0	0.0	0.0	0.0	0.0	0.0	0.0
Greece / Grèce[1]	0.8	1.8	0.7	0.0	0.0	0.0	0.0	0.0	0.0	0.0
Hungary / Hongrie	..	..	..	3.6	1.5	1.4	1.4	1.3	1.4	1.5
Iceland / Islande	0.9	3.8	3.5	0.1	0.3	0.4	0.5	0.5	0.9	1.0
Ireland / Irlande	0.0	0.2	1.3	0.0	0.7	0.8	0.8	0.7	0.6	0.6
Israel / Israël	..	..	..	3.7	4.0	3.8	4.0	3.8	3.9	3.9
Italy / Italie	0.0	0.6	0.3	0.0	0.0	0.0	0.0	0.0	0.0	0.0
Japan / Japon	0.0	0.0	0.0	0.0	0.0	0.0	0.0	0.0	0.0	0.0
Korea / Corée	..	0.5	0.4	0.2	0.2	0.3	0.2	0.2	0.3	0.3
Luxembourg	0.9	0.6	0.0	0.0	0.0	0.0	0.0	0.0	0.0	0.0
Mexico / Mexique	..	1.0	1.4	1.1	1.4	1.2	1.5	1.5	1.6	1.7
Netherlands / Pays-Bas	0.0	0.0	0.0	0.0	0.0	0.0	0.0	0.0	0.0	0.0
New Zealand / Nouvelle-Zélande	0.0	0.0	0.0	0.0	0.0	0.0	0.0	0.0	0.0	0.0
Norway / Norvège	0.0	0.0	0.0	0.0	0.0	0.0	0.0	0.0	0.0	0.0
Poland / Pologne	..	..	..	0.7	0.7	0.8	0.9	0.8	0.8	0.8
Portugal	0.9	2.6	0.0	0.0	0.0	0.0	0.0	0.0	0.0	0.0
Slovak Republic / République slovaque	..	..	..	0.0	0.0	0.0	0.0	0.0	0.0	0.0
Slovenia / Slovénie	..	..	..	4.2	3.2	1.9	0.2	0.2	0.2	0.2
Spain / Espagne[1]	0.0	0.0	0.0	0.0	0.0	0.0	0.0	0.0	0.0	0.0
Sweden / Suède	0.0	2.6	2.5	4.3	5.6	8.4	8.5	10.0	10.2	10.6
Switzerland / Suisse	0.0	0.0	0.0	0.0	0.0	0.0	0.0	0.0	0.0	0.0
Turkey / Turquie	0.0	0.0	0.0	0.0	0.0	0.0	0.0	0.0	0.0	0.0
United Kingdom / Royaume-Uni	0.0	4.3	0.0	0.0	0.0	0.0	0.0	0.0	0.0	0.0
United States / États-Unis	0.0	0.0	0.0	0.0	0.0	0.0	0.0	0.0	0.0	0.0
Unweighted average / Moyenne non pondérée										
OECD Average / Moyenne OCDE	**1.0**	**1.3**	**1.0**	**1.0**	**1.0**	1.1	1.1	1.1	1.1	1.1

1. The total tax revenue has been reduced by the amount of any capital transfer that represents uncollected taxes. The capital transfer has been allocated between tax headings in proportion to the reported tax revenue.
2. From 1991 the figures relate to the united Germany.
1. Le total des recettes fiscales a été diminué du montant de tout transfert en capital représentant les impôts non perçus. Le transfert en capital a été réparti entre les différentes rubriques en proportion des recettes fiscales.
2. Depuis 1991, les chiffres se rapportent à l'Allemagne unifiée.

StatLink http://dx.doi.org/10.1787/888933276828

Table 21. **Taxes on property (4000) as % of GDP**
Tableau 21. **Impôts sur le patrimoine (4000) en % du PIB**

	1965	1980	1990	2000	2007	2008	2009	2011	2012	2013
Australia / Australie	2.4	2.0	2.5	2.7	2.6	2.2	2.5	2.3	2.4	2.6
Austria / Autriche	1.3	1.1	1.1	0.6	0.6	0.5	0.5	0.5	0.6	0.7
Belgium / Belgique	1.1	1.3	1.6	2.1	3.1	3.0	2.9	3.1	3.3	3.5
Canada	3.6	2.8	3.5	3.3	3.4	3.4	3.5	3.3	3.3	3.2
Chile / Chili	..	..	1.0	1.3	1.1	1.2	0.8	0.8	0.9	0.8
Czech Republic / République tchèque	..	..	..	0.5	0.4	0.4	0.4	0.5	0.5	0.5
Denmark / Danemark[1]	2.4	2.4	1.9	1.6	1.8	1.9	1.8	1.9	1.8	1.8
Estonia / Estonie	..	..	..	0.4	0.2	0.3	0.3	0.3	0.3	0.3
Finland / Finlande	1.2	0.7	1.1	1.1	1.1	1.1	1.1	1.1	1.2	1.3
France[1]	1.4	1.9	2.6	2.9	3.3	3.2	3.3	3.6	3.8	3.8
Germany / Allemagne[2]	1.8	1.2	1.2	0.8	0.9	0.8	0.8	0.8	0.9	0.9
Greece / Grèce[1]	1.6	1.0	1.2	2.0	1.7	1.7	1.9	2.3	2.5	2.6
Hungary / Hongrie	..	..	..	0.7	0.8	0.9	0.8	1.1	1.2	1.3
Iceland / Islande	1.0	1.8	2.5	2.8	2.4	2.1	2.1	2.3	2.5	2.5
Ireland / Irlande	3.7	1.6	1.5	1.8	2.4	1.8	1.5	1.7	1.8	2.1
Israel / Israël	..	..	..	3.0	3.0	2.9	2.8	2.9	2.7	2.7
Italy / Italie	1.8	1.1	0.8	1.9	2.0	1.8	2.6	2.2	2.7	2.7
Japan / Japon	1.4	2.0	2.7	2.8	2.6	2.7	2.7	2.8	2.7	2.7
Korea / Corée	..	1.4	2.2	2.7	3.2	2.9	2.8	2.7	2.6	2.5
Luxembourg	1.6	1.9	2.8	3.9	3.5	2.8	2.6	2.6	2.8	2.8
Mexico / Mexique	..	0.3	0.2	0.2	0.3	0.3	0.3	0.3	0.3	0.3
Netherlands / Pays-Bas	1.4	1.4	1.5	2.0	1.7	1.5	1.4	1.2	1.1	1.2
New Zealand / Nouvelle-Zélande	2.7	2.3	2.5	1.7	1.8	2.0	2.0	2.0	2.0	1.9
Norway / Norvège	0.9	0.7	1.2	1.0	1.2	1.2	1.2	1.2	1.2	1.2
Poland / Pologne	..	..	..	1.4	1.4	1.4	1.4	1.3	1.3	1.4
Portugal	0.8	0.3	0.7	1.1	1.3	1.2	1.1	1.1	1.1	1.1
Slovak Republic / République slovaque	..	..	..	0.6	0.4	0.4	0.4	0.4	0.4	0.4
Slovenia / Slovénie	..	..	..	0.6	0.6	0.6	0.6	0.6	0.6	0.6
Spain / Espagne[1]	0.9	1.0	1.7	2.1	2.9	2.3	2.0	1.9	2.0	2.2
Sweden / Suède	0.6	0.4	1.7	1.7	1.1	1.0	1.0	1.0	1.0	1.1
Switzerland / Suisse	1.6	1.9	2.0	2.5	2.1	2.0	2.0	1.9	1.8	1.8
Turkey / Turquie	1.1	0.7	0.3	0.8	0.9	0.9	0.9	1.1	1.2	1.4
United Kingdom / Royaume-Uni	4.3	4.0	2.7	4.0	4.3	4.0	3.9	3.9	3.9	4.0
United States / États-Unis	3.7	2.7	3.0	2.9	3.1	3.1	3.2	3.0	2.9	2.9
Unweighted average / Moyenne non pondérée										
OECD Average / Moyenne OCDE	**1.9**	**1.5**	**1.8**	**1.8**	**1.9**	**1.7**	**1.7**	**1.8**	**1.8**	**1.9**

1. The total tax revenue has been reduced by the amount of any capital transfer that represents uncollected taxes. The capital transfer has been allocated between tax headings in proportion to the reported tax revenue.
2. From 1991 the figures relate to the united Germany.
1. Le total des recettes fiscales a été diminué du montant de tout transfert en capital représentant les impôts non perçus. Le transfert en capital a été réparti entre les différentes rubriques en proportion des recettes fiscales.
2. Depuis 1991, les chiffres se rapportent à l'Allemagne unifiée.

StatLink http://dx.doi.org/10.1787/888933276839

Table 22. **Taxes on property (4000) as % of total taxation**
Tableau 22. **Impôts sur le patrimoine (4000) en % du total des recettes fiscales**

	1965	1980	1990	2000	2007	2008	2009	2011	2012	2013
Australia / Australie	11.5	7.8	9.0	8.8	8.9	8.2	9.5	8.6	8.7	9.4
Austria / Autriche	4.0	2.9	2.7	1.3	1.4	1.3	1.3	1.2	1.3	1.7
Belgium / Belgique	3.7	3.1	3.8	4.7	7.2	7.0	7.0	7.3	7.4	7.8
Canada	14.3	9.1	10.0	9.5	10.6	10.8	11.3	10.9	10.6	10.4
Chile / Chili	..	..	6.2	7.0	4.9	5.4	4.8	4.0	4.3	4.1
Czech Republic / République tchèque	..	..	..	1.4	1.2	1.1	1.1	1.5	1.5	1.4
Denmark / Danemark[1]	8.1	5.9	4.3	3.3	3.9	4.2	4.0	4.2	3.9	3.9
Estonia / Estonie	..	..	..	1.3	0.7	0.9	1.0	1.0	1.0	1.0
Finland / Finlande	4.0	1.9	2.4	2.4	2.6	2.6	2.6	2.6	2.8	2.9
France[1]	4.3	4.8	6.3	6.9	7.9	7.6	8.0	8.4	8.5	8.4
Germany / Allemagne[2]	5.8	3.3	3.4	2.3	2.5	2.3	2.3	2.4	2.4	2.5
Greece / Grèce[1]	9.7	4.6	4.6	6.1	5.3	5.5	6.2	7.0	7.2	7.6
Hungary / Hongrie	..	..	..	1.7	2.0	2.2	2.1	3.1	3.2	3.4
Iceland / Islande	4.0	6.3	8.4	7.9	6.1	6.1	6.5	6.7	7.1	6.9
Ireland / Irlande	15.1	5.3	4.6	5.7	8.0	6.2	5.3	6.1	6.4	7.1
Israel / Israël	..	..	..	8.5	8.9	9.1	9.4	9.4	9.0	8.8
Italy / Italie	7.2	3.7	2.3	4.6	4.9	4.3	6.2	5.3	6.2	6.2
Japan / Japon	8.1	8.2	9.4	10.5	9.0	9.4	10.1	9.7	9.1	8.8
Korea / Corée	..	8.0	11.8	12.4	12.8	11.9	11.6	11.4	10.6	10.3
Luxembourg	6.2	5.7	8.3	10.6	9.7	7.4	6.7	7.0	7.1	7.3
Mexico / Mexique	..	1.9	1.5	1.4	1.7	1.4	1.7	1.5	1.5	1.5
Netherlands / Pays-Bas	4.4	3.6	3.7	5.3	4.7	4.2	4.0	3.4	3.0	3.4
New Zealand / Nouvelle-Zélande	11.5	7.9	6.8	5.3	5.3	5.9	6.5	6.6	6.3	6.1
Norway / Norvège	3.1	1.7	2.9	2.3	2.8	2.8	2.9	2.8	2.9	3.0
Poland / Pologne	..	..	..	4.3	4.1	4.2	4.3	4.0	4.2	4.4
Portugal	5.0	1.4	2.7	3.7	4.1	3.7	3.6	3.4	3.3	3.3
Slovak Republic / République slovaque	..	..	..	1.8	1.3	1.3	1.5	1.4	1.5	1.5
Slovenia / Slovénie	..	..	..	1.7	1.6	1.5	1.6	1.6	1.7	1.7
Spain / Espagne[1]	6.4	4.6	5.5	6.3	8.0	7.0	6.6	6.0	6.3	6.7
Sweden / Suède	1.8	0.9	3.5	3.4	2.4	2.3	2.4	2.4	2.4	2.5
Switzerland / Suisse	9.9	8.3	8.4	9.0	7.9	7.4	7.4	7.0	6.6	6.7
Turkey / Turquie	10.5	5.4	2.3	3.2	3.8	3.6	3.6	4.1	4.2	4.6
United Kingdom / Royaume-Uni	14.5	12.0	8.2	11.6	12.6	11.6	12.2	11.6	11.8	12.3
United States / États-Unis	15.9	10.7	11.6	10.2	11.5	12.3	14.1	12.6	12.1	11.3
Unweighted average / Moyenne non pondérée										
OECD Average / Moyenne OCDE	**7.9**	**5.3**	**5.7**	**5.5**	**5.6**	**5.4**	**5.6**	**5.5**	**5.5**	**5.6**

1. The total tax revenue has been reduced by the amount of any capital transfer that represents uncollected taxes. The capital transfer has been allocated between tax headings in proportion to the reported tax revenue.
2. From 1991 the figures relate to the united Germany.

1. Le total des recettes fiscales a été diminué du montant de tout transfert en capital représentant les impôts non perçus. Le transfert en capital a été réparti entre les différentes rubriques en proportion des recettes fiscales.
2. Depuis 1991, les chiffres se rapportent à l'Allemagne unifiée.

StatLink http://dx.doi.org/10.1787/888933276845

Table 23. **Taxes on goods and services (5000) as % of GDP**
Tableau 23. **Impôts sur les biens et services (5000) en % du PIB**

	1965	1980	1990	2000	2007	2008	2009	2011	2012	2013
Australia / Australie	7.2	8.2	7.8	8.7	7.9	7.5	7.6	7.1	7.7	7.8
Austria / Autriche	12.6	12.2	12.4	12.1	11.2	11.3	11.6	11.6	11.8	11.7
Belgium / Belgique	11.4	10.9	10.8	10.9	10.7	10.5	10.6	10.7	11.0	10.8
Canada	10.2	9.9	9.1	8.5	7.7	7.4	7.5	7.4	7.5	7.4
Chile / Chili	..	..	10.7	12.0	10.0	10.8	9.6	10.5	10.8	10.8
Czech Republic / République tchèque	..	..	..	10.2	10.3	10.6	10.8	11.3	11.5	11.7
Denmark / Danemark[1]	12.2	15.8	15.1	15.5	16.2	15.2	15.2	15.1	15.2	15.4
Estonia / Estonie	..	..	..	11.9	12.9	11.6	14.2	13.2	13.5	13.0
Finland / Finlande	12.7	12.5	14.0	13.3	12.6	12.4	12.9	13.8	14.1	14.5
France[1]	12.9	12.0	11.6	11.1	10.5	10.4	10.4	10.7	10.8	10.8
Germany / Allemagne[2]	10.4	9.9	9.3	10.2	10.2	10.2	10.8	10.4	10.4	10.2
Greece / Grèce[1]	8.3	8.5	11.2	12.1	11.4	11.2	11.0	13.2	12.9	13.5
Hungary / Hongrie	..	..	..	15.7	14.9	14.7	15.5	16.0	17.0	16.9
Iceland / Islande	16.0	17.3	15.5	16.0	15.6	13.0	11.4	12.0	12.3	12.0
Ireland / Irlande	12.9	13.2	13.6	11.8	11.1	10.7	9.9	9.4	9.6	9.7
Israel / Israël	..	..	..	11.6	12.1	11.9	11.6	12.2	11.6	11.9
Italy / Italie	9.7	7.6	10.2	11.3	10.5	10.3	10.4	11.2	11.6	11.5
Japan / Japon	4.7	4.0	3.9	5.1	5.1	5.1	5.1	5.3	5.3	5.3
Korea / Corée	..	10.6	8.3	8.2	7.8	7.8	7.6	7.5	7.7	7.5
Luxembourg	6.5	7.4	8.5	10.1	10.2	10.4	10.9	10.6	11.0	10.9
Mexico / Mexique	..	7.4	8.6	8.8	9.3	12.3	8.6	10.5	10.6	9.8
Netherlands / Pays-Bas	8.8	10.2	10.6	10.8	11.2	11.1	10.8	10.8	10.7	10.9
New Zealand / Nouvelle-Zélande	6.5	6.6	12.1	11.3	10.8	11.2	11.1	12.3	12.4	12.0
Norway / Norvège	12.1	14.8	14.3	13.3	12.0	10.8	11.5	11.1	10.9	11.1
Poland / Pologne	..	..	..	11.6	13.1	13.1	11.7	12.6	11.8	11.5
Portugal	7.5	10.2	11.7	12.5	13.3	12.9	11.6	12.9	12.9	12.9
Slovak Republic / République slovaque	..	..	..	12.2	11.1	10.5	10.4	10.5	9.9	10.4
Slovenia / Slovénie	..	..	..	13.8	13.0	13.0	13.3	13.8	14.2	14.7
Spain / Espagne[1]	5.8	4.6	9.0	9.9	9.2	8.0	6.8	8.2	8.6	9.2
Sweden / Suède	9.8	10.5	12.4	12.1	12.0	12.2	12.7	12.4	12.3	12.2
Switzerland / Suisse	5.7	5.4	4.9	6.2	5.8	5.9	5.9	6.0	6.2	6.0
Turkey / Turquie	5.7	3.4	4.2	10.1	11.5	11.0	11.2	12.6	12.4	13.5
United Kingdom / Royaume-Uni	9.7	9.7	10.2	11.1	9.9	9.8	9.4	10.9	10.9	10.8
United States / États-Unis	5.3	4.5	4.6	4.6	4.5	4.4	4.2	4.4	4.4	4.4
Unweighted average / Moyenne non pondérée										
OECD Average / Moyenne OCDE	**9.4**	**9.5**	**10.2**	**11.0**	**10.8**	**10.6**	**10.4**	**10.8**	**10.9**	**11.0**

1. The total tax revenue has been reduced by the amount of any capital transfer that represents uncollected taxes. The capital transfer has been allocated between tax headings in proportion to the reported tax revenue.
2. From 1991 the figures relate to the united Germany.
1. Le total des recettes fiscales a été diminué du montant de tout transfert en capital représentant les impôts non perçus. Le transfert en capital a été réparti entre les différentes rubriques en proportion des recettes fiscales.
2. Depuis 1991, les chiffres se rapportent à l'Allemagne unifiée.

StatLink *http://dx.doi.org/10.1787/888933276851*

Table 24. **Taxes on goods and services (5000) as % of total taxation**
Tableau 24. **Impôts sur les biens et services (5000) en % du total des recettes fiscales**

	1965	1980	1990	2000	2007	2008	2009	2011	2012	2013
Australia / Australie	34.7	31.1	27.8	28.7	26.8	27.6	29.4	27.1	28.1	28.4
Austria / Autriche	37.4	31.5	31.5	28.7	27.7	27.2	28.2	28.3	28.2	27.5
Belgium / Belgique	37.2	27.0	26.1	25.1	25.1	24.5	25.0	24.9	25.1	24.2
Canada	40.5	32.6	25.8	24.2	24.0	23.3	23.8	24.5	24.3	24.2
Chile / Chili	..	..	62.9	63.8	43.8	50.6	55.9	49.3	50.1	54.0
Czech Republic / République tchèque	..	..	..	31.5	29.9	31.5	33.3	33.7	33.9	34.3
Denmark / Danemark[1]	41.9	38.1	33.9	33.1	34.9	33.9	33.6	33.2	32.9	32.3
Estonia / Estonie	..	..	..	38.6	41.6	37.2	40.6	41.5	42.2	41.0
Finland / Finlande	42.5	35.3	32.5	29.0	30.2	30.2	31.6	32.9	33.1	33.2
France[1]	38.4	30.4	28.4	25.9	24.9	24.7	25.2	24.9	24.6	24.1
Germany / Allemagne[2]	33.0	27.1	26.7	28.1	29.3	28.9	29.8	29.1	28.5	28.0
Greece / Grèce[1]	48.8	41.2	44.5	36.3	36.6	36.2	35.8	39.4	37.3	39.1
Hungary / Hongrie	..	..	..	40.5	37.7	37.2	39.8	43.7	44.1	44.0
Iceland / Islande	62.7	59.9	51.3	44.1	40.4	37.0	35.5	34.7	35.1	33.5
Ireland / Irlande	52.6	43.7	41.9	38.2	36.4	37.4	35.7	34.3	34.3	33.6
Israel / Israël	..	..	..	33.3	35.2	37.3	39.3	39.4	39.2	39.0
Italy / Italie	39.5	26.5	28.0	27.9	25.3	24.9	24.8	26.8	26.5	26.1
Japan / Japon	26.2	16.3	13.7	19.3	18.0	17.9	19.1	18.4	18.0	17.6
Korea / Corée	..	62.7	44.3	38.4	31.3	31.6	31.8	31.2	31.2	30.7
Luxembourg	24.7	21.8	25.1	27.1	27.9	28.0	28.0	28.1	28.3	28.4
Mexico / Mexique	..	51.2	55.3	53.0	53.1	59.2	50.2	54.1	54.5	49.8
Netherlands / Pays-Bas	28.6	25.3	26.4	29.2	31.0	30.3	30.6	30.0	29.7	29.6
New Zealand / Nouvelle-Zélande	27.9	22.3	33.6	34.7	31.7	33.7	36.6	39.7	38.3	38.4
Norway / Norvège	41.1	35.3	35.5	31.8	28.5	26.0	27.9	26.4	26.3	27.4
Poland / Pologne	..	..	..	35.2	37.6	38.1	37.0	39.3	36.4	35.9
Portugal	47.6	46.5	44.2	40.1	41.4	40.5	38.6	39.7	40.5	37.3
Slovak Republic / République slovaque	..	..	..	36.2	37.8	35.9	36.1	36.7	35.0	34.4
Slovenia / Slovénie	..	..	..	37.6	35.0	35.6	36.7	37.7	38.4	40.1
Spain / Espagne[1]	40.8	20.7	28.4	29.6	25.3	24.8	22.9	26.1	26.6	28.1
Sweden / Suède	31.2	24.0	25.0	24.8	26.6	27.7	28.9	29.1	28.9	28.6
Switzerland / Suisse	34.2	23.0	20.7	22.3	22.3	22.3	21.8	22.1	22.9	22.2
Turkey / Turquie	54.0	25.6	27.9	42.0	47.7	45.5	45.7	45.2	45.0	46.1
United Kingdom / Royaume-Uni	33.1	29.2	31.0	31.9	29.2	28.9	29.1	32.5	32.9	32.9
United States / États-Unis	22.8	17.6	17.6	16.2	16.8	17.4	18.5	18.8	18.3	17.4
Unweighted average / Moyenne non pondérée										
OECD Average / Moyenne OCDE	**38.4**	**32.5**	**33.0**	**33.1**	**32.1**	**32.1**	**32.5**	**33.0**	**32.9**	**32.7**

1. The total tax revenue has been reduced by the amount of any capital transfer that represents uncollected taxes. The capital transfer has been allocated between tax headings in proportion to the reported tax revenue.
2. From 1991 the figures relate to the united Germany.
1. Le total des recettes fiscales a été diminué du montant de tout transfert en capital représentant les impôts non perçus. Le transfert en capital a été réparti entre les différentes rubriques en proportion des recettes fiscales.
2. Depuis 1991, les chiffres se rapportent à l'Allemagne unifiée.

StatLink *http://dx.doi.org/10.1787/888933276864*

Table 25. **Consumption taxes (5100) as % of GDP**
Tableau 25. **Impôts sur la consommation (5100) en % du PIB**

	1965	1980	1990	2000	2007	2008	2009	2011	2012	2013
Australia / Australie	6.2	7.3	6.6	8.0	7.2	6.7	6.8	6.3	6.4	6.6
Austria / Autriche	12.3	11.7	11.8	11.4	10.6	10.6	10.9	10.9	11.1	11.0
Belgium / Belgique	10.4	10.4	10.2	10.1	10.0	9.9	9.9	10.0	10.4	10.2
Canada	8.8	7.5	8.6	8.0	7.2	6.8	6.9	6.9	7.0	6.9
Chile / Chili	..	..	10.2	11.4	9.5	10.3	9.0	9.9	10.1	10.1
Czech Republic / République tchèque	..	..	..	9.5	9.6	9.9	10.1	10.6	10.8	11.1
Denmark / Danemark[1]	11.5	15.0	14.4	14.7	15.1	14.2	14.1	14.0	14.1	14.1
Estonia / Estonie	..	..	..	11.6	12.5	11.3	13.7	12.9	13.2	12.7
Finland / Finlande	12.6	12.3	13.8	13.0	12.2	12.1	12.5	13.4	13.7	14.1
France[1]	12.6	11.6	11.3	10.8	10.2	10.1	10.1	10.4	10.5	10.5
Germany / Allemagne[2]	9.8	9.4	9.0	9.8	9.9	9.9	10.4	10.0	10.0	9.8
Greece / Grèce[1]	7.5	7.9	10.7	11.0	10.5	10.3	9.7	12.0	11.7	11.9
Hungary / Hongrie	..	..	..	15.4	14.6	14.4	15.1	15.6	16.6	16.5
Iceland / Islande	15.7	16.9	14.8	14.3	14.0	11.9	10.7	11.4	11.8	11.4
Ireland / Irlande	12.0	13.0	13.1	11.3	10.5	10.0	9.1	8.6	8.8	8.9
Israel / Israël	..	..	..	10.8	11.2	11.0	10.8	11.3	10.8	11.1
Italy / Italie	9.1	7.2	9.2	10.1	9.5	9.3	9.3	10.1	10.4	10.1
Japan / Japon	4.4	3.5	3.4	4.5	4.5	4.5	4.5	4.7	4.8	4.8
Korea / Corée	..	10.4	8.1	7.9	7.5	7.6	7.3	7.1	7.2	7.0
Luxembourg	6.2	7.2	8.3	9.9	10.0	10.2	10.7	10.5	10.8	10.7
Mexico / Mexique	..	7.3	8.5	8.6	9.1	12.1	8.4	10.4	10.5	9.7
Netherlands / Pays-Bas	8.4	9.3	9.7	9.7	10.1	10.0	9.7	9.5	9.5	9.7
New Zealand / Nouvelle-Zélande	6.1	6.3	11.4	10.5	10.0	10.5	10.4	11.5	11.6	11.3
Norway / Norvège	11.7	14.4	13.7	12.3	11.3	10.1	10.9	10.6	10.4	10.5
Poland / Pologne	..	..	..	11.4	12.7	12.7	11.3	12.2	11.4	11.2
Portugal	6.9	9.9	11.5	12.2	12.9	12.5	11.2	12.4	12.4	12.1
Slovak Republic / République slovaque	..	..	..	11.5	10.3	9.7	9.6	9.8	9.2	9.6
Slovenia / Slovénie	..	..	..	13.1	12.3	12.4	12.7	13.2	13.5	13.8
Spain / Espagne[1]	5.8	4.6	8.4	9.1	8.6	7.4	6.3	7.6	8.0	8.6
Sweden / Suède	9.3	9.9	11.9	11.8	11.6	11.7	12.2	11.9	11.9	11.8
Switzerland / Suisse	5.3	5.0	4.5	5.6	5.1	5.3	5.2	5.2	5.4	5.2
Turkey / Turquie	5.6	3.4	4.1	9.8	11.0	10.5	10.7	12.1	11.9	13.0
United Kingdom / Royaume-Uni	9.1	9.3	9.7	10.6	9.5	9.4	8.9	10.5	10.5	10.4
United States / États-Unis	4.7	3.9	3.9	3.9	3.7	3.7	3.6	3.7	3.7	3.7
Unweighted average / Moyenne non pondérée										
OECD Average / Moyenne OCDE	**8.8**	**9.0**	**9.7**	**10.4**	**10.1**	**10.0**	**9.8**	**10.2**	**10.3**	**10.3**

1. The total tax revenue has been reduced by the amount of any capital transfer that represents uncollected taxes. The capital transfer has been allocated between tax headings in proportion to the reported tax revenue.
2. From 1991 the figures relate to the united Germany.
1. Le total des recettes fiscales a été diminué du montant de tout transfert en capital représentant les impôts non perçus. Le transfert en capital a été réparti entre les différentes rubriques en proportion des recettes fiscales.
2. Depuis 1991, les chiffres se rapportent à l'Allemagne unifiée.

StatLink http://dx.doi.org/10.1787/888933276871

Table 26. **Consumption taxes (5100) as % of total taxation**
Tableau 26. **Impôts sur la consommation (5100) en % du total des recettes fiscales**

	1965	1980	1990	2000	2007	2008	2009	2011	2012	2013
Australia / Australie	30.0	27.8	23.4	26.2	24.3	24.9	26.5	24.1	23.3	23.8
Austria / Autriche	36.6	30.3	29.9	27.1	26.1	25.6	26.6	26.7	26.5	25.8
Belgium / Belgique	34.1	25.7	24.7	23.2	23.4	23.0	23.5	23.3	23.7	22.8
Canada	34.7	24.6	24.4	22.8	22.4	21.7	22.1	22.7	22.6	22.5
Chile / Chili	..	..	60.4	60.6	41.6	48.1	52.6	46.4	47.1	50.7
Czech Republic / République tchèque	..	..	..	29.3	27.9	29.5	31.2	31.8	32.0	32.5
Denmark / Danemark[1]	39.6	36.4	32.3	31.4	32.6	31.6	31.1	30.8	30.5	29.7
Estonia / Estonie	..	..	..	37.4	40.2	35.9	39.3	40.4	41.1	39.9
Finland / Finlande	41.9	35.0	32.1	28.3	29.4	29.3	30.6	31.9	32.1	32.1
France[1]	37.5	29.5	27.5	25.2	24.2	23.9	24.4	24.2	23.8	23.4
Germany / Allemagne[2]	31.1	25.9	25.8	27.1	28.2	27.9	28.7	28.1	27.4	26.9
Greece / Grèce[1]	44.1	38.2	42.5	33.0	33.5	33.2	31.4	35.9	33.8	34.7
Hungary / Hongrie	..	..	..	39.9	36.9	36.4	38.7	42.6	43.0	42.9
Iceland / Islande	61.7	58.7	49.2	39.5	36.1	33.9	33.3	33.1	33.5	31.8
Ireland / Irlande	49.1	43.0	40.3	36.5	34.6	35.0	33.1	31.4	31.5	30.6
Israel / Israël	..	..	..	30.9	32.6	34.5	36.5	36.6	36.4	36.3
Italy / Italie	37.0	25.2	25.3	25.0	22.8	22.3	22.2	24.0	23.6	23.0
Japan / Japon	25.0	14.1	12.0	17.0	15.9	15.8	16.9	16.5	16.2	15.9
Korea / Corée	..	61.5	43.0	36.7	30.3	30.6	30.7	29.2	29.2	28.8
Luxembourg	23.5	21.2	24.6	26.8	27.4	27.5	27.4	27.6	27.9	28.0
Mexico / Mexique	..	50.3	54.8	52.1	52.0	58.3	49.1	53.3	53.9	49.2
Netherlands / Pays-Bas	27.1	23.2	24.0	26.4	28.0	27.3	27.3	26.6	26.3	26.4
New Zealand / Nouvelle-Zélande	26.2	21.4	31.6	32.4	29.4	31.4	34.1	37.3	35.9	35.9
Norway / Norvège	39.9	34.4	34.1	29.4	26.8	24.3	26.4	25.2	25.1	25.9
Poland / Pologne	..	..	..	34.4	36.5	36.9	35.8	38.1	35.3	35.1
Portugal	44.0	45.0	43.4	39.0	40.2	39.3	37.1	38.2	38.9	35.2
Slovak Republic / République slovaque	..	..	..	34.1	35.2	33.2	33.4	34.0	32.3	31.6
Slovenia / Slovénie	..	..	..	35.8	33.3	34.1	35.1	36.0	36.6	37.5
Spain / Espagne[1]	40.6	20.7	26.5	27.2	23.5	23.0	21.0	24.2	24.8	26.4
Sweden / Suède	29.5	22.6	24.0	24.1	25.7	26.6	27.7	28.1	27.9	27.5
Switzerland / Suisse	31.9	21.3	18.9	20.4	19.5	19.8	19.3	19.4	20.2	19.5
Turkey / Turquie	53.5	25.2	27.5	40.6	45.6	43.5	43.6	43.5	43.2	44.3
United Kingdom / Royaume-Uni	31.1	27.9	29.4	30.5	28.0	27.6	27.6	31.2	31.6	31.7
United States / États-Unis	19.9	15.3	15.2	14.0	14.1	14.5	15.5	15.7	15.3	14.6
Unweighted average / Moyenne non pondérée										
OECD Average / Moyenne OCDE	**36.2**	**30.9**	**31.4**	**31.3**	**30.2**	**30.3**	**30.6**	**31.1**	**31.0**	**30.7**

1. The total tax revenue has been reduced by the amount of any capital transfer that represents uncollected taxes. The capital transfer has been allocated between tax headings in proportion to the reported tax revenue.
2. From 1991 the figures relate to the united Germany.
1. Le total des recettes fiscales a été diminué du montant de tout transfert en capital représentant les impôts non perçus. Le transfert en capital a été réparti entre les différentes rubriques en proportion des recettes fiscales.
2. Depuis 1991, les chiffres se rapportent à l'Allemagne unifiée.

StatLink http://dx.doi.org/10.1787/888933276884

Table 27. **Taxes on general consumption (5110) as % of GDP**
Tableau 27. **Impôts généraux sur la consommation (5110) en % du PIB**

	1965	1980	1990	2000	2007	2008	2009	2011	2012	2013
Australia / Australie	1.5	1.4	2.3	3.7	3.9	3.5	3.7	3.4	3.4	3.6
Austria / Autriche	6.3	7.8	8.2	7.9	7.4	7.5	7.8	7.6	7.8	7.7
Belgium / Belgique	6.5	6.8	6.8	7.1	7.0	6.9	6.8	6.9	7.0	7.0
Canada	4.5	3.5	5.0	4.9	4.5	4.2	4.2	4.3	4.4	4.3
Chile / Chili	..	..	6.3	7.9	7.5	8.4	7.3	7.9	8.1	8.2
Czech Republic / République tchèque	..	..	..	6.0	6.1	6.5	6.6	6.9	7.1	7.5
Denmark / Danemark[1]	3.0	9.4	9.4	9.2	10.0	9.6	9.7	9.6	9.7	9.6
Estonia / Estonie	..	..	..	8.4	8.8	7.8	8.7	8.4	8.6	8.3
Finland / Finlande	5.5	6.1	8.3	8.0	8.2	8.1	8.4	8.8	9.0	9.3
France[1]	7.8	8.3	7.7	7.4	7.3	7.2	7.0	7.1	7.1	7.1
Germany / Allemagne[2]	5.2	6.1	5.8	6.7	6.8	6.9	7.2	7.0	7.1	7.0
Greece / Grèce[1]	1.8	2.7	6.7	7.1	7.4	7.5	6.6	7.6	7.4	7.3
Hungary / Hongrie	..	..	..	10.1	10.3	10.1	10.9	11.0	11.7	11.4
Iceland / Islande	4.3	8.3	9.7	10.3	10.0	8.7	7.6	7.7	8.0	8.0
Ireland / Irlande	1.4	4.5	6.6	7.1	7.3	7.0	6.1	5.7	5.9	5.9
Israel / Israël	..	..	..	9.3	9.3	9.1	8.9	9.3	8.9	9.3
Italy / Italie	3.2	4.5	5.3	6.2	5.9	5.7	5.5	6.0	6.0	5.8
Japan / Japon	0.0	0.0	1.3	2.4	2.5	2.5	2.6	2.7	2.7	2.8
Korea / Corée	..	3.7	3.5	3.7	3.9	4.0	4.1	4.1	4.3	4.1
Luxembourg	3.3	3.9	4.7	5.3	6.1	6.2	6.7	6.8	7.1	7.4
Mexico / Mexique	..	2.3	3.2	3.1	3.6	3.7	3.4	3.7	3.7	3.5
Netherlands / Pays-Bas	3.8	6.4	6.6	6.4	7.0	6.8	6.5	6.5	6.5	6.5
New Zealand / Nouvelle-Zélande	1.8	3.0	8.1	8.1	8.0	8.4	8.4	9.6	9.7	9.4
Norway / Norvège	6.3	7.7	7.6	8.3	8.1	7.1	7.7	7.6	7.6	7.7
Poland / Pologne	..	..	..	6.9	8.2	8.0	7.3	7.9	7.2	7.0
Portugal	0.0	3.5	5.2	7.6	8.2	8.1	6.8	8.1	8.3	8.1
Slovak Republic / République slovaque	..	..	..	6.9	6.6	6.8	6.6	6.7	6.0	6.4
Slovenia / Slovénie	..	..	..	8.7	8.3	8.3	7.9	8.1	8.0	8.4
Spain / Espagne[1]	3.2	2.2	5.1	5.9	5.8	4.9	3.8	5.1	5.3	5.8
Sweden / Suède	3.3	5.8	7.4	8.4	8.7	8.9	9.2	9.2	9.0	9.1
Switzerland / Suisse	1.8	2.4	2.8	3.6	3.4	3.4	3.3	3.5	3.5	3.5
Turkey / Turquie	0.0	0.0	3.0	5.8	5.1	4.9	4.9	6.1	5.8	6.4
United Kingdom / Royaume-Uni	1.7	4.9	5.5	6.3	6.2	6.1	5.4	6.9	6.9	6.9
United States / États-Unis	1.1	1.8	2.1	2.2	2.1	2.0	2.0	2.0	2.0	2.0
Unweighted average / Moyenne non pondérée										
OECD Average / Moyenne OCDE	**3.2**	**4.5**	**5.7**	**6.7**	**6.7**	**6.6**	**6.5**	**6.8**	**6.8**	**6.8**

1. The total tax revenue has been reduced by the amount of any capital transfer that represents uncollected taxes. The capital transfer has been allocated between tax headings in proportion to the reported tax revenue.
2. From 1991 the figures relate to the united Germany.

1. Le total des recettes fiscales a été diminué du montant de tout transfert en capital représentant les impôts non perçus. Le transfert en capital a été réparti entre les différentes rubriques en proportion des recettes fiscales.
2. Depuis 1991, les chiffres se rapportent à l'Allemagne unifiée.

StatLink *http://dx.doi.org/10.1787/888933276894*

Table 28. **Taxes on general consumption (5110) as % of total taxation**
Tableau 28. **Impôts généraux sur la consommation (5110) en % du total des recettes fiscales**

	1965	1980	1990	2000	2007	2008	2009	2011	2012	2013
Australia / Australie	7.4	5.3	8.0	12.0	13.0	12.9	14.3	12.8	12.4	13.1
Austria / Autriche	18.7	20.1	20.8	18.8	18.3	18.2	19.0	18.6	18.6	18.2
Belgium / Belgique	21.1	16.9	16.4	16.3	16.5	15.9	16.2	16.1	15.9	15.6
Canada	17.8	11.5	14.1	14.2	13.9	13.2	13.4	14.2	14.3	14.2
Chile / Chili	..	..	37.4	41.8	32.9	39.4	42.5	37.0	37.7	40.8
Czech Republic / République tchèque	..	..	..	18.3	17.7	19.3	20.4	20.6	20.9	21.8
Denmark / Danemark[1]	10.3	22.7	21.1	19.5	21.6	21.5	21.6	21.1	20.9	20.2
Estonia / Estonie	..	..	..	27.3	28.2	24.9	24.8	26.4	26.7	26.1
Finland / Finlande	18.5	17.3	19.3	17.4	19.6	19.6	20.5	20.9	21.1	21.3
France[1]	23.3	21.1	18.8	17.1	17.1	17.0	16.9	16.5	16.1	15.7
Germany / Allemagne[2]	16.5	16.6	16.6	18.4	19.4	19.4	20.1	19.7	19.4	19.2
Greece / Grèce[1]	10.3	13.2	26.5	21.5	23.8	24.1	21.5	22.7	21.4	21.2
Hungary / Hongrie	..	..	..	26.1	26.0	25.6	28.0	30.0	30.4	29.8
Iceland / Islande	16.7	28.9	32.3	28.5	25.9	24.7	23.7	22.4	22.8	22.2
Ireland / Irlande	5.7	14.8	20.4	22.9	24.0	24.5	22.2	20.8	21.2	20.4
Israel / Israël	..	..	..	26.6	27.1	28.4	29.9	30.0	30.0	30.4
Italy / Italie	12.9	15.6	14.7	15.4	14.2	13.8	13.1	14.4	13.6	13.3
Japan / Japon	0.0	0.0	4.4	9.1	8.8	8.9	9.6	9.4	9.2	9.2
Korea / Corée	..	22.0	18.7	17.0	15.8	16.1	17.2	17.0	17.2	17.0
Luxembourg	12.4	11.6	13.8	14.3	16.6	16.7	17.3	17.8	18.4	19.2
Mexico / Mexique	..	15.7	20.8	18.7	20.4	18.0	19.7	19.0	19.0	17.6
Netherlands / Pays-Bas	12.4	15.8	16.5	17.5	19.4	18.6	18.3	18.0	17.9	17.8
New Zealand / Nouvelle-Zélande	7.7	10.2	22.4	24.9	23.5	25.4	27.6	31.0	30.0	30.0
Norway / Norvège	21.5	18.2	18.8	19.8	19.1	17.2	18.7	18.0	18.2	19.0
Poland / Pologne	..	..	..	20.9	23.7	23.2	23.2	24.7	22.3	22.0
Portugal	0.0	16.2	19.6	24.3	25.5	25.3	22.7	24.9	26.0	23.5
Slovak Republic / République slovaque	..	..	..	20.4	22.6	23.3	22.9	23.4	21.1	21.0
Slovenia / Slovénie	..	..	..	23.7	22.4	22.9	21.9	22.3	21.8	22.9
Spain / Espagne[1]	22.2	10.2	16.0	17.6	16.0	15.1	12.6	16.4	16.6	17.8
Sweden / Suède	10.4	13.4	14.9	17.1	19.3	20.3	20.9	21.5	21.3	21.1
Switzerland / Suisse	10.6	10.3	11.7	13.1	13.0	12.7	12.3	12.8	13.0	13.1
Turkey / Turquie	0.0	0.0	20.1	24.2	21.3	20.3	20.0	21.8	20.8	22.0
United Kingdom / Royaume-Uni	5.9	14.7	16.9	18.1	18.2	17.8	16.7	20.5	20.8	20.9
United States / États-Unis	4.8	7.0	8.1	7.6	7.9	8.1	8.5	8.4	8.2	7.8
Unweighted average / Moyenne non pondérée										
OECD Average / Moyenne OCDE	**11.9**	**14.2**	**18.1**	**19.7**	**19.8**	**19.8**	**19.9**	**20.3**	**20.2**	**20.2**

1. The total tax revenue has been reduced by the amount of any capital transfer that represents uncollected taxes. The capital transfer has been allocated between tax headings in proportion to the reported tax revenue.
2. From 1991 the figures relate to the united Germany.
1. Le total des recettes fiscales a été diminué du montant de tout transfert en capital représentant les impôts non perçus. Le transfert en capital a été réparti entre les différentes rubriques en proportion des recettes fiscales.
2. Depuis 1991, les chiffres se rapportent à l'Allemagne unifiée.

StatLink http://dx.doi.org/10.1787/888933276900

Table 29. **Taxes on specific goods and services (5120) as % of GDP**
Tableau 29. **Impôts sur les biens et services déterminés (5120) en % du PIB**

	1965	1980	1990	2000	2007	2008	2009	2011	2012	2013
Australia / Australie	4.7	5.9	4.3	4.3	3.4	3.3	3.1	3.0	3.0	3.0
Austria / Autriche	6.0	3.9	3.6	3.5	3.1	3.1	3.1	3.3	3.3	3.2
Belgium / Belgique	4.0	3.6	3.4	3.0	3.0	3.0	3.1	3.1	3.4	3.2
Canada	4.3	4.0	3.6	3.0	2.7	2.7	2.7	2.6	2.6	2.5
Chile / Chili	..	..	3.9	3.5	2.0	1.9	1.7	2.0	2.0	2.0
Czech Republic / République tchèque	..	..	..	3.6	3.5	3.4	3.5	3.7	3.8	3.7
Denmark / Danemark[1]	8.5	5.7	5.0	5.5	5.1	4.5	4.3	4.4	4.4	4.6
Estonia / Estonie	..	..	..	3.1	3.8	3.5	5.1	4.5	4.6	4.4
Finland / Finlande	7.0	6.2	5.5	5.0	4.0	4.0	4.2	4.6	4.7	4.7
France[1]	4.8	3.3	3.6	3.5	3.0	2.9	3.1	3.3	3.4	3.5
Germany / Allemagne[2]	4.6	3.4	3.2	3.2	3.1	3.0	3.1	3.0	2.9	2.8
Greece / Grèce[1]	5.8	5.2	3.9	3.8	3.0	2.8	3.0	4.2	4.1	4.4
Hungary / Hongrie	..	..	..	5.4	4.3	4.3	4.2	4.6	4.9	5.0
Iceland / Islande	11.5	8.6	5.1	4.0	4.0	3.2	3.1	3.7	3.8	3.5
Ireland / Irlande	10.6	8.5	6.5	4.2	3.2	3.0	3.0	2.9	2.9	3.0
Israel / Israël	..	..	..	1.5	1.9	1.9	2.0	2.0	1.9	1.8
Italy / Italie	5.9	2.8	3.8	3.9	3.6	3.5	3.8	4.0	4.4	4.3
Japan / Japon	4.4	3.5	2.2	2.1	2.0	2.0	2.0	2.0	2.0	2.0
Korea / Corée	..	6.7	4.6	4.2	3.6	3.6	3.2	2.9	3.0	2.9
Luxembourg	2.9	3.2	3.6	4.6	4.0	4.0	4.0	3.7	3.7	3.4
Mexico / Mexique	..	5.0	5.3	5.5	5.6	8.4	5.1	6.7	6.8	6.2
Netherlands / Pays-Bas	4.5	2.9	3.0	3.3	3.1	3.2	3.2	3.1	3.0	3.2
New Zealand / Nouvelle-Zélande	4.3	3.3	3.3	2.5	2.0	2.0	2.0	1.9	1.9	1.8
Norway / Norvège	5.4	6.8	6.2	4.0	3.2	3.0	3.2	3.0	2.8	2.8
Poland / Pologne	..	..	..	4.5	4.4	4.8	4.0	4.3	4.2	4.2
Portugal	6.9	6.3	6.3	4.6	4.7	4.5	4.3	4.3	4.1	4.0
Slovak Republic / République slovaque	..	..	..	4.6	3.7	2.9	3.0	3.1	3.2	3.2
Slovenia / Slovénie	..	..	..	4.4	4.1	4.1	4.8	5.0	5.5	5.4
Spain / Espagne[1]	2.6	2.3	3.3	3.2	2.7	2.5	2.5	2.4	2.6	2.8
Sweden / Suède	6.0	4.0	4.5	3.4	2.9	2.8	3.0	2.8	2.8	2.7
Switzerland / Suisse	3.5	2.6	1.7	2.0	1.7	1.9	1.9	1.8	1.9	1.7
Turkey / Turquie	5.6	3.4	1.1	4.0	5.8	5.6	5.8	6.0	6.2	6.5
United Kingdom / Royaume-Uni	7.4	4.4	4.1	4.3	3.3	3.3	3.5	3.6	3.6	3.5
United States / États-Unis	3.6	2.1	1.8	1.8	1.6	1.6	1.6	1.7	1.7	1.7
Unweighted average / Moyenne non pondérée										
OECD Average / Moyenne OCDE	**5.6**	**4.5**	**3.9**	**3.7**	**3.4**	**3.4**	**3.3**	**3.5**	**3.5**	**3.5**

1. The total tax revenue has been reduced by the amount of any capital transfer that represents uncollected taxes. The capital transfer has been allocated between tax headings in proportion to the reported tax revenue.
2. From 1991 the figures relate to the united Germany.
1. Le total des recettes fiscales a été diminué du montant de tout transfert en capital représentant les impôts non perçus. Le transfert en capital a été réparti entre les différentes rubriques en proportion des recettes fiscales.
2. Depuis 1991, les chiffres se rapportent à l'Allemagne unifiée.

StatLink http://dx.doi.org/10.1787/888933276913

Table 30. **Taxes on specific goods and services (5120) as % of total taxation**
Tableau 30. **Impôts sur les biens et services déterminés (5120) en % du total des recettes fiscales**

	1965	1980	1990	2000	2007	2008	2009	2011	2012	2013
Australia / Australie	22.7	22.6	15.3	14.1	11.3	12.1	12.2	11.3	11.0	10.8
Austria / Autriche	18.0	10.1	9.0	8.2	7.7	7.5	7.6	8.1	7.9	7.6
Belgium / Belgique	13.0	8.8	8.3	6.9	7.0	7.0	7.3	7.2	7.8	7.2
Canada	16.8	13.0	10.3	8.6	8.5	8.4	8.7	8.6	8.3	8.3
Chile / Chili	..	..	23.0	18.8	8.7	8.7	10.1	9.4	9.4	9.9
Czech Republic / République tchèque	..	..	..	11.0	10.2	10.1	10.8	11.2	11.1	10.7
Denmark / Danemark[1]	29.3	13.7	11.2	11.8	11.0	10.1	9.6	9.7	9.6	9.6
Estonia / Estonie	..	..	..	10.1	12.1	11.0	14.5	14.0	14.4	13.8
Finland / Finlande	23.4	17.6	12.9	10.9	9.7	9.7	10.2	11.0	11.0	10.8
France[1]	14.3	8.4	8.7	8.0	7.0	7.0	7.5	7.7	7.7	7.7
Germany / Allemagne[2]	14.6	9.3	9.2	8.8	8.8	8.4	8.6	8.3	7.9	7.8
Greece / Grèce[1]	33.8	25.1	15.6	11.5	9.6	8.9	9.8	12.5	11.8	12.7
Hungary / Hongrie	..	..	..	13.8	10.9	10.8	10.7	12.6	12.6	13.1
Iceland / Islande	45.0	29.8	16.9	11.0	10.2	9.1	9.6	10.7	10.7	9.7
Ireland / Irlande	43.4	28.3	19.9	13.6	10.6	10.5	10.8	10.6	10.3	10.2
Israel / Israël	..	..	..	4.3	5.4	6.1	6.6	6.6	6.5	5.9
Italy / Italie	24.1	9.7	10.6	9.6	8.5	8.5	9.1	9.7	10.0	9.7
Japan / Japon	25.0	14.1	7.5	8.0	7.1	6.9	7.3	7.1	6.9	6.7
Korea / Corée	..	39.5	24.3	19.7	14.5	14.5	13.6	12.2	12.0	11.8
Luxembourg	11.1	9.6	10.8	12.5	10.8	10.7	10.2	9.8	9.5	8.7
Mexico / Mexique	..	34.4	34.0	33.4	31.6	40.3	29.4	34.3	34.9	31.6
Netherlands / Pays-Bas	14.7	7.3	7.5	8.9	8.7	8.8	8.9	8.6	8.4	8.6
New Zealand / Nouvelle-Zélande	18.5	11.2	9.2	7.5	5.9	6.1	6.4	6.3	6.0	5.8
Norway / Norvège	18.4	16.1	15.3	9.6	7.7	7.2	7.8	7.1	6.9	6.9
Poland / Pologne	..	..	..	13.5	12.8	13.8	12.6	13.4	13.0	13.1
Portugal	44.0	28.9	23.8	14.7	14.7	14.0	14.4	13.3	12.9	11.7
Slovak Republic / République slovaque	..	..	..	13.7	12.7	9.9	10.4	10.7	11.2	10.6
Slovenia / Slovénie	..	..	..	12.1	10.9	11.2	13.2	13.8	14.8	14.6
Spain / Espagne[1]	18.4	10.5	10.5	9.6	7.5	7.8	8.4	7.8	8.2	8.6
Sweden / Suède	19.2	9.2	9.2	7.0	6.4	6.4	6.8	6.6	6.7	6.4
Switzerland / Suisse	21.3	11.0	7.2	7.3	6.5	7.0	7.0	6.6	7.2	6.4
Turkey / Turquie	53.5	25.2	7.3	16.4	24.3	23.2	23.6	21.7	22.4	22.4
United Kingdom / Royaume-Uni	25.2	13.3	12.5	12.4	9.7	9.8	11.0	10.7	10.8	10.7
United States / États-Unis	15.1	8.3	7.1	6.3	6.1	6.4	7.0	7.3	7.1	6.8
Unweighted average / Moyenne non pondérée										
OECD Average / Moyenne OCDE	**24.3**	**16.7**	**13.2**	**11.6**	**10.5**	**10.5**	**10.6**	**10.8**	**10.8**	**10.5**

1. The total tax revenue has been reduced by the amount of any capital transfer that represents uncollected taxes. The capital transfer has been allocated between tax headings in proportion to the reported tax revenue.
2. From 1991 the figures relate to the united Germany.
1. Le total des recettes fiscales a été diminué du montant de tout transfert en capital représentant les impôts non perçus. Le transfert en capital a été réparti entre les différentes rubriques en proportion des recettes fiscales.
2. Depuis 1991, les chiffres se rapportent à l'Allemagne unifiée.

StatLink http://dx.doi.org/10.1787/888933276928

Table 31. Total tax revenue in millions of US dollars at market exchange rates
Tableau 31. Total des recettes fiscales en millions de dollars des É-U au taux de change du marché

	1965	1980	1990	2000	2007	2008	2009	2011	2012	2013
Australia / Australie	5 625	45 465	90 886	124 326	292 354	283 977	260 535	403 111	430 543	419 702
Austria / Autriche	..	41 355	68 606	82 751	156 698	176 704	162 878	176 048	169 848	182 101
Belgium / Belgique	..	52 031	89 387	103 414	201 171	223 409	204 756	226 945	219 489	234 337
Canada	14 208	86 383	209 202	262 765	477 199	480 532	436 948	547 385	567 345	567 080
Chile / Chili	..	..	5 829	14 650	39 445	38 357	29 691	53 292	57 028	55 285
Czech Republic / République tchèque	..	..	..	19 971	64 752	78 828	66 605	75 914	69 986	71 403
Denmark / Danemark[1]	3 011	29 274	61 400	76 903	148 319	158 155	144 481	155 300	149 576	159 835
Estonia / Estonie	..	..	..	1 760	6 915	7 561	6 857	7 280	7 274	7 920
Finland / Finlande	..	16 529	49 576	57 539	106 021	116 703	102 949	115 065	109 599	117 733
France[1]	..	248 154	550 698	589 281	1 128 960	1 230 919	1 113 178	1 227 355	1 183 677	1 265 267
Germany / Allemagne[2]	..	399 174	577 350	706 891	1 200 351	1 326 069	1 233 516	1 341 751	1 288 224	1 367 726
Greece / Grèce[1]	..	2 050	14 564	43 422	99 338	109 593	101 618	96 899	86 229	83 372
Hungary / Hongrie	..	..	..	18 211	54 890	61 771	50 545	50 998	49 004	51 224
Iceland / Islande	139	989	1 969	3 229	8 299	6 177	4 104	5 049	5 007	5 535
Ireland / Irlande	..	5 623	15 565	30 723	81 992	78 064	64 536	65 112	61 993	67 365
Israel / Israël	..	..	..	45 924	60 615	68 348	61 319	79 768	76 460	88 872
Italy / Italie	..	83 964	336 581	463 642	918 826	993 349	919 540	954 441	910 832	937 523
Japan / Japon	17 074	275 448	903 504	1 262 348	1 241 928	1 350 408	1 365 456	1 702 088	1 748 801	1 500 394
Korea / Corée	..	11 008	52 630	120 547	278 198	247 262	214 634	290 720	303 158	317 220
Luxembourg	..	2 144	4 756	7 927	18 406	20 470	19 654	22 235	21 703	23 625
Mexico / Mexique	..	33 627	45 044	107 333	183 266	227 702	153 422	227 645	231 826	247 925
Netherlands / Pays-Bas	..	97 249	132 567	152 130	302 717	340 620	304 009	320 586	299 055	316 917
New Zealand / Nouvelle-Zélande	1 386	7 393	16 372	18 037	47 059	43 743	37 192	51 777	56 783	60 188
Norway / Norvège	2 355	27 041	48 226	71 798	169 015	191 227	159 036	209 462	211 705	211 474
Poland / Pologne	..	..	..	56 853	149 188	182 589	137 689	167 841	160 370	167 902
Portugal	..	2 498	18 821	36 909	76 863	83 414	73 243	79 623	69 230	77 593
Slovak Republic / République slovaque	..	..	..	9 793	25 140	28 995	25 588	28 023	26 396	29 667
Slovenia / Slovénie	..	..	..	6 381	17 837	20 190	18 194	18 713	17 050	17 650
Spain / Espagne[1]	..	30 574	131 605	198 962	540 493	527 218	447 207	468 082	435 989	455 509
Sweden / Suède	7 755	61 292	127 730	127 285	219 400	225 963	189 440	239 523	231 683	248 343
Switzerland / Suisse	2 596	27 674	60 826	75 134	124 783	147 129	146 644	188 299	179 204	184 068
Turkey / Turquie	1 265	12 343	30 200	64 490	156 208	177 278	151 706	216 045	218 560	240 846
United Kingdom / Royaume-Uni	30 605	188 624	359 508	537 234	1 009 903	945 374	746 906	870 894	866 799	881 857
United States / États-Unis	167 022	730 672	1 550 453	2 896 222	3 862 089	3 708 617	3 311 367	3 656 166	3 887 222	4 260 050
Unweighted average / Moyenne non pondérée										
OECD Average / Moyenne OCDE	..	**96 868**	**205 698**	**246 905**	**396 136**	**409 021**	**366 631**	**421 748**	**423 754**	**438 927**

1. The total tax revenue has been reduced by the amount of any capital transfer that represents uncollected taxes. The capital transfer has been allocated between tax headings in proportion to the reported tax revenue.
2. From 1991 the figures relate to the united Germany.
1. Le total des recettes fiscales a été diminué du montant de tout transfert en capital représentant les impôts non perçus. Le transfert en capital a été réparti entre les différentes rubriques en proportion des recettes fiscales.
2. Depuis 1991, les chiffres se rapportent à l'Allemagne unifiée.

StatLink http://dx.doi.org/10.1787/888933276938

Table 32. **Tax revenue of individual countries as % of total OECD tax revenue**
Tableau 32. **Recettes fiscales de chaque pays en % du total des recettes des pays membres de l'OCDE**

	1965	1980	1990	2000	2007	2008	2009	2011	2012	2013
Australia / Australie	..	1.8	1.6	1.5	2.2	2.0	2.1	2.8	3.0	2.8
Austria / Autriche	..	1.6	1.2	1.0	1.2	1.3	1.3	1.2	1.2	1.2
Belgium / Belgique	..	2.1	1.6	1.2	1.5	1.6	1.6	1.6	1.5	1.6
Canada	..	3.4	3.8	3.1	3.5	3.5	3.5	3.8	3.9	3.8
Chile / Chili	..	..	0.1	0.2	0.3	0.3	0.2	0.4	0.4	0.4
Czech Republic / République tchèque	..	..	..	0.2	0.5	0.6	0.5	0.5	0.5	0.5
Denmark / Danemark[1]	..	1.2	1.1	0.9	1.1	1.1	1.2	1.1	1.0	1.1
Estonia / Estonie	..	..	..	0.0	0.1	0.1	0.1	0.1	0.1	0.1
Finland / Finlande	..	0.7	0.9	0.7	0.8	0.8	0.8	0.8	0.8	0.8
France[1]	..	9.9	9.9	7.0	8.4	8.9	8.9	8.6	8.2	8.5
Germany / Allemagne[2]	..	15.8	10.4	8.4	8.9	9.5	9.9	9.4	8.9	9.2
Greece / Grèce[1]	..	0.1	0.3	0.5	0.7	0.8	0.8	0.7	0.6	0.6
Hungary / Hongrie	..	..	..	0.2	0.4	0.4	0.4	0.4	0.3	0.3
Iceland / Islande	..	0.0	0.0	0.0	0.1	0.0	0.0	0.0	0.0	0.0
Ireland / Irlande	..	0.2	0.3	0.4	0.6	0.6	0.5	0.5	0.4	0.5
Israel / Israël	..	..	..	0.5	0.5	0.5	0.5	0.6	0.5	0.6
Italy / Italie	..	3.3	6.1	5.5	6.8	7.1	7.4	6.7	6.3	6.3
Japan / Japon	..	10.9	16.3	15.0	9.2	9.7	11.0	11.9	12.1	10.1
Korea / Corée	..	0.4	0.9	1.4	2.1	1.8	1.7	2.0	2.1	2.1
Luxembourg	..	0.1	0.1	0.1	0.1	0.1	0.2	0.2	0.2	0.2
Mexico / Mexique	..	1.3	0.8	1.3	1.4	1.6	1.2	1.6	1.6	1.7
Netherlands / Pays-Bas	..	3.9	2.4	1.8	2.2	2.4	2.4	2.2	2.1	2.1
New Zealand / Nouvelle-Zélande	..	0.3	0.3	0.2	0.3	0.3	0.3	0.4	0.4	0.4
Norway / Norvège	..	1.1	0.9	0.9	1.3	1.4	1.3	1.5	1.5	1.4
Poland / Pologne	..	..	..	0.7	1.1	1.3	1.1	1.2	1.1	1.1
Portugal	..	0.1	0.3	0.4	0.6	0.6	0.6	0.6	0.5	0.5
Slovak Republic / République slovaque	..	..	..	0.1	0.2	0.2	0.2	0.2	0.2	0.2
Slovenia / Slovénie	..	..	..	0.1	0.1	0.1	0.1	0.1	0.1	0.1
Spain / Espagne[1]	..	1.2	2.4	2.4	4.0	3.8	3.6	3.3	3.0	3.1
Sweden / Suède	..	2.4	2.3	1.5	1.6	1.6	1.5	1.7	1.6	1.7
Switzerland / Suisse	..	1.1	1.1	0.9	0.9	1.1	1.2	1.3	1.2	1.2
Turkey / Turquie	..	0.5	0.5	0.8	1.2	1.3	1.2	1.5	1.5	1.6
United Kingdom / Royaume-Uni	..	7.5	6.5	6.4	7.5	6.8	6.0	6.1	6.0	5.9
United States / États-Unis	..	29.0	27.9	34.5	28.7	26.7	26.6	25.5	27.0	28.5
Cumulative sum / Somme cumulative										
OECD Total / Total OCDE	..	**100.0**	**100.0**	**100.0**	**100.0**	**100.0**	**100.0**	**100.0**	**100.0**	**100.0**

1. The total tax revenue has been reduced by the amount of any capital transfer that represents uncollected taxes. The capital transfer has been allocated between tax headings in proportion to the reported tax revenue.
2. From 1991 the figures relate to the united Germany.
1. Le total des recettes fiscales a été diminué du montant de tout transfert en capital représentant les impôts non perçus. Le transfert en capital a été réparti entre les différentes rubriques en proportion des recettes fiscales.
2. Depuis 1991, les chiffres se rapportent à l'Allemagne unifiée.

StatLink http://dx.doi.org/10.1787/888933276944

Table 33. **Tax revenue in US dollars per capita at market exchange rates**
Tableau 33. **Recettes fiscales en dollars des É-U par habitant, au taux de change du marché**

	1965	1980	1990	2000	2007	2008	2009	2011	2012	2013
Australia / Australie	496	3 094	5 326	6 534	14 037	13 363	12 012	18 044	18 947	18 144
Austria / Autriche	..	5 478	8 936	10 329	18 890	21 235	19 526	20 987	20 157	21 503
Belgium / Belgique	..	5 277	8 968	10 088	18 933	20 860	18 965	20 542	19 724	20 930
Canada	711	3 523	7 555	8 563	14 492	14 423	12 955	15 874	16 265	16 057
Chile / Chili	..	..	442	951	2 376	2 288	1 754	3 090	3 277	3 149
Czech Republic / République tchèque	..	..	..	1 944	6 273	7 558	6 348	7 232	6 659	6 793
Denmark / Danemark[1]	633	5 714	11 943	14 402	27 157	28 789	26 159	27 879	26 738	28 635
Estonia / Estonie	..	..	..	1 276	5 151	5 642	5 123	5 453	5 472	5 999
Finland / Finlande	..	3 458	9 941	11 119	20 042	21 966	19 286	21 364	20 247	21 642
France[1]	..	4 606	9 711	9 977	18 219	19 758	17 778	19 413	18 636	19 836
Germany / Allemagne[2]	..	5 099	7 268	8 598	14 591	16 150	15 061	16 403	15 723	16 873
Greece / Grèce[1]	..	213	1 434	3 977	8 899	9 797	9 085	8 711	7 775	7 338
Hungary / Hongrie	..	..	..	1 783	5 459	6 154	5 043	5 121	4 940	5 181
Iceland / Islande	721	4 334	7 727	11 483	26 652	19 343	12 855	15 826	15 668	17 184
Ireland / Irlande	..	1 653	4 440	8 107	18 737	17 405	14 236	14 233	13 520	14 666
Israel / Israël	..	..	..	7 302	8 442	9 352	8 192	10 272	9 666	11 031
Italy / Italie	..	1 488	5 934	8 142	15 475	16 602	15 277	15 743	14 952	15 324
Japan / Japon	174	2 353	7 309	9 945	9 720	10 576	10 709	13 318	13 714	11 787
Korea / Corée	..	289	1 228	2 564	5 725	5 051	4 364	5 840	6 063	6 317
Luxembourg	..	5 888	12 454	18 170	38 346	41 890	39 483	42 897	40 876	47 997
Mexico / Mexique	..	504	517	1 064	1 669	2 046	1 359	1 968	1 981	2 094
Netherlands / Pays-Bas	..	6 873	8 866	9 553	18 479	20 712	18 391	19 205	17 849	18 807
New Zealand / Nouvelle-Zélande	525	2 332	4 829	4 675	11 129	10 240	8 615	11 757	12 809	13 459
Norway / Norvège	633	6 619	11 370	15 987	35 891	40 105	32 935	42 298	42 189	41 629
Poland / Pologne	..	..	..	1 486	3 914	4 790	3 609	4 357	4 162	4 412
Portugal	..	256	1 885	3 587	7 290	7 900	6 931	7 542	6 584	7 236
Slovak Republic / République slovaque	..	..	..	1 817	4 678	5 390	4 750	5 191	4 881	5 478
Slovenia / Slovénie	..	..	..	3 208	8 873	9 989	8 920	9 116	8 288	8 465
Spain / Espagne[1]	..	817	3 387	4 942	12 043	11 573	9 741	10 137	9 448	9 892
Sweden / Suède	1 003	7 375	14 924	14 347	23 983	24 509	20 373	25 348	24 338	25 842
Switzerland / Suisse	443	4 379	9 062	10 458	16 525	19 238	18 937	23 798	22 527	22 957
Turkey / Turquie	41	278	548	1 003	2 227	2 495	2 106	2 911	2 907	3 167
United Kingdom / Royaume-Uni	563	3 348	6 281	9 123	16 794	15 615	12 259	13 761	13 606	14 094
United States / États-Unis	860	3 216	6 211	10 264	12 821	12 196	10 794	11 734	12 385	13 476
Unweighted average / Moyenne non pondérée										
OECD Average / Moyenne OCDE	..	**3 402**	**6 611**	**7 258**	**13 939**	**14 559**	**12 763**	**14 628**	**14 205**	**14 923**

1. The total tax revenue has been reduced by the amount of any capital transfer that represents uncollected taxes. The capital transfer has been allocated between tax headings in proportion to the reported tax revenue.
2. From 1991 the figures relate to the united Germany.
1. Le total des recettes fiscales a été diminué du montant de tout transfert en capital représentant les impôts non perçus. Le transfert en capital a été réparti entre les différentes rubriques en proportion des recettes fiscales.
2. Depuis 1991, les chiffres se rapportent à l'Allemagne unifiée.

StatLink http://dx.doi.org/10.1787/888933276952

Table 34. **Annual % change in total tax revenue**
Tableau 34. **Variation annuelle en % des recettes fiscales totales**

	1966	1980	1990	2000	2007	2008	2009	2011	2012	2013
Australia / Australie	7.3	18.0	3.0	8.9	9.0	-2.7	-1.8	8.5	6.5	4.6
Austria / Autriche	11.2	8.8	8.4	2.9	6.4	5.6	-3.0	5.2	4.4	3.8
Belgium / Belgique	14.7	4.5	7.2	4.9	4.9	4.0	-3.6	5.2	4.6	3.4
Canada	15.5	15.9	5.2	6.6	4.7	0.1	-2.8	5.5	4.7	3.0
Chile / Chili	..	..	..	14.3	14.2	-2.5	-17.4	18.8	7.6	-1.2
Czech Republic / République tchèque	..	..	..	3.4	9.9	2.5	-5.7	4.3	1.9	2.1
Denmark / Danemark[1]	17.5	10.2	1.0	4.6	3.3	-0.1	-4.0	2.1	4.1	3.7
Estonia / Estonie	..	..	..	9.5	22.9	2.4	-4.6	7.2	8.1	5.4
Finland / Finlande	11.3	16.2	9.4	11.1	6.4	3.1	-7.2	8.4	3.0	4.0
France[1]	7.6	17.4	5.7	3.5	3.3	2.1	-4.8	6.2	4.3	3.5
Germany / Allemagne[2]	8.3	7.1	4.5	2.7	6.2	3.4	-2.1	6.9	3.9	2.8
Greece / Grèce[1]	19.8	16.8	32.5	12.2	9.8	3.3	-2.4	-3.9	-3.7	-6.4
Hungary / Hongrie	..	..	..	15.4	14.2	5.7	-4.1	1.9	7.5	4.0
Iceland / Islande	..	..	14.8	9.1	9.7	2.2	-6.6	8.5	6.9	7.9
Ireland / Irlande	13.8	29.2	7.3	16.5	5.1	-10.9	-13.0	3.4	3.0	5.2
Israel / Israël	..	..	..	13.5	6.6	-1.6	-1.7	7.7	3.3	9.0
Italy / Italie	7.4	42.0	13.6	4.9	6.8	1.2	-2.6	2.2	3.2	-0.3
Japan / Japon	14.1	13.4	5.8	3.6	2.3	-4.5	-8.5	2.4	2.9	4.9
Korea / Corée	..	23.0	39.5	19.8	13.6	5.3	0.5	8.8	6.0	1.8
Luxembourg	4.1	11.5	8.8	12.8	11.0	4.1	1.0	6.3	5.6	5.4
Mexico / Mexique	..	..	35.6	27.4	6.4	26.8	-18.4	15.1	7.7	3.9
Netherlands / Pays-Bas	13.6	8.4	5.8	6.9	5.0	5.4	-6.1	1.0	0.9	2.6
New Zealand / Nouvelle-Zélande	7.6	17.2	-0.7	7.3	3.4	-2.6	-4.6	5.2	6.9	4.8
Norway / Norvège	12.2	23.1	7.2	19.2	4.4	9.1	-7.4	8.1	4.9	0.9
Poland / Pologne	..	..	..	4.3	14.3	6.7	-2.4	10.1	4.9	1.7
Portugal	12.4	39.3	18.5	7.8	7.3	1.6	-7.6	4.0	-5.9	8.5
Slovak Republic / République slovaque	..	..	..	6.9	11.7	8.0	-7.1	6.6	1.9	8.8
Slovenia / Slovénie	..	..	..	7.9	9.7	6.0	-5.2	0.6	-1.4	0.2
Spain / Espagne[1]	7.6	18.9	10.7	9.0	8.5	-8.7	-10.7	4.1	0.8	1.2
Sweden / Suède	11.2	13.2	10.6	6.8	4.1	0.5	-2.8	2.2	0.9	3.1
Switzerland / Suisse	11.4	6.4	6.2	10.0	5.6	6.5	-0.1	4.0	0.6	1.6
Turkey / Turquie	20.0	109.1	85.4	66.3	9.2	13.4	1.9	25.5	8.4	17.1
United Kingdom / Royaume-Uni	9.1	27.6	8.2	6.8	4.4	2.2	-7.2	6.3	0.7	3.1
United States / États-Unis	11.4	10.3	7.1	7.8	4.7	-4.0	-10.7	5.4	6.3	9.6
Unweighted average / Moyenne non pondérée										
OECD Average / Moyenne OCDE	**11.7**	**21.1**	**13.9**	**11.0**	**7.9**	**2.8**	**-5.4**	**6.3**	**3.7**	**3.9**

1. The total tax revenue has been reduced by the amount of any capital transfer that represents uncollected taxes. The capital transfer has been allocated between tax headings in proportion to the reported tax revenue.
2. From 1991 the figures relate to the united Germany.
1. Le total des recettes fiscales a été diminué du montant de tout transfert en capital représentant les impôts non perçus. Le transfert en capital a été réparti entre les différentes rubriques en proportion des recettes fiscales.
2. Depuis 1991, les chiffres se rapportent à l'Allemagne unifiée.

StatLink http://dx.doi.org/10.1787/888933276960

Table 35. **Gross domestic product for tax reporting years at market prices, in billions of national currency units**
Tableau 35. **Produit intérieur brut pour les années de déclaration fiscale au prix du marché, en milliards de monnaie nationale**

	1965	1980	1990	2000	2007	2008	2009	2011	2012	2013
Australia / Australie[1]	24	152	415	705	1 178	1 258	1 296	1 488	1 521	1 582
Austria / Autriche	18	77	137	213	282	292	286	309	317	323
Belgium / Belgique	21	92	171	258	345	355	350	380	388	395
Canada[1]	61	331	691	1 118	1 589	1 627	1 590	1 790	1 845	1 913
Chile / Chili	..	..	10 482	42 095	90 429	93 848	96 444	121 319	129 028	137 029
Czech Republic / République tchèque	..	..	..	2 373	3 832	4 015	3 922	4 023	4 042	4 077
Denmark / Danemark	71	399	855	1 327	1 739	1 798	1 714	1 833	1 867	1 886
Estonia / Estonie	..	..	..	6	16	17	14	16	18	19
Finland / Finlande	5	34	91	136	187	194	181	197	200	203
France	77	453	1 059	1 485	1 946	1 996	1 939	2 059	2 087	2 117
Germany / Allemagne	235	789	1 307	2 116	2 513	2 562	2 460	2 703	2 755	2 821
Greece / Grèce	1	7	46	142	233	242	237	208	194	182
Hungary / Hongrie	..	..	..	13 294	25 447	26 949	26 175	28 035	28 549	29 846
Iceland / Islande	0	16	381	703	1 374	1 548	1 586	1 703	1 780	1 881
Ireland / Irlande	1	13	38	108	197	187	168	171	173	175
Israel / Israël	..	..	..	536	726	768	812	925	992	1 049
Italy / Italie	22	210	729	1 240	1 610	1 633	1 574	1 639	1 615	1 609
Japan / Japon[1]	34 708	252 254	458 413	510 835	513 023	489 520	473 996	474 171	474 636	483 075
Korea / Corée	..	39 471	197 712	635 185	1 043 258	1 104 492	1 151 708	1 332 681	1 377 457	1 429 445
Luxembourg	1	5	11	23	37	38	36	42	44	46
Mexico / Mexique	..	5	825	6 132	11 399	12 257	12 073	14 527	15 600	16 083
Netherlands / Pays-Bas	35	174	260	448	613	639	618	643	645	651
New Zealand / Nouvelle-Zélande[1]	4	26	76	122	188	188	195	212	217	234
Norway / Norvège	57	318	750	1 508	2 350	2 605	2 430	2 792	2 965	3 069
Poland / Pologne	..	..	..	747	1 187	1 277	1 362	1 554	1 616	1 662
Portugal	1	8	56	128	175	179	175	176	168	169
Slovak Republic / République slovaque	..	..	..	32	63	68	64	70	72	74
Slovenia / Slovénie	..	..	..	19	35	38	36	37	36	36
Spain / Espagne	9	100	328	646	1 081	1 116	1 079	1 075	1 055	1 049
Sweden / Suède	128	593	1 528	2 380	3 297	3 388	3 289	3 657	3 685	3 775
Switzerland / Suisse	68	199	358	459	573	597	587	618	625	635
Turkey / Turquie	0	0	1	167	843	951	953	1 298	1 417	1 567
United Kingdom / Royaume-Uni	37	243	616	1 024	1 481	1 519	1 482	1 618	1 655	1 713
United States / États-Unis	711	2 863	5 980	10 285	14 478	14 719	14 419	15 518	16 163	16 768

1. GDP is fiscal year. The year Y is calculated (at annual rate) as the average of: Q2(Y) to Q1(Y+1) for Canada and Japan; and Q3(Y) to Q2(Y+1) for Australia and New Zealand.

Source: OECD National Accounts.

1. PIB se référant á l'année fiscale.L'année A est calculée (taux annuel) comme la moyenne de: T2(A) á T1(A+1) pour le Canada et le Japon; et T3(A) á T2(A+1) pour l'Australie et la Nouvelle-Zélande.

Source : Comptes nationaux de l'OCDE.

StatLink *http://dx.doi.org/10.1787/888933276978*

Table 36. **Exchange rates used, national currency per US dollar at market exchange rates**
Tableau 36. **Taux de change utilisés, unités de monnaie nationale par dollar des É-U au taux de change du marché**

	1965	1980	1990	2000	2007	2008	2009	2011	2012	2013
Australia / Australie	0.893	0.877	1.282	1.727	1.195	1.198	1.282	0.969	0.966	1.036
Austria / Autriche	..	0.720	0.788	1.085	0.730	0.684	0.720	0.719	0.778	0.753
Belgium / Belgique	..	0.720	0.788	1.085	0.730	0.684	0.720	0.719	0.778	0.753
Canada	1.078	1.169	1.167	1.485	1.074	1.068	1.141	0.989	0.999	1.030
Chile / Chili	..	..	304.903	539.388	522.228	523.542	558.942	483.421	485.984	495.282
Czech Republic / République tchèque	..	..	..	38.637	20.289	17.078	19.050	17.672	19.538	19.560
Denmark / Danemark	6.915	5.636	6.186	8.088	5.443	5.099	5.359	5.357	5.790	5.618
Estonia / Estonie	..	..	..	1.085	0.730	0.684	0.720	0.719	0.778	0.753
Finland / Finlande	..	0.720	0.788	1.085	0.730	0.684	0.720	0.719	0.778	0.753
France	..	0.720	0.788	1.085	0.730	0.684	0.720	0.719	0.778	0.753
Germany / Allemagne	..	0.720	0.788	1.085	0.730	0.684	0.720	0.719	0.778	0.753
Greece / Grèce	..	0.720	0.788	1.085	0.730	0.684	0.720	0.719	0.778	0.753
Hungary / Hongrie	..	..	..	282.286	183.595	172.465	202.062	200.907	224.823	223.582
Iceland / Islande	0.431	4.785	58.378	78.845	64.075	87.999	123.665	116.058	125.118	122.167
Ireland / Irlande	..	0.720	0.788	1.085	0.730	0.684	0.720	0.719	0.778	0.753
Israel / Israël	..	..	..	4.077	4.109	3.585	3.927	3.574	3.850	3.609
Italy / Italie	..	0.720	0.788	1.085	0.730	0.684	0.720	0.719	0.778	0.753
Japan / Japon	361.491	226.696	144.796	107.835	117.755	103.388	93.572	79.707	79.814	97.598
Korea / Corée	..	607.446	707.995	1 130.640	929.450	1 100.862	1 274.947	1 107.302	1 125.935	1 094.926
Luxembourg	..	0.720	0.788	1.085	0.730	0.684	0.720	0.719	0.778	0.753
Mexico / Mexique	..	0.023	2.841	9.453	10.929	11.153	13.504	12.434	13.150	12.770
Netherlands / Pays-Bas	..	0.720	0.788	1.085	0.730	0.684	0.720	0.719	0.778	0.753
New Zealand / Nouvelle-Zélande	0.722	1.027	1.678	2.205	1.361	1.425	1.600	1.266	1.235	1.220
Norway / Norvège	7.151	4.937	6.258	8.797	5.858	5.648	6.290	5.605	5.815	5.877
Poland / Pologne	..	..	..	4.346	2.765	2.410	3.119	2.962	3.252	3.160
Portugal	..	0.720	0.788	1.085	0.730	0.684	0.720	0.719	0.778	0.753
Slovak Republic / République slovaque	..	..	..	1.085	0.730	0.684	0.720	0.719	0.778	0.753
Slovenia / Slovénie	..	..	..	1.085	0.730	0.684	0.720	0.719	0.778	0.753
Spain / Espagne	..	0.720	0.788	1.085	0.730	0.684	0.720	0.719	0.778	0.753
Sweden / Suède	5.158	4.229	5.918	9.161	6.758	6.597	7.653	6.489	6.769	6.513
Switzerland / Suisse	4.328	1.676	1.389	1.688	1.200	1.084	1.086	0.887	0.937	0.927
Turkey / Turquie	0.000	0.000	0.003	0.624	1.300	1.299	1.547	1.672	1.792	1.905
United Kingdom / Royaume-Uni	0.358	0.430	0.563	0.661	0.500	0.546	0.641	0.624	0.631	0.640
United States / États-Unis	1.000	1.000	1.000	1.000	1.000	1.000	1.000	1.000	1.000	1.000

Source: OECD Financial indicators data. / Indicateurs financiers de l'OCDE.

StatLink *http://dx.doi.org/10.1787/888933276982*

Revenue Statistics 1965-2014
Statistiques des recettes publiques 1965-2014

PART II/PARTIE II

B. Comparative charts, 1965-2013

B. Graphiques comparatifs, 1965-2013

Chart 1. **Total tax revenue as % of GDP, 2013**
Graphique 1. **Total des recettes fiscales en % du PIB, 2013**

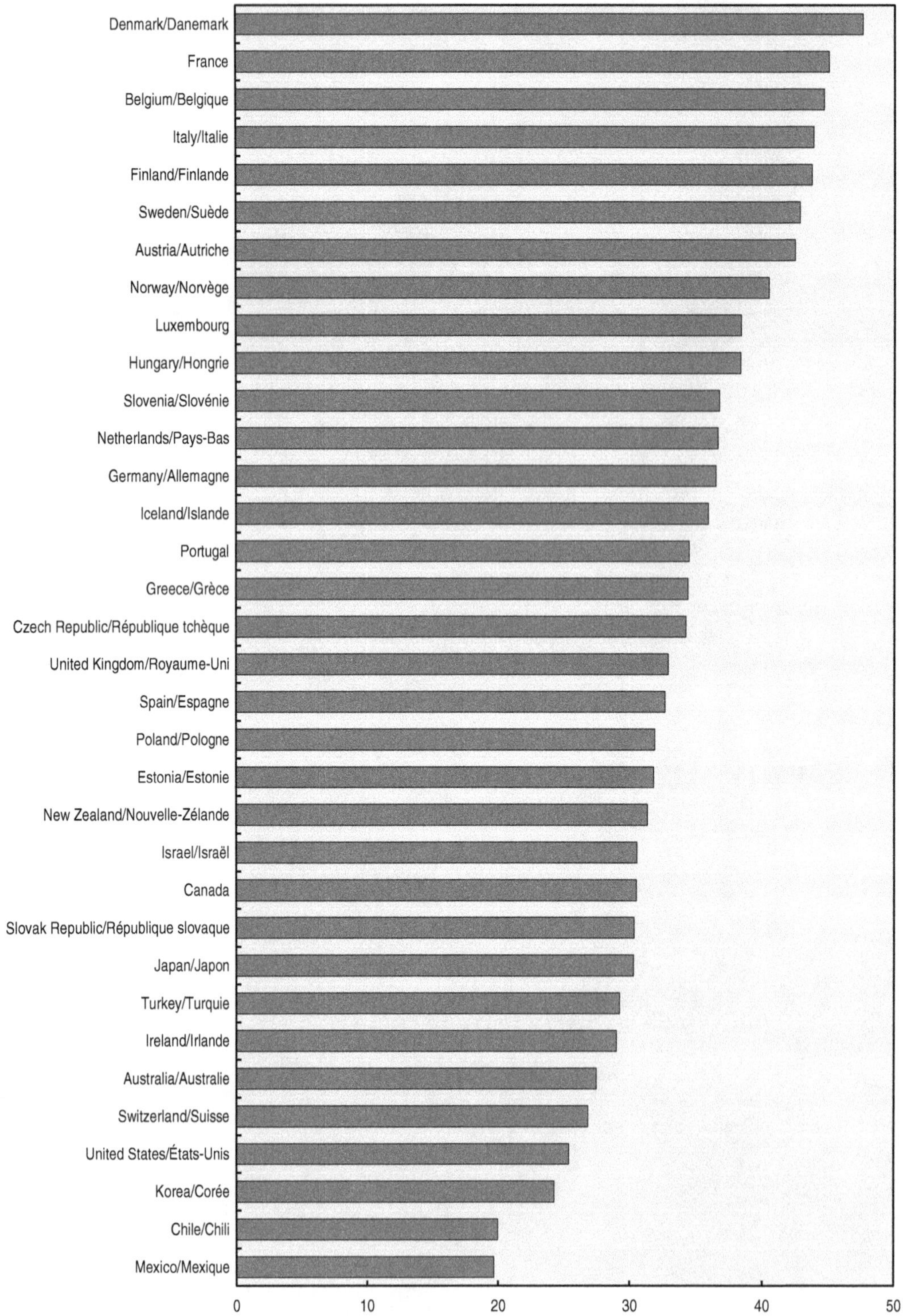

Note: Countries have been ranked by their total tax revenue to GDP ratios./Le classement des pays a été fait en fonction du total des recettes par rapport au PIB.
Source: Table 1/Tableau 1.

StatLink http://dx.doi.org/10.1787/888933276453

Chart 2. **Tax revenue of main headings as % of total revenue, 2013**
Graphique 2. **Recettes fiscales sous les principales rubriques en % du total des recettes fiscales, 2013**

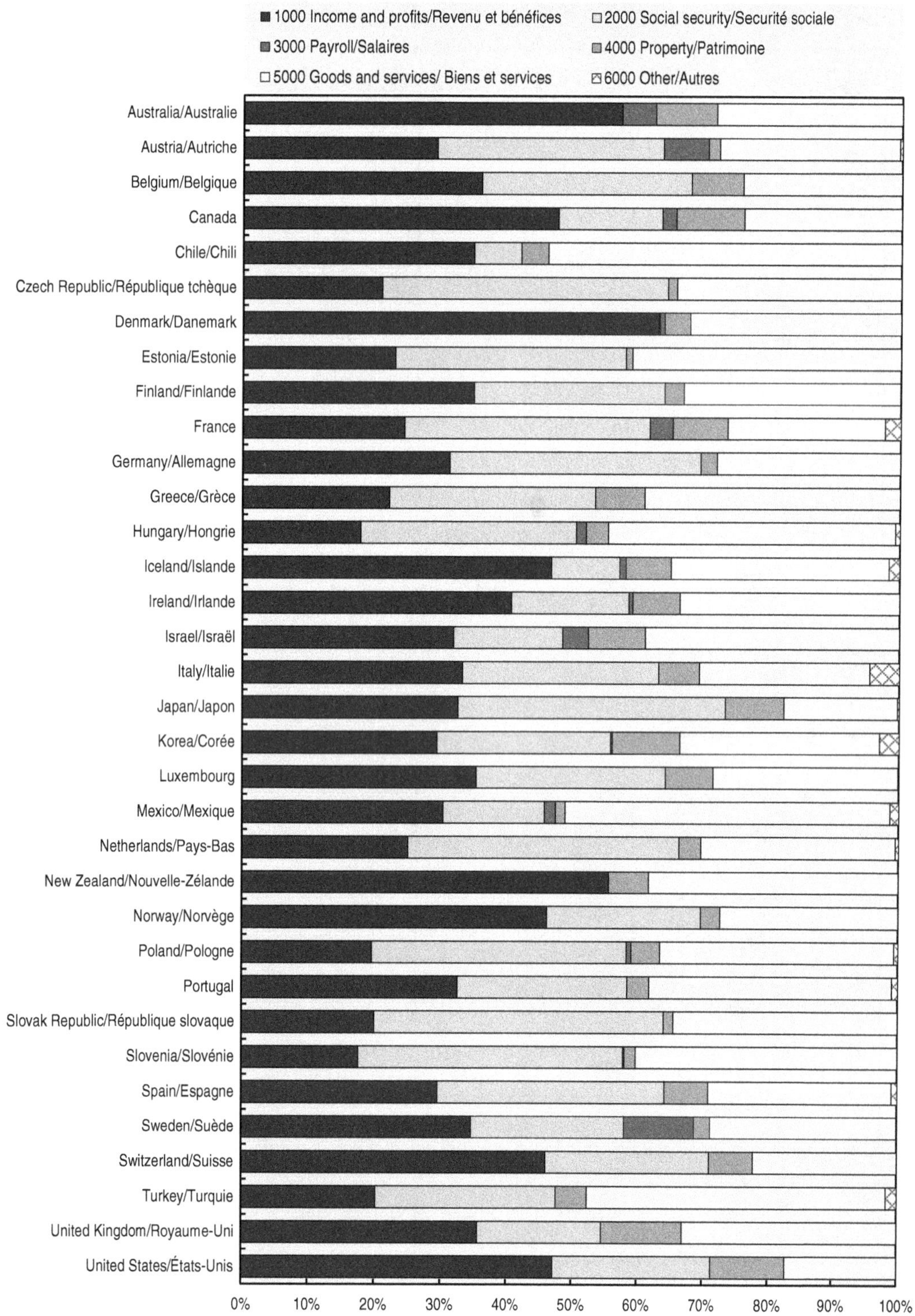

Source: Table 6/Tableau 6.

StatLink http://dx.doi.org/10.1787/888933276467

Chart 3. **Total tax revenue as % of GDP, 1965-2013**
Graphique 3. **Total des recettes fiscales en % du PIB, 1965-2013**

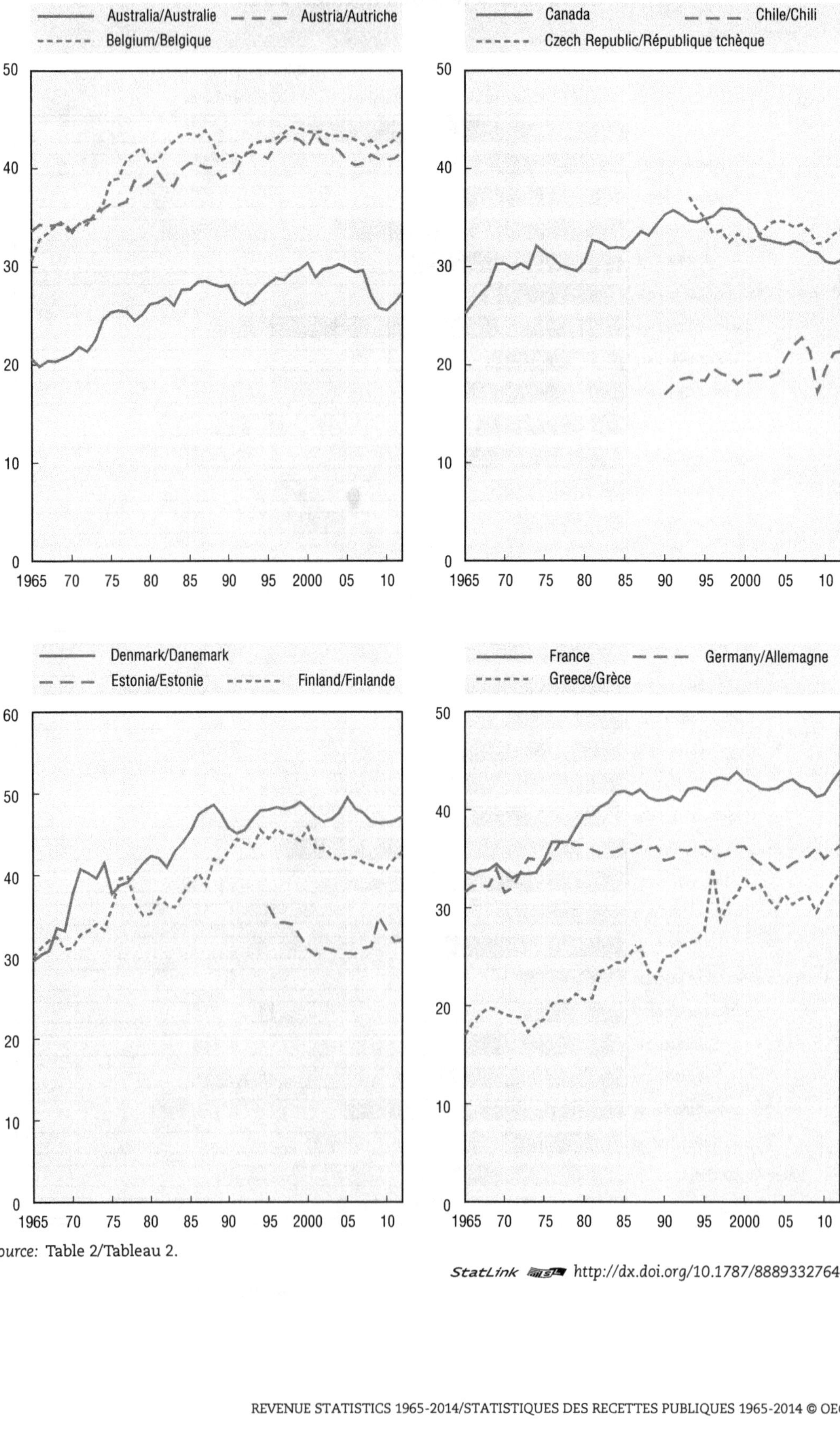

Source: Table 2/Tableau 2.

StatLink http://dx.doi.org/10.1787/888933276473

Chart 3. **Total tax revenue as % of GDP, 1965-2013** *(cont.)*
Graphique 3. **Total des recettes fiscales en % du PIB, 1965-2013** *(suite)*

Source: Table 2/Tableau 2.

StatLink http://dx.doi.org/10.1787/888933276473

Chart 3. **Total tax revenue as % of GDP, 1965-2012** *(cont.)*
Graphique 3. **Total des recettes fiscales en % du PIB, 1965-2012** *(suite)*

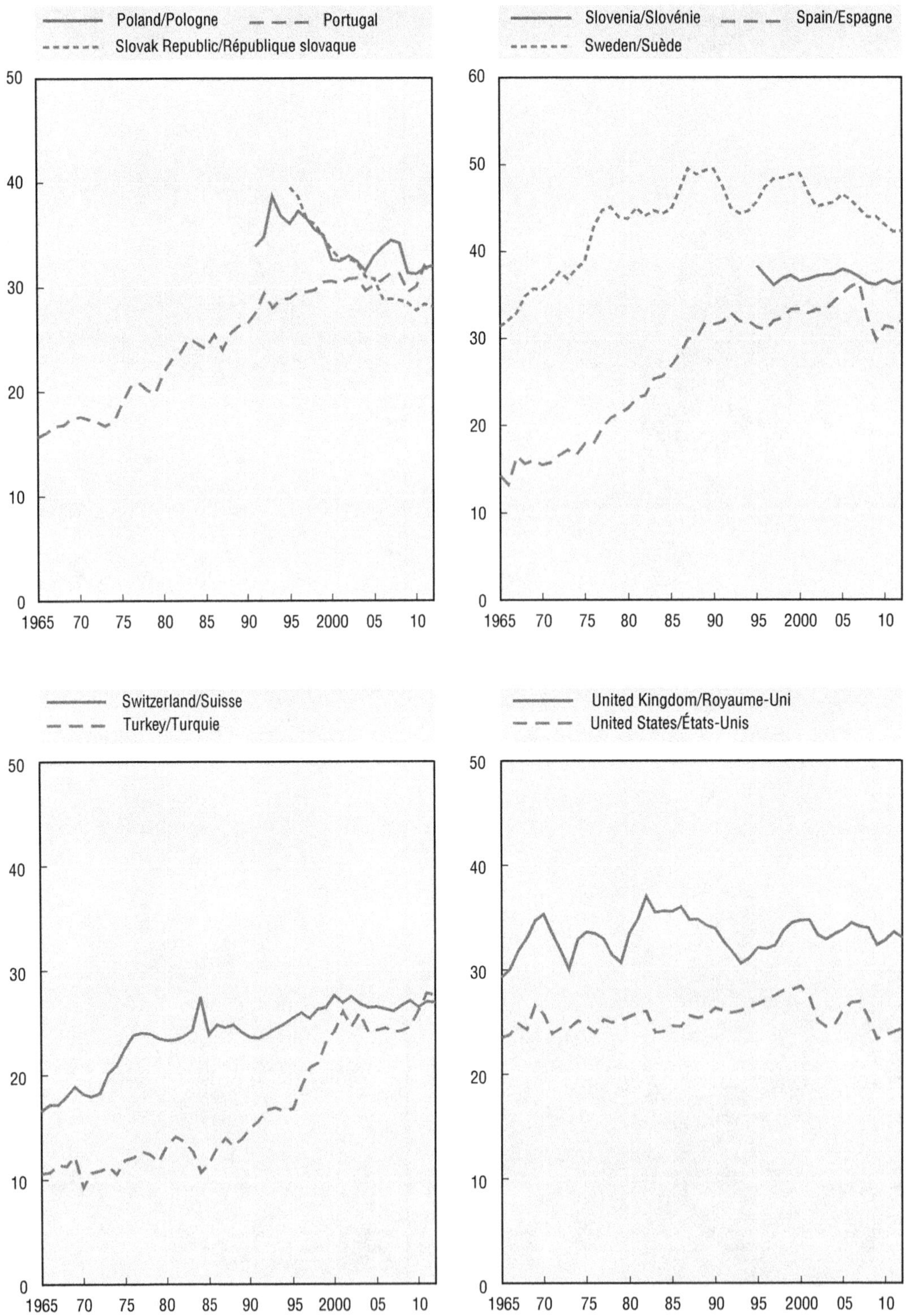

Source: Table 2/Tableau 2.

StatLink http://dx.doi.org/10.1787/888933276473

Chart 4. **Tax structures in OECD member countries, 1965-2013**
Graphique 4. **Structure de la fiscalité dans les pays membres de l'OCDE, 1965-2013**

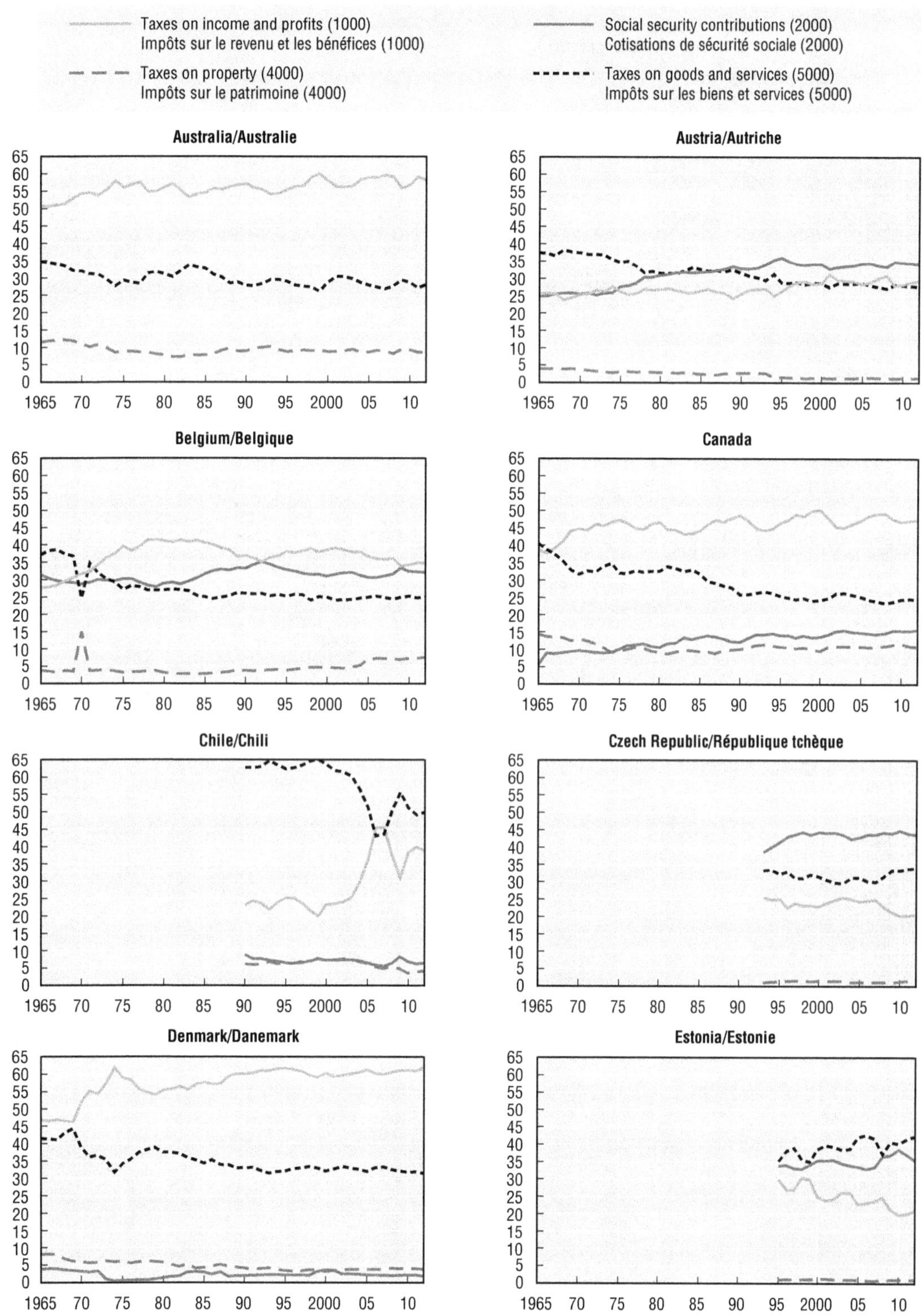

Source: Table 2/Tableau 2

StatLink http://dx.doi.org/10.1787/888933276484

Chart 4. **Tax structures in OECD member countries, 1965-2013** *(cont.)*
Graphique 4. **Structure de la fiscalité dans les pays membres de l'OCDE, 1965-2013** *(suite)*

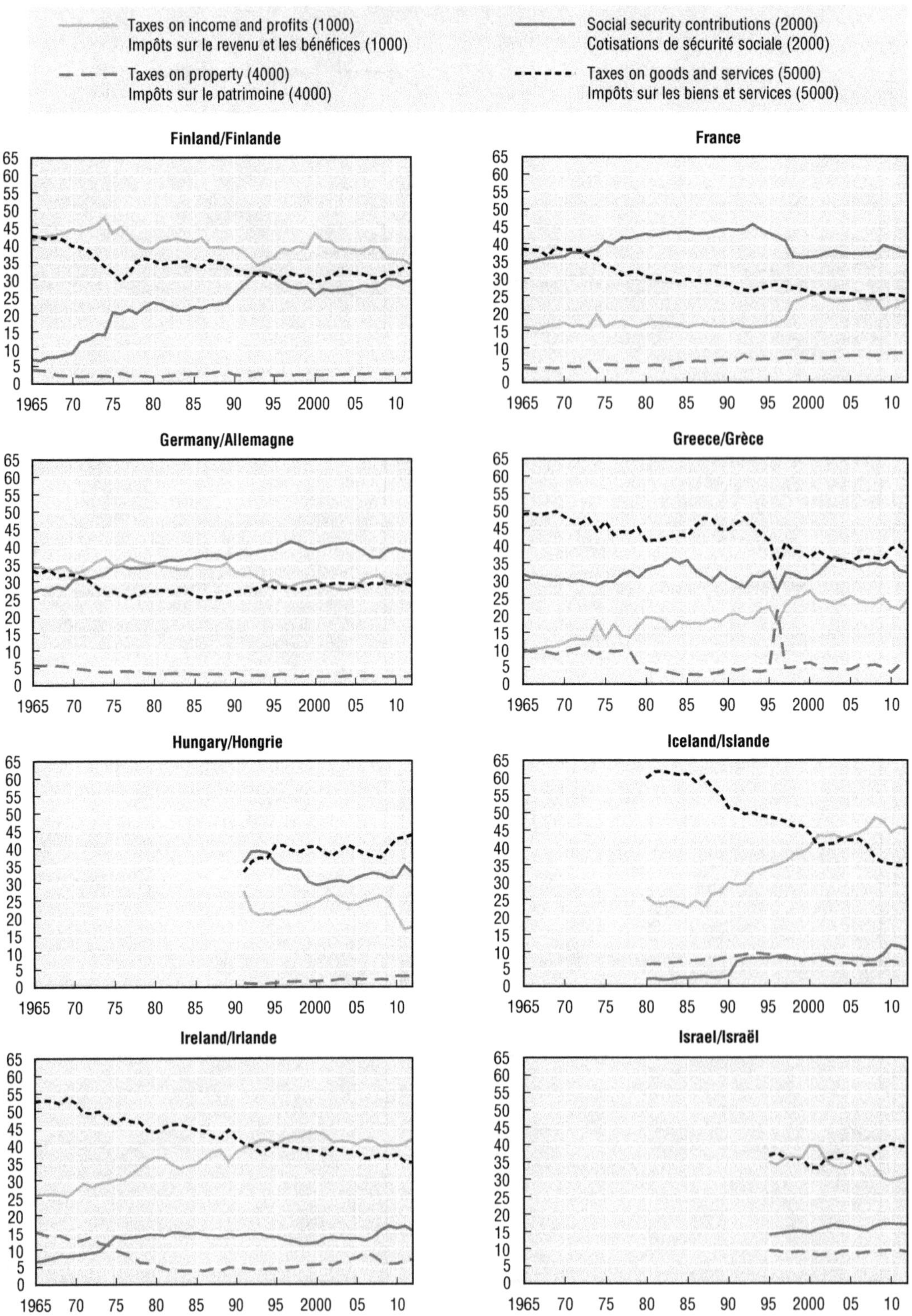

Source: Table 2/Tableau 2

StatLink http://dx.doi.org/10.1787/888933276484

Chart 4. **Tax structures in OECD member countries, 1965-2012** *(cont.)*
Graphique 4. **Structure de la fiscalité dans les pays membres de l'OCDE, 1965-2012** *(suite)*

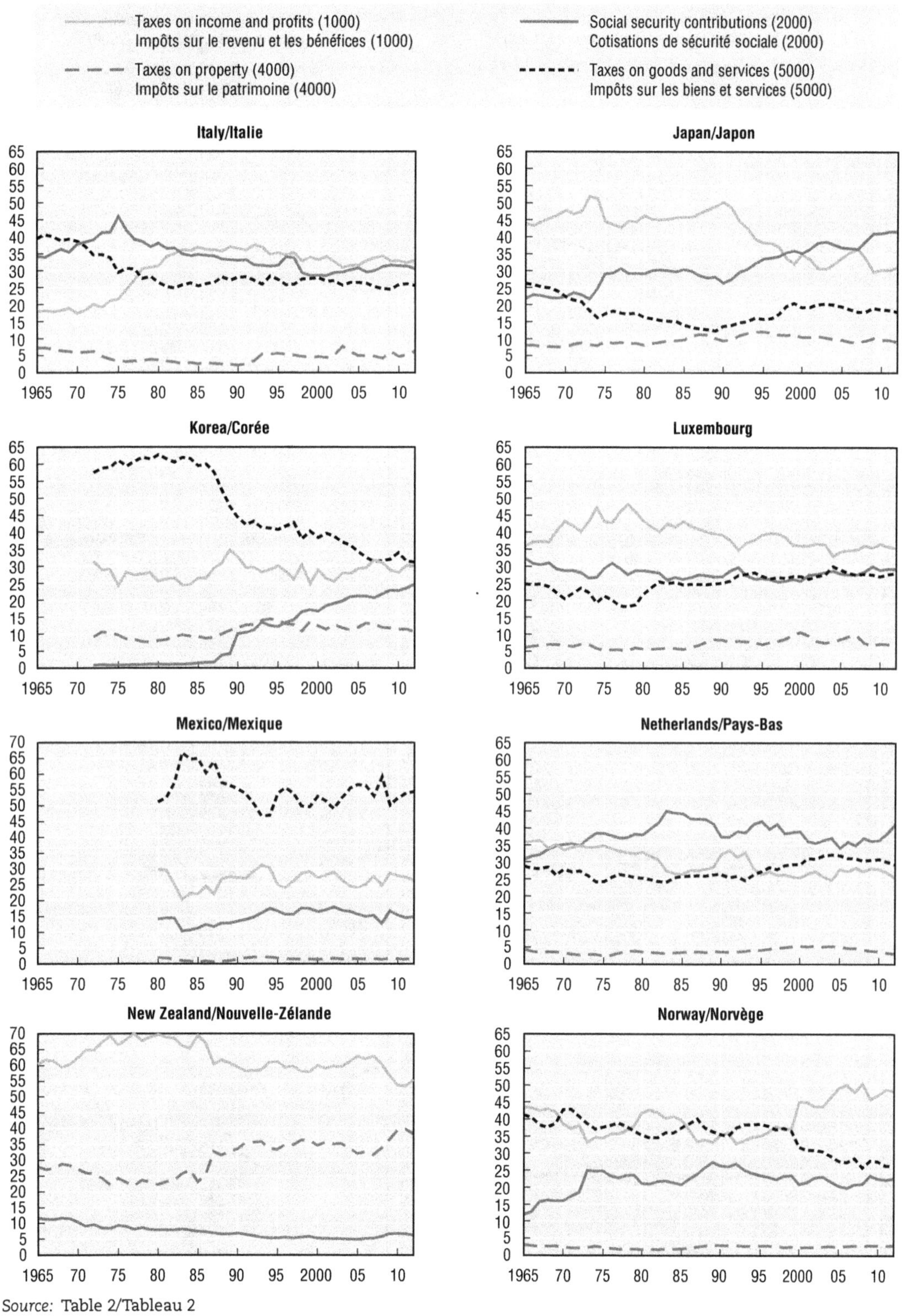

Source: Table 2/Tableau 2

StatLink http://dx.doi.org/10.1787/888933276484

Chart 4. **Tax structures in OECD member countries, 1965-2013** *(cont.)*
Graphique 4. **Structure de la fiscalité dans les pays membres de l'OCDE, 1965-2013** *(suite)*

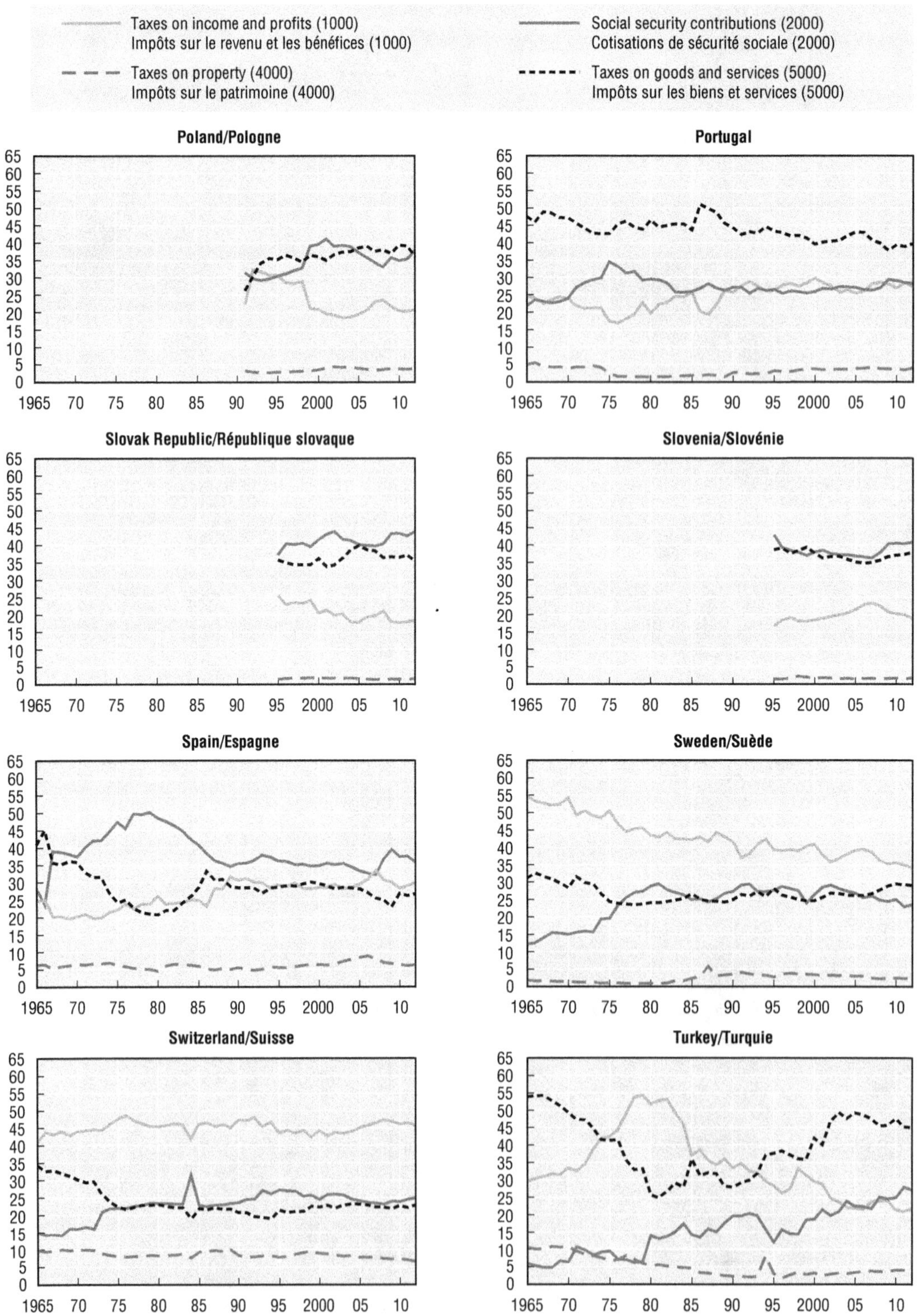

Source: Table 2/Tableau 2

StatLink http://dx.doi.org/10.1787/888933276484

Chart 4. **Tax structures in OECD member countries, 1965-2013** *(cont.)*
Graphique 4. **Structure de la fiscalité dans les pays membres de l'OCDE, 1965-2013** *(suite)*

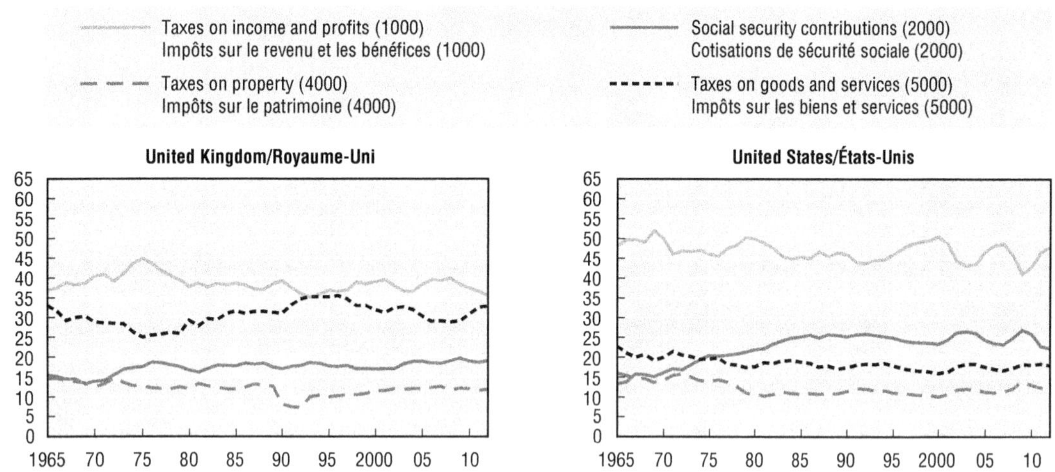

Source: Table 2/Tableau 2.

StatLink http://dx.doi.org/10.1787/888933276484

PART II/PARTIE II

C. Estimates of tax revenues, 2014

Data provided in the preceding sections II.A (Tables) and II.B (Charts) cover the years 1965 to 2013 because most countries are unable to provide definitive figures for the most recent year. However, provisional estimates of tax revenues in 2014 for the main headings in the OECD list of tax categories were available for most OECD countries at the time of publication. Two countries exclude revenues for specific levels of government and so their revenues cannot be compared with earlier years. Mexico excludes those for state and local government and Japan excludes social security contributions.

C. Estimations des recettes fiscales pour 2014

Les données rassemblées dans les sections II.A (tableaux) et II.B (graphiques) concernent les années 1965 à 2013, car la plupart des pays ne sont pas en mesure de fournir des chiffres définitifs pour la période la plus récente. Cependant, des estimations provisoires des recettes fiscales en 2014 concernant les principales rubriques de la liste de l'OCDE de catégories fiscales étaient disponibles pour la plupart des pays de l'OCDE au moment de la publication. Deux pays ne fournissent pas d'estimations des recettes fiscales pour des niveaux d'administration spécifiques, par conséquent leurs recettes fiscales ne sont pas comparables aux chiffres des années précédentes. Le Mexique ne donne pas d'estimations pour les administrations d'États et les administrations locales et le Japon ne donne pas d'estimations pour les cotisations de sécurité sociale.

Table 37. **Estimates of tax revenues in billions of national currency units, 2014**
Tableau 37. **Estimations des recettes fiscales en milliards de monnaie nationale, 2014**

	Australia	Austria	Belgium	Canada	Chile	Czech Republic	Denmark[1]	Estonia	Finland
1000 Taxes on income, profits and capital gains	..	**41.7**	**64.5**	**290.7**	**9 628.0**	**304.2**	**637.1**	**1.5**	**31.5**
1100 Of individuals	..	33.4	51.7	223.3	2 114.3	149.6	531.1	1.1	27.5
1200 Corporate	..	7.0	12.8	60.6	6 196.1	154.6	51.7	0.3	4.0
1300 Unallocable between 1100 and 1200	..	1.3	0.0	6.8	1 317.7	0.0	54.3	0.0	0.0
2000 Social security contributions	..	**48.6**	**56.5**	**98.2**	**2 110.1**	**625.5**	**1.4**	**2.2**	**26.0**
2100 Employees	..	19.6	16.7	39.5	2 044.4	126.9	0.7	0.1	6.1
2200 Employers	..	22.7	34.7	55.6	65.7	396.0	0.7	2.0	17.9
2300 Self-employed or non-employed	..	6.3	5.1	3.2	0.0	102.6	0.0	0.0	2.0
2400 Unallocable between 2100, 2200 and 2300	..	0.0	0.0	0.0	0.0	0.0	0.0	0.0	0.0
3000 Taxes on payroll and workforce	..	**9.8**	**0.0**	**12.6**	**0.0**	**0.0**	**6.3**	**0.0**	**0.0**
4000 Taxes on property	..	**2.0**	**14.2**	**61.7**	**1 256.0**	**19.2**	**36.2**	**0.1**	**2.7**
4100 Recurrent taxes on immovable property	..	0.8	5.3	53.3	951.1	9.6	27.1	0.1	1.5
4200 Recurrent taxes on net wealth	..	0.0	0.6	0.6	0.0	0.0	0.0	0.0	0.0
4300 Estate, inheritance and gift taxes	..	0.0	2.8	0.0	31.3	0.0	3.8	0.0	0.5
4400 Taxes on financial and capital transactions	..	0.9	4.1	4.0	273.6	9.6	5.2	0.0	0.7
4500 Non-recurrent taxes	..	0.3	1.1	3.9	0.0	0.0	0.0	0.0	0.0
4600 Other recurrent taxes on property	..	0.0	0.3	0.0	0.0	0.0	0.0	0.0	0.0
5000 Taxes on goods and services	..	**38.7**	**42.9**	**147.2**	**16 126.7**	**469.8**	**292.3**	**2.7**	**29.5**
5100 Taxes on production, sale, transfer, etc	..	36.0	40.5	137.5	15 131.3	444.7	269.4	2.6	28.5
5110 General taxes	..	25.5	27.8	87.0	12 133.7	319.5	185.5	1.7	18.9
5120 Taxes on specific goods and services	..	10.5	12.7	50.5	2 997.6	125.2	83.9	0.9	9.6
5130 Unallocable between 5110 and 5120	..	0.0	0.0	0.0	0.0	0.0	0.0	0.0	0.0
5200 Taxes on use of goods and perform activities	..	2.7	2.4	9.8	995.4	25.2	16.0	0.1	1.0
5300 Unallocable between 5100 and 5200	..	0.0	0.0	0.0	0.0	0.0	6.8	0.0	0.0
6000 Other taxes	..	**0.5**	**0.0**	**0.3**	**50.3**	**0.3**	**0.2**	**0.0**	**0.1**
Customs duties collected for the EU	..	**0.4**	**1.3**	..	..	**7.0**	**3.0**	**0.0**	**0.2**
Total tax revenue	..	**141.6**	**179.5**	**610.8**	**29 171.1**	**1 425.9**	**976.5**	**6.4**	**90.0**

	France[1]	Germany[2]	Greece	Hungary[3]	Iceland	Ireland	Israel	Italy	Japan[4]
1000 Taxes on income, profits and capital gains	**223.2**	**321.6**	**15.5**	**2 064.1**	**358.7**	**22.4**	**105.7**	**230.2**	**48 175.0**
1100 Of individuals	179.7	277.3	..	1 589.1	274.5	17.8	63.4	187.9	28 347.4
1200 Corporate	43.5	44.3	..	475.0	59.3	4.6	35.0	44.4	19 827.5
1300 Unallocable between 1100 and 1200	0.0	0.0	..	0.0	24.9	0.0	7.3	-2.1	0.0
2000 Social security contributions	**363.6**	**408.0**	**18.7**	**4 135.8**	**74.0**	**9.6**	**56.1**	**211.8**	..
2100 Employees	90.3	181.7	..	1 602.0	..	3.4	36.5	39.6	..
2200 Employers	244.8	191.7	..	2 533.8	..	5.8	16.2	142.2	..
2300 Self-employed or non-employed	28.5	34.7	..	0.0	..	0.4	3.4	29.9	..
2400 Unallocable between 2100, 2200 and 2300	0.0	0.0	..	0.0	74.0	0.0	0.0	0.0	..
3000 Taxes on payroll and workforce	**34.1**	**0.0**	**0.0**	**178.4**	**6.8**	**0.3**	**12.9**	**0.0**	**0.0**
4000 Taxes on property	**83.0**	**25.2**	**3.4**	**415.6**	**49.1**	**4.2**	**29.5**	**41.3**	**13 100.0**
4100 Recurrent taxes on immovable property	55.1	9.9	..	191.0	32.0	1.9	23.1	20.1	9 936.5
4200 Recurrent taxes on net wealth	5.1	0.5	..	136.6	9.6	0.7	0.0	0.6	0.0
4300 Estate, inheritance and gift taxes	10.2	5.5	..	6.2	2.6	0.4	0.0	0.6	1 748.0
4400 Taxes on financial and capital transactions	12.6	9.3	..	81.9	4.3	1.2	3.7	18.3	1 415.5
4500 Non-recurrent taxes	0.0	0.0	..	0.0	0.3	0.0	2.7	0.1	0.0
4600 Other recurrent taxes on property	0.0	0.0	..	0.0	0.3	0.0	0.0	1.6	0.0
5000 Taxes on goods and services	**234.9**	**293.9**	**26.5**	**5 374.3**	**240.7**	**18.6**	**134.5**	**189.5**	**30 168.6**
5100 Taxes on production, sale, transfer, etc	228.0	283.3	..	5 260.7	228.9	17.0	125.6	167.5	27 744.8
5110 General taxes	153.4	203.4	..	3 744.1	161.2	11.5	105.7	97.1	18 285.9
5120 Taxes on specific goods and services	74.6	79.6	..	1 516.6	67.8	5.5	19.9	70.4	9 458.9
5130 Unallocable between 5110 and 5120	0.0	0.3	..	0.0	0.0	0.0	0.0	0.0	0.0
5200 Taxes on use of goods and perform activities	6.9	10.6	..	113.6	11.8	1.6	8.9	11.0	2 423.7
5300 Unallocable between 5100 and 5200	0.0	0.0	..	0.0	0.0	0.0	0.0	11.0	0.0
6000 Other taxes	**23.6**	**0.1**	**0.0**	**60.8**	**41.5**	**0.0**	**0.0**	**30.4**	**396.5**
Customs duties collected for the EU	**1.8**	**4.6**	**0.2**	**31.9**	..	**0.3**	..	**2.0**	..
Total tax revenue	**964.2**	**1 053.5**	**64.3**	**12 261.0**	**770.8**	**55.4**	**338.7**	**705.3**	..

Table 37. **Estimates of tax revenues in billions of national currency units, 2014** *(cont.)*
Tableau 37. **Estimations des recettes fiscales en milliards de monnaie nationale, 2014** *(suite)*

	Korea	Luxembourg	Mexico[5]	Netherlands	New Zealand	Norway	Poland	Portugal	Slovak Republic
1000 Taxes on income, profits and capital gains	**106 353.0**	**6.5**	**979.3**	..	**43.2**	**533.2**	..	**18.5**	**4.7**
1100 Of individuals	59 457.0	4.4	514.2	..	29.8	308.7	..	13.4	2.3
1200 Corporate	46 896.0	2.1	441.3	..	10.6	224.4	..	5.2	2.3
1300 Unallocable between 1100 and 1200	0.0	0.0	23.7	..	2.8	0.0	..	0.0	0.2
2000 Social security contributions	**98 184.0**	**5.4**	**538.2**	..	**0.0**	**312.0**	..	**15.6**	**10.1**
2100 Employees	41 355.0	2.4	..	..	0.0	126.7	..	6.7	2.4
2200 Employers	44 806.0	2.3	..	..	0.0	185.4	..	8.9	5.8
2300 Self-employed or non-employed	12 023.0	0.6	..	..	0.0	0.0	..	0.0	2.0
2400 Unallocable between 2100, 2200 and 2300	0.0	0.0	538.2	..	0.0	0.0	..	0.0	0.0
3000 Taxes on payroll and workforce	**1 042.0**	**0.0**	..	..	**0.0**	**0.0**	..	**0.0**	**0.0**
4000 Taxes on property	**40 305.0**	**1.5**	..	..	**4.7**	**34.5**	..	**2.2**	**0.3**
4100 Recurrent taxes on immovable property	11 654.0	0.0	..	..	4.6	13.6	..	1.5	0.3
4200 Recurrent taxes on net wealth	0.0	1.1	..	..	0.0	13.3	..	0.0	0.0
4300 Estate, inheritance and gift taxes	4 625.0	0.1	..	..	0.0	0.0	..	0.0	0.0
4400 Taxes on financial and capital transactions	24 026.0	0.3	..	..	0.1	7.6	..	0.7	0.0
4500 Non-recurrent taxes	0.0	0.0	..	..	0.0	0.0	..	0.0	0.0
4600 Other recurrent taxes on property	0.0	0.0	..	..	0.0	0.0	..	0.0	0.0
5000 Taxes on goods and services	**109 451.0**	**5.3**	..	..	**29.8**	**351.0**	..	**22.5**	**8.0**
5100 Taxes on production, sale, transfer, etc	102 531.0	5.3	..	..	27.9	331.5	..	21.5	7.4
5110 General taxes	62 975.0	3.6	667.1	..	23.3	245.2	..	14.7	5.0
5120 Taxes on specific goods and services	39 556.0	1.6	..	..	4.6	86.3	..	6.8	2.4
5130 Unallocable between 5110 and 5120	0.0	0.0	..	..	0.0	0.0	..	0.0	0.0
5200 Taxes on use of goods and perform activities	6 920.0	0.1	..	..	1.9	19.5	..	1.0	0.5
5300 Unallocable between 5100 and 5200	0.0	0.0	..	..	0.0	0.0	..	0.0	0.1
6000 Other taxes	**10 093.0**	**0.0**	..	..	**0.0**	**0.0**	..	**0.6**	**0.0**
Customs duties collected for the EU	..	**0.0**	..	..	..	..	..	**0.1**	**0.1**
Total tax revenue	**365 428.0**	**18.7**	..	..	**77.7**	**1 230.7**	..	**59.6**	**23.3**

	Slovenia	Spain[1]	Sweden	Switzerland	Turkey	United Kingdom	United States		
1000 Taxes on income, profits and capital gains	**2.4**	**102.1**	**579.7**	**79.6**	**106.2**	**204.5**	**2 183.6**	..	..
1100 Of individuals	1.9	78.5	478.5	54.5	73.9	160.6	1 730.8	..	..
1200 Corporate	0.5	20.6	101.2	18.2	32.3	43.9	452.7	..	..
1300 Unallocable between 1100 and 1200	0.0	2.9	0.0	7.0	0.0	0.0	0.0	..	..
2000 Social security contributions	**5.4**	**121.0**	**389.0**	**43.4**	**143.4**	**109.0**	**1 085.4**	..	..
2100 Employees	2.8	19.0	104.1	20.3	54.3	42.6	479.8	..	..
2200 Employers	2.0	84.8	280.1	20.4	80.0	63.8	543.0	..	..
2300 Self-employed or non-employed	0.6	17.2	5.4	2.7	9.1	2.6	62.7	..	..
2400 Unallocable between 2100, 2200 and 2300	0.0	0.0	-0.5	0.0	0.0	0.0	0.0	..	..
3000 Taxes on payroll and workforce	**0.0**	**0.0**	**178.9**	**0.0**	**0.0**	**0.0**	**0.0**	..	..
4000 Taxes on property	**0.2**	**24.5**	**41.6**	**11.5**	**24.5**	**73.6**	**483.9**	..	..
4100 Recurrent taxes on immovable property	0.2	12.1	31.7	1.0	5.0	55.7	450.4	..	..
4200 Recurrent taxes on net wealth	0.0	1.2	0.0	7.3	0.0	0.0	0.0	..	..
4300 Estate, inheritance and gift taxes	0.0	2.7	0.0	1.0	0.4	3.9	26.1	..	..
4400 Taxes on financial and capital transactions	0.0	6.3	9.9	2.2	19.0	14.1	0.0	..	..
4500 Non-recurrent taxes	0.0	2.2	0.0	0.0	0.0	0.0	0.0	..	..
4600 Other recurrent taxes on property	0.0	0.1	0.0	0.0	0.0	0.0	7.4	..	..
5000 Taxes on goods and services	**5.5**	**100.1**	**475.0**	**38.1**	**221.6**	**193.4**	**776.7**	..	..
5100 Taxes on production, sale, transfer, etc	5.2	94.1	458.2	33.4	213.2	186.3	658.1	..	..
5110 General taxes	3.2	63.8	356.7	22.4	102.5	124.0	350.8	..	..
5120 Taxes on specific goods and services	2.0	30.4	101.5	11.0	110.7	62.4	307.3	..	..
5130 Unallocable between 5110 and 5120	0.0	0.0	0.0	0.0	0.0	0.0	0.0	..	..
5200 Taxes on use of goods and perform activities	0.3	5.0	16.8	4.7	8.4	7.1	118.6	..	..
5300 Unallocable between 5100 and 5200	0.0	1.0	0.0	0.0	0.0	0.0	0.0	..	..
6000 Other taxes	**0.0**	**2.2**	**1.4**	**0.0**	**6.9**	**0.3**	**0.0**	..	..
Customs duties collected for the EU	**0.1**	**1.5**	**5.7**	..	..	**2.9**	..	..	..
Total tax revenue	**13.6**	**351.4**	**1 671.4**	**172.7**	**502.5**	**583.7**	**4 529.5**	..	..

1. The total tax revenues have been reduced by the amount of any capital transfer that represents uncollected taxes. / Le total des recettes fiscales a été diminué du montant de tout transfert en capital représentant les impôts non perçus.
2. From 1991 the figures relate to the united Germany. / Depuis 1991, les chiffres se rapportent à l'Allemagne unifiée.
3. The figures are on a cash basis. / Les données sont sur la base de la trésorerie.
4. The tax revenue figures exclude revenue from Social security funds, figures are not available. / Les données excluent les chiffres de l'administration de sécurité sociale, les données n'étant pas disponibles.
5. Central government and Social security funds only. / Administration centrale et administrations de sécurité sociale seulement.

StatLink *http://dx.doi.org/10.1787/888933276997*

Table 38. **Estimates of tax revenues as % of GDP, 2014**
Tableau 38. **Estimations des recettes fiscales en % du PIB, 2014**

	Total tax revenue / Total des recettes fiscales	1000 Income & profits / Revenu & bénéfices	2000 Social security / Sécurité sociale	3000 Payroll / Salaires	4000 Property / Patrimoine	5000 Goods & services / Biens & services	6000 Other / Autres	EU Custom Duties / UE droits de douane
Australia / Australie	..	..	..	..	..	..	..	..
Austria / Autriche	43.0	12.7	14.8	3.0	0.6	11.7	0.2	0.1
Belgium / Belgique	44.7	16.1	14.1	0.0	3.5	10.7	0.0	0.3
Canada	30.8	14.7	5.0	0.6	3.1	7.4	0.0	..
Chile / Chili	19.8	6.5	1.4	0.0	0.9	11.0	0.0	..
Czech Republic / République tchèque	33.5	7.1	14.7	0.0	0.5	11.0	0.0	0.2
Denmark / Danemark[1]	50.9	33.2	0.1	0.3	1.9	15.2	0.0	0.2
Estonia / Estonie	32.9	7.6	11.2	0.0	0.3	13.7	0.0	0.2
Finland / Finlande	43.9	15.3	12.7	0.0	1.3	14.4	0.0	0.1
France[1]	45.2	10.5	17.1	1.6	3.9	11.0	1.1	0.1
Germany / Allemagne[2]	36.1	11.0	14.0	0.0	0.9	10.1	0.0	0.2
Greece / Grèce	35.9	8.7	10.4	0.0	1.9	14.8	0.0	0.1
Hungary / Hongrie[3]	38.5	6.5	13.0	0.6	1.3	16.9	0.2	0.1
Iceland / Islande	38.7	18.0	3.7	0.3	2.5	12.1	2.1	..
Ireland / Irlande	29.9	12.1	5.2	0.2	2.3	10.0	0.0	0.1
Israel / Israël	31.1	9.7	5.2	1.2	2.7	12.4	0.0	..
Italy / Italie	43.6	14.2	13.1	0.0	2.6	11.7	1.9	0.1
Japan / Japon[4]	..	9.8	..	0.0	2.7	6.1	0.1	..
Korea / Corée	24.6	7.2	6.6	0.1	2.7	7.4	0.7	..
Luxembourg	37.8	13.1	10.8	0.0	3.0	10.8	0.0	0.0
Mexico / Mexique[5]	19.5	5.8	3.2	..	..	..	..	..
Netherlands / Pays-Bas	..	..	..	..	..	..	..	..
New Zealand / Nouvelle-Zélande	32.4	18.0	0.0	0.0	1.9	12.4	0.0	..
Norway / Norvège	39.1	16.9	9.9	0.0	1.1	11.1	0.0	..
Poland / Pologne	..	..	..	..	..	..	..	..
Portugal	34.4	10.7	9.0	0.0	1.3	13.0	0.3	0.1
Slovak Republic / République slovaque	31.0	6.3	13.5	0.0	0.4	10.7	0.0	0.2
Slovenia / Slovénie	36.6	6.5	14.5	0.1	0.6	14.8	0.0	0.1
Spain / Espagne[1]	33.2	9.6	11.4	0.0	2.3	9.5	0.2	0.1
Sweden / Suède	42.7	14.8	9.9	4.6	1.1	12.1	0.0	0.1
Switzerland / Suisse	26.6	12.3	6.7	0.0	1.8	5.9	0.0	..
Turkey / Turquie	28.7	6.1	8.2	0.0	1.4	12.7	0.4	..
United Kingdom / Royaume-Uni	32.6	11.4	6.1	0.0	4.1	10.8	0.0	0.2
United States / États-Unis	26.0	12.5	6.2	0.0	2.8	4.5	0.0	..

1. The total tax revenue has been reduced by the amount of any capital transfer that represents uncollected taxes. The capital transfer has been allocated between tax headings in proportion to the reported tax revenue.
2. From 1991 the figures relate to the united Germany.
3. The tax revenue figures are on a cash basis.
4. The tax revenue figures exclude revenue for Social Security funds, figures are not available.
5. Central government and Social security funds only.

1. Le total des recettes fiscales a été diminué du montant de tout transfert en capital représentant les impôts non perçus. Le transfert en capital a été réparti entre les différentes rubriques en proportion des recettes fiscales.
2. Depuis 1991, les chiffres se rapportent à l'Allemagne unifiée.
3. Les chiffres relatifs aux recettes fiscales sont sur la base de la trésorerie.
4. Les données excluent les chiffres de l'administration de sécurité sociale, les données n'étant pas disponibles.
5. Administration centrale et administrations de sécurité sociale seulement.

StatLink http://dx.doi.org/10.1787/888933277004

Table 39. **Tax revenue of main headings as % of total taxation, 2014**
Tableau 39. **Recettes fiscales sous les principales rubriques en % du total des recettes fiscales, 2014**

	Total tax revenue / Total des recettes fiscales	1000 Income & profits / Revenu & bénéfices	2000 Social security / Sécurité sociale	3000 Payroll / Salaires	4000 Property / Patrimoine	5000 Goods & services / Biens & services	6000 Other / Autres	EU Custom Duties / UE droits de douane
Australia / Australie	..	..	..	..	..	..	..	..
Austria / Autriche	100.0	29.4	34.3	6.9	1.4	27.3	0.4	0.3
Belgium / Belgique	100.0	35.9	31.5	0.0	7.9	23.9	0.0	0.7
Canada	100.0	47.6	16.1	2.1	10.1	24.1	0.0	..
Chile / Chili	100.0	33.0	7.2	0.0	4.3	55.3	0.2	..
Czech Republic / République tchèque	100.0	21.3	43.9	0.0	1.3	32.9	0.0	0.5
Denmark / Danemark[1]	100.0	65.2	0.1	0.6	3.7	29.9	0.0	0.3
Estonia / Estonie	100.0	23.0	33.9	0.0	0.9	41.6	0.0	0.5
Finland / Finlande	100.0	35.0	28.9	0.0	3.0	32.8	0.1	0.2
France[1]	100.0	23.1	37.7	3.5	8.6	24.4	2.4	0.2
Germany / Allemagne[2]	100.0	30.5	38.7	0.0	2.4	27.9	0.0	0.4
Greece / Grèce	100.0	24.1	29.0	0.0	5.4	41.2	0.0	0.3
Hungary / Hongrie[3]	100.0	16.8	33.7	1.5	3.4	43.8	0.5	0.3
Iceland / Islande	100.0	46.5	9.6	0.9	6.4	31.2	5.4	..
Ireland / Irlande	100.0	40.4	17.3	0.6	7.6	33.5	0.0	0.5
Israel / Israël	100.0	31.2	16.6	3.8	8.7	39.7	0.0	..
Italy / Italie	100.0	32.6	30.0	0.0	5.9	26.9	4.3	0.3
Japan / Japon	..	..	..	..	..	..	..	..
Korea / Corée	100.0	29.1	26.9	0.3	11.0	30.0	2.8	..
Luxembourg	100.0	34.8	28.7	0.0	7.8	28.5	0.1	0.1
Mexico / Mexique	..	..	..	..	..	..	..	..
Netherlands / Pays-Bas	..	..	..	..	..	..	..	..
New Zealand / Nouvelle-Zélande	100.0	55.6	0.0	0.0	6.0	38.4	0.0	..
Norway / Norvège	100.0	43.3	25.4	0.0	2.8	28.5	0.0	..
Poland / Pologne	..	..	..	..	..	..	..	..
Portugal	100.0	31.1	26.2	0.0	3.6	37.8	1.0	0.2
Slovak Republic / République slovaque	100.0	20.3	43.4	0.0	1.4	34.4	0.0	0.5
Slovenia / Slovénie	100.0	17.8	39.6	0.1	1.7	40.4	0.0	0.4
Spain / Espagne[1]	100.0	29.0	34.4	0.0	7.0	28.5	0.6	0.4
Sweden / Suède	100.0	34.7	23.3	10.7	2.5	28.4	0.1	0.3
Switzerland / Suisse	100.0	46.1	25.1	0.0	6.7	22.1	0.0	..
Turkey / Turquie	100.0	21.1	28.5	0.0	4.9	44.1	1.4	..
United Kingdom / Royaume-Uni	100.0	35.0	18.7	0.0	12.6	33.1	0.0	0.5
United States / États-Unis	100.0	48.2	24.0	0.0	10.7	17.1	0.0	..

1. The total tax revenue has been reduced by the amount of any capital transfer that represents uncollected taxes. The capital transfer has been allocated between tax headings in proportion to the reported tax revenue.
2. From 1991 the figures relate to the united Germany.
3. The tax revenue figures are on a cash basis.
1. Le total des recettes fiscales a été diminué du montant de tout transfert en capital représentant les impôts non perçus. Le transfert en capital a été réparti entre les différentes rubriques en proportion des recettes fiscales.
2. Depuis 1991, les chiffres se rapportent à l'Allemagne unifiée.
3. Les chiffres relatifs aux recettes fiscales sont sur la base de la trésorerie.

StatLink *http://dx.doi.org/10.1787/888933277012*

Table 40. **Gross domestic product at market prices, in billions of national currency units**
Tableau 40. **Produit intérieur brut au prix du marché, en milliards de monnaie nationale**

	2014
Australia / Australie[1]	1 608
Austria / Autriche	329
Belgium / Belgique	402
Canada[1]	1 982
Chile / Chili	147 185
Czech Republic / République tchèque	4 261
Denmark / Danemark	1 919
Estonia / Estonie	20
Finland / Finlande	205
France	2 132
Germany / Allemagne	2 916
Greece / Grèce	179
Hungary / Hongrie	31 864
Iceland / Islande	1 993
Ireland / Irlande	185
Israel / Israël	1 088
Italy / Italie	1 616
Japan / Japon[1]	490 779
Korea / Corée	1 485 078
Luxembourg	49
Mexico / Mexique	17 009
Netherlands / Pays-Bas	663
New Zealand / Nouvelle-Zélande[1]	240
Norway / Norvège	3 150
Poland / Pologne	1 725
Portugal	173
Slovak Republic / République slovaque	75
Slovenia / Slovénie	37
Spain / Espagne	1 058
Sweden / Suède	3 915
Switzerland / Suisse	648
Turkey / Turquie	1 750
United Kingdom / Royaume-Uni	1 792
United States / États-Unis	17 419

1. GDP is fiscal year. The year Y is calculated (at annual rate) as the average of: Q2(Y) to Q1(Y+1) for Canada and Japan; and Q3(Y) to Q2(Y+1) for Australia and New Zealand.

Source: OECD National Accounts.

1. PIB se référant à l'année fiscale. L'année A est calculée (taux annuel) comme la moyenne de : T2(A) à T1(A+1) pour le Canada et le Japon ; et T3(A) à T2(A+1) pour l'Australie et la Nouvelle-Zélande.

Source : Comptes nationaux de l'OCDE.

StatLink *http://dx.doi.org/10.1787/888933277028*

PART III

Country tables, 1965-2013

PARTIE III

Tableaux par pays, 1965-2013

Revenue Statistics 1965-2014
Statistiques des recettes publiques 1965-2014

PART III/PARTIE III

A. Tax revenues

A. Recettes fiscales

Table 41. **Australia / Australie**
Details of tax revenue / Recettes fiscales détaillées

Million AUD

	1965	1980	1990	2000	2007	2008	2009	2011	2012	2013
Total tax revenue	**5 024**	**39 878**	**116 500**	**214 651**	**349 416**	**340 063**	**334 047**	**390 690**	**415 889**	**434 981**
1000 Taxes on income, profits and capital gains	**2 547**	**22 383**	**66 542**	**124 602**	**208 234**	**200 998**	**186 659**	**230 870**	**241 728**	**248 448**
1100 Of individuals	1 729	17 532	50 062	81 166	127 993	127 639	124 941	153 760	162 993	170 313
1110 On income and profits	1 729	17 532	49 888	81 166	127 993	127 639	124 941	153 760	162 993	170 313
1120 On capital gains	0	0	174	0	0	0	0	0	0	0
1200 Corporate	818	4 851	16 480	43 436	80 241	73 359	61 718	77 110	78 735	78 135
1210 On profits	818	4 851	16 315	43 436	80 241	73 359	61 718	77 110	78 735	78 135
Income tax on companies	791	4 574	15 220	42 221	78 577	71 986	60 654	75 856	77 691	76 682
Dividend and interest taxes	17	161	899	846	1 664	1 373	1 064	1 254	1 044	1 453
Other withholding taxes	0	116	196	369	0	0	0	0	0	0
1220 On capital gains	0	0	165	0	0	0	0	0	0	0
1300 Unallocable between 1100 and 1200	0	0	0	0	0	0	0	0	0	0
2000 Social security contributions	**0**	**0**	**0**	**0**	**0**	**0**	**0**	**0**	**0**	**0**
2100 Employees	0	0	0	0	0	0	0	0	0	0
2110 On a payroll basis	..	..	..	..	..	..	..	..	..	..
2120 On an income tax basis	..	..	..	..	..	..	..	..	..	..
2200 Employers	0	0	0	0	0	0	0	0	0	0
2210 On a payroll basis	..	..	..	..	..	..	..	..	..	..
2220 On an income tax basis	..	..	..	..	..	..	..	..	..	..
2300 Self-employed or non-employed	0	0	0	0	0	0	0	0	0	0
2310 On a payroll basis	..	..	..	..	..	..	..	..	..	..
2320 On an income tax basis	..	..	..	..	..	..	..	..	..	..
2400 Unallocable between 2100, 2200 and 2300	0	0	0	0	0	0	0	0	0	0
2410 On a payroll basis	..	..	..	..	..	..	..	..	..	..
2420 On an income tax basis	..	..	..	..	..	..	..	..	..	..
3000 Taxes on payroll and workforce	**157**	**1 988**	**7 115**	**9 624**	**16 407**	**17 303**	**17 303**	**20 307**	**21 443**	**22 222**
4000 Taxes on property	**576**	**3 105**	**10 427**	**18 818**	**31 130**	**27 908**	**31 897**	**33 582**	**36 006**	**40 795**
4100 Recurrent taxes on immovable property	341	1 886	6 148	9 067	15 615	17 667	18 685	20 759	21 806	23 471
4110 Households	..	0	0	0	0	0	0	0	0	0
4120 Others	..	1 886	6 148	9 067	15 615	17 667	18 685	20 759	21 806	23 471
4200 Recurrent taxes on net wealth	0	0	0	0	0	0	0	0	0	0
4210 Individual	..	..	..	..	..	..	..	..	..	..
4220 Corporate	..	..	..	..	..	..	..	..	..	..
4300 Estate, inheritance and gift taxes	137	175	0	0	0	0	0	0	0	0
4310 Estate and inheritance taxes	131	174	..	..	..	..	..	..	..	..
Estate duty central government	36	17	..	..	..	..	..	..	..	..
St. and loc. estate probate and succession	95	157	..	..	..	..	..	..	..	..
4320 Gift taxes	7	1	..	..	..	..	..	..	..	..
4400 Taxes on financial and capital transactions	98	1 044	4 279	9 751	15 515	10 241	13 212	12 823	14 200	17 324
4500 Non-recurrent taxes	0	0	0	0	0	0	0	0	0	0
4510 On net wealth	..	..	..	..	..	..	..	..	..	..
4520 Other non-recurrent taxes	..	..	..	..	..	..	..	..	..	..
4600 Other recurrent taxes on property	0	0	0	0	0	0	0	0	0	0
5000 Taxes on goods and services	**1 744**	**12 402**	**32 416**	**61 607**	**93 645**	**93 854**	**98 188**	**105 931**	**116 712**	**123 516**
5100 Taxes on production, sale, transfer, etc	1 508	11 097	27 213	56 180	85 022	84 744	88 585	94 210	97 072	103 678
5110 General taxes	370	2 102	9 365	25 830	45 486	43 716	47 800	50 004	51 462	56 819
5111 Value added taxes	0	0	0	23 854	44 381	42 626	46 553	48 849	50 313	55 517
5112 Sales tax	370	2 102	9 365	1 976	1 105	1 090	1 247	1 155	1 149	1 302
5113 Other	0	0	0	0	0	0	0	0	0	0
5120 Taxes on specific goods and services	1 138	8 995	17 848	30 350	39 536	41 028	40 785	44 206	45 610	46 859
5121 Excises	781	6 183	11 975	19 768	24 357	25 206	25 372	26 325	26 425	26 472
Excises central government	752	5 834	10 359	19 019	23 526	24 319	24 547	25 480	25 710	25 648
Statutory corporate payments	0	83	378	295	231	279	444	436	248	343
Primary production charges	29	266	1 238	454	600	608	381	409	467	481
5122 Profits of fiscal monopolies	0	0	0	0	0	0	0	0	0	0
5123 Customs and import duties	271	1 799	3 319	4 606	6 070	6 276	5 748	7 105	8 172	9 280
Customs duties central government	271	1 799	3 319	4 606	6 070	6 276	5 748	7 105	8 172	9 280
5124 Taxes on exports	1	117	57	0	10	13	14	12	9	10
Customs duties on coal exports	0	85	54	..	0	0	0	0	0	0
Other	1	32	3	..	10	13	14	12	9	10
5125 Taxes on investment goods	0	0	0	0	0	0	0	0	0	0
5126 Taxes on specific services	85	896	2 497	5 976	9 099	9 533	9 651	10 764	11 004	11 097
Taxes race meetings	31	240	651	300	358	381	376	359	325	318
Poker machines	16	140	295	2 064	2 985	3 034	2 976	3 161	3 195	3 220
Lotteries	7	122	325	890	1 118	1 184	1 230	1 256	1 354	1 257
Levies on fire insurance companies	16	157	363	574	937	1 028	1 109	1 395	1 279	740
Other	15	237	863	2 148	3 701	3 906	3 960	4 593	4 851	5 562
5127 Other taxes on internat. trade and transactions	0	0	0	0	0	0	0	0	0	0
5128 Other taxes	0	0	0	0	0	0	0	0	0	0
5130 Unallocable between 5110 and 5120	0	0	0	0	0	0	0	0	0	0

Table 41. **Australia / Australie** *(cont.)*
Details of tax revenue / Recettes fiscales détaillées

Million AUD

	1965	1980	1990	2000	2007	2008	2009	2011	2012	2013
5200 Taxes on use of goods and perform activities	236	1 305	5 203	5 427	8 623	9 110	9 603	11 721	19 640	19 838
5210 Recurrent taxes	197	1 260	5 109	5 427	8 623	9 110	9 603	11 721	19 640	19 838
5211 Paid by households: motor vehicles	65	448	1 373	3 908	6 196	6 276	6 787	7 631	8 246	8 591
5212 Paid by others: motor vehicles	65	351	937	125	189	182	205	254	285	301
Fees on motor vehicle registry	46	312	794	0	0	0	0	0	0	0
Drivers licences	12	30	111	0	0	0	0	0	0	0
Stamp duty on vehicle registry	6	9	32	125	189	182	205	254	285	301
5213 Paid in respect of other goods	67	461	2 799	1 394	2 238	2 652	2 611	3 836	11 109	10 946
Broadcasting tv licences	37	21	125	210	288	341	241	231	167	157
Business franchise lic. tobac. fuel	0	221	2 016	227	0	2	3	1	1	2
Other taxes	2	12	33	860	1 948	2 308	2 366	3 580	10 917	10 763
Liquor taxes	28	206	603	97	2	1	1	24	24	24
Dog licenses	0	1	22	0	0	0	0	0	0	0
5220 Non-recurrent taxes	39	45	94	0	0	0	0	0	0	0
5300 Unallocable between 5100 and 5200	0	0	0	0	0	0	0	0	0	0
6000 Other taxes	**0**	**0**	**0**	**0**	**0**	**0**	**0**	**0**	**0**	**0**
6100 Paid solely by business	..	..	..	..	..	..	..	..	..	..
6200 Other	..	..	..	..	..	..	..	..	..	..
Non wastable tax credits										
Non-wastable tax credits against 1110	..	..	..	195	2 585	2 563	840	973	326	323
Tax expenditure component	..	..	..	175	178	127	67	581	232	215
Transfer component	..	..	..	20	2 407	2 436	773	392	94	108
Non-wastable tax credits against 1210	..	..	..	0	4 534	5 504	5 793	6 406	7 218	7 914
Tax expenditure component	..	..	..	..	1 922	2 213	2 227	2 426	2 736	3 091
Transfer component	..	..	..	..	2 642	3 291	3 566	3 980	4 482	4 823
Total tax revenue on cash basis	**5 024**	**39 878**	**116 500**	..	..	..	..	..	..	**0**
Total tax revenue on accrual basis	..	..	..	**214 651**	**349 416**	**340 063**	**334 047**	**390 690**	**415 889**	**434 981**
Conciliation with National Accounts										
Additional taxes included in National Accounts	..	..	..	..	..	..	..	..	..	..
Taxes excluded from National Accounts	..	..	..	..	..	..	..	..	..	..
Difference in treatment of tax credits	..	..	..	..	..	..	..	..	..	..
Capital transfer for uncollected revenue	..	..	..	..	..	..	..	..	..	..
Voluntary social security contributions	..	..	..	..	..	..	..	..	..	..
Miscellaneous differences	..	..	..	..	..	..	..	..	..	..
National Accounts: Taxes and actual social contributions	..	..	..	..	..	..	..	..	..	..
Imputed social contributions	..	..	..	..	..	..	..	..	..	..
National Accounts: Taxes and all social contributions	..	..	..	..	..	..	..	..	..	..

Note:

Data are on a fiscal year basis beginning 1st July.

From 1998 taxes are recorded on an accrual basis; prior to that they were on a cash basis.

Direct taxes paid by public trading enterprises are excluded from receipts.

The figures for total tax revenue do not match the published totals in Taxation Revenue Australia. The latter is based on an accrual IMF GFS methodology and there are some differences between that and the OECD equivalent.

Heading 5213 includes radio and television licenses fees, though these are usually not regarded as a tax revenue in the OECD list.

Headings for non-wastable tax credits 1110 and 1210 include the private health insurance tax offset, family benefit, baby bonus tax offsets (paid during the 2003-04 budget year), film tax offset, and research and development tax offsets. The estimation of non-wastable credits into the expenditure and transfer components is in accordance with the OECD guidelines on the treatment and the data for this memorandum item has been provided by the Australian Taxation Office.

Source: Australian Bureau of Statistics.

StatLink http://dx.doi.org/10.1787/888933277036

Table 42. **Austria / Autriche**
Details of tax revenue / Recettes fiscales détaillées

Million EUR

	1965	1980	1990	2000	2007	2008	2009	2011	2012	2013
Total tax revenue	**6 210**	**29 759**	**54 040**	**89 793**	**114 465**	**120 863**	**117 240**	**126 607**	**132 143**	**137 176**
Total tax revenue exclusive of custom duties	..	..	..	**89 436**	**114 068**	**120 492**	**116 920**	**126 229**	**131 799**	**136 848**
1000 Taxes on income, profits and capital gains	**1 584**	**7 959**	**13 797**	**25 553**	**34 319**	**37 221**	**32 780**	**36 074**	**38 067**	**39 792**
1100 Of individuals	1 240	6 899	11 326	19 890	25 741	28 008	26 151	28 546	30 289	31 474
1110 On income and profits	1 240	6 899	11 326	19 890	25 741	28 008	26 151	28 546	30 289	31 474
Income tax	415	1 576	2 501	3 202	3 253	3 387	3 314	3 374	3 537	3 737
Special income tax	0	0	0	0	0	0	0	0	0	0
Wage tax	417	4 626	7 823	15 630	20 607	22 467	20 997	23 031	24 759	25 669
Tax on industry and trade	196	402	454	7	0	0	0	0	1	0
Tax on capital yields	2	14	46	354	970	1 180	858	1 087	884	981
Contribution to chambers	60	279	501	697	910	974	983	1 054	1 107	1 087
Water supply fund	151	0	0	0	0	0	0	0	0	0
Contribution emergency fund	0	0	0	0	0	0	0	0	0	0
1120 On capital gains	0	0	0	0	0	0	0	0	0	0
1200 Corporate	334	1 049	1 930	4 157	6 622	6 953	4 683	6 180	6 379	6 963
1210 On profits	334	1 049	1 930	4 157	6 622	6 953	4 683	6 180	6 379	6 963
Corporation tax	195	698	998	3 865	6 094	6 335	4 177	5 582	5 835	6 377
Tax on industry and trade	83	254	624	10	0	0	1	0	1	0
Special tax on income	0	0	0	0	0	0	0	0	0	0
Tax on capital yields	5	33	108	118	346	424	323	388	328	370
Water supply fund	35	0	0	0	0	0	0	0	0	0
Contribution emergency fund	0	0	0	0	0	0	0	0	0	0
Contribution to chambers	14	58	200	164	182	195	182	210	216	216
Directors tax	2	6	0	0	0	0	0	0	0	0
1220 On capital gains	0	0	0	0	0	0	0	0	0	0
1300 Unallocable between 1100 and 1200	10	12	540	1 506	1 956	2 259	1 946	1 348	1 398	1 354
Fines related to tax offences	10	12	18	33	77	82	75	84	66	73
Tax on interest	0	0	522	1 473	1 879	2 177	1 871	1 263	1 332	1 282
2000 Social security contributions	**1 548**	**9 200**	**17 763**	**30 613**	**38 583**	**40 300**	**40 771**	**43 486**	**45 058**	**46 988**
2100 Employees	686	3 792	7 512	12 524	15 671	16 439	16 534	17 596	18 169	18 997
2110 On a payroll basis	..	..	..	12 524	15 671	16 439	16 534	17 596	18 169	18 997
Health insurance contributions	..	..	..	2 606	3 326	3 572	3 599	3 824	3 940	4 082
Pension insurance contributions	..	..	..	6 410	8 274	8 692	8 771	9 406	9 777	10 183
Pension contributions, civil servants	..	..	..	1 536	1 638	1 664	1 693	1 674	1 627	1 738
Unemployment insurance contributions	..	..	..	1 854	2 284	2 355	2 308	2 510	2 637	2 803
Health insurance contributions, local government employees	..	..	..	100	130	137	144	161	167	169
Special unemployment insurance contributions	..	..	..	17	19	19	19	20	21	22
2120 On an income tax basis	..	..	..	0	0	0	0	0	0	0
2200 Employers	721	4 563	8 768	14 707	18 162	18 928	19 023	20 377	21 158	21 998
2210 On a payroll basis	..	..	..	14 707	18 162	18 928	19 023	20 377	21 158	21 998
Health insurance contributions	..	..	..	2 667	3 395	3 565	3 593	3 818	3 934	4 075
Pension insurance contributions	..	..	..	7 888	10 214	10 752	10 859	11 684	12 154	12 642
Pension contributions, civil servants	..	..	..	494	446	449	445	424	417	374
Accident insurance contributions	..	..	..	952	1 157	1 214	1 223	1 307	1 355	1 409
Unemployment insurance contributions	..	..	..	1 854	2 284	2 355	2 308	2 510	2 637	2 803
Health insurance contributions, local government employees	..	..	..	101	141	148	155	161	167	170
Contributions to sickness benefit fund	..	..	..	341	0	0	0	0	0	0
Special pension contributions, nightshift workers	..	..	..	11	18	18	16	15	18	31
Contributions to insolvency fund	..	..	..	381	488	408	406	437	455	473
Special unemployment insurance contributions construction workers	..	..	..	17	19	19	19	20	21	22
2220 On an income tax basis	..	..	..	0	0	0	0	0	0	0
2300 Self-employed or non-employed	141	845	1 482	3 382	4 750	4 934	5 214	5 514	5 732	5 993
2310 On a payroll basis	..	..	..	3 382	4 750	4 934	5 214	5 514	5 732	5 993
Health insurance contributions	..	..	..	1 971	2 724	2 835	3 020	3 186	3 315	3 441
Pension insurance contributions	..	..	..	1 117	1 527	1 584	1 661	1 778	1 830	1 973
Pension contributions, civil servants (retired)	..	..	..	116	274	281	291	300	329	315
Accident insurance contributions	..	..	..	77	85	86	87	88	91	95
Health insurance contributions, local government employees	..	..	..	101	140	147	154	161	167	169
2320 On an income tax basis	..	..	..	0	0	0	0	0	0	0
2400 Unallocable between 2100, 2200 and 2300	0	0	0	0	0	0	0	0	0	0
2410 On a payroll basis	..	..	..	..	..	..	..	..	..	..
2420 On an income tax basis	..	..	..	..	..	..	..	..	..	..

Table 42. **Austria / Autriche** *(cont.)*
Details of tax revenue / Recettes fiscales détaillées

Million EUR

	1965	1980	1990	2000	2007	2008	2009	2011	2012	2013
3000 Taxes on payroll and workforce	**472**	**2 097**	**3 259**	**5 788**	**7 266**	**7 922**	**8 143**	**8 756**	**9 156**	**9 489**
Emplr. contr. equaliz. of family.burdens	318	1 397	2 147	3 140	3 915	4 399	4 624	4 977	5 157	5 319
Tax on sum of wages	82	375	669	1 735	2 238	2 359	2 342	2 533	2 650	2 742
Promotion residential buildings	44	217	389	595	754	785	796	844	876	915
Tax on employment (Vienna undergr.)	0	20	21	21	22	23	24	22	42	67
Special levy for households allowances	26	80	0	0	0	0	0	0	0	0
Disabled persons equalization levy	2	8	34	54	83	86	93	92	131	138
Contributions to chambers	0	0	0	242	253	270	265	288	300	308
4000 Taxes on property	**246**	**858**	**1 473**	**1 206**	**1 572**	**1 534**	**1 511**	**1 576**	**1 765**	**2 341**
4100 Recurrent taxes on immovable property	92	231	355	526	626	651	667	693	709	736
4110 Households	47	66	84	87	92	93	94	93	96	105
Duty on farms	9	15	20	20	20	20	20	20	20	29
Farm contr. equaliz. of family burdens	5	6	6	6	6	6	6	6	6	6
Farm contribution to chambers	14	23	32	32	39	40	41	40	44	43
Contr. residential buildings reconstruction	4	0	0	0	0	0	0	0	0	0
Land tax A	16	22	25	28	26	27	27	26	26	26
4120 Others	45	165	271	440	534	558	573	601	613	631
Tax on vacant plots	1	4	5	5	5	6	5	6	6	6
Land tax B	44	161	266	435	529	552	568	595	607	625
4200 Recurrent taxes on net wealth	103	401	642	1	0	0	0	0	0	0
4210 Individual	37	140	189	1	..	..	..	..	..	..
Capital tax	25	109	189	1	..	..	..	..	..	..
Contribution emergency fund	0	0	0	0	..	..	..	..	..	..
Tax on industry and trade	10	26	0	0	..	..	..	..	..	..
Contribution to chambers	2	6	0	0	..	..	..	..	..	..
4220 Corporate	66	260	453	0	..	..	..	..	..	..
Capital tax	24	139	322	0	..	..	..	..	..	..
Capital death duty	20	53	131	0	..	..	..	..	..	..
Contribution emergency fund	0	0	0	0	..	..	..	..	..	..
Tax on industry and trade	19	56	0	0	..	..	..	..	..	..
Contribution to chambers	3	13	0	0	..	..	..	..	..	..
4300 Estate, inheritance and gift taxes	16	50	77	111	155	136	116	33	21	19
4310 Estate and inheritance taxes	..	..	..	..	..	..	..	..	..	..
4320 Gift taxes	..	..	..	..	..	..	..	..	..	..
4400 Taxes on financial and capital transactions	35	176	399	568	791	741	714	831	1 025	858
Land transfer tax	30	150	251	452	644	652	623	754	935	790
Capital transfer tax	5	27	148	115	147	89	91	77	89	67
4500 Non-recurrent taxes	0	0	0	0	0	6	14	18	11	728
4510 On net wealth	..	..	..	..	..	0	0	0	0	717
Withholding tax	..	..	..	..	..	0	0	0	0	717
4520 Other non-recurrent taxes	..	..	..	..	..	6	14	18	11	11
Foundation tax	..	..	..	..	..	6	14	18	11	11
4600 Other recurrent taxes on property	0	0	0	0	0	0	0	0	0	0
5000 Taxes on goods and services	**2 321**	**9 379**	**17 034**	**25 727**	**31 688**	**32 870**	**33 088**	**35 881**	**37 263**	**37 745**
5100 Taxes on production, sale, transfer, etc	2 275	9 006	16 169	24 297	29 830	30 986	31 141	33 771	35 056	35 442
5110 General taxes	1 160	5 984	11 229	16 894	20 988	21 957	22 231	23 498	24 601	24 978
5111 Value added taxes	0	5 984	11 229	16 894	20 988	21 957	22 231	23 498	24 601	24 978
5112 Sales tax	0	0	0	0	0	0	0	0	0	0
5113 Other	1 160	0	0	0	0	0	0	0	0	0
Turnover tax	664	..	..	..	..	..	..	..	..	..
Additional federal levy-turnover	332	..	..	..	..	..	..	..	..	..
Additional lieu invoice stp.	164	..	..	..	..	..	..	..	..	..
5120 Taxes on specific goods and services	1 115	2 996	4 873	7 365	8 839	9 027	8 907	10 270	10 453	10 462

Table 42. **Austria / Autriche** *(cont.)*
Details of tax revenue / Recettes fiscales détaillées

Million EUR

	1965	1980	1990	2000	2007	2008	2009	2011	2012	2013
5121 Excises	610	2 219	3 290	5 484	6 760	6 866	6 714	7 472	7 562	7 588
Tax on beer	39	44	56	161	200	190	193	189	191	193
Tax on wine	7	0	0	0	0	0	0	0	0	0
Tax on sparkling wine	1	7	25	25	1	1	1	1	1	1
Tax on tobacco	188	519	820	1 197	1 446	1 424	1 458	1 568	1 621	1 662
Tax on mineral oils	50	136	1 426	2 726	3 689	3 894	3 800	4 213	4 181	4 165
Additional federal levy mineral oils	202	876	0	0	0	0	0	0	0	0
Special duty alcoholic drinks	0	142	193	0	0	0	0	0	0	0
Special duty vehicles	0	0	0	0	0	0	0	0	0	0
Duty on starch products	0	4	13	0	0	0	0	0	0	0
Beverage tax	46	216	364	178	3	-1	-21	-2	0	-1
Other receipts-Market Organisation Act	26	35	9	0	1	0	0	0	0	0
Transport equality levy	0	5	1	0	0	0	0	0	0	0
Market Organisation Act - milk	35	177	192	0	0	0	0	0	0	0
Market Organisation Act - livestock	0	0	0	0	0	0	0	0	0	0
Market Organisation Act - grain	16	23	142	0	0	0	0	0	0	0
Duty promotion milk distrib.	0	34	13	0	0	0	0	0	0	0
Special tax on mineral oils	0	0	37	0	0	0	0	0	0	0
Duty on vehicles (fuel consumption)	0	0	0	433	457	467	450	484	505	455
Agricultural fund	0	0	0	23	16	16	17	18	18	18
Tax on energy	0	0	0	562	764	709	655	792	831	886
Social contributions to the artists' fund	0	0	0	0	11	7	6	7	8	7
Duty on exceeding milk-quota	0	0	0	36	24	9	0	33	29	26
Car registration taxes	0	0	0	143	148	150	153	168	177	175
5122 Profits of fiscal monopolies	37	57	52	130	122	124	130	318	332	324
Duty on spirits	5	14	17	130	122	124	130	132	128	130
Federal monopolies salt	1	0	0	0	0	0	0	0	0	0
Federal monopolies spirits	30	43	35	0	0	0	0	0	0	0
Federal monopolies gambling	0	0	0	0	0	0	0	186	204	194
5123 Customs and import duties	332	354	677	-5	-8	-21	0	0	0	0
Customs duties	310	237	418	-5	-8	-21	0	0	0	0
Other import duties	0	21	61	0	0	0	0	0	0	0
Contribution promote foreign trade	10	63	171	0	0	0	0	0	0	0
Import equalization duties	12	33	27	0	0	0	0	0	0	0
5124 Taxes on exports	8	36	1	0	0	0	0	0	0	0
Contribution to promote foreign trade	8	36	1	..	..	..	..	..	..	..
5125 Taxes on investment goods	0	33	0	0	0	0	0	0	0	0
5126 Taxes on specific services	129	297	854	1 720	1 967	2 039	2 059	2 475	2 551	2 545
Insurance tax	25	135	384	745	993	1 022	1 033	1 071	1 053	1 056
Transport tax	63	0	0	0	0	0	0	0	0	0
Duty on casinos	2	28	64	105	71	73	67	47	47	45
Fire protection tax	5	24	50	45	54	57	57	57	57	57
Advertisement tax	7	31	65	62	0	0	0	0	0	0
Entertainment tax	2	2	2	5	8	9	9	12	18	21
Tax on tourism	8	43	71	103	142	150	153	166	180	182
Amusement tax	13	17	51	73	94	96	101	98	86	84
Announcement tax	3	18	40	81	0	0	0	0	0	0
Tax on interest yields	0	0	0	0	0	0	0	0	0	0
Tax on gambling stakes - licenses	0	0	116	197	202	215	232	268	257	251
Tax on advertisement	0	0	0	33	108	114	105	111	110	110
Levy on dangerous waste	0	0	10	71	72	64	57	53	53	53
Duty for airways security	0	0	0	28	56	64	62	5	0	0
Tax on gambling stakes - gains	0	0	0	171	166	174	183	16	0	0
Flight Charge	0	0	0	0	0	0	0	59	107	98
Financial Institutions Stability Fee	0	0	0	0	0	0	0	510	583	588
5127 Other taxes on internat. trade and transactions	0	0	0	0	0	0	0	0	0	0
5128 Other taxes	0	0	0	34	-3	18	4	4	8	4
Levy on sugar	..	..	..	34	-3	18	4	4	8	4
5130 Unallocable between 5110 and 5120	0	26	66	38	3	2	2	3	3	2
Fines related to tax offenses	..	26	66	38	3	2	2	3	3	2
5200 Taxes on use of goods and perform activities	46	373	865	1 430	1 858	1 884	1 948	2 110	2 207	2 303
5210 Recurrent taxes	38	335	757	1 283	1 683	1 699	1 742	1 881	1 952	2 017
5211 Paid by households: motor vehicles	22	156	366	811	1 173	1 227	1 265	1 382	1 437	1 482
5212 Paid by others: motor vehicles	13	41	97	298	370	328	327	342	340	352
5213 Paid in respect of other goods	3	138	294	174	140	144	149	157	175	183
Hunting and fishing duties	1	4	7	10	10	10	10	10	17	19
Dog tax	1	4	6	8	10	10	11	12	15	17
Contribution to promotion of arts	1	3	8	11	16	17	17	17	18	18
Tax on radio and tv - licenses	0	15	46	61	104	107	112	117	125	129
Road transport duty	0	112	226	84	0	0	0	0	0	0

Table 42. **Austria / Autriche** *(cont.)*
Details of tax revenue / Recettes fiscales détaillées

Million EUR

	1965	1980	1990	2000	2007	2008	2009	2011	2012	2013
5220 Non-recurrent taxes	8	38	108	147	175	185	206	229	255	286
Certain user fees	8	38	108	147	175	185	206	229	255	286
5300 Unallocable between 5100 and 5200	0	0	0	0	0	0	0	0	0	0
6000 Other taxes	**38**	**266**	**714**	**548**	**641**	**645**	**626**	**457**	**489**	**493**
Tax on financial institutions	0	0	123	-3	0	0	0	0	0	0
Administration duties	4	17	32	57	79	75	75	74	82	79
Stamp fees	7	46	76	135	92	84	79	78	88	27
Contributions of interested persons	0	0	130	0	0	0	0	0	0	0
Parking duty	0	0	6	0	0	0	0	0	0	0
Contrbutions to students' associations	0	0	0	4	8	8	9	11	11	12
Duty on contribution to political parties	0	0	0	0	-1	0	1	1	1	0
Other fees, taxes on production n.e.c.	0	0	0	272	346	355	336	160	161	227
Embossing fee	0	0	0	0	1	1	1	1	1	1
Other taxes	28	202	347	83	115	122	125	133	145	146
6100 Paid solely by business	..	..	..	..	..	..	..	..	..	..
6200 Other	..	..	..	..	..	..	..	..	..	..
Custom duties collected for the EU	..	..	..	**356**	**397**	**371**	**320**	**378**	**344**	**328**
Non wastable tax credits										
Non-wastable tax credits against 1110	..	..	..	650	650	650	650	570	560	570
Tax expenditure component	..	..	..	590	450	440	447	344	330	341
Transfer component	..	..	..	60	200	210	203	226	230	229
Non-wastable tax credits against 1210	..	..	..	0	0	0	0	0	0	0
Tax expenditure component	..	..	..	..	..	..	..	..	..	..
Transfer component	..	..	..	..	..	..	..	..	..	..
Total tax revenue on cash basis	**6 210**	**29 759**	**54 040**	**89 768**	**114 364**	**120 630**	**116 701**	**126 408**	**131 912**	**45 950**
Total tax revenue on accrual basis	..	..	..	**89 793**	**114 465**	**120 863**	**117 240**	**126 607**	**132 143**	**137 176**
Conciliation with National Accounts										
Additional taxes included in National Accounts	..	..	..	0	0	0	0	0	0	0
VAT collected for the EU	..	..	..	..	..	..	..	..	..	..
Taxes excluded from National Accounts	..	..	..	0	0	0	0	0	0	0
Difference in treatment of tax credits	..	..	..	590	450	440	447	344	330	341
Capital transfer for uncollected revenue	..	..	..	0	0	0	0	0	0	0
Voluntary social security contributions	..	..	..	206	256	270	300	343	310	299
Miscellaneous differences	..	..	..	0	0	0	0	0	0	0
National Accounts: Taxes and actual social contributions	..	..	..	90 589	115 172	121 572	117 987	127 293	132 782	137 816
Imputed social contributions	..	..	..	2 420	2 133	2 116	2 084	2 026	1 964	1 915
National Accounts: Taxes and all social contributions	..	..	..	93 009	117 305	123 689	120 071	129 319	134 746	139 731

Note:

Year ending 31st December.

From 1995 data are on accrual basis.

Following national practice, one-third of the revenues from stamp fees (heading 6000) and fifty percent of the revenues from administration duties (heading 6000) are treated as tax revenues, the remainder being treated as non-tax revenue.

From 1988 onwards promoting residential building is being mainly financed by capital transfers from the Federal Government to the Länder. For the years 1985 to 1987 legally fixed shares of some taxes have been transmitted automatically from Federal Government to the Länder for this purpose and these funds have been classified as tax receipts of the Länder in those years. From 1988, they are classified as Federal Government tax revenues. This break in the time series (1987/1988) affects only the shares of the different subsectors and not total tax revenues.

From 1998 contributions of interested persons and parking duties are classified as non-tax revenues (sales) and no longer reported under heading 6000.

Source: Statistics Austria.

StatLink http://dx.doi.org/10.1787/888933277045

Table 43. **Belgium / Belgique**
Details of tax revenue / Recettes fiscales détaillées

Million EUR

	1965	1980	1990	2000	2007	2008	2009	2011	2012	2013
Recettes fiscales totales	**6 421**	**37 443**	**70 408**	**112 214**	**146 953**	**152 808**	**147 383**	**163 209**	**170 764**	**176 525**
Recettes fiscales totales excluant les droits de douane	..	..	..	**111 254**	**145 565**	**151 388**	**146 237**	**161 893**	**169 481**	**175 295**
1000 Impôts sur revenu, bénéfices et gains en capital	**1 774**	**15 379**	**25 983**	**43 421**	**52 805**	**55 197**	**50 094**	**56 772**	**59 274**	**62 784**
1100 Des personnes physiques	1 317	13 626	22 538	35 260	40 971	43 583	41 956	46 068	47 621	50 524
1110 Sur le revenu et les bénéfices	1 317	13 626	22 538	35 260	40 971	43 583	41 956	46 068	47 621	50 524
Précompte immobilier	148	532	1 053	1 857	0	0	0	0	0	0
Précompte mobilier	119	1 062	3 014	1 737	2 351	2 605	2 295	2 691	3 377	4 298
Précompte professionnel	740	9 119	15 422	28 119	36 626	39 012	39 714	42 824	44 091	45 442
Impôt versé par non-salariés	125	1 776	2 144	1 968	1 756	1 728	1 547	1 520	1 420	1 516
Impôt des non-résidents	0	-2	4	195	130	112	131	96	84	45
Impôt sur revenu global	183	1 128	878	774	-915	-884	-2 871	-2 157	-2 475	-1 934
Cotisation spéciale séc. sociale	0	0	19	602	957	970	1 048	1 069	1 094	1 117
Autres (personnes physiques)	0	12	2	8	65	40	93	25	30	41
1120 Sur les gains en capital	0	0	0	0	0	0	0	0	0	0
1200 Des sociétés	397	1 744	3 405	8 085	11 760	11 598	8 113	10 688	11 635	12 222
1210 Sur les bénéfices	397	1 744	3 405	8 085	11 760	11 598	8 113	10 688	11 635	12 222
Précompte immobilier	33	0	0	0	0	0	0	0	0	0
Précompte mobilier	41	367	1 206	545	688	680	297	393	365	497
Versements anticipés (sociétés)	262	1 273	2 735	7 114	9 742	9 634	6 844	7 870	7 926	7 939
Impôt sur revenu global	60	79	-553	404	1 270	1 224	870	2 379	3 211	3 662
Impôt des non-résidents (sociétés)	0	-6	18	17	41	46	62	36	120	113
Autres (sociétés)	0	32	-2	5	19	14	39	10	12	10
1220 Sur les gains en capital	0	0	0	0	0	0	0	0	0	0
1300 Non-ventilables entre 1100 et 1200	61	9	40	76	74	15	25	17	18	38
Anciens impôts sur revenu	51	0	0	0	0	0	0	0	0	0
Amendes	3	0	0	0	0	0	0	0	0	0
Autres	7	9	40	76	74	15	25	17	18	38
2000 Cotisations de sécurité sociale	**2 018**	**10 798**	**23 386**	**34 411**	**45 321**	**47 940**	**48 933**	**52 560**	**54 633**	**55 975**
2100 A la charge des salariés	569	3 130	7 152	10 936	13 851	14 406	14 647	15 699	16 246	16 484
2110 Sur la base du salaire	..	3 130	7 152	10 936	13 851	14 406	14 647	15 699	16 246	16 484
Sur les salaires et traitements bruts	..	3 130	7 062	10 936	13 851	14 406	14 647	15 699	16 246	16 484
Sur les prestations sociales	..	0	89	0	0	0	0	0	0	0
2120 Sur la base de l'impôt sur les revenus	..	0	0	0	0	0	0	0	0	0
2200 A la charge des employeurs	1 320	6 791	14 689	20 569	27 605	29 185	29 715	32 153	33 524	34 428
2210 Sur la base du salaire	..	6 791	14 689	20 569	27 605	29 185	29 715	32 153	33 524	34 428
A la charge des administrations publiques	..	1 059	1 769	2 845	4 086	4 327	4 619	5 117	5 683	6 187
A la charge des autres secteurs	..	5 732	12 920	17 724	23 519	24 858	25 096	27 035	27 841	28 241
2220 Sur la base de l'impôt sur les revenus	..	0	0	0	0	0	0	0	0	0
2300 A charge des travailleurs indép. ou sans emploi	129	877	1 546	2 906	3 866	4 350	4 572	4 709	4 863	5 063
Travailleurs indépendants	..	803	1 230	2 053	2 678	3 066	3 234	3 400	3 539	3 700
Sans emploi	..	0	0	0	0	0	0	0	0	0
Pensionnés, retraités	..	29	198	709	1 012	1 084	1 156	1 203	1 225	1 262
Autres	..	45	118	144	176	199	182	106	99	102
2310 Sur la base du salaire	..	877	1 546	2 906	3 866	4 350	4 572	4 709	4 863	5 063
2320 Sur la base de l'impôt sur les revenus	..	0	0	0	0	0	0	0	0	0
2400 Non-ventilables entre 2100, 2200 et 2300	0	0	0	0	0	0	0	0	0	0
2410 Sur la base du salaire	..	..	..	..	..	..	..	..	..	..
2420 Sur la base de l'impôt sur les revenus	..	..	..	..	..	..	..	..	..	..
3000 Sur salaires ou main d'oeuvre	**0**	**0**	**0**	**0**	**6**	**6**	**6**	**9**	**8**	**8**
Cotisation mandats publics	..	..	..	..	6	6	6	9	8	8
4000 Impôts sur le patrimoine	**240**	**1 161**	**2 679**	**5 282**	**10 550**	**10 764**	**10 247**	**11 938**	**12 645**	**13 805**
4100 Impôts périodiques sur la propriété immobilière	2	210	599	1 164	4 146	4 326	4 439	4 854	4 899	5 187
4110 Ménages	0	26	63	102	2 779	2 904	2 981	3 252	3 289	3 478
4120 Autres agents	2	184	536	1 063	1 367	1 421	1 458	1 602	1 610	1 710
Taxes sur associations sans but lucratif	2	7	17	41	32	32	28	35	36	38
Précompte immobilier (soc.)	0	177	519	929	1 269	1 315	1 358	1 485	1 499	1 584
Taxe régionale (Br.)	0	0	0	94	66	75	72	81	76	88
4200 Impôts périodiques sur l'actif net	0	0	0	92	253	243	209	254	328	451
4210 Personnes physiques	..	..	..	0	0	0	0	0	0	0
4220 Sociétés	..	..	..	92	253	243	209	254	328	451
4300 Impôts sur mut. par décès, succ. et donations	75	309	504	1 101	2 053	2 199	2 050	2 434	2 728	3 096
4310 Impôts sur mut. par décès et successions	69	281	475	1 042	1 702	1 882	1 780	2 064	2 332	2 634
4320 Impôts sur les donations	6	29	29	59	351	317	270	370	397	463

Table 43. **Belgium / Belgique** *(cont.)*
Details of tax revenue / Recettes fiscales détaillées

Million EUR

	1965	1980	1990	2000	2007	2008	2009	2011	2012	2013
4400 Impôts sur transact. mobilières et immob.	163	633	1 478	2 669	3 704	3 545	3 096	3 771	3 782	3 886
Droits d'enregistrement	153	527	1 213	1 967	3 325	3 271	2 820	3 496	3 467	3 542
Droits d'hypothèque	2	10	29	37	76	70	74	75	74	72
Droits de greffe	2	8	29	38	31	32	34	34	35	37
Fonds d'expansion économique	0	0	0	0	0	0	0	0	0	0
Taxe sur opérations de bourse	4	31	92	386	234	129	129	128	164	193
Taxe sur titres cotés en bourse	2	4	21	0	0	0	0	0	0	0
Taxe sur les titres au porteur	0	0	0	79	3	0	0	0	4	6
Droits de timbre, droits d'écriture	0	53	94	161	35	43	39	39	39	36
4500 Impôts non-périodiques	0	0	0	74	163	172	185	337	590	877
4510 Sur l'actif net	..	..	..	0	0	0	0	0	0	0
4520 Autres non-périodiques	..	..	..	74	163	172	185	337	590	877
Taxe sur l'épargne à long terme	..	..	..	74	163	172	185	203	400	207
Déclaration libératoire unique (DLU)	..	..	..	0	0	0	0	0	0	0
Déclaration libératoire unique (Diamant)	..	..	..	0	0	0	0	0	0	0
Régularisation fiscale (DLU bis)	..	..	..	0	0	0	0	134	74	614
Régularisation fiscale (DLU ter)	..	..	..	0	0	0	0	0	0	54
Contr. spéciale associations de crédit	..	..	..	0	0	0	0	0	116	2
4600 Autres impôts périodiques sur patrimoine	0	8	99	182	232	280	269	287	318	309
5000 Impôts sur les biens et services	**2 386**	**10 105**	**18 360**	**28 140**	**36 823**	**37 423**	**36 898**	**40 571**	**42 876**	**42 678**
5100 Impôts sur production, vente, transfert, etc.	2 187	9 606	17 387	26 037	34 453	35 104	34 574	38 025	40 437	40 183
5110 Impôts généraux	1 355	6 321	11 570	18 256	24 179	24 364	23 832	26 297	27 122	27 499
5111 Taxes sur la valeur ajoutée	0	6 321	11 547	18 130	23 908	24 126	23 600	26 019	26 896	27 259
T V A	..	6 293	11 491	18 130	23 908	24 126	23 600	26 019	26 896	27 259
Droits de timbre	..	0	0	0	0	0	0	0	0	0
Taxe d'immatriculation	..	28	56	0	0	0	0	0	0	0
5112 Impôts sur les ventes	0	0	23	126	271	238	232	278	226	240
5113 Autres impôts	1 355	0	0	0	0	0	0	0	0	0
Taxes assimilées au timbre	1 355	..	..	..	..	..	..	..	..	..
5120 Impôts sur biens et services déterminés	832	3 285	5 818	7 781	10 274	10 740	10 743	11 727	13 315	12 683
5121 Accises	531	1 997	3 478	5 690	7 344	7 252	7 287	7 850	7 947	8 036
Huiles minérales	278	1 109	2 017	3 392	3 869	3 902	3 929	4 330	4 209	4 072
Gaz de pétrole, hydroc. liquéfiés, benzoles	0	4	0	0	0	0	0	0	0	0
Sur le tabac	132	501	868	1 342	1 821	1 742	1 811	1 696	1 909	2 197
Eaux de vie	23	123	191	206	225	230	229	239	249	272
Taxe consommation alcools, eaux de vie	26	54	0	0	0	0	0	0	0	0
Boissons fermentées mousseuses	1	7	11	24	39	42	50	61	66	77
Boissons fermentées de fruits	18	57	88	101	115	114	115	116	115	132
Bières	38	93	170	208	191	185	183	184	181	183
Eaux de boisson et limonades	10	44	113	148	49	50	53	56	54	58
Sucres et sirops de raffinage + café	5	5	22	13	12	13	13	14	14	15
Cotisation sur l'énergie	0	0	0	193	341	331	335	341	328	337
Produits intermédiaires alcoolisés	0	0	0	32	28	28	26	24	24	26
Redevance de contrôle fuel domestique	0	0	0	29	43	51	44	40	39	41
Ecotaxes	0	0	0	2	1	1	0	2	2	1
Cotisation d'emballage	0	0	0	0	296	308	310	320	318	332
Cotisation fédérale sur l'électricité et le gaz naturel	0	0	0	0	311	242	175	414	426	281
Cotisation environnementale	0	0	0	0	5	14	12	12	14	14
5122 Bénéfices des monopoles fiscaux	0	0	0	0	0	0	0	0	0	0
5123 Droits de douane et droits à l'importation	272	627	809	0	0	0	0	0	0	0
Droits d'entrée	206	0	0	..	..	..	..	..	..	..
Prélèvements agricoles	63	0	0	..	..	..	..	..	..	..
Prélèvements CECA	2	0	0	..	..	..	..	..	..	..
Prélèvements UE, droit d'entrée	0	383	716	..	..	..	..	..	..	..
Prélèvements agricoles UE	0	244	93	..	..	..	..	..	..	..
5124 Taxes à l'exportation	0	1	0	0	0	0	0	0	0	0
5125 Impôts sur biens d'équipement	0	0	0	0	0	0	0	0	0	0
5126 Impôts sur services déterminés	29	452	937	1 365	2 044	2 117	2 241	2 951	3 528	3 137
Taxes jeux et paris	9	47	51	45	64	68	74	58	63	73
Taxe annuelle contrats assurances	19	404	885	1 282	1 930	1 970	2 019	2 109	2 223	2 285
Taxe d'affichage	0	0	1	1	3	2	3	3	3	3
Protection des dépots	0	0	0	36	48	76	145	780	1 000	609
Fonds de résolution	0	0	0	0	0	0	0	0	238	167
5127 Autres impôts sur commerce et transact. internat.	0	0	0	0	0	0	0	0	0	0
5128 Autres impôts	0	208	593	726	885	1 371	1 215	927	1 840	1 510
5130 Non-ventilables entre 5110 et 5120	0	0	0	0	0	0	0	0	0	0
5200 Impôts sur utilisation des biens et exerc. activités	199	496	966	2 096	2 363	2 308	2 315	2 540	2 431	2 485
5210 Impôts périodiques	199	496	966	1 887	2 032	1 950	1 972	2 161	2 061	2 113
Taxe de circulation	100	368	712	1 413	1 693	1 616	1 705	1 898	1 791	1 830
5211 A la charge des ménages : véhicules à moteur	0	204	458	889	1 051	996	1 037	1 178	1 121	1 148

Table 43. **Belgium / Belgique** *(cont.)*
Details of tax revenue / Recettes fiscales détaillées

Million EUR

	1965	1980	1990	2000	2007	2008	2009	2011	2012	2013
5212 A la charge autres agents : véhicules à moteur	0	164	254	525	642	620	667	720	670	683
5213 Autres impôts périodiques	99	127	254	474	338	334	267	263	270	283
Taxe appareils de divertissement	6	20	20	71	56	54	49	53	47	74
Taxe débits de boissons	1	5	24	18	0	0	0	0	0	0
Taxe sur la chasse	2	0	0	0	0	0	0	0	0	0
Collectivités locales	90	15	19	38	99	110	107	113	113	100
Radio, TV	0	87	191	347	184	170	111	97	111	108
5220 Impôts non-périodiques	0	0	0	209	332	358	343	379	371	372
Taxe de mise en circulation	..	..	..	209	332	358	343	379	371	360
Ménages	..	..	..	139	221	239	229	252	247	240
Autres agents	..	..	..	70	111	119	114	126	124	120
Droits d'émission	..	..	..	0	0	0	0	0	0	12
5300 Non-ventilables entre 5100 et 5200	0	3	7	7	7	11	9	7	7	10
6000 Autres impôts	**2**	**0**	**0**	**0**	**61**	**58**	**59**	**43**	**45**	**46**
6100 A la charge exclusive des entreprises	0	..	..	..	0	0	0	0	0	0
6200 A la charge d'autres agents	2	..	..	..	61	58	59	43	45	46
Amendes et intérets	2	..	..	..	0	0	0	0	0	0
Droits de douane perçus pour l'UE	**..**	**..**	**..**	**960**	**1 388**	**1 420**	**1 147**	**1 316**	**1 284**	**1 230**
Crédits d'impôts récupérables										
Crédits d'impôts récupérables contre 1110	..	..	..	..	348	426	937	1 446	1 640	1 795
Composante fiscale	..	..	..	..	78	83	161	1 000	1 198	1 325
Composante transfert	..	..	..	..	270	344	776	445	441	470
Crédits d'impôts récupérables contre 1210	..	..	..	..	0	0	0	0	0	0
Composante fiscale	..	..	..	..	..	..	..	..	..	..
Composante transfert	..	..	..	..	..	..	..	..	..	..
Recettes fiscales totales sur la base d'encaissements	**6 421**	**37 438**	**70 268**	**..**	**..**	**..**	**..**	**..**	**..**	**..**
Recettes fiscales totales sur la base des droits constatés	**..**	**37 443**	**70 408**	**112 214**	**146 953**	**152 808**	**147 383**	**163 209**	**170 764**	**176 525**
Conciliation avec les Comptes nationaux										
Impôts additionnels inclus dans les comptes nationaux	..	107	447	1 300	1 387	1 423	1 505	1 612	1 617	1 596
Bénéfices de la loterie nationale	..	107	262	279	225	240	240	231	242	214
Taxes sur les eaux (RF, RW et RB-C)	..	0	66	378	119	108	122	117	122	122
Cot. producteurs produits animaux (Sanitel)	..	0	0	14	13	12	11	13	14	14
Taxe sur les déchets industriels	..	0	27	74	68	72	56	59	53	46
Taxe sur le lisier (RF)	..	0	0	11	11	8	4	5	5	5
Taxe sur les déchets ménagers (RW)	..	0	0	20	0	0	0	0	0	0
Retenue à la source sur salaires (UE)	..	0	93	174	270	285	311	330	335	339
Cotisations de sécurité sociale (UE)	..	0	0	136	250	260	275	327	331	335
Cotisations sociales imputées (UE)	..	0	0	213	431	440	485	530	517	522
Impôt exclus des comptes nationaux	..	0	0	0	0	0	0	0	0	0
Protection des dépots	..	..	..	..	..	..	..	..	..	..
Différence dans les traitements des crédits d'impôts	..	0	0	0	78	83	161	1 000	1 198	1 325
Transfert en capital des recettes non collectées	..	0	0	0	0	0	0	0	0	0
Cotisations de sécurité sociale volontaires	..	41	52	54	55	62	62	67	71	75
Différences diverses	..	0	0	0	0	0	0	0	0	0
Ré-allocation niveaux d'administration nationaux	..	..	..	..	..	..	..	..	..	..
Ré-allocation UE	..	..	..	..	..	..	..	..	..	..
Comptes nationaux: impôts et cotisations sociales effectives	..	37 590	70 907	113 355	148 041	153 936	148 627	165 358	173 134	179 000
Cotisations sociales imputées	..	1 497	2 886	5 375	7 565	7 989	8 422	9 262	9 659	10 148
Comptes nationaux: impôts et toutes les cotisations sociales	..	39 087	73 793	118 729	155 606	161 924	157 048	174 620	182 794	189 148

Note:

Données établies sur la base de l'année civile se terminant le 31 décembre.

A partir de 1970, les données sont sur la base des droits constatés.

La rubrique 5100 comprend des taxes sur la fourniture d'eau, de gaz et d'éléctricité, sur le téléphone et les transports, taxes qui seraient classées dans d'autres postes de la rubrique 5100 si elles ne faisaient pas partie de la taxe de transmission (impôt sur le chiffre d'affaires) qui a été remplacée au 1er janvier 1971 par une taxe sur la valeur ajoutée.

Source: Ministère des Finances, Service d'Étude et de Documentation.

StatLink http://dx.doi.org/10.1787/888933277057

Table 44. **Canada**
Details of tax revenue / Recettes fiscales détaillées

Million CAD

	1965	1980	1990	2000	2007	2008	2009	2011	2012	2013
Total tax revenue	**15 318**	**101 015**	**244 152**	**390 234**	**512 663**	**512 996**	**498 722**	**541 432**	**566 913**	**584 164**
1000 Taxes on income, profits and capital gains	**5 910**	**47 064**	**118 566**	**195 320**	**251 198**	**251 646**	**236 416**	**255 509**	**268 829**	**277 602**
1100 Of individuals	3 464	34 451	99 722	143 652	190 025	190 514	177 941	193 793	205 411	213 636
1110 On income and profits	3 464	34 451	99 722	143 652	190 025	190 514	177 941	193 793	205 411	213 636
Taxes federal government	2 635	21 231	60 252	90 694	116 395	117 181	109 547	118 840	124 668	129 452
Taxes on individuals - province	829	13 220	39 470	52 958	73 630	73 333	68 394	74 953	80 743	84 184
1120 On capital gains	0	0	0	0	0	0	0	0	0	0
1200 Corporate	2 276	11 741	17 190	47 643	54 272	53 346	52 607	55 812	57 209	56 682
1210 On profits	2 276	11 741	17 190	47 643	54 272	53 346	52 607	55 812	57 209	56 682
Taxes federal government	1 752	8 110	11 726	31 570	37 093	35 300	32 739	35 201	35 313	34 665
Taxes on corporations - province	524	3 631	5 464	16 073	17 179	18 046	19 868	20 611	21 896	22 017
1220 On capital gains	0	0	0	0	0	0	0	0	0	0
1300 Unallocable between 1100 and 1200	170	872	1 654	4 025	6 901	7 786	5 868	5 904	6 209	7 284
Non-resident withhold taxes - federal	170	872	1 654	4 025	6 901	7 786	5 868	5 904	6 209	7 284
2000 Social security contributions	**854**	**10 649**	**29 653**	**53 109**	**73 722**	**75 347**	**76 882**	**82 508**	**87 897**	**92 257**
2100 Employees	318	3 756	10 634	21 361	29 361	30 197	30 745	32 887	35 133	36 955
Canada pension plan	47	1 265	3 745	9 401	16 194	16 338	17 258	17 971	19 175	20 009
Quebec pension plan	15	431	1 108	2 897	4 124	4 730	4 868	5 303	5 690	5 949
Employment insurance	164	1 393	5 284	7 782	7 084	6 943	6 996	7 758	8 393	9 031
Hospital insurance premiums	92	667	496	1 281	1 959	2 187	1 624	1 856	1 876	1 966
2110 On a payroll basis	..	..	10 634	20 976	28 654	29 153	29 923	31 991	34 281	36 068
2120 On an income tax basis	..	..	0	385	707	1 044	822	896	852	887
2200 Employers	536	6 697	18 449	30 307	41 922	42 641	43 497	46 852	49 807	52 216
Canada pension plan	48	1 266	3 745	9 401	16 194	16 338	17 258	17 971	19 175	20 009
Quebec pension plan	15	432	1 108	2 897	4 124	4 730	4 868	5 303	5 690	5 949
Employment insurance	164	2 006	7 398	10 894	9 917	9 720	9 794	10 861	11 750	12 643
Hospital insurance premiums	92	1 270	496	897	1 252	1 143	802	960	1 024	1 079
Social insurance levies	217	1 723	5 702	6 218	10 434	10 710	10 775	11 758	12 169	12 536
2210 On a payroll basis	..	..	18 449	30 307	41 922	42 641	43 497	46 852	49 807	52 216
2220 On an income tax basis	..	..	0	0	0	0	0	0	0	0
2300 Self-employed or non-employed	0	196	570	1 442	2 440	2 509	2 640	2 768	2 956	3 086
Canada pension plan	..	153	478	1 200	2 096	2 114	2 233	2 325	2 481	2 589
Quebec pension plan	..	43	92	242	344	395	406	443	475	497
2310 On a payroll basis	..	196	570	1 442	2 440	2 509	2 640	2 768	2 956	3 086
2320 On an income tax basis	..	0	0	0	0	0	0	0	0	0
2400 Unallocable between 2100, 2200 and 2300	0	0	0	0	0	0	0	0	0	0
2410 On a payroll basis	..	..	..	..	..	..	..	..	..	..
2420 On an income tax basis	..	..	..	..	..	..	..	..	..	..
3000 Taxes on payroll and workforce	**0**	**0**	**5 499**	**8 013**	**10 038**	**10 364**	**10 412**	**11 557**	**11 939**	**12 293**
4000 Taxes on property	**2 186**	**9 195**	**24 467**	**37 157**	**54 507**	**55 538**	**56 150**	**59 042**	**60 065**	**60 628**
4100 Recurrent taxes on immovable property	1 830	8 315	20 189	30 242	44 567	46 497	48 370	51 019	52 197	52 648
On property provincial government	11	133	1 645	3 078	3 164	3 008	3 445	3 740	3 952	3 977
Personal property local government	17	0	18 544	27 165	41 403	43 489	44 925	47 279	48 245	48 671
Real property local government	1 802	8 182	0	0	0	0	0	0	0	0
4110 Households	..	..	..	..	..	..	..	..	..	..
4120 Others	..	..	..	..	..	..	..	..	..	..
4200 Recurrent taxes on net wealth	25	512	1 911	4 171	2 970	2 322	1 827	1 013	719	661
4210 Individual	0	0	0	0	0	0	0	0	0	0
4220 Corporate	25	512	1 911	4 171	2 970	2 322	1 827	1 013	719	661
4300 Estate, inheritance and gift taxes	223	75	3	2	0	0	0	0	0	0
4310 Estate and inheritance taxes	216	75	3	2	..	..	..	..	..	..
On inheritances federal government	108	0	0	0	..	..	..	..	..	..
Succession duties provincial government	108	75	3	2	..	..	..	..	..	..
4320 Gift taxes	7	0	0	0	..	..	..	..	..	..
On gifts federal government	7	..	..	..	..	..	..	..	..	..
4400 Taxes on financial and capital transactions	0	0	0	0	2 868	2 594	2 700	3 402	3 307	3 656
4500 Non-recurrent taxes	108	293	2 365	2 742	4 102	4 125	3 253	3 607	3 841	3 663
4510 On net wealth	0	0	0	0	0	0	0	0	0	0
4520 Other non-recurrent taxes	108	293	2 365	2 742	4 102	4 125	3 253	3 607	3 841	3 663
Special assessments and charges local govt.	108	293	2 365	2 742	4 102	4 125	3 253	3 607	3 841	3 663
4600 Other recurrent taxes on property	0	0	0	0	0	0	0	0	0	0
5000 Taxes on goods and services	**6 202**	**32 909**	**63 092**	**94 468**	**122 855**	**119 765**	**118 583**	**132 542**	**137 900**	**141 097**
5100 Taxes on production, sale, transfer, etc	5 310	24 808	59 627	88 879	114 701	111 086	110 439	123 068	128 292	131 473
5110 General taxes	2 730	11 658	34 475	55 313	71 242	67 744	66 843	76 663	81 098	82 978
5111 Value added taxes	0	0	0	35 884	46 072	42 056	41 891	71 952	76 498	77 333
5112 Sales tax	2 730	11 658	34 475	19 429	25 170	25 688	24 952	4 711	4 600	5 645
Sales taxes federal government	813	5 429	16 866	0	0	0	0	0	0	0
Sales taxes provincial, local govt.	1 917	6 229	17 609	19 429	25 170	25 688	24 952	4 711	4 600	5 645
5113 Other	0	0	0	0	0	0	0	0	0	0
5120 Taxes on specific goods and services	2 580	13 150	25 153	33 565	43 459	43 342	43 596	46 406	47 193	48 496

Table 44. **Canada** *(cont.)*
Details of tax revenue / Recettes fiscales détaillées

Million CAD

	1965	1980	1990	2000	2007	2008	2009	2011	2012	2013
5121 Excises	1 499	6 805	14 473	18 417	22 759	22 877	23 224	25 208	25 368	26 302
Excises federal government	740	3 850	6 405	8 377	9 249	9 406	9 420	10 065	10 092	10 396
Liquor	..	..	926	1 103	1 224	1 402	1 376	1 529	1 578	1 565
Tobacco	..	..	2 247	2 176	2 466	2 468	2 346	2 912	2 864	2 937
Gasoline and motive fuel	..	..	2 472	4 807	5 272	5 248	5 440	5 359	5 380	5 604
Remitted gaming profits	..	..	45	0	0	0	0	0	0	0
Miscellaneous consumption taxes	..	..	715	291	287	288	258	265	270	290
Excises provincial government	759	2 955	8 067	10 039	13 510	13 472	13 805	15 143	15 276	15 906
Motor fuel	680	1 863	4 674	7 031	8 065	7 836	7 937	8 583	8 625	8 983
Tobacco	53	772	2 776	2 279	4 181	4 085	4 201	4 612	4 610	4 851
Other	26	320	617	730	1 264	1 551	1 667	1 948	2 041	2 072
5122 Profits of fiscal monopolies	294	1 406	3 758	8 756	11 565	11 387	11 472	11 935	12 257	12 313
Own enterprises contributions	294	1 406	3 758	8 756	11 565	11 387	11 472	11 935	12 257	12 313
5123 Customs and import duties	686	3 199	4 021	2 824	3 829	4 011	3 662	3 695	3 902	4 078
Customs and import duties federal govt.	686	3 199	4 021	2 824	3 829	4 011	3 662	3 695	3 902	4 078
5124 Taxes on exports	0	842	0	0	0	0	0	0	0	0
5125 Taxes on investment goods	0	0	0	0	0	0	0	0	0	0
5126 Taxes on specific services	84	575	2 385	2 524	4 088	4 203	4 380	4 633	4 841	5 087
Tax on insurance premiums, provincial govt.	45	261	1 141	1 740	2 796	2 910	3 139	3 485	3 691	3 891
Tax on insurance premiums, federal govt.	0	1	1	1	11	5	18	13	10	10
Amusement and admission taxes	4	25	126	538	537	548	517	292	279	298
Air transportation taxes	0	166	488	0	403	387	375	631	636	656
Racetrack betting	35	122	155	55	36	35	42	35	34	32
Tax on meals and hotels	0	0	473	191	305	318	289	177	191	200
5127 Other taxes on internat. trade and transactions	0	0	0	0	0	0	0	0	0	0
5128 Other taxes	17	323	517	1 045	1 217	864	859	935	825	715
Other taxes federal government	0	98	272	758	762	546	542	575	500	396
Other taxes provincial government	17	225	245	287	455	318	317	360	325	319
5130 Unallocable between 5110 and 5120	0	0	0	0	0	0	0	0	0	0
5200 Taxes on use of goods and perform activities	892	8 101	3 465	5 589	8 154	8 679	8 144	9 474	9 608	9 624
5210 Recurrent taxes	306	1 500	2 393	3 644	4 368	4 401	4 765	5 045	5 300	5 640
5211 Paid by households: motor vehicles	103	666	1 056	1 696	2 241	2 287	2 372	2 490	2 612	2 796
5212 Paid by others: motor vehicles	141	509	697	1 039	1 242	1 218	1 204	1 245	1 326	1 411
5213 Paid in respect of other goods	62	325	640	909	885	896	1 189	1 310	1 362	1 433
5220 Non-recurrent taxes	586	6 601	1 072	1 945	3 786	4 278	3 379	4 429	4 308	3 984
Licences and permits local govt.	36	132	317	499	889	908	859	1 041	1 058	1 058
Licences and permits provincial govt.	550	6 469	755	1 446	2 897	3 370	2 520	3 388	3 250	2 926
5300 Unallocable between 5100 and 5200	0	0	0	0	0	0	0	0	0	0
6000 Other taxes	**166**	**1 198**	**2 875**	**2 167**	**342**	**335**	**279**	**275**	**284**	**286**
6100 Paid solely by business	139	943	2 386	1 280	0	0	0	0	0	0
6200 Other	27	255	489	887	342	335	279	275	284	286
Poll tax local government	5	0	0	0	0	0	0	0	0	0
Miscellaneous local government	11	358	489	887	342	335	279	275	284	286
Other federal government	11	-103	0	0	0	0	0	0	0	0
Non wastable tax credits										
Non-wastable tax credits against 1110	..	..	..	1 633	5 550	5 951	6 552	6 867	6 983	6 962
Tax expenditure component	..	..	..	276	824	830	878	938	924	922
Transfer component	..	..	..	1 357	4 726	5 121	5 674	5 929	6 059	6 040
Non-wastable tax credits against 1210	..	..	..	1 758	3 445	4 119	4 184	4 863	3 863	3 840
Tax expenditure component	..	..	..	20	12	14	17	18	13	13
Transfer component	..	..	..	1 738	3 433	4 105	4 167	4 845	3 850	3 827
Total tax revenue on cash basis	**15 318**	**101 015**	**244 152**	**388 833**	**527 734**	**507 407**	**..**	**..**	**..**	**..**
Total tax revenue on accrual basis	**..**	**..**	**..**	**390 234**	**512 663**	**512 996**	**498 722**	**541 432**	**566 913**	**584 164**
Conciliation with National Accounts										
Additional taxes included in National Accounts	..	..	..	0	0	0	0	0	0	0
Taxes excluded from National Accounts	..	..	..	0	0	0	0	0	0	0
Difference in treatment of tax credits	..	..	..	0	0	0	0	0	0	0
Capital transfer for uncollected revenue	..	..	..	0	0	0	0	0	0	0
Voluntary social security contributions	..	..	..	0	0	0	0	0	0	0
Miscellaneous differences	..	..	..	0	0	0	0	0	0	0
National Accounts: Taxes and actual social contributions	..	..	..	390 234	512 663	512 996	498 722	541 432	566 913	584 164
Imputed social contributions	..	..	..	0	0	0	0	0	0	0
National Accounts: Taxes and all social contributions	..	..	..	390 234	512 663	512 996	498 722	541 432	566 913	584 164

Note:

From 2001, all data are for the year ending 31st December. For 2005 and and earlier years, data for the Federal, Provincial, and Territorial governments are on a fiscal year basis commencing 1st April. Data for local government are on a fiscal year basis commencing 1st January.

From 1999 data are on accrual basis except that personal income taxes are on a modified cash basis.

There are some minor differences between the data for the years 1965 to 1978 and those for subsequent years. These mostly relate to the inclusion of fines and penalities or late payment of taxes and deductions for the child tax credits in the data for the years 1979 to 1983.

Heading 1210 - Taxes federal government: Federal corporate taxes include capital taxes.

Heading 2000: Includes receipts from the Canadian Pension Plan, Quebec Pension Plan, Unemployement Insurance Fund and Provincial Health Insurance. Premiums, Medicare Premiums and Social Insurance levies but excludes that part of the taxes on income and sales taxes earmarked for old age security. The practice of earmarking these taxes was discontinued in June 1975.

Heading 4400: From 2002 onward includes land transfer taxes of the provincial, territorial and local governments. Prior to 2002 land transfer taxes of the local government were included in line 6000 and those provincial and territorial governments were included in line 4520.

Heading 5121: The large increase in this heading between 1980 and 1981 is due to the introduction of a 'special petroleum compensation charge', a 'Canadian ownership special charge' and to an increase in the natural gas tax of C$ 2399 millions.

Heading 5122: From 1988, profits on fiscal monopolies include lottery profits.

Heading 5128: From 1988, other taxes of Federal Government include the annual fees for managing the spectrum (airwaves) allocation to the cellular industry.

Heading 5211: Some Québec motor vehicle licence administrative fees are included in sales of goods and services for the period 1988-89 to 1997-98. From 1998-99 onward, these fees are included under other taxes - motor vehicle licences.

Source: Statistics Canada.

StatLink http://dx.doi.org/10.1787/888933277064

Table 45. **Chile / Chili**
Details of tax revenue / Recettes fiscales détaillées

Million CLP

	1965	1980	1990	2000	2007	2008	2009	2011	2012	2013
Total tax revenue	..	..	**1 777 218**	**7 901 998**	**20 599 131**	**20 081 681**	**16 595 349**	**25 762 449**	**27 714 772**	**27 381 686**
1000 Taxes on income, profits and capital gains	..	..	**412 974**	**1 841 630**	**9 412 056**	**7 536 172**	**5 162 043**	**10 322 824**	**10 803 031**	**9 520 709**
1100 Of individuals	..	..	99 154	604 100	989 348	1 146 546	1 252 672	1 690 230	1 893 620	1 964 172
Second category tax	..	..	65 552	490 980	993 129	1 110 643	1 239 815	1 663 293	1 917 675	1 981 699
Global complementary tax	..	..	33 603	113 120	-3 781	35 903	12 857	26 936	-24 055	-17 527
1110 On income and profits	..	..	..	..	..	..	..	..	..	..
1120 On capital gains	..	..	..	..	..	..	..	..	..	..
1200 Corporate	..	..	219 586	882 896	6 054 487	4 805 522	4 110 485	6 021 408	7 560 906	6 041 089
First category tax	..	..	200 891	815 747	5 084 996	4 252 551	3 729 488	5 254 907	6 770 329	5 473 355
Surtax on state owned enterprises	..	..	16 074	47 634	113 334	92 949	44 974	116 725	80 084	124 220
Mining tax	..	..	0	0	835 452	417 214	312 473	598 790	619 150	324 577
Other	..	..	2 621	19 516	20 705	42 808	23 550	50 987	91 343	118 937
1210 On profits	..	..	..	..	..	..	..	..	..	..
1220 On capital gains	..	..	..	..	..	..	..	..	..	..
1300 Unallocable between 1100 and 1200	..	..	94 233	354 634	2 368 221	1 584 104	-201 113	2 611 186	1 348 506	1 515 449
Adicionel tax	..	..	59 082	350 301	1 462 715	1 363 357	1 023 497	1 187 866	1 178 917	1 337 721
Other	..	..	35 151	4 332	905 507	220 747	-1 224 610	1 423 320	169 589	177 727
2000 Social security contributions	..	..	**159 559**	**576 758**	**1 148 647**	**1 289 225**	**1 371 750**	**1 623 818**	**1 802 468**	**1 968 973**
2100 Employees	..	..	154 021	553 937	1 098 620	1 229 912	1 312 793	1 565 828	1 742 526	1 906 340
2110 On a payroll basis	..	..	154 021	553 937	1 098 620	1 229 912	1 312 793	1 565 828	1 742 526	1 906 340
2120 On an income tax basis	..	..	0	0	0	0	0	0	0	0
2200 Employers	..	..	5 538	22 821	50 027	59 313	58 957	57 990	59 942	62 633
2210 On a payroll basis	..	..	5 538	22 821	50 027	59 313	58 957	57 990	59 942	62 633
2220 On an income tax basis	..	..	0	0	0	0	0	0	0	0
2300 Self-employed or non-employed	..	..	0	0	0	0	0	0	0	0
2310 On a payroll basis	..	..	..	..	..	..	..	..	..	..
2320 On an income tax basis	..	..	..	..	..	..	..	..	..	..
2400 Unallocable between 2100, 2200 and 2300	..	..	0	0	0	0	0	0	0	0
2410 On a payroll basis	..	..	..	..	..	..	..	..	..	..
2420 On an income tax basis	..	..	..	..	..	..	..	..	..	..
3000 Taxes on payroll and workforce	..	..	**0**	**0**	**0**	**0**	**0**	**0**	**0**	**0**
4000 Taxes on property	..	..	**109 319**	**554 037**	**1 013 571**	**1 080 090**	**795 084**	**1 027 627**	**1 180 307**	**1 133 765**
4100 Recurrent taxes on immovable property	..	..	59 968	302 244	496 311	541 268	532 279	731 191	788 919	840 842
4110 Households	..	..	..	..	..	..	..	..	..	..
4120 Others	..	..	..	..	..	..	..	..	..	..
4200 Recurrent taxes on net wealth	..	..	0	0	0	0	0	0	0	0
4210 Individual	..	..	..	..	..	..	..	..	..	..
4220 Corporate	..	..	..	..	..	..	..	..	..	..
4300 Estate, inheritance and gift taxes	..	..	3 444	10 906	28 501	35 554	200 203	30 876	66 719	45 550
4310 Estate and inheritance taxes	..	..	..	..	..	..	..	..	..	..
4320 Gift taxes	..	..	..	..	..	..	..	..	..	..
4400 Taxes on financial and capital transactions	..	..	45 907	240 886	488 759	503 269	62 602	265 560	324 669	247 373
4500 Non-recurrent taxes	..	..	0	0	0	0	0	0	0	0
4510 On net wealth	..	..	..	..	..	..	..	..	..	..
4520 Other non-recurrent taxes	..	..	..	..	..	..	..	..	..	..
4600 Other recurrent taxes on property	..	..	0	0	0	0	0	0	0	0
5000 Taxes on goods and services	..	..	**1 118 722**	**5 041 769**	**9 023 834**	**10 166 189**	**9 271 910**	**12 700 180**	**13 873 611**	**14 779 915**
5100 Taxes on production, sale, transfer, etc	..	..	1 074 009	4 789 827	8 578 804	9 650 260	8 724 696	11 963 914	13 052 989	13 869 529
5110 General taxes	..	..	664 421	3 306 350	6 781 501	7 912 009	7 051 079	9 536 786	10 447 374	11 170 794
5111 Value added taxes	..	..	664 421	3 306 350	6 781 501	7 912 009	7 051 079	9 536 786	10 447 374	11 170 794
5112 Sales tax	..	..	0	0	0	0	0	0	0	0
5113 Other	..	..	0	0	0	0	0	0	0	0
5120 Taxes on specific goods and services	..	..	409 588	1 483 477	1 797 303	1 738 251	1 673 617	2 427 128	2 605 615	2 698 735
5121 Excises	..	..	166 050	816 160	1 300 012	1 190 726	1 248 243	1 750 916	1 892 713	1 987 475
Cigarettes and tobacco	..	..	60 604	283 275	455 595	504 480	556 651	744 302	783 995	815 991
Gasolene and diesel	..	..	105 445	532 885	844 249	661 380	684 698	1 006 614	1 108 718	1 171 483
Oil stabilisation fund	..	..	0	0	168	24 866	6 894	0	0	0
Fisheries Law Extraction Rights	..	..	0	0	0	0	0	0	0	0
5122 Profits of fiscal monopolies	..	..	0	0	0	0	0	0	0	0
5123 Customs and import duties	..	..	222 486	548 571	300 416	307 265	162 987	301 828	314 441	303 393
5124 Taxes on exports	..	..	0	0	0	0	0	0	0	0
5125 Taxes on investment goods	..	..	0	0	0	0	0	0	0	0
5126 Taxes on specific services	..	..	21 052	118 746	196 875	240 260	262 387	374 384	398 461	407 867
5127 Other taxes on internat. trade and transactions	..	..	0	0	0	0	0	0	0	0
5128 Other taxes	..	..	0	0	0	0	0	0	0	0
5130 Unallocable between 5110 and 5120	..	..	0	0	0	0	0	0	0	0
5200 Taxes on use of goods and perform activities	..	..	44 714	251 942	445 030	515 929	547 214	736 266	820 622	910 386
5210 Recurrent taxes	..	..	44 714	251 942	445 030	515 929	547 214	736 266	820 622	910 386
Motor vehicles	..	..	24 469	93 880	155 158	177 167	171 141	267 116	301 895	330 754
5211 Paid by households: motor vehicles	..	..	0	0	0	0	0	0	0	0

Table 45. **Chile / Chili** *(cont.)*
Details of tax revenue / Recettes fiscales détaillées

Million CLP

	1965	1980	1990	2000	2007	2008	2009	2011	2012	2013
5212 Paid by others: motor vehicles	..	..	0	0	0	0	0	0	0	0
5213 Paid in respect of other goods	..	..	20 245	158 062	289 872	338 762	376 073	469 150	518 727	579 632
Municipal permits	..	..	18 401	136 138	263 996	307 349	342 861	425 138	468 938	527 955
Mining patents	..	..	3 374	34 730	25 184	30 391	32 690	42 944	47 899	50 094
Other	..	..	-1 530	-12 806	692	1 022	522	1 068	1 890	1 583
5220 Non-recurrent taxes	..	..	0	0	0	0	0	0	0	0
5300 Unallocable between 5100 and 5200	..	..	0	0	0	0	0	0	0	0
6000 Other taxes	**..**	**..**	**-23 356**	**-112 195**	**1 023**	**10 005**	**-5 438**	**88 000**	**55 355**	**-21 676**
6100 Paid solely by business	..	..	0	0	0	0	0	0	0	0
6200 Other	..	..	-23 356	-112 195	1 023	10 005	-5 438	88 000	55 355	-21 676
Total tax revenue on cash basis	**..**	**..**	**1 777 218**	**7 901 998**	**20 599 131**	**20 081 681**	**16 595 349**	**25 762 449**	**27 714 772**	**27 381 686**
Total tax revenue on accrual basis	..	..	..	..	..	..	..	..	..	..
Conciliation with National Accounts										
Additional taxes included in National Accounts	..	..	..	..	..	..	..	..	..	..
Taxes excluded from National Accounts	..	..	..	..	..	..	..	..	..	..
Difference in treatment of tax credits	..	..	..	..	..	..	..	..	..	..
Capital transfer for uncollected revenue	..	..	..	..	..	..	..	..	..	..
Voluntary social security contributions	..	..	..	..	..	..	..	..	..	..
Miscellaneous differences	..	..	..	..	..	..	..	..	..	..
National Accounts: Taxes and actual social contributions	..	..	..	..	..	..	..	..	..	..
Imputed social contributions	..	..	..	..	..	..	..	..	..	..
National Accounts: Taxes and all social contributions	..	..	..	..	..	..	..	..	..	..

Note:

Year ending 31st December.

The data are on a cash basis.

Source: Servicio de Impuestos internos (Chile's Tax Service).

StatLink http://dx.doi.org/10.1787/888933277074

Table 46. **Czech Republic / République tchèque**
Details of tax revenue / Recettes fiscales détaillées

Million CZK

	1965	1980	1990	2000	2007	2008	2009	2011	2012	2013
Total tax revenue	..	..	..	**771 596**	**1 313 753**	**1 346 208**	**1 268 851**	**1 341 575**	**1 367 409**	**1 396 684**
Total tax revenue exclusive of custom duties	..	..	..	..	**1 307 310**	**1 339 885**	**1 263 303**	**1 334 614**	**1 361 237**	**1 391 140**
1000 Taxes on income, profits and capital gains	..	..	..	**175 846**	**325 328**	**305 082**	**269 343**	**272 467**	**280 058**	**290 263**
1100 Of individuals	..	..	..	99 668	153 374	142 269	136 023	142 752	144 831	149 831
1110 On income and profits	..	..	..	99 668	153 374	142 269	136 023	142 752	144 831	149 831
Wages and salaries withholding	..	..	..	73 474	126 736	116 034	113 119	122 569	124 005	129 793
Of unincorporated individuals	..	..	..	17 254	17 825	16 052	12 750	7 866	7 767	7 437
Withheld on interest and dividends paid to individuals	..	..	..	8 940	8 813	10 184	10 154	12 317	13 059	12 602
1120 On capital gains	..	..	..	0	0	0	0	0	0	0
1200 Corporate	..	..	..	76 178	171 954	162 813	133 319	129 715	135 227	140 432
1210 On profits	..	..	..	76 178	171 954	162 813	133 319	129 715	135 227	140 432
Profit tax	..	..	..	68 945	164 016	153 051	123 301	120 320	119 978	124 820
Withheld on interest and dividends paid to corporations	..	..	..	7 233	7 162	8 897	9 027	8 710	7 503	7 736
Levy on lottery revenue	..	..	..	0	776	865	992	685	7 747	7 876
1220 On capital gains	..	..	..	0	0	0	0	0	0	0
1300 Unallocable between 1100 and 1200	..	..	..	0	0	0	0	0	0	0
2000 Social security contributions	..	..	..	**341 544**	**573 417**	**595 552**	**557 702**	**588 996**	**596 841**	**603 072**
2100 Employees	..	..	..	77 272	127 662	133 235	112 156	120 070	121 892	123 353
2110 On a payroll basis	..	..	..	77 272	127 662	133 235	112 156	120 070	121 892	123 353
Retirement	..	..	..	40 489	66 644	69 707	66 042	70 999	71 647	71 871
State employment policy	..	..	..	2 492	4 101	4 291	0	0	0	0
Sick leave	..	..	..	6 852	11 279	11 797	0	0	0	0
Health insurance	..	..	..	27 439	45 638	47 440	46 114	49 071	50 245	51 482
2120 On an income tax basis	..	..	..	0	0	0	0	0	0	0
2200 Employers	..	..	..	220 207	359 493	375 356	345 361	372 760	377 834	382 498
2210 On a payroll basis	..	..	..	220 207	359 493	375 356	345 361	372 760	377 834	382 498
Retirement	..	..	..	121 547	220 591	230 729	218 310	235 129	237 277	239 248
State employment policy	..	..	..	19 933	12 303	12 870	11 836	13 054	13 236	13 345
Sick leave	..	..	..	20 555	33 834	35 390	21 500	24 904	25 234	25 454
Health insurance	..	..	..	54 879	91 275	94 881	92 229	98 141	100 491	102 964
Penalties	..	..	..	3 293	1 490	1 486	1 486	1 532	1 596	1 487
2220 On an income tax basis	..	..	..	0	0	0	0	0	0	0
2300 Self-employed or non-employed	..	..	..	44 065	86 262	86 961	100 185	96 166	97 114	97 221
2310 On a payroll basis	..	..	..	44 065	86 262	86 961	100 185	96 166	97 114	97 221
Retirement	..	..	..	7 819	19 508	19 110	25 320	22 225	22 334	21 262
State employment policy	..	..	..	1 082	1 114	1 092	1 446	976	957	911
Sick leave	..	..	..	0	0	0	0	0	0	0
Health insurance	..	..	..	34 992	65 483	66 608	73 241	72 815	73 671	74 908
Self-employed	..	..	..	7 328	15 921	17 208	20 572	17 632	18 352	18 732
Non-employed	..	..	..	200	2 103	2 147	3 996	2 466	2 451	2 500
Government	..	..	..	27 464	47 459	47 253	48 673	52 717	52 867	53 676
Penalties	..	..	..	172	157	151	178	150	153	140
2320 On an income tax basis	..	..	..	0	0	0	0	0	0	0
2400 Unallocable between 2100, 2200 and 2300	..	..	..	0	0	0	0	0	0	0
2410 On a payroll basis	..	..	..	..	..	..	..	..	..	..
2420 On an income tax basis	..	..	..	..	..	..	..	..	..	..
3000 Taxes on payroll and workforce	..	..	..	**0**	**0**	**0**	**0**	**0**	**0**	**0**
4000 Taxes on property	..	..	..	**10 890**	**15 495**	**15 216**	**14 085**	**20 439**	**20 554**	**19 210**
4100 Recurrent taxes on immovable property	..	..	..	4 469	5 126	5 200	6 366	8 484	9 546	9 852
4110 Households	..	..	..	1 452	2 228	2 347	2 912	4 344	4 837	4 993
Real property tax	..	..	..	1 452	2 228	2 347	2 912	4 344	4 837	4 993
4120 Others	..	..	..	3 017	2 898	2 853	3 454	4 140	4 708	4 859
Levy collected by Winery Fund	..	..	..	0	2	4	5	5	5	5
Real property tax	..	..	..	3 017	2 895	2 849	3 448	4 135	4 703	4 855
4200 Recurrent taxes on net wealth	..	..	..	0	0	0	0	0	0	0
4210 Individual	..	..	..	..	..	..	..	..	..	..
4220 Corporate	..	..	..	..	..	..	..	..	..	..
4300 Estate, inheritance and gift taxes	..	..	..	587	460	249	225	4 401	3 392	215
4310 Estate and inheritance taxes	..	..	..	112	115	88	87	71	76	76
Inheritance tax	..	..	..	112	115	88	87	71	76	76
4320 Gift taxes	..	..	..	475	345	162	138	4 330	3 316	139
Gift tax	..	..	..	475	345	162	138	4 330	3 316	139
4400 Taxes on financial and capital transactions	..	..	..	5 834	9 909	9 767	7 495	7 554	7 617	9 143
Real property transfer tax	..	..	..	5 834	9 909	9 767	7 495	7 554	7 617	9 143
4500 Non-recurrent taxes	..	..	..	0	0	0	0	0	0	0
4510 On net wealth	..	..	..	..	..	..	..	..	..	..
4520 Other non-recurrent taxes	..	..	..	..	..	..	..	..	..	..
4600 Other recurrent taxes on property	..	..	..	0	0	0	0	0	0	0
5000 Taxes on goods and services	..	..	..	**242 960**	**393 041**	**424 026**	**421 958**	**452 578**	**463 459**	**478 386**
5100 Taxes on production, sale, transfer, etc	..	..	..	226 354	365 998	396 639	396 042	426 528	438 090	453 863

Table 46. **Czech Republic / République tchèque** *(cont.)*
Details of tax revenue / Recettes fiscales détaillées

Million CZK

	1965	1980	1990	2000	2007	2008	2009	2011	2012	2013
5110 General taxes	..	..	..	141 235	232 288	260 366	258 627	276 533	286 116	303 822
5111 Value added taxes	..	..	..	141 235	232 288	260 366	258 627	276 533	286 116	303 822
5112 Sales tax	..	..	..	0	0	0	0	0	0	0
5113 Other	..	..	..	0	0	0	0	0	0	0
Previous turnover tax	..	..	..	..	..	..	..	..	..	..
5120 Taxes on specific goods and services	..	..	..	85 119	133 710	136 273	137 414	149 995	151 975	150 041
5121 Excises	..	..	..	71 404	133 492	136 050	137 203	149 757	151 719	149 760
On mineral oils	..	..	..	46 998	81 661	81 164	80 867	80 561	77 991	77 160
On alcohol and liquor	..	..	..	5 629	7 201	7 025	7 689	6 870	5 998	6 658
On beer	..	..	..	3 410	3 564	3 579	3 478	4 553	4 611	4 545
On wine	..	..	..	350	342	324	366	296	308	288
On tobacco products	..	..	..	14 984	40 713	41 200	41 581	48 203	53 334	52 193
Duty on CFC	..	..	..	33	0	0	0	0	0	0
Levy collected by Winery Fund	..	..	..	0	11	22	26	19	29	21
On electricity	..	..	..	0	0	1 126	1 391	1 368	1 342	1 305
On natural gas	..	..	..	0	0	1 136	1 299	1 299	1 261	1 256
On solid fuels	..	..	..	0	0	473	507	476	447	469
Fee on electricity from solar radiation	..	..	..	0	0	0	0	6 111	6 397	5 866
5122 Profits of fiscal monopolies	..	..	..	0	0	0	0	0	0	0
5123 Customs and import duties	..	..	..	13 572	0	0	0	0	0	0
Customs duties	..	..	..	13 572	..	..	..	..	..	..
Previous import surcharge	..	..	..	0	..	..	..	..	..	..
5124 Taxes on exports	..	..	..	0	0	0	0	0	0	0
5125 Taxes on investment goods	..	..	..	0	0	0	0	0	0	0
5126 Taxes on specific services	..	..	..	143	218	223	211	238	256	281
Fees on entry tickets	..	..	..	65	61	65	63	60	58	56
Fees on recreational units (based on capacity)	..	..	..	69	144	146	135	166	188	213
Fees on advertising facilities	..	..	..	0	0	0	0	0	0	0
Restaurant sale alcoh. beverages and tobac. products	..	..	..	0	0	0	0	0	0	0
Fees collected by the cinematography EBF	..	..	..	9	13	12	13	11	11	12
5127 Other taxes on internat. trade and transactions	..	..	..	0	0	0	0	0	0	0
5128 Other taxes	..	..	..	0	0	0	0	0	0	0
5130 Unallocable between 5110 and 5120	..	..	..	0	0	0	0	0	0	0
5200 Taxes on use of goods and perform activities	..	..	..	16 606	27 043	27 387	25 916	26 049	25 368	24 523
5210 Recurrent taxes	..	..	..	10 788	18 100	18 363	18 132	19 002	18 342	18 176
Highway fee	..	..	..	1 753	2 429	2 819	2 845	3 186	3 872	3 803
5211 Paid by households: motor vehicles	..	..	..	0	0	0	0	0	0	0
5212 Paid by others: motor vehicles	..	..	..	5 456	5 882	5 777	4 944	5 256	5 224	5 323
Road tax (commercial)	..	..	..	5 456	5 882	5 777	4 944	5 256	5 224	5 323
5213 Paid in respect of other goods	..	..	..	3 579	9 790	9 767	10 343	10 560	9 246	9 050
Resort and recreation fees on visitors	..	..	..	232	312	309	282	302	304	301
Dog fees	..	..	..	191	277	287	287	287	286	281
Motor vehicle entry fees	..	..	..	32	25	24	22	11	13	14
Water pollution fee	..	..	..	520	404	244	192	224	215	208
Air pollution fee	..	..	..	685	525	553	376	439	408	268
Waste deposit fee	..	..	..	454	5 728	5 777	6 002	5 172	5 864	6 162
Levy on temp. withdrawal of land from agriculture	..	..	..	94	40	39	40	32	51	52
Radioactive waste fee	..	..	..	642	1 310	1 341	1 375	1 479	1 543	1 563
Fees on operated gambling machines	..	..	..	722	1 145	1 164	1 055	1 305	188	131
Fees on registration and recording of packaging	..	..	..	0	17	18	17	17	17	16
Levy on temp. withdrawal of land from forestry	..	..	..	7	6	6	7	7	5	6
Other environmental fees	..	..	..	0	0	4	688	1 284	353	47
5220 Non-recurrent taxes	..	..	..	5 818	8 943	9 024	7 784	7 048	7 027	6 348
Levy on withdrawal of land from agriculture	..	..	..	532	361	352	361	290	457	469
Levy on withdrawal of land from forestry	..	..	..	40	57	50	63	59	49	55
Tax on use of public space	..	..	..	645	639	710	632	682	655	629
Misc. licence and permit fees	..	..	..	4 601	7 881	7 905	6 715	6 000	5 855	5 187
Land betterment fee	..	..	..	0	4	6	11	16	10	7
Licence for lorry transport	..	..	..	0	1	1	2	1	1	0
5300 Unallocable between 5100 and 5200	..	..	..	0	0	0	0	0	0	0
6000 Other taxes	**..**	**..**	**..**	**356**	**29**	**9**	**216**	**135**	**325**	**208**
Unallocated previous taxes and levies	..	..	..	0	0	0	0	0	0	0
6100 Paid solely by business	..	..	..	0	0	0	0	0	0	0
6200 Other	..	..	..	356	29	9	216	135	325	208
Other taxes, fees and related payments	..	..	..	356	29	9	216	135	325	208
Custom duties collected for the EU	**..**	**..**	**..**	**..**	**6 443**	**6 323**	**5 548**	**6 961**	**6 172**	**5 544**
Non wastable tax credits										
Non-wastable tax credits against 1110	..	..	..	0	16 022	26 188	26 074	28 277	33 077	29 493
Tax expenditure component	..	..	..	..	13 416	20 615	19 110	21 032	24 506	21 000
Transfer component	..	..	..	..	2 606	5 573	6 964	7 245	8 571	8 493

Table 46. **Czech Republic / République tchèque** *(cont.)*
Details of tax revenue / Recettes fiscales détaillées

Million CZK

	1965	1980	1990	2000	2007	2008	2009	2011	2012	2013
Total tax revenue on cash basis	..	..	..	**772 272**	**1 310 618**	**1 364 086**	**1 242 426**	**1 316 448**	**1 342 342**	**1 353 469**
Total tax revenue on accrual basis	..	..	..	**771 596**	**1 313 753**	**1 346 208**	**1 268 851**	**1 341 575**	**1 367 409**	**1 396 684**
Conciliation with National Accounts										
Additional taxes included in National Accounts	..	..	..	2 837	5 757	6 302	6 140	6 286	6 408	6 424
Compulsory injury insurance	..	..	..	2 837	5 757	6 222	6 140	6 286	6 408	6 424
Driving licence fees	..	..	..	0	0	0	0	0	0	0
Taxes excluded from National Accounts	..	..	..	-9 488	-17 797	-18 385	-20 129	-18 714	-19 143	-18 893
Tax on use of public space	..	..	..	-645	-639	-710	-710	-682	-655	-629
Waste deposit fee	..	..	..	-454	-5 728	-5 777	-6 002	-5 172	-5 864	-6 162
Misc. licence and permit fees	..	..	..	-2 301	-3 940	-3 953	-3 357	-3 000	-2 928	-2 593
Radioactive waste fee	..	..	..	-642	-1 310	-1 341	-1 375	-1 479	-1 543	-1 563
Health insurance: non-employed	..	..	..	-200	-2 103	-2 147	-3 996	-2 466	-2 451	-2 500
Health insurance: government	..	..	..	0	0	0	0	0	0	0
Soc. Security contr. employers: Penalties	..	..	..	-3 293	-1 490	-1 486	-1 486	-1 532	-1 596	-1 487
Soc. Security contr. Self-employed or non-employed: Penalties	..	..	..	-200	-157	-151	-178	-150	-153	-140
Licence for lorry transport	..	..	..	0	-1	-1	-2	-1	-1	0
Highway fee	..	..	..	-1 753	-2 429	-2 819	-2 845	-3 186	-3 872	-3 803
Other environmental fees	..	..	..	0	0	0	-18	-829	-19	-14
Levy on loterry revenue	..	..	..	0	0	0	-158	-218	-63	0
Value added taxes	..	..	..	0	0	0	0	0	0	0
Difference in treatment of tax credits	..	..	..	0	0	0	0	0	0	0
Capital transfer for uncollected revenue	..	..	..	0	0	0	0	0	0	0
Voluntary social security contributions	..	..	..	1 099	974	882	635	423	313	326
Miscellaneous differences	..	..	..	2 162	0	0	0	0	0	0
National Accounts: Taxes and actual social contributions	..	..	..	768 206	1 302 688	1 335 008	1 255 498	1 329 570	1 354 987	1 384 541
Imputed social contributions	..	..	..	423	299	285	828	739	806	654
National Accounts: Taxes and all social contributions	..	..	..	768 629	1 302 987	1 335 293	1 256 326	1 330 309	1 355 793	1 385 195

Note:

Year ending 31st December.

From 1995 data are on accrual basis.

Source: Ministry of Finance, Economic Department.

StatLink http://dx.doi.org/10.1787/888933277085

Table 47. **Denmark / Danemark**
Details of tax revenue / Recettes fiscales détaillées

Million DKK

	1965	1980	1990	2000	2007	2008	2009	2011	2012	2013
Total tax revenue	**20 821**	**166 358**	**382 232**	**623 911**	**809 988**	**808 883**	**777 375**	**835 834**	**870 047**	**901 928**
Total tax revenue exclusive of custom duties	..	..	..	**621 586**	**806 707**	**805 777**	**774 728**	**832 657**	**867 085**	**899 001**
1000 Taxes on income, profits and capital gains	**9 712**	**92 404**	**233 739**	**383 244**	**486 845**	**491 450**	**476 879**	**513 117**	**539 861**	**565 020**
1100 Of individuals	8 758	86 958	206 478	328 532	427 412	435 866	435 208	434 783	447 246	494 651
1110 On income and profits	8 758	86 909	206 335	328 305	427 070	435 503	434 874	434 479	446 945	494 391
Central government income tax	5 020	33 351	91 638	77 491	155 540	154 128	136 756	134 200	138 781	145 281
County income tax	0	10 742	31 361	56 135	0	0	0	0	0	0
Municipality income tax	2 948	33 555	77 571	121 975	173 114	177 940	176 284	196 751	203 137	209 343
Seaman's income tax	66	457	0	0	0	0	0	0	0	0
Old-age pension fund contributions	592	2 163	0	0	0	0	0	0	0	0
Social pension fund contributions	0	3 340	0	0	0	0	0	0	0	0
Sickness benefit fund contributions	0	1 804	0	0	0	0	0	0	0	0
Pension schemes and annuity insurance	22	355	2 627	6 923	8 948	9 479	28 294	9 269	9 269	42 974
Special income tax	101	1 054	2 810	0	0	0	0	0	0	0
Duty on canceled pension schemes	9	82	0	0	0	0	0	0	0	0
Duty on feed rent increases	0	8	5	0	0	0	0	0	0	0
Duty on employees' remuneration compens. fund releases	0	0	325	654	1 144	1 547	1 552	1 089	1 224	1 129
Duty on interest on consumer loans	0	0	0	0	0	0	0	0	0	0
Labour market contributions	0	0	0	56 729	76 609	80 286	79 626	80 357	81 518	82 450
Imputed income from owner-occupied dwelling	0	0	0	8 399	11 716	12 123	12 361	12 814	13 016	13 216
1120 On capital gains	0	49	144	226	343	363	335	305	301	260
Tax on winnings from lotteries, pools, etc.	0	49	144	226	343	363	335	305	301	260
1200 Corporate	954	5 446	14 660	42 279	54 871	46 050	32 886	40 286	49 063	50 385
1210 On profits	954	5 446	14 660	42 279	54 871	46 050	32 886	40 286	49 063	50 385
1220 On capital gains	0	0	0	0	0	0	0	0	0	0
1300 Unallocable between 1100 and 1200	0	0	12 601	12 434	4 562	9 535	8 784	38 048	43 552	19 984
2000 Social security contributions	**690**	**710**	**101**	**8 453**	**1 286**	**1 087**	**1 018**	**2 040**	**1 824**	**1 618**
2100 Employees	567	1	98	8 209	1 057	909	877	1 049	1 078	879
Sickness benefit fund contributions	30	0	0	0	0	0	0	0	0	0
Sickday benefit contributions, ordinary	534	0	0	0	0	0	0	0	0	0
Sickday benefit contributions, special	3	0	0	0	0	0	0	0	0	0
Contribution to merchant marine's welf. board	0	1	1	0	0	0	0	0	0	0
Special pension scheme savings	0	0	0	6 846	0	0	0	0	0	0
Contr. to pension funds from officials in companies	0	0	0	879	555	506	463	448	644	476
Contr. to pension funds from officials in non-profit institutions	0	0	96	485	502	403	414	601	434	403
2110 On a payroll basis	..	..	..	..	..	..	..	..	..	..
2120 On an income tax basis	..	..	..	..	..	..	..	..	..	..
2200 Employers	123	709	3	244	229	177	141	991	746	739
Unemployment insurance contributions	41	598	0	0	0	0	0	0	0	0
Disablement insurance contributions	21	58	0	0	0	0	0	0	0	0
Sickness benefit fund contributions	61	0	0	0	0	0	0	0	0	0
Contribution to employee's wage guarantee fund	0	50	0	241	227	170	135	982	733	731
Contribution to merchant marine's welf. board	0	1	1	0	0	0	0	0	0	0
Shipping owners contr. sickness assist. seamen	0	1	2	3	2	7	6	9	13	8
2210 On a payroll basis	..	..	..	..	..	..	..	..	..	..
2220 On an income tax basis	..	..	..	..	..	..	..	..	..	..
2300 Self-employed or non-employed	0	0	0	0	0	0	0	0	0	0
2310 On a payroll basis	..	..	..	..	..	..	..	..	..	..
2320 On an income tax basis	..	..	..	..	..	..	..	..	..	..
2400 Unallocable between 2100, 2200 and 2300	0	0	0	0	0	0	0	0	0	0
2410 On a payroll basis	..	..	..	..	..	..	..	..	..	..
2420 On an income tax basis	..	..	..	..	..	..	..	..	..	..
3000 Taxes on payroll and workforce	**0**	**0**	**2 494**	**2 258**	**3 975**	**4 205**	**4 153**	**4 635**	**5 547**	**6 197**
4000 Taxes on property	**1 691**	**9 806**	**16 269**	**20 738**	**31 556**	**34 364**	**31 472**	**34 910**	**33 772**	**34 995**
4100 Recurrent taxes on immovable property	1 029	5 676	8 891	13 565	18 996	21 494	22 562	25 018	24 821	26 370
Central government land tax	130	264	0	0	0	0	0	0	0	0
County land tax	169	2 315	2 915	4 070	0	0	0	0	0	0
Municipal land tax	408	2 257	4 123	7 049	15 601	17 000	18 102	20 547	20 947	22 580
Centr. Govt. fixed tax on real property	32	11	0	0	0	0	0	0	0	0
County fixed tax on real property	45	0	0	0	0	0	0	0	0	0
Municipal fixed tax on real property	190	91	0	0	0	0	0	0	0	0
County duty on land (public property)	4	22	22	25	0	0	0	0	0	0
County duty on buildings (public property)	0	53	88	97	0	0	0	0	0	0
Municipal duty on land (public property)	26	103	244	383	393	641	601	420	360	359
Municipal duty on buildings (residential)	0	195	335	381	757	945	916	768	664	641
Municipal duty on buildings (business)	25	366	1 165	1 560	2 244	2 907	2 943	3 284	2 851	2 789
4110 Households	..	..	..	..	..	..	..	..	..	..
4120 Others	..	..	..	..	..	..	..	..	..	..

Table 47. **Denmark / Danemark** *(cont.)*
Details of tax revenue / Recettes fiscales détaillées

Million DKK

	1965	1980	1990	2000	2007	2008	2009	2011	2012	2013
4200 Recurrent taxes on net wealth	306	963	934	0	0	0	0	0	0	0
4210 Individual	306	963	934	..	..	..	..	..	..	..
4220 Corporate	0	0	0	..	..	..	..	..	..	..
4300 Estate, inheritance and gift taxes	137	738	2 197	2 863	3 896	4 754	3 669	4 792	4 042	3 940
4310 Estate and inheritance taxes	..	..	..	..	..	..	..	..	..	..
4320 Gift taxes	..	..	..	..	..	..	..	..	..	..
4400 Taxes on financial and capital transactions	219	2 313	4 166	4 171	8 659	8 110	5 232	5 100	4 910	4 685
Stamp duties	214	2 243	2 829	4 125	8 574	8 049	5 181	5 069	4 883	4 664
Duty on share capital creation	0	32	500	0	0	0	0	0	0	0
Duty to land registry office	5	38	28	46	85	62	51	31	27	21
Duty on transfers of shares	0	0	809	0	0	0	0	0	0	0
4500 Non-recurrent taxes	0	116	81	140	6	6	9	0	0	0
4510 On net wealth	..	0	0	0	0	0	0	0	..	..
4520 Other non-recurrent taxes	..	116	81	140	6	6	9	0	..	..
4600 Other recurrent taxes on property	0	0	0	0	0	0	0	0	0	0
5000 Taxes on goods and services	**8 727**	**63 437**	**129 630**	**206 502**	**282 855**	**274 453**	**261 019**	**277 780**	**285 889**	**291 021**
5100 Taxes on production, sale, transfer, etc	8 239	60 545	123 645	195 666	264 043	255 587	242 044	257 292	265 047	268 054
5110 General taxes	2 139	37 727	80 650	121 955	174 639	173 872	167 530	176 448	181 618	181 759
5111 Value added taxes	2 139	37 727	72 120	121 955	174 639	173 872	167 530	176 448	181 618	181 759
5112 Sales tax	0	0	0	0	0	0	0	0	0	0
5113 Other	0	0	8 530	0	0	0	0	0	0	0
Labour market contrib. concerning imports	..	..	4 903	..	..	..	..	..	..	..
Labour market contrib. concerning value added	..	..	3 627	..	..	..	..	..	..	..
5120 Taxes on specific goods and services	6 100	22 817	42 995	73 711	89 405	81 715	74 514	80 844	83 429	86 295

Table 47. **Denmark / Danemark** *(cont.)*
Details of tax revenue / Recettes fiscales détaillées

Million DKK

	1965	1980	1990	2000	2007	2008	2009	2011	2012	2013
5121 Excises	5 466	20 473	38 339	68 977	82 861	75 168	68 727	75 392	78 796	81 897
Duty on petrol	1 016	3 713	5 637	10 005	9 154	8 898	8 700	7 731	7 392	7 286
Motor vehicle registration duty	818	2 989	7 917	13 858	24 289	19 109	11 864	13 613	13 075	15 218
Cigarettes and tobacco duties	1 469	4 472	6 516	7 489	7 201	7 036	7 119	7 448	8 163	8 417
Duties on cigars, cheroots and cigarillos	234	220	128	80	40	40	33	32	52	47
Sale of revenue labels	0	3	10	13	13	15	8	3	3	4
Sales duties on chocolate and sugar	254	331	801	1 205	1 289	1 221	1 196	1 530	1 735	2 023
Raw material duty on chocolate and sugar	11	14	54	60	93	113	125	159	193	181
Special tax on chocolate and sugar	0	2	13	76	46	47	31	58	91	68
Duty on ice-cream	33	58	135	168	180	180	175	217	265	297
Duty on coffee	5	249	224	266	250	246	253	248	259	271
Duty on mineral water	68	195	466	505	418	407	413	397	505	374
Duty on beer	622	1 983	3 100	1 510	1 080	1 031	949	885	1 037	977
Duty on wine	122	611	1 448	1 166	1 032	1 066	1 054	1 133	1 519	1 674
Duty on spirits	412	1 432	1 982	1 756	1 213	1 159	1 065	1 062	1 074	1 127
Duty on restaurant sales of alcoholic bev.	150	0	0	0	0	0	0	0	0	0
Duty on wireless sets	55	67	0	0	0	0	0	0	0	0
Duty on television sets	0	93	-18	0	0	0	0	0	0	0
Duty on video recorders	0	17	-15	0	0	0	0	0	0	0
Duty on major household appliances	0	199	-10	0	0	0	0	0	0	0
Duty on grammophone records	10	46	84	0	0	0	0	0	0	0
Duty on playing cards	1	2	0	0	0	0	0	0	0	0
Duty on matches	5	3	-1	0	0	0	0	0	0	0
Duty on lighters	1	8	-4	0	0	0	0	0	0	0
Duty on electric bulbs	36	67	152	176	211	178	144	117	103	95
Duty on perfumery and toilet articles	91	214	506	0	0	0	0	0	0	0
Duty on almanacs	3	0	0	0	0	0	0	0	0	0
Duty on salmon	0	1	0	0	0	0	0	0	0	0
Duty on paper and cardboard	45	0	0	0	0	0	0	0	0	0
Duty on sugar	0	174	-8	0	0	0	0	0	0	0
Duty on tea	0	12	10	8	8	8	8	7	8	8
Duty on electricity	0	1 222	4 317	7 430	8 665	8 729	8 600	11 944	11 167	10 013
Duty on certain oil products	0	1 719	2 938	6 757	8 549	8 934	8 970	9 557	9 231	9 306
Duty on certain retail containers	0	100	397	594	727	732	693	640	690	715
Duty on gas	0	56	47	0	0	0	0	0	0	0
Duty on extraction and import of raw materials	0	16	129	172	220	184	121	149	133	132
Duty on disposable tableware	0	0	72	65	126	129	124	121	121	122
Duty on insecticides, herbicides, etc.	0	0	13	366	449	570	436	480	553	656
Duty on videotapes	0	0	0	0	0	0	0	0	0	0
Duty on coal, etc.	0	0	849	1 217	1 450	1 481	1 583	2 357	2 583	2 991
Other duties on goods and services	5	186	20	53	147	134	149	152	51	-13
Duty on waste	0	0	404	1 025	1 225	1 113	961	178	164	167
Duty on CFC	0	0	27	0	53	57	55	70	72	82
Duty on CO2	0	0	0	4 883	5 108	5 056	5 006	5 882	5 709	5 762
Duty on cigarette paper	0	0	0	68	32	30	28	29	35	36
Duty on rechargeable Ni-Cd batteries	0	0	0	21	17	12	6	3	1	3
Duty on piped water	0	0	0	1 357	1 371	1 372	1 371	1 333	1 516	1 584
Duty on carrier bags made of paper, plastic, etc.	0	0	0	178	210	212	202	197	194	186
Duty on tires	0	0	0	29	45	38	44	57	49	50
Duty on sulpher	0	0	0	165	108	82	68	48	44	51
Duty on chlorinated solvents	0	0	0	2	0	0	0	0	0	0
Duty on natural gas	0	0	0	2 532	3 375	3 610	3 515	4 324	4 033	5 255
Duty on nitrogen	0	0	0	30	27	25	22	17	13	21
Duty on specific growth stimulants	0	0	0	0	0	0	0	0	0	0
Duty on PVC-film	0	0	0	7	12	13	11	11	10	10
Duty on PVC and phathalates	0	0	0	31	42	36	26	21	21	18
Duty on lead accumulators	0	0	0	14	0	0	0	0	0	0
Duty on mineral phosphorus	0	0	0	0	51	39	40	51	47	49
Surcharge on alcoholic soft drinks	0	0	0	0	17	14	12	49	37	33
Duty on nitrogen oxides	0	0	0	0	0	0	0	197	505	870
Duty on saturated fat	0	0	0	0	0	0	0	283	1 223	0
Duty on PSO (Public Service Obligations)	0	0	0	3 641	4 319	1 814	3 549	2 601	5 121	5 734
5122 Profits of fiscal monopolies	16	183	404	1 402	1 648	1 543	1 429	1 576	1 413	1 339
5123 Customs and import duties	556	1 113	1 849	0	0	0	0	0	0	0
Customs duties	0	1 032	1 779	..	..	..	..	..	..	..
Temporary import surcharge	556	0	0	..	..	..	..	..	..	..
Import duties on agricultural produce	0	81	70	..	..	..	..	..	..	..
5124 Taxes on exports	0	0	0	0	0	0	0	0	0	0
5125 Taxes on investment goods	0	0	0	0	0	0	0	0	0	0

Table 47. **Denmark / Danemark** *(cont.)*
Details of tax revenue / Recettes fiscales détaillées

Million DKK

	1965	1980	1990	2000	2007	2008	2009	2011	2012	2013
5126 Taxes on specific services	62	771	1 567	3 019	4 525	4 284	4 011	3 843	3 187	3 008
Sales tax on gambling stakes races	17	28	20	12	18	18	16	16	16	15
Tax on football pools	31	152	284	942	1 143	1 120	1 039	1 102	39	0
Tax on cinema tickets	14	0	0	0	0	0	0	0	0	0
Duty on motor vehicle compl. insurance	0	470	923	1 327	2 104	1 976	1 898	1 746	1 732	1 598
Duty on insurance on pleasure boats	0	13	57	66	100	116	115	112	102	127
Duty on charter flight	0	109	283	0	0	0	0	0	0	0
Turnover tax on 6-win horse race betting	0	0	0	0	0	0	0	0	0	0
Duty on casinos	0	0	0	180	261	222	185	186	197	192
Passenger duty	0	0	0	477	6	0	0	0	0	0
Duty on the Danish State Lottery	0	0	0	16	35	38	40	42	42	42
Duty on slot machines	0	0	0	0	858	795	718	638	651	545
Duty on gambling	0	0	0	0	0	0	0	0	235	288
Duty on online casinos	0	0	0	0	0	0	0	0	173	202
5127 Other taxes on internat. trade and transactions	0	0	0	0	0	0	0	0	0	0
5128 Other taxes	0	277	837	312	370	720	348	33	33	51
Duty paid to ECSC	...	4	5	0	0	0	0	0	0	0
Sugar storing duty	...	83	113	62	0	0	0	0	0	0
Duty on the production of sugar	...	81	145	249	-26	213	33	33	33	51
Duty on milk co-reponsibility levy	...	109	255	0	0	0	0	0	0	0
Grain co-reponsibility levy	...	0	319	0	0	0	0	0	0	0
Restructuring scheme for EU sugar system	...	0	0	0	397	507	314	0	0	0
5130 Unallocable between 5110 and 5120	0	0	0	0	0	0	0	0	0	0
5200 Taxes on use of goods and perform activities	488	2 893	4 410	7 468	14 088	14 301	14 510	14 719	15 010	16 470
5210 Recurrent taxes	488	2 893	4 410	7 468	14 088	14 301	14 510	14 719	15 010	15 966
5211 Paid by households: motor vehicles	199	1 874	2 922	5 485	7 105	7 484	7 384	7 538	7 568	7 867
Weight duty automobiles	199	1 874	2 922	5 318	6 954	7 330	7 224	7 385	7 424	7 709
Recycling fee on cars	0	0	0	167	151	154	160	153	144	158
5212 Paid by others: motor vehicles	287	1 014	1 441	1 919	3 125	2 917	3 080	2 919	3 028	3 563
Weight duty automobiles	287	1 014	1 441	1 612	2 652	2 504	2 650	2 547	2 651	3 180
Road charges	0	0	0	307	473	413	430	372	378	383
5213 Paid in respect of other goods	2	5	47	64	3 858	3 900	4 046	4 262	4 414	4 537
5220 Non-recurrent taxes	0	0	0	0	0	0	0	0	0	504
5300 Unallocable between 5100 and 5200	0	0	1 575	3 368	4 724	4 565	4 465	5 769	5 831	6 497
6000 Other taxes	**0**	**0**	**0**	**391**	**190**	**219**	**187**	**174**	**193**	**152**
6100 Paid solely by business	...	...	...	391	190	219	187	174	193	152
6200 Other	...	...	...	0	0	0	0	0	0	0
Custom duties collected for the EU	**..**	**..**	**..**	**2 325**	**3 282**	**3 106**	**2 647**	**3 177**	**2 962**	**2 926**
Total tax revenue on cash basis	..	..	..	..	..	..	..	..	..	..
Total tax revenue on accrual basis	**20 821**	**166 358**	**382 232**	**623 911**	**809 988**	**808 883**	**777 375**	**835 834**	**870 047**	**901 928**
Conciliation with National Accounts										
Additional taxes included in National Accounts	0	0	0	0	0	0	0	0	0	0
Taxes excluded from National Accounts	0	0	0	0	0	0	0	0	0	0
Difference in treatment of tax credits	0	0	0	0	0	0	0	0	0	0
Capital transfer for uncollected revenue	0	-1 374	-2 387	-1 917	-2 726	-2 458	-3 043	-3 905	-4 013	-4 013
Voluntary social security contributions	0	1 673	8 087	16 633	17 061	17 166	16 816	17 610	16 320	14 655
Miscellaneous differences	0	0	0	0	0	0	0	0	0	0
National Accounts: Taxes and actual social contributions	20 821	166 657	387 932	638 626	824 324	823 591	791 148	849 539	882 354	912 570
Imputed social contributions	0	5 958	4 592	6 223	5 693	5 504	5 453	5 100	4 842	4 847
National Accounts: Taxes and all social contributions	20 821	172 615	392 525	644 849	830 017	829 095	796 601	854 639	887 197	917 417

Note:

Year ending 31st December.

The figures are on an accrual basis.

Heading 2300 includes a small amount of voluntary contributions which cannot be isolated.

Source: Danmarks Statistik.

StatLink http://dx.doi.org/10.1787/888933277093

Table 48. **Estonia / Estonie**
Details of tax revenue / Recettes fiscales détaillées

Million EUR

	1965	1980	1990	2000	2007	2008	2009	2011	2012	2013
Total tax revenue	..	..	..	**1 910**	**5 051**	**5 172**	**4 936**	**5 235**	**5 659**	**5 966**
Total tax revenue exclusive of customs duties	..	..	..	..	**5 016**	**5 139**	**4 916**	**5 206**	**5 630**	**5 937**
1000 Taxes on income, profits and capital gains	..	..	..	**476**	**1 197**	**1 277**	**1 045**	**1 047**	**1 184**	**1 357**
1100 Of individuals	..	..	..	421	936	1 011	789	846	931	1 031
1110 On income and profits	..	..	..	421	936	1 011	789	846	931	1 031
1120 On capital gains	..	..	..	0	0	0	0	0	0	0
1200 Corporate	..	..	..	55	261	266	256	201	252	327
1210 On profits	..	..	..	55	65	59	39	37	56	62
1220 On capital gains	..	..	..	0	196	208	218	164	197	265
1300 Unallocable between 1100 and 1200	..	..	..	0	0	0	0	0	0	0
2000 Social security contributions	..	..	..	**674**	**1 683**	**1 891**	**1 819**	**1 935**	**2 000**	**2 077**
2100 Employees	..	..	..	0	28	31	75	127	137	109
2110 On a payroll basis	..	..	..	..	28	31	75	127	137	109
2120 On an income tax basis	..	..	..	..	0	0	0	0	0	0
2200 Employers	..	..	..	662	1 635	1 836	1 720	1 789	1 845	1 949
2210 On a payroll basis	..	..	..	662	1 635	1 836	1 720	1 789	1 845	1 949
2220 On an income tax basis	..	..	..	0	0	0	0	0	0	0
2300 Self-employed or non-employed	..	..	..	12	21	24	25	19	18	19
2310 On a payroll basis	..	..	..	12	21	24	25	19	18	19
2320 On an income tax basis	..	..	..	0	0	0	0	0	0	0
2400 Unallocable between 2100, 2200 and 2300	..	..	..	0	0	0	0	0	0	0
2410 On a payroll basis	..	..	..	..	..	..	..	..	..	..
2420 On an income tax basis	..	..	..	..	..	..	..	..	..	..
3000 Taxes on payroll and workforce	..	..	..	**0**	**0**	**0**	**0**	**0**	**0**	**0**
4000 Taxes on property	..	..	..	**24**	**35**	**48**	**48**	**51**	**59**	**57**
4100 Recurrent taxes on immovable property	..	..	..	24	35	48	48	51	59	57
Land tax	..	..	..	24	35	48	48	51	59	57
4110 Households	..	..	..	..	..	..	..	..	..	..
4120 Others	..	..	..	..	..	..	..	..	..	..
4200 Recurrent taxes on net wealth	..	..	..	0	0	0	0	0	0	0
4210 Individual	..	..	..	..	..	..	..	..	..	..
4220 Corporate	..	..	..	..	..	..	..	..	..	..
4300 Estate, inheritance and gift taxes	..	..	..	0	0	0	0	0	0	0
4310 Estate and inheritance taxes	..	..	..	..	..	..	..	..	..	..
4320 Gift taxes	..	..	..	..	..	..	..	..	..	..
4400 Taxes on financial and capital transactions	..	..	..	0	0	0	0	0	0	0
4500 Non-recurrent taxes	..	..	..	0	0	0	0	0	0	0
4510 On net wealth	..	..	..	..	..	..	..	..	..	..
4520 Other non-recurrent taxes	..	..	..	..	..	..	..	..	..	..
4600 Other recurrent taxes on property	..	..	..	0	0	0	0	0	0	0
5000 Taxes on goods and services	..	..	..	**736**	**2 101**	**1 923**	**2 004**	**2 173**	**2 387**	**2 445**
5100 Taxes on production, sale, transfer, etc	..	..	..	714	2 033	1 859	1 942	2 113	2 328	2 380
5110 General taxes	..	..	..	521	1 423	1 288	1 224	1 380	1 513	1 558
5111 Value added taxes	..	..	..	520	1 423	1 288	1 224	1 363	1 508	1 558
5112 Sales tax	..	..	..	0	0	0	0	17	5	0
5113 Other	..	..	..	0	0	0	0	0	0	0
5120 Taxes on specific goods and services	..	..	..	194	610	571	718	734	815	822
5121 Excises	..	..	..	183	577	537	697	711	791	796
Alcohol	..	..	..	62	153	151	174	181	204	212
Tobacco	..	..	..	36	134	68	171	139	160	169
Fuel	..	..	..	76	290	295	331	359	394	383
Motor vehicle	..	..	..	9	0	0	0	0	0	0
Package	..	..	..	0	0	0	0	0	0	0
Fur	..	..	..	0	0	0	0	0	0	0
Electricity	..	..	..	0	0	23	22	32	33	33
5122 Profits of fiscal monopolies	..	..	..	0	0	0	0	0	0	0
5123 Customs and import duties	..	..	..	2	0	0	0	0	0	0
5124 Taxes on exports	..	..	..	0	0	0	0	0	0	0
5125 Taxes on investment goods	..	..	..	0	0	0	0	0	0	0
5126 Taxes on specific services	..	..	..	8	33	34	20	22	24	25
Gambling tax	..	..	..	7	30	31	18	19	21	22
Advertising tax	..	..	..	1	3	3	2	3	3	4
Postal service payment	..	..	..	0	0	0	0	0	0	0
5127 Other taxes on internat. trade and transactions	..	..	..	0	0	0	0	0	0	0
5128 Other taxes	..	..	..	0	0	0	0	0	0	0
5130 Unallocable between 5110 and 5120	..	..	..	0	0	0	0	0	0	0
5200 Taxes on use of goods and perform activities	..	..	..	22	68	64	62	60	59	66
5210 Recurrent taxes	..	..	..	22	68	64	62	60	59	66
Car registration fee	..	..	..	2	5	3	3	6	7	7
Heavy vehicle tax	..	..	..	0	4	4	4	4	4	4

Table 48. **Estonia / Estonie** *(cont.)*
Details of tax revenue / Recettes fiscales détaillées

Million EUR

	1965	1980	1990	2000	2007	2008	2009	2011	2012	2013
5211 Paid by households: motor vehicles	..	..	..	..	..	..	..	..	..	..
5212 Paid by others: motor vehicles	..	..	..	..	..	..	..	..	..	..
5213 Paid in respect of other goods	..	..	..	20	58	57	55	50	49	55
Business and professional licenses	..	..	..	3	2	1	1	1	1	1
Pollution fee	..	..	..	10	44	43	41	34	32	37
Specific use of water	..	..	..	4	9	10	11	13	13	14
Fees for closure of roads, streets and squares	..	..	..	0	1	1	1	1	1	1
Fishing fees	..	..	..	1	1	1	1	1	2	2
Tax on motor vehicle	..	..	..	2	0	0	0	0	0	0
Boat tax	..	..	..	0	0	0	0	0	0	0
Animal tax	..	..	..	0	0	0	0	0	0	0
5220 Non-recurrent taxes	..	..	..	0	0	0	0	0	0	0
Revenue from the sale of emission permits	..	..	..	..	..	..	..	..	..	..
5300 Unallocable between 5100 and 5200	..	..	..	0	0	0	0	0	0	0
6000 Other taxes	..	..	..	**0**	**0**	**0**	**0**	**0**	**0**	**0**
6100 Paid solely by business	..	..	..	..	..	..	..	..	..	..
6200 Other	..	..	..	..	..	..	..	..	..	..
Custom duties collected for the EU	..	..	..	..	**35**	**33**	**20**	**29**	**29**	**29**
Total tax revenue on cash basis	..	..	..	**1 898**	**4 972**	**5 233**	**4 828**	**5 212**	**5 620**	**5 942**
Total tax revenue on accrual basis	..	..	..	**1 910**	**5 051**	**5 172**	**4 936**	**5 235**	**5 659**	**5 966**
Conciliation with National Accounts										
Additional taxes included in National Accounts	..	..	..	0	0	0	0	0	0	0
Taxes excluded from National Accounts	..	..	..	0	0	0	0	0	0	0
Difference in treatment of tax credits	..	..	..	0	0	0	0	0	0	0
Capital transfer for uncollected revenue	..	..	..	0	0	0	0	0	0	0
Voluntary social security contributions	..	..	..	0	0	0	0	0	0	0
Miscellaneous differences	..	..	..	0	0	0	0	0	0	0
National Accounts: Taxes and actual social contributions	..	..	..	1 910	5 051	5 172	4 936	5 235	5 659	5 966
Imputed social contributions	..	..	..	2	16	21	23	26	28	31
National Accounts: Taxes and all social contributions	..	..	..	1 911	5 067	5 193	4 959	5 261	5 687	5 997

Note:

Year ending 31st December.

Data on an accrual basis.

Source: Statistics Estonia.

StatLink http://dx.doi.org/10.1787/888933277103

Table 49. **Finland / Finlande**
Details of tax revenue / Recettes fiscales détaillées

Million EUR

	1965	1980	1990	2000	2007	2008	2009	2011	2012	2013
Total tax revenue	**1 362**	**11 895**	**39 050**	**62 435**	**77 447**	**79 823**	**74 103**	**82 750**	**85 269**	**88 688**
Total tax revenue exclusive of custom duties	..	..	..	**62 306**	**77 248**	**79 618**	**73 951**	**82 561**	**85 085**	**88 522**
1000 Taxes on income, profits and capital gains	**564**	**4 654**	**15 323**	**26 911**	**30 358**	**31 064**	**26 505**	**29 334**	**29 202**	**30 797**
1100 Of individuals	453	4 248	13 562	19 118	23 396	24 593	23 011	24 181	24 989	25 998
1110 On income and profits	453	4 234	13 521	19 118	23 396	24 593	23 011	24 181	24 989	25 998
Tax on income	125	1 827	5 918	9 036	9 086	9 039	7 103	7 682	7 890	7 903
The final withdrawal tax on interest income	0	0	0	92	254	432	493	198	237	207
Communal tax	279	2 376	7 603	9 990	14 056	15 122	15 415	16 301	16 862	17 888
Seaman's tax	3	31	0	0	0	0	0	0	0	0
National pension contributions	32	0	0	0	0	0	0	0	0	0
National health insurance contributions	15	0	0	0	0	0	0	0	0	0
1120 On capital gains	0	14	42	0	0	0	0	0	0	0
Tax on lottery prizes	..	14	42	..	..	..	..	..	..	..
1200 Corporate	111	405	1 761	7 792	6 962	6 471	3 494	5 153	4 213	4 799
1210 On profits	111	405	1 761	7 792	6 962	6 471	3 494	5 153	4 213	4 799
Tax on income	72	202	1 001	4 758	5 298	4 922	2 222	3 375	2 906	3 227
Communal tax	36	187	699	2 900	1 541	1 435	1 184	1 647	1 208	1 456
Church tax	3	16	61	134	123	114	88	131	99	116
1220 On capital gains	0	0	0	0	0	0	0	0	0	0
1300 Unallocable between 1100 and 1200	0	0	0	0	0	0	0	0	0	0
2000 Social security contributions	**93**	**2 776**	**10 012**	**15 756**	**21 384**	**22 335**	**22 055**	**23 776**	**25 261**	**25 632**
2100 Employees	1	394	1 152	2 926	4 050	4 042	4 141	5 124	5 724	5 811
For employment pension schemes	1	10	23	2 120	2 950	2 997	3 093	3 692	4 190	4 235
For unemployment schemes	0	0	0	435	369	268	188	427	459	457
2110 On a payroll basis	..	10	23	2 565	3 319	3 265	3 281	4 119	4 649	4 692
2120 On an income tax basis	..	384	1 129	361	731	777	860	1 005	1 075	1 119
National pension contributions	..	251	502	2	0	0	0	0	0	0
National health insurance contributions	..	133	627	359	731	777	860	1 005	1 075	1 119
2200 Employers	93	2 230	8 127	11 571	15 715	16 682	16 261	16 937	17 674	17 888
For national pension schemes	29	685	1 502	1 566	1 331	1 076	632	0	0	0
For national health insurance	10	244	792	839	1 142	1 407	1 418	1 592	1 658	1 612
For unemployment schemes	3	106	206	1 143	1 346	1 343	1 296	1 610	1 736	1 775
For employment pension schemes	50	1 195	5 627	8 023	11 896	12 856	12 915	13 735	14 280	14 501
For accident and group life insurance premiums	0	0	0	0	0	0	0	0	0	0
2210 On a payroll basis	..	2 230	8 127	11 571	15 715	16 682	16 261	16 937	17 674	17 888
2220 On an income tax basis	..	0	0	0	0	0	0	0	0	0
2300 Self-employed or non-employed	0	152	733	1 259	1 619	1 611	1 653	1 715	1 863	1 933
For employment pension schemes	..	84	394	576	817	848	888	1 045	1 147	1 187
2310 On a payroll basis	..	84	394	576	817	848	888	1 045	1 147	1 187
2320 On an income tax basis	..	68	339	683	802	763	765	670	716	746
National pension contributions	..	43	151	5	0	0	0	0	0	0
National health insurance contributions	..	25	188	678	802	763	765	670	716	746
2400 Unallocable between 2100, 2200 and 2300	0	0	0	0	0	0	0	0	0	0
2410 On a payroll basis	..	..	..	..	..	..	..	..	..	..
2420 On an income tax basis	..	..	..	..	..	..	..	..	..	..
3000 Taxes on payroll and workforce	**70**	**22**	**0**	**0**	**0**	**0**	**0**	**0**	**0**	**0**
Soc. Sec. contr. for children allowance	70	22	..	..	..	..	..	..	..	..
4000 Taxes on property	**54**	**221**	**956**	**1 518**	**2 012**	**2 048**	**1 903**	**2 138**	**2 361**	**2 599**
4100 Recurrent taxes on immovable property	0	0	76	569	855	914	974	1 199	1 270	1 363
4110 Households	..	..	46	273	405	437	462	592	628	623
4120 Others	..	..	30	296	450	477	512	607	642	740
4200 Recurrent taxes on net wealth	24	24	26	179	0	0	0	0	0	0
4210 Individual	11	23	25	175	..	..	..	..	..	..
4220 Corporate	13	2	1	4	..	..	..	..	..	..
4300 Estate, inheritance and gift taxes	3	26	146	368	459	651	440	395	509	646
4310 Estate and inheritance taxes	3	21	121	307	384	545	368	330	426	541
4320 Gift taxes	1	5	25	61	75	106	72	65	83	105
4400 Taxes on financial and capital transactions	27	170	707	401	698	483	489	544	582	590
Stamp duty excluded entertainment	27	170	688	-20	0	0	0	0	0	0
Credit tax	0	0	19	0	0	0	0	0	0	0
Transfer tax	0	0	0	421	698	483	489	544	582	590
4500 Non-recurrent taxes	0	0	0	0	0	0	0	0	0	0
4510 On net wealth	..	..	..	..	..	..	..	..	..	..
4520 Other non-recurrent taxes	..	..	..	..	..	..	..	..	..	..
4600 Other recurrent taxes on property	0	0	0	0	0	0	0	0	0	0
5000 Taxes on goods and services	**578**	**4 202**	**12 710**	**18 091**	**23 425**	**24 098**	**23 419**	**27 240**	**28 186**	**29 430**
5100 Taxes on production, sale, transfer, etc	570	4 158	12 553	17 651	22 754	23 393	22 700	26 407	27 355	28 496
5110 General taxes	251	2 062	7 519	10 869	15 207	15 658	15 176	17 315	17 987	18 888

Table 49. **Finland / Finlande** *(cont.)*
Details of tax revenue / Recettes fiscales détaillées

Million EUR

	1965	1980	1990	2000	2007	2008	2009	2011	2012	2013
5111 Value added taxes	251	2 062	7 519	10 869	15 207	15 658	15 176	17 315	17 987	18 888
Value added taxes	251	2 062	7 519	9 616	13 657	13 976	13 434	15 281	15 814	16 561
VAT repayments of local government	0	0	0	849	1 550	1 682	1 742	2 034	2 173	2 327
Social Insur. Institutions' part of VAT revenue	0	0	0	404	0	0	0	0	0	0
5112 Sales tax	0	0	0	0	0	0	0	0	0	0
5113 Other	0	0	0	0	0	0	0	0	0	0
Suppl. sales tax on consumer durables	..	..	..	..	..	..	..	..	..	..
5120 Taxes on specific goods and services	319	2 096	5 034	6 782	7 547	7 735	7 524	9 092	9 368	9 608
5121 Excises	183	1 615	3 811	5 613	6 013	6 150	5 888	7 319	7 514	7 511
Excise on tobacco products	52	206	473	561	622	627	693	718	749	852
Excise on sweetments	6	23	26	0	0	0	0	0	0	0
Excise on medium, strong beer	3	109	419	0	0	0	0	0	0	0
Excise on non-alcoholic beverages	2	17	22	32	35	35	35	134	197	204
Excise on certain foodstuffs	3	218	36	0	0	0	0	0	0	0
Excise on liquid fuels	58	504	983	2 582	2 907	3 162	3 052	3 875	3 956	3 925
Excise on motor cars	28	238	697	1 059	1 217	1 016	687	1 068	1 006	931
Tax on alcoholic beverages	29	353	813	1 239	1 016	1 114	1 223	1 291	1 374	1 355
Levies on pharmacy	2	16	46	86	113	120	129	144	145	153
Levies for price reduction on butter	0	3	0	0	0	0	0	0	0	0
Levies for marketing of milk	0	12	58	0	0	0	0	0	0	0
Excise on margarines	0	18	55	0	0	0	0	0	0	0
Stock-building levies on liquid fuels	0	15	44	46	50	49	45	46	44	45
Excise on sugar products	0	18	34	0	0	0	0	0	0	0
Excise on feeding stuffs	0	0	0	0	0	0	0	0	0	0
Excise on fertilizers	0	21	21	0	0	0	0	0	0	0
Excise on oil-based concentrated feed	0	1	0	0	0	0	0	0	0	0
Excise on protein feed	0	0	0	0	0	0	0	0	0	0
Equalization fee agricultural products	0	8	29	0	0	0	0	0	0	0
Excise on albumen	0	0	30	0	0	0	0	0	0	0
Tax on electricity	0	65	0	0	0	0	0	0	0	0
Oil damage levy	0	0	7	5	8	8	8	24	24	27
Oil waste levy	0	0	4	3	4	4	4	4	4	4
Price difference compensations	0	-231	0	0	0	0	0	0	0	0
The milk quota charge	0	0	6	0	0	0	0	0	0	0
Levies for marketing of special agric. prod.	0	0	0	0	0	0	0	0	0	0
Excise on phosphorous fertilizers	0	0	7	0	0	0	0	0	0	0
Excise on certain beverage packages	0	0	0	0	41	15	12	15	15	15
5122 Profits of fiscal monopolies	38	86	202	0	0	0	0	0	0	0
Excess profits on alcohol	38	86	202	..	..	..	..	..	..	..
5123 Customs and import duties	88	235	423	0	0	0	0	0	0	0
Import duties	62	126	232	..	..	..	..	..	..	..
Import levies on agricultural products	26	6	12	..	..	..	..	..	..	..
Local import duties (Town dues)	1	0	0	..	..	..	..	..	..	..
Import levies price stabilisation fund	0	3	0	..	..	..	..	..	..	..
Custom duties and levies on agricultural goods	0	0	0	..	..	..	..	..	..	..
Equalization tax	0	100	179	..	..	..	..	..	..	..
5124 Taxes on exports	0	0	0	0	0	0	0	0	0	0
Export duties	..	..	..	..	..	..	..	..	..	..
Levies on export	..	..	..	..	..	..	..	..	..	..
Counter-cyclical tax exports	..	..	..	..	..	..	..	..	..	..
5125 Taxes on investment goods	0	0	0	0	0	0	0	0	0	0
Investment tax on buildings	..	..	..	..	..	..	..	..	..	..
5126 Taxes on specific services	9	161	599	1 160	1 533	1 584	1 635	1 772	1 853	2 096
Net revenue of betting	8	94	329	703	807	829	868	883	901	948
Tax on motion pictures	0	0	0	0	0	0	0	0	0	0
Stamp duties on entertainment	2	5	0	0	0	0	0	0	0	0
Fire protection levy	0	3	7	6	8	8	9	9	10	10
Tax on waste	0	0	0	33	56	52	45	64	56	56
Rail tax	0	0	0	0	18	21	17	18	16	19
Tax on insurance premiums	0	58	263	337	509	536	557	626	660	712
Tax on lottery prizes	0	0	0	80	135	138	139	172	210	217
Tax on telecommunications	0	0	0	0	0	0	0	0	0	0
Bank tax	0	0	0	0	0	0	0	0	0	134
5127 Other taxes on internat. trade and transactions	0	0	0	0	0	0	0	0	0	0
Tax on charter flights	..	..	..	..	..	..	..	..	..	..
5128 Other taxes	0	0	0	9	1	1	1	1	1	1
Sugar levy	..	..	..	9	1	1	1	1	1	1
Steel and coal levy	..	..	..	0	0	0	0	0	0	0
5130 Unallocable between 5110 and 5120	0	0	0	0	0	0	0	0	0	0
5200 Taxes on use of goods and perform activities	8	44	157	440	671	705	719	833	831	934

Table 49. **Finland / Finlande** *(cont.)*
Details of tax revenue / Recettes fiscales détaillées

Million EUR

	1965	1980	1990	2000	2007	2008	2009	2011	2012	2013
5210 Recurrent taxes	8	44	157	423	637	669	686	792	791	897
5211 Paid by households: motor vehicles	0	2	5	165	486	500	511	585	615	696
5212 Paid by others: motor vehicles	7	32	135	235	126	137	144	174	143	170
5213 Paid in respect of other goods	1	10	17	22	25	32	31	33	33	31
Dog licenses	1	2	4	5	3	3	2	1	2	2
Hunting and fishing licenses	1	7	13	17	17	24	23	24	23	23
Seamens welfare and rescue levy	0	0	0	1	1	1	1	1	1	1
Nuclear energy research levy	0	0	0	0	4	4	5	7	7	5
5220 Non-recurrent taxes	0	0	0	17	34	36	33	41	40	37
Vehicle registration tax	..	..	..	17	34	36	33	41	40	37
Income from auction of emission allowances	...	...	...	0	0	0	0	0	0	0
5300 Unallocable between 5100 and 5200	0	0	0	0	0	0	0	0	0	0
6000 Other taxes	**2**	**21**	**50**	**30**	**69**	**73**	**69**	**73**	**75**	**64**
6100 Paid solely by business	0	0	0	0	0	0	0	0	0	0
6200 Other	2	21	50	30	69	73	69	73	75	64
Custom duties collected for the EU	**..**	**..**	**..**	**129**	**199**	**205**	**152**	**189**	**184**	**166**
Total tax revenue on cash basis	**1 362**	**11 895**	**39 398**	**61 639**	**77 110**	**79 969**	**74 057**	**82 474**	**85 244**	**88 416**
Total tax revenue on accrual basis	**..**	**..**	**39 050**	**62 435**	**77 447**	**79 823**	**74 103**	**82 750**	**85 269**	**88 688**
Conciliation with National Accounts										
Additional taxes included in National Accounts	...	0	0	0	0	0	0	0	0	0
Taxes excluded from National Accounts	...	0	0	0	0	0	0	0	0	0
Difference in treatment of tax credits	...	0	0	0	0	0	0	0	0	0
Capital transfer for uncollected revenue	...	0	0	0	0	0	0	0	0	0
Voluntary social security contributions	...	262	632	235	228	224	220	261	267	270
Miscellaneous differences	...	0	0	0	0	0	0	0	0	0
National Accounts: Taxes and actual social contributions	...	12 157	39 682	62 671	77 675	80 047	74 323	83 011	85 536	88 958
Imputed social contributions	...	513	688	30	0	0	0	0	0	0
National Accounts: Taxes and all social contributions	...	12 670	40 370	62 701	77 675	80 047	74 323	83 011	85 536	88 958

Note:

Year ending 31st December.

From 1988 data are on accrual basis.

Finland has an imputation system where the full credit is taken into account in shareholders taxation. According to estimates made by the National Board of Taxation, the credit given to shareholders was 193 millions euros in 1991; the effects on personal income taxation are estimated.

Headings 2120 and 2320: The breakdown of contributions paid by employees and self-employed or non-employed is estimated.

Heading 4200: All figures in this subheading are estimated.

Heading 4400: Stamp duties include payment for some government services where the levy can be regarded as requited (the levy is linked to the cost of providing the service). However they are classified as taxes and recorded under this subheading as taxes on financial and capital transactions because the amounts involved cannot be identified.

Heading 5121: The negative item under the title 'Price difference compensations' refers to the subsidies paid out on agricultural products under the price compensation scheme which can be offset against any positive tax liability which arising under the same scheme. From 1983 this item has been offset against revenues from excises on certain foodstuffs, on medium and stronger beer and on non-alcoholic beverages.

Heading 5126: Prior to 1979, no figures are available for amounts paid under the Fire protection levy .

Heading 5212: Prior to 1990, a part of the tax is paid by 'households'.

Source: Bulletin of Statistics; Central Statistical Office (for Central Government revenues); the Annual report of the National Pension Institute and Official Statistics of Finland Series XXIIA published by the Ministry and Social Affairs (for the Social Security and private pension respectively); supplementary information from unpublished sources.

StatLink http://dx.doi.org/10.1787/888933277116

Table 50. **France**
Details of tax revenue / Recettes fiscales détaillées

Million EUR

	1965	1980	1990	2000	2007	2008	2009	2011	2012	2013
Recettes fiscales totales	**25 776**	**178 576**	**433 771**	**643 309**	**828 971**	**846 614**	**806 916**	**888 970**	**925 905**	**960 166**
Recettes fiscales totales excluant les droits de douane	..	..	..	**641 796**	**827 314**	**844 999**	**805 455**	**887 104**	**924 022**	**958 324**
1000 Impôts sur revenu, bénéfices et gains en capital	**4 095**	**30 019**	**69 649**	**160 363**	**197 939**	**204 424**	**167 118**	**202 235**	**219 090**	**232 630**
1100 Des personnes physiques	2 736	20 734	46 272	115 885	141 405	147 438	139 193	151 431	166 986	178 294
1110 Sur le revenu et les bénéfices	2 723	20 674	46 252	115 884	141 405	147 437	139 193	151 431	166 986	178 294
Impôt sur revenu personnes physiques	..	18 207	39 237	49 548	48 597	50 957	46 113	50 765	59 514	68 677
Retenue source sur B.N.C.	..	51	189	293	559	499	416	530	621	598
Retenue sur capitaux mobiliers	..	2 333	3 971	0	0	0	0	0	0	0
CSG, FSV, CRDS	..	0	0	65 953	92 204	95 902	92 564	99 877	106 123	108 251
Taxe forfaitaire sur métaux précieux,	..	70	58	47	37	40	39	88	100	69
Ressources sur cumuls rémunérations	..	7	20	38	0	1	0	0	0	0
Contribution sociale de solidarité	..	0	2 207	5	0	29	30	109	386	377
Autres	..	6	571	0	8	9	31	62	242	322
1120 Sur les gains en capital	14	59	20	1	0	1	0	0	0	0
Sur les gains en capital	..	0	0	0	..	0	..	..	..	..
Prélèv. sur bénéf. construction immobilière	..	59	20	1	..	1	..	..	..	..
1200 Des sociétés	1 358	9 158	23 117	44 478	56 534	56 986	27 925	50 804	52 104	54 336
1210 Sur les bénéfices	1 358	9 158	23 117	44 478	56 534	56 986	27 925	50 804	52 104	54 336
Impôts sur les sociétés (émission de rôles)	..	8 524	20 804	39 755	51 063	48 787	20 286	42 424	42 310	44 561
3% dividendes	..	0	0	0	0	0	0	0	193	1 943
Retenue sur capitaux mobiliers	..	487	1 333	1 460	3 492	5 314	5 480	6 916	8 057	5 894
Précomptes sur bénéfices distribués (devenu prélèvement exceptionnel de 25% en 2005)	..	36	247	1 135	88	17	63	13	1	-6
Prélèv. except. entrep. travail temporaire	..	0	0	0	0	0	0	0	0	0
Contribution sociale sur bénéfices des sociétés	..	0	0	589	158	938	601	776	769	1 160
Imposition annuelle forfaitaire	..	111	658	1 484	1 656	1 720	1 399	592	662	680
Prélèvement except. assurances	..	0	61	55	64	71	96	83	112	104
Autres (prélèv. except. entrep. pétrol.)	..	0	14	0	13	139	0	0	0	0
1220 Sur les gains en capital	0	0	0	0	0	0	0	0	0	0
1300 Non-ventilables entre 1100 et 1200	0	127	260	0	0	0	0	0	0	0
2000 Cotisations de sécurité sociale	**8 804**	**76 235**	**191 141**	**231 875**	**307 663**	**315 789**	**317 560**	**336 595**	**346 137**	**356 941**
2100 A la charge des salariés	1 701	19 851	57 347	57 686	76 815	77 511	77 172	80 987	83 669	87 965
Cotisations effectives	..	19 851	57 347	57 686	76 815	77 511	77 172	80 987	83 669	87 965
2110 Sur la base du salaire	..	..	..	57 686	76 815	77 511	77 172	80 987	83 669	87 965
2120 Sur la base de l'impôt sur les revenus	..	..	..	0	0	0	0	0	0	0
2200 A la charge des employeurs	6 525	50 742	118 079	159 476	208 688	214 746	215 326	229 873	235 530	240 848
Cotisations effectives	..	50 742	118 079	159 476	208 688	214 746	215 326	229 873	235 530	240 848
2210 Sur la base du salaire	..	..	..	159 476	208 688	214 746	215 326	229 873	235 530	240 848
2220 Sur la base de l'impôt sur les revenus	..	..	..	0	0	0	0	0	0	0
2300 A charge des travailleurs indép. ou sans emploi	578	5 642	15 714	14 713	22 160	23 532	25 062	25 735	26 938	28 128
Cotisations effectives	..	5 642	15 714	14 713	22 160	23 532	25 062	25 735	26 938	28 128
2310 Sur la base du salaire	..	..	..	14 713	22 160	23 532	25 062	25 735	26 938	28 128
2320 Sur la base de l'impôt sur les revenus	..	..	..	0	0	0	0	0	0	0
2400 Non-ventilables entre 2100, 2200 et 2300	0	0	0	0	0	0	0	0	0	0
2410 Sur la base du salaire	..	..	..	..	..	..	..	..	..	..
2420 Sur la base de l'impôt sur les revenus	..	..	..	..	..	..	..	..	..	..
3000 Sur salaires ou main d'oeuvre	**1 189**	**3 935**	**8 254**	**14 916**	**22 874**	**24 375**	**25 676**	**27 807**	**29 707**	**33 597**
Taxe sur les salaires	..	2 413	5 208	7 583	10 272	11 239	11 201	11 675	12 094	13 128
Forfait social	..	0	0	0	0	0	314	1 150	2 716	4 654
Taxe d'apprentissage	..	172	101	102	964	1 120	474	459	515	554
Divers contributions directes	..	263	379	551	736	542	1 111	1 498	1 418	1 435
Taxe de formation professionnelle	..	236	30	97	19	23	16	14	17	17
Fonds national d'aide au logement	..	120	754	1 506	2 412	2 383	2 438	2 570	2 663	3 123
Taxe au profit des syndicats de transports	..	731	1 600	3 786	5 738	5 977	6 793	7 358	7 780	8 091
Versement au profit de l'UNEDIC	..	0	23	24	0	0	0	0	0	0
Taxe sur salaires retraités réemployés	..	0	0	0	0	0	0	0	0	0
Cotisation de prévoyance	..	0	0	415	773	735	1 427	1 081	470	515
Autres	..	0	159	851	100	435	6	30	20	29
Caisse nationale de solidarité pour l'autonomie (CNSA)	..	0	0	0	1 860	1 921	1 896	1 972	2 014	2 051
Contribution employeurs pour le FCAATA	..	0	0	0	0	0	0	0	0	0
Taxe exceptionnelle de solidarité sur les hautes rémunérations	..	0	0	0	0	0	0	0	0	0
4000 Impôts sur le patrimoine	**1 105**	**8 591**	**27 434**	**44 070**	**65 318**	**64 726**	**64 429**	**75 043**	**78 882**	**81 099**
4100 Impôts périodiques sur la propriété immobilière	506	5 358	14 808	27 340	39 875	41 666	45 099	49 782	52 184	54 257

Table 50. **France** *(cont.)*
Details of tax revenue / Recettes fiscales détaillées

Million EUR

	1965	1980	1990	2000	2007	2008	2009	2011	2012	2013
4110 Ménages	198	4 454	11 493	20 186	30 584	31 970	34 562	38 110	39 964	41 529
Taxe d'habitation	...	2 306	5 100	8 366	12 433	13 036	14 407	15 894	16 780	17 462
Contributions foncieres (bâti)	...	1 034	4 040	8 460	11 983	12 525	13 647	15 145	15 868	16 541
Taxe d'enlèvement ordures ménagères	...	534	1 219	3 103	5 117	5 370	5 411	5 910	6 101	6 266
Imposition foncier non-bâti	...	506	979	172	851	863	895	917	933	955
Taxe au profit chambre d'agriculture	...	0	0	53	59	59	61	62	62	62
Taxe de balayage	...	0	0	68	74	74	71	75	109	109
Autres	...	74	156	-36	67	43	70	107	111	134
4120 Autres agents	308	904	3 315	7 154	9 291	9 696	10 537	11 672	12 220	12 728
Contribution foncière propriété bâtie	...	759	3 032	6 256	9 054	9 458	10 295	11 425	11 971	12 478
Impositions foncier non-bâti	...	127	245	688	0	0	0	0	0	0
Taxe au profit chambre d'agriculture	...	18	39	210	237	238	242	247	249	250
Autres	...	0	0	0	0	0	0	0	0	0
4200 Impôts périodiques sur l'actif net	0	0	2 615	2 440	4 390	4 155	3 580	4 305	5 030	4 372
4210 Personnes physiques	...	...	938	2 440	4 390	4 155	3 580	4 305	5 030	4 372
4220 Sociétés	...	...	1 677	0	0	0	0	0	0	0
4300 Impôts sur mut. par décès, succ. et donations	145	1 010	4 124	6 907	8 910	7 894	7 462	8 668	9 616	10 456
4310 Impôts sur mut. par décès et successions	140	875	3 490	5 508	7 853	7 111	6 887	7 075	8 225	9 368
Mutations à titre gratuit	...	861	3 453	5 428	7 794	6 996	6 782	6 881	7 596	8 433
Recettes diverses et pénalités	...	14	37	80	59	115	105	194	629	935
4320 Impôts sur les donations	5	135	634	1 399	1 057	783	575	1 593	1 391	1 088
Donations	...	113	568	1 399	1 057	783	575	1 593	1 391	1 088
Recettes diverses et pénalités	...	0	0	0	0	0	0	0	0	0
Autres	...	22	66	0	0	0	0	0	0	0
4400 Impôts sur transact. mobilières et immob.	447	2 224	5 886	7 383	12 143	11 011	8 288	12 288	12 052	12 014
Créances rentes offices	...	30	209	279	443	323	224	358	384	359
Fonds de commerce	...	253	518	199	268	228	135	161	159	135
Meubles corporels	...	14	18	0	0	0	1	1	1	0
Immeubles et droits immobiliers	...	63	4	2	2	0	2	0	0	1
Sociétés	...	95	218	4	5	9	7	7	7	7
Recettes diverses et pénalités	...	35	60	367	179	165	183	260	54	4
Actes judiciaires et extra-judiciaires	...	6	10	0	0	0	0	0	0	0
Taxe de publicité foncière	...	781	38	68	130	151	135	122	161	703
Droits et timbres divers	...	94	242	0	0	0	0	0	0	0
Impôts sur opérations de bourse	...	168	525	407	271	0	0	0	0	0
Taxe sur les transactions financières	...	0	0	0	0	0	0	0	245	697
Taxe additionnelle droits d'enregistrement	...	679	4 002	5 339	10 396	9 691	7 188	10 909	10 489	9 540
Autres droits et recettes	...	5	44	718	449	444	413	470	552	568
4500 Impôts non-périodiques	8	0	0	0	0	0	0	0	0	0
4510 Sur l'actif net	8	...	...	...	...	...	...	...	...	...
4520 Autres non-périodiques	0	...	...	...	...	...	...	...	...	...
4600 Autres impôts périodiques sur patrimoine	0	0	0	0	0	0	0	0	0	0
5000 Impôts sur les biens et services	**9 902**	**54 317**	**123 235**	**166 608**	**206 293**	**208 962**	**203 264**	**221 478**	**227 362**	**231 228**
5100 Impôts sur production, vente, transfert, etc.	9 676	52 719	119 201	162 007	200 452	202 571	197 004	214 729	220 156	224 581
5110 Impôts généraux	5 994	37 760	81 341	110 296	142 033	143 610	136 313	146 489	148 768	150 755
5111 Taxes sur la valeur ajoutée	5 173	37 282	79 972	107 511	137 137	138 378	130 861	141 160	143 168	145 084
TVA (budget général)	...	36 895	78 902	103 054	136 927	137 835	130 303	140 552	142 527	144 301
TVA (BAPSA)	...	62	101	4 111	0	0	0	0	0	0
Autres TVA	...	325	969	0	0	0	0	0	0	0
Sous-compensation TVA agriculture	...	0	0	346	138	333	330	376	406	471
TVA sur subventions	...	0	0	0	72	210	228	232	235	312
5112 Impôts sur les ventes	822	0	0	0	0	0	0	0	0	0
5113 Autres impôts	0	477	1 369	2 784	4 896	5 232	5 452	5 329	5 600	5 671
Contribution sociale de solidarité	...	477	1 369	2 784	4 896	5 232	5 452	5 329	5 600	5 671
5120 Impôts sur biens et services déterminés	3 682	14 960	37 860	51 712	58 419	58 961	60 691	68 240	71 388	73 826

Table 50. **France** *(cont.)*
Details of tax revenue / Recettes fiscales détaillées

Million EUR

	1965	1980	1990	2000	2007	2008	2009	2011	2012	2013
5121 Accises	2 775	11 013	26 834	39 850	44 013	44 226	44 636	48 513	49 656	52 339
Taxe sur les produits pétroliers	..	7 136	17 476	23 493	24 318	23 897	23 547	23 923	23 564	23 691
Prélèv. except. sur entrep. produits pétroliers	..	0	0	0	0	0	0	0	0	0
Droits sur vins, cidres et hydromels	..	97	174	0	121	113	117	122	281	486
Droits sur alcools	..	1 238	1 593	3 025	484	352	2 564	2 987	2 625	2 950
Droits sur bière et eaux minérales	..	58	91	20	409	392	397	395	413	803
Autres droits et recettes	..	136	38	19	2 169	2 163	136	97	103	90
Impôts et taxes sur tabacs et allumettes	..	1 188	2 989	7 965	9 659	9 931	10 295	11 768	12 149	12 227
Amendes et confiscations	..	2	1	0	0	0	0	0	0	0
Garantie matières or et argent	..	6	19	29	2	0	0	0	0	0
Taxes au profit de l'ANDA	..	84	147	89	0	0	0	0	0	0
Taxe sanitaire et d'org. marché des viandes	..	0	0	48	46	43	46	42	40	41
Taxe sur les céréales	..	147	275	19	19	0	18	18	17	14
Redevances débits de tabac	..	0	0	0	0	0	0	0	0	0
Redevances sur sel de potasse	..	0	0	0	0	0	0	0	0	0
Taxe sur les farines	..	0	0	38	0	0	0	0	0	0
Redevances incluses dans prix carburants	..	36	32	453	485	467	489	492	482	499
Taxe au profit du Fonds National du Livre	..	7	17	0	0	0	0	0	0	0
Taxe sur produit exploitations forestières	..	11	0	0	0	0	0	0	0	0
Redevances des mines	..	16	59	43	23	23	25	24	23	22
Taxe sur électricité et chauffage	..	426	1 340	1 061	2 990	3 249	3 390	4 778	5 573	7 255
Surtaxe sur les apéritifs	..	12	17	0	0	0	0	0	0	0
Vignettes pharmaceutiques	..	4	559	0	0	0	0	0	0	0
Taxe sur betterave, sucre et alcool	..	22	400	0	0	0	0	0	0	0
Taxe solidarité sur graines oléagineuses	..	8	41	0	0	0	0	0	0	0
Taxe sur corps gras alimentaires	..	32	89	99	0	0	0	0	0	0
Taxe au profit Caisse Nationale des Lettres	..	23	0	0	0	0	0	0	0	0
Taxe sur consommation eau au profit FNAE	..	34	51	74	5	5	4	7	1	1
Taxe sur les viandes	..	25	36	0	19	2	18	157	278	1
Taxe au profit agences financières de bassin	..	217	609	1 624	1 821	1 959	1 905	2 051	2 212	2 175
Taxe au profit du FIRS (marché du sucre)	..	0	0	0	0	0	0	0	0	0
Contrib. except. pharmacies et laboratoires	..	16	0	522	0	0	0	0	0	0
Taxe locale	..	5	8	241	247	268	303	352	138	127
Contrib. distributeurs énergie élec. au profit du FACE	..	0	0	183	322	344	346	354	349	374
Taxe au profit de l'ADEME	..	0	0	80	212	313	387	479	491	499
Octroi de mer	..	0	0	449	544	587	589	376	378	386
Taxe générale sur les activités polluantes	..	0	0	6	16	12	3	36	123	205
Stocks sur les produits pétroliers	..	0	0	0	0	0	0	0	354	367
Autres	..	30	772	78	102	106	57	55	62	126
Institut français du pétrole (IFP)	..	0	0	193	0	0	0	0	0	0
5122 Bénéfices des monopoles fiscaux	0	0	0	0	0	0	0	0	0	0
5123 Droits de douane et droits à l'importation	471	966	1 669	297	386	374	378	771	655	763
Droits à l'importation (Etat)	..	0	0	0	0	0	0	0	0	0
Droits à l'importation (UE)	..	873	1 623	0	0	0	0	0	0	0
Octroi de mer	..	0	0	267	327	313	299	614	607	627
Autres	..	94	46	30	59	61	79	157	48	136
5124 Taxes à l'exportation	0	75	15	0	0	0	0	0	0	0
Prélèv. agricoles (part de l'Etat)	..	0	0	..	..	..	..	..	..	..
Prélèv. agricoles (part UE)	..	75	15	..	..	..	..	..	..	..
5125 Impôts sur biens d'équipement	0	0	0	0	0	0	0	0	0	0

Table 50. **France** *(cont.)*
Details of tax revenue / Recettes fiscales détaillées

Million EUR

	1965	1980	1990	2000	2007	2008	2009	2011	2012	2013
5126 Impôts sur services déterminés	431	2 690	8 373	11 204	14 007	14 043	15 623	18 902	21 019	20 657
Prélèvements sur le PMU	..	446	545	502	719	672	688	449	429	434
Prélèv. produit jeux et casinos	..	0	0	727	1 022	955	793	760	742	708
Prélèv. sur loterie nationale et loto	..	200	702	1 305	1 982	1 756	1 721	2 143	2 050	1 941
Prélèv. except. sur banque et établ. crédit	..	0	0	0	0	0	0	0	0	0
Taxe sur convention d'assurance	..	1 292	4 782	5 097	6 571	6 769	6 846	8 429	9 826	9 973
Baux enregistrement	..	264	633	573	29	3	-3	-4	0	0
Taxes funéraires	..	11	32	14	11	11	12	11	11	12
Droits de timbre contrat transport	..	9	77	10	0	0	0	0	0	0
Expertises et vérifications techniques	..	0	0	0	0	0	0	0	0	0
Taxe au profit de l'ANAEM	..	0	0	33	58	45	108	141	149	145
Taxe sur l'utilisation des voies navigables	..	0	0	104	157	165	171	175	187	191
Autres taxes diverses	..	98	272	273	449	312	983	947	905	551
Taxes sur les jeux et spectacles	..	75	195	274	372	335	309	788	808	799
Taxe sur fonds de garantie automobile (FGAC)	..	32	135	223	274	306	321	384	372	387
Taxes assurance auto. (Etat + Séc. Soc.)	..	0	0	55	0	0	0	0	0	0
Taxe Fonds National Calamités Agricoles	..	0	0	261	96	96	97	106	114	120
Prélèv. 5% Fonds Nat. Amélioration Habitat	..	114	258	678	604	621	595	619	663	726
Cotisat. des entrep. au Centre Nat. du Cinéma	..	52	207	397	144	148	612	818	733	735
Taxe alimentation au Fonds Assurances Agricoles	..	0	0	0	0	0	0	0	0	0
Taxe au profit du Fonds National Sportif	..	3	0	0	0	0	0	0	0	0
Taxe Fonds de Revalorisation Rentes et Pensions	..	15	0	0	0	0	0	0	0	0
Taxe annuelle sur encours de crédits	..	0	0	0	0	0	0	0	0	0
Taxe sur la publicité	..	0	26	52	38	59	152	190	205	219
Prélèv. sur salaires des conserv. hypothèques	..	67	188	0	0	0	0	0	0	0
Taxe de sécurité et sûreté	..	0	0	220	353	552	450	477	521	521
Taxe de risque systémique	..	0	0	0	0	0	0	495	1 026	898
Taxe sur les mutuelles au profit de la CMU	..	0	0	247	560	396	1 566	1 735	1 862	1 851
Taxe au profit du FPRNM (Fonds de prévention des risques naturels majeurs)	..	0	0	0	0	0	0	0	193	197
Autres	..	10	320	159	568	842	202	239	223	249
5127 Autres impôts sur commerce et transact. internat.	0	0	0	0	0	0	0	0	0	0
5128 Autres impôts	5	215	970	360	13	318	54	54	58	67
Taxe de co-responsabilité sur le lait	..	48	119	0	0	0	0	0	0	0
Taxe de co-responsabilité sur les céréales	..	0	520	0	0	0	0	0	0	0
Prélèvement pour la CECA	..	14	0	0	0	0	0	0	0	0
Receveur des douanes	..	9	24	0	0	0	0	0	0	0
Divers (collect. locales)	..	0	0	0	0	0	0	0	0	0
Cotisations sur les sucres	..	68	185	270	0	305	41	41	45	54
Taxe au profit du FIRS (marché du sucre)	..	76	120	76	0	0	0	0	0	0
Autres	..	0	2	14	13	13	13	13	13	13
5130 Non-ventilables entre 5110 et 5120	0	0	0	0	0	0	0	0	0	0
5200 Impôts sur utilisation des biens et exerc. activités	226	1 598	4 034	4 601	5 841	6 391	6 260	6 749	7 206	6 647
5210 Impôts périodiques	178	1 226	3 024	2 810	3 009	3 108	2 821	2 888	3 139	2 849
5211 A la charge des ménages : véhicules à moteur	27	545	1 236	126	0	0	0	0	0	0
Taxe différentielle (budget gén. et collect. loc.)	..	545	1 236	126	0	0	0	0	0	0
5212 A la charge autres agents : véhicules à moteur	79	545	1 086	1 280	1 559	1 505	1 376	1 215	1 255	1 181
Taxe sur les véhicules des sociétés	..	197	345	644	891	1 086	1 098	927	983	876
Taxe sur les véhicules (budg. gén. et coll. loc.)	..	348	741	636	668	419	278	288	272	305
5213 Autres impôts périodiques	72	136	702	1 404	1 450	1 603	1 445	1 673	1 884	1 668
Taxe spéciale usage des routes	..	0	0	420	526	521	528	612	570	573
Droit de pesage	..	17	14	0	0	0	0	0	0	0
Divers taxes (collectivités locales)	..	7	33	0	0	0	0	0	0	0
Taxe magnétoscopes	..	0	0	0	0	0	0	0	0	0
Redev. pour surveillance centrales nucléaires	..	8	41	0	0	0	0	0	0	0
Taxe d'usage des abattoirs	..	19	13	0	0	0	0	0	0	0
Contrib. des entrepr. à la prépa. médicaments	..	0	20	238	0	429	284	362	318	213
Taxe sur les pylones électriques	..	1	66	128	183	190	190	223	233	244
Licence débit de boisson	..	8	22	23	0	2	0	0	0	0
Droit annuel de francisation et de navigation	..	0	0	0	0	37	37	39	37	37
Redevances d'usage des fréquences radioélectriques	..	0	0	191	280	268	244	177	325	262
Autres	..	75	493	404	461	156	162	260	401	339

Table 50. **France** *(cont.)*
Details of tax revenue / Recettes fiscales détaillées

Million EUR

	1965	1980	1990	2000	2007	2008	2009	2011	2012	2013
5220 Impôts non-périodiques	47	372	1 010	1 791	2 832	3 283	3 439	3 861	4 067	3 798
Récépissés de mise en circulation	..	75	0	0	0	0	0	0	0	0
Taxes et licences débits de boissons	..	0	0	3	0	0	0	0	0	0
Redevance pour droit de construire	..	79	53	72	0	68	1	18	18	18
Taxe locale d'équipement	..	146	263	305	848	928	1 239	1 483	1 614	1 379
Taxe sur les certificats d'immatriculation des véhicules	..	0	0	1 373	1 939	1 968	1 917	2 080	2 117	2 042
Dépassement plafond légal de densité	..	38	270	38	45	94	82	82	82	82
Taxe additionnelle sur certif. d'immatric. des véhicules	..	0	0	0	0	225	200	198	236	277
Autres	..	35	423	0	0	0	0	0	0	0
5300 Non-ventilables entre 5100 et 5200	0	0	0	0	0	0	0	0	0	0
6000 Autres impôts	**681**	**5 480**	**14 060**	**23 964**	**27 227**	**26 723**	**27 408**	**23 946**	**22 844**	**22 829**
6100 A la charge exclusive des entreprises	678	5 480	14 060	22 278	27 219	26 701	27 383	23 940	22 838	22 823
Taxes au profit de l'INPI	..	43	67	115	156	165	160	170	171	180
Taxe sur les frais généraux	..	0	0	0	0	0	0	0	0	0
Taxe professionnelle	..	5 152	13 381	19 641	22 035	21 100	21 885	0	0	0
Taxe des prestations des syndicats (collect. loc.)	..	36	197	293	0	0	0	0	0	0
Taxes diverses (budget gén. et org. div. adm. cent.)	..	0	0	61	236	254	219	232	293	310
Taxe annuelle sur les encours de crédits	..	110	0	0	0	0	0	0	0	0
Prélèv. except. sur entreprises d'assurances	..	0	0	0	0	0	0	0	0	0
Produit de l'imposition (Chambre des Métiers)	..	36	125	155	203	205	217	187	205	232
Contribution au FNE	..	4	240	204	33	35	12	4	4	3
Autres	..	98	50	1 007	3 721	3 938	3 824	2 212	1 182	951
Taxe ANDA - ADAR	..	0	0	32	0	0	0	0	0	0
Cotisation foncière des entreprises	..	0	0	0	0	0	0	5 160	5 465	5 897
Cotisation sur la valeur ajoutée des entreprises	..	0	0	0	0	0	0	11 703	12 584	12 132
Imposition forfaitaire sur les entreprises de réseaux	..	0	0	0	0	0	0	1 085	1 142	1 217
Exit taxe sur les assurances	..	0	0	0	0	0	0	1 670	0	0
Produit imposition Chambre de Commerce	..	0	0	770	835	784	937	1 180	1 328	1 321
Contribution patronale sur stock-options	..	0	0	0	0	220	129	262	309	380
Taxe sur le résultat des entreprises ferroviaires	..	0	0	0	0	0	0	75	155	200
6200 A la charge d'autres agents	3	0	0	1 686	8	22	25	6	6	6
Autres	..	..	..	1 686	8	22	25	6	6	6
Ecart aux comptes de secteurs	..	..	..	0	0	0	0	0	0	0
Droits de douane perçus pour l'UE	..	..	..	**1 513**	**1 657**	**1 615**	**1 461**	**1 866**	**1 883**	**1 842**
Crédits d'impôts récupérables										
Crédits d'impôts récupérables contre 1110	..	..	..	0	7 663	9 689	10 966	9 750	9 030	8 092
Composante fiscale	..	..	..	..	..	..	..	..	..	..
Composante transfert	..	..	..	..	..	..	..	..	..	..
Crédits d'impôts récupérables contre 1210	..	..	..	457	1 860	2 667	7 633	5 180	5 563	5 548
Composante fiscale	..	..	..	..	..	..	..	..	..	..
Composante transfert	..	..	..	..	..	..	..	..	..	..
Recettes fiscales totales sur la base d'encaissements	**25 776**	**178 576**	**433 771**	**639 427**	**824 688**	**841 927**	**801 266**	**882 663**	**920 908**	**953 123**
Recettes fiscales totales sur la base des droits constatés	..	..	..	**643 309**	**828 971**	**846 614**	**806 916**	**888 970**	**925 905**	**960 166**
Conciliation avec les comptes nationaux										
Impôts additionnels inclus dans les comptes nationaux	..	..	..	0	0	0	0	0	0	0
Impôt exclus des comptes nationaux	..	..	..	-3 171	-5 191	-5 444	-5 482	-5 985	-6 210	-6 375
Taxe d'enlèvement des ordures ménagères	..	..	..	-3 103	-5 117	-5 370	-5 411	-5 910	-6 101	-6 266
Taxe sur les pylônes	..	..	..	0	0	0	0	0	0	0
Taxe de balayage	..	..	..	-68	-74	-74	-71	-75	-109	-109
Différence dans les traitements des crédits d'impôts	..	..	..	0	0	0	0	0	0	0
Transfert en capital des recettes non collectées	..	..	..	-3 882	-4 283	-4 687	-5 650	-6 307	-4 997	-7 043
Cotisations de sécurité sociale volontaires	..	..	..	0	0	0	0	0	0	0
Différences diverses	..	..	..	0	0	0	0	0	0	0
Comptes nationaux: impôts et cotisations sociales effectives	..	..	..	636 256	819 497	836 483	795 784	876 678	914 698	946 748
Cotisations sociales imputées	..	..	..	25 875	33 510	34 875	36 723	39 560	40 980	41 961
Comptes nationaux: impôts et toutes les cotisations sociales	..	..	..	662 131	853 007	871 358	832 507	916 238	955 678	988 709

Note:

Année civile se terminant le 31 décembre.

A partir de 1992, les données sont sur la base des droits constatés.

A partir de 1970 les chiffres ont été calculés selon le nouveau Système de Comptes Nationaux et ne sont pas, de ce fait, comparables à ceux des années précédentes.

La rubrique 2000 comprend certaines contributions volontaires.

La rubrique 4220 correspond à la rémunération de la garantie de l'État accordée aux caisses d'épargne.

Source: Compte général de l'Administration des finances pour les chiffres de recettes fiscales. OSCE pour les chiffres de sécurité sociale de 1965 à 1969 et SEC pourles années suivantes.

StatLink http://dx.doi.org/10.1787/888933277128

Table 51. **Germany / Allemagne**
Details of tax revenue / Recettes fiscales détaillées

Million EUR

	1965	1980	1990	2000	2007	2008	2009	2011	2012	2013
Total tax revenue	**74 190**	**287 252**	**454 764**	**767 045**	**876 839**	**907 008**	**887 885**	**964 932**	**1 002 246**	**1 030 305**
Total tax revenue exclusive of customs duties	..	..	..	**763 651**	**872 867**	**902 972**	**884 107**	**960 376**	**997 829**	**1 026 054**
1000 Taxes on income, profits and capital gains	**25 059**	**100 821**	**147 257**	**231 249**	**273 596**	**288 808**	**256 478**	**284 168**	**304 598**	**319 389**
1100 Of individuals	19 254	85 134	125 296	194 173	218 848	240 294	223 325	238 747	257 122	268 856
1110 On income and profits	19 254	85 134	125 296	194 173	218 848	240 294	223 325	238 747	257 122	268 856
Taxes on wages and salaries	8 558	57 039	90 801	135 733	146 365	156 109	150 423	155 518	165 122	173 668
Assessed income tax	7 567	18 813	18 672	12 225	25 341	32 986	30 675	32 577	37 777	42 896
Withholding tax on dividends	691	2 135	5 538	13 515	13 572	15 640	11 850	18 136	20 060	17 258
Supplementary tax	0	0	0	10 347	10 907	11 678	11 245	11 660	12 479	13 083
Enterprise tax	2 438	7 147	10 285	16 486	14 630	14 966	11 824	15 623	16 256	16 518
Stabilisation tax	0	0	0	0	0	0	0	0	0	0
Withholding tax on interest	0	0	0	5 867	8 033	8 915	7 308	5 233	5 428	5 433
1120 On capital gains	0	0	0	0	0	0	0	0	0	0
1200 Corporate	5 806	15 686	21 961	37 076	54 748	48 514	33 153	45 421	47 476	50 533
1210 On profits	5 806	15 686	21 961	37 076	54 748	48 514	33 153	45 421	47 476	50 533
Corporation tax	4 177	10 902	15 385	23 575	23 386	16 374	7 864	16 348	17 250	19 762
Supplementary tax	0	20	1	1 494	1 550	1 269	758	1 170	1 215	1 337
Sacrifice for Berlin	3	0	0	0	0	0	0	0	0	0
Enterprise tax	1 625	4 765	6 576	10 540	25 486	26 071	20 597	25 085	26 089	26 508
Stabilisation tax	0	0	0	0	0	0	0	0	0	0
Withholding tax on interest	0	0	0	1 467	4 326	4 800	3 934	2 818	2 922	2 926
1220 On capital gains	0	0	0	0	0	0	0	0	0	0
1300 Unallocable between 1100 and 1200	0	0	0	0	0	0	0	0	0	0
2000 Social security contributions	**19 876**	**98 659**	**170 449**	**299 440**	**320 594**	**330 453**	**342 658**	**372 040**	**383 487**	**392 548**
2100 Employees	8 723	43 833	73 580	131 610	141 079	144 182	150 578	164 966	170 562	174 334
Payments by employees total	8 723	43 833	73 580	131 610	141 079	144 182	150 578	164 966	170 562	174 334
2110 On a payroll basis	...	...	...	131 610	141 079	144 182	150 578	164 966	170 562	174 334
2120 On an income tax basis	...	...	...	0	0	0	0	0	0	0
2200 Employers	10 693	52 985	86 659	147 410	152 198	155 468	160 936	173 794	179 856	184 429
Payments by employers total	10 693	52 985	86 659	147 410	152 198	155 468	160 936	173 794	179 856	184 429
2210 On a payroll basis	...	...	...	147 410	152 198	155 468	160 936	173 794	179 856	184 429
2220 On an income tax basis	...	...	...	0	0	0	0	0	0	0
2300 Self-employed or non-employed	460	1 841	10 210	20 420	27 317	30 803	31 144	33 280	33 069	33 785
Payments total	460	1 841	10 210	20 420	27 317	30 803	31 144	33 280	33 069	33 785
2310 On a payroll basis	...	...	...	20 420	27 317	30 803	31 144	33 280	33 069	33 785
2320 On an income tax basis	...	...	...	0	0	0	0	0	0	0
2400 Unallocable between 2100, 2200 and 2300	0	0	0	0	0	0	0	0	0	0
2410 On a payroll basis	...	...	...	...	...	...	...	...	...	...
2420 On an income tax basis	...	...	...	...	...	...	...	...	...	...
3000 Taxes on payroll and workforce	**477**	**445**	**0**	**0**	**0**	**0**	**0**	**0**	**0**	**0**
Payroll tax	477	445	...	...	...	...	...	...	...	...
4000 Taxes on property	**4 313**	**9 414**	**15 321**	**17 505**	**21 873**	**21 300**	**20 350**	**22 874**	**24 404**	**25 925**
4100 Recurrent taxes on immovable property	1 079	2 968	4 461	8 849	10 713	10 807	10 936	11 674	12 017	12 377
4110 Households	644	1 187	1 784	3 540	4 285	4 323	4 374	4 670	4 807	4 951
4120 Others	435	1 780	2 676	5 309	6 428	6 484	6 562	7 004	7 210	7 426
4200 Recurrent taxes on net wealth	2 530	4 362	6 213	433	5	-7	7	588	693	521
4210 Individual	973	977	1 425	191	2	-3	3	-2	0	0
General wealth tax	471	954	1 425	191	2	-3	3	-2	0	0
Equalization of war burden	502	23	0	0	0	0	0	0	0	0
4220 Corporate	1 557	3 385	4 788	242	3	-4	4	590	693	521
General wealth tax	490	1 431	1 813	242	3	-4	4	-2	-1	0
Equalization of war burden	350	15	0	0	0	0	0	0	0	0
Enterprise tax	717	1 939	2 975	0	0	0	0	0	0	0
Bank levy	0	0	0	0	0	0	0	592	694	521
4300 Estate, inheritance and gift taxes	162	520	1 545	2 982	4 203	4 772	4 550	4 246	4 305	4 633
4310 Estate and inheritance taxes	134	416	1 359	2 624	3 699	4 199	4 004	3 736	3 788	4 077
4320 Gift taxes	28	104	186	358	504	573	546	510	517	556
4400 Taxes on financial and capital transactions	542	1 564	3 103	5 241	6 952	5 728	4 857	6 366	7 389	8 394
Real property transfer tax	150	521	1 999	5 081	6 952	5 728	4 857	6 366	7 389	8 394
Additional real property transfer	198	680	148	160	0	0	0	0	0	0
Capital transfer tax	111	200	807	0	0	0	0	0	0	0
Bill of exchange tax	83	163	149	0	0	0	0	0	0	0
4500 Non-recurrent taxes	0	0	0	0	0	0	0	0	0	0
4510 On net wealth	...	...	...	...	...	...	...	...	...	...
4520 Other non-recurrent taxes	...	...	...	...	...	...	...	...	...	...
4600 Other recurrent taxes on property	0	0	0	0	0	0	0	0	0	0
5000 Taxes on goods and services	**24 462**	**77 863**	**121 577**	**215 292**	**256 708**	**262 314**	**264 523**	**281 180**	**285 221**	**288 064**
5100 Taxes on production, sale, transfer, etc	23 079	74 406	117 209	208 050	247 547	253 205	254 971	271 046	274 219	277 659
5110 General taxes	12 235	47 779	75 459	140 871	170 387	176 188	178 020	190 229	194 353	197 326
5111 Value added taxes	0	47 779	75 459	140 871	170 387	176 188	178 020	190 229	194 353	197 326

Table 51. **Germany / Allemagne** *(cont.)*
Details of tax revenue / Recettes fiscales détaillées

Million EUR

	1965	1980	1990	2000	2007	2008	2009	2011	2012	2013
5112 Sales tax	0	0	0	0	0	0	0	0	0	0
5113 Other	12 235	0	0	0	0	0	0	0	0	0
Turnover tax old	11 028	..	..	..	..	..	..	..	..	..
Old turnover tax on import	1 208	..	..	..	..	..	..	..	..	..
5120 Taxes on specific goods and services	10 844	26 627	41 750	67 179	76 808	76 637	76 587	80 501	79 582	80 049
5121 Excises	8 213	20 566	31 158	57 224	63 811	63 583	63 684	66 343	64 868	64 624
Duty on mineral oils	3 798	10 917	17 701	37 826	38 877	39 415	39 693	40 279	39 351	39 260
Duty on power	0	0	0	3 356	6 439	6 262	6 251	7 278	6 970	6 987
Duty on tobacco	2 402	5 771	8 898	11 443	14 108	13 588	13 503	14 455	14 249	14 131
Duty on alcohol	771	1 986	2 162	2 151	2 169	2 121	2 042	2 144	2 097	2 098
Duty on beer	501	645	693	843	750	744	730	702	690	675
Duty on coffee	488	756	986	1 087	1 016	1 002	1 007	1 021	1 046	1 033
Duty on sugar	59	72	79	0	0	0	0	0	0	0
Duty on tea	16	32	31	0	0	0	0	0	0	0
Duty on salt	20	20	23	0	0	0	0	0	0	0
Duty on electric lamps	34	63	83	0	0	0	0	0	0	0
Duty on playing cards	2	4	0	0	0	0	0	0	0	0
Duty on beverages	46	22	8	6	1	1	0	0	0	0
Duty on acetic acid	3	2	0	0	0	0	0	0	0	0
Duty on champagne	69	274	494	512	451	450	458	464	465	440
Duty on matches	5	2	0	0	0	0	0	0	0	0
Duty on ice cream	1	0	0	0	0	0	0	0	0	0
5122 Profits of fiscal monopolies	8	2	0	0	0	0	0	0	0	0
5123 Customs and import duties	1 658	3 125	3 847	0	0	0	0	0	0	0
Monetary compensation accounts	0	368	1	..	..	..	..	..	..	..
Customs (mainly EU)	1 294	2 353	3 662	..	..	..	..	..	..	..
Agricultural levies EU	364	404	184	..	..	..	..	..	..	..
5124 Taxes on exports	0	0	0	0	0	0	0	0	0	0
5125 Taxes on investment goods	0	0	0	0	0	0	0	0	0	0
5126 Taxes on specific services	942	2 689	6 443	9 599	13 025	12 834	12 864	14 120	14 663	15 359
Duty transport goods on residents	0	0	0	0	0	0	0	0	0	0
Transport tax	452	0	0	0	0	0	0	0	0	0
Insurance tax	198	910	2 266	7 243	10 410	10 476	10 555	10 767	11 165	11 588
Fire insurance tax	33	124	200	288	319	327	323	365	380	392
Entertainment tax	55	44	140	267	210	260	302	480	617	708
Taxes on betting and gambling	204	655	1 046	1 801	1 702	1 536	1 511	1 420	1 432	1 635
Tax on electricity bills	0	956	2 792	0	0	0	0	0	0	0
Aviation tax	0	0	0	0	0	0	0	959	954	955
Gaming casinos levy	0	0	0	0	384	235	173	129	115	81
5127 Other taxes on internat. trade and transactions	0	0	4	5	1	2	3	2	2	2
5128 Other taxes	24	244	298	351	-29	218	36	36	49	64
Levies CECA	24	56	36	0	0	0	0	0	0	0
Cotisation sugar EU	0	112	224	351	-29	218	36	36	49	64
Levy on milk	0	75	38	0	0	0	0	0	0	0
5130 Unallocable between 5110 and 5120	0	0	0	0	352	380	364	316	284	284
Contributions to the German National Petroleum Stockpiling Agency	..	..	..	..	352	380	364	316	284	284
5200 Taxes on use of goods and perform activities	1 383	3 457	4 368	7 242	9 161	9 109	9 552	10 134	11 002	10 405
5210 Recurrent taxes	1 369	3 454	4 368	7 239	9 161	9 109	8 470	9 481	10 474	10 084
5211 Paid by households: motor vehicles	614	1 892	2 950	5 177	6 823	6 779	6 288	6 404	6 405	6 393
5212 Paid by others: motor vehicles	728	1 475	1 300	1 838	2 075	2 063	1 913	2 018	2 037	2 097
5213 Paid in respect of other goods	27	87	118	224	263	267	269	1 059	2 032	1 594
Dog taxes	24	75	101	198	240	244	247	275	288	299
Hunting and fishing taxes	4	13	17	26	23	23	22	16	13	10
Nuclear fuel tax	0	0	0	0	0	0	0	768	1 731	1 285
5220 Non-recurrent taxes	14	3	1	3	0	0	1 082	653	528	321
Non-recurrent taxes	..	..	..	..	..	..	0	0	0	0
CO2 emission certificates	..	..	..	..	..	..	1 082	653	528	321
5300 Unallocable between 5100 and 5200	0	0	0	0	0	0	0	0	0	0
6000 Other taxes	**4**	**51**	**160**	**165**	**96**	**97**	**98**	**114**	**119**	**128**
6100 Paid solely by business	0	0	0	0	0	0	0	0	0	0
6200 Other	4	51	160	165	96	97	98	114	119	128
Custom duties collected for the EU	..	..	..	**3 394**	**3 972**	**4 036**	**3 778**	**4 556**	**4 417**	**4 251**
Non-wastable tax credits										
Non-wastable tax credits against 1110	..	..	..	38 356	43 602	41 849	45 035	43 647	42 802	41 890
Tax expenditure component	..	..	..	..	29 499	28 071	28 466	27 939	27 548	27 120
Transfer component	..	..	..	..	14 104	13 779	16 569	15 708	15 254	14 772
Non-wastable tax credits against 1210	..	..	..	962	804	876	1 106	594	540	426
Tax expenditure component	..	..	..	..	348	370	414	238	224	172
Transfer component	..	..	..	..	456	506	690	356	316	254

Table 51. **Germany / Allemagne** *(cont.)*
Details of tax revenue / Recettes fiscales détaillées

Million EUR

	1965	1980	1990	2000	2007	2008	2009	2011	2012	2013
Total tax revenue on cash basis	**74 190**	**287 252**	**454 764**	**767 045**	**874 109**	**906 717**	**888 746**	**964 168**	**1 000 995**	**1 029 007**
Total tax revenue on accrual basis	..	..	..	..	**876 839**	**907 008**	**887 885**	**964 932**	**1 002 246**	**1 030 305**
Conciliation with National Accounts										
Additional taxes included in National Accounts	..	..	..	..	2 348	2 419	2 096	2 244	2 280	2 356
Several duties, administrative fees and other revenues	..	..	..	..	2 348	2 419	2 096	2 244	2 280	2 356
Taxes excluded from National Accounts	..	..	..	..	0	0	0	0	0	0
Difference in treatment of tax credits	..	..	..	..	12 623	11 120	11 019	8 433	7 452	6 701
Capital transfer for uncollected revenue	..	..	..	..	0	0	0	0	0	0
Voluntary social security contributions	..	..	..	..	20 930	20 734	7 763	6 237	6 913	7 353
Miscellaneous differences	..	..	..	..	33 538	31 629	33 923	31 110	31 090	31 928
National Accounts: Taxes and actual social contributions	..	..	..	..	946 278	972 910	942 686	1 012 956	1 049 981	1 078 643
Imputed social contributions	..	..	..	..	29 424	30 175	31 400	32 827	32 909	33 511
National Accounts: Taxes and all social contributions	..	..	..	..	975 702	1 003 085	974 086	1 045 783	1 082 890	1 112 154

Note:

Year ending 31st December.

From 2002 data are on accrual basis.

The tax revenues for Germany refer to the old Länder until 1990 and to all Germany beginning in 1991.

Heading 1000: In the years up to 2000, the revenues shown take into account the whole amount of non-wastable tax credits including that part paid out by the tax authorities which should, under the OECD criteria, be treated as expenditure. From 2001, the data necessary to make the adjustment have become available and the revenue figures comply with the OECD criteria from that year. The impact of this change is shown in Table D in Part I of this Report.

Heading for non-wastable tax credits against 1110 comprise child tax credits (paid out of wage tax revenue), tax credits for owner occupied housing (paid out of assessed income tax revenue) and investment tax credits for unincorporated businesses (for investment in former East Germany; paid out of assessed income tax revenue).

Heading for non-wastable tax credits against 1210 are investment tax credits for incorporated businesses (for investment in former East Germany; paid out of corporate income tax revenue).

Source: Finanzbericht, Bonn; Tax Statistics. Unpublished estimates by the Ministry of Finance.

StatLink http://dx.doi.org/10.1787/888933277130

Table 52. **Greece / Grèce**
Details of tax revenue / Recettes fiscales détaillées

Million EUR

	1965	1980	1990	2000	2007	2008	2009	2011	2012	2013
Total tax revenue	**116**	**1 475**	**11 472**	**47 178**	**72 565**	**74 960**	**73 145**	**69 686**	**67 087**	**62 804**
Total tax revenue exclusive of custom duties	..	..	..	**46 968**	**72 258**	**74 655**	**72 893**	**69 500**	**66 925**	**62 656**
1000 Taxes on income, profits and capital gains	**11**	**286**	**2 283**	**12 664**	**16 890**	**17 432**	**17 693**	**14 793**	**16 048**	**13 795**
1100 Of individuals	8	220	1 619	6 827	10 821	11 284	11 528	10 019	13 572	11 084
1110 On income and profits	8	220	1 619	6 802	10 767	11 226	11 469	9 954	13 500	11 000
Personal income tax	..	..	1 414	6 802	..	..	..	..	..	..
Receipts from previous years	..	..	62	0	..	..	..	..	..	..
Agricultural social security fund	..	..	143	0	..	..	..	..	..	..
1120 On capital gains	0	0	0	25	54	58	59	65	72	84
1200 Corporate	2	56	631	5 642	5 704	5 875	5 960	4 589	2 314	2 429
1210 On profits	2	56	631	5 642	5 704	5 875	5 960	4 589	2 314	2 429
Corporation income tax	2	39	553	5 642	..	..	..	..	..	..
Receipts from previous years	0	8	33	0	..	..	..	..	..	..
Agricultural social security fund	0	9	46	0	..	..	..	..	..	..
1220 On capital gains	0	0	0	0	0	0	0	0	0	0
1300 Unallocable between 1100 and 1200	1	10	32	195	365	273	205	185	162	282
Extraordinary taxes	0	10	32	0	..	..	..	..	..	..
Other taxes on income and profits	1	0	0	195	..	..	..	..	..	..
2000 Social security contributions	**37**	**485**	**3 466**	**14 299**	**24 941**	**25 985**	**24 453**	**22 410**	**20 988**	**19 542**
2100 Employees	15	214	1 735	5 608	9 428	9 798	9 797	8 918	8 402	7 942
2110 On a payroll basis	..	..	..	..	..	..	..	..	..	..
2120 On an income tax basis	..	..	..	..	..	..	..	..	..	..
2200 Employers	14	213	1 728	6 664	11 516	12 207	11 044	9 928	9 270	8 473
2210 On a payroll basis	..	..	..	..	..	..	..	..	..	..
2220 On an income tax basis	..	..	..	..	..	..	..	..	..	..
2300 Self-employed or non-employed	0	0	3	2 027	3 997	3 980	3 612	3 564	3 316	3 127
2310 On a payroll basis	..	..	..	..	..	..	..	..	..	..
2320 On an income tax basis	..	..	..	..	..	..	..	..	..	..
2400 Unallocable between 2100, 2200 and 2300	7	58	0	0	0	0	0	0	0	0
2410 On a payroll basis	..	..	..	..	..	..	..	..	..	..
2420 On an income tax basis	..	..	..	..	..	..	..	..	..	..
3000 Taxes on payroll and workforce	**1**	**27**	**79**	**0**	**0**	**0**	**0**	**0**	**0**	**0**
4000 Taxes on property	**11**	**68**	**532**	**2 875**	**3 861**	**4 089**	**4 526**	**4 853**	**4 853**	**4 759**
4100 Recurrent taxes on immovable property	0	4	22	236	367	424	793	2 226	2 476	2 314
4110 Households	0	3	22	..	..	..	..	..	..	..
4120 Others	0	1	0	..	..	..	..	..	..	..
Taxes on immovable property	0	0	..	..	..	..	..	..	..	..
4200 Recurrent taxes on net wealth	0	0	0	65	488	496	1 294	1 255	1 224	1 081
4210 Individual	..	..	..	..	..	..	..	..	..	..
4220 Corporate	..	..	..	..	..	..	..	..	..	..
4300 Estate, inheritance and gift taxes	1	18	141	372	224	149	147	123	92	99
4310 Estate and inheritance taxes	1	13	85	..	..	..	..	..	..	..
4320 Gift taxes	0	4	55	..	..	..	..	..	..	..
4400 Taxes on financial and capital transactions	10	44	368	2 049	2 550	2 653	1 938	880	749	622
Stamp and transaction taxes	10	41	368	2 049	2 550	2 653	1 938	880	749	622
Receipts from previous years	0	3	0	0	0	0	0	0	0	0
4500 Non-recurrent taxes	0	2	1	0	0	0	0	0	0	0
4510 On net wealth	0	0	0	..	..	..	..	..	..	..
4520 Other non-recurrent taxes	0	2	1	..	..	..	..	..	..	..
4600 Other recurrent taxes on property	0	0	0	153	232	367	354	369	312	643
5000 Taxes on goods and services	**57**	**608**	**5 109**	**17 130**	**26 566**	**27 149**	**26 221**	**27 444**	**25 036**	**24 560**
5100 Taxes on production, sale, transfer, etc	51	564	4 881	15 576	24 332	24 890	22 950	24 984	22 701	21 766
5110 General taxes	12	194	3 040	10 128	17 253	18 102	15 699	15 837	14 356	13 284
5111 Value added taxes	0	0	2 821	9 824	16 611	17 020	14 876	15 021	13 712	12 594
5112 Sales tax	9	185	123	36	147	360	348	286	155	183
5113 Other	2	9	96	268	495	722	475	530	489	507
Other taxes on goods and services	1	9	34	268	495	722	475	530	489	507
Receipts from previous years	1	0	62	0	0	0	0	0	0	0
5120 Taxes on specific goods and services	39	370	1 789	5 405	6 972	6 698	7 166	8 684	7 885	7 980
5121 Excises	20	165	1 372	4 178	5 748	5 391	5 956	7 740	7 022	6 822
Duty on tobacco products	8	45	357	1 764	2 650	2 385	2 797	3 052	2 443	2 500
Duty on alcohol and spirits	1	7	50	252	353	323	369	467	421	418
Duty on mineral oil	7	75	637	2 151	2 739	2 680	2 784	4 027	3 973	3 725
Duty on sugar	3	6	0	0	0	0	0	0	0	0
Duty on coton and other products	0	30	328	11	6	3	6	194	185	179
5122 Profits of fiscal monopolies	2	6	0	0	0	0	0	0	0	0
5123 Customs and import duties	12	94	112	-7	7	2	1	2	0	0
Import duties	11	90	111	-7	7	2	1	2	0	0
Agricultural social security fund	1	5	1	0	0	0	0	0	0	0
5124 Taxes on exports	0	1	1	5	0	0	0	0	0	0

Table 52. **Greece / Grèce** *(cont.)*
Details of tax revenue / Recettes fiscales détaillées

Million EUR

	1965	1980	1990	2000	2007	2008	2009	2011	2012	2013
5125 Taxes on investment goods	0	0	0	0	0	0	0	0	0	0
5126 Taxes on specific services	2	47	293	1 229	1 217	1 305	1 209	942	863	1 158
5127 Other taxes on internat. trade and transactions	0	0	0	0	0	0	0	0	0	0
5128 Other taxes	4	58	10	0	0	0	0	0	0	0
Agricultural social security fund	2	..	..	..	..	..	..	..	..	..
Other taxes	2	..	..	..	..	..	..	..	..	..
5130 Unallocable between 5110 and 5120	0	0	52	43	107	90	85	463	460	502
5200 Taxes on use of goods and perform activities	6	44	228	1 254	2 146	2 163	2 308	1 671	1 728	2 357
5210 Recurrent taxes	5	24	219	1 254	2 146	2 163	2 308	1 671	1 728	2 357
Motor vehicle tax	5	0	..	..	..	..	..	..	..	..
5211 Paid by households: motor vehicles	..	23	210	227	606	737	1 129	872	978	1 430
5212 Paid by others: motor vehicles	..	0	8	750	1 190	1 016	696	155	107	119
5213 Paid in respect of other goods	0	1	1	277	350	410	483	644	643	808
Taxes on boats/ships	0	0	1	0	..	..	..	..	..	..
5220 Non-recurrent taxes	1	20	9	0	0	0	0	0	0	0
Exceptional tax on construction of buildings	0	..	9	..	..	..	..	..	..	..
Building permits	0	..	0	..	..	..	..	..	..	..
5300 Unallocable between 5100 and 5200	0	0	0	300	88	96	963	789	607	437
6000 Other taxes	**0**	**1**	**3**	**0**	**0**	**0**	**0**	**0**	**0**	**0**
6100 Paid solely by business	..	0	0	..	..	..	..	..	..	..
6200 Other	..	1	3	..	..	..	..	..	..	..
Custom duties collected for the EU	..	..	..	**210**	**307**	**305**	**252**	**186**	**162**	**148**
Total tax revenue on cash basis	**116**	**1 475**	**11 472**	**46 548**	**72 311**	**75 709**	**71 824**	**68 074**	**67 062**	**62 411**
Total tax revenue on accrual basis	..	..	..	**47 178**	**72 565**	**74 960**	**73 145**	**69 686**	**67 087**	**62 804**
Conciliation with National Accounts										
Additional taxes included in National Accounts	..	..	..	0	0	0	0	0	0	0
Taxes excluded from National Accounts	..	..	..	0	0	0	0	0	0	0
Difference in treatment of tax credits	..	..	..	0	0	0	0	0	0	0
Capital transfer for uncollected revenue	..	..	..	-61	0	0	0	0	0	0
Tax (Employer's actual social contributions)	..	..	..	-30	..	..	..	..	..	..
Tax (Employee's actual social contributions)	..	..	..	-31	..	..	..	..	..	..
Voluntary social security contributions	..	..	..	0	0	0	0	0	0	0
Miscellaneous differences	..	..	..	0	0	0	0	0	0	0
National Accounts: Taxes and actual social contributions	..	..	..	47 117	72 565	74 960	73 145	69 686	67 087	62 804
Imputed social contributions	..	..	..	2 690	4 021	4 764	5 202	5 134	5 486	4 972
National Accounts: Taxes and all social contributions	..	..	..	49 807	76 586	79 724	78 347	74 820	72 573	67 776

Note:

Year ending 31st December.

From 1998 data are on accrual basis.

Source: Ministry of Finance, General accounting Office, 20th Directorate of Budget except the heading 2000 provided by the National Statistics Bureau.

StatLink http://dx.doi.org/10.1787/888933277147

Table 53. **Hungary / Hongrie**
Details of tax revenue / Recettes fiscales détaillées

Million HUF

	1965	1980	1990	2000	2007	2008	2009	2011	2012	2013
Total tax revenue	..	..	..	**5 140 592**	**10 077 488**	**10 653 379**	**10 213 265**	**10 245 857**	**11 017 213**	**11 452 701**
Total tax revenue exclusive of custom duties	..	..	..	..	**10 049 508**	**10 626 690**	**10 187 608**	**10 218 395**	**10 990 007**	**11 426 364**
1000 Taxes on income, profits and capital gains	..	..	..	**1 247 420**	**2 539 389**	**2 767 798**	**2 507 179**	**1 760 627**	**1 990 265**	**2 026 518**
1100 Of individuals	...	...	...	954 698	1 838 563	2 067 806	1 928 107	1 422 112	1 622 030	1 610 329
1110 On income and profits	...	...	...	954 698	1 838 563	2 067 806	1 928 107	1 422 112	1 622 030	1 610 329
1120 On capital gains	...	...	...	0	0	0	0	0	0	0
1200 Corporate	...	...	...	292 722	700 826	699 992	579 072	338 515	368 235	416 189
Corporate income tax	...	...	...	292 722	510 781	487 524	385 543	316 620	342 305	322 467
Research and development fund levy	...	...	...	0	0	0	0	0	0	0
Credit institutions' special tax	...	...	...	0	10 890	11 849	12 255	20 921	19 783	27 686
Separate tax for companies	...	...	...	0	178 598	200 493	156 859	-16 100	0	0
Medicine tax	...	...	...	0	558	127	245	188	537	111
Energy corporations' special tax	...	...	...	0	0	0	24 170	16 886	5 610	54 060
Small business tax	...	...	...	0	0	0	0	0	0	11 865
1210 On profits	...	...	...	...	...	...	...	...	...	...
1220 On capital gains	...	...	...	...	...	...	...	...	...	...
1300 Unallocable between 1100 and 1200	...	...	...	0	0	0	0	0	0	0
Interest withholding	...	...	...	...	...	...	...	...	...	...
2000 Social security contributions	..	..	..	**1 506 755**	**3 292 206**	**3 449 129**	**3 198 477**	**3 480 809**	**3 581 998**	**3 727 979**
2100 Employees	...	...	...	275 323	862 082	891 868	850 428	1 319 803	1 452 892	1 568 322
Pensions	...	...	...	150 585	283 938	347 893	330 631	754 870	789 363	852 332
Health	...	...	...	81 874	486 950	445 990	423 659	452 284	545 862	589 590
Unemployment	...	...	...	42 864	91 194	97 985	96 138	112 649	117 667	126 400
2110 On a payroll basis	...	...	...	...	...	...	...	...	...	...
2120 On an income tax basis	...	...	...	...	...	...	...	...	...	...
2200 Employers	...	...	...	1 213 190	2 378 224	2 496 038	2 273 909	2 115 624	2 099 672	2 134 343
Pensions	...	...	...	734 456	1 534 352	1 834 744	1 773 357	1 879 114	1 837 096	2 108 029
Health	...	...	...	385 019	643 126	448 024	336 704	161 410	191 537	26 314
Unemployment	...	...	...	93 715	200 746	213 270	163 847	75 100	71 039	0
2210 On a payroll basis	...	...	...	...	...	...	...	...	...	...
2220 On an income tax basis	...	...	...	...	...	...	...	...	...	...
2300 Self-employed or non-employed	...	...	...	873	2 534	4 277	17 310	22 882	0	0
Pensions: of which	...	...	...	0	0	0	0	0	...	...
Self-employed	...	...	...	...	...	...	...	...	...	...
Unemployed	...	...	...	...	...	...	...	...	...	...
Retired	...	...	...	...	...	...	...	...	...	...
Other	...	...	...	...	...	...	...	...	...	...
Health: of which	...	...	...	873	2 534	4 277	17 310	22 882	...	...
Self-employed	...	...	...	873	2 534	4 277	17 310	22 882	...	...
Unemployed	...	...	...	0	0	0	0	0	...	...
Retired	...	...	...	0	0	0	0	0	...	...
Other	...	...	...	0	0	0	0	0	...	...
2310 On a payroll basis	...	...	...	...	...	...	...	...	...	...
2320 On an income tax basis	...	...	...	...	...	...	...	...	...	...
2400 Unallocable between 2100, 2200 and 2300	...	...	...	17 368	49 366	56 946	56 830	22 500	29 434	25 314
2410 On a payroll basis	...	...	...	...	...	...	...	...	...	...
2420 On an income tax basis	...	...	...	...	...	...	...	...	...	...
3000 Taxes on payroll and workforce	..	..	..	**183 430**	**155 223**	**148 134**	**146 973**	**128 417**	**156 392**	**168 749**
Rehabilitation contribution	...	...	...	2 184	13 559	14 778	14 951	66 427	63 409	64 400
Training levy	...	...	...	13 186	36 612	42 760	43 516	49 647	80 157	63 536
Wage guarantee contribution	...	...	...	0	0	0	0	0	0	0
Communal tax on enterprises	...	...	...	1 192	1 261	1 325	1 291	102	16	2
Health contribution	...	...	...	166 869	93 581	84 730	78 997	4	0	0
Medicine tax	...	...	...	0	10 209	4 540	8 219	12 232	12 799	9 547
Tax on home-workers	...	...	...	0	0	0	0	5	11	23
Lump sum tax for small taxpayers	...	...	...	0	0	0	0	0	0	31 241
4000 Taxes on property	..	..	..	**89 024**	**202 711**	**230 861**	**215 068**	**317 081**	**351 136**	**388 824**
4100 Recurrent taxes on immovable property	...	...	...	30 810	72 071	81 645	87 328	102 454	127 032	190 249
Land tax	...	...	...	0	0	0	0	0	0	0
Building tax	...	...	...	22 262	54 556	61 916	66 683	80 987	96 318	102 719
Development land tax	...	...	...	3 099	6 900	8 328	9 114	10 310	17 523	19 395
Communal tax on recreational howes	...	...	...	893	1 412	1 491	1 450	58	30	21
Communal tax on households	...	...	...	4 557	9 069	9 739	10 077	11 099	13 161	13 175
Luxury tax	...	...	...	0	134	171	3	0	0	0
Public utility tax	...	...	...	0	0	0	0	0	0	54 939
4110 Households	...	...	...	...	...	...	...	...	...	...
4120 Others	...	...	...	...	...	...	...	...	...	...
4200 Recurrent taxes on net wealth	...	...	...	0	0	0	0	139 222	138 581	128 560
Surtax payable by financial institutions	...	...	...	...	...	...	...	139 222	138 581	128 560
4210 Individual	...	...	...	...	...	...	...	...	...	...

Table 53. **Hungary / Hongrie** *(cont.)*
Details of tax revenue / Recettes fiscales détaillées

Million HUF

	1965	1980	1990	2000	2007	2008	2009	2011	2012	2013
4220 Corporate	..	..	..	..	..	..	..	..	..	..
4300 Estate, inheritance and gift taxes	..	..	..	5 460	13 175	11 276	9 259	6 500	5 654	5 307
4310 Estate and inheritance taxes	..	..	..	4 020	10 775	8 937	5 871	5 201	4 591	4 097
Inheritance tax-local	..	..	..	2 010	4 658	3 875	2 561	2 244	616	0
Inheritance tax-central	..	..	..	2 010	6 117	5 062	3 310	2 957	3 975	4 097
4320 Gift taxes	..	..	..	1 440	2 400	2 338	3 387	1 298	1 063	1 210
Gift tax-local	..	..	..	720	1 038	1 014	1 478	560	143	0
Gift tax-central	..	..	..	720	1 363	1 325	1 910	738	920	1 210
4400 Taxes on financial and capital transactions	..	..	..	52 754	117 465	137 940	118 482	68 905	79 869	64 708
Property transfer tax-local	..	..	..	26 349	50 783	59 811	51 689	29 733	10 720	0
Property transfer tax-central	..	..	..	26 405	66 682	78 129	66 792	39 172	69 149	64 708
4500 Non-recurrent taxes	..	..	..	0	0	0	0	0	0	0
4510 On net wealth	..	..	..	..	..	..	..	..	..	..
4520 Other non-recurrent taxes	..	..	..	..	..	..	..	..	..	..
4600 Other recurrent taxes on property	..	..	..	0	0	0	0	0	0	0
5000 Taxes on goods and services	**..**	**..**	**..**	**2 081 107**	**3 803 630**	**3 963 094**	**4 061 730**	**4 476 168**	**4 858 734**	**5 038 129**
5100 Taxes on production, sale, transfer, etc	..	..	..	2 052 380	3 722 487	3 874 486	3 954 201	4 365 926	4 741 036	4 915 333
5110 General taxes	..	..	..	1 340 572	2 622 027	2 725 438	2 857 504	3 077 927	3 353 969	3 414 342
5111 Value added taxes	..	..	..	1 153 750	2 013 271	2 068 438	2 192 234	2 379 253	2 627 571	2 693 555
5112 Sales tax	..	..	..	0	0	0	0	43 598	55 040	47 927
Public health product tax	..	..	..	..	..	..	..	4 643	19 208	19 090
Hydrocarbons stockholding fee	..	..	..	..	..	..	..	38 955	35 832	28 837
5113 Other	..	..	..	186 823	608 756	657 000	665 270	655 076	671 358	672 860
Local tax on company sales	..	..	..	186 823	427 134	465 075	472 155	457 308	471 031	500 868
Simplified business tax	..	..	..	0	152 812	166 537	169 704	172 273	146 531	110 021
Research and development contribution	..	..	..	0	28 810	25 388	23 411	25 495	53 796	61 971
5120 Taxes on specific goods and services	..	..	..	711 808	1 100 461	1 149 048	1 096 698	1 287 999	1 387 067	1 500 991
5121 Excises	..	..	..	533 502	969 730	1 003 342	971 431	959 962	1 022 624	992 270
Road fund petrol tax	..	..	..	0	0	0	0	0	0	0
Alcohol production duty	..	..	..	3 848	5 621	5 785	8 272	180	183	196
Water fund tax	..	..	..	6 017	13 171	14 336	14 708	14 282	13 640	13 164
Forestry fund tax	..	..	..	2 858	3 353	2 915	108	36	319	0
Environment petrol tax	..	..	..	14 837	19 447	23 185	27 704	18 368	55 031	46 711
Budget excises (central budget)	..	..	..	505 942	916 869	941 510	906 910	909 775	937 288	915 547
Coffee	..	..	..	3 200	0	0	0	0	0	0
Alcohol	..	..	..	53 500	88 600	86 900	83 300	85 779	85 974	85 487
Tobacco	..	..	..	107 000	252 400	275 200	307 200	285 346	339 845	312 509
Petrol	..	..	..	156 000	218 200	215 900	215 400	203 997	189 984	189 755
Diesel	..	..	..	157 000	256 600	274 600	264 900	297 242	302 561	308 736
Other oil	..	..	..	6 000	2 200	2 100	2 600	2 932	5 253	3 451
Other budget excises	..	..	..	30 343	93 442	86 775	33 552	34 479	13 671	15 608
Energy tax	..	..	..	0	11 269	15 610	13 729	17 321	16 163	16 652
5122 Profits of fiscal monopolies	..	..	..	0	0	0	0	0	0	0
5123 Customs and import duties	..	..	..	137 730	9 193	9 211	7 995	9 380	8 999	8 970
Customs duties	..	..	..	137 730	9 193	9 211	7 995	9 380	8 999	8 970
5124 Taxes on exports	..	..	..	0	0	0	0	0	0	0
5125 Taxes on investment goods	..	..	..	0	0	0	0	0	0	0
5126 Taxes on specific services	..	..	..	40 576	105 879	117 760	109 627	317 613	354 640	498 871
Gambling tax	..	..	..	27 935	71 804	73 109	65 050	64 088	61 452	41 316
Tourism tax	..	..	..	4 379	0	0	0	0	0	0
Communal tourism tax	..	..	..	2 943	4 935	5 468	5 481	6 761	7 682	8 411
Cultural contribution	..	..	..	4 387	8 432	8 676	7 433	136	207	105
Pork slaughterhouse tax	..	..	..	32	0	0	0	0	0	0
Breeding contribution	..	..	..	899	919	185	0	0	0	0
Medicine tax	..	..	..	0	19 789	30 322	31 663	40 055	41 441	40 496
Surtax payable by financial institutions	..	..	..	0	0	0	0	34 630	33 964	1 217
Specific sectors' surtax	..	..	..	0	0	0	0	171 943	165 645	9 815
Telecommunication services tax	..	..	..	0	0	0	0	0	18 322	50 176
Accident tax	..	..	..	0	0	0	0	0	25 927	23 313
Insurance tax	..	..	..	0	0	0	0	0	0	28 088
Financial transaction levy	..	..	..	0	0	0	0	0	0	289 321
Waste dumping contribution	..	..	..	0	0	0	0	0	0	6 613
Advertising tax	..	..	..	0	0	0	0	0	0	0
5127 Other taxes on internat. trade and transactions	..	..	..	0	0	0	0	0	0	0
Previous differential producer's turnover tax	..	..	..	..	..	..	..	..	..	..
5128 Other taxes	..	..	..	0	15 659	18 736	7 645	1 044	804	881
Sugar duty	..	..	..	..	15 659	18 736	7 645	1 044	804	881
5130 Unallocable between 5110 and 5120	..	..	..	0	0	0	0	0	0	0
5200 Taxes on use of goods and perform activities	..	..	..	28 727	81 143	88 607	107 529	110 242	117 698	122 796

Table 53. **Hungary / Hongrie** *(cont.)*
Details of tax revenue / Recettes fiscales détaillées

Million HUF

	1965	1980	1990	2000	2007	2008	2009	2011	2012	2013
5210 Recurrent taxes	...	...	...	25 454	74 268	80 712	100 861	106 512	113 675	119 226
Tax on domestically registered vehicles-local	...	...	...	12 622	62 432	65 713	63 754	72 073	70 660	69 248
Tax on domestically registered vehicles-extra budget	...	...	...	0	0	0	0	0	0	0
Tax on domestically registered vehicles-central	...	...	...	8 250	0	0	0	37	0	0
Tax on foreign registered vehicles extra budget fund	...	...	...	0	0	0	0	0	0	0
Tax on foreign registered vehicles-central	...	...	...	3 078	1 655	1 652	1 630	1 422	0	0
Company car tax	...	...	...	0	0	0	23 060	25 239	34 293	32 935
5211 Paid by households: motor vehicles	...	...	...	0	0	0	0	0	0	0
5212 Paid by others: motor vehicles	...	...	...	0	0	0	0	0	0	0
5213 Paid in respect of other goods	...	...	...	1 504	10 181	13 347	12 417	7 741	8 722	17 043
Environmental protection fee	...	...	...	5	13	32	20	0	0	0
Fishing development contribution	...	...	...	40	104	0	0	0	0	0
Environmental protection charge	...	...	...	0	8 785	11 412	11 787	7 292	8 272	7 861
Air pollution levy	...	...	...	751	610	455	38	0	0	0
Water pollution levy	...	...	...	225	186	748	1	0	0	0
Toxic waste levy	...	...	...	65	42	24	18	0	0	0
Noise abatement levy	...	...	...	13	8	9	12	0	0	0
Unidentified environmental protection levies paid to local governments	...	...	...	404	433	667	541	449	450	521
Sale of emission allowances	...	...	...	0	0	0	0	0	0	8 661
5220 Non-recurrent taxes	...	...	...	3 273	6 875	7 895	6 667	3 730	4 023	3 570
Land protection levy	...	...	...	1 640	3 777	5 079	4 408	962	1 856	1 881
Vehicle weight fee	...	...	...	805	1 288	1 324	676	1 037	1 161	624
Game protection contribution	...	...	...	178	176	0	0	0	-1	0
Casino license fee	...	...	...	650	1 635	1 492	1 583	1 731	1 007	1 065
5300 Unallocable between 5100 and 5200	...	...	...	0	0	0	0	0	0	0
6000 Other taxes	**..**	**..**	**..**	**32 857**	**56 348**	**67 675**	**58 181**	**55 293**	**51 482**	**76 165**
Unallocable tax penalties	...	...	...	23 546	33 321	44 806	35 354	32 165	32 153	56 836
6100 Paid solely by business	...	...	...	...	...	...	...	...	...	...
Nuclear contribution	...	...	...	...	...	...	...	...	...	...
Medicine tax	...	...	...	...	...	...	...	...	...	...
6200 Other	...	...	...	...	...	...	...	...	...	...
Custom duties collected for the EU	**..**	**..**	**..**	**..**	**27 981**	**26 689**	**25 657**	**27 462**	**27 206**	**26 337**
Total tax revenue on cash basis	**..**	**..**	**..**	**5 140 592**	**10 020 734**	**10 689 304**	**10 158 013**	**10 033 880**	**11 017 202**	**11 451 047**
Total tax revenue on accrual basis	**..**	**..**	**..**	**..**	**10 077 488**	**10 653 379**	**10 213 265**	**10 245 857**	**11 017 213**	**11 452 701**
Conciliation with National Accounts										
Additional taxes included in National Accounts	...	...	...	...	81 952	122 366	119 236	159 867	57 221	84 753
Social security contributions	...	...	...	...	36 832	74 910	78 022	126 258	20 924	47 251
Duty for state procedures	...	...	...	...	45 084	47 418	41 176	33 545	36 234	37 417
Other taxes	...	...	...	...	36	38	38	64	63	85
Taxes excluded from National Accounts	...	...	...	...	-49 439	-62 729	-52 322	-49 360	-47 415	-77 779
Water fund tax	...	...	...	...	-13 171	-14 336	-14 708	-14 282	-13 640	-13 164
Tax on foreign registered vehicles	...	...	...	...	-1 655	-1 652	-1 630	-1 422	0	0
Environmental protection fee	...	...	...	...	-446	-699	-561	-449	-450	-520
Air pollution levy	...	...	...	...	-610	-455	-38	0	0	0
Water pollution levy	...	...	...	...	-186	-748	-1	0	0	0
Toxic waste levy	...	...	...	...	-42	-24	-18	0	0	0
Noise abatement levy	...	...	...	...	-8	-9	-12	0	0	0
Vehicle weight fee	...	...	...	...	0	0	0	-1 037	-1 161	-624
Unallocable tax penalties	...	...	...	...	-33 320	-44 806	-35 354	-32 165	-32 153	-56 836
Waste dumping contribution	...	...	...	...	0	0	0	0	0	-6 612
Tax on home-workers	...	...	...	...	0	0	0	-5	-11	-23
Difference in treatment of tax credits	...	...	...	...	0	0	0	0	0	0
Capital transfer for uncollected revenue	...	...	...	...	0	0	0	0	0	0
Voluntary social security contributions	...	...	...	...	1 762	1 792	1 626	1 676	1 590	1 503
Miscellaneous differences	...	...	...	...	-2 685	-4 104	308	0	1	-1
Inheritance tax	...	...	...	...	0	0	0	0	0	0
Gift tax	...	...	...	...	0	0	0	0	0	0
Property transfer tax	...	...	...	...	0	0	0	0	0	0
Rounding	...	...	...	...	6	3	-1	0	1	-1
Taxes on income and profits	...	...	...	...	-2 087	0	0	0	0	0
Corporate income tax	...	...	...	...	0	-5 000	0	0	0	0
Customs duties	...	...	...	...	-603	893	-56	0	0	0
Vehicle weight fee	...	...	...	...	0	0	0	0	0	0
Environment petrol tax	...	...	...	...	0	0	0	0	0	0
Social security contributions	...	...	...	...	0	0	0	0	0	0
Credit institutions' special tax	...	...	...	...	0	0	364	0	0	0
National Accounts: Taxes and actual social contributions	...	...	...	..	10 109 079	10 710 704	10 282 113	10 358 040	11 028 610	11 461 177
Imputed social contributions	...	...	...	..	21 113	23 150	23 835	23 039	20 664	21 669
National Accounts: Taxes and all social contributions	...	...	...	..	10 130 192	10 733 854	10 305 948	10 381 079	11 049 274	11 482 846

Note:

Year ending 31st December.

From 2002, data are on accrual basis.

Heading 5121: the aggregate figure for excise tax revenues is on a cash basis. Revenue from specific excises is in several cases reported on an accrual basis.

Tax base for "Environment petrol tax" is broader than petrol only.

Heading 5123: part of environmentally related payments is attributable to Local government. It is not possible to present a more detailed breakdown of these figures.

Source: Ministry of Finance, Economic Department.

StatLink http://dx.doi.org/10.1787/888933277157

Table 54. **Iceland / Islande**
Details of tax revenue / Recettes fiscales détaillées

Million ISK

	1965	1980	1990	2000	2007	2008	2009	2011	2012	2013
Total tax revenue	**60**	**4 731**	**114 932**	**254 556**	**531 760**	**543 584**	**507 481**	**585 936**	**626 450**	**676 142**
1000 Taxes on income, profits and capital gains	**13**	**1 211**	**34 106**	**101 473**	**241 378**	**263 455**	**239 890**	**266 823**	**283 239**	**315 577**
1100 Of individuals	12	1 092	30 908	88 492	180 070	195 636	192 275	220 571	234 475	258 623
1110 On income and profits	..	..	..	88 492	180 070	195 636	192 275	220 571	234 475	258 623
1120 On capital gains	..	..	..	0	0	0	0	0	0	0
1200 Corporate	1	119	3 198	8 356	32 555	28 476	26 499	29 480	33 980	40 479
1210 On profits	..	..	..	8 356	32 555	28 476	26 499	29 480	33 980	40 479
1220 On capital gains	..	..	..	0	0	0	0	0	0	0
1300 Unallocable between 1100 and 1200	0	0	0	4 625	28 754	39 343	21 116	16 772	14 784	16 475
2000 Social security contributions	**5**	**102**	**3 607**	**19 680**	**39 594**	**41 644**	**45 912**	**66 820**	**64 882**	**69 899**
2100 Employees	0	0	315	..	..	..	..	..	..	..
2110 On a payroll basis	..	..	..	..	..	..	..	..	..	..
2120 On an income tax basis	..	..	..	..	..	..	..	..	..	..
2200 Employers	5	102	3 292	..	..	..	..	..	..	..
2210 On a payroll basis	..	..	..	..	..	..	..	..	..	..
2220 On an income tax basis	..	..	..	..	..	..	..	..	..	..
2300 Self-employed or non-employed	0	0	0	..	..	..	..	..	..	..
2310 On a payroll basis	..	..	..	..	..	..	..	..	..	..
2320 On an income tax basis	..	..	..	..	..	..	..	..	..	..
2400 Unallocable between 2100, 2200 and 2300	0	0	0	19 680	39 594	41 644	45 912	66 820	64 882	69 899
2410 On a payroll basis	..	..	..	19 680	39 594	41 644	45 912	66 820	64 882	69 899
2420 On an income tax basis	..	..	..	0	0	0	0	0	0	0
3000 Taxes on payroll and workforce	**1**	**180**	**4 071**	**184**	**1 519**	**2 243**	**2 470**	**2 900**	**5 402**	**6 534**
4000 Taxes on property	**2**	**297**	**9 689**	**19 983**	**32 523**	**33 206**	**32 806**	**39 282**	**44 304**	**46 493**
4100 Recurrent taxes on immovable property	1	138	4 131	10 107	20 567	25 879	27 647	28 348	29 129	30 664
4110 Households	0	50	1 862	..	..	..	..	..	..	..
4120 Others	1	88	2 269	..	..	..	..	..	..	..
4200 Recurrent taxes on net wealth	0	69	2 402	5 173	-8	-18	12	6 312	9 396	8 886
4210 Individual	..	29	1 476	..	..	..	..	..	..	..
4220 Corporate	..	40	926	..	..	..	..	..	..	..
4300 Estate, inheritance and gift taxes	0	6	235	765	1 663	1 167	1 643	1 292	1 916	2 437
4310 Estate and inheritance taxes	0	6	235	765	1 663	1 167	1 643	1 292	1 916	2 437
4320 Gift taxes	0	0	0	0	0	0	0	0	0	0
4400 Taxes on financial and capital transactions	1	84	2 921	3 143	9 484	5 646	2 934	2 890	3 352	3 973
4500 Non-recurrent taxes	0	0	0	113	460	465	311	177	227	233
4510 On net wealth	..	..	..	0	0	0	0	0	0	0
4520 Other non-recurrent taxes	..	..	..	113	460	465	311	177	227	233
4600 Other recurrent taxes on property	0	0	0	681	356	66	260	263	284	299
5000 Taxes on goods and services	**37**	**2 834**	**58 943**	**112 245**	**214 988**	**200 882**	**180 199**	**203 545**	**219 681**	**226 619**
5100 Taxes on production, sale, transfer, etc	37	2 778	56 564	100 669	191 957	184 053	168 932	193 705	209 755	215 271
5110 General taxes	10	1 368	37 084	72 667	137 593	134 391	120 241	131 057	142 814	149 828
5111 Value added taxes	0	0	32 698	72 667	137 593	134 391	120 241	131 057	142 814	149 828
5112 Sales tax	10	1 368	4 386	0	0	0	0	0	0	0
5113 Other	0	0	0	0	0	0	0	0	0	0
5120 Taxes on specific goods and services	27	1 410	19 480	28 002	54 364	49 662	48 692	62 648	66 941	65 444
5121 Excises	1	311	2 346	23 585	45 891	40 364	39 935	50 239	53 930	55 171
5122 Profits of fiscal monopolies	5	263	5 986	0	0	0	0	0	0	0
5123 Customs and import duties	20	715	9 181	2 702	5 446	5 858	5 303	7 288	7 682	5 815
5124 Taxes on exports	1	2	0	1	0	6	5	0	0	0
5125 Taxes on investment goods	0	0	0	0	0	0	0	0	0	0
5126 Taxes on specific services	1	69	1 404	1 715	3 026	3 435	3 448	5 122	5 329	4 457
5127 Other taxes on internat. trade and transactions	0	50	563	0	0	0	0	0	0	0
5128 Other taxes	0	0	0	0	0	0	0	0	0	0
5130 Unallocable between 5110 and 5120	0	0	0	0	0	0	0	0	0	0
5200 Taxes on use of goods and perform activities	1	56	2 379	11 576	23 032	16 829	11 267	9 839	9 926	11 347
5210 Recurrent taxes	1	56	2 379	..	..	..	..	..	..	..
5211 Paid by households: motor vehicles	0	10	970	..	..	..	..	..	..	..
5212 Paid by others: motor vehicles	0	41	1 331	..	..	..	..	..	..	..
5213 Paid in respect of other goods	0	5	78	..	..	..	..	..	..	..
5220 Non-recurrent taxes	0	0	0	..	..	..	..	..	..	..
5300 Unallocable between 5100 and 5200	0	0	0	0	0	0	0	0	0	0
6000 Other taxes	**2**	**107**	**4 516**	**991**	**1 758**	**2 153**	**6 203**	**6 567**	**8 942**	**11 020**
6100 Paid solely by business	2	107	4 145	418	628	846	1 049	1 370	3 332	5 255
6200 Other	0	0	371	573	1 130	1 307	5 154	5 196	5 610	5 766

Table 54. **Iceland / Islande** *(cont.)*
Details of tax revenue / Recettes fiscales détaillées

Million ISK

	1965	1980	1990	2000	2007	2008	2009	2011	2012	2013
Non wastable tax credits										
Non-wastable tax credits against 1110	..	..	..	..	..	..	..	..	..	..
Tax expenditure component	..	..	..	..	..	..	..	..	..	..
Transfer component	..	..	..	..	..	..	..	..	..	..
Non-wastable tax credits against 1210	..	..	..	..	..	..	..	..	..	..
Tax expenditure component	..	..	..	..	..	..	..	..	..	..
Transfer component	..	..	..	..	..	..	..	..	..	..
Total tax revenue on cash basis	**60**	**4 731**	**114 932**	..	..	..	..	..	..	..
Total tax revenue on accrual basis	..	..	..	**254 556**	**531 760**	**543 584**	**507 481**	**585 936**	**626 450**	**676 142**
Conciliation with National Accounts										
Additional taxes included in National Accounts	..	..	..	0	0	0	0	0	0	0
Taxes excluded from National Accounts	..	..	..	-765	-1 663	-1 167	-1 643	-1 292	-1 916	-2 437
Estate and inheritance taxes (4310)	..	..	..	-765	-1 663	-1 167	-1 643	-1 292	-1 916	-2 437
Difference in treatment of tax credits	..	..	..	0	0	0	0	0	0	0
Capital transfer for uncollected revenue	..	..	..	0	0	0	0	0	0	0
Voluntary social security contributions	..	..	..	0	0	0	0	0	0	0
Miscellaneous differences	..	..	..	0	0	0	0	0	0	0
National Accounts: Taxes and actual social contributions	..	..	..	253 791	530 097	542 417	505 837	584 644	624 534	673 704
Imputed social contributions	..	..	..	0	0	0	0	0	0	0
National Accounts: Taxes and all social contributions	..	..	..	253 791	530 097	542 417	505 837	584 644	624 534	673 704

Note:

Year ending 31st December.

From 1998 data are on accrual basis.

Source: Ministry of Finance, Economic Department.

StatLink http://dx.doi.org/10.1787/888933277168

Table 55. **Ireland / Irlande**
Details of tax revenue / Recettes fiscales détaillées

Million EUR

	1965	1980	1990	2000	2007	2008	2009	2011	2012	2013
Total tax revenue	**317**	**4 046**	**12 260**	**33 337**	**59 894**	**53 395**	**46 453**	**46 826**	**48 231**	**50 746**
Total tax revenue exclusive of custom duties	..	..	..	**33 130**	**59 621**	**53 150**	**46 245**	**46 586**	**47 989**	**50 499**
1000 Taxes on income, profits and capital gains	**82**	**1 478**	**4 662**	**14 551**	**24 521**	**21 141**	**18 043**	**18 339**	**19 613**	**20 483**
1100 Of individuals	53	1 294	4 059	10 650	18 127	16 066	14 147	14 582	15 643	16 205
1110 On income and profits	53	1 286	4 023	9 876	15 029	14 642	13 602	14 166	15 230	15 836
Income tax	66	1 286	4 023	9 876	15 029	14 642	13 602	14 166	15 230	15 836
Surtax	3	0	0	0	0	0	0	0	0	0
Income tax paid by corporations	-17	0	0	0	0	0	0	0	0	0
1120 On capital gains	0	8	36	774	3 097	1 424	545	416	413	369
1200 Corporate	29	184	603	3 900	6 395	5 075	3 892	3 753	3 965	4 273
1210 On profits	29	184	603	3 900	6 395	5 075	3 892	3 753	3 965	4 273
Corporation profits tax	12	2	0	0	0	0	0	0	0	0
Corporation tax	0	176	603	3 885	6 393	5 071	3 889	3 751	3 964	4 272
Income tax paid by corporation	17	0	0	0	0	0	0	0	0	0
Agricultural produce duty	0	6	0	14	1	3	2	1	1	1
1220 On capital gains	0	0	0	0	0	0	0	0	0	0
1300 Unallocable between 1100 and 1200	0	0	0	2	0	0	4	4	4	4
2000 Social security contributions	**21**	**578**	**1 729**	**3 941**	**8 118**	**8 325**	**8 795**	**9 002**	**8 474**	**9 025**
2100 Employees	10	190	570	937	1 901	2 023	3 183	3 289	3 142	3 296
2110 On a payroll basis	..	..	570	937	1 901	2 023	3 183	3 289	3 142	3 296
2120 On an income tax basis	..	..	0	0	0	0	0	0	0	0
2200 Employers	10	380	1 092	2 814	5 796	5 896	5 297	5 365	5 008	5 326
2210 On a payroll basis	..	..	1 092	2 814	5 796	5 896	5 297	5 365	5 008	5 326
2220 On an income tax basis	..	..	0	0	0	0	0	0	0	0
2300 Self-employed or non-employed	0	8	67	190	421	406	315	348	324	403
2310 On a payroll basis	..	..	67	190	421	406	315	348	324	403
2320 On an income tax basis	..	..	0	0	0	0	0	0	0	0
2400 Unallocable between 2100, 2200 and 2300	0	0	0	0	0	0	0	0	0	0
2410 On a payroll basis	..	..	..	..	..	..	..	..	..	..
2420 On an income tax basis	..	..	..	..	..	..	..	..	..	..
3000 Taxes on payroll and workforce	**0**	**9**	**159**	**15**	**411**	**414**	**368**	**318**	**295**	**314**
4000 Taxes on property	**48**	**213**	**569**	**1 902**	**4 762**	**3 313**	**2 453**	**2 842**	**3 070**	**3 619**
4100 Recurrent taxes on immovable property	39	139	312	587	1 233	1 276	1 322	1 342	1 478	1 720
4110 Households	..	..	..	..	..	..	..	..	..	..
4120 Others	..	..	..	..	..	..	..	..	..	..
4200 Recurrent taxes on net wealth	0	1	0	0	0	0	0	460	483	536
4210 Individual	..	..	..	..	..	..	..	0	0	0
4220 Corporate	..	..	..	..	..	..	..	460	483	536
4300 Estate, inheritance and gift taxes	6	14	48	225	405	349	258	242	282	278
4310 Estate and inheritance taxes	6	14	45	210	337	302	210	215	256	259
Estate duty	5	..	..	..	..	..	..	..	..	..
Legacy duty	1	..	..	..	..	..	..	..	..	..
Succession duty	0	..	..	..	..	..	..	..	..	..
4320 Gift taxes	0	0	3	15	68	47	48	27	26	20
4400 Taxes on financial and capital transactions	3	59	209	1 090	3 124	1 688	874	798	827	1 084
Stamp duty	3	59	209	1 090	3 124	1 688	874	798	827	1 084
4500 Non-recurrent taxes	0	0	0	0	0	0	0	0	0	0
4510 On net wealth	..	..	..	..	..	..	..	..	..	..
4520 Other non-recurrent taxes	..	..	..	..	..	..	..	..	..	..
4600 Other recurrent taxes on property	0	0	0	0	0	0	0	0	0	0
5000 Taxes on goods and services	**167**	**1 769**	**5 141**	**12 721**	**21 809**	**19 957**	**16 582**	**16 075**	**16 528**	**17 034**
5100 Taxes on production, sale, transfer, etc	155	1 741	4 940	12 166	20 710	18 710	15 354	14 719	15 169	15 546
5110 General taxes	18	597	2 500	7 643	14 355	13 084	10 324	9 755	10 219	10 372
5111 Value added taxes	0	597	2 500	7 643	14 355	13 084	10 324	9 755	10 219	10 372
Value added tax	..	597	2 500	7 643	14 355	13 084	10 324	9 755	10 219	10 372
5112 Sales tax	18	0	0	0	0	0	0	0	0	0
Turnover tax	18	..	..	..	..	..	..	..	..	..
Wholesale tax	0	..	..	..	..	..	..	..	..	..
5113 Other	0	0	0	0	0	0	0	0	0	0
5120 Taxes on specific goods and services	137	1 143	2 440	4 523	6 354	5 626	5 029	4 963	4 949	5 174
5121 Excises	124	1 045	2 084	4 402	6 103	5 367	4 870	4 855	4 774	5 013
Beer	19	192	356	475	459	431	397	309	309	363
Oils	31	330	745	1 491	2 204	2 168	2 170	2 119	2 035	2 035
Spirits	16	148	153	241	363	337	267	251	263	282
Table waters	0	11	23	0	0	0	0	0	0	0
Tobacco	50	187	419	1 035	1 192	1 171	1 217	1 127	1 072	1 064
Wine, cider, perry	1	18	46	154	297	290	297	270	280	354
Motor vehicle (incl. tyres)	7	148	331	985	1 554	938	373	394	384	459
Others	1	11	11	20	34	32	149	385	431	457
5122 Profits of fiscal monopolies	0	0	0	0	0	0	0	0	0	0

Table 55. **Ireland / Irlande** *(cont.)*
Details of tax revenue / Recettes fiscales détaillées

Million EUR

	1965	1980	1990	2000	2007	2008	2009	2011	2012	2013
5123 Customs and import duties	10	62	147	0	0	0	0	0	0	0
5124 Taxes on exports	0	0	0	0	0	0	0	0	0	0
UE agriculture levies	..	..	..	..	..	..	..	..	..	..
5125 Taxes on investment goods	0	0	0	0	0	0	0	0	0	0
5126 Taxes on specific services	3	21	171	122	252	258	160	109	176	161
Duty on betting	2	19	37	59	36	35	31	28	27	26
Sweepstakes duty	1	1	0	0	0	0	0	0	0	0
Bank levy	0	0	46	61	66	83	-1	-103	-32	-23
Other	0	1	88	2	150	140	130	184	181	159
5127 Other taxes on internat. trade and transactions	0	0	0	0	0	0	0	0	0	0
5128 Other taxes	0	14	37	0	0	0	0	0	0	0
5130 Unallocable between 5110 and 5120	0	0	0	0	0	0	0	0	0	0
5200 Taxes on use of goods and perform activities	11	28	201	555	1 100	1 246	1 228	1 357	1 359	1 488
5210 Recurrent taxes	11	28	201	555	1 100	1 246	1 228	1 357	1 359	1 488
5211 Paid by households: motor vehicles	6	14	100	373	723	800	793	758	791	853
5212 Paid by others: motor vehicles	5	11	82	124	239	265	264	253	264	284
5213 Paid in respect of other goods	0	3	20	58	138	182	170	347	304	351
5220 Non-recurrent taxes	0	0	0	0	0	0	0	0	0	0
5300 Unallocable between 5100 and 5200	0	0	0	0	0	0	0	0	0	0
6000 Other taxes	**0**	**0**	**0**	**0**	**0**	**0**	**4**	**10**	**10**	**23**
6100 Paid solely by business	..	..	..	..	..	..	0	0	0	0
6200 Other	..	..	..	..	..	..	4	10	10	23
Custom duties collected for the EU	..	..	..	**208**	**273**	**245**	**208**	**240**	**242**	**247**
Non wastable tax credits										
Non-wastable tax credits against 1110	..	..	..	..	..	..	..	..	..	..
Tax expenditure component	..	..	..	..	..	..	..	..	..	..
Transfer component	..	..	..	..	843	1 026	1 076	1 096	1 224	816
Total tax revenue on cash basis	**317**	**4 046**	**12 260**	**33 055**	**59 940**	**53 987**	**47 018**	**46 485**	**48 491**	**50 779**
Total tax revenue on accrual basis	..	..	..	**33 337**	**59 894**	**53 395**	**46 453**	**46 826**	**48 231**	**50 746**
Conciliation with National Accounts										
Additional taxes included in National Accounts	..	..	..	0	0	0	196	180	180	180
Taxes excluded from National Accounts	..	..	..	0	0	0	0	0	0	0
Difference in treatment of tax credits	..	..	..	0	843	1 026	1 076	1 096	1 224	816
Capital transfer for uncollected revenue	..	..	..	0	0	0	0	0	0	0
Voluntary social security contributions	..	..	..	0	0	0	0	0	0	0
Miscellaneous differences	..	..	..	0	0	0	0	0	0	0
National Accounts: Taxes and actual social contributions	..	..	..	33 337	60 737	54 420	47 724	48 101	49 635	51 741
Imputed social contributions	..	..	..	1 366	2 579	2 659	1 448	971	1 177	1 276
National Accounts: Taxes and all social contributions	..	..	..	34 704	63 316	57 079	49 172	49 072	50 812	53 017

Note:

The data for personal income tax revenues differs from the ESA2010 presentation as payable tax credits are excluded in accordance with the presentation in earlier editions of the publication.

The data for years 1965 to 1973 are on fiscal year basis (commencing on 1st April) and are therefore not strictly comparable with the data for later years, which are on a calendar year basis.

From 1998, data are on accrual basis.

Heading 1200: Capital gains taxes paid by corporations are included in heading 1210.

Heading 2100: Includes contributions by self-employed and certain voluntary contributions.

Heading 2200: Since 1976 income tax paid by corporations and corporation profits tax have been replaced by corporation tax.

Heading 5111: Includes arrears of the wholesale and turnover taxes.

Tax receipts in 1988 were inflated by the success of the new arrangements for assessment and collection of tax.These arrangements included an amnesty for tax arrears paid by 30th September. This amnesty waived penalities and interest charge tax. It resulted in payments of 631 millons of euros spread across the main tax headings.

Source: Annual Report of he Revenue Commissioners, Financial Accounts and National Income and Expenditure Accounts.

StatLink http://dx.doi.org/10.1787/888933277173

Table 56. **Israel / Israël**
Details of tax revenue / Recettes fiscales détaillées

Million ILS

	1965	1980	1990	2000	2007	2008	2009	2011	2012	2013
Total tax revenue	..	..	..	**187 215**	**249 065**	**245 014**	**240 786**	**285 102**	**294 374**	**320 748**
1000 Taxes on income, profits and capital gains	..	..	..	**74 551**	**91 522**	**81 672**	**72 816**	**86 190**	**90 669**	**101 797**
1100 Of individuals	..	..	..	54 753	56 426	53 409	47 572	51 866	53 460	57 627
1110 On income and profits	..	..	..	53 698	55 205	52 488	46 965	50 981	52 721	56 137
On wages – deduction at source	..	..	..	45 278	45 507	43 215	39 141	42 817	43 345	46 774
On self employement income – deduction at source	..	..	..	2 655	3 676	3 509	2 699	3 149	3 372	3 891
On self employement income – other	..	..	..	5 764	6 022	5 764	5 125	5 015	6 004	5 472
1120 On capital gains	..	..	..	1 055	1 221	921	608	886	739	1 490
1200 Corporate	..	..	..	18 001	30 210	24 689	20 663	27 636	27 054	36 639
1210 On profits	..	..	..	16 109	27 582	22 899	20 049	26 860	26 083	33 939
deduction at source	..	..	..	1 991	2 550	2 488	2 090	2 308	2 423	2 611
In lieu of VAT on the profits of Financial Institutions	..	..	..	1 181	1 049	819	685	917	897	1 215
Other	..	..	..	12 937	23 983	19 592	17 273	23 635	22 763	30 113
1220 On capital gains	..	..	..	1 892	2 628	1 790	614	776	971	2 700
1300 Unallocable between 1100 and 1200	..	..	..	1 797	4 886	3 574	4 580	6 688	10 155	7 531
Tax deducted at the source on the capital market	..	..	..	1 797	4 886	3 574	4 580	6 688	10 155	7 531
2000 Social security contributions	..	..	..	**27 565**	**37 909**	**40 445**	**41 227**	**48 759**	**50 296**	**53 364**
2100 Employees	..	..	..	17 895	25 729	27 705	28 236	32 922	33 936	35 134
2110 On a payroll basis	..	..	..	17 895	25 729	27 705	28 236	32 922	33 936	35 134
2120 On an income tax basis	..	..	..	0	0	0	0	0	0	0
2200 Employers	..	..	..	8 182	9 960	10 190	10 278	12 805	13 313	15 026
2210 On a payroll basis	..	..	..	8 182	9 960	10 190	10 278	12 805	13 313	15 026
2220 On an income tax basis	..	..	..	0	0	0	0	0	0	0
2300 Self-employed or non-employed	..	..	..	1 488	2 220	2 550	2 712	3 033	3 047	3 204
2310 On a payroll basis	..	..	..	1 488	2 220	2 550	2 712	3 033	3 047	3 204
2320 On an income tax basis	..	..	..	0	0	0	0	0	0	0
2400 Unallocable between 2100, 2200 and 2300	..	..	..	0	0	0	0	0	0	0
2410 On a payroll basis	..	..	..	..	..	..	..	..	..	..
2420 On an income tax basis	..	..	..	..	..	..	..	..	..	..
3000 Taxes on payroll and workforce	..	..	..	**6 850**	**9 920**	**9 250**	**9 570**	**10 850**	**11 600**	**12 355**
Employers tax on the the non-profit sector other than govt	..	..	..	1 250	1 500	400	300	350	400	392
In lieu of VAT on the wage-bill in the non-profit sector	..	..	..	4 260	6 580	7 000	7 250	8 050	8 550	9 012
In lieu VAT on the wage-bill in Financial Institutions	..	..	..	1 340	1 840	1 850	2 020	2 450	2 650	2 951
4000 Taxes on property	..	..	..	**15 852**	**22 051**	**22 238**	**22 606**	**26 880**	**26 417**	**28 111**
4100 Recurrent taxes on immovable property	..	..	..	11 803	16 761	17 480	18 620	20 691	21 525	22 156
Land tax	..	..	..	442	52	53	45	82	57	59
4110 Households	..	..	..	0	0	0	0	0	0	0
4120 Others	..	..	..	11 361	16 709	17 427	18 575	20 609	21 468	22 097
4200 Recurrent taxes on net wealth	..	..	..	0	0	0	0	0	0	0
4210 Individual	..	..	..	..	..	..	..	..	..	..
4220 Corporate	..	..	..	..	..	..	..	..	..	..
4300 Estate, inheritance and gift taxes	..	..	..	0	0	0	0	0	0	0
4310 Estate and inheritance taxes	..	..	..	..	..	..	..	..	..	..
4320 Gift taxes	..	..	..	..	..	..	..	..	..	..
4400 Taxes on financial and capital transactions	..	..	..	2 845	3 087	2 411	2 229	3 113	2 788	3 398
Transaction tax on the buyer of real estate	..	..	..	1 632	2 616	2 284	2 166	3 086	2 786	3 398
Transaction tax on the seller of real estate	..	..	..	210	404	109	43	21	1	0
Stamp tax	..	..	..	1 003	67	17	20	7	1	0
4500 Non-recurrent taxes	..	..	..	1 204	2 203	2 347	1 757	3 075	2 104	2 557
4510 On net wealth	..	..	..	0	0	0	0	0	0	0
4520 Other non-recurrent taxes	..	..	..	1 204	2 203	2 347	1 757	3 075	2 104	2 557
Capital gains tax on real estate	..	..	..	1 204	2 203	2 347	1 757	3 075	2 104	2 557
4600 Other recurrent taxes on property	..	..	..	0	0	0	0	0	0	0
5000 Taxes on goods and services	..	..	..	**62 397**	**87 663**	**91 409**	**94 568**	**112 423**	**115 391**	**125 121**
5100 Taxes on production, sale, transfer, etc	..	..	..	57 887	81 109	84 642	87 834	104 407	107 155	116 335
5110 General taxes	..	..	..	49 876	67 571	69 687	71 954	85 586	88 167	97 357
5111 Value added taxes	..	..	..	39 805	53 984	56 737	59 223	70 197	72 777	81 524
5112 Sales tax	..	..	..	10 071	13 587	12 950	12 731	15 389	15 390	15 833
On domestic production	..	..	..	662	287	233	229	307	305	457
On imports	..	..	..	9 409	13 300	12 717	12 502	15 082	15 085	15 376
5113 Other	..	..	..	0	0	0	0	0	0	0
5120 Taxes on specific goods and services	..	..	..	8 011	13 538	14 955	15 880	18 821	18 988	18 978
5121 Excises	..	..	..	6 595	11 323	12 580	13 478	15 910	16 445	16 680
On domestically refined fuel	..	..	..	5 666	10 590	11 852	12 714	15 118	15 628	15 876
On domestically processed tobacco products	..	..	..	929	733	728	764	792	817	804
5122 Profits of fiscal monopolies	..	..	..	0	0	0	0	0	0	0
5123 Customs and import duties	..	..	..	1 417	2 215	2 375	2 402	2 911	2 543	2 298
5124 Taxes on exports	..	..	..	0	0	0	0	0	0	0
5125 Taxes on investment goods	..	..	..	0	0	0	0	0	0	0

Table 56. **Israel / Israël** (*cont.*)
Details of tax revenue / Recettes fiscales détaillées

Million ILS

	1965	1980	1990	2000	2007	2008	2009	2011	2012	2013
5126 Taxes on specific services	..	..	..	0	0	0	0	0	0	0
5127 Other taxes on internat. trade and transactions	..	..	..	0	0	0	0	0	0	0
5128 Other taxes	..	..	..	0	0	0	0	0	0	0
5130 Unallocable between 5110 and 5120	..	..	..	0	0	0	0	0	0	0
5200 Taxes on use of goods and perform activities	..	..	..	4 510	6 555	6 767	6 734	8 016	8 236	8 786
5210 Recurrent taxes	..	..	..	4 510	6 555	6 767	6 734	8 016	8 236	8 786
5211 Paid by households: motor vehicles	..	..	..	1 436	1 895	1 935	2 047	2 424	2 533	2 872
5212 Paid by others: motor vehicles	..	..	..	479	632	645	682	808	844	957
5213 Paid in respect of other goods	..	..	..	2 596	4 029	4 187	4 005	4 784	4 859	4 957
Licences collected by the Ministry of Transportation	..	..	..	257	535	457	357	287	345	132
Licences collected by the Ministry of Communication	..	..	..	151	332	281	282	148	269	299
Licences collected by other ministries	..	..	..	1 600	2 262	2 482	2 346	3 134	2 952	3 195
Business and professional licences paid locally	..	..	..	537	814	879	917	1 113	1 183	1 218
Other local authority fees	..	..	..	51	86	88	102	102	110	113
5220 Non-recurrent taxes	..	..	..	0	0	0	0	0	0	0
5300 Unallocable between 5100 and 5200	..	..	..	0	0	0	0	0	0	0
6000 Other taxes	..	..	..	**0**	**0**	**0**	**0**	**0**	**0**	**0**
6100 Paid solely by business	..	..	..	..	..	..	..	..	..	..
6200 Other	..	..	..	..	..	..	..	..	..	..
Total tax revenue on cash basis	..	..	..	**187 215**	**249 065**	**245 014**	**240 786**	**285 102**	**294 374**	**320 748**
Total tax revenue on accrual basis	..	..	..	..	..	..	..	..	..	..
Conciliation with National Accounts										
Additional taxes included in National Accounts	..	..	..	719	582	495	473	214	240	247
Taxes excluded from National Accounts	..	..	..	0	0	0	0	0	0	0
Difference in treatment of tax credits	..	..	..	0	0	0	0	0	0	0
Capital transfer for uncollected revenue	..	..	..	0	0	0	0	0	0	0
Voluntary social security contributions	..	..	..	0	0	0	0	0	0	0
Miscellaneous differences	..	..	..	0	0	0	0	0	0	0
National Accounts: Taxes and actual social contributions	..	..	..	187 934	249 647	245 509	241 259	285 316	294 614	320 995
Imputed social contributions	..	..	..	6 283	6 933	7 541	7 560	8 300	8 773	9 190
National Accounts: Taxes and all social contributions	..	..	..	194 217	256 579	253 050	248 819	293 616	303 387	330 186

Note:

Year ending 31st December.

Data are on a cash basis.

The statistical data for Israel are supplied by and under the resposibility of the relevant Israeli authorities. The use of such data by the OECD is without prejudice to the status of the Golan Heights, East Jerusalem and Israeli settlements in the West Bank under the terms of International law.

Source: Israel Central Bureau of Statistics and Israel Ministry of Finance.

StatLink http://dx.doi.org/10.1787/888933277187

Table 57. **Italy / Italie**
Details of tax revenue / Recettes fiscales détaillées

Million EUR

	1965	1980	1990	2000	2007	2008	2009	2011	2012	2013
Recettes fiscales totales	**5 505**	**60 422**	**265 116**	**503 096**	**671 189**	**679 433**	**661 885**	**686 395**	**708 633**	**706 234**
Recettes fiscales totales excluant les droits de douane	..	..	..	**501 560**	**668 928**	**677 233**	**659 877**	**684 076**	**706 556**	**704 344**
1000 Impôts sur revenu, bénéfices et gains en capital	**982**	**18 821**	**96 707**	**166 912**	**226 498**	**233 020**	**215 396**	**219 107**	**231 035**	**233 462**
1100 Des personnes physiques	603	13 940	69 654	124 918	171 938	182 186	176 991	182 440	189 433	187 508
1110 Sur le revenu et les bénéfices	603	13 796	68 786	124 233	171 924	182 176	176 981	182 433	189 428	187 503
Impôt sur le revenu des personnes physiques	0	11 538	57 318	121 211	166 859	176 468	171 610	179 155	184 987	182 576
Impôt sur revenu local (40%)	0	829	4 492	67	6	10	9	4	6	5
Impôt revenu richesse mobilière (60%)	319	55	15	0	0	1	0	0	8	11
Impôt complémentaire progressif	94	37	5	0	0	0	0	0	0	0
Centime additionnel de 10%	1	0	0	0	0	0	0	0	0	0
Retenue d'acompte sur bénéf. sociétés (40%)	23	51	496	110	217	275	171	178	258	226
Centime additionnel et loi 1177 (60%)	39	0	1	0	0	0	0	0	0	0
5% sur impôts directs centime additionnel (60%)	0	8	72	0	0	0	0	0	0	0
Majoration additionnelle du Trésor (60%)	23	6	1	0	0	0	0	0	0	0
Recettes du décret-loi 1132 (60%)	0	0	0	0	0	0	0	0	0	0
Impôt de famille	65	7	0	0	0	0	0	0	0	0
Impôt sur valeur locative	2	0	0	0	0	0	0	0	0	0
Impôt de patente	1	0	0	0	0	0	0	0	0	0
ICAP (provincial et communal) (40%)	37	5	0	22	0	0	0	0	0	0
Impôt sur le revenu des dépôts (40%)	0	1 206	6 223	2 823	4 308	4 846	4 489	2 478	3 658	4 184
Remises fiscales impôts directs (60%)	0	0	41	0	0	0	0	0	0	0
Autres	0	53	123	0	534	576	702	618	511	501
1120 Sur les gains en capital	0	144	867	685	14	10	10	7	5	5
Impôt sur les plus-value des terrains	..	0	0	0	0	0	0	0	0	0
Impôt sur les plus-value sur immeubles (60%)	..	144	867	685	14	10	10	7	5	5
1200 Des sociétés	379	4 710	26 605	34 699	58 943	58 102	46 523	42 886	47 586	50 773
1210 Sur les bénéfices	379	4 494	26 027	34 242	58 934	58 095	46 517	42 882	47 583	50 769
Impôt sur personnes morales	0	1 245	9 042	28 877	51 193	48 542	38 803	38 551	40 925	43 596
ICAP (provincial et communal) (60%)	37	8	0	32	0	0	0	0	0	0
Richesse mobilière (40%)	213	37	10	0	0	1	0	0	5	8
Impôt sur sociétés et obligations	88	12	2	0	0	0	0	0	0	0
Centimes additionnels et loi 1177 (40%)	26	0	0	0	0	0	0	0	0	0
5% sur centime additionnel impôts directs (40%)	0	20	48	0	0	0	0	0	0	0
Recettes décret-loi 1132 (40%)	0	0	0	0	0	0	0	0	0	0
Majoration additionnelle du Trésor (40 %)	15	4	0	0	0	0	0	0	0	0
Retenue d'acompte bénéfices sociétés (60%)	0	77	745	166	325	413	257	267	386	338
Impôt revenus des dépôts (60%)	0	1 810	9 334	4 235	6 464	7 270	6 732	3 718	5 487	6 274
Impôt local sur revenu (60%)	0	1 245	6 738	100	9	16	13	6	9	7
Remises fiscales impôts directs (40%)	0	0	27	0	0	0	0	0	0	0
Autres	0	36	82	832	943	1 853	712	340	771	546
1220 Sur les gains en capital	0	216	578	457	9	7	6	4	3	4
Impôt plus-value sur immeubles (40%)	..	216	578	457	9	7	6	4	3	4
1300 Non-ventilables entre 1100 et 1200	0	171	448	7 295	-4 383	-7 268	-8 118	-6 219	-5 984	-4 819
Remboursements impôts directs	..	-240	-1 768	-5 175	-9 433	-10 910	-11 164	-10 088	-12 466	-12 397
Autres	..	412	2 216	12 470	5 050	3 642	3 046	3 869	6 482	7 578
2000 Cotisations de sécurité sociale	**1 881**	**22 976**	**87 256**	**143 629**	**200 772**	**209 736**	**207 637**	**211 647**	**211 158**	**210 625**
2100 A la charge des salariés	..	4 171	16 753	27 333	35 715	38 454	37 866	37 607	36 689	39 284
2110 Sur la base du salaire	..	..	..	27 333	35 715	38 454	37 866	37 607	36 689	39 284
2120 Sur la base de l'impôt sur les revenus	..	..	..	0	0	0	0	0	0	0
2200 A la charge des employeurs	..	17 152	62 540	99 904	137 924	144 298	142 787	145 555	143 325	141 626
2210 Sur la base du salaire	..	..	..	99 904	137 924	144 298	142 787	145 555	143 325	141 626
2220 Sur la base de l'impôt sur les revenus	..	..	..	0	0	0	0	0	0	0
2300 A charge des travailleurs indép. ou sans emploi	..	1 654	7 962	16 392	27 133	26 984	26 984	28 485	31 144	29 715
2310 Sur la base du salaire	..	..	..	16 392	27 133	26 984	26 984	28 485	31 144	29 715
2320 Sur la base de l'impôt sur les revenus	..	..	..	0	0	0	0	0	0	0
2400 Non-ventilables entre 2100, 2200 et 2300	1 881	0	0	0	0	0	0	0	0	0
2410 Sur la base du salaire	..	..	..	..	..	..	..	..	..	..
2420 Sur la base de l'impôt sur les revenus	..	..	..	..	..	..	..	..	..	..
3000 Sur salaires ou main d'oeuvre	**0**	**387**	**890**	**0**	**0**	**0**	**0**	**0**	**0**	**0**
Cotisations GESCAL	..	387	890	..	..	..	..	..	..	..
4000 Impôts sur le patrimoine	**397**	**2 248**	**5 983**	**23 360**	**32 646**	**29 246**	**40 985**	**36 098**	**43 643**	**43 889**
4100 Impôts périodiques sur la propriété immobilière	96	7	1	9 354	12 778	9 683	9 461	9 848	23 942	20 729
Impôt sur revenu propriétaires de terres	2	0	0	0	0	0	0	0	0	0
Impôt sur revenu bâtiments	12	2	1	0	0	0	0	0	0	0
Impôt sur revenu bâtiments de luxe	1	0	0	0	0	0	0	0	0	0
Surtaxe terrains (province)	16	0	0	0	0	0	0	0	0	0
Surtaxe terrains (commune)	18	0	0	0	0	0	0	0	0	0
Surtaxe bâtiments (province)	26	2	0	0	0	0	0	0	0	0
Surtaxe bâtiments (commune)	21	3	0	0	0	0	0	0	0	0
Impôt communal immeubles	0	0	0	9 354	12 778	9 683	9 461	9 848	23 942	20 729

Table 57. **Italy / Italie** *(cont.)*
Details of tax revenue / Recettes fiscales détaillées

Million EUR

	1965	1980	1990	2000	2007	2008	2009	2011	2012	2013
4110 Ménages	..	..	..	..	..	..	..	..	..	..
4120 Autres agents	..	..	..	..	..	..	..	..	..	..
4200 Impôts périodiques sur l'actif net	0	0	0	14	1	1	6 575	5 117	778	2 547
4210 Personnes physiques	..	..	..	5	0	0	0	0	0	0
4220 Sociétés	..	..	..	9	1	1	6 575	5 117	778	2 547
4300 Impôts sur mut. par décès, succ. et donations	47	128	376	1 005	149	388	462	510	592	622
Impôt sur successions, donations	33	119	376	1 005	149	388	462	510	592	622
Valeur nette globale successions	11	9	0	0	0	0	0	0	0	0
Centimes additionnels et majoration	3	0	0	0	0	0	0	0	0	0
4310 Impôts sur mut. par décès et successions	..	..	..	..	..	..	..	..	..	..
4320 Impôts sur les donations	..	..	..	..	..	..	..	..	..	..
4400 Impôts sur transact. mobilières et immob.	255	2 113	5 606	12 320	18 256	17 533	17 349	16 798	15 317	17 091
Droit d'enregistrement	120	1 048	2 421	6 794	9 410	9 015	8 833	8 411	7 557	7 353
Impôts hypothécaires	22	190	469	1 067	2 525	2 341	2 076	2 112	1 854	1 841
Centimes additionnels de 5%	6	0	0	0	0	0	0	0	0	0
Majoration additionnelle	4	0	0	0	0	0	0	0	0	0
Droit de timbre	104	751	2 185	4 459	6 321	6 177	6 440	6 275	5 906	7 897
Autres	0	123	530	0	0	0	0	0	0	0
4500 Impôts non-périodiques	0	0	0	98	151	98	5 219	1 354	154	985
4510 Sur l'actif net	..	..	..	0	0	0	0	0	0	0
4520 Autres non-périodiques	..	..	..	98	151	98	5 219	1 354	154	985
4600 Autres impôts périodiques sur patrimoine	0	0	0	569	1 311	1 543	1 919	2 471	2 860	1 915
5000 Impôts sur les biens et services	**2 173**	**15 990**	**74 280**	**140 316**	**169 608**	**168 838**	**164 207**	**184 275**	**187 524**	**184 382**
5100 Impôts sur production, vente, transfert, etc.	2 037	15 251	67 083	125 745	152 930	151 709	146 855	164 900	167 312	162 694
Remboursements impôts indirects	0	-73	-86	0	0	0	0	0	0	0
5110 Impôts généraux	710	9 438	38 940	77 473	95 623	93 753	86 544	98 650	96 170	93 921
5111 Taxes sur la valeur ajoutée	0	9 438	38 940	77 473	95 623	93 753	86 544	98 650	96 170	93 921
TVA	..	9 438	38 940	77 473	95 623	93 753	86 544	98 650	96 170	93 921
5112 Impôts sur les ventes	0	0	0	0	0	0	0	0	0	0
5113 Autres impôts	710	0	0	0	0	0	0	0	0	0
Impôt général sur recettes	662	..	..	..	..	..	..	..	..	..
Impôt compensation sur produits importés	48	..	..	..	..	..	..	..	..	..
5120 Impôts sur biens et services déterminés	1 327	5 886	28 048	48 272	57 307	57 956	60 311	66 250	71 142	68 773
5121 Accises	816	4 088	20 304	31 479	32 904	33 431	35 639	41 088	46 796	45 720
Sur huiles minérales	465	3 462	15 928	22 172	23 252	23 448	23 157	23 771	27 680	26 332
Sur spiritueux	27	87	206	486	595	607	569	552	545	571
Sur bière	12	54	172	242	489	553	463	528	494	532
Sur sucre et matières édulcorantes	22	25	68	120	0	11	6	5	7	10
Sur énergie électrique	20	51	2 018	3 079	3 034	5 509	5 960	10 361	13 099	13 542
Sur bananes	9	53	97	0	0	0	0	0	0	0
Sur café	31	60	74	0	0	0	0	0	0	0
Sur cacao	3	4	7	0	0	0	0	0	0	0
Sur huile d'olive	0	0	0	0	0	0	0	0	0	0
Autres accises	44	190	1 037	5 201	5 385	3 230	5 425	5 816	4 910	4 659
Alcool, eaux de vie, liqueur	5	0	0	0	0	0	0	0	0	0
Sur allumettes et pierres à briquets	13	22	47	0	0	0	0	0	0	0
Viandes	26	0	0	0	0	0	0	0	0	0
Surtaxe sur douane	0	81	650	174	143	67	59	48	54	67
Combustibles	39	0	0	0	0	0	0	0	0	0
Matériaux de construction	30	0	0	0	0	0	0	0	0	0
Taxe de radiodiffusion	3	0	0	0	0	0	0	0	0	0
Impôt sur disques phonographiques	1	0	0	0	0	0	0	0	0	0
Droit de timbre cartes a jouer	1	0	0	0	0	0	0	0	0	0
Autres	66	0	0	5	6	6	0	7	7	7
5122 Bénéfices des monopoles fiscaux	303	1 033	3 248	7 718	10 440	10 781	10 945	11 247	11 362	10 683
Sur tabac	292	1 033	3 248	7 712	10 436	10 775	10 941	11 243	11 358	10 679
Sur sel	10	0	0	0	0	0	0	0	0	0
Sur papiers et tubes à cigarettes	1	0	0	6	4	6	4	4	4	4
5123 Droits de douane et droits à l'importation	142	261	1 164	0	0	0	0	0	0	0
Tarif douanier commune (Ress. pr. CEE)	0	0	836	..	..	..	..	..	..	..
Douanes et droits maritimes	115	14	0	..	..	..	..	..	..	..
Droit services administration	11	0	0	..	..	..	..	..	..	..
Prélèvement dans l'agriculture	15	228	207	..	..	..	..	..	..	..
Recettes diverses	0	9	68	..	..	..	..	..	..	..
Montants compensatoires	0	9	53	..	..	..	..	..	..	..
5124 Taxes à l'exportation	0	0	0	0	0	0	0	0	0	0
5125 Impôts sur biens d'équipement	0	0	0	0	0	0	0	0	0	0

Table 57. **Italy / Italie** *(cont.)*
Details of tax revenue / Recettes fiscales détaillées

Million EUR

	1965	1980	1990	2000	2007	2008	2009	2011	2012	2013
5126 Impôts sur services déterminés	67	483	3 141	9 029	13 932	13 744	13 727	13 915	12 984	12 370
Taxes entrées spectacles	20	59	167	118	68	66	56	52	44	42
Droit de timbres	6	0	0	0	0	0	0	0	0	0
Impôt sur la publicité	6	56	168	389	392	403	393	440	424	422
Loto, loterie et concours dotés de prix	3	123	617	4 164	7 144	7 247	7 980	8 090	7 477	7 088
Droit d'état sur spectacles, jeux et paris	0	0	0	158	152	155	151	192	191	130
Taxe sur concours de pronostics et jeux d'adresse	9	74	476	487	405	330	237	186	144	85
Droit spécial péages autoroutes	0	0	0	0	0	0	0	0	5	7
Impôts subst. (compris sur l'assurance)	23	171	1 714	3 713	5 771	5 543	4 910	4 955	4 699	4 596
5127 Autres impôts sur commerce et transact. internat.	0	0	0	0	0	0	0	0	0	0
Droit spéc. paiements et ventes devises à l'étranger	..	..	..	..	..	..	..	..	..	..
5128 Autres impôts	0	21	192	46	31	0	0	0	0	0
Prélèvements CECA cotisation sucre et autres	..	21	121	0	0	..	..	..	..	..
Autres	..	0	70	46	31	..	..	..	..	..
5130 Non-ventilables entre 5110 et 5120	0	0	180	0	0	0	0	0	0	0
5200 Impôts sur utilisation des biens et exerc. activités	136	456	4 474	8 479	10 550	10 471	10 407	10 907	11 185	10 930
5210 Impôts périodiques	136	456	4 474	8 479	10 550	10 471	10 407	10 907	11 185	10 930
Taxe sur les voitures	64	152	967	1 034	1 326	1 249	1 192	1 242	1 368	1 359
Centime additionnel de 5% sur imp. de circulation	3	13	450	0	0	0	0	0	0	0
Surtaxe sur voitures diesel	0	66	683	0	0	0	0	0	0	0
Surtaxe sur voitures à gaz	0	0	171	0	0	0	0	0	0	0
5211 A la charge des ménages : véhicules à moteur	..	..	..	3 433	4 652	4 595	4 497	4 658	4 803	4 487
5212 A la charge autres agents : véhicules à moteur	..	..	..	1 006	1 332	1 311	1 293	1 392	1 382	1 395
Impôt de licence	3	..	..	1 006	1 332	1 311	1 293	1 392	1 382	1 395
5213 Autres impôts périodiques	67	225	2 203	3 006	3 240	3 316	3 425	3 615	3 632	3 689
Centimes additionnels loi 1177	22	0	0	0	0	0	0	0	0	0
Taxes sur enseignes	2	4	0	0	0	0	0	0	0	0
Plaques de chien	0	7	12	0	0	0	0	0	0	0
Taxe sur chasse et pêche	0	0	0	0	0	0	0	0	0	0
Taxes concessions gouvernementales	43	215	2 191	3 006	3 240	3 316	3 425	3 615	3 632	3 689
5220 Impôts non-périodiques	0	0	0	0	0	0	0	0	0	0
Véhicules a moteur, aéroplanes	..	..	..	..	..	..	..	..	..	..
Pro.friuli sur les voitures	..	..	..	..	..	..	..	..	..	..
5300 Non-ventilables entre 5100 et 5200	0	283	2 724	6 092	6 128	6 658	6 945	8 468	9 027	10 758
Remise fiscale impôts indirects	..	0	160	288	616	614	523	684	769	473
Autres	..	283	2 564	5 804	5 512	6 044	6 422	7 784	8 258	10 285
6000 Autres impôts	**72**	**0**	**0**	**27 343**	**39 404**	**36 393**	**31 652**	**32 949**	**33 196**	**31 986**
6100 A la charge exclusive des entreprises	0	..	..	27 343	39 404	36 393	31 652	32 949	33 196	31 986
6200 A la charge d'autres agents	72	..	..	0	0	0	0	0	0	0
Impôt extraordinaire sur patrimoine	2	..	..	..	..	..	..	..	..	..
Autres recettes	71	..	..	..	..	..	..	..	..	..
Droits de douane perçus pour l'UE	**..**	**..**	**..**	**1 536**	**2 261**	**2 200**	**2 008**	**2 319**	**2 077**	**1 890**
Recettes fiscales totales sur la base d'encaissements	**5 505**	**60 422**	**265 116**	**488 738**	**653 836**	**664 703**	**647 496**	**664 769**	**679 758**	**673 580**
Recettes fiscales totales sur la base des droits constatés	**..**	**..**	**..**	**503 096**	**671 189**	**679 433**	**661 885**	**686 395**	**708 633**	**706 234**
Conciliation avex les Comptes nationaux										
Impôts additionnels inclus dans les comptes nationaux	..	..	..	0	0	0	0	0	0	0
Impôt exclus des comptes nationaux	..	..	..	-5 416	-5 470	-5 704	-6 137	-7 517	-7 997	-10 003
Taxe sur les déchets ménagers urbains	..	..	..	-4 387	-4 443	-4 689	-5 133	-6 404	-6 802	-8 644
Autres	..	..	..	-1 029	-1 027	-1 015	-1 004	-1 113	-1 195	-1 359
Différence dans les traitements des crédits d'impôts	..	..	..	0	0	0	0	0	0	0
Transfert en capital des recettes non collectées	..	..	..	0	0	0	0	0	0	0
Cotisations de sécurité sociale volontaires	..	..	..	464	567	500	529	569	575	575
Différences diverses	..	..	..	0	0	0	0	0	0	0
Comptes nationaux: impôts et cotisations sociales effectives	..	..	..	498 144	666 286	674 229	656 277	679 447	701 211	696 806
Cotisations sociales imputées	..	..	..	3 884	3 980	3 873	3 959	4 108	4 089	4 092
Comptes nationaux: impôts et toutes les cotisations sociales	..	..	..	502 028	670 266	678 102	660 236	683 555	705 300	700 898

Note:

Année civile se terminant le 31 décembre.

A partir de l'année 2000, les données sont sur la base des droits constatés.

A partir de 1997, les données tiennent compte des statistiques communiquées à l'Union européenne aux fins de la procédure sur les déficits excessifs du traité de Maastricht.

Rubrique 6000 : Impôt régional sur les activités productives (IRAP); il s'agit d'un impôt sur la valeur ajoutée de la production prélevé sur une base différente de celle indiquée pour les autres groupes. La ventilation entre l'IRAP à la charge des personnes morales et l'IRAP à la charge des personnes physiques est fondée sur des estimations.

Rubrique Impôts exclus des comptes nationaux, ligne « autres » : Taxes sur l'occupation des lieux publics et sur la collecte et le traitement des eaux usées.

Source: Rendiconto Generale della Administrazione dello Stato; Relazione generale sulla Situazione Economica del Paese et Ministerio delle Finanze, Direzione Centrale per la Fiscalita Locale.

StatLink http://dx.doi.org/10.1787/888933277196

Table 58. **Japan / Japon**
Details of tax revenue / Recettes fiscales détaillées

Billion JPY

	1965	1980	1990	2000	2007	2008	2009	2011	2012	2013
Total tax revenue	**6 172**	**62 443**	**130 823**	**136 125**	**146 243**	**139 616**	**127 768**	**135 668**	**139 578**	**146 436**
1000 Taxes on income, profits and capital gains	**2 708**	**28 800**	**65 682**	**47 398**	**53 174**	**46 850**	**37 739**	**40 910**	**43 352**	**47 534**
1100 Of individuals	1 338	15 180	36 394	28 677	28 600	27 790	25 518	24 951	25 946	28 150
1110 On income and profits	1 338	15 180	36 394	28 677	28 600	27 790	25 518	24 951	25 946	28 150
Income tax	970	10 800	25 996	18 789	16 080	14 985	12 914	13 476	14 044	15 865
Prefectural inhabitants tax	123	1 415	3 675	3 621	5 008	5 143	5 052	4 608	4 783	5 089
Municipal inhabitants tax	220	2 890	6 475	6 044	7 294	7 445	7 349	6 688	6 942	7 015
Enterprise tax	25	75	249	223	218	217	204	179	178	181
1120 On capital gains	0	0	0	0	0	0	0	0	0	0
1200 Corporate	1 370	13 620	29 288	18 721	24 573	19 061	12 221	15 959	17 406	19 384
1210 On profits	1 370	13 620	29 288	18 721	24 573	19 061	12 221	15 959	17 406	19 384
Corporation tax	927	8 923	18 384	11 747	14 744	10 011	6 356	9 351	10 408	11 698
Prefectural inhabitants tax	53	557	1 414	879	1 206	1 096	715	800	846	854
Municipal inhabitants tax	85	1 297	3 198	2 176	3 015	2 752	1 775	2 011	2 129	2 157
Enterprise tax	305	2 843	6 293	3 918	5 608	5 203	2 701	2 240	2 354	2 674
Local special corporate tax	0	0	0	0	0	0	674	1 556	1 670	2 001
1220 On capital gains	0	0	0	0	0	0	0	0	0	0
1300 Unallocable between 1100 and 1200	0	0	0	0	0	0	0	0	0	0
2000 Social security contributions	**1 344**	**18 178**	**34 593**	**47 857**	**53 321**	**54 227**	**52 342**	**56 321**	**58 068**	**59 834**
2100 Employees	446	6 393	13 883	19 786	21 972	23 250	22 484	24 431	25 182	25 972
2110 On a payroll basis	..	..	13 883	19 786	21 972	23 250	22 484	24 431	25 182	25 972
2120 On an income tax basis	..	..	0	0	0	0	0	0	0	0
2200 Employers	588	9 267	16 642	22 388	24 240	24 663	23 575	25 735	26 333	27 186
2210 On a payroll basis	..	..	16 642	22 388	24 240	24 663	23 575	25 735	26 333	27 186
2220 On an income tax basis	..	..	0	0	0	0	0	0	0	0
2300 Self-employed or non-employed	107	2 518	4 069	5 683	7 108	6 314	6 282	6 156	6 553	6 676
2310 On a payroll basis	..	..	4 069	5 683	7 108	6 314	6 282	6 156	6 553	6 676
2320 On an income tax basis	..	..	0	0	0	0	0	0	0	0
2400 Unallocable between 2100, 2200 and 2300	203	0	0	0	0	0	0	0	0	0
2410 On a payroll basis	..	..	..	..	..	..	..	..	..	..
2420 On an income tax basis	..	..	..	..	..	..	..	..	..	..
3000 Taxes on payroll and workforce	**0**	**0**	**0**	**0**	**0**	**0**	**0**	**0**	**0**	**0**
4000 Taxes on property	**498**	**5 114**	**12 296**	**14 294**	**13 138**	**13 111**	**12 949**	**13 100**	**12 716**	**12 940**
4100 Recurrent taxes on immovable property	319	3 326	7 099	10 414	9 949	10 123	10 128	10 237	9 799	9 882
Prefectural property tax	4	8	15	11	14	18	19	3	2	2
Municipal property tax	296	2 784	6 023	9 041	8 729	8 876	8 874	8 966	8 580	8 653
City planning tax	19	469	942	1 318	1 202	1 225	1 233	1 268	1 216	1 227
Special landholding tax	0	65	118	43	4	4	2	1	1	1
Water and land utilization tax	0	0	0	0	0	0	0	0	0	0
Land value tax	0	0	0	1	0	0	0	0	0	0
4110 Households	..	..	..	..	..	..	..	..	..	..
4120 Others	..	..	..	..	..	..	..	..	..	..
4200 Recurrent taxes on net wealth	0	0	0	0	0	0	0	0	0	0
4210 Individual	..	..	..	..	..	..	..	..	..	..
4220 Corporate	..	..	..	..	..	..	..	..	..	..
4300 Estate, inheritance and gift taxes	44	441	1 918	1 782	1 503	1 455	1 350	1 474	1 504	1 574
4310 Estate and inheritance taxes	34	375	..	..	..	..	..	..	..	..
Inheritance tax	34	375	..	..	..	..	..	..	..	..
4320 Gift taxes	10	65	..	..	..	..	..	..	..	..
Tax on gifts	10	65	..	..	..	..	..	..	..	..
4400 Taxes on financial and capital transactions	135	1 347	3 280	2 099	1 686	1 534	1 472	1 388	1 413	1 483
Bourse tax	3	15	41	0	0	0	0	0	0	0
Securities transaction	8	209	748	0	0	0	0	0	0	0
Bank of Japan note issue tax	0	0	0	0	0	0	0	0	0	0
Stamp revenues	83	841	1 894	1 532	1 202	1 088	1 068	1 047	1 078	1 126
Real property acquisition tax	41	282	596	567	485	445	404	342	336	357
4500 Non-recurrent taxes	0	0	0	0	0	0	0	0	0	0
4510 On net wealth	..	..	..	..	..	..	..	..	..	..
4520 Other non-recurrent taxes	..	..	..	..	..	..	..	..	..	..
4600 Other recurrent taxes on property	0	0	0	0	0	0	0	0	0	0
5000 Taxes on goods and services	**1 620**	**10 200**	**17 917**	**26 227**	**26 256**	**25 060**	**24 364**	**24 966**	**25 056**	**25 744**
5100 Taxes on production, sale, transfer, etc	1 544	8 822	15 647	23 180	23 241	22 111	21 561	22 410	22 592	23 313
5110 General taxes	0	0	5 778	12 350	12 841	12 443	12 221	12 745	12 902	13 479
5111 Value added taxes	..	..	5 778	12 350	12 841	12 443	12 221	12 745	12 902	13 479
5112 Sales tax	..	..	0	0	0	0	0	0	0	0
5113 Other	..	..	0	0	0	0	0	0	0	0
5120 Taxes on specific goods and services	1 544	8 822	9 868	10 830	10 400	9 668	9 340	9 665	9 690	9 834

Table 58. **Japan / Japon** *(cont.)*
Details of tax revenue / Recettes fiscales détaillées

Billion JPY

	1965	1980	1990	2000	2007	2008	2009	2011	2012	2013
5121 Excises	1 062	6 674	8 637	9 837	9 374	8 702	8 527	8 719	8 721	8 728
Liquor tax	353	1 424	1 935	1 816	1 524	1 461	1 417	1 369	1 350	1 371
Sugar excises	29	43	0	0	0	0	0	0	0	0
Local gasoline tax	46	278	361	296	302	286	291	283	281	275
Gasoline tax	254	1 547	2 007	2 769	2 820	2 572	2 715	2 648	2 622	2 574
Liquefied petroleum gas tax	0	30	31	28	27	26	25	23	21	21
Aviation fuel tax	0	58	76	104	104	99	94	60	64	67
Commodity tax	138	1 038	5	0	0	0	0	0	0	0
Playing-card tax	1	1	0	0	0	0	0	0	0	0
Prefectural tobacco tax	44	229	361	282	278	263	250	293	289	173
Municipal tobacco tax	73	402	636	865	853	808	767	900	887	983
Timber delivery tax	3	3	0	0	0	0	0	0	0	0
Mineral product tax	2	5	3	2	2	2	2	2	2	2
Electricity and gas tax	54	386	0	0	0	0	0	0	0	0
Diesel oil tax	65	447	834	1 208	1 034	919	908	932	925	943
Vehicle acquisition tax	0	270	613	464	425	366	231	168	210	193
Promotion of power resources development tax	0	109	295	375	352	341	329	331	328	328
Petroleum and coal tax	0	404	487	489	513	511	487	519	567	599
Tobacco tax	0	0	996	876	925	851	822	1 032	1 018	1 038
Special tobacco tax	0	0	0	264	214	197	190	160	158	161
5122 Profits of fiscal monopolies	179	808	0	0	0	0	0	0	0	0
Monopoly profits	179	808	..	..	..	..	..	..	..	..
5123 Customs and import duties	222	786	928	877	941	883	732	874	897	1 034
Customs duty	222	786	928	877	941	883	732	874	897	1 034
5124 Taxes on exports	0	0	0	0	0	0	0	0	0	0
5125 Taxes on investment goods	0	0	0	0	0	0	0	0	0	0
5126 Taxes on specific services	81	554	303	116	85	84	81	72	73	71
Travel tax	4	64	0	0	0	0	0	0	0	0
Admission tax	10	5	0	0	0	0	0	0	0	0
Local entertainment tax	10	74	0	0	0	0	0	0	0	0
Golf course utilization tax	0	0	90	81	60	60	58	51	51	49
Meal and lodging tax	56	398	0	0	0	0	0	0	0	0
Special local consumption tax	0	0	195	12	0	0	0	0	0	0
Bathing tax	1	13	18	23	25	24	23	21	22	22
5127 Other taxes on internat. trade and transactions	0	0	0	0	0	0	0	0	0	0
5128 Other taxes	0	0	0	0	0	0	0	0	0	0
5130 Unallocable between 5110 and 5120	0	0	0	0	0	0	0	0	0	0
5200 Taxes on use of goods and perform activities	76	1 378	2 270	3 047	3 015	2 949	2 803	2 557	2 464	2 431
5210 Recurrent taxes	69	1 358	2 250	3 027	2 993	2 928	2 783	2 535	2 442	2 409
Automobile tax	55	781	1 276	1 765	1 717	1 681	1 654	1 597	1 586	1 574
Light vehicle tax	13	43	88	125	164	169	174	180	184	189
Motor vehicle tonnage tax	0	527	881	1 134	1 110	1 076	953	755	669	643
Hunter licence tax	0	3	2	2	0	0	0	0	0	0
Hunting tax	0	3	2	1	2	2	2	2	2	2
Mine lot tax	1	1	1	1	0	0	0	0	0	0
5211 Paid by households: motor vehicles	..	..	..	..	..	..	..	..	..	..
5212 Paid by others: motor vehicles	..	..	..	..	..	..	..	..	..	..
5213 Paid in respect of other goods	..	..	..	..	..	..	..	..	..	..
5220 Non-recurrent taxes	7	20	20	20	22	21	20	22	22	22
5300 Unallocable between 5100 and 5200	0	0	0	0	0	0	0	0	0	0
6000 Other taxes	**2**	**151**	**335**	**348**	**356**	**367**	**374**	**371**	**386**	**384**
6100 Paid solely by business	0	139	288	324	313	323	328	339	350	348
Business office tax	..	139	288	324	313	323	328	339	350	348
6200 Other	2	12	47	24	43	45	46	32	36	35
Taxes not in local tax law	2	12	47	24	43	45	46	32	36	35
Other	0	0	0	0	0	0	0	0	0	0
Total tax revenue on cash basis	**6 172**	**62 443**	..	..	..	..	..	..	..	..
Total tax revenue on accrual basis	..	..	**130 823**	**136 125**	**146 243**	**139 616**	**127 768**	**135 668**	**139 578**	**146 436**
Conciliation with National Accounts										
Additional taxes included in National Accounts	..	..	..	..	..	..	..	..	..	..
Taxes excluded from National Accounts	..	..	..	..	..	..	..	..	..	..
Difference in treatment of tax credits	..	..	..	..	..	..	..	..	..	..
Capital transfer for uncollected revenue	..	..	..	..	..	..	..	..	..	..
Voluntary social security contributions	..	..	..	..	..	..	..	..	..	..
Miscellaneous differences	..	..	..	..	..	..	..	..	..	..
National Accounts: Taxes and actual social contributions	..	..	..	..	..	..	..	..	..	..
Imputed social contributions	..	..	..	..	..	..	..	..	..	..
National Accounts: Taxes and all social contributions	..	..	..	..	..	..	..	..	..	..

Note:

Data are on a fiscal year basis beginning 1st April.

From 1990, data are on accrual basis.

The figures for different groups of taxes are reported on different reporting bases, namely: Social security contributions (heading 2000) : in principle accrual basis, Central government taxes : accrual basis (revenues accrued during the fiscal year plus cash receipts collected before the end of May (the end of April until 1977), Local government taxes : accrual basis (due to be paid during the fiscal year and cash receipts collected before the end of May).

The Japanese authorities take the view that the Enterprise tax (classified in 1100 and 1200) and the Mineral product tax (classified in 5121) should be classified in heading 6000 since under articles 72 and 519 of the Local Tax Law these taxes are regarded as levies on the business or mining activity itself.

Heading 2000 includes some unidentifiable voluntary contributions.

Heading 2300: Includes contibutions to the National pension, National Health Insurance and the Farmer's pension fund. Contributions to the Farmer's pension fund are not available for the years before 1999.

Heading 4100: Municipal property tax, includes Prefectural property tax from 1990 to 1994 because data is not available to provide a breakdown.

Heading 5121: Municipal tobacco tax, includes Prefectural tobacco tax from 1990 to 1994 because data is not available to provide a breakdown.

Heading 5121: In sub-item Petroleum and coal tax, the data before 2003 refer to petroleum tax.

Source: Tax Bureau, Ministry of Finance.

StatLink http://dx.doi.org/10.1787/888933277206

Table 59. **Korea / Corée**
Details of tax revenue / Recettes fiscales détaillées

Billion KRW

	1965	1980	1990	2000	2007	2008	2009	2011	2012	2013
Total tax revenue	..	**6 687**	**37 262**	**136 295**	**258 571**	**272 201**	**273 647**	**321 915**	**341 336**	**347 332**
1000 Taxes on income, profits and capital gains	..	**1 704**	**12 203**	**39 254**	**82 239**	**84 321**	**77 897**	**96 845**	**101 944**	**101 792**
1100 Of individuals	..	766	7 440	19 950	43 276	40 910	38 618	47 299	51 185	53 311
Income tax	..	0	0	0	0	0	0	0	0	0
Dividends and interest income tax	..	0	0	0	4 682	4 659	4 762	4 896	5 152	4 889
Wages and salaries income tax	..	0	0	0	14 124	15 595	13 407	18 337	19 627	21 931
Other income tax	..	0	0	0	2 607	2 698	2 829	3 365	3 595	3 432
Global income tax	..	661	4 723	16 128	6 151	4 078	6 117	8 300	9 938	10 901
Defence tax on income tax	..	105	938	0	0	0	0	0	0	0
Education tax on income tax	..	0	325	0	0	0	0	0	0	0
Rural development tax on interest, bus. Inc. & cap.gains relief	..	0	0	156	160	148	199	156	125	124
Inhabitant tax on income tax (local)	..	0	341	2 285	4 260	4 407	3 996	4 856	5 293	5 377
1110 On income and profits	..	766	6 327	18 569	31 984	31 585	31 310	39 910	43 730	46 654
1120 On capital gains	..	0	1 113	1 381	11 292	9 325	7 308	7 389	7 455	6 657
Capital gains tax	..	..	1 113	1 381	11 292	9 325	7 308	7 389	7 455	6 657
1200 Corporate	..	738	4 757	19 271	38 963	43 409	39 279	49 546	50 759	48 481
Corporation tax - withholding	..	..	677	8 577	8 360	7 417	4 681	10 534	11 516	12 176
Corporation tax - final returns	..	..	2 549	9 302	27 057	31 737	30 570	34 339	34 416	31 679
Defence tax on corporation tax	..	..	1 323	0	0	0	0	0	0	0
Inhabitant tax on corporation tax (local)	..	..	207	1 142	3 152	3 756	3 556	3 953	4 258	4 118
Rural development tax corporate income	..	..	0	251	394	498	472	720	569	508
1210 On profits	..	738	4 757	19 271	38 963	43 409	39 279	49 546	50 759	48 481
Excess profit tax	..	0	0	0	0	0	0	0	0	0
1220 On capital gains	..	0	0	0	0	0	0	0	0	0
Capital gains tax	..	..	..	..	..	..	..	..	..	..
1300 Unallocable between 1100 and 1200	..	199	6	33	0	2	0	0	0	0
Business income tax	..	0	0	0	..	0	..	..	..	..
Real estate income tax	..	0	0	0	..	0	..	..	..	..
Defence tax on real estate & business income	..	0	0	0	..	0	..	..	..	..
Rural dev. tax on bus. inc. & cap. gains relief	..	0	0	30	..	2	..	..	..	..
Inhabitant tax before 1990 (local)	..	117	0	0	..	0	..	..	..	..
Farm land tax (local)	..	83	6	3	..	0	..	..	..	..
Inhabitant tax on farm land tax (local)	..	0	0	0	..	0	..	..	..	..
2000 Social security contributions	..	**73**	**3 760**	**22 759**	**53 588**	**59 415**	**63 939**	**77 234**	**84 380**	**91 596**
2100 Employees	..	0	1 464	8 578	21 773	24 236	25 638	31 875	35 670	38 396
Veterans' relief fund	..	0	0	0	0	0	0	0	0	0
Soldiers' annuity fund	..	0	0	0	0	0	0	0	0	0
Unemployment assurance	..	0	0	598	1 164	1 288	1 346	1 698	2 138	2 418
National welfare pension fund	..	0	429	4 325	9 338	9 976	10 358	11 832	12 867	13 890
Social benefit fund	..	0	0	0	0	0	0	0	0	0
Health Insurance	..	0	483	2 066	8 180	9 702	10 581	13 954	15 718	17 128
Teachers' pensions	..	0	86	279	581	612	621	940	1 229	1 077
Government employees pensions	..	0	406	1 144	2 202	2 345	2 308	3 106	3 345	3 435
Military personal pensions	..	0	60	166	308	313	313	345	373	448
2110 On a payroll basis	..	..	..	8 578	21 773	24 236	25 638	31 875	35 670	38 396
2120 On an income tax basis	..	..	..	0	0	0	0	0	0	0
2200 Employers	..	73	1 694	9 409	23 557	26 194	28 981	34 366	36 911	41 518
Ind. works' insurance fund	..	73	550	1 876	4 431	4 844	4 732	4 632	5 508	5 436
Soldiers' annuity fund	..	0	0	0	0	0	0	0	0	0
Pneumoconiosis fund	..	0	0	0	0	0	0	0	0	0
Unemployment insurance	..	0	0	1 449	2 474	2 681	2 843	3 347	4 166	4 545
Veterans' relief fund	..	0	0	0	0	0	0	0	0	0
National welfare pension fund	..	0	430	4 340	9 383	10 009	10 393	11 833	12 930	13 958
Social benefit fund	..	0	0	0	0	0	0	0	0	0
Health Insurance	..	0	658	1 547	6 844	8 213	8 980	13 889	13 576	16 826
Teachers' pensions	..	0	56	197	425	447	456	665	731	753
Government employees pensions	..	0	0	0	0	0	0	0	0	0
2210 On a payroll basis	..	..	..	9 409	23 557	26 194	28 981	34 366	36 911	41 518
2220 On an income tax basis	..	..	..	0	0	0	0	0	0	0
2300 Self-employed or non-employed	..	0	602	4 772	8 258	8 985	9 320	10 993	11 799	11 682
2310 On a payroll basis	..	..	0	0	0	0	0	0	0	0
2320 On an income tax basis	..	..	602	4 772	8 258	8 985	9 234	10 993	11 799	11 682
2400 Unallocable between 2100, 2200 and 2300	..	0	0	0	0	0	0	0	0	0
2410 On a payroll basis	..	..	..	..	..	..	..	..	..	..
2420 On an income tax basis	..	..	..	..	..	..	..	..	..	..
3000 Taxes on payroll and workforce	..	**34**	**153**	**258**	**619**	**682**	**681**	**803**	**868**	**981**
Workshop tax on workforce (local)	..	31	124	258	619	682	681	803	868	981
Vocational training promotion fund	..	3	29	0	0	0	0	0	0	0
4000 Taxes on property	..	**537**	**4 389**	**16 846**	**33 109**	**32 468**	**31 803**	**36 555**	**36 213**	**35 847**

Table 59. **Korea / Corée** *(cont.)*
Details of tax revenue / Recettes fiscales détaillées

Billion KRW

	1965	1980	1990	2000	2007	2008	2009	2011	2012	2013
4100 Recurrent taxes on immovable property	..	183	980	3 385	9 196	9 859	8 859	9 779	10 315	10 809
Property tax (local)	..	119	227	728	3 755	4 411	4 423	7 617	8 049	8 267
City planning tax on urban real estate (local)	..	51	244	815	1 883	2 183	2 269	5	3	0
Community facilities tax (local)	..	13	86	341	543	589	591	705	766	912
Tax on excessive land holdings (local)	..	0	1	0	0	0	0	0	0	0
Tax on aggregate land holdings (local)	..	0	400	1 282	5	0	0	0	0	0
Rural dev. tax on local agg. land holdings tax	..	0	0	81	1	0	0	0	0	0
Tax on excessively increased land value	..	0	0	0	0	0	0	0	0	0
Comprehensive real estate tax	..	0	0	0	2 414	2 130	1 207	1 102	1 131	1 224
Rural dev. tax on comprehensive real estate tax	..	0	0	0	483	428	242	223	228	250
4110 Households	..	..	0	0	0	0	0	0	0	0
4120 Others	..	..	22	138	112	118	127	127	138	156
Workshop tax on property (local)	..	..	22	138	112	118	127	127	138	156
4200 Recurrent taxes on net wealth	..	0	0	0	0	0	0	0	0	0
4210 Individual	..	..	..	..	..	..	..	..	..	..
4220 Corporate	..	..	..	..	..	..	..	..	..	..
4300 Estate, inheritance and gift taxes	..	12	354	989	2 842	2 777	2 431	3 333	4 021	4 290
4310 Estate and inheritance taxes	..	5	85	449	1 059	1 182	1 221	1 259	1 719	1 587
Inheritance tax	..	3	71	449	1 059	1 182	1 221	1 259	1 719	1 587
Defence tax on inheritance tax	..	2	14	0	0	0	0	0	0	0
4320 Gift taxes	..	7	269	540	1 783	1 595	1 210	2 074	2 302	2 703
Gift tax	..	7	225	540	1 783	1 595	1 210	2 074	2 302	2 703
Defence tax on gift tax	..	0	44	0	0	0	0	0	0	0
4400 Taxes on financial and capital transactions	..	319	2 960	11 935	21 071	19 832	20 513	23 443	21 877	20 748
Registration tax (local)	..	122	1 378	4 528	7 254	7 143	7 131	7 680	7 645	1 312
Registration tax	..	0	0	0	0	0	0	0	0	0
Defence tax on registration tax	..	0	0	0	0	0	0	0	0	0
Rural dev. tax on local acquisition tax	..	0	0	246	627	635	621	982	853	874
Rural dev. tax on local registration tax	..	0	0	66	143	142	169	2	2	1
Securities transactions tax	..	0	224	2 736	3 469	2 788	3 534	4 279	3 681	3 077
Rural dev. tax on securities transaction tax	..	0	0	823	1 729	1 635	1 870	2 515	1 769	1 529
Acquisition tax (local)	..	163	1 165	3 148	7 261	6 916	6 644	7 361	7 326	13 318
Stamp tax	..	34	193	388	588	573	544	624	601	637
4500 Non-recurrent taxes	..	22	95	537	0	0	0	0	0	0
Asset revaluation tax	..	22	95	537	..	..	..	..	..	..
4510 On net wealth	..	..	..	..	..	..	..	..	..	..
4520 Other non-recurrent taxes	..	..	..	..	..	..	..	..	..	..
4600 Other recurrent taxes on property	..	0	0	0	0	0	0	0	0	0
5000 Taxes on goods and services	..	**4 190**	**16 497**	**52 271**	**80 861**	**86 096**	**87 043**	**100 551**	**106 402**	**106 717**
5100 Taxes on production, sale, transfer, etc	..	4 114	16 024	50 023	78 414	83 412	84 135	93 983	99 731	99 970
5110 General taxes	..	1 471	6 964	23 212	40 942	43 820	46 992	54 868	58 702	59 105
5111 Value added taxes	..	1 471	6 964	23 212	40 942	43 820	46 992	54 868	58 702	59 105
Value added tax	..	1 471	6 964	23 212	40 942	43 820	46 992	54 868	58 702	59 105
5112 Sales tax	..	0	0	0	0	0	0	0	0	0
Business tax	..	..	..	..	..	..	..	..	..	..
5113 Other	..	0	0	0	0	0	0	0	0	0
5120 Taxes on specific goods and services	..	2 643	9 059	26 811	37 472	39 592	37 143	39 115	41 029	40 865
5121 Excises	..	1 029	4 924	18 155	27 880	28 344	25 341	25 401	28 410	27 661
Commodity tax	..	0	0	0	0	0	0	0	0	0
Defence tax on commodity tax	..	0	0	0	0	0	0	0	0	0
Liquor tax	..	298	1 022	1 963	2 268	2 831	2 771	2 529	2 999	2 947
Defence tax on liquor tax	..	78	0	0	0	0	0	0	0	0
Education tax on liquor tax	..	0	81	516	580	739	713	644	774	764
Textile tax	..	0	0	0	0	0	0	0	0	0
Petroleum tax	..	0	0	0	0	0	0	0	0	0
Transport tax on petrol products	..	0	0	8 404	11 464	11 909	10 092	11 546	13 809	13 248
Education tax on transport tax	..	0	0	1 247	1 715	1 782	1 483	1 726	2 030	1 895
Electricity and gas tax	..	0	0	0	0	0	0	0	0	0
Special excise tax	..	583	1 912	2 985	5 161	4 499	3 642	5 537	5 336	5 484
Defence tax on special excise tax	..	70	337	0	0	0	0	0	0	0
Education tax on special excise tax	..	0	0	498	607	536	322	589	525	485
Rural development on special excise tax	..	0	0	37	54	47	20	45	56	56
Tobacco sales tax (local)	..	0	0	0	0	0	0	0	0	0
Tobacco consumption tax (local)	..	0	1 572	2 251	2 761	2 920	3 011	2 785	2 881	2 782
Motor fuel tax (local)	..	0	0	254	3 270	3 081	3 287	0	0	0
5122 Profits of fiscal monopolies	..	510	0	0	0	0	0	0	0	0
Monopoly profit	..	510	..	..	..	..	..	..	..	..

Table 59. **Korea / Corée** *(cont.)*
Details of tax revenue / Recettes fiscales détaillées

Billion KRW

	1965	1980	1990	2000	2007	2008	2009	2011	2012	2013
5123 Customs and import duties	..	1 014	3 692	5 936	7 690	9 068	9 486	11 350	10 220	11 012
Customs duties	..	762	2 765	5 800	7 411	8 776	9 169	10 990	9 816	10 562
Defence tax on customs duties	..	248	919	0	0	0	0	0	0	0
Special customs duties	..	0	0	0	0	0	0	0	0	0
Tonnage tax	..	0	0	0	0	0	0	0	0	0
Education tax on imports	..	0	7	99	234	246	273	322	375	429
Rural dev. tax on customs exemptions	..	0	0	37	45	46	44	38	29	21
Previous year receipts	..	4	0	0	0	0	0	0	0	0
5124 Taxes on exports	..	0	0	0	0	0	0	0	0	0
5125 Taxes on investment goods	..	0	0	0	0	0	0	0	0	0
5126 Taxes on specific services	..	90	444	2 720	1 902	2 180	2 316	2 364	2 399	2 192
Telephone tax	..	50	262	1 457	0	0	0	0	0	0
Defence tax on telephone tax	..	33	0	0	0	0	0	0	0	0
Entertainment tax	..	0	0	0	0	0	0	0	0	0
Defence tax on entertainment tax	..	0	0	0	0	0	0	0	0	0
Entertainment tax (local)	..	0	0	0	0	0	0	0	0	0
Travel tax	..	0	0	0	0	0	0	0	0	0
Admission tax	..	0	0	0	0	0	0	0	0	0
Defence tax on admission tax	..	0	0	0	0	0	0	0	0	0
Education tax on banking & insurance	..	0	108	473	721	872	964	966	932	938
Horse race tax (local)	..	3	56	566	864	989	1 002	1 072	1 129	1 042
Rural dev. tax on horse race tax	..	0	0	84	165	174	203	214	221	212
Butchery tax (local)	..	5	18	51	52	52	56	5	0	0
Regional development tax (local)	..	0	0	89	100	93	91	107	117	0
5127 Other taxes on internat. trade and transactions	..	0	0	0	0	0	0	0	0	0
5128 Other taxes	..	0	0	0	0	0	0	0	0	0
5130 Unallocable between 5110 and 5120	..	0	0	0	0	0	0	0	0	0
5200 Taxes on use of goods and perform activities	..	75	474	2 248	2 447	2 684	2 908	6 568	6 671	6 747
5210 Recurrent taxes	..	75	474	2 248	2 447	2 684	2 908	6 568	6 671	6 747
License tax (local)	..	18	48	241	77	73	74	78	78	0
Automobile tax (local)	..	57	426	2 007	2 370	2 611	2 834	6 490	6 593	6 747
5211 Paid by households: motor vehicles	..	..	..	..	..	..	..	..	..	..
5212 Paid by others: motor vehicles	..	..	..	..	..	..	..	..	..	..
5213 Paid in respect of other goods	..	..	..	..	..	..	..	..	..	..
5220 Non-recurrent taxes	..	0	0	0	0	0	0	0	0	0
5300 Unallocable between 5100 and 5200	..	0	0	0	0	0	0	0	0	0
6000 Other taxes	..	**150**	**259**	**4 907**	**8 155**	**9 219**	**12 284**	**9 927**	**11 529**	**10 399**
6100 Paid solely by business	..	0	0	0	0	0	0	0	0	0
6200 Other	..	150	259	4 907	8 155	9 219	12 284	9 927	11 529	10 399
Unallocable tax revenue	..	143	0	0	0	0	0	0	0	0
Previous year tax	..	0	213	1 474	2 965	3 759	6 890	4 232	5 768	4 774
Previous year tax (local)	..	6	47	474	672	592	600	728	680	601
Unallocable defence tax	..	0	0	-3	0	0	0	0	0	0
Education tax on local taxes	..	0	0	2 962	4 518	4 868	4 794	4 967	5 081	5 024
Total tax revenue on cash basis	..	**6 687**	**37 262**	**136 295**	**258 571**	**272 201**	**273 647**	**321 915**	**341 336**	**347 332**
Total tax revenue on accrual basis	..	..	..	..	..	..	..	..	..	..
Conciliation with National Accounts										
Additional taxes included in National Accounts	..	..	..	..	..	..	..	..	..	..
Taxes excluded from National Accounts	..	..	..	..	..	..	..	..	..	..
Difference in treatment of tax credits	..	..	..	..	..	..	..	..	..	..
Capital transfer for uncollected revenue	..	..	..	..	..	..	..	..	..	..
Voluntary social security contributions	..	..	..	..	..	..	..	..	..	..
Miscellaneous differences	..	..	..	..	..	..	..	..	..	..
National Accounts: Taxes and actual social contributions	..	..	..	..	..	..	..	..	..	..
Imputed social contributions	..	..	..	..	..	..	..	..	..	..
National Accounts: Taxes and all social contributions	..	..	..	..	..	..	..	..	..	..

Note:

Year ending 31st December.

Data are on cash basis.

Heading 2000: From 1997 the contributions to the three funds (civil servant pension fund, private school teachers pension fund and medical insurance fund) are classified as security social contributions. The reasons for the change are that the contributions either became mandatory or the fund started to be managed by public authorities in that year, thereby meeting the OECD definition of social security contributions.

Heading 2200: From 2007, this includes long-term care insurance.

Source: Ministry of Finance and Economy, Ministry of Home Affairs.

StatLink http://dx.doi.org/10.1787/888933277210

Table 60. **Luxembourg**

Details of tax revenue / Recettes fiscales détaillées

Million EUR

	1965	1980	1990	2000	2007	2008	2009	2011	2012	2013
Recettes fiscales totales	**266**	**1 543**	**3 746**	**8 602**	**13 445**	**14 001**	**14 147**	**15 991**	**16 885**	**17 797**
Recettes fiscales totales excluant les droits de douane	..	..	..	**8 575**	**13 422**	**13 982**	**14 134**	**15 973**	**16 870**	**17 781**
1000 Impôts sur revenu, bénéfices et gains en capital	**95**	**667**	**1 476**	**3 107**	**4 655**	**5 040**	**4 992**	**5 693**	**5 956**	**6 275**
1100 Des personnes physiques	66	417	884	1 573	2 678	3 036	2 917	3 545	3 699	4 062
1110 Sur le revenu et les bénéfices	66	417	884	1 573	2 678	3 036	2 917	3 545	3 699	4 062
Impôt sur le revenu des personnes physiques	27	106	184	258	389	411	480	597	609	666
Impôt solidarité majoration personnes physiques	0	10	41	37	59	65	64	128	148	268
Impôt sur traitements et salaires	36	287	601	1 178	1 910	2 125	1 996	2 327	2 504	2 797
Impôt sur le revenu des capitaux	2	11	52	88	188	280	271	271	315	223
Impôt sur les tantièmes	1	2	5	11	20	22	23	32	38	38
Impôt sur le revenu de certains non-résidents	0	1	1	2	1	1	1	1	1	1
Impôt retenu sur revenus épargne (non résidents)	0	0	0	0	51	58	41	43	47	40
Retenu libératoire nationale sur les intérêts	0	0	0	0	60	74	42	37	37	28
Contribution à la crise	0	0	0	0	0	0	0	110	0	0
1120 Sur les gains en capital	0	0	0	0	0	0	0	0	0	0
Prélèvement sur gains des paris	..	..	..	..	..	..	..	..	..	..
1200 Des sociétés	29	250	592	1 533	1 977	2 003	2 075	2 148	2 257	2 213
1210 Sur les bénéfices	29	250	592	1 533	1 977	2 003	2 075	2 148	2 257	2 213
Impôt sur le revenu des collectivites	18	168	376	1 031	1 381	1 370	1 431	1 378	1 557	1 530
Impôt de solidarité sur le revenu des collectivités	0	2	8	43	58	57	59	83	83	113
Impôt commercial communal	0	80	209	460	538	576	585	687	617	569
1220 Sur les gains en capital	0	0	0	0	0	0	0	0	0	0
1300 Non-ventilables entre 1100 et 1200	0	0	0	0	0	0	0	0	0	0
2000 Cotisations de sécurité sociale	**86**	**443**	**1 011**	**2 212**	**3 696**	**3 971**	**4 223**	**4 654**	**4 911**	**5 130**
2100 A la charge des salariés	32	175	388	982	1 676	1 816	1 917	2 122	2 238	2 337
2110 Sur la base du salaire	..	175	388	982	1 676	1 816	1 917	2 122	2 238	2 337
2120 Sur la base de l'impôt sur les revenus	..	0	0	0	0	0	0	0	0	0
2200 A la charge des employeurs	49	243	494	964	1 584	1 699	1 812	2 006	2 093	2 174
2210 Sur la base du salaire	..	243	494	964	1 584	1 699	1 812	2 006	2 093	2 174
2220 Sur la base de l'impôt sur les revenus	..	0	0	0	0	0	0	0	0	0
2300 A charge des travailleurs indép. ou sans emploi	5	25	129	266	436	456	493	527	579	619
2310 Sur la base du salaire	..	25	129	266	436	456	493	527	579	619
2320 Sur la base de l'impôt sur les revenus	..	0	0	0	0	0	0	0	0	0
2400 Non-ventilables entre 2100, 2200 et 2300	0	0	0	0	0	0	0	0	0	0
2410 Sur la base du salaire	..	..	..	..	..	..	..	..	..	..
2420 Sur la base de l'impôt sur les revenus	..	..	..	..	..	..	..	..	..	..
3000 Sur salaires ou main d'oeuvre	**2**	**10**	**0**	**0**	**0**	**0**	**0**	**0**	**0**	**0**
Impôt sur la somme des salaires	2	10	..	..	..	..	..	..	..	..
4000 Impôts sur le patrimoine	**16**	**87**	**311**	**912**	**1 301**	**1 041**	**944**	**1 119**	**1 199**	**1 304**
4100 Impôts périodiques sur la propriété immobilière	4	9	14	21	27	28	29	31	33	33
Impôt foncier	4	9	14	21	27	28	29	31	33	33
4110 Ménages	..	..	..	..	..	..	..	..	..	..
4120 Autres agents	..	..	..	..	..	..	..	..	..	..
4200 Impôts périodiques sur l'actif net	7	44	172	633	878	725	716	858	898	980
4210 Personnes physiques	2	15	58	152	172	169	211	256	267	269
Impôt sur la fortune	2	15	58	152	172	169	211	256	267	269
4220 Sociétés	5	29	114	481	706	557	505	602	630	710
Impôt sur la fortune	3	29	114	481	706	557	505	602	630	710
Taxe d'abonnement	3	0	0	0	0	0	0	0	0	0
4300 Impôts sur mut. par décès, succ. et donations	1	5	11	23	47	53	52	43	71	72
4310 Impôts sur mut. par décès et successions	1	5	11	23	47	53	52	43	71	72
4320 Impôts sur les donations	0	0	0	0	0	0	0	0	0	0
4400 Impôts sur transact. mobilières et immob.	4	30	114	235	350	235	147	187	197	220
Droits d'enregistrement	4	26	94	208	288	188	103	137	145	164
Droits d'hypothèque	1	3	9	12	29	19	19	24	26	28
Droits de timbre	0	2	4	7	14	13	12	12	12	13
Taxe pour construction dans secteurs centraux	0	0	0	0	1	1	1	1	2	1
Surtaxe sur les mutations immobilières	0	0	6	7	17	13	11	11	10	12
Hypothèques salaires	0	0	1	1	1	1	1	1	1	1
Autorisations à bâtir	0	0	0	0	0	0	0	0	0	0
Taxe d'infrastructure	0	0	0	0	0	0	0	0	0	0
Taxes d'autorisation sur les réservoirs de mazout	0	0	0	0	0	0	0	0	0	0
Taxe sur les résidences secondaires	0	0	0	0	0	0	0	0	1	0
4500 Impôts non-périodiques	0	0	0	0	0	0	0	0	0	0
4510 Sur l'actif net	..	..	..	..	..	..	..	..	..	..
4520 Autres non-périodiques	..	..	..	..	..	..	..	..	..	..
4600 Autres impôts périodiques sur patrimoine	0	0	0	0	0	0	0	0	0	0
5000 Impôts sur les biens et services	**66**	**336**	**939**	**2 332**	**3 756**	**3 917**	**3 957**	**4 487**	**4 779**	**5 050**
5100 Impôts sur production, vente, transfert, etc.	62	327	921	2 304	3 688	3 848	3 882	4 421	4 715	4 978
5110 Impôts généraux	33	179	519	1 229	2 233	2 344	2 441	2 853	3 114	3 425

Table 60. **Luxembourg** *(cont.)*
Details of tax revenue / Recettes fiscales détaillées

Million EUR

	1965	1980	1990	2000	2007	2008	2009	2011	2012	2013
5111 Taxes sur la valeur ajoutée	0	179	519	1 229	2 233	2 344	2 441	2 853	3 114	3 425
TVA ressources propres UE	..	18	75	92	50	46	35	42	42	43
5112 Impôts sur les ventes	0	0	0	0	0	0	0	0	0	0
5113 Autres impôts	33	0	0	0	0	0	0	0	0	0
Impôt sur chiffre d'affaires	33	..	..	..	..	..	..	..	..	..
5120 Impôts sur biens et services déterminés	30	148	403	1 075	1 455	1 505	1 441	1 568	1 601	1 553
5121 Accises	26	134	365	1 036	1 394	1 438	1 371	1 499	1 530	1 484
Droits d'accises autonomes huiles minérales	1	1	10	100	135	135	126	174	200	197
Droits d'accises autonomes tabac	..	0	8	24	66	64	67	76	83	85
Droits d'accises sur les huiles minérales (R203)	..	76	173	414	559	564	526	562	558	530
Taxe sur la consommation d'alcool	1	5	19	20	21	21	21	23	22	25
Droits d'accises sur le tabac	..	40	141	407	418	433	423	447	454	445
Produit de la contrib.sociale prélevée sur les carburants	..	0	0	59	145	144	133	137	134	126
Redevance de contrôle sur le fuel domestique	..	0	0	2	3	3	3	2	2	2
Droits d'accises sur gaz liquéfiés (R203)	..	0	0	0	0	0	0	0	0	0
Droits d'accises sur benzols (R203)	..	0	0	1	1	1	1	1	1	1
Droits d'accises sur alcools étrangers (R203)	..	3	5	5	6	6	6	6	6	7
Droits d'accises sur bières indigènes	..	4	2	3	4	4	4	4	4	4
Droits d'accises sur boissons fermentées fruits (R203)	..	2	3	0	0	0	0	0	0	0
Droits d'accises boissons fermentées mousseuses (R203)	..	0	1	0	0	0	0	0	0	0
Droits d'accises sur sucres et sirops raffinés (R203)	..	0	1	0	0	0	0	0	0	0
Ajustement accises U.E.B.L.	..	0	0	0	0	0	0	0	0	0
Droits d'accises sur alcools indigènes	..	1	1	0	0	0	0	0	0	0
Accise "Kyoto"	..	0	0	0	37	64	61	65	65	62
Surtaxe sur les boissons confectionnées (alcopops)	..	0	0	0	0	0	0	0	0	0
5122 Bénéfices des monopoles fiscaux	0	0	0	0	0	0	0	0	0	0
5123 Droits de douane et droits à l'importation	1	5	11	0	1	1	1	1	1	0
Prélèvements agricoles UE	1	0	0	0	1	1	1	1	1	0
Droits de douane	0	0	0	0	0	0	0	0	0	0
Droits de douane + mobiles + C.E.C.A.	0	4	11	0	0	0	0	0	0	0
Montants compensatoires agricoles communautaires	0	0	0	0	0	0	0	0	0	0
5124 Taxes à l'exportation	0	0	0	0	0	0	0	0	0	0
5125 Impôts sur biens d'équipement	0	0	0	0	0	0	0	0	0	0
5126 Impôts sur services déterminés	2	6	22	39	60	66	69	69	71	69
Prélèv. sommes engagées dans les paris	0	0	0	0	0	0	0	0	0	0
Taxe sur les assurances	1	5	15	23	32	36	39	38	42	45
Taxe sur les transports	1	0	0	0	0	0	0	0	0	0
Taxe de séjour	0	0	1	1	2	2	2	2	2	2
Taxe sur le loto	0	0	3	4	3	3	3	3	3	0
Prélèvement sur les jeux du casino	0	0	3	9	21	23	24	23	22	21
Impôts sur les billets de banque	0	0	0	0	0	0	0	0	0	0
Taxe sur amusements publics (nuits blanches)	0	1	1	2	2	2	1	2	2	1
5127 Autres impôts sur commerce et transact. internat.	0	0	0	0	0	0	0	0	0	0
5128 Autres impôts	0	4	4	0	0	0	0	0	0	0
C.E.C.A.	..	3	4	..	..	..	..	..	..	..
Taxe de coresponsabilité sur le lait	..	1	0	..	..	..	..	..	..	..
Taxe de coresponsabilité sur les céréales	..	0	0	..	..	..	..	..	..	..
5130 Non-ventilables entre 5110 et 5120	0	0	0	0	0	0	0	0	0	0
5200 Impôts sur utilisation des biens et exerc. activités	3	9	18	28	68	69	75	66	64	72
5210 Impôts périodiques	3	8	17	26	65	66	72	63	61	68
5211 A la charge des ménages : véhicules à moteur	2	4	9	16	39	40	43	38	36	40
5212 A la charge autres agents : véhicules à moteur	1	4	7	11	26	27	29	26	25	27
5213 Autres impôts périodiques	0	0	1	2	2	2	3	3	3	4
Taxe sur les cabarets	0	0	0	0	1	1	1	1	1	1
Taxes d'immatriculation (Com. aux affaires maritimes)	0	0	0	1	1	1	1	1	1	2
Taxe sur les chiens	0	0	1	1	1	1	1	1	1	1
Taxe de colportage	0	0	0	0	0	0	0	0	0	0
Taxe sur les navires	0	0	0	0	0	0	0	0	0	0
5220 Impôts non-périodiques	0	0	0	0	0	0	0	0	0	0
5300 Non-ventilables entre 5100 et 5200	0	0	0	0	0	0	0	0	0	0
6000 Autres impôts	**0**	**0**	**8**	**12**	**14**	**14**	**19**	**20**	**25**	**22**

Table 60. **Luxembourg** *(cont.)*
Details of tax revenue / Recettes fiscales détaillées

Million EUR

	1965	1980	1990	2000	2007	2008	2009	2011	2012	2013
6100 A la charge exclusive des entreprises	..	0	6	11	13	13	18	19	24	21
Taxe supplémentaire sur l'électricité	..	0	0	2	2	2	2	2	2	2
Taxe sur la distribution d'électricité	..	0	3	4	1	1	1	1	1	1
Taxe sur la production d'électricité	..	0	2	2	1	1	1	1	1	1
Taxe sur la consommation de gaz naturel	..	0	0	0	3	4	4	8	13	11
Registre aux firmes: taxes	..	0	1	1	0	0	0	0	0	0
Recettes conc. les dép. des affaires étrangères	..	0	0	0	2	1	7	4	5	5
Timbres de chancellerie	..	0	1	2	4	4	3	3	3	1
TVA reclassée et autres impôts sur la production	..	0	0	1	1	1	1	1	1	1
Sous-compensation TVA	..	0	2	0	0	0	0	0	0	0
6200 A la charge d'autres agents	..	0	0	0	0	0	0	0	0	0
Droits de douane perçus pour l'UE	..	..	..	**27**	**23**	**18**	**13**	**17**	**15**	**15**
Recettes fiscales totales sur la base d'encaissements	..	..	..	..	..	..	..	..	..	..
Recettes fiscales totales sur la base des droits constatés	..	..	**3 746**	**8 602**	**13 445**	**14 001**	**14 147**	**15 991**	**16 885**	**17 797**
Conciliation avec les comptes nationaux										
Impôts additionnels inclus dans les comptes nationaux	..	..	0	0	0	0	0	0	0	0
Impôt exclus des comptes nationaux	..	..	0	0	0	0	0	0	0	0
Différence dans les traitements des crédits d'impôts	..	..	0	0	0	0	0	0	0	0
Transfert en capital des recettes non collectées	..	..	0	0	0	0	0	0	0	0
Cotisations de sécurité sociale volontaires	..	..	4	18	18	19	25	31	34	35
Différences diverses	..	..	0	0	0	0	0	0	0	0
Comptes nationaux: impôts et cotisations sociales effectives	..	..	3 749	8 620	13 463	14 020	14 172	16 022	16 919	17 832
Cotisations sociales imputées	..	..	128	177	291	311	339	385	416	414
Comptes nationaux: impôts et toutes les cotisations sociales	..	..	3 878	8 797	13 754	14 331	14 511	16 407	17 335	18 246

Note:

Année civile se terminant le 31 décembre.

A partir de 1990, les données sont sur la base des droits constatés.

A la rubrique 2000, la différence entre le total des cotisations de sécurité sociale et celles recueillies par les parastataux de la sécurité sociale correspond au prélèvement pour la péréquation des pensions opéré sur les rémunérations et les pensions des salariés et anciens agents de P&T de la Caisse d'épargne de l'État; ces établissements ressortissant l'un au secteur "sociétés et quasi-sociétés non financières" et l'autre à celui des institutions de crédit.

Source: Compte Général de l'État.

StatLink http://dx.doi.org/10.1787/888933277222

Table 61. **Mexico / Mexique**
Details of tax revenue / Recettes fiscales détaillées

Million MXN

	1965	1980	1990	2000	2007	2008	2009	2011	2012	2013
Total tax revenue	..	**771**	**127 959**	**1 014 625**	**2 002 846**	**2 539 615**	**2 071 854**	**2 830 477**	**3 048 561**	**3 165 976**
1000 Taxes on income, profits and capital gains	..	**230**	**34 673**	**276 548**	**554 099**	**629 135**	**591 942**	**772 704**	**803 071**	**957 213**
1100 Of individuals	..	..	..	..	238 938	285 270	280 230	352 386	397 701	425 621
Tax on income of individuals	..	..	..	..	238 938	285 270	280 230	352 386	397 701	425 621
1110 On income and profits	..	..	..	..	..	..	..	..	..	..
1120 On capital gains	..	..	..	..	..	..	..	..	..	..
1200 Corporate	..	..	..	..	217 790	214 611	191 685	303 176	288 360	392 199
Tax on income of corporations	..	..	..	..	217 790	214 611	191 685	303 176	288 360	392 199
1210 On profits	..	..	..	..	..	..	..	..	..	..
1220 On capital gains	..	..	..	..	..	..	..	..	..	..
1300 Unallocable between 1100 and 1200	..	230	34 673	276 548	97 370	129 254	120 027	117 143	117 010	139 393
Tax on income of other individuals and corporations	..	..	..	244 841	54 785	61 208	64 816	66 004	74 042	89 028
Tax on asset	..	..	..	13 913	15 670	1 134	-2 540	-1 120	-1 192	-1 325
Credit on salary	..	..	..	17 794	23 177	15 886	12 113	2 076	1 387	1 274
Oil yields tax	..	..	..	0	3 738	4 441	921	3 019	573	3 210
IETU	..	..	..	0	0	46 586	44 718	47 165	42 199	47 205
2000 Social security contributions	..	**109**	**17 165**	**167 292**	**307 026**	**321 843**	**346 031**	**411 289**	**454 778**	**490 918**
2100 Employees	..	..	..	..	..	..	..	..	..	..
2110 On a payroll basis	..	..	..	..	..	..	..	..	..	..
2120 On an income tax basis	..	..	..	..	..	..	..	..	..	..
2200 Employers	..	..	..	..	..	..	..	..	..	..
2210 On a payroll basis	..	..	..	..	..	..	..	..	..	..
2220 On an income tax basis	..	..	..	..	..	..	..	..	..	..
2300 Self-employed or non-employed	..	..	..	..	..	..	..	..	..	..
2310 On a payroll basis	..	..	..	..	..	..	..	..	..	..
2320 On an income tax basis	..	..	..	..	..	..	..	..	..	..
2400 Unallocable between 2100, 2200 and 2300	..	109	17 165	167 292	307 026	321 843	346 031	411 289	454 778	490 918
2410 On a payroll basis	..	..	..	167 292	307 026	321 843	346 031	411 289	454 778	490 918
2420 On an income tax basis	..	..	..	0	0	0	0	0	0	0
3000 Taxes on payroll and workforce	..	**8**	**1 797**	**11 217**	**28 071**	**31 123**	**31 965**	**41 980**	**48 033**	**53 042**
Substitute tax on salary	..	..	..	0	0	0	0	0	0	0
Payroll tax	..	..	..	11 101	20 277	22 919	23 530	31 817	35 480	41 184
Tax on remuneration to the personal work	..	..	..	65	7 578	7 992	8 180	9 990	12 333	11 645
Tax on professions and fees	..	..	..	36	68	72	70	58	48	50
Tax on operations by contract	..	..	..	15	148	140	186	116	173	163
4000 Taxes on property	..	**15**	**1 914**	**13 964**	**33 161**	**35 847**	**35 484**	**41 186**	**45 186**	**46 238**
4100 Recurrent taxes on immovable property	..	10	1 036	9 948	19 425	21 394	22 862	28 728	31 544	31 338
4110 Households	..	0	0	0	0	0	0	0	0	0
4120 Others	..	10	1 036	9 948	19 425	21 394	22 862	28 728	31 544	31 338
Property tax	..	..	..	9 948	19 425	21 394	22 862	28 728	31 544	31 338
4200 Recurrent taxes on net wealth	..	0	0	0	0	0	0	0	0	0
4210 Individual	..	..	..	..	..	..	..	..	..	..
4220 Corporate	..	..	..	..	..	..	..	..	..	..
4300 Estate, inheritance and gift taxes	..	0	8	0	0	0	0	0	0	0
4310 Estate and inheritance taxes	..	..	8	..	..	..	..	..	..	..
4320 Gift taxes	..	..	0	..	..	..	..	..	..	..
4400 Taxes on financial and capital transactions	..	5	870	4 017	13 736	14 452	12 622	12 458	13 642	14 900
Alienation of immovable property	..	..	..	1 763	1 076	1 310	1 163	1 379	1 341	1 271
Transfer of ownership of real estate	..	..	..	2 236	8 147	5 825	5 005	3 923	4 575	4 518
Purchasing property	..	..	..	18	4 513	7 318	6 454	7 157	7 725	9 110
4500 Non-recurrent taxes	..	0	0	0	0	0	0	0	0	0
4510 On net wealth	..	..	..	..	..	..	..	..	..	..
4520 Other non-recurrent taxes	..	..	..	..	..	..	..	..	..	..
4600 Other recurrent taxes on property	..	0	0	0	0	0	0	0	0	0
5000 Taxes on goods and services	..	**395**	**70 791**	**537 953**	**1 063 584**	**1 502 941**	**1 039 344**	**1 530 906**	**1 660 413**	**1 576 887**
5100 Taxes on production, sale, transfer, etc	..	388	70 125	528 666	1 042 372	1 480 972	1 017 627	1 508 269	1 643 337	1 557 226
5110 General taxes	..	121	26 635	189 606	409 013	457 248	407 795	537 143	579 988	556 794
5111 Value added taxes	..	120	26 635	189 606	409 013	457 248	407 795	537 143	579 988	556 794
5112 Sales tax	..	0	0	0	0	0	0	0	0	0
5113 Other	..	1	0	0	0	0	0	0	0	0
5120 Taxes on specific goods and services	..	265	43 473	339 060	633 359	1 023 723	609 832	971 126	1 063 349	1 000 432
5121 Excises	..	45	10 072	86 163	47 008	60 462	69 770	94 623	98 490	104 111
Special tax on production and services	..	..	..	81 544	41 532	55 391	65 708	89 544	92 620	97 860
Tax on new automobiles	..	..	..	4 619	5 476	5 071	4 063	5 079	5 870	6 252
Tax on luxury goods and services	..	..	..	0	0	0	0	0	0	0
5122 Profits of fiscal monopolies	..	0	0	0	0	0	0	0	0	0
5123 Customs and import duties	..	45	6 998	33 285	33 344	37 831	31 732	29 946	31 161	32 324
Step customs officer	..	..	..	423	1 156	2 048	1 535	3 065	3 255	3 065
Import taxes	..	..	..	32 861	32 188	35 783	30 196	26 881	27 906	29 260

Table 61. **Mexico / Mexique** *(cont.)*
Details of tax revenue / Recettes fiscales détaillées

Million MXN

	1965	1980	1990	2000	2007	2008	2009	2011	2012	2013
5124 Taxes on exports	..	2	75	4	3	1	1	2	1	1
Tax on exports	..	..	..	4	3	1	1	2	1	1
5125 Taxes on investment goods	..	0	0	0	0	0	0	0	0	0
5126 Taxes on specific services	..	8	132	1 042	2 146	20 097	18 461	-5 610	7 169	-1 441
IDE	..	8	..	0	0	17 700	15 888	-8 442	2 786	-5 988
Tax on lodging	..	0	..	504	1 059	1 178	1 147	1 375	1 702	1 890
Public entertainment tax	..	0	..	240	365	383	486	360	625	566
Tax on lotteries, raffles and gambling	..	0	..	267	705	717	789	952	1 329	1 213
Tax on commercials	..	0	..	4	17	118	150	145	16	203
Various indirect taxes	..	0	..	28	0	0	0	0	711	674
5127 Other taxes on internat. trade and transactions	..	0	0	0	0	0	0	0	0	0
5128 Other taxes	..	165	26 196	218 567	550 858	905 332	489 869	852 166	926 528	865 438
Ordinary fee on oil production	..	..	..	125 329	0	0	0	0	0	0
Extraordinary fee on oil production	..	..	..	68 235	0	0	0	0	0	0
Additional fee on oil production	..	..	..	2 576	3 233	3 715	149	0	0	0
Tax on oil yields	..	..	..	22 201	1 255	0	0	0	0	0
Mining fees	..	..	..	226	414	68	1 782	2 858	3 243	3 886
Ordinary	..	..	..	0	478 609	794 030	410 437	721 209	769 489	721 790
Stabilization Fund	..	..	..	0	55 402	71 536	63 839	81 247	106 151	106 401
Extraordinary on crude petroleum export	..	..	..	0	11 517	33 640	-556	24 152	19 594	10 313
Scientific research and technological Fund in the matter of energy	..	..	..	0	403	1 583	2 046	5 635	8 441	8 422
For oil control	..	..	..	0	24	37	23	35	42	39
Rights on the extraction of mineral oils	..	..	..	0	0	158	2 663	5 601	7 185	6 178
Special rights on mineral oils for fields in the "Paleoncanal icontepec"	..	..	..	0	0	565	7 676	6 117	7 521	5 450
Special right on hydrocarbons	..	..	..	0	0	0	1 813	1 308	0	0
Special right on hydrocarbons in deep water fields	..	..	..	0	0	0	0	4 003	4 493	2 574
Right to register for exploration and exploitation of hydrocarbons	..	..	..	0	0	0	0	0	370	385
Additional rights on the extraction of mineral oils	..	..	..	0	0	0	0	0	0	0
5130 Unallocable between 5110 and 5120	..	2	17	0	0	0	0	0	0	0
5200 Taxes on use of goods and perform activities	..	7	666	9 287	21 212	21 970	21 717	22 637	17 076	19 660
5210 Recurrent taxes	..	7	666	9 287	21 212	21 970	21 717	22 637	17 076	19 660
5211 Paid by households: motor vehicles	..	3	567	8 878	20 692	21 492	21 301	22 186	16 464	19 174
Tax on motor vehicules	..	..	..	8 878	20 692	21 492	21 301	22 186	16 464	19 174
5212 Paid by others: motor vehicles	..	0	0	301	275	311	270	296	370	357
Tax on federal auto transport	..	..	..	301	275	311	270	296	370	357
5213 Paid in respect of other goods	..	4	99	108	246	166	147	155	242	129
Sport fishing	..	..	..	40	98	85	68	50	55	50
Sport hunting	..	..	..	3	0	1	0	0	0	0
Tax on commercial activities	..	..	..	63	147	33	42	66	42	26
Trade in books and magazines	..	..	..	0	0	0	0	0	0	3
Tax on industrial activities	..	..	..	2	0	47	35	38	145	49
Mining	..	..	..	0	0	0	1	0	0	0
5220 Non-recurrent taxes	..	0	0	0	0	0	0	0	0	0
5300 Unallocable between 5100 and 5200	..	0	0	0	0	0	0	0	0	0
6000 Other taxes	..	**14**	**1 619**	**7 651**	**16 906**	**18 726**	**27 087**	**32 412**	**37 080**	**41 679**
6100 Paid solely by business	..	0	0	0	0	0	0	0	0	0
6200 Other	..	14	1 619	7 651	16 906	18 726	27 087	32 412	37 080	41 679
Accessories	..	..	..	5 504	12 403	13 744	21 710	24 059	24 077	25 301
Unallocable between 1000 and 5000 caused in exercices fiscal previous liquidation slopes or of payment	..	..	..	374	222	58	7	-118	2 260	1 618
Additional state and local taxes	..	..	..	1 773	4 280	4 924	5 361	8 471	10 743	14 760
Non-wastable tax credits										
Non-wastable tax credits against 1000	..	..	..	..	..	..	..	..	..	..
Tax expenditure component	..	..	..	..	..	..	..	..	..	..
Transfer component	..	..	..	..	..	..	..	..	..	..
Total tax revenue on cash basis	..	**771**	**127 959**	**1 014 625**	**2 002 846**	**2 539 615**	**2 071 854**	**2 830 477**	**3 048 561**	**3 165 976**
Total tax revenue on accrual basis	..	..	..	..	..	..	..	..	..	..
Conciliation with National Accounts										
Additional taxes included in National Accounts	..	..	..	..	..	..	..	..	..	..
Taxes excluded from National Accounts	..	..	..	..	..	..	..	..	..	..
Difference in treatment of tax credits	..	..	..	..	..	..	..	..	..	..
Capital transfer for uncollected revenue	..	..	..	..	..	..	..	..	..	..
Voluntary social security contributions	..	..	..	..	..	..	..	..	..	..
Miscellaneous differences	..	..	..	..	..	..	..	..	..	..
National Accounts: Taxes and actual social contributions	..	..	..	..	..	..	..	..	..	..
Imputed social contributions	..	..	..	..	..	..	..	..	..	..
National Accounts: Taxes and all social contributions	..	..	..	..	..	..	..	..	..	..

Note:

Year ending 31st December.

Data are on cash basis.

Source: Ministry of Finance, Economic Department.

StatLink http://dx.doi.org/10.1787/888933277238

Table 62. **Netherlands / Pays-Bas**
Details of tax revenue / Recettes fiscales détaillées

Million EUR

	1965	1980	1990	2000	2007	2008	2009	2011	2012	2013
Total tax revenue	**10 860**	**69 982**	**104 419**	**165 076**	**221 130**	**232 978**	**218 826**	**230 552**	**232 667**	**238 733**
Total tax revenue exclusive of custom duties	..	..	..	**163 766**	**219 433**	**231 190**	**217 308**	**228 555**	**230 508**	**236 523**
1000 Taxes on income, profits and capital gains	**3 884**	**22 998**	**33 689**	**41 804**	**62 463**	**63 418**	**61 489**	**61 929**	**58 869**	**59 085**
1100 Of individuals	3 008	18 383	25 806	25 068	43 911	44 604	49 885	49 520	47 015	46 638
1110 On income and profits	3 007	18 364	25 757	25 009	43 773	44 445	49 663	49 283	46 786	46 400
Income tax	1 359	2 895	2 455	-880	2 294	-142	535	-533	-902	-1 337
Wage tax	1 466	14 984	22 258	23 033	37 729	40 636	47 044	47 226	45 207	45 546
Dividend tax	123	486	1 044	2 856	3 750	3 951	2 084	2 590	2 481	2 191
Directors tax	14	0	0	0	0	0	0	0	0	0
Inhabited house tax	45	0	0	0	0	0	0	0	0	0
1120 On capital gains	1	18	50	59	138	159	222	237	229	238
Tax on games of chance	1	18	50	59	138	159	222	237	229	238
1200 Corporate	876	4 615	7 882	16 736	18 552	18 814	11 604	12 409	11 854	12 447
1210 On profits	876	4 615	7 882	16 736	18 552	18 814	11 604	12 409	11 854	12 447
Corporation tax	876	4 615	7 882	16 736	18 552	18 814	11 604	12 409	11 854	12 447
1220 On capital gains	0	0	0	0	0	0	0	0	0	0
1300 Unallocable between 1100 and 1200	0	0	0	0	0	0	0	0	0	0
2000 Social security contributions	**3 342**	**26 641**	**39 075**	**64 464**	**77 063**	**86 264**	**79 188**	**88 551**	**94 845**	**97 512**
2100 Employees	1 659	11 018	24 109	32 108	34 766	39 455	33 729	38 399	41 095	43 258
2110 On a payroll basis	..	..	..	7 213	34 766	39 455	33 729	38 399	41 095	43 258
2120 On an income tax basis	..	..	..	24 895	0	0	0	0	0	0
2200 Employers	1 371	12 465	7 837	18 668	25 925	28 472	28 348	30 241	32 628	32 020
2210 On a payroll basis	..	..	..	18 668	25 925	28 472	28 348	30 241	32 628	32 020
2220 On an income tax basis	..	..	..	0	0	0	0	0	0	0
2300 Self-employed or non-employed	311	3 158	7 129	13 688	16 372	18 337	17 111	19 911	21 122	22 234
2310 On a payroll basis	..	..	..	0	0	0	0	0	0	0
2320 On an income tax basis	..	..	..	13 688	16 372	18 337	17 111	19 911	21 122	22 234
2400 Unallocable between 2100, 2200 and 2300	0	0	0	0	0	0	0	0	0	0
2410 On a payroll basis	..	..	..	..	..	..	..	..	..	..
2420 On an income tax basis	..	..	..	..	..	..	..	..	..	..
3000 Taxes on payroll and workforce	**0**	**0**	**0**	**0**	**0**	**0**	**0**	**0**	**0**	**0**
4000 Taxes on property	**476**	**2 509**	**3 816**	**8 794**	**10 353**	**9 893**	**8 671**	**7 911**	**7 061**	**8 083**
4100 Recurrent taxes on immovable property	111	1 021	1 711	3 090	3 473	3 683	4 082	4 434	4 549	5 248
Municipal immovable property tax	-59	821	1 398	..	..	..	..	..	..	..
Tax on land	59	0	0	..	..	..	..	..	..	..
Other municipal taxes	66	5	18	..	..	..	..	..	..	..
Contributions polder boards	44	195	295	..	..	..	..	..	..	..
4110 Households	..	..	..	892	267	279	403	450	466	478
Municipal immovable property tax	..	..	..	737	0	0	0	0	0	0
Contributions polder boards	..	..	..	155	267	279	403	450	466	478
4120 Others	..	..	..	2 198	3 206	3 404	3 679	3 984	4 083	4 770
Municipal immovable property tax	..	..	..	1 803	2 690	2 792	2 940	3 173	3 337	3 474
Contributions polder boards	..	..	..	395	516	535	666	705	721	740
Levies on social housing corporations	..	..	..	0	0	77	73	106	25	556
4200 Recurrent taxes on net wealth	86	517	554	824	30	20	25	11	2	1
4210 Individual	86	517	554	824	30	20	25	11	2	1
Property tax of individuals	86	517	554	824	30	20	25	11	2	1
4220 Corporate	0	0	0	0	0	0	0	0	0	0
4300 Estate, inheritance and gift taxes	117	336	522	1 484	1 882	1 795	1 813	1 536	1 382	1 730
4310 Estate and inheritance taxes	..	304	472	1 304	1 882	1 795	1 813	1 536	1 382	1 730
Estate tax	..	0	0	0	0	0	0	0	0	0
Inheritance tax	..	304	472	1 304	1 882	1 795	1 813	1 536	1 382	1 730
4320 Gift taxes	..	32	50	180	0	0	0	0	0	0
4400 Taxes on financial and capital transactions	162	635	1 030	3 396	4 968	4 395	2 751	1 930	1 128	1 104
Stamp duties	44	0	0	0	0	0	0	0	0	0
Registration duties	118	0	0	0	0	0	0	0	0	0
Tax on legal transactions	0	635	1 030	0	0	0	0	0	0	0
Tax on the sale of immovable property	0	0	0	2 804	4 925	4 375	2 745	1 935	1 128	1 104
Tax on capital formation	0	0	0	592	43	20	6	-5	0	0
4500 Non-recurrent taxes	0	0	0	0	0	0	0	0	0	0
4510 On net wealth	..	..	..	..	..	..	..	..	..	..
4520 Other non-recurrent taxes	..	..	..	..	..	..	..	..	..	..
4600 Other recurrent taxes on property	0	0	0	0	0	0	0	0	0	0
5000 Taxes on goods and services	**3 110**	**17 675**	**27 585**	**48 261**	**68 555**	**70 643**	**66 929**	**69 187**	**69 127**	**70 720**
5100 Taxes on production, sale, transfer, etc	2 943	16 204	25 067	43 567	62 015	63 620	59 635	61 390	61 290	63 046
5110 General taxes	1 344	11 081	17 216	28 849	42 873	43 221	40 086	41 610	41 699	42 424
5111 Value added taxes	0	11 081	17 216	28 849	42 873	43 221	40 086	41 610	41 699	42 424
5112 Sales tax	0	0	0	0	0	0	0	0	0	0
5113 Other	1 344	0	0	0	0	0	0	0	0	0
Turnover tax	1 344	..	..	..	..	..	..	..	..	..

Table 62. **Netherlands / Pays-Bas** *(cont.)*
Details of tax revenue / Recettes fiscales détaillées

Million EUR

	1965	1980	1990	2000	2007	2008	2009	2011	2012	2013
5120 Taxes on specific goods and services	1 600	5 123	7 850	14 718	19 142	20 399	19 549	19 780	19 591	20 622
5121 Excises	880	3 789	5 985	13 705	17 659	18 662	17 802	18 009	17 165	16 994
Excise on spirits	129	463	422	397	335	328	306	314	348	306
Excise on beer	34	123	259	281	310	318	390	383	387	413
Excise on sugar	45	9	27	0	0	0	0	0	0	0
Excise on tobacco	307	839	948	1 590	2 136	2 360	2 318	2 527	2 653	2 228
Excise on wine	14	82	91	171	257	285	285	299	316	348
Special excise on motor vehicles	0	613	1 189	2 875	3 647	3 236	2 145	1 978	1 500	1 159
Excise on soft drinks	0	59	186	216	155	158	158	159	158	154
Levies for nuclear reactor	0	0	0	0	0	0	0	0	0	0
Excise on petrol	310	1 280	1 684	3 151	4 010	4 049	4 028	4 054	3 928	3 825
Excise on mineral oil	41	295	808	2 139	2 965	3 176	3 369	3 691	3 657	3 765
Levies on noise pollution	0	0	0	36	55	56	49	35	49	39
Levies on air pollution	0	27	304	0	0	0	0	0	0	0
Levies on petroleum products	0	0	68	0	0	0	0	0	0	0
Levies on environmental basis	0	0	0	2 849	3 789	4 624	4 479	4 281	3 885	4 754
Other excise duties and consumption taxes	0	0	0	0	0	72	0	0	0	0
Packaging tax	0	0	0	0	0	0	275	288	284	3
5122 Profits of fiscal monopolies	0	0	0	0	0	0	0	0	0	0
5123 Customs and import duties	702	971	1 375	0	0	0	0	0	0	0
Agriculture levy	338	295	168	..	..	..	..	..	..	..
MCA levy	0	9	0	..	..	..	..	..	..	..
Remaining import duties	364	667	1 207	..	..	..	..	..	..	..
5124 Taxes on exports	0	0	0	0	0	0	0	0	0	0
5125 Taxes on investment goods	0	77	0	0	0	0	0	0	0	0
Selective investment regulation levy	..	77	..	..	..	..	..	..	..	..
5126 Taxes on specific services	16	222	372	658	1 053	1 136	1 326	1 425	2 090	3 275
Tax on fire insurance	2	0	0	0	0	0	0	0	0	0
Entertainment tax	14	0	0	0	0	0	0	0	0	0
Tax on insurances	0	209	340	512	807	795	849	1 020	1 145	2 343
Tourist tax	0	14	32	79	126	137	121	148	159	165
Tax on games of chance	0	0	0	67	109	174	222	238	230	239
Taxes on outside advertising	0	0	0	0	11	10	16	19	20	21
Flight tax	0	0	0	0	0	20	118	0	0	0
Bank levies	0	0	0	0	0	0	0	0	536	507
5127 Other taxes on internat. trade and transactions	0	0	0	0	0	0	0	0	0	0
5128 Other taxes	1	64	118	355	430	601	421	346	336	353
ESCC levy	1	5	0	0	0	0	0	0	0	0
Sugar contribution	0	23	36	0	0	0	0	0	0	0
Milk levy	0	36	82	0	0	0	0	0	0	0
EU levies on food products	0	0	0	273	345	377	302	257	250	252
Petroleum storage duty	0	0	0	68	85	83	94	89	86	101
Sugar storage duty	0	0	0	14	0	141	25	0	0	0
5130 Unallocable between 5110 and 5120	0	0	0	0	0	0	0	0	0	0
5200 Taxes on use of goods and perform activities	167	1 470	2 518	4 694	6 540	7 023	7 294	7 797	7 837	7 674
5210 Recurrent taxes	165	1 470	2 518	4 694	6 540	7 023	7 294	7 797	7 837	7 674
5211 Paid by households: motor vehicles	27	463	799	2 304	3 205	3 550	3 835	4 072	4 047	4 008
Motor vehicle tax	27	427	744	2 304	3 205	3 550	3 835	4 072	4 047	4 008
Motor vehicle licence	0	36	54	0	0	0	0	0	0	0
5212 Paid by others: motor vehicles	132	604	1 044	651	891	959	1 023	1 103	1 097	959
Motor vehicle tax	132	590	1 026	552	760	844	907	976	968	959
Motor vehicle licence	0	14	18	0	0	0	0	0	0	0
Heavy motor vehicle tax	0	0	0	99	131	115	116	127	129	0
5213 Paid in respect of other goods	6	404	676	1 739	2 444	2 514	2 436	2 622	2 693	2 707
Dog licences	3	23	27	42	54	55	58	61	65	69
Non-residence tax	0	5	5	14	21	23	24	26	28	26
Levies on water pollution	1	372	644	1 013	1 273	1 269	1 105	1 165	1 175	1 209
Permission to sell spirits	2	5	0	0	0	0	0	0	0	0
Sewerage charges	0	0	0	650	1 097	1 163	1 246	1 366	1 419	1 399
Levies on manure surplus	0	0	0	18	-4	2	1	2	4	4
Hunting and shooting permits	0	0	0	2	3	2	2	2	2	0
5220 Non-recurrent taxes	2	0	0	0	0	0	0	0	0	0
5300 Unallocable between 5100 and 5200	0	0	0	0	0	0	0	0	0	0
6000 Other taxes	**48**	**159**	**254**	**443**	**999**	**972**	**1 031**	**977**	**606**	**1 123**
6100 Paid solely by business	48	159	254	407	353	350	368	335	315	139
Administrative levies	48	159	254	407	353	350	368	335	315	139
6200 Other	0	0	0	36	646	622	663	642	291	984
Wage Tax reductions	..	..	..	0	497	527	616	541	165	804
Other taxes	..	..	..	36	149	95	47	101	126	180
Custom duties collected for the EU	..	..	..	**1 310**	**1 697**	**1 788**	**1 518**	**1 997**	**2 159**	**2 210**

Table 62. **Netherlands / Pays-Bas** *(cont.)*
Details of tax revenue / Recettes fiscales détaillées

Million EUR

	1965	1980	1990	2000	2007	2008	2009	2011	2012	2013
Total tax revenue on cash basis	**10 860**	**69 982**	**104 419**	**165 503**	**220 162**	**232 925**	..	..	..	..
Total tax revenue on accrual basis	..	..	..	**165 076**	**221 130**	**232 978**	**218 826**	**230 552**	**232 667**	**238 733**
Conciliation with National Accounts										
Additional taxes included in National Accounts	..	..	..	1 668	312	341	233	244	323	305
Wage Tax reductions	..	..	..	1 400	0	0	0	0	0	0
Dividend tax to foreign countries	..	..	..	268	312	341	233	244	323	305
Taxes excluded from National Accounts	..	..	..	0	0	0	0	0	0	0
Difference in treatment of tax credits	..	..	..	0	0	0	0	0	0	0
Capital transfer for uncollected revenue	..	..	..	0	0	0	0	0	0	0
Voluntary social security contributions	..	..	..	0	0	0	0	0	0	0
Miscellaneous differences	..	..	..	-70	0	0	0	0	0	0
National Accounts: Taxes and actual social contributions	..	..	..	166 674	221 442	233 319	219 059	230 796	232 990	239 038
Imputed social contributions	..	..	..	0	4 405	4 178	4 277	3 860	3 829	3 248
National Accounts: Taxes and all social contributions	..	..	..	166 674	225 847	237 497	223 336	234 656	236 819	242 286

Note:

Year ending 31st December.

From 1999 data are on accrual basis.

Heading 2000: From 1998 the figures include some violuntary contributions and the breakdown between premiums paid by employees (2100) and by self-employed / non-employed has been estimated. This is also the case for the breakdown between premiums paid on a payroll or on an income tax basis for those years where both apply.

Heading 4100: From 1992, there was a structural break in the data for the 'municipal immovable property tax'. The tax ceased to be collected by the central government at that time and the figures are presented on a different type of statistical registration (no longer cash basis).

Heading 5110: Includes 358 millions of euros (1969) and 186 millions of euros (1970) in respect of deduction of turnover tax on stocks existing at 1st January 1969.

Heading 5213: Small amounts (less than 2.3 millions euros) of hunting and fishing licence receipts which should be classified here have been omitted.

Source: Social security contributions and local taxes: Central Bureau of Statistics. Other taxes: Ministry of Finance.

StatLink http://dx.doi.org/10.1787/888933277242

Table 63. **New Zealand / Nouvelle-Zélande**
Details of tax revenue / Recettes fiscales détaillées

Million NZD

	1965	1980	1990	2000	2007	2008	2009	2011	2012	2013
Total tax revenue	**1 001**	**7 594**	**27 471**	**39 765**	**64 046**	**62 355**	**59 508**	**65 573**	**70 121**	**73 453**
1000 Taxes on income, profits and capital gains	**606**	**5 299**	**16 370**	**23 861**	**40 308**	**37 622**	**33 860**	**35 208**	**38 876**	**40 764**
1100 Of individuals	394	4 679	13 177	17 126	26 965	25 356	24 475	24 259	26 426	27 904
1110 On income and profits	394	4 679	13 177	17 126	26 965	25 356	24 475	24 259	26 426	27 904
1120 On capital gains	0	0	0	0	0	0	0	0	0	0
1200 Corporate	207	589	1 780	4 914	9 069	8 179	6 568	8 484	9 889	10 344
1210 On profits	207	589	1 780	4 914	9 069	8 179	6 568	8 484	9 889	10 344
1220 On capital gains	0	0	0	0	0	0	0	0	0	0
1300 Unallocable between 1100 and 1200	5	31	1 413	1 821	4 274	4 087	2 817	2 465	2 561	2 516
NRWT	5	24	277	760	1 506	1 451	884	497	417	427
Property speculation	0	0	0	0	0	0	0	0	0	0
Absentee income tax	0	7	0	0	0	0	0	0	0	0
Interest	0	0	1 028	990	2 699	2 571	1 803	1 676	1 628	1 643
Dividends	0	0	83	71	69	65	130	292	516	446
Other	0	0	25	0	0	0	0	0	0	0
2000 Social security contributions	**0**	**0**	**0**	**0**	**0**	**0**	**0**	**0**	**0**	**0**
2100 Employees	0	0	0	0	0	0	0	0	0	0
2110 On a payroll basis	..	..	..	..	..	..	..	..	..	..
2120 On an income tax basis	..	..	..	..	..	..	..	..	..	..
2200 Employers	0	0	0	0	0	0	0	0	0	0
2210 On a payroll basis	..	..	..	..	..	..	..	..	..	..
2220 On an income tax basis	..	..	..	..	..	..	..	..	..	..
2300 Self-employed or non-employed	0	0	0	0	0	0	0	0	0	0
2310 On a payroll basis	..	..	..	..	..	..	..	..	..	..
2320 On an income tax basis	..	..	..	..	..	..	..	..	..	..
2400 Unallocable between 2100, 2200 and 2300	0	0	0	0	0	0	0	0	0	0
2410 On a payroll basis	..	..	..	..	..	..	..	..	..	..
2420 On an income tax basis	..	..	..	..	..	..	..	..	..	..
3000 Taxes on payroll and workforce	**0**	**0**	**0**	**0**	**0**	**0**	**0**	**0**	**0**	**0**
4000 Taxes on property	**116**	**602**	**1 880**	**2 112**	**3 417**	**3 683**	**3 858**	**4 297**	**4 386**	**4 516**
4100 Recurrent taxes on immovable property	84	515	1 722	2 049	3 322	3 592	3 774	4 208	4 302	4 423
Local govt rates and services	81	503	1 550	2 049	3 322	3 592	3 774	4 208	4 302	4 423
Land tax	3	12	172	0	0	0	0	0	0	0
4110 Households	..	..	0	..	..	..	..	..	..	..
4120 Others	..	..	172	..	..	..	..	..	..	..
4200 Recurrent taxes on net wealth	0	0	0	0	0	0	0	0	0	0
4210 Individual	..	..	..	..	..	..	..	..	..	..
4220 Corporate	..	..	..	..	..	..	..	..	..	..
4300 Estate, inheritance and gift taxes	23	39	80	2	3	1	2	0	0	0
4310 Estate and inheritance taxes	21	37	74	0	0	0	0	..	..	..
4320 Gift taxes	2	2	6	2	3	1	2	..	..	..
4400 Taxes on financial and capital transactions	9	48	78	61	92	90	82	89	84	93
Instrument duty	7	40	62	51	85	83	77	85	82	91
Cheque duty	2	8	16	10	7	7	5	4	3	2
4500 Non-recurrent taxes	0	0	0	0	0	0	0	0	0	0
4510 On net wealth	..	..	..	..	..	..	..	..	..	..
4520 Other non-recurrent taxes	..	..	..	..	..	..	..	..	..	..
4600 Other recurrent taxes on property	0	0	0	0	0	0	0	0	0	0
5000 Taxes on goods and services	**280**	**1 693**	**9 220**	**13 792**	**20 290**	**21 042**	**21 781**	**26 063**	**26 856**	**28 170**
5100 Taxes on production, sale, transfer, etc	262	1 624	8 680	12 887	18 832	19 606	20 278	24 437	25 193	26 346
5110 General taxes	77	776	6 163	9 885	15 046	15 824	16 449	20 314	21 004	22 063
5111 Value added taxes	0	0	6 163	9 885	15 046	15 824	16 449	20 314	21 004	22 063
5112 Sales tax	77	776	0	0	0	0	0	0	0	0
Motor vehicles	..	231	..	..	..	..	..	..	..	..
Other sales tax	..	544	..	..	..	..	..	..	..	..
5113 Other	0	0	0	0	0	0	0	0	0	0
5120 Taxes on specific goods and services	186	849	2 517	3 002	3 786	3 782	3 829	4 123	4 189	4 283

Table 63. **New Zealand / Nouvelle-Zélande** *(cont.)*
Details of tax revenue / Recettes fiscales détaillées

Million NZD

	1965	1980	1990	2000	2007	2008	2009	2011	2012	2013
5121 Excises	124	548	1 929	2 148	1 627	1 638	1 691	1 814	1 866	1 856
On alcoholic beverages	37	84	411	436	573	617	600	656	664	650
Beer	33	64	0	201	290	312	304	252	251	250
Wine	0	0	0	100	163	176	171	213	220	204
Spirits	4	20	0	135	120	129	125	191	193	196
Tobacco	33	99	568	764	159	172	217	244	281	273
Motor vehicles	0	0	7	0	0	0	0	0	0	0
Refined sugar	2	0	0	0	0	0	0	0	0	0
CA petroleum fuels	0	140	835	810	819	781	805	847	855	865
NRF fuel excise	49	121	0	0	0	0	0	0	0	0
Local petroleum fuels	0	18	21	27	30	29	30	31	32	33
CA mileage tax	0	0	0	0	0	0	0	0	0	0
NRF mileage tax	3	0	0	0	0	0	0	0	0	0
Road user charges	0	68	0	0	0	0	0	0	0	0
Energy resources levy	0	20	87	111	46	39	39	36	34	35
5122 Profits of fiscal monopolies	0	0	0	0	0	0	0	0	0	0
5123 Customs and import duties	49	231	505	648	1 857	1 880	1 873	2 038	2 056	2 160
5124 Taxes on exports	0	0	0	0	0	0	0	0	0	0
5125 Taxes on investment goods	0	0	0	0	0	0	0	0	0	0
5126 Taxes on specific services	13	57	83	206	302	264	265	271	267	267
Lottery (national)	1	6	26	167	290	252	252	258	253	254
Lottery (overseas)	0	0	0	0	0	0	0	0	0	0
Racing	12	46	57	39	12	12	13	13	14	13
Film hire tax	0	1	0	0	0	0	0	0	0	0
Domestic air travel tax	0	3	0	0	0	0	0	0	0	0
5127 Other taxes on internat. trade and transactions	0	12	0	0	0	0	0	0	0	0
Foreign fishing vessels tax	..	0	..	..	..	..	..	..	..	..
Foreign travel tax	..	0	..	..	..	..	..	..	..	..
International departure tax	..	12	..	..	..	..	..	..	..	..
5128 Other taxes	0	0	0	0	0	0	0	0	0	0
5130 Unallocable between 5110 and 5120	0	0	0	0	0	0	0	0	0	0
5200 Taxes on use of goods and perform activities	18	69	539	905	1 458	1 436	1 503	1 626	1 663	1 824
5210 Recurrent taxes	18	69	539	905	1 458	1 436	1 503	1 626	1 663	1 824
Motor vehicle registration	7	47	154	181	226	171	171	175	174	187
Heavy traffic fees	8	0	285	532	851	868	910	1 045	1 066	1 205
Accident compensation levies	0	0	0	0	0	0	0	0	0	0
5211 Paid by households: motor vehicles	0	0	0	0	0	0	0	0	0	0
5212 Paid by others: motor vehicles	0	0	0	0	0	0	0	0	0	0
5213 Paid in respect of other goods	3	23	100	192	381	397	422	406	423	432
Local authority fees and charges	3	23	100	192	381	397	422	406	423	432
5220 Non-recurrent taxes	0	0	0	0	0	0	0	0	0	0
5300 Unallocable between 5100 and 5200	0	0	0	0	0	0	0	0	0	0
6000 Other taxes	**0**	**0**	**1**	**0**	**31**	**8**	**9**	**5**	**3**	**3**
6100 Paid solely by business	..	..	0	..	0	0	0	0	0	0
6200 Other	..	..	1	..	31	8	9	5	3	3
Non wastable tax credits										
Non-wastable tax credits against 1110	..	..	..	1 057	2 568	2 728	2 835	2 707	2 636	2 582
Tax expenditure component	..	..	..	311	873	927	964	920	896	878
Transfer component	..	..	..	746	1 695	1 801	1 871	1 787	1 740	1 704
Non-wastable tax credits against 1210	..	..	..	0	0	0	0	0	0	0
Tax expenditure component	..	..	..	..	..	..	..	..	..	..
Transfer component	..	..	..	..	..	..	..	..	..	..
Total tax revenue on cash basis	**1 001**	**7 594**	**27 471**	**39 276**	**64 273**	**60 336**	**60 029**	**65 153**	**69 162**	**73 089**
Total tax revenue on accrual basis	..	..	..	**39 765**	**64 046**	**62 355**	**59 508**	**65 573**	**70 121**	**73 453**
Conciliation with National Accounts										
Additional taxes included in National Accounts	..	..	..	..	0	0	0	0	0	0
Taxes excluded from National Accounts	..	..	..	..	0	0	0	0	0	0
Difference in treatment of tax credits	..	..	..	..	0	0	0	0	0	0
Capital transfer for uncollected revenue	..	..	..	..	0	0	0	0	0	0
Voluntary social security contributions	..	..	..	..	0	0	0	0	0	0
Miscellaneous differences	..	..	..	..	0	0	0	0	0	0
National Accounts: Taxes and actual social contributions	..	..	..	..	64 046	62 355	59 508	65 573	70 121	73 453
Imputed social contributions	..	..	..	..	0	0	0	0	0	0
National Accounts: Taxes and all social contributions	..	..	..	..	64 046	62 355	59 508	65 573	70 121	73 453

Note:

For the years before 1989 data are on a fiscal year basis ending 31st March. The figures provided for 1989 and onwards relate to the financial year ending 30th June of the following year.

From 1993, data are on accrual basis.

Heading 1000: Tax credits to exporters under the export incentives schemes are non-wastable, but that part of the excess of tax liability paid out to taxpayers is not identifiable.

Heading 1100: The figures up to 1969 include revenues collected by a social security income tax. The base of this tax was the same as the ordinary income tax base and the two have now been incorporated into a single income tax.

Heading 5121: From October 1986 incorporates that portion of the selective impost on wine, spirits, tobacco and motor vehicles which was formerly collected and reported as sales tax. The revenue collected on those imported goods which are subject to the equivalent of the domestic excise has been classified as excise duty. In this respect, there is a discontinuity between the excises recorded before and after October 1986.

Heading 5210: The other local authority licence fees include some small items which could be regarded as non-tax revenues.

Heading for non-wastable tax credits 1110 comprises four Family assistance tax credits. The total in item 1100 is net of the tax expenditure component but not net of the transfer component.

Source: Local Authorities Statistics, Department of Statistics, Wellington.

StatLink http://dx.doi.org/10.1787/888933277251

Table 64. **Norway / Norvège**
Details of tax revenue / Recettes fiscales détaillées

Million NOK

	1965	1980	1990	2000	2007	2008	2009	2011	2012	2013
Total tax revenue	**16 842**	**133 499**	**301 812**	**631 581**	**990 168**	**1 080 018**	**1 000 352**	**1 173 944**	**1 231 048**	**1 242 734**
1000 Taxes on income, profits and capital gains	**7 316**	**55 837**	**106 290**	**284 189**	**473 816**	**544 731**	**459 156**	**572 225**	**594 666**	**573 530**
1100 Of individuals	6 671	38 018	79 068	152 013	219 726	231 842	241 108	271 322	288 119	304 364
1110 On income and profits	6 671	38 018	79 068	152 013	219 726	231 842	241 108	271 322	288 119	304 364
Employee social security contributions	1 305	0	0	0	0	0	0	0	0	0
Income taxes	5 366	38 018	79 068	152 013	219 726	231 842	241 108	271 322	288 119	304 364
1120 On capital gains	0	0	0	0	0	0	0	0	0	0
1200 Corporate	645	17 819	27 222	132 176	254 090	312 889	218 048	300 903	306 547	269 166
1210 On profits	...	...	..	132 176	254 090	312 889	218 048	300 903	306 547	269 166
1220 On capital gains	...	...	..	0	0	0	0	0	0	0
1300 Unallocable between 1100 and 1200	0	0	0	0	0	0	0	0	0	0
2000 Social security contributions	**2 009**	**28 205**	**79 362**	**132 170**	**206 314**	**224 384**	**233 083**	**258 760**	**276 790**	**291 781**
2100 Employees	0	6 639	25 345	45 162	68 707	74 828	77 766	87 838	93 196	114 994
2110 On a payroll basis	...	...	...	45 162	68 707	74 828	77 766	87 838	93 196	114 994
2120 On an income tax basis	...	...	...	0	0	0	0	0	0	0
2200 Employers	1 716	20 454	50 116	79 242	125 902	136 689	141 949	155 813	167 553	176 787
2210 On a payroll basis	...	...	..	79 242	125 902	136 689	141 949	155 813	167 553	176 787
2220 On an income tax basis	...	...	..	0	0	0	0	0	0	0
2300 Self-employed or non-employed	293	1 112	3 901	7 766	11 705	12 867	13 368	15 109	16 041	0
2310 On a payroll basis	...	...	...	7 766	11 705	12 867	13 368	15 109	16 041	...
2320 On an income tax basis	...	...	...	0	0	0	0	0	0	...
2400 Unallocable between 2100, 2200 and 2300	0	0	0	0	0	0	0	0	0	0
2410 On a payroll basis	...	...	...	...	...	...	...	...	...	...
2420 On an income tax basis	...	...	...	...	...	...	...	...	...	...
3000 Taxes on payroll and workforce	**0**	**0**	**0**	**0**	**0**	**0**	**0**	**0**	**0**	**0**
4000 Taxes on property	**523**	**2 295**	**8 887**	**14 546**	**27 709**	**30 168**	**29 112**	**32 798**	**35 306**	**37 262**
4100 Recurrent taxes on immovable property	100	431	2 216	2 848	6 335	8 036	7 970	9 083	9 803	10 573
4110 Households	...	431	2 216	2 724	5 571	6 194	6 500	7 566	8 022	8 873
4120 Others	...	0	0	124	764	1 842	1 470	1 517	1 781	1 700
4200 Recurrent taxes on net wealth	341	1 450	5 118	7 703	13 244	15 034	13 635	15 250	16 417	17 134
4210 Individual	235	907	3 692	6 869	10 746	11 308	11 913	12 742	13 329	14 039
4220 Corporate	106	543	1 426	834	2 498	3 726	1 722	2 508	3 088	3 095
4300 Estate, inheritance and gift taxes	45	122	446	1 273	2 576	1 973	2 431	1 754	1 887	2 246
4310 Estate and inheritance taxes	0	122	446	1 273	2 576	1 973	2 431	1 754	1 887	2 246
4320 Gift taxes	0	0	0	0	0	0	0	0	0	0
4400 Taxes on financial and capital transactions	37	292	1 107	2 722	5 554	5 125	5 076	6 711	7 199	7 309
4500 Non-recurrent taxes	0	0	0	0	0	0	0	0	0	0
4510 On net wealth	...	...	...	...	...	...	...	...	...	...
4520 Other non-recurrent taxes	...	...	...	...	...	...	...	...	...	...
4600 Other recurrent taxes on property	0	0	0	0	0	0	0	0	0	0
5000 Taxes on goods and services	**6 928**	**47 154**	**107 262**	**200 676**	**282 329**	**280 735**	**279 001**	**310 161**	**324 286**	**340 161**
5100 Taxes on production, sale, transfer, etc	6 720	45 882	102 901	185 926	265 669	262 621	264 495	295 394	308 450	321 353
5110 General taxes	3 622	24 350	56 656	124 985	189 424	185 341	186 759	211 689	224 062	235 610
5111 Value added taxes	0	24 350	56 656	124 166	188 705	184 843	186 211	211 037	223 425	234 941
Value added tax	...	24 350	56 656	124 166	188 705	184 843	186 211	211 037	223 425	234 941
5112 Sales tax	3 622	0	0	819	719	498	548	652	637	669
Turnover tax	3 622	...	..	819	719	498	548	652	637	669
5113 Other	0	0	0	0	0	0	0	0	0	0
5120 Taxes on specific goods and services	3 098	21 532	46 245	60 941	76 245	77 280	77 736	83 705	84 388	85 743
5121 Excises	2 338	14 914	37 453	54 876	71 047	71 426	71 764	76 966	77 303	78 423
Stamp duty on tobacco	392	1 076	3 750	6 806	6 815	7 457	8 061	7 488	7 403	6 375
Taxes on spirits and wines	449	2 013	3 454	5 217	0	0	0	0	0	0
Excise on beer	162	605	2 195	3 650	0	0	0	0	0	0
Excise on petrol	480	2 310	7 057	14 558	14 556	15 185	15 492	16 034	15 774	16 923
Vehicles transfer tax	395	2 761	4 554	10 956	22 898	20 661	18 672	22 564	23 409	22 229
Chocolate and sweets	123	247	551	789	1 078	1 102	1 123	1 155	1 223	1 261
Sugar	0	0	217	230	192	194	197	183	193	201
Non-alcoholic beverages	38	120	487	1 113	1 024	1 085	1 696	1 742	1 866	1 803
Electric energy	89	1 515	3 414	5 091	7 079	7 122	7 579	8 116	7 913	8 656
Oil and gas products	0	3 703	8 729	88	92	96	88	100	102	108
Sales of radio and tv sets	0	163	220	920	0	0	0	0	0	0
Mineral oil	0	113	1 098	4 015	5 154	5 710	5 718	6 058	5 650	6 296
Cosmetics	0	0	0	159	0	0	0	0	0	0
Recording equipment	0	0	92	35	0	0	0	0	0	0
Others	210	288	1 635	1 249	1 821	1 863	1 850	1 918	1 923	1 969
Taxes on alcoholic beverages	0	0	0	0	10 338	10 951	11 288	11 608	11 847	12 602
5122 Profits of fiscal monopolies	31	395	751	2 534	2 115	2 704	3 070	3 651	3 780	3 800
Profits state wine monopoly	31	30	67	41	32	36	51	36	27	36
Norsk tipping	0	365	684	2 493	2 083	2 668	3 019	3 615	3 753	3 764

Table 64. **Norway / Norvège** *(cont.)*
Details of tax revenue / Recettes fiscales détaillées

Million NOK

	1965	1980	1990	2000	2007	2008	2009	2011	2012	2013
5123 Customs and import duties	634	697	1 360	1 944	2 132	2 173	2 120	2 649	2 921	3 111
Customs revenue	615	689	1 305	1 944	2 132	2 173	2 120	2 649	2 921	3 111
Loading and lighthouse dues	11	0	0	0	0	0	0	0	0	0
Other import duties	8	8	55	0	0	0	0	0	0	0
5124 Taxes on exports	7	105	227	0	112	115	128	174	184	177
5125 Taxes on investment goods	0	4 274	4 454	0	0	0	0	0	0	0
5126 Taxes on specific services	88	195	1 233	1 386	131	137	135	140	144	140
Excise on race tracks	9	25	15	88	119	137	135	140	144	140
Taxes on specific services	34	49	150	1 298	0	0	0	0	0	0
Pengelotteriet (national lotteries)	45	121	462	0	0	0	0	0	0	0
Excise on lotto games	0	0	606	0	12	0	0	0	0	0
5127 Other taxes on internat. trade and transactions	0	0	0	0	0	0	0	0	0	0
5128 Other taxes	0	952	767	201	708	725	519	125	56	92
5130 Unallocable between 5110 and 5120	0	0	0	0	0	0	0	0	0	0
5200 Taxes on use of goods and perform activities	208	1 272	4 361	14 750	16 660	18 114	14 506	14 767	15 836	18 808
5210 Recurrent taxes	208	1 272	4 361	14 750	16 660	15 699	14 506	14 767	15 165	18 308
5211 Paid by households: motor vehicles	88	458	1 789	4 435	6 699	6 589	6 872	7 462	7 734	8 007
5212 Paid by others: motor vehicles	108	696	2 072	1 346	712	642	520	520	496	494
5213 Paid in respect of other goods	12	118	500	8 969	9 249	8 468	7 114	6 785	6 935	9 807
CO2 tax	0	0	0	3 047	3 385	3 392	2 215	2 189	2 251	3 293
Excise on pharmacies	6	32	59	105	153	138	97	67	81	78
Others	6	86	441	5 817	4 504	4 307	4 677	4 395	4 485	6 442
Tax on emissions of NOX	0	0	0	0	1 207	631	125	134	118	-6
5220 Non-recurrent taxes	0	0	0	0	0	2 415	0	0	671	500
5300 Unallocable between 5100 and 5200	0	0	0	0	0	0	0	0	0	0
6000 Other taxes	**66**	**8**	**11**	**0**	**0**	**0**	**0**	**0**	**0**	**0**
6100 Paid solely by business	0	3	2	..	..	..	..	..	..	..
6200 Other	66	5	9	..	..	..	..	..	..	..
Non wastable tax credits										
Non-wastable tax credits against 1210	..	..	..	..	952	1 011	1 184	1 311	1 397	1 398
Tax expenditure component	..	..	..	..	..	..	..	..	..	..
Transfer component	..	..	..	..	..	..	..	..	..	..
Total tax revenue on cash basis	**16 842**	**133 499**	**301 812**	**575 989**	**967 171**	**1 078 572**	**1 015 366**	**1 156 926**	**1 220 956**	**1 248 965**
Total tax revenue on accrual basis	..	..	..	**631 581**	**990 168**	**1 080 018**	**1 000 352**	**1 173 944**	**1 231 048**	**1 242 734**
Conciliation with National Accounts										
Additional taxes included in National Accounts	..	..	..	0	0	0	0	0	0	0
Taxes excluded from National Accounts	..	..	..	0	0	0	0	0	0	0
Difference in treatment of tax credits	..	..	..	0	0	0	0	0	0	0
Capital transfer for uncollected revenue	..	..	..	0	0	0	0	0	0	0
Voluntary social security contributions	..	..	..	0	0	0	0	0	0	0
Miscellaneous differences	..	..	..	0	0	0	0	0	0	0
National Accounts: Taxes and actual social contributions	..	..	..	631 581	990 168	1 080 018	1 000 352	1 173 944	1 231 048	1 242 734
Imputed social contributions	..	..	..	400	656	486	350	253	225	243
National Accounts: Taxes and all social contributions	..	..	..	631 981	990 824	1 080 504	1 000 702	1 174 197	1 231 273	1 242 977

Note:

Year ending 31st December.

From 2000, data are on accrual basis.

Heading 5211: Up to 1971 this item contains motor vehicle licences paid by both households and enterprises.

Heading 5121: From 2005, taxes on alcoholic beverages include both 'taxes on spirits and wines' and 'excise on beer'.

Heading 5125: From 1998, revenue from taxes on investments goods is included in item 5121 "Others".

Source: Statistics Norway; National Accounts.

StatLink http://dx.doi.org/10.1787/888933277260

Table 65. **Poland / Pologne**
Details of tax revenue / Recettes fiscales détaillées

Million PLN

	1965	1980	1990	2000	2007	2008	2009	2011	2012	2013
Total tax revenue	..	..	..	**247 064**	**412 546**	**440 056**	**429 470**	**497 161**	**521 498**	**530 618**
Total tax revenue exclusive of custom duties	..	..	..	..	**411 263**	**438 484**	**428 162**	**495 714**	**519 887**	**529 005**
1000 Taxes on income, profits and capital gains	..	..	..	**50 268**	**93 795**	**102 513**	**92 877**	**99 510**	**106 480**	**103 567**
1100 Of individuals	..	..	..	32 415	61 471	68 028	62 161	67 861	72 617	74 216
Individual income tax	..	..	..	32 415	61 403	67 940	62 078	67 768	72 516	74 124
Tax on winnings from lottery or gambling	..	..	..	0	68	88	83	93	101	92
Tax on salaries	..	..	..	0	0	0	0	0	0	0
Tax on salaries-local	..	..	..	0	0	0	0	0	0	0
Presumptive income tax-local	..	..	..	0	0	0	0	0	0	0
Income equalization tax	..	..	..	0	0	0	0	0	0	0
Income equalization tax-local	..	..	..	0	0	0	0	0	0	0
Health contribution	..	..	..	0	0	0	0	0	0	0
1110 On income and profits	..	..	..	..	..	..	..	..	..	..
1120 On capital gains	..	..	..	..	..	..	..	..	..	..
1200 Corporate	..	..	..	17 853	32 324	34 485	30 716	31 649	33 863	29 351
Income from legal entities	..	..	..	..	..	..	..	..	..	..
Income from legal entities-local	..	..	..	..	..	..	..	..	..	..
1210 On profits	..	..	..	..	..	..	..	..	..	..
1220 On capital gains	..	..	..	..	..	..	..	..	..	..
1300 Unallocable between 1100 and 1200	..	..	..	0	0	0	0	0	0	0
2000 Social security contributions	..	..	..	**97 411**	**141 457**	**145 451**	**153 386**	**175 827**	**196 620**	**204 634**
2100 Employees	..	..	..	40 902	56 192	55 962	57 264	69 798	77 594	81 128
2110 On a payroll basis	..	..	..	..	..	..	..	..	..	..
2120 On an income tax basis	..	..	..	..	..	..	..	..	..	..
2200 Employers	..	..	..	43 201	57 156	59 528	63 640	72 275	79 579	86 300
2210 On a payroll basis	..	..	..	..	..	..	..	..	..	..
2220 On an income tax basis	..	..	..	..	..	..	..	..	..	..
2300 Self-employed or non-employed	..	..	..	13 308	28 109	29 961	32 482	33 754	39 447	37 206
2310 On a payroll basis	..	..	..	..	..	..	..	..	..	..
2320 On an income tax basis	..	..	..	..	..	..	..	..	..	..
2400 Unallocable between 2100, 2200 and 2300	..	..	..	0	0	0	0	0	0	0
2410 On a payroll basis	..	..	..	..	..	..	..	..	..	..
2420 On an income tax basis	..	..	..	..	..	..	..	..	..	..
3000 Taxes on payroll and workforce	..	..	..	**1 628**	**3 081**	**3 628**	**3 787**	**4 182**	**4 290**	**3 998**
Tax on wages	..	..	..	0	0	0	0	0	0	0
Tax on wages-local	..	..	..	0	0	0	0	0	0	0
Penalties for excessive payroll increases	..	..	..	0	0	0	0	0	0	0
Excessive wage tax	..	..	..	0	0	0	0	0	0	0
Rehabilitation fund contribution	..	..	..	1 508	2 860	3 373	3 429	3 819	3 915	3 633
Wage guarantee fund contribution	..	..	..	120	221	255	358	363	375	365
4000 Taxes on property	..	..	..	**10 584**	**17 116**	**18 329**	**18 434**	**20 089**	**21 744**	**23 120**
4100 Recurrent taxes on immovable property	..	..	..	8 404	13 515	15 070	15 908	17 492	19 468	20 747
Agricultural tax-local	..	..	..	720	906	1 227	1 227	1 055	1 573	1 666
Forest tax-local	..	..	..	96	157	179	183	188	227	228
Real estate tax-local	..	..	..	7 588	12 452	13 664	14 498	16 249	17 668	18 853
4110 Households	..	..	..	2 348	3 613	4 233	4 553	4 925	5 878	6 289
4120 Others	..	..	..	6 056	9 902	10 837	11 355	12 567	13 590	14 458
4200 Recurrent taxes on net wealth	..	..	..	0	0	0	0	0	0	0
4210 Individual	..	..	..	..	..	..	..	..	..	..
4220 Corporate	..	..	..	..	..	..	..	..	..	..
4300 Estate, inheritance and gift taxes	..	..	..	172	328	344	313	279	293	252
Inheritance and gift tax-local	..	..	..	172	328	344	313	279	293	252
4310 Estate and inheritance taxes	..	..	..	..	..	..	..	..	..	..
4320 Gift taxes	..	..	..	..	..	..	..	..	..	..
4400 Taxes on financial and capital transactions	..	..	..	2 008	3 273	2 915	2 213	2 318	1 983	2 121
Tax on public sale of shares	..	..	..	2 008	3 273	2 915	2 213	2 318	1 983	2 121
4500 Non-recurrent taxes	..	..	..	0	0	0	0	0	0	0
4510 On net wealth	..	..	..	..	..	..	..	..	..	..
4520 Other non-recurrent taxes	..	..	..	..	..	..	..	..	..	..
4600 Other recurrent taxes on property	..	..	..	0	0	0	0	0	0	0
5000 Taxes on goods and services	..	..	..	**86 863**	**155 239**	**167 821**	**158 967**	**195 393**	**189 953**	**190 618**
5100 Taxes on production, sale, transfer, etc	..	..	..	84 885	150 570	162 555	153 543	189 215	184 109	186 112
5110 General taxes	..	..	..	51 615	97 848	101 876	99 562	122 647	116 265	116 607
5111 Value added taxes	..	..	..	51 615	97 848	101 876	99 562	122 647	116 265	116 607
Taxes on goods and services (VAT)	..	..	..	..	..	..	..	..	..	..
VAT on imported goods	..	..	..	..	..	..	..	..	..	..

Table 65. **Poland / Pologne** *(cont.)*
Details of tax revenue / Recettes fiscales détaillées

Million PLN

	1965	1980	1990	2000	2007	2008	2009	2011	2012	2013
5112 Sales tax	..	..	..	0	0	0	0	0	0	0
Turnover tax, of which:	..	..	..	..	..	..	..	..	..	..
On spirits	..	..	..	..	..	..	..	..	..	..
On fuels	..	..	..	..	..	..	..	..	..	..
On tobacco	..	..	..	..	..	..	..	..	..	..
5113 Other	..	..	..	0	0	0	0	0	0	0
5120 Taxes on specific goods and services	..	..	..	33 270	52 722	60 679	53 981	66 568	67 844	69 505
5121 Excises	..	..	..	27 170	49 376	56 716	50 962	63 019	64 438	65 764
On domestic excise products, of which:	..	..	..	24 213	45 752	53 345	48 001	59 724	60 075	60 228
On spirits	..	..	..	..	..	..	..	..	..	..
On fuels	..	..	..	..	..	..	..	..	..	..
On tobacco	..	..	..	..	..	..	..	..	..	..
On beer	..	..	..	..	..	..	..	..	..	..
On wine	..	..	..	..	..	..	..	..	..	..
On other products	..	..	..	..	..	..	..	..	..	..
On imported excise products, of which:	..	..	..	2 957	3 624	3 371	2 961	3 295	4 363	5 536
On spirits	..	..	..	..	..	..	..	..	..	..
On fuels	..	..	..	..	..	..	..	..	..	..
On tobacco	..	..	..	..	..	..	..	..	..	..
On beer	..	..	..	..	..	..	..	..	..	..
On wine	..	..	..	..	..	..	..	..	..	..
On other products	..	..	..	..	..	..	..	..	..	..
5122 Profits of fiscal monopolies	..	..	..	0	0	0	0	0	0	0
5123 Customs and import duties	..	..	..	5 038	477	173	281	508	339	428
Customs duties	..	..	..	5 038	..	..	..	..	..	..
Import tax	..	..	..	0	..	..	..	..	..	..
Compensatory fees on agricultural imports	..	..	..	0	..	..	..	..	..	..
5124 Taxes on exports	..	..	..	0	0	0	0	0	0	0
5125 Taxes on investment goods	..	..	..	0	0	0	0	0	0	0
5126 Taxes on specific services	..	..	..	1 062	1 297	1 619	1 895	2 251	2 145	2 410
Lump sum tax occasional passenger transp. serv.	..	..	..	443	189	215	319	747	844	953
Gambling tax	..	..	..	619	1 108	1 404	1 576	1 504	1 301	1 457
5127 Other taxes on internat. trade and transactions	..	..	..	0	0	0	0	0	0	0
5128 Other taxes	..	..	..	0	1 572	2 171	843	790	922	903
5130 Unallocable between 5110 and 5120	..	..	..	0	0	0	0	0	0	0
5200 Taxes on use of goods and perform activities	..	..	..	1 978	4 669	5 266	5 424	6 178	5 844	4 506
Local fees	..	..	..	..	..	..	..	..	..	..
Tax on means of transportation-local	..	..	..	..	..	..	..	..	..	..
5210 Recurrent taxes	..	..	..	1 978	4 669	5 266	5 424	6 178	5 844	4 506
5211 Paid by households: motor vehicles	..	..	..	0	0	0	0	0	0	0
5212 Paid by others: motor vehicles	..	..	..	0	0	0	0	0	0	0
5213 Paid in respect of other goods	..	..	..	1 978	4 669	5 266	5 424	6 178	5 844	4 506
5220 Non-recurrent taxes	..	..	..	0	0	0	0	0	0	0
5300 Unallocable between 5100 and 5200	..	..	..	0	0	0	0	0	0	0
6000 Other taxes	**..**	**..**	**..**	**310**	**575**	**742**	**711**	**713**	**800**	**3 068**
Abolished taxes	..	..	..	..	..	..	..	..	..	..
Abolished taxes-local	..	..	..	..	..	..	..	..	..	..
6100 Paid solely by business	..	..	..	0	0	0	0	0	0	0
6200 Other	..	..	..	310	575	742	711	713	800	3 068
Custom duties collected for the EU	**..**	**..**	**..**	**..**	**1 283**	**1 572**	**1 308**	**1 447**	**1 611**	**1 613**
Total tax revenue on cash basis	**..**	**..**	**..**	**..**	**..**	**..**	**..**	**..**	**..**	**..**
Total tax revenue on accrual basis	**..**	**..**	**..**	**247 064**	**412 546**	**440 056**	**429 470**	**497 161**	**521 498**	**530 618**
Conciliation with National Accounts										
Additional taxes included in National Accounts	..	..	..	..	..	..	..	..	..	..
Taxes excluded from National Accounts	..	..	..	..	..	..	..	..	..	..
Difference in treatment of tax credits	..	..	..	..	..	..	..	..	..	..
Capital transfer for uncollected revenue	..	..	..	..	..	..	..	..	..	..
Voluntary social security contributions	..	..	..	..	..	..	..	..	..	..
Miscellaneous differences	..	..	..	..	..	..	..	..	..	..
National Accounts: Taxes and actual social contributions	..	..	..	..	..	..	..	..	..	..
Imputed social contributions	..	..	..	..	..	..	..	..	..	..
National Accounts: Taxes and all social contributions	..	..	..	..	..	..	..	..	..	..

Note:

Year ending 31st December.

From 2002, data are on accrual basis.

Source: Ministry of Finance, Economic Department.

StatLink http://dx.doi.org/10.1787/888933277275

Table 66. **Portugal**
Details of tax revenue / Recettes fiscales détaillées

Million EUR

	1965	1980	1990	2000	2007	2008	2009	2011	2012	2013
Total tax revenue	**99**	**1 798**	**14 825**	**40 050**	**56 147**	**57 054**	**52 721**	**57 262**	**53 862**	**58 451**
Total tax revenue exclusive of customs duties	**..**	**..**	**..**	**39 846**	**55 962**	**56 877**	**52 567**	**57 094**	**53 706**	**58 307**
1000 Taxes on income, profits and capital gains	**24**	**355**	**3 805**	**11 852**	**15 766**	**16 262**	**14 750**	**16 306**	**14 992**	**18 950**
1100 Of individuals	..	..	2 350	7 022	9 424	9 740	9 764	10 569	9 859	13 188
Individual income tax	..	..	2 350	7 022	9 424	9 740	9 764	10 569	9 859	13 188
1110 On income and profits	..	..	..	..	..	..	..	..	..	..
1120 On capital gains	..	..	..	..	..	..	..	..	..	..
1200 Corporate	..	..	1 182	4 830	6 342	6 523	4 986	5 736	4 875	5 762
Corporate income tax>	..	..	1 088	4 543	6 029	6 263	4 673	5 488	4 587	5 554
Local corporate income tax ("Derrama")	..	..	84	287	313	260	312	248	288	208
Other	..	..	11	0	0	0	0	0	0	0
1210 On profits	..	..	..	..	..	..	..	..	..	..
1220 On capital gains	..	..	..	..	..	..	..	..	..	..
1300 Unallocable between 1100 and 1200	24	355	273	0	0	0	0	0	258	0
Tax on wages and professional income	2	93	9	..	..	..	..	..	0	..
Industrial tax	7	108	129	..	..	..	..	..	0	..
Tax on income from movable capital	2	71	1	..	..	..	..	..	0	..
Property income tax	3	23	17	..	..	..	..	..	0	..
Agricultural income tax	0	0	1	..	..	..	..	..	0	..
Complementary income ax	4	43	58	..	..	..	..	..	0	..
Tax on capital gains	0	3	1	..	..	..	..	..	258	..
Taxes abolished by DL 442-A/88 and DL 442-B/88	0	0	0	..	..	..	..	..	0	..
Other	6	15	58	..	..	..	..	..	0	..
2000 Social security contributions	**22**	**531**	**4 026**	**10 168**	**14 274**	**14 970**	**14 998**	**15 671**	**14 621**	**15 115**
2100 Employees	8	203	1 470	4 286	6 344	6 711	6 718	6 666	6 194	6 403
2110 On a payroll basis	8	203	1 470	4 286	6 344	6 711	6 718	6 666	6 194	6 403
Compulsory employee's social contributions	8	203	1 470	4 286	6 344	6 711	6 718	6 666	6 194	6 403
2120 On an income tax basis	0	0	0	0	0	0	0	0	0	0
2200 Employers	13	318	2 413	5 882	7 930	8 258	8 281	9 005	8 428	8 712
2210 On a payroll basis	13	318	2 413	5 882	7 930	8 258	8 281	9 005	8 428	8 712
Employers' social contributions	13	318	2 413	5 882	7 930	8 258	8 281	9 005	8 428	8 712
2220 On an income tax basis	0	0	0	0	0	0	0	0	0	0
2300 Self-employed or non-employed	0	10	143	0	0	0	0	0	0	0
Compulsory social contributions by self-employed	0	10	143	..	..	..	..	..	..	..
2310 On a payroll basis	..	..	..	..	..	..	..	..	..	..
2320 On an income tax basis	..	..	..	..	..	..	..	..	..	..
2400 Unallocable between 2100, 2200 and 2300	0	0	0	0	0	0	0	0	0	0
2410 On a payroll basis	..	..	..	..	..	..	..	..	..	..
2420 On an income tax basis	..	..	..	..	..	..	..	..	..	..
3000 Taxes on payroll and workforce	**1**	**47**	**0**	**0**	**0**	**0**	**0**	**0**	**0**	**0**
Contributions for Unemployment Fund	1	47	..	..	..	..	..	..	..	..
Stamp duty on wages and salaries	0	0	..	..	..	..	..	..	..	..
4000 Taxes on property	**5**	**26**	**402**	**1 468**	**2 284**	**2 133**	**1 905**	**1 946**	**1 768**	**1 937**
4100 Recurrent taxes on immovable property	0	0	133	508	1 008	1 102	1 055	1 205	1 140	1 269
Real estate tax	..	..	133	508	1 008	1 102	1 055	1 205	1 140	1 269
4110 Households	..	..	..	..	..	..	..	..	..	..
4120 Others	..	..	..	..	..	..	..	..	..	..
4200 Recurrent taxes on net wealth	0	0	0	0	0	0	0	0	0	0
4210 Individual	..	..	..	..	..	..	..	..	..	..
4220 Corporate	..	..	..	..	..	..	..	..	..	..
4300 Estate, inheritance and gift taxes	2	4	74	103	10	8	0	0	0	2
Inheritance and gift taxes	2	4	74	103	10	8	0	0	..	2
4310 Estate and inheritance taxes	..	..	..	..	..	..	..	..	..	..
4320 Gift taxes	..	..	..	..	..	..	..	..	..	..
4400 Taxes on financial and capital transactions	2	21	195	857	1 266	1 023	850	741	628	666
Real estate transfer tax	2	21	195	674	973	775	635	513	417	450
Stamp duty on registrations and mortgages	0	0	0	34	35	29	19	33	32	32
Stamp duty on the raising of capital	0	0	0	0	10	6	14	0	0	0
Stamp duty on real estate transactions	0	0	0	150	249	213	182	195	179	184
4500 Non-recurrent taxes	0	0	0	0	0	0	0	0	0	0
4510 On net wealth	..	..	..	..	..	..	..	..	..	..
4520 Other non-recurrent taxes	..	..	..	..	..	..	..	..	..	..
4600 Other recurrent taxes on property	0	0	0	0	0	0	0	0	0	0
5000 Taxes on goods and services	**47**	**837**	**6 555**	**16 070**	**23 253**	**23 099**	**20 340**	**22 706**	**21 802**	**21 776**
5100 Taxes on production, sale, transfer, etc	44	810	6 440	15 634	22 583	22 407	19 576	21 865	20 952	20 567
5110 General taxes	0	290	2 906	9 734	14 333	14 424	11 971	14 265	13 995	13 710
5111 Value added taxes	0	0	2 899	9 734	14 333	14 424	11 971	14 265	13 995	13 710
VAT	..	..	2 899	9 734	14 333	14 424	11 971	14 265	13 995	13 710
5112 Sales tax	0	290	7	0	0	0	0	0	0	0
General sales tax	..	290	7	..	..	..	..	..	..	..

Table 66. **Portugal** *(cont.)*
Details of tax revenue / Recettes fiscales détaillées

Million EUR

	1965	1980	1990	2000	2007	2008	2009	2011	2012	2013
5113 Other	0	0	0	0	0	0	0	0	0	0
5120 Taxes on specific goods and services	44	519	3 534	5 901	8 249	7 983	7 604	7 600	6 957	6 857
5121 Excises	15	295	2 052	4 501	5 941	5 619	5 316	5 367	4 775	4 675
Excise duties on tobacco	3	62	362	1 077	1 165	1 281	1 232	1 530	1 432	1 387
Excise duties on beer	1	0	55	90	100	92	84	79	75	77
Tax on motor vehicle sales	1	59	304	1 239	1 221	946	714	644	370	360
Tax on oil products	6	166	1 251	1 969	3 325	3 189	3 177	3 002	2 790	2 741
Excise duties on alcoholic beverages	0	0	23	126	128	111	108	111	107	108
Excise duties on alcohol	0	0	0	1	1	1	1	1	0	1
Other	4	7	59	0	0	0	0	0	0	0
5122 Profits of fiscal monopolies	0	0	0	261	521	462	467	470	522	516
5123 Customs and import duties	21	96	511	1	1	1	1	1	1	0
Import levies	14	36	392	1	1	1	1	1	1	0
Import surtax	0	26	1	0	0	0	0	0	0	0
Other	6	34	119	0	0	0	0	0	0	0
5124 Taxes on exports	0	0	0	0	0	0	0	0	0	0
Taxes on Oporto wine exports	0	0	..	..	..	..	..	..	..	..
Other	0	0	..	..	..	..	..	..	..	..
5125 Taxes on investment goods	0	0	0	0	0	0	0	0	0	0
5126 Taxes on specific services	1	38	547	1 102	1 744	1 861	1 762	1 655	1 560	1 563
Tax on insurance premiums	0	6	47	131	170	199	209	214	208	205
Stamp duty on bank transactions	1	24	405	330	734	786	796	580	534	548
Stamp duty on debt related operations, interest and leasing of buildings	0	0	22	258	384	408	259	298	275	251
Stamp duty on insurance premiums	0	0	0	248	347	350	378	314	288	296
Bank levies	0	0	0	100	81	85	91	231	238	245
Other	2	8	73	33	29	33	29	18	17	19
5127 Other taxes on internat. trade and transactions	0	0	0	0	0	0	0	0	0	0
5128 Other taxes	6	91	424	36	43	40	58	107	99	101
Stamp taxes (miscellaneous)	6	91	424	36	43	40	58	107	99	101
Other	0	0	0	0	0	0	0	0	0	0
5130 Unallocable between 5110 and 5120	0	0	0	0	0	0	0	0	0	0
5200 Taxes on use of goods and perform activities	4	27	115	383	615	641	724	815	819	1 004
5210 Recurrent taxes	4	27	115	383	615	641	724	815	819	1 004
5211 Paid by households: motor vehicles	0	4	15	55	94	100	133	130	138	177
Local tax on vehicles	..	4	15	55	94	100	133	130	138	177
5212 Paid by others: motor vehicles	2	10	20	67	132	149	188	234	262	339
Local tax on vehicles	0	2	6	0	0	0	0	0	0	0
Road taxes	2	8	14	67	132	149	188	234	262	339
5213 Paid in respect of other goods	2	13	80	260	390	392	403	451	419	489
Gambling tax	0	3	72	110	140	152	148	141	113	140
Tax on the use, carrying and possession of weapons	0	0	1	3	6	8	7	4	7	7
Tax on motor vehicles - compensation	2	8	0	0	0	0	0	0	0	0
Hunting and fishery licenses	0	1	4	1	1	3	0	1	0	0
Fee for the use of water resources	0	0	0	0	2	2	9	18	25	25
Other	0	1	2	146	241	227	240	287	274	317
5220 Non-recurrent taxes	0	0	0	0	0	0	0	0	0	0
Special tax on motor vehicles	..	..	0	..	..	..	..	..	..	..
5300 Unallocable between 5100 and 5200	0	0	0	53	55	50	40	26	31	206
Miscellneous taxes on production	..	..	..	53	55	50	40	26	31	206
6000 Other taxes	**0**	**3**	**37**	**288**	**385**	**413**	**574**	**465**	**522**	**528**
6100 Paid solely by business	0	2	17	105	184	201	207	224	216	210
General services and licenses granted to corporations	0	2	17	105	184	201	207	224	216	210
6200 Other	0	0	20	183	200	212	367	242	306	318
Fees collected by courts of justice	0	0	0	177	189	203	363	233	232	210
Miscellaneous taxes	0	0	20	6	11	9	4	8	74	108
Custom duties collected for the EU	..	..	..	**204**	**185**	**177**	**154**	**168**	**155**	**144**
Import duties	..	..	..	170	156	157	135	155	120	119
Agricultural levies	..	..	..	30	29	19	19	13	35	25
Levy on sugar and isoglucose	..	..	..	4	0	0	0	0	0	0
Total tax revenue on cash basis	**99**	**1 798**	**14 825**	..	..	..	..	..	..	..
Total tax revenue on accrual basis	..	..	..	**40 050**	**56 147**	**57 054**	**52 721**	**57 262**	**53 862**	**58 451**

Table 66. **Portugal** *(cont.)*
Details of tax revenue / Recettes fiscales détaillées

Million EUR

	1965	1980	1990	2000	2007	2008	2009	2011	2012	2013
Conciliation with National Accounts										
Additional taxes included in National Accounts	..	..	..	0	0	0	0	0	0	0
Taxes excluded from National Accounts	..	..	..	0	0	0	0	0	0	0
Difference in treatment of tax credits	..	..	..	0	0	0	0	0	0	0
Capital transfer for uncollected revenue	..	..	..	0	0	0	0	0	0	0
Voluntary social security contributions	..	..	..	0	0	0	0	0	0	0
Miscellaneous differences	..	..	..	0	0	0	0	0	0	0
National Accounts: Taxes and actual social contributions	..	..	..	40 050	56 147	57 054	52 721	57 262	53 862	58 451
Imputed social contributions	..	..	..	3 292	5 592	5 729	6 192	5 530	4 521	4 936
National Accounts: Taxes and all social contributions	..	..	..	43 342	61 738	62 783	58 913	62 792	58 383	63 387

Note:

Fiscal year ending 31 December.

From 1995, data are on accrual basis.

Source: Instituto Nacionale de Estatistica; Conta do Estado, Contas de Gerência dos Fundos e Serviços Autonomos da Administraçao Central; Estatisticas das Financas publicas; Relatorio do Instituto de Gestao Financeira da Seguranta Social, Contas de Gerência das Regioes Autonomas da Madeira e dos Atores.

StatLink http://dx.doi.org/10.1787/888933277284

Table 67. **Slovak Republic / République slovaque**
Details of tax revenue / Recettes fiscales détaillées

Million EUR

	1965	1980	1990	2000	2007	2008	2009	2011	2012	2013
Total tax revenue	..	..	..	**10 626**	**18 365**	**19 832**	**18 418**	**20 153**	**20 536**	**22 348**
Total tax revenue exclusive of custom duties	..	..	..	..	**18 229**	**19 677**	**18 307**	**19 997**	**20 408**	**22 233**
1000 Taxes on income, profits and capital gains	..	..	..	**2 181**	**3 844**	**4 389**	**3 526**	**3 842**	**4 005**	**4 440**
1100 Of individuals	..	..	..	1 055	1 820	2 095	1 794	2 000	2 123	2 144
1110 On income and profits	..	..	..	1 055	1 820	2 095	1 794	2 000	2 123	2 144
Wages and salaries withholding	..	..	..	..	..	..	..	..	..	..
Of unicorporated individuals	..	..	..	..	..	..	..	..	..	..
1120 On capital gains	..	..	..	0	0	0	0	0	0	0
1200 Corporate	..	..	..	813	1 835	2 087	1 577	1 699	1 715	2 118
1210 On profits	..	..	..	..	..	..	..	..	..	..
1220 On capital gains	..	..	..	..	..	..	..	..	..	..
1300 Unallocable between 1100 and 1200	..	..	..	314	189	206	156	143	167	178
2000 Social security contributions	..	..	..	**4 409**	**7 192**	**7 909**	**7 858**	**8 479**	**8 907**	**9 783**
2100 Employees	..	..	..	901	1 700	1 899	1 886	2 016	2 138	2 238
Retirement	..	..	..	..	..	..	..	..	..	..
State employment policy	..	..	..	..	..	..	..	..	..	..
Health insurance	..	..	..	..	..	..	..	..	..	..
Sick leave	..	..	..	..	..	..	..	..	..	..
2110 On a payroll basis	..	..	..	901	1 700	1 899	1 886	2 016	2 138	2 238
2120 On an income tax basis	..	..	..	0	0	0	0	0	0	0
2200 Employers	..	..	..	2 850	3 861	4 428	4 243	4 591	4 810	5 492
Retirement	..	..	..	..	..	..	..	..	..	..
State employment policy	..	..	..	..	..	..	..	..	..	..
Health insurance	..	..	..	..	..	..	..	..	..	..
Sick leave	..	..	..	..	..	..	..	..	..	..
2210 On a payroll basis	..	..	..	2 850	3 861	4 428	4 243	4 591	4 810	5 492
2220 On an income tax basis	..	..	..	0	0	0	0	0	0	0
2300 Self-employed or non-employed	..	..	..	658	1 631	1 582	1 729	1 872	1 960	2 054
Retirement	..	..	..	..	..	..	..	..	..	..
State employment policy	..	..	..	..	..	..	..	..	..	..
Health insurance	..	..	..	..	..	..	..	..	..	..
Sick leave	..	..	..	..	..	..	..	..	..	..
2310 On a payroll basis	..	..	..	658	1 631	1 582	1 729	1 872	1 960	2 054
2320 On an income tax basis	..	..	..	0	0	0	0	0	0	0
2400 Unallocable between 2100, 2200 and 2300	..	..	..	0	0	0	0	0	0	0
2410 On a payroll basis	..	..	..	..	..	..	..	..	..	..
2420 On an income tax basis	..	..	..	..	..	..	..	..	..	..
3000 Taxes on payroll and workforce	..	..	..	**0**	**0**	**0**	**0**	**0**	**0**	**0**
4000 Taxes on property	..	..	..	**194**	**245**	**251**	**267**	**286**	**316**	**327**
4100 Recurrent taxes on immovable property	..	..	..	143	243	250	267	286	316	327
4110 Households	..	..	..	55	76	79	84	91	101	105
4120 Others	..	..	..	88	168	172	182	195	215	223
4200 Recurrent taxes on net wealth	..	..	..	0	0	0	0	0	0	0
4210 Individual	..	..	..	..	..	..	..	..	..	..
4220 Corporate	..	..	..	..	..	..	..	..	..	..
4300 Estate, inheritance and gift taxes	..	..	..	8	0	0	0	0	0	0
4310 Estate and inheritance taxes	..	..	..	3	0	0	0	0	0	0
4320 Gift taxes	..	..	..	5	0	0	0	0	0	0
4400 Taxes on financial and capital transactions	..	..	..	43	1	1	0	0	0	0
Real property transfer tax	..	..	..	30	1	1	0	0	0	0
4500 Non-recurrent taxes	..	..	..	0	0	0	0	0	0	0
4510 On net wealth	..	..	..	..	..	..	..	..	..	..
4520 Other non-recurrent taxes	..	..	..	..	..	..	..	..	..	..
4600 Other recurrent taxes on property	..	..	..	0	0	0	0	0	0	0
5000 Taxes on goods and services	..	..	..	**3 842**	**6 948**	**7 127**	**6 656**	**7 389**	**7 179**	**7 683**
5100 Taxes on production, sale, transfer, etc	..	..	..	3 621	6 471	6 588	6 143	6 859	6 635	7 072
5110 General taxes	..	..	..	2 168	4 147	4 621	4 221	4 711	4 328	4 696
5111 Value added taxes	..	..	..	2 168	4 147	4 621	4 221	4 711	4 328	4 696
5112 Sales tax	..	..	..	0	0	0	0	0	0	0
5113 Other	..	..	..	0	0	0	0	0	0	0
5120 Taxes on specific goods and services	..	..	..	1 453	2 324	1 967	1 921	2 148	2 307	2 376
5121 Excises	..	..	..	971	2 171	1 809	1 762	1 999	1 973	1 985
On hydrocarbon fuels and lubricants	..	..	..	617	1 118	1 185	1 047	1 071	1 036	1 045
On alcohol and liquers	..	..	..	143	201	220	197	205	195	201
On beer	..	..	..	43	66	64	58	58	56	56
On wine	..	..	..	12	4	4	4	4	4	4
On tobacco products	..	..	..	156	783	325	436	623	640	636
On electricity	..	..	..	0	0	5	8	16	17	17
On coal	..	..	..	0	0	0	1	1	1	1
On natural gas	..	..	..	0	0	6	11	21	23	25

Table 67. **Slovak Republic / République slovaque** *(cont.)*
Details of tax revenue / Recettes fiscales détaillées

Million EUR

	1965	1980	1990	2000	2007	2008	2009	2011	2012	2013
5122 Profits of fiscal monopolies	...	...	...	0	0	0	0	0	0	0
5123 Customs and import duties	...	...	...	437	1	0	0	0	0	0
Customs duties	...	...	...	122	0	0	0	0	0	0
Import surcharges	...	...	...	315	0	0	0	0	0	0
Other customs revenues	...	...	...	0	0	0	0	0	0	0
5124 Taxes on exports	...	...	...	0	0	0	0	0	0	0
5125 Taxes on investment goods	...	...	...	0	0	0	0	0	0	6
5126 Taxes on specific services	...	...	...	45	152	158	160	149	334	385
5127 Other taxes on internat. trade and transactions	...	...	...	0	0	0	0	0	0	0
5128 Other taxes	...	...	...	0	0	0	0	0	0	0
5130 Unallocable between 5110 and 5120	...	...	...	0	0	0	0	0	0	0
5200 Taxes on use of goods and perform activities	...	...	...	219	372	412	384	392	400	466
5210 Recurrent taxes	...	...	...	219	372	412	384	392	400	466
5211 Paid by households: motor vehicles	...	...	...	0	0	0	0	0	0	0
5212 Paid by others: motor vehicles	...	...	...	76	124	136	124	140	138	153
5213 Paid in respect of other goods	...	...	...	143	248	276	260	253	261	313
5220 Non-recurrent taxes	...	...	...	0	0	0	0	0	0	0
5300 Unallocable between 5100 and 5200	...	...	...	2	105	127	129	138	145	145
6000 Other taxes	**...**	**...**	**...**	**0**	**0**	**0**	**0**	**0**	**0**	**0**
6100 Paid solely by business	...	...	...	...	...	...	...	...	...	...
6200 Other	...	...	...	...	...	...	...	...	...	...
Custom duties collected for the EU	**..**	**..**	**..**	**..**	**136**	**156**	**111**	**157**	**129**	**115**
Total tax revenue on cash basis	**..**	**..**	**..**	**10 821**	**17 941**	**19 637**	**18 536**	**19 558**	**20 073**	**21 810**
Total tax revenue on accrual basis	**..**	**..**	**..**	**10 626**	**18 365**	**19 832**	**18 418**	**20 153**	**20 536**	**22 348**
Conciliation with National Accounts										
Additional taxes included in National Accounts	...	...	...	0	0	0	0	0	0	0
Taxes excluded from National Accounts	...	...	...	0	-103	-124	-126	-135	-142	148
Difference in treatment of tax credits	...	...	...	0	0	0	0	0	0	0
Capital transfer for uncollected revenue	...	...	...	0	0	0	0	0	0	0
Voluntary social security contributions	...	...	...	0	22	25	26	34	23	17
Miscellaneous differences	...	...	...	0	0	0	0	0	0	0
National Accounts: Taxes and actual social contributions	...	...	...	10 626	18 284	19 732	18 318	20 053	20 417	22 513
Imputed social contributions	...	...	...	19	73	82	88	121	96	131
National Accounts: Taxes and all social contributions	...	...	...	10 646	18 357	19 814	18 406	20 174	20 513	22 644

Note:

Year ending 31st December.

Data are on accrual basis.

Source: Ministry of Finance.

StatLink http://dx.doi.org/10.1787/888933277290

Table 68. **Slovenia / Slovénie**
Details of tax revenue / Recettes fiscales détaillées

Million EUR

	1965	1980	1990	2000	2007	2008	2009	2011	2012	2013
Total tax revenue	..	..	..	**6 924**	**13 030**	**13 810**	**13 096**	**13 458**	**13 265**	**13 296**
Total tax revenue exclusive of customs duties	..	..	..	..	**12 945**	**13 733**	**13 039**	**13 396**	**13 211**	**13 244**
1000 Taxes on income, profits and capital gains	..	..	..	**1 280**	**3 041**	**3 120**	**2 722**	**2 670**	**2 494**	**2 325**
1100 Of individuals	..	..	..	1 041	1 919	2 181	2 066	2 056	2 045	1 889
1110 On income and profits	..	..	..	1 039	1 916	2 178	2 063	2 053	2 040	1 887
Personal income tax	..	..	..	1 039	1 916	2 178	2 063	2 053	2 040	1 887
Special contribution for the reconstruction of the Posocje region	..	..	..	0	0	0	0	0	0	0
1120 On capital gains	..	..	..	2	3	4	4	3	4	3
Taxes on winnings from lottery and gambling	..	..	..	2	3	4	4	3	4	3
1200 Corporate	..	..	..	216	1 116	933	652	611	446	433
1210 On profits	..	..	..	216	1 116	933	652	611	446	433
1220 On capital gains	..	..	..	0	0	0	0	0	0	0
1300 Unallocable between 1100 and 1200	..	..	..	24	5	5	4	3	4	3
Tax on income - copy rights, patents and trademarks	..	..	..	24	5	5	4	3	3	2
Tax on profits due to changes in land use	..	..	..	0	0	0	0	0	0	0
2000 Social security contributions	..	..	..	**2 631**	**4 724**	**5 221**	**5 276**	**5 407**	**5 365**	**5 332**
2100 Employees	..	..	..	1 446	2 488	2 752	2 736	2 767	2 698	2 673
2110 On a payroll basis	..	..	..	1 446	2 488	2 752	2 736	2 767	2 698	2 673
2120 On an income tax basis	..	..	..	0	0	0	0	0	0	0
2200 Employers	..	..	..	1 008	1 844	2 042	2 032	2 064	2 054	2 049
2210 On a payroll basis	..	..	..	1 008	1 844	2 042	2 032	2 064	2 054	2 049
2220 On an income tax basis	..	..	..	0	0	0	0	0	0	0
2300 Self-employed or non-employed	..	..	..	177	392	427	508	575	614	610
2310 On a payroll basis	..	..	..	177	392	427	508	575	614	610
2320 On an income tax basis	..	..	..	0	0	0	0	0	0	0
2400 Unallocable between 2100, 2200 and 2300	..	..	..	0	0	0	0	0	0	0
2410 On a payroll basis	..	..	..	..	..	..	..	..	..	..
2420 On an income tax basis	..	..	..	..	..	..	..	..	..	..
3000 Taxes on payroll and workforce	..	..	..	**289**	**418**	**258**	**27**	**29**	**26**	**23**
Payroll tax	..	..	..	272	391	230	0	0	0	0
Tax on work contracts	..	..	..	18	27	28	27	29	26	23
4000 Taxes on property	..	..	..	**120**	**206**	**214**	**210**	**219**	**227**	**232**
4100 Recurrent taxes on immovable property	..	..	..	81	140	154	169	177	188	199
4110 Households	..	..	..	17	38	40	46	46	54	61
Property tax on weekend cottages	..	..	..	1	1	1	1	1	1	1
Compensation on the use of building ground - paid by individuals	..	..	..	16	37	39	45	45	52	48
Tax on immovable property of higher value	..	..	..	0	0	0	0	0	1	13
4120 Others	..	..	..	65	102	114	123	131	135	138
Property tax on buildings	..	..	..	2	3	3	3	4	4	4
Compensation on the use of building ground - paid by legal entities	..	..	..	63	100	111	120	127	131	134
4200 Recurrent taxes on net wealth	..	..	..	4	0	0	0	0	0	0
4210 Individual	..	..	..	0	..	..	..	..	..	..
4220 Corporate	..	..	..	4	..	..	..	..	..	..
Tax on balance wealth paid by banks	..	..	..	4	..	..	..	..	..	..
4300 Estate, inheritance and gift taxes	..	..	..	2	9	11	11	10	9	8
4310 Estate and inheritance taxes	..	..	..	..	..	..	..	..	..	..
4320 Gift taxes	..	..	..	..	..	..	..	..	..	..
4400 Taxes on financial and capital transactions	..	..	..	23	57	49	30	29	27	23
Taxes on the sale of immovable property - from legal entities	..	..	..	11	19	13	7	6	5	5
Taxes on the sale of immovable property - from individuals	..	..	..	12	38	36	22	23	21	18
4500 Non-recurrent taxes	..	..	..	10	0	0	0	4	2	1
4510 On net wealth	..	..	..	0	..	..	..	0	0	0
4520 Other non-recurrent taxes	..	..	..	10	..	..	..	4	2	1
Payments for the change of use of agricultural and forest land	..	..	..	10	..	..	..	2	0	1
Granting of easements and the creation of building rights	..	..	..	0	..	..	..	2	2	1
4600 Other recurrent taxes on property	..	..	..	0	0	0	0	0	0	0
Property tax on boats	..	..	..	0	0	0	0	0	0	0
5000 Taxes on goods and services	..	..	..	**2 602**	**4 556**	**4 920**	**4 804**	**5 070**	**5 099**	**5 331**
5100 Taxes on production, sale, transfer, etc	..	..	..	2 481	4 341	4 704	4 597	4 850	4 853	4 990
5110 General taxes	..	..	..	1 641	2 916	3 159	2 862	2 995	2 889	3 048
5111 Value added taxes	..	..	..	1 610	2 916	3 159	2 862	2 995	2 889	3 048
Value added tax	..	..	..	1 598	2 898	3 140	2 849	2 994	2 886	3 047
Negative compensation of farmers in a VAT flat rate system	..	..	..	12	18	19	13	1	3	1

Table 68. **Slovenia / Slovénie** *(cont.)*
Details of tax revenue / Recettes fiscales détaillées

Million EUR

	1965	1980	1990	2000	2007	2008	2009	2011	2012	2013
5112 Sales tax	..	..	..	31	0	0	0	0	0	0
Turnover tax on goods	..	..	..	11	..	..	..	..	..	..
Turnover tax on services	..	..	..	12	..	..	..	..	..	..
Special turnover tax on alcohol	..	..	..	0	..	..	..	..	..	..
Customs duties paid by individuals	..	..	..	1	..	..	..	..	..	..
Special import duties and customs charges	..	..	..	7	..	..	..	..	..	..
5113 Other	..	..	..	0	0	0	0	0	0	0
5120 Taxes on specific goods and services	..	..	..	841	1 425	1 545	1 735	1 855	1 964	1 942
5121 Excises	..	..	..	581	1 196	1 318	1 502	1 548	1 637	1 579
Alcohol and alcoholic drinks	..	..	..	39	71	72	86	92	93	96
Mineral oil and gas	..	..	..	405	758	824	1 005	955	1 035	998
Tobacco	..	..	..	97	301	343	363	429	442	425
Duty free shops - alcohol and alcoholic drinks	..	..	..	3	0	0	0	0	0	0
Duty free shops - tobacco	..	..	..	17	0	0	0	0	0	0
Electric power and coal	..	..	..	0	4	7	7	33	33	31
Tax on the sales of new motor vehicles	..	..	..	18	60	70	41	38	34	26
Tax on the sales of used motor vehicles	..	..	..	2	2	1	0	0	0	0
Additional tax on motor vehicles	..	..	..	0	0	0	0	0	1	3
5122 Profits of fiscal monopolies	..	..	..	0	0	0	0	0	0	0
5123 Customs and import duties	..	..	..	158	0	0	0	0	0	0
Import duties	..	..	..	151	..	..	..	..	..	..
Levies on imported agricultural products	..	..	..	7	..	..	..	..	..	..
5124 Taxes on exports	..	..	..	0	0	0	0	0	0	0
5125 Taxes on investment goods	..	..	..	0	0	0	0	0	0	0
5126 Taxes on specific services	..	..	..	102	230	227	233	308	327	363
Tax on special gambling (gambling in casinos)	..	..	..	25	64	61	57	51	45	41
Tax on classical gambling (lottery...)	..	..	..	1	3	4	4	3	4	3
Special tax on slot machines	..	..	..	4	0	0	0	0	0	0
Tax on insurance services	..	..	..	37	65	66	69	71	70	65
Sojourn tax	..	..	..	3	7	7	7	7	8	8
Concessions	..	..	..	1	29	30	40	42	60	90
Concessions duties on special gambling (gambling in casinos)	..	..	..	26	55	52	49	45	41	32
Fire protection tax	..	..	..	4	6	7	7	8	8	8
Tax on lottery tickets	..	..	..	0	0	0	0	0	0	3
Tax on financial services	..	..	..	0	0	0	0	0	0	32
FIHO, FSO	..	..	..	0	0	0	0	23	37	26
SOS	..	..	..	0	0	0	0	27	17	10
Tax on balace wealth paid by banks	..	..	..	0	0	0	0	0	7	18
Commodity reserve fund	..	..	..	0	0	0	0	31	31	27
5127 Other taxes on internat. trade and transactions	..	..	..	0	0	0	0	0	0	0
5128 Other taxes	..	..	..	0	0	0	0	0	0	0
Sugar levy	..	..	..	..	0	..	..	..	..	..
5130 Unallocable between 5110 and 5120	..	..	..	0	0	0	0	0	0	0
5200 Taxes on use of goods and perform activities	..	..	..	121	215	217	207	220	245	340
5210 Recurrent taxes	..	..	..	121	215	217	207	220	245	323
5211 Paid by households: motor vehicles	..	..	..	49	87	80	83	87	88	109
Registration fees on motor vehicles, boats and airplanes paid by individuals	..	..	..	49	87	80	83	87	88	109
5212 Paid by others: motor vehicles	..	..	..	12	21	25	22	20	20	24
Registration fees on motor vehicles, boats and airplanes paid by legal entities	..	..	..	12	21	25	22	20	20	24
Registration fees on tractors	..	..	..	0	0	0	0	0	0	0
5213 Paid in respect of other goods	..	..	..	59	107	112	102	113	137	189
Charges on the use of water	..	..	..	4	22	23	22	25	26	29
Taxes on waste pollution	..	..	..	7	10	9	4	4	4	4
Taxes on air pollution - caused by gas and hard fuels	..	..	..	3	8	9	9	10	8	10
Contribution of Nuclear power plant to finance its de-composition	..	..	..	16	8	9	8	9	8	8
Indemnity for the restricted use of area on the territory of Nuclear power plant	..	..	..	0	7	8	7	11	11	11
Taxes on air pollution	..	..	..	29	21	23	23	21	49	98
Special water tax	..	..	..	0	30	30	29	33	30	29
5220 Non-recurrent taxes	..	..	..	0	0	0	0	0	0	18
Emission permits	..	..	..	0	0	0	0	0	0	18
5300 Unallocable between 5100 and 5200	..	..	..	0	0	0	0	0	0	0
6000 Other taxes	..	..	..	**0**	**0**	**0**	**0**	**0**	**0**	**0**
6100 Paid solely by business	..	..	..	..	..	..	..	..	..	..
6200 Other	..	..	..	..	..	..	..	..	..	..
Custom duties collected for the EU	..	..	..	..	**85**	**77**	**57**	**62**	**54**	**52**
Total tax revenue on cash basis	..	..	..	**6 990**	**12 937**	**14 196**	**13 344**	**13 690**	**13 612**	**13 219**

Table 68. **Slovenia / Slovénie** *(cont.)*
Details of tax revenue / Recettes fiscales détaillées

Million EUR

	1965	1980	1990	2000	2007	2008	2009	2011	2012	2013
Total tax revenue on accrual basis	..	..	..	**6 924**	**13 030**	**13 810**	**13 096**	**13 458**	**13 265**	**13 296**
Conciliation with National Accounts										
Additional taxes included in National Accounts	...	...	...	0	0	79	85	81	92	90
Radio and television licence fee	...	...	...	...	...	79	85	81	92	90
Taxes excluded from National Accounts	...	...	...	0	0	0	0	0	0	0
Difference in treatment of tax credits	...	...	...	0	0	0	0	0	0	0
Capital transfer for uncollected revenue	...	...	...	0	0	0	0	0	0	0
Voluntary social security contributions	...	...	...	0	0	0	0	0	0	0
Miscellaneous differences	..	...	...	0	0	0	0	0	0	0
National Accounts: Taxes and actual social contributions	...	...	...	6 924	13 030	13 889	13 181	13 539	13 357	13 386
Imputed social contributions	...	...	...	39	80	90	97	101	100	101
National Accounts: Taxes and all social contributions	...	...	...	6 962	13 110	13 979	13 278	13 641	13 456	13 487

Note:

Year ending 31st December.

Data are on accrual basis.

Source: Statistical Office of the Republic of Slovenia.

StatLink http://dx.doi.org/10.1787/888933277306

Table 69. **Spain / Espagne**
Details of tax revenue / Recettes fiscales détaillées

Million EUR

	1965	1980	1990	2000	2007	2008	2009	2011	2012	2013
Total tax revenue	**1 238**	**22 002**	**103 662**	**219 347**	**399 659**	**366 776**	**331 251**	**345 436**	**347 157**	**349 665**
Total tax revenue exclusive of custom duties	..	..	..	**218 377**	**397 937**	**365 198**	**329 923**	**343 882**	**345 721**	**348 349**
1000 Taxes on income, profits and capital gains	**304**	**5 714**	**31 763**	**62 405**	**134 137**	**112 738**	**99 371**	**100 638**	**104 234**	**102 777**
1100 Of individuals	177	4 481	22 527	40 969	80 757	78 521	71 833	78 297	78 893	78 321
1110 On income and profits	169	4 393	22 527	40 969	80 757	78 521	71 833	78 297	78 893	78 321
Personal income tax	..	..	22 527	40 969	80 757	78 521	71 833	78 297	78 893	78 321
1120 On capital gains	8	88	0	0	0	0	0	0	0	0
1200 Corporate	114	1 119	9 146	19 616	49 750	30 682	23 845	18 853	22 098	21 509
1210 On profits	114	1 089	9 146	19 616	49 750	30 682	23 845	18 853	22 098	21 123
Tax on commercial activity	33	5	0	0	0	0	0	0	0	0
Special tax 4 percent	0	0	0	0	0	0	0	0	0	0
Taxes on profits	81	1 084	0	0	0	0	0	0	0	0
Corporate income tax	0	0	9 146	19 616	49 750	30 682	23 845	18 853	22 098	21 123
1220 On capital gains	0	29	0	0	0	0	0	0	0	386
1300 Unallocable between 1100 and 1200	13	114	91	1 820	3 630	3 535	3 693	3 488	3 243	2 947
Local taxes	13	114	0	0	0	0	0	0	0	0
Non residente income tax	0	0	0	1 184	2 645	2 499	2 481	2 147	1 781	1 428
Other taxes	0	0	91	636	985	1 036	1 212	1 341	1 462	1 519
2000 Social security contributions	**350**	**10 682**	**36 722**	**76 421**	**129 170**	**134 372**	**130 843**	**129 535**	**123 967**	**120 750**
2100 Employees	81	2 376	5 976	12 336	20 582	21 351	20 451	20 491	19 393	18 819
2110 On a payroll basis	..	..	5 976	12 336	20 582	21 351	20 451	20 491	19 393	18 819
2120 On an income tax basis	..	..	0	0	0	0	0	0	0	0
2200 Employers	269	8 306	26 385	55 090	94 102	96 968	91 297	90 874	85 701	83 488
2210 On a payroll basis	..	..	26 385	55 090	94 102	96 968	91 297	90 874	85 701	83 488
2220 On an income tax basis	..	..	0	0	0	0	0	0	0	0
2300 Self-employed or non-employed	0	0	4 361	8 995	14 486	16 053	19 095	18 170	18 873	18 443
Self-employment	..	..	2 492	7 037	10 335	10 682	10 503	10 633	10 712	10 639
Unemployment	..	..	1 869	1 958	4 151	5 371	8 592	7 537	8 161	7 804
2310 On a payroll basis	..	..	..	..	..	..	..	..	..	..
2320 On an income tax basis	..	..	..	..	..	..	..	..	..	..
2400 Unallocable between 2100, 2200 and 2300	0	0	0	0	0	0	0	0	0	0
2410 On a payroll basis	..	..	..	..	..	..	..	..	..	..
2420 On an income tax basis	..	..	..	..	..	..	..	..	..	..
3000 Taxes on payroll and workforce	**0**	**0**	**0**	**0**	**0**	**0**	**0**	**0**	**0**	**0**
4000 Taxes on property	**79**	**1 004**	**5 718**	**13 873**	**32 150**	**25 626**	**21 848**	**20 816**	**21 753**	**23 566**
4100 Recurrent taxes on immovable property	6	41	1 478	3 990	7 274	7 941	8 853	10 176	11 182	11 944
4110 Households	..	40	1 478	3 990	7 274	7 941	8 853	10 176	11 182	11 944
Real State tax	..	..	1 478	3 990	7 274	7 941	8 853	10 176	11 182	11 944
Real State tax. Surchage	..	..	0	0	0	0	0	0	0	0
4120 Others	..	1	0	0	0	0	0	0	0	0
4200 Recurrent taxes on net wealth	0	107	637	1 200	2 059	2 416	93	56	784	1 370
4210 Individual	..	107	637	1 200	2 059	2 416	93	56	784	1 370
Wealth tax	..	..	637	1 200	2 059	2 416	93	56	784	1 370
4220 Corporate	..	0	0	0	0	0	0	0	0	0
4300 Estate, inheritance and gift taxes	13	90	440	1 381	2 905	2 915	2 667	2 220	2 285	2 518
4310 Estate and inheritance taxes	..	90	440	1 381	2 905	2 915	2 667	2 220	2 285	2 518
Inheritance and gift tax	..	..	440	1 381	2 905	2 915	2 667	2 220	2 285	2 518
4320 Gift taxes	..	0	0	0	0	0	0	0	0	0
4400 Taxes on financial and capital transactions	60	767	2 478	6 140	17 399	10 344	8 483	6 574	5 777	5 657
Taxes on property transactions	60	767	2 478	6 140	17 399	10 344	8 483	6 574	5 777	5 657
4500 Non-recurrent taxes	0	0	646	1 108	2 447	1 934	1 651	1 676	1 595	1 946
4510 On net wealth	..	..	467	705	1 911	1 488	1 290	1 357	1 382	1 801
Tax on land holding gains	..	..	467	705	1 911	1 488	1 290	1 357	1 382	1 801
4520 Other non-recurrent taxes	..	..	179	403	536	446	361	319	213	145
Special duties	..	..	179	180	168	147	135	134	94	85
Land development contributions	..	..	0	223	368	299	226	185	119	60
4600 Other recurrent taxes on property	0	0	38	54	66	76	101	114	130	131
5000 Taxes on goods and services	**506**	**4 553**	**29 437**	**64 892**	**101 020**	**90 963**	**75 913**	**90 083**	**92 411**	**98 233**
5100 Taxes on production, sale, transfer, etc	503	4 552	27 508	59 582	93 926	84 208	69 530	83 508	86 074	92 185
5110 General taxes	275	2 234	16 611	38 546	63 943	55 457	41 830	56 733	57 584	62 179
5111 Value added taxes	0	0	16 304	38 546	63 943	55 457	41 830	56 733	57 584	62 179
Value added tax (VAT)	..	..	16 304	37 806	62 672	54 231	41 093	55 904	56 652	61 071
Canary Islands general indirect tax	..	..	0	740	1 271	1 226	737	829	932	1 108
5112 Sales tax	0	0	0	0	0	0	0	0	0	0
5113 Other	275	2 234	307	0	0	0	0	0	0	0
Cascade tax	118	1 483	197	..	..	..	..	..	..	..
Excises on luxury expenditure	96	939	15	..	..	..	..	..	..	..
Other import duties	94	832	128	..	..	..	..	..	..	..
Refund of internal taxes	-33	-1 020	-33	..	..	..	..	..	..	..
5120 Taxes on specific goods and services	228	2 317	10 896	21 036	29 983	28 751	27 700	26 775	28 490	30 006

Table 69. **Spain / Espagne** *(cont.)*
Details of tax revenue / Recettes fiscales détaillées

Million EUR

	1965	1980	1990	2000	2007	2008	2009	2011	2012	2013
5121 Excises	69	1 239	6 048	16 489	23 174	22 950	22 610	22 256	21 710	24 052
Special excises	69	1 239	10	0	0	0	0	0	0	0
On beer	0	0	87	202	307	309	299	302	303	300
On wine	0	0	0	0	0	0	0	0	0	0
On alcohol	0	0	481	821	1 032	1 006	907	830	827	779
On hydrocarbon	0	0	4 222	9 997	11 785	11 207	10 859	10 226	9 460	11 788
On tobacco	0	0	1 123	4 505	7 250	7 528	7 717	7 845	7 737	7 127
On electricity bills	0	0	0	703	1 153	1 281	1 363	1 499	1 632	1 561
On carbon	0	0	0	0	0	0	0	0	0	148
Tax on retail sales of specific hydrocarbons	0	0	0	0	1 356	1 330	1 232	1 315	1 489	466
Tax on oil derived fuels	0	0	120	237	263	263	233	216	240	267
Petrol tax	0	0	0	6	5	6	0	5	4	13
Production and storage of electricity	0	0	0	0	0	0	0	0	0	1 587
Tax Greenhouse Effect Flourinated	0	0	0	0	0	0	0	0	0	0
Other taxes	0	0	5	18	23	20	0	18	18	16
5122 Profits of fiscal monopolies	66	132	546	0	0	0	0	0	0	0
Tobacco	21	77	0	..	..	..	..	..	..	..
Petroleum	45	55	546	..	..	..	..	..	..	..
5123 Customs and import duties	87	561	2 078	103	145	140	120	127	118	127
Import duties	87	561	1 394	0	0	0	0	0	0	0
Canary Islands taxes on imported products	0	0	137	33	51	52	36	48	46	47
Taxes on imported products in Ceuta and Melilla	0	0	36	41	42	40	39	41	28	40
Customs duties paid to EU	0	0	511	0	0	0	0	0	0	0
Special duties and other taxes on importes products	0	0	0	29	52	48	45	38	44	40
5124 Taxes on exports	0	0	0	0	0	0	0	0	0	0
5125 Taxes on investment goods	0	0	0	0	0	0	0	0	0	0
5126 Taxes on specific services	7	385	2 203	2 913	4 311	4 192	3 977	3 637	6 080	5 315
Taxes on betting and gambling	0	232	1 307	1 699	2 062	1 893	1 747	1 475	1 495	1 282
Taxes on other specific services	6	153	120	0	0	0	0	0	0	0
Taxes on insurance premiums	0	0	0	849	1 581	1 608	1 498	1 517	1 473	1 417
Compensation for local taxes	0	0	86	140	176	185	178	158	144	131
Parafiscal taxes	0	0	690	225	492	506	554	487	451	674
Deposit Guarantee Fund (DGF)	0	0	0	0	0	0	0	0	2 517	1 811
5127 Other taxes on internat. trade and transactions	0	0	0	0	0	0	0	0	0	0
5128 Other taxes	0	0	22	1 531	2 353	1 469	993	755	582	512
Duty on specific means of transport	..	..	0	1 323	2 159	1 273	819	563	426	325
Canary Islands taxes on national products	..	..	0	51	86	83	63	76	72	73
Taxes on national products in Ceuta and Melilla	..	..	0	108	110	105	103	109	73	107
Duty on the production of sugar	..	..	22	49	-2	8	8	7	11	7
5130 Unallocable between 5110 and 5120	0	0	0	0	0	0	0	0	0	0
5200 Taxes on use of goods and perform activities	3	1	1 857	5 032	6 721	6 009	5 442	5 233	5 043	4 917
5210 Recurrent taxes	3	1	1 530	3 464	4 004	4 136	4 204	4 240	4 378	4 139
5211 Paid by households: motor vehicles	..	0	461	1 129	1 698	1 769	1 800	1 799	1 805	1 851
Car registration tax	..	..	461	1 129	1 698	1 769	1 800	1 799	1 805	1 851
5212 Paid by others: motor vehicles	..	0	117	286	430	448	456	456	457	469
Car registration tax	..	..	117	286	430	448	456	456	457	469
5213 Paid in respect of other goods	..	1	952	2 049	1 876	1 919	1 948	1 985	2 116	1 819
Hunting and fishing taxes	..	..	0	28	28	30	30	30	29	35
Economic activity tax	..	..	925	1 934	1 635	1 690	1 790	1 732	1 764	1 587
Economic activity tax. Surchage	..	..	0	0	0	0	0	0	0	0
Advertising	..	..	27	0	0	0	0	0	0	0
Tax on environment and pollution	..	..	0	0	0	0	0	0	0	0
Other taxes on environment	..	..	0	42	131	129	85	162	241	82
Tax on effluent, use of hydrocarbon and mines	..	..	0	45	82	70	43	61	82	115
5220 Non-recurrent taxes	0	0	327	1 568	2 717	1 873	1 238	993	665	778
Tax and building permits	..	..	327	1 117	2 227	1 507	988	773	500	486
Urban licenses	..	..	0	451	490	366	250	220	165	154
Greenhouse gas emission trading	..	..	0	0	0	0	0	0	0	138
5300 Unallocable between 5100 and 5200	0	0	72	278	373	746	941	1 342	1 294	1 131
6000 Other taxes	**0**	**49**	**22**	**785**	**1 460**	**1 499**	**1 947**	**2 810**	**3 356**	**3 022**
6100 Paid solely by business	..	49	0	510	886	957	958	1 211	1 258	1 244
Municipal fees for private use of public space	..	..	..	510	886	957	958	1 211	1 258	1 244
6200 Other	..	0	22	275	574	542	989	1 599	2 098	1 778
Custom duties collected for the EU	..	..	..	**970**	**1 722**	**1 578**	**1 328**	**1 554**	**1 436**	**1 316**
Total tax revenue on cash basis	**1 238**	**22 002**	**103 662**	**215 212**	**394 169**	**360 256**	**320 592**	**352 331**	**352 213**	**352 093**
Total tax revenue on accrual basis	..	..	..	**219 347**	**399 659**	**366 776**	**331 251**	**345 436**	**347 157**	**349 665**

Table 69. **Spain / Espagne** *(cont.)*
Details of tax revenue / Recettes fiscales détaillées

Million EUR

	1965	1980	1990	2000	2007	2008	2009	2011	2012	2013
Conciliation with National Accounts										
Additional taxes included in National Accounts	..	..	..	0	0	0	0	0	0	0
Taxes excluded from National Accounts	..	..	..	-2 201	-3 334	-3 303	-5 046	-4 029	-4 226	-4 007
Fines and penalties	..	..	..	-1 182	-1 614	-1 717	-2 182	-2 468	-2 779	-2 684
VAT for EU	..	..	..	0	0	0	-1 528	0	0	0
Duty on the production of sugar	..	..	..	-49	2	-8	-8	-7	-11	-7
Customs duties collected for the EU	..	..	..	-970	-1 722	-1 578	-1 328	-1 554	-1 436	-1 316
Difference in treatment of tax credits	..	..	..	0	0	0	0	0	0	0
Capital transfer for uncollected revenue	..	..	..	-3 454	-4 837	-6 168	-9 351	-8 811	-7 955	-6 531
Voluntary social security contributions	..	..	..	0	0	0	0	0	0	0
Miscellaneous differences	..	..	..	0	0	0	0	0	0	0
National Accounts: Taxes and actual social contributions	..	..	..	213 692	391 488	357 305	316 854	332 596	334 976	339 127
Imputed social contributions	..	..	..	5 379	7 702	8 155	9 851	8 814	8 534	8 012
National Accounts: Taxes and all social contributions	..	..	..	219 071	399 190	365 460	326 705	341 410	343 510	347 139

Note:

Year ending 31st December.

From 2000, data are on accrual basis.

From 1981 the figures take into account the classification procedures set out in the OECD Interpretative Guide. Consequently they are not completely comparable with the figures for earlier years though the amounts involved are quite small.

Heading 1000: Includes a tax on property 'Contribucion Rustica' which would be more appropriately classified in 4110, and the 'Licencia fiscal industrial and professionales' which, because it is a tax levied by reference to the size of the firm, energy input, etc, would be more appropriately classified in 6000. The data necessary to provide a breakdown is not available.

All subdivisions are estimated.

Heading 2300: Contributions paid by self-employed were shown under heading 2100 until 1982.

Heading 4100: Most of these receipts fall under 4110.

Heading 4400: In 1988 revenues from taxes on legal Acts issued by Autonomous Communities (Local) are included in 4400.

Heading 5121 comprises certain local levies which may include non-tax revenues.

Source: Informacion Estatistica del Ministerio de Hacienda (for national taxes). Cuentas de las Administraciones Publicas (for local taxes and social security) both published by Secretaria General Tecnica del Ministerio de Hacienda.

StatLink http://dx.doi.org/10.1787/888933277313

Table 70. **Sweden / Suède**
Details of tax revenue / Recettes fiscales détaillées

Million SEK

	1965	1980	1990	2000	2007	2008	2009	2011	2012	2013
Total tax revenue	**40 003**	**259 216**	**755 953**	**1 166 006**	**1 482 649**	**1 490 704**	**1 449 712**	**1 554 311**	**1 568 247**	**1 617 457**
Total tax revenue exclusive of custom duties	..	..	..	**1 162 556**	**1 477 550**	**1 485 493**	**1 444 948**	**1 548 912**	**1 563 252**	**1 612 481**
1000 Taxes on income, profits and capital gains	**21 956**	**112 730**	**314 797**	**475 304**	**573 698**	**539 262**	**510 372**	**540 942**	**534 404**	**558 683**
1100 Of individuals	19 500	106 376	291 146	387 531	457 760	443 638	417 337	427 894	439 623	459 078
1110 On income and profits	19 390	105 866	289 598	353 106	408 054	417 337	392 416	399 118	411 899	426 777
Coupon tax	9	44	233	2 040	6 306	5 480	3 063	4 536	3 722	4 108
Duties on foreign artists	4	3	3	50	86	103	127	85	6	-1
National income tax individual	8 676	31 682	70 755	32 486	44 326	47 003	39 935	44 636	44 080	44 664
Local income tax individual	9 294	78 134	220 072	336 304	479 068	503 423	511 150	538 227	560 766	581 934
Tax reduction individual	0	-3 997	-1 465	-18 872	-122 029	-139 190	-162 550	-189 120	-197 423	-204 632
Other	1 407	0	0	1 098	296	518	690	753	748	704
1120 On capital gains	110	510	1 548	34 425	49 707	26 301	24 921	28 776	27 724	32 301
Lottery prize tax	110	510	1 548	60	0	0	0	0	0	0
1200 Corporate	2 456	6 354	23 651	87 772	115 937	95 624	93 035	113 048	94 781	99 605
1210 On profits	2 456	6 354	23 651	87 772	115 937	95 624	93 035	113 048	94 781	99 605
Tax on profits not distributed	1	10	3	0	0	0	0	0	0	0
National income tax b.c. list	1 425	2 078	19 774	74 501	103 150	80 390	80 718	101 186	84 635	92 755
Local income tax b.c. list	1 030	4 266	0	0	0	0	0	0	0	0
Special tax on profits	0	0	3 874	0	0	0	0	0	0	0
Taxes on pension insurance savings	0	0	0	13 271	12 787	15 234	12 317	11 862	10 146	6 850
1220 On capital gains	0	0	0	0	0	0	0	0	0	0
1300 Unallocable between 1100 and 1200	0	0	0	0	0	0	0	0	0	0
2000 Social security contributions	**4 851**	**74 647**	**205 867**	**306 974**	**388 505**	**372 762**	**357 289**	**361 987**	**375 628**	**376 684**
2100 Employees	743	254	823	63 074	81 088	85 162	86 845	93 500	97 561	100 861
Health insurance fees	743	9	5	0	0	0	0	0	0	0
Unemployment insurance fees	0	245	818	0	0	0	0	0	0	0
Pension fees	0	0	0	63 074	81 088	85 162	86 845	93 500	97 561	100 861
2110 On a payroll basis	..	..	..	63 074	81 088	85 162	86 845	93 500	97 561	100 861
2120 On an income tax basis	..	..	..	0	0	0	0	0	0	0
2200 Employers	3 568	71 602	196 905	237 527	300 010	279 771	264 807	263 272	272 511	271 449
Survivors pension fees	0	20 343	44 181	14 847	19 611	20 351	19 905	14 771	15 250	15 693
Health insurance fees	717	26 005	58 334	74 097	100 979	92 340	78 631	63 318	65 434	58 365
Unemployment insurance fees	0	0	0	0	0	0	28 325	0	0	0
Labour market fees	0	982	12 516	45 975	48 471	29 012	7 964	36 752	37 919	39 007
Industrial injury insurance fees	132	1 201	4 663	12 030	7 844	8 139	0	8 571	3 914	4 022
Seamen's pension fees	0	10	26	30	0	0	0	0	0	0
Part pension fees	0	1 119	2 897	0	0	0	0	0	0	0
Supplementary pension fees	2 719	21 458	73 129	71 335	97 748	103 597	104 219	112 130	116 116	119 508
Parent insurance fees	0	484	1 159	19 215	25 356	26 331	25 764	27 729	33 878	34 854
2210 On a payroll basis	..	..	..	237 527	300 010	279 771	264 807	263 272	272 511	271 449
2220 On an income tax basis	..	..	..	0	0	0	0	0	0	0
2300 Self-employed or non-employed	540	2 791	8 139	5 618	8 391	8 205	7 721	6 252	5 881	5 607
Survivors pension fees	0	943	1 580	451	662	668	643	482	452	442
Health insurance fees	260	992	1 702	1 988	3 297	2 910	2 609	840	751	550
Industrial injury insurance fees	0	64	191	365	264	267	258	279	116	113
Parent insurance fees	0	58	106	573	856	865	834	903	1 008	960
Supplementary pension fees	280	734	4 560	2 241	3 312	3 495	3 377	3 747	3 554	3 542
Reduction	0	0	0	0	0	0	0	0	0	0
2310 On a payroll basis	..	..	..	5 618	8 391	8 205	7 721	6 252	5 881	5 607
2320 On an income tax basis	..	..	..	0	0	0	0	0	0	0
2400 Unallocable between 2100, 2200 and 2300	0	0	0	756	-984	-377	-2 084	-1 036	-324	-1 233
2410 On a payroll basis	..	..	..	756	-984	-377	-2 084	-1 036	-324	-1 233
2420 On an income tax basis	..	..	..	0	0	0	0	0	0	0
3000 Taxes on payroll and workforce	**13**	**6 759**	**18 686**	**50 106**	**83 279**	**124 610**	**122 591**	**155 341**	**160 326**	**172 170**
Special wage tax	0	61	0	22 391	30 225	32 570	32 462	36 218	37 400	36 832
Child care fees	0	4 740	13 080	0	0	0	0	0	0	0
Adult education fees	0	614	1 555	0	0	0	0	0	0	0
Building research fees	13	105	0	0	0	0	0	0	0	0
Labour welfare fees	0	257	2 033	0	0	0	0	0	0	0
Labour education fees	0	982	0	0	0	0	0	0	0	0
Labour market fees	0	0	0	112	156	198	189	14	2	7
General wage fees	0	0	2 018	27 603	52 898	91 842	89 939	119 109	122 924	135 331
4000 Taxes on property	**712**	**2 424**	**26 630**	**39 890**	**36 228**	**34 618**	**34 288**	**36 529**	**37 558**	**41 182**
4100 Recurrent taxes on immovable property	10	16	8 946	23 286	25 899	23 994	25 352	27 584	28 743	31 596
4110 Households	0	0	3 877	13 321	13 474	10 017	11 571	11 866	13 071	13 422
Special tax on real estate	..	..	3 877	13 321	13 474	10 017	11 571	11 866	13 071	13 422
4120 Others	10	16	5 069	9 965	12 424	13 977	13 781	15 718	15 672	18 174
Forestry levy	10	16	423	22	34	41	25	44	51	37
Special tax on real estate	0	0	4 646	9 943	12 390	13 937	13 756	15 673	15 621	18 137
4200 Recurrent taxes on net wealth	366	717	3 200	8 223	0	0	0	0	0	0

Table 70. **Sweden / Suède** *(cont.)*
Details of tax revenue / Recettes fiscales détaillées

Million SEK

	1965	1980	1990	2000	2007	2008	2009	2011	2012	2013
4210 Individual	361	702	3 135	8 043	..	..	..	..	..	..
4220 Corporate	5	15	65	180	..	..	..	..	..	..
4300 Estate, inheritance and gift taxes	155	545	1 433	2 549	23	16	2	4	-5	-4
4310 Estate and inheritance taxes	143	495	1 118	2 088	15	14	2	4	-5	-4
4320 Gift taxes	12	50	315	460	8	2	0	0	0	0
4400 Taxes on financial and capital transactions	181	1 146	13 051	5 833	10 305	10 608	8 934	8 942	8 819	9 590
Taxes on financial and capital transactions	181	1 146	6 946	4 878	9 414	9 423	8 064	7 989	7 961	8 913
Turnover tax on securities	0	0	6 105	0	0	0	0	0	0	0
Tax on life group insurances	0	0	0	955	891	1 184	870	953	859	678
4500 Non-recurrent taxes	0	0	0	0	0	0	0	0	0	0
4510 On net wealth	..	..	..	..	..	..	..	..	..	..
4520 Other non-recurrent taxes	..	..	..	..	..	..	..	..	..	..
4600 Other recurrent taxes on property	0	0	0	0	0	0	0	0	0	0
5000 Taxes on goods and services	**12 471**	**62 234**	**188 709**	**288 803**	**394 073**	**412 628**	**418 419**	**452 359**	**453 503**	**461 955**
5100 Taxes on production, sale, transfer, etc	11 808	58 474	181 587	281 370	380 990	396 601	402 042	436 635	437 900	445 453
5110 General taxes	4 147	34 643	112 399	199 606	286 211	301 935	303 095	334 708	333 342	341 952
5111 Value added taxes	0	34 643	112 399	197 483	282 586	297 504	299 452	330 769	329 311	337 822
5112 Sales tax	4 147	0	0	0	0	0	0	0	0	0
5113 Other	0	0	0	2 123	3 625	4 431	3 643	3 939	4 031	4 130
5120 Taxes on specific goods and services	7 661	23 831	69 188	81 764	94 779	94 667	98 947	101 927	104 558	103 500
5121 Excises	5 953	19 941	55 332	70 313	84 818	86 252	89 173	89 715	89 772	88 485
Taxes on petrol and fuel	1 420	4 229	17 171	39 011	44 501	45 454	46 274	45 723	45 099	43 869
Special sales tax	390	585	1 098	0	0	0	0	0	0	0
Sales tax on motor vehicles	325	553	1 983	195	3	0	0	0	0	0
Tobacco tax	1 150	3 087	5 636	7 747	9 742	9 926	10 604	11 261	11 799	11 136
Tax on spirits	1 548	4 431	6 205	4 902	4 249	4 162	4 437	4 349	4 328	4 001
Tax on wine	149	930	2 922	3 567	4 001	4 093	4 449	4 678	4 767	4 887
Tax on beer and soft drinks	242	964	2 532	2 355	2 773	3 131	3 271	3 186	3 237	3 329
Tax on energy consumption	729	5 162	16 352	11 451	18 939	19 154	19 949	20 314	20 343	21 144
Taxes on electricity from certain sources	0	0	1 018	0	0	0	0	0	0	0
Tax on wastes	0	0	0	1 085	609	333	189	205	198	119
Tax on cassette tapes	0	0	194	0	0	0	0	0	0	0
Tax on videorecorders	0	0	221	0	0	0	0	0	0	0
5122 Profits of fiscal monopolies	72	204	332	3 641	3 952	3 788	4 822	5 165	5 227	5 385
Alcohol monopoly wholesale	23	116	98	0	0	0	0	0	0	0
Alcohol monopoly retailing	49	88	234	80	296	201	345	159	90	116
Gaming monopoly retailing	0	0	0	3 561	3 657	3 587	4 477	5 006	5 137	5 269
5123 Customs and import duties	1 419	2 433	8 308	0	0	0	0	0	0	0
Customs	1 080	1 300	3 115	0	0	0	0	0	0	0
Agricultural levies	339	1 133	5 193	0	0	0	0	0	0	0
5124 Taxes on exports	0	0	0	0	0	0	0	0	0	0
5125 Taxes on investment goods	0	0	40	0	0	0	0	0	0	0
Investment tax	..	..	40	..	..	..	..	..	..	..
5126 Taxes on specific services	217	1 253	5 176	6 472	4 341	3 396	4 075	6 224	8 915	9 072
Betting tax	79	223	616	0	0	0	0	0	0	0
Advertisement tax	0	202	1 073	1 116	657	213	292	390	290	244
Tax on gambling	0	69	88	1 245	1 315	1 289	1 370	1 411	1 335	1 309
Other specific services	138	656	2 938	4 111	2 369	1 895	2 412	4 422	7 291	7 520
Tax on charter travelling	0	103	461	0	0	0	0	0	0	0
5127 Other taxes on internat. trade and transactions	0	0	0	0	0	0	0	0	0	0
5128 Other taxes	0	0	0	1 339	1 668	1 230	878	824	644	559
5130 Unallocable between 5110 and 5120	0	0	0	0	0	0	0	0	0	0
5200 Taxes on use of goods and perform activities	663	3 760	7 122	7 433	13 083	16 027	16 376	15 724	15 603	16 502
5210 Recurrent taxes	663	3 760	7 122	7 433	13 083	16 027	16 376	15 724	15 603	16 502
5211 Paid by households: motor vehicles	336	1 241	2 003	4 969	7 451	8 127	8 411	8 090	8 058	8 275
5212 Paid by others: motor vehicles	313	2 476	5 055	2 464	5 632	7 900	7 965	7 633	7 545	8 227
5213 Paid in respect of other goods	14	43	64	0	0	0	0	0	0	0
5220 Non-recurrent taxes	0	0	0	0	0	0	0	0	0	0
5300 Unallocable between 5100 and 5200	0	0	0	0	0	0	0	0	0	0
6000 Other taxes	**0**	**422**	**1 264**	**1 479**	**1 768**	**1 613**	**1 990**	**1 754**	**1 832**	**1 806**
6100 Paid solely by business	..	0	0	0	0	0	0	0	0	0
6200 Other	..	422	1 264	1 479	1 768	1 613	1 990	1 754	1 832	1 806
Custom duties collected for the EU	..	..	..	**3 450**	**5 099**	**5 212**	**4 764**	**5 399**	**4 995**	**4 976**
Total tax revenue on cash basis	**40 003**	**259 216**	**755 953**	**1 144 233**	**1 465 382**	**1 520 520**	**1 437 531**	**1 574 357**	**1 584 780**	**1 611 794**
Total tax revenue on accrual basis	..	..	..	**1 166 006**	**1 482 649**	**1 490 704**	**1 449 712**	**1 554 311**	**1 568 247**	**1 617 457**

Table 70. **Sweden / Suède** *(cont.)*
Details of tax revenue / Recettes fiscales détaillées

Million SEK

	1965	1980	1990	2000	2007	2008	2009	2011	2012	2013
Conciliation with National Accounts										
Additional taxes included in National Accounts	..	..	..	0	0	0	0	0	0	0
Taxes excluded from National Accounts	..	..	..	0	0	0	0	0	0	0
Difference in treatment of tax credits	..	..	..	0	0	0	0	0	0	0
Capital transfer for uncollected revenue	..	..	..	0	0	0	0	0	0	0
Voluntary social security contributions	..	..	..	0	0	0	0	0	0	0
Miscellaneous differences	..	..	..	0	0	0	0	0	0	0
National Accounts: Taxes and actual social contributions	..	..	..	1 166 006	1 482 649	1 490 704	1 449 712	1 554 311	1 568 247	1 617 457
Imputed social contributions	..	..	..	5 941	6 121	6 500	6 749	7 032	7 091	7 614
National Accounts: Taxes and all social contributions	..	..	..	1 171 947	1 488 770	1 497 204	1 456 461	1 561 343	1 575 338	1 625 071

Note:

Year ending 31st December.

From 2000 data are on accrual basis.

Figures prior to 1970 are not strictly comparable with those of later years, though the amounts involved are insignificant.

Heading 1000: Receipts are on accrual and not on a cash basis for all years.

Heading 2000 includes some voluntary contributions.

Source: Monthly reports of central Government Revenues (unpublished) National Audit Bureau, Stockholm. Local Government Finance (SOS), Tax assessment statistics (SOS) , National Central Bureau of Statistics, Stockholm.National Accounts (Statistical Reports), National Bureau of Statistics, Stockholm.

StatLink http://dx.doi.org/10.1787/888933277326

Table 71. **Switzerland / Suisse**
Details of tax revenue / Recettes fiscales détaillées

Million CHF

	1965	1980	1990	2000	2007	2008	2009	2011	2012	2013
Recettes fiscales totales	**11 237**	**46 385**	**84 479**	**126 822**	**149 724**	**159 433**	**159 270**	**167 061**	**168 000**	**170 634**
1000 Impôts sur revenu, bénéfices et gains en capital	**4 616**	**21 022**	**39 873**	**56 043**	**69 482**	**75 242**	**74 634**	**77 480**	**76 583**	**78 570**
1100 Des personnes physiques	3 748	18 056	27 792	37 703	47 712	49 516	51 028	52 251	53 319	53 691
1110 Sur le revenu et les bénéfices	3 547	17 622	27 792	37 703	47 712	49 516	51 028	52 251	53 319	53 691
Impôt fédéral direct	245	2 525	4 526	5 827	8 625	9 147	9 894	9 684	9 866	9 769
Taxe d'exemption service militaire	35	103	40	49	41	42	44	47	48	49
Impôt cantonal personnes physiques	1 473	7 510	12 785	17 337	22 820	23 704	24 016	25 157	25 816	26 055
Impôt communal personnes physiques	1 322	6 235	10 440	14 490	16 224	16 623	17 074	17 363	17 589	17 817
Impôt anticipé	358	1 249	0	0	0	0	0	0	0	0
Coupons	114	0	0	0	0	0	0	0	0	0
1120 Sur les gains en capital	201	434	0	0	0	0	0	0	0	0
Impôt cantonal personnes physiques	84	229	..	..	..	..	..	..	..	..
Impôt communal personnes physiques	112	190	..	..	..	..	..	..	..	..
Impôt fédéral direct	5	15	..	..	..	..	..	..	..	..
1200 Des sociétés	868	2 966	6 002	11 204	16 117	17 734	16 707	17 545	17 531	17 966
1210 Sur les bénéfices	801	2 818	6 002	11 204	16 117	17 734	16 707	17 545	17 531	17 966
Impôt fédéral direct	153	781	1 941	4 891	6 860	8 464	8 087	8 317	8 588	8 698
Impôt cantonal personnes morales	363	1 230	2 561	3 934	6 031	5 990	5 500	5 791	5 662	5 944
Impôt communal personnes morales	285	807	1 500	2 378	3 225	3 280	3 120	3 437	3 281	3 323
1220 Sur les gains en capital	67	148	0	0	0	0	0	0	0	0
Impôt sur gains personnes morales	2	7	..	..	..	..	..	..	..	..
Impôt cantonal personnes morales	28	77	..	..	..	..	..	..	..	..
Impôt communal personnes morales	37	64	..	..	..	..	..	..	..	..
1300 Non-ventilables entre 1100 et 1200	0	0	6 079	7 136	5 654	7 992	6 899	7 684	5 732	6 914
2000 Cotisations de sécurité sociale	**1 670**	**10 844**	**19 961**	**31 059**	**35 115**	**36 860**	**38 142**	**40 941**	**41 840**	**42 758**
2100 A la charge des salariés	716	4 833	9 051	14 311	16 187	17 056	17 700	19 104	19 554	19 989
2110 Sur la base du salaire	716	4 833	9 051	14 311	16 187	17 056	17 700	19 104	19 554	19 989
2120 Sur la base de l'impôt sur les revenus	0	0	0	0	0	0	0	0	0	0
2200 A la charge des employeurs	747	4 897	9 051	14 311	16 200	17 070	17 715	19 121	19 570	20 007
2210 Sur la base du salaire	747	4 897	9 051	14 311	16 200	17 070	17 715	19 121	19 570	20 007
2220 Sur la base de l'impôt sur les revenus	0	0	0	0	0	0	0	0	0	0
2300 A charge des travailleurs indép. ou sans emploi	208	1 046	1 859	2 437	2 728	2 733	2 727	2 716	2 716	2 762
2310 Sur la base du salaire	209	1 046	1 859	2 437	2 728	2 733	2 727	2 716	2 716	2 762
2320 Sur la base de l'impôt sur les revenus	0	0	0	0	0	0	0	0	0	0
2400 Non-ventilables entre 2100, 2200 et 2300	0	68	0	0	0	0	0	0	0	0
2410 Sur la base du salaire	..	68	..	..	..	..	..	..	..	..
2420 Sur la base de l'impôt sur les revenus	..	0	..	..	..	..	..	..	..	..
3000 Sur salaires ou main d'oeuvre	**0**	**0**	**0**	**0**	**0**	**0**	**0**	**0**	**0**	**0**
4000 Impôts sur le patrimoine	**1 108**	**3 830**	**7 119**	**11 383**	**11 764**	**11 824**	**11 750**	**11 672**	**11 048**	**11 363**
4100 Impôts périodiques sur la propriété immobilière	78	304	223	735	895	913	936	967	1 027	1 024
4110 Ménages	78	304	223	735	895	913	936	967	1 027	1 024
Impôt sur immeubles canton	20	71	62	187	265	262	265	266	315	303
Impôt sur immeubles commune	58	233	161	548	630	651	671	701	712	721
4120 Autres agents	0	0	0	0	0	0	0	0	0	0
4200 Impôts périodiques sur l'actif net	692	2 201	3 640	5 232	6 943	6 997	6 946	6 913	6 918	7 166
4210 Personnes physiques	420	1 383	2 184	3 930	5 267	5 429	5 538	5 421	5 462	5 629
Impôt fortune canton	206	739	1 225	2 207	3 109	3 200	3 245	3 301	3 348	3 487
Impôt fortune commune	214	644	959	1 723	2 158	2 230	2 293	2 120	2 114	2 142
4220 Sociétés	272	818	1 456	1 302	1 676	1 567	1 408	1 492	1 456	1 537
Impôt capital fédéral direct	21	92	273	37	0	0	0	0	0	0
Impôt capital canton	142	436	756	807	1 094	1 014	898	958	949	1 023
Impôt capital commune	109	290	426	458	582	554	510	534	507	513
4300 Impôts sur mut. par décès, succ. et donations	142	393	1 120	1 212	869	875	995	862	898	970
4310 Impôts sur mut. par décès et successions	142	393	1 120	1 212	869	875	995	862	898	970
Impôt successions cantons	128	361	883	1 115	773	771	910	775	783	853
Impôt successions commune	14	32	237	97	96	104	85	88	115	117
4320 Impôts sur les donations	0	0	0	0	0	0	0	0	0	0
4400 Impôts sur transact. mobilières et immob.	196	932	2 137	4 205	3 057	3 039	2 873	2 930	2 205	2 203
Impôt mutations canton	48	245	34	43	54	51	55	59	56	55
Impôt mutations commune	21	103	12	16	13	14	13	15	15	15
Emissions de titres	99	175	621	906	598	584	672	874	353	182
Négociation de titres	19	409	1 470	3 240	2 392	2 390	2 133	1 981	1 781	1 952
Effets de change	9	0	0	0	0	0	0	0	0	0
4500 Impôts non-périodiques	0	0	0	0	0	0	0	0	0	0
4510 Sur l'actif net	..	..	..	..	..	..	..	..	..	..
4520 Autres non-périodiques	..	..	..	..	..	..	..	..	..	..
4600 Autres impôts périodiques sur patrimoine	0	0	0	0	0	0	0	0	0	0
5000 Impôts sur les biens et services	**3 843**	**10 689**	**17 525**	**28 337**	**33 363**	**35 507**	**34 744**	**36 968**	**38 529**	**37 943**
5100 Impôts sur production, vente, transfert, etc.	3 582	9 863	15 980	25 878	29 146	31 526	30 731	32 433	33 913	33 325
5110 Impôts généraux	1 191	4 772	9 871	16 594	19 472	20 311	19 656	21 449	21 799	22 336

Table 71. **Switzerland / Suisse** *(cont.)*
Details of tax revenue / Recettes fiscales détaillées

Million CHF

	1965	1980	1990	2000	2007	2008	2009	2011	2012	2013
5111 Taxes sur la valeur ajoutée	0	0	0	16 594	19 472	20 311	19 656	21 449	21 799	22 336
5112 Impôts sur les ventes	1 191	4 772	9 871	0	0	0	0	0	0	0
5113 Autres impôts	0	0	0	0	0	0	0	0	0	0
5120 Impôts sur biens et services déterminés	2 391	5 091	6 109	9 284	9 674	11 215	11 075	10 984	12 114	10 989
5121 Accises	1 016	3 427	4 359	6 948	7 239	8 133	7 866	7 988	8 187	8 023
Impôt sur bière	26	33	59	84	95	220	110	113	113	113
Impôt sur tabac	190	634	879	1 492	1 988	2 073	1 987	2 208	2 397	2 295
Supplément de prix autres	104	542	400	47	4	6	4	0	0	0
Droits carburants	467	955	1 176	2 643	2 724	3 110	3 087	2 995	3 005	2 988
Droits supplémentaires carburants	229	1 263	1 553	1 795	1 836	2 089	2 072	2 006	2 007	1 994
Taxes routières	0	0	292	576	287	293	308	288	282	285
Impôt sur les huiles minérales grèvant les combustibles	0	0	0	21	24	22	24	19	20	23
Impôt sur les automobiles	0	0	0	289	282	320	274	359	363	324
5122 Bénéfices des monopoles fiscaux	158	472	431	1 026	494	1 063	1 172	994	1 992	1 045
Monopole d'alcool	111	354	343	270	223	235	246	0	0	0
Régale des sels	16	25	0	0	0	0	0	0	0	0
Régale des eaux	30	90	0	0	0	0	0	0	0	0
Autres	1	3	88	756	271	828	926	994	1 992	1 045
5123 Droits de douane et droits à l'importation	1 104	953	1 069	937	961	1 017	1 033	1 046	1 044	1 059
Droits d'entrée	972	923	1 035	930	961	1 017	1 033	1 046	1 044	1 059
Droits tabac	114	6	7	6	0	0	0	0	0	0
Autres droits supplémentaires	18	24	27	0	0	0	0	0	0	0
5124 Taxes à l'exportation	0	0	0	0	0	0	0	0	0	0
5125 Impôts sur biens d'équipement	0	0	0	0	0	0	0	0	0	0
5126 Impôts sur services déterminés	113	239	250	374	980	1 002	1 003	956	891	862
Jeux dans kursaals confédération	2	2	0	0	449	455	415	376	329	308
Impôt sur divertissement canton	17	37	205	347	513	532	571	565	547	539
Impôt sur divertissement commune	11	19	46	26	18	16	17	15	15	15
Autres impôts dépenses canton	24	63	0	0	0	0	0	0	0	0
Autres impôts dépenses commune	19	6	0	0	0	0	0	0	0	0
Quittances de primes	40	112	0	0	0	0	0	0	0	0
5127 Autres impôts sur commerce et transact. internat.	0	0	0	0	0	0	0	0	0	0
5128 Autres impôts	0	0	0	0	0	0	0	0	0	0
5130 Non-ventilables entre 5110 et 5120	0	0	0	0	0	0	0	0	0	0
5200 Impôts sur utilisation des biens et exerc. activités	261	826	1 545	2 459	4 217	3 981	4 013	4 535	4 616	4 618
5210 Impôts périodiques	261	826	1 545	2 459	4 217	3 981	4 013	4 535	4 616	4 618
Impôt sur véhicules à moteur	227	752	1 479	2 313	3 984	3 529	3 573	3 793	3 817	3 715
5211 A la charge des ménages : véhicules à moteur	152	501	921	1 336	1 579	1 608	1 637	1 703	1 741	1 671
5212 A la charge autres agents : véhicules à moteur	76	251	558	977	2 405	1 921	1 936	2 090	2 075	2 043
5213 Autres impôts périodiques	33	74	66	145	233	452	440	742	800	903
Chasse et pêche	9	20	46	47	44	36	36	42	43	46
Impôt sur chiens canton	3	9	6	9	8	9	8	9	9	10
Impôt sur chiens commune	2	8	14	21	25	25	28	31	31	32
Auberges canton	12	24	0	0	0	0	0	0	0	0
Patentes canton	5	12	0	0	0	0	0	0	0	0
Autres	2	1	0	68	156	382	368	660	716	816
5220 Impôts non-périodiques	0	0	0	0	0	0	0	0	0	0
5300 Non-ventilables entre 5100 et 5200	0	0	0	0	0	0	0	0	0	0
6000 Autres impôts	**0**	**0**	**0**	**0**	**0**	**0**	**0**	**0**	**0**	**0**
6100 A la charge exclusive des entreprises	..	..	..	..	..	..	..	..	..	..
6200 A la charge d'autres agents	..	..	..	..	..	..	..	..	..	..
Recettes fiscales totales sur la base d'encaissements	**11 237**	**46 385**	**84 479**	**86 522**	**149 724**	**159 433**	**159 270**	**167 061**	**168 000**	**170 634**
Recettes fiscales totales sur la base des droits constatés	**..**	**..**	**..**	**..**	**..**	**..**	**..**	**..**	**..**	**..**
Conciliation avec les comptes nationaux										
Impôts additionnels inclus dans les comptes nationaux	..	..	..	..	..	..	..	..	..	..
Impôt exclus des comptes nationaux	..	..	..	..	..	..	..	..	..	..
Différence dans les traitements des crédits d'impôts	..	..	..	..	..	..	..	..	..	..
Transfert en capital des recettes non collectées	..	..	..	..	..	..	..	..	..	..
Cotisations de sécurité sociale volontaires	..	..	..	..	..	..	..	..	..	..
Différences diverses	..	..	..	..	..	..	..	..	..	..
Comptes nationaux: impôts et cotisations sociales effectives	..	..	..	..	..	..	..	..	..	..
Cotisations sociales imputées	..	..	..	..	..	..	..	..	..	..
Comptes nationaux: impôts et toutes les cotisations sociales	..	..	..	..	..	..	..	..	..	..

Note:

Année civile se terminant le 31 décembre.

Les données sont sur la base des encaissements.

Les chiffres antérieurs à 1970 ne sont pas strictement comparables avec ceux des années suivantes qui ont été légèrement révisés.

A compter de 1985 les "Impôts paroissiaux" ne sont plus reportés dans ces statistiques.

A la rubrique 1100: les paiements effectués en contrepartie de l'exemption du service militaire pourraient être classés dans les recettes non fiscales.

La rubrique 2000 (Cotisations de sécurité sociale) a été révisée depuis 1985 pour tenir compte de la sectorisation des administrations publiques retenue dans le cadre du passage aux Comptes nationaux SEC95. De ce fait, les cotisations à l'assurance maladie et à la Caisse nationale suisse contre les accidents sont maintenant exclues de la rubrique 2000.

Source: Statistique financière, Administration fédérale des finances.

StatLink http://dx.doi.org/10.1787/888933277335

Table 72. **Turkey / Turquie**
Details of tax revenue / Recettes fiscales détaillées

Million TRY

	1965	1980	1990	2000	2007	2008	2009	2011	2012	2013
Total tax revenue	**0**	**1**	**79**	**40 263**	**203 053**	**230 245**	**234 669**	**361 153**	**391 572**	**458 698**
1000 Taxes on income, profits and capital gains	**0**	**0**	**26**	**11 890**	**48 197**	**54 935**	**56 469**	**75 800**	**85 511**	**92 749**
1100 Of individuals	0	0	21	8 954	34 447	38 030	38 446	48 807	56 494	63 761
1110 On income and profits	0	0	21	8 954	34 447	38 030	38 446	48 807	56 494	63 761
Income tax	0	0	21	8 954	34 447	38 030	38 446	48 807	56 494	63 761
1120 On capital gains	0	0	0	0	0	0	0	0	0	0
1200 Corporate	0	0	5	2 935	13 751	16 905	18 023	26 993	29 017	28 988
1210 On profits	0	0	5	2 935	13 751	16 905	18 023	26 993	29 017	28 988
Corporation tax	0	0	5	2 935	13 751	16 905	18 023	26 993	29 017	28 988
1220 On capital gains	0	0	0	0	0	0	0	0	0	0
1300 Unallocable between 1100 and 1200	0	0	0	0	0	0	0	0	0	0
Fiscal balance tax	...	0	...	...	...	...	...	...	...	...
Capital gains tax on real estate sales	...	0	...	...	...	...	...	...	...	...
2000 Social security contributions	**0**	**0**	**15**	**7 543**	**44 052**	**57 637**	**57 595**	**100 687**	**106 405**	**125 871**
2100 Employees	0	0	6	2 712	17 867	19 255	21 059	36 230	40 714	49 831
2110 On a payroll basis	...	...	...	2 712	17 867	19 255	21 059	36 230	40 714	49 831
2120 On an income tax basis	...	...	...	0	0	0	0	0	0	0
2200 Employers	0	0	9	3 619	20 442	28 858	31 477	53 162	58 272	71 184
2210 On a payroll basis	...	...	...	3 619	20 442	28 858	31 477	53 162	58 272	71 184
2220 On an income tax basis	...	...	...	0	0	0	0	0	0	0
2300 Self-employed or non-employed	0	0	1	1 211	5 743	9 523	5 059	11 295	7 419	4 856
2310 On a payroll basis	...	...	...	1 211	5 743	9 523	5 059	11 295	7 419	4 856
2320 On an income tax basis	...	...	...	0	0	0	0	0	0	0
2400 Unallocable between 2100, 2200 and 2300	0	0	0	0	0	0	0	0	0	0
2410 On a payroll basis	...	...	...	...	...	...	...	...	...	...
2420 On an income tax basis	...	...	...	...	...	...	...	...	...	...
3000 Taxes on payroll and workforce	**0**	**0**	**0**	**0**	**0**	**0**	**0**	**0**	**0**	**0**
4000 Taxes on property	**0**	**0**	**2**	**1 272**	**7 621**	**8 366**	**8 518**	**14 661**	**16 511**	**21 280**
4100 Recurrent taxes on immovable property	0	0	0	191	1 464	1 717	1 854	3 464	3 528	3 847
Real estate tax	0	0	...	191	1 464	1 717	1 854	3 464	3 528	3 847
4110 Households	...	...	...	...	...	...	...	...	...	...
4120 Others	...	...	...	...	...	...	...	...	...	...
4200 Recurrent taxes on net wealth	0	0	0	0	0	0	0	0	0	0
4210 Individual	...	...	...	...	...	...	...	...	...	...
4220 Corporate	...	...	...	...	...	...	...	...	...	...
4300 Estate, inheritance and gift taxes	0	0	0	15	125	144	168	253	293	340
Gift and inheritance tax	0	0	0	15	125	144	168	253	293	340
4310 Estate and inheritance taxes	...	...	...	...	...	...	...	...	...	...
4320 Gift taxes	...	...	...	...	...	...	...	...	...	...
4400 Taxes on financial and capital transactions	0	0	2	1 065	6 032	6 504	6 496	10 943	12 690	17 093
Stamp tax	0	0	2	818	3 642	3 945	4 169	6 464	7 360	9 416
Real estate purchase tax	0	0	0	0	0	0	0	0	0	0
Title deed fees	0	0	0	207	2 000	2 169	1 889	4 042	4 844	7 072
Notary fees	0	0	0	40	389	390	437	437	486	606
4500 Non-recurrent taxes	0	0	0	0	0	0	0	0	0	0
4510 On net wealth	...	...	...	...	...	...	...	...	...	...
4520 Other non-recurrent taxes	...	...	...	...	...	...	...	...	...	...
4600 Other recurrent taxes on property	0	0	0	0	0	0	0	0	0	0
5000 Taxes on goods and services	**0**	**0**	**22**	**16 901**	**96 766**	**104 678**	**107 128**	**163 347**	**176 305**	**211 257**
5100 Taxes on production, sale, transfer, etc	0	0	22	16 328	92 605	100 091	102 384	156 944	169 226	203 364
5110 General taxes	0	0	16	9 735	43 285	46 777	46 987	78 642	81 572	100 723
5111 Value added taxes	...	...	14	9 735	43 285	46 777	46 987	78 642	81 572	100 723
5112 Sales tax	...	...	0	0	0	0	0	0	0	0
5113 Other	...	...	1	0	0	0	0	0	0	0
5120 Taxes on specific goods and services	0	0	6	6 593	49 320	53 314	55 397	78 302	87 653	102 641
5121 Excises	0	0	1	4 718	39 111	41 832	43 620	64 189	71 706	85 462
Sales taxes	0	0	0	0	0	0	0	0	0	0
Domestic production tax	0	0	0	0	0	0	0	0	0	0
Domestic production tax on petrol	0	0	0	0	0	0	0	0	0	0
Production tax on monopoly goods	0	0	0	0	0	0	0	0	0	0
Sugar consumption taxes	0	0	0	0	0	0	0	0	0	0
Motor vehicles purchase tax (Total)	0	0	1	916	4 293	3 805	3 353	8 568	8 409	10 565
Motor vehicles purchase tax	0	0	0	498	4 293	3 805	3 353	8 568	8 409	10 565
Additional motor vehicle purchase tax	0	0	0	418	0	0	0	0	0	0
Revenue from other excises	0	0	0	533	12 765	14 085	14 742	22 048	27 362	29 739
Petroleum consumption tax	0	0	0	3 269	22 052	23 941	25 525	33 573	35 935	45 158
5122 Profits of fiscal monopolies	0	0	0	0	0	0	0	0	0	0

Table 72. **Turkey / Turquie** *(cont.)*
Details of tax revenue / Recettes fiscales détaillées

Million TRY

	1965	1980	1990	2000	2007	2008	2009	2011	2012	2013
5123 Customs and import duties	0	0	4	462	2 478	2 809	2 517	4 767	5 310	5 542
Customs duty	0	0	1	449	2 441	2 770	2 466	4 653	5 195	5 409
Customs duty on petrol	0	0	0	0	0	0	0	0	0	0
Production tax on imports	0	0	0	0	0	0	0	0	0	0
Production tax on petrol imports	0	0	0	0	0	0	0	0	0	0
Stamp duty on imports	0	0	2	0	0	0	0	0	0	0
Wharf duty	0	0	1	0	0	0	0	0	0	0
Other	0	0	0	13	37	39	51	113	115	133
5124 Taxes on exports	0	0	0	0	0	0	0	0	0	0
5125 Taxes on investment goods	0	0	0	0	0	0	0	0	0	0
5126 Taxes on specific services	0	0	1	997	7 686	4 071	4 399	4 816	6 086	6 853
Bank, insurance transaction tax	0	0	1	997	3 149	3 695	4 003	4 288	5 471	6 160
Transportation tax	0	0	0	0	0	0	0	0	0	0
PTT service tax	0	0	0	0	4 211	0	0	0	0	0
Tax on football pool	0	0	0	0	0	0	0	0	0	0
Lottery tax	0	0	0	0	327	376	396	528	616	692
5127 Other taxes on internat. trade and transactions	0	0	0	0	0	0	0	0	0	0
Foreign travel expenditures tax	0	0	..	..	..	..	..	..	..	..
5128 Other taxes	0	0	0	416	46	4 602	4 861	4 531	4 551	4 785
5130 Unallocable between 5110 and 5120	0	0	0	0	0	0	0	0	0	0
5200 Taxes on use of goods and perform activities	0	0	0	572	4 161	4 587	4 744	6 403	7 079	7 894
5210 Recurrent taxes	0	0	0	359	4 161	4 587	4 744	6 403	7 079	7 894
Motor vehicles tax	0	0	0	359	0	4 587	4 744	6 403	7 079	7 894
5211 Paid by households: motor vehicles	..	..	..	0	0	0	0	0	0	0
5212 Paid by others: motor vehicles	..	..	..	359	4 161	4 587	4 744	6 403	7 079	7 894
Motor vehicles tax	..	..	..	302	3 521	3 944	4 496	6 004	6 716	7 353
Traffic fees	..	..	..	58	640	643	248	399	363	540
5213 Paid in respect of other goods	..	..	..	0	0	0	0	0	0	0
5220 Non-recurrent taxes	0	0	0	213	0	0	0	0	0	0
Building construction tax	..	0	..	..	..	..	..	..	..	..
5300 Unallocable between 5100 and 5200	0	0	0	0	0	0	0	0	0	0
6000 Other taxes	**0**	**0**	**13**	**2 658**	**6 417**	**4 630**	**4 959**	**6 658**	**6 840**	**7 541**
6100 Paid solely by business	..	0	0	0	0	0	0	0	0	0
6200 Other	..	0	13	2 658	6 417	4 630	4 959	6 658	6 840	7 541
Funds	..	..	..	1 938	0	0	0	0	0	0
Vocatial Train Pro.F.	..	..	..	67	0	0	0	0	0	0
Tax penalties and fines	..	..	..	548	4 191	2 157	3 037	3 221	3 119	3 175
Municipalities revenue	..	..	..	106	2 227	2 473	1 922	3 437	3 722	4 366
Total tax revenue on cash basis	**0**	**1**	**79**	**40 263**	**203 053**	**230 245**	**234 669**	**361 153**	**391 572**	**458 698**
Total tax revenue on accrual basis	..	..	..	..	..	..	..	..	..	..
Conciliation with National Accounts										
Additional taxes included in National Accounts	..	..	..	..	..	..	..	..	..	..
Taxes excluded from National Accounts	..	..	..	..	..	..	..	..	..	..
Difference in treatment of tax credits	..	..	..	..	..	..	..	..	..	..
Capital transfer for uncollected revenue	..	..	..	..	..	..	..	..	..	..
Voluntary social security contributions	..	..	..	..	..	..	..	..	..	..
Miscellaneous differences	..	..	..	..	..	..	..	..	..	..
National Accounts: Taxes and actual social contributions	..	..	..	..	..	..	..	..	..	..
Imputed social contributions	..	..	..	..	..	..	..	..	..	..
National Accounts: Taxes and all social contributions	..	..	..	..	..	..	..	..	..	..

Note:

From 1982 the data are based on the fiscal year ending 31st December. Before that the data are on a fiscal year basis beginning 1st March.

Revenue is reported on a cash basis except for social security contributions which are reported on an assessment basis.

The figures under the local tax collections include taxes under "Municipalities Revenues Law" and Property tax. They also include transfers to the local authorities from central budget tax revenues under the revenue sharing system.

Heading 2000: Before 2003, contributions to some private social security schemes are included in this heading.

Source: Bulletin of national accounts and the Budget revenue Bulletin.

StatLink http://dx.doi.org/10.1787/888933277346

Table 73. **United Kingdom / Royaume-Uni**
Details of tax revenue / Recettes fiscales détaillées

Million GBP

	1965	1980	1990	2000	2007	2008	2009	2011	2012	2013
Total tax revenue	**10 945**	**81 153**	**202 414**	**354 881**	**504 697**	**515 887**	**479 001**	**543 272**	**547 017**	**564 164**
Total tax revenue exclusive of custom duties	..	..	..	**353 081**	**502 623**	**513 590**	**476 566**	**540 347**	**544 132**	**561 250**
1000 Taxes on income, profits and capital gains	**4 050**	**30 651**	**79 576**	**138 591**	**198 918**	**206 299**	**184 475**	**199 360**	**194 878**	**199 816**
1100 Of individuals	3 618	23 868	59 506	104 136	151 219	154 863	145 779	152 692	150 454	156 299
1110 On income and profits	3 615	23 376	57 614	101 925	147 371	149 575	137 964	149 093	146 120	152 397
Income tax	..	23 370	57 614	101 925	147 371	149 575	137 964	149 093	146 120	152 397
Surtax	..	6	0	0	0	0	0	0	0	0
1120 On capital gains	3	492	1 892	2 211	3 848	5 288	7 815	3 599	4 334	3 902
1200 Corporate	484	6 783	20 070	34 455	47 699	51 436	38 696	46 668	44 424	43 517
1210 On profits	484	6 510	18 994	32 087	44 336	48 605	37 405	45 439	42 370	41 346
Petroleum revenue tax	..	1 799	941	1 540	1 387	2 663	1 047	1 775	2 106	1 296
Supplementary petroleum duty	..	0	0	0	0	0	0	0	0	0
Corporation tax	..	4 712	18 053	30 547	42 235	45 166	35 662	43 039	39 637	39 383
Corporation tax overspill relief	..	-1	0	0	0	0	0	0	0	0
Profits tax	..	0	0	0	0	0	0	0	0	0
Windfall tax	..	0	0	0	0	0	0	0	0	0
Betting tax	..	0	0	0	590	569	543	539	565	605
Non fossil fuel obligation levy	..	0	0	0	124	207	153	86	62	62
1220 On capital gains	0	273	1 076	2 368	3 363	2 831	1 291	1 229	2 054	2 171
1300 Unallocable between 1100 and 1200	-52	0	0	0	0	0	0	0	0	0
2000 Social security contributions	**1 685**	**13 531**	**34 457**	**60 252**	**93 210**	**98 319**	**94 445**	**101 441**	**104 319**	**106 085**
2100 Employees	770	5 228	13 296	24 175	36 585	38 186	37 184	40 196	41 037	41 587
2110 On a payroll basis	..	..	13 296	24 175	36 585	38 186	37 184	40 196	41 037	41 587
2120 On an income tax basis	..	..	0	0	0	0	0	0	0	0
2200 Employers	831	8 210	19 984	34 028	53 765	57 080	54 411	58 604	60 689	61 912
2210 On a payroll basis	..	..	19 984	34 028	53 765	57 080	54 411	58 604	60 689	61 912
2220 On an income tax basis	..	..	0	0	0	0	0	0	0	0
2300 Self-employed or non-employed	75	317	1 177	2 049	2 860	3 053	2 850	2 641	2 593	2 586
2310 On a payroll basis	..	..	1 177	2 049	2 860	3 053	2 850	2 641	2 593	2 586
2320 On an income tax basis	..	..	0	0	0	0	0	0	0	0
2400 Unallocable between 2100, 2200 and 2300	9	-224	0	0	0	0	0	0	0	0
2410 On a payroll basis	..	..	..	..	..	..	..	..	..	..
2420 On an income tax basis	..	..	..	..	..	..	..	..	..	..
3000 Taxes on payroll and workforce	**0**	**3 498**	**0**	**0**	**0**	**0**	**0**	**0**	**0**	**0**
Selective employment tax	..	0	..	..	..	..	..	..	..	..
National insurance surcharge	..	3 498	..	..	..	..	..	..	..	..
4000 Taxes on property	**1 591**	**9 774**	**16 538**	**41 134**	**63 378**	**60 064**	**58 387**	**62 813**	**64 613**	**69 358**
4100 Recurrent taxes on immovable property	1 228	8 665	13 462	30 552	44 877	47 308	48 845	51 046	52 566	54 439
4110 Households	539	3 687	2 373	14 205	23 609	24 718	25 419	26 263	26 610	27 624
Northern Ireland rates paid to CG	..	37	113	141	265	329	355	391	416	406
Council tax	..	0	0	13 991	23 217	24 267	24 933	25 715	26 030	27 048
Rates paid to LA	..	3 650	2 260	73	127	122	131	157	164	170
4120 Others	689	4 978	11 089	16 347	21 268	22 590	23 426	24 783	25 956	26 815
National non-domestic rates	..	0	7 542	14 966	19 344	20 607	21 361	22 426	23 581	24 380
Rates paid to LA	..	4 925	2 869	149	267	301	317	352	360	363
Northern Ireland rates paid to CG	..	53	115	207	353	328	325	368	366	373
London Regional Transport levy	..	0	47	0	0	0	0	0	0	0
LA payments of NNDR	..	0	469	889	1 111	1 147	1 189	1 356	1 389	1 389
NPISH payments of NNDR	..	0	47	136	193	207	234	281	260	310
4200 Recurrent taxes on net wealth	0	0	0	0	0	0	0	0	0	0
4210 Individual	..	..	..	..	..	..	..	..	..	..
4220 Corporate	..	..	..	..	..	..	..	..	..	..
4300 Estate, inheritance and gift taxes	287	479	1 321	2 215	3 867	3 257	2 401	2 936	3 129	3 379
4310 Estate and inheritance taxes	287	479	1 321	2 215	3 867	3 257	2 401	2 936	3 129	3 379
Death duties	..	423	1 278	2 156	3 764	3 130	2 305	2 856	3 041	3 293
Development land tax	..	42	6	0	0	0	0	0	0	0
Taxes on other capital transfers	..	14	37	59	50	50	50	50	50	50
Special tax on bank deposits	..	0	0	0	0	0	0	0	0	0
Betterment duty	..	0	0	0	0	0	0	0	0	0
Special charges	..	0	0	0	0	0	0	0	0	0
Special contribution	..	0	0	0	0	0	0	0	0	0
Equal pay on capital transfers	..	0	0	0	53	77	46	30	38	36
4320 Gift taxes	0	0	0	0	0	0	0	0	0	0
4400 Taxes on financial and capital transactions	76	630	1 755	8 367	14 634	9 499	7 141	8 831	8 918	11 540
Stamp duties	..	630	1 755	8 367	14 634	9 499	7 141	8 831	8 918	11 540
4500 Non-recurrent taxes	0	0	0	0	0	0	0	0	0	0
4510 On net wealth	..	..	..	..	..	..	..	..	..	..
4520 Other non-recurrent taxes	..	..	..	..	..	..	..	..	..	..
4600 Other recurrent taxes on property	0	0	0	0	0	0	0	0	0	0
5000 Taxes on goods and services	**3 619**	**23 699**	**62 826**	**113 104**	**147 117**	**148 908**	**139 259**	**176 521**	**180 105**	**185 787**

Table 73. **United Kingdom / Royaume-Uni** *(cont.)*
Details of tax revenue / Recettes fiscales détaillées

Million GBP

	1965	1980	1990	2000	2007	2008	2009	2011	2012	2013
5100 Taxes on production, sale, transfer, etc	3 406	22 677	59 425	108 121	141 151	142 563	132 412	169 668	173 113	178 585
5110 General taxes	647	11 897	34 136	64 202	92 025	92 002	79 900	111 461	113 895	118 106
5111 Value added taxes	0	11 897	34 136	64 202	92 025	92 002	79 900	111 461	113 895	118 106
Value added tax	..	11 893	33 620	64 202	92 025	92 002	79 900	111 437	113 892	118 296
Adj. to VAT contribution	..	4	516	0	0	0	0	24	3	-190
Purchase tax	..	0	0	0	0	0	0	0	0	0
5112 Sales tax	647	0	0	0	0	0	0	0	0	0
5113 Other	0	0	0	0	0	0	0	0	0	0
5120 Taxes on specific goods and services	2 759	10 780	25 289	43 919	49 126	50 561	52 512	58 207	59 218	60 479
5121 Excises	2 383	8 616	19 707	37 271	40 424	41 666	43 867	46 152	46 800	46 577
Beer	..	1 029	2 220	2 813	3 042	3 140	3 189	3 429	3 425	3 337
Wines, spirits, cider and perry	..	1 513	2 627	3 751	5 008	5 533	5 728	6 439	6 775	7 063
Tobacco	..	2 735	5 541	7 666	7 862	8 203	9 056	9 361	9 897	9 479
Hydrocarbon oil	..	3 327	9 302	23 041	24 512	24 790	25 894	26 923	26 703	26 698
Other excise duties	..	12	17	0	0	0	0	0	0	0
5122 Profits of fiscal monopolies	0	0	0	0	0	0	0	0	0	0
5123 Customs and import duties	343	1 109	1 837	286	338	339	210	0	0	0
Custom duties	..	0	0	0	0	0	0	..	..	..
Import duties	..	855	1 722	0	0	0	0	..	..	..
Agricultural levies	..	254	115	286	338	339	210	..	..	..
Temporary charges of import	..	0	0	0	0	0	0	..	..	..
5124 Taxes on exports	0	-1	36	0	0	0	0	0	0	0
Levies on exports	..	-1	36	..	..	..	..	..	..	..
5125 Taxes on investment goods	0	0	0	0	0	0	0	0	0	0
5126 Taxes on specific services	33	456	1 022	5 759	6 458	6 551	6 625	10 000	10 436	11 331
Betting and gaming	..	456	1 022	1 522	959	989	1 013	1 206	1 207	1 538
National Lottery contributions to fund	..	0	0	1 590	1 310	1 405	1 553	1 793	1 832	1 644
Air passenger duty	..	0	0	940	1 883	1 876	1 800	2 605	2 766	2 960
Insurance premium tax	..	0	0	1 707	2 306	2 281	2 259	2 942	3 022	3 018
Bank Levy - Stability Fee Scheme	..	0	0	0	0	0	0	1 454	1 609	2 171
5127 Other taxes on internat. trade and transactions	0	0	0	0	0	0	0	0	0	0
5128 Other taxes	0	600	2 687	603	1 906	2 005	1 810	2 055	1 982	2 571
Fossil fuel levy	..	0	875	56	0	0	0	0	0	0
Sugar levy	..	21	46	44	0	0	0	0	0	0
European coal and steel levy	..	12	11	0	0	0	0	0	0	0
Gas levy	..	83	291	0	0	0	0	0	0	0
Car tax	..	484	1 464	0	0	0	0	0	0	0
Landfill tax	..	0	0	461	877	954	842	1 090	1 094	1 191
Climate change levy	..	0	0	0	690	717	693	675	624	1 098
Aggregates levy	..	0	0	0	339	334	275	290	264	282
Hydro benefit	..	0	0	42	0	0	0	0	0	0
Renewable energy obligations	..	0	0	0	0	0	0	0	0	0
Channel 4 advertising formula	..	0	0	0	0	0	0	0	0	0
Milk super levy	..	0	0	0	0	0	0	0	0	0
5130 Unallocable between 5110 and 5120	0	0	0	0	0	0	0	0	0	0
5200 Taxes on use of goods and perform activities	212	1 378	3 401	4 983	5 966	6 345	6 847	6 853	6 992	7 202
5210 Recurrent taxes	212	1 378	3 401	4 983	5 966	6 345	6 847	6 853	6 992	7 202
5211 Paid by households: motor vehicles	118	729	1 841	3 195	4 506	4 639	4 722	4 889	4 933	5 124
Motor vehicle duty	..	726	1 837	3 191	4 506	4 639	4 722	4 889	4 933	5 124
Boat licences	..	3	4	4	0	0	0	0	0	0
5212 Paid by others: motor vehicles	74	588	1 134	1 415	878	885	908	931	940	977
Motor vehicle levy	..	588	1 134	1 415	878	885	908	931	940	977
5213 Paid in respect of other goods	20	61	426	373	582	821	1 217	1 033	1 119	1 101
IBA levy	..	..	134	0	0	0	0	0	0	0
Telecommunications regulator fees	..	..	7	12	17	9	12	12	3	0
Gas regulator fees	..	..	2	0	0	0	0	0	0	0
Electricity regulator fees	..	..	5	0	0	0	0	0	0	0
Water regulator fees	..	..	6	11	11	13	12	21	24	24
Rail regulator fees	..	..	0	14	12	12	12	12	12	12
Company registration surplus fees	..	..	12	0	0	0	0	0	0	0
Consumer and credit act fees	..	..	163	119	281	328	435	480	480	480
Levy funded bodies	..	..	97	217	261	459	746	508	600	585
1936 Tithe Act payments	..	..	0	0	0	0	0	0	0	0
5220 Non-recurrent taxes	0	0	0	0	0	0	0	0	0	0
5300 Unallocable between 5100 and 5200	1	-356	0	0	0	0	0	0	0	0
6000 Other taxes	**0**	**0**	**9 017**	**0**	**0**	**0**	**0**	**212**	**217**	**204**
6100 Paid solely by business	..	..	0	..	..	..	..	0	0	0
6200 Other	..	..	9 017	..	..	..	..	212	217	204
Community charge	..	..	9 017	..	..	..	..	..	..	..
Custom duties collected for the EU	..	..	..	**1 800**	**2 074**	**2 297**	**2 435**	**2 925**	**2 885**	**2 914**

Table 73. **United Kingdom / Royaume-Uni** *(cont.)*
Details of tax revenue / Recettes fiscales détaillées

Million GBP

	1965	1980	1990	2000	2007	2008	2009	2011	2012	2013
Non wastable tax credits										
Non-wastable tax credits against 1110	...	...	7 454	4 651	19 586	23 005	26 935	29 615	29 934	29 833
Tax expenditure component	...	...	6 973	1 233	4 352	5 239	5 659	4 973	3 338	2 809
Transfer component	...	...	481	3 418	15 234	17 766	21 276	24 642	26 596	27 024
Non-wastable tax credits against 1210	...	...	0	1	762	865	1 079	1 309	1 349	1 470
Tax expenditure component	...	...	...	0	549	616	778	973	869	979
Transfer component	...	...	...	1	213	249	301	336	480	491
Total tax revenue on cash basis	**10 945**	**81 153**	**202 400**	**351 778**	**508 997**	**522 748**	**483 036**	**540 465**	**542 656**	**561 127**
Total tax revenue on accrual basis	**..**	**..**	**202 414**	**354 881**	**504 697**	**515 887**	**479 001**	**543 272**	**547 017**	**564 164**
Conciliation with National Accounts										
Additional taxes included in National Accounts	...	...	1 323	2 062	4 072	4 321	4 459	4 879	5 525	5 813
Taxes excluded from National Accounts	...	...	0	0	0	0	0	0	0	0
Difference in treatment of tax credits	...	...	308	1 204	575	635	795	982	877	987
Capital transfer for uncollected revenue	...	...	0	0	0	0	0	0	0	0
Voluntary social security contributions	...	...	3 288	5 907	14 478	15 282	16 089	16 786	19 217	16 759
Miscellaneous differences	...	...	0	0	0	0	0	0	0	0
National Accounts: Taxes and actual social contributions	...	...	207 333	364 054	523 822	536 125	500 344	565 919	572 636	587 723
Imputed social contributions	...	...	3 966	8 252	8 413	8 896	10 049	9 853	9 514	9 526
National Accounts: Taxes and all social contributions	...	...	211 299	372 306	532 235	545 021	510 393	575 772	582 150	597 249

Note:

Year ending 31st December.

From 1990 data are on accrual basis.

Heading 1210: The corporate tax figures include company income tax from 1990 onwards.

Heading 2000: Includes some voluntary contributions which cannot be separately identified.

Heading 6200: The community charge replaced domestic rates in Scotland in April 1989 and was extended to England and Wales in April 1990. This tax has been classified in heading 6200 as it is a lump-sum tax levied on ach adult in a household (domestic rates are classified in heading 4100).

Headings for non-wastable tax credits 1110 and 1210 are consistent with the guidelines, and the figures in the data are treated accordingly. The following method is adopted separately for Working Families 'Tax Credit and Disabled Persons Tax Credit' paid from 1999 to 2003. For each calendar, a random sample of awards over-lapping the quarter is taken. Each recipient family's income tax liability for the fiscal year within which the quarter falls is calculated , based on the earned income reported for the award (uprated to the middle of the overlap period). And the result multiplied by the number of days in the overlap period divided by 365. The tax expenditure component is defined as the minimum of this amount and the total amount of award paid in the overlap period. The total amount of award paid and the tax expenditure component are each summed over the sample cases, and the ratio is taken as the tax expenditure ration for the quarter. From 2003, the equivalent breakdown for Child and Working tax credits is based on household survey data. Survey data is used to estimate the breakdown into the tax expenditure and the transfer components for the other smaller tax credits.

Source: National Income and Expenditure; Central Statistical Office; Annual reports of Her Majesty's Revenue and Customs.

StatLink http://dx.doi.org/10.1787/888933277356

Table 74. **United States / État-Unis**
Details of tax revenue / Recettes fiscales détaillées

Million USD

	1965	1980	1990	2000	2007	2008	2009	2011	2012	2013
Total tax revenue	**167 022**	**730 672**	**1 550 453**	**2 896 222**	**3 862 089**	**3 708 617**	**3 311 367**	**3 656 166**	**3 887 222**	**4 260 050**
1000 Taxes on income, profits and capital gains	**80 284**	**364 137**	**699 771**	**1 449 568**	**1 862 171**	**1 676 876**	**1 330 054**	**1 660 319**	**1 824 010**	**2 009 241**
1100 Of individuals	52 894	285 513	582 773	1 220 241	1 476 052	1 427 482	1 131 496	1 386 162	1 489 759	1 648 674
1110 On income and profits	50 401	272 879	550 874	1 084 567	1 323 356	1 301 610	1 056 624	1 314 311	1 384 288	1 527 744
Individual income tax federal	46 492	233 269	447 279	891 380	1 057 640	1 021 663	814 291	1 036 618	1 084 409	1 210 178
Individual income tax state and local govt.	3 909	39 610	103 595	193 187	265 716	279 947	242 333	277 693	299 879	317 566
1120 On capital gains	2 493	12 634	31 899	135 674	152 696	125 872	74 872	71 851	105 471	120 930
Capital gains federal	2 300	10 800	25 900	111 507	122 036	98 800	57 700	56 670	82 623	95 793
Capital gains tax state and local govt.	193	1 834	5 999	24 167	30 660	27 072	17 172	15 181	22 848	25 137
1200 Corporate	27 390	78 624	116 998	229 327	386 119	249 394	198 558	274 157	334 251	360 567
1210 On profits	26 745	73 586	106 134	170 835	330 596	218 893	179 866	240 737	295 128	322 183
Corporate income tax federal	24 861	60 525	85 736	144 590	281 040	177 260	138 562	196 653	248 184	272 793
Corporate income tax state and local govt.	1 884	13 061	20 398	26 245	49 556	41 633	41 304	44 084	46 944	49 390
1220 On capital gains	645	5 038	10 864	58 492	55 523	30 501	18 692	33 420	39 123	38 384
Capital gains tax corp. federal	600	4 143	8 776	49 506	47 200	24 700	14 400	27 300	32 900	32 500
Capital gains tax corp. state and local govt.	45	895	2 088	8 986	8 323	5 801	4 292	6 120	6 223	5 884
1300 Unallocable between 1100 and 1200	0	0	0	0	0	0	0	0	0	0
2000 Social security contributions	**22 192**	**159 763**	**396 972**	**683 104**	**907 433**	**930 086**	**902 632**	**848 299**	**880 925**	**1 030 633**
2100 Employees	8 459	67 022	173 860	305 555	400 940	413 833	401 239	315 703	327 957	456 902
Federal insurance contribution Act tax	8 084	66 221	..	..	..	..	..	..	..	..
Less refund federal	-192	-507	..	..	..	..	..	..	..	..
Railroad retirement taxes federal	322	590	..	..	..	..	..	..	..	..
Fed. hosp. insur. recpts from railroad retir.	0	111	..	..	..	..	..	..	..	..
Unemployment state tax federal	20	127	..	..	..	..	..	..	..	..
Temp. disability insurance state and local	225	480	..	..	..	..	..	..	..	..
2110 On a payroll basis	..	..	..	..	..	..	..	..	..	..
2120 On an income tax basis	..	..	..	..	..	..	..	..	..	..
2200 Employers	12 703	87 019	204 102	343 184	456 655	465 817	451 475	485 865	505 946	519 074
Federal insurance contributions act tax	7 802	64 768	..	..	..	..	..	..	..	..
Railroad retirement taxes federal	314	1 722	..	..	..	..	..	..	..	..
Fed. hosp. insur. recpts from railroad retir.	0	111	..	..	..	..	..	..	..	..
Military service credit federal	14	652	..	..	..	..	..	..	..	..
Old-age dis. hosp. insur. fed. employer contr.	282	1 453	..	..	..	..	..	..	..	..
Unemployment state tax federal	3 032	11 788	..	..	..	..	..	..	..	..
Federal unemployment tax Act	615	3 246	..	..	..	..	..	..	..	..
Railroad unempl. insurance Act tax federal	152	175	..	..	..	..	..	..	..	..
Workmen's compensation state and local	484	3 039	..	..	..	..	..	..	..	..
Temp. disability insurance state and local	8	65	..	..	..	..	..	..	..	..
2210 On a payroll basis	..	..	..	..	..	..	..	..	..	..
2220 On an income tax basis	..	..	..	..	..	..	..	..	..	..
2300 Self-employed or non-employed	1 030	5 722	19 010	34 365	49 838	50 436	49 918	46 731	47 022	54 657
Federal old-age survivors trust	0	4 250	..	..	..	..	..	..	..	..
Federal disability insurance trust	1 030	733	..	..	..	..	..	..	..	..
Federal hospital insurance trust	0	739	..	..	..	..	..	..	..	..
2310 On a payroll basis	..	..	..	..	..	..	..	..	..	..
2320 On an income tax basis	..	..	..	..	..	..	..	..	..	..
2400 Unallocable between 2100, 2200 and 2300	0	0	0	0	0	0	0	0	0	0
2410 On a payroll basis	..	..	..	..	..	..	..	..	..	..
2420 On an income tax basis	..	..	..	..	..	..	..	..	..	..
3000 Taxes on payroll and workforce	**0**	**0**	**0**	**0**	**0**	**0**	**0**	**0**	**0**	**0**
4000 Taxes on property	**26 529**	**77 913**	**180 260**	**295 157**	**442 276**	**454 662**	**467 458**	**460 902**	**470 096**	**479 880**
4100 Recurrent taxes on immovable property	22 918	68 499	164 505	259 517	410 767	420 799	442 541	439 178	443 739	446 358
4110 Households	8 548	28 975	..	..	..	..	..	..	..	..
Property tax state and local	8 548	28 975	..	..	..	..	..	..	..	..
Other	0	0	..	..	..	..	..	..	..	..
4120 Others	14 370	39 524	..	..	..	..	..	..	..	..
Property tax state and local	14 370	39 524	..	..	..	..	..	..	..	..
Other	0	0	..	..	..	..	..	..	..	..
4200 Recurrent taxes on net wealth	0	0	0	0	0	0	0	0	0	0
4210 Individual	..	..	..	..	..	..	..	..	..	..
4220 Corporate	..	..	..	..	..	..	..	..	..	..
4300 Estate, inheritance and gift taxes	3 447	8 425	15 755	35 640	31 509	33 863	24 917	14 379	19 006	26 150
4310 Estate and inheritance taxes	3 080	8 149	..	..	..	..	..	..	..	..
Estate tax less refund federal	2 427	6 181	..	..	..	..	..	..	..	..
Estate tax state and local govt.	653	1 968	..	..	..	..	..	..	..	..
4320 Gift taxes	367	276	..	..	..	..	..	..	..	..
Gift tax less refund federal	289	209	..	..	..	..	..	..	..	..
Gift tax calculate state and local govt.	78	67	..	..	..	..	..	..	..	..

Table 74. **United States / État-Unis** *(cont.)*
Details of tax revenue / Recettes fiscales détaillées

Million USD

	1965	1980	1990	2000	2007	2008	2009	2011	2012	2013
4400 Taxes on financial and capital transactions	164	989	0	0	0	0	0	0	0	0
Interest equalisation tax federal	15	0	..	..	..	..	..	..	..	..
Document and stock transfer state and local	149	989	..	..	..	..	..	..	..	..
4500 Non-recurrent taxes	0	0	0	0	0	0	0	0	0	0
4510 On net wealth	..	..	..	..	..	..	..	..	..	..
4520 Other non-recurrent taxes	..	..	..	..	..	..	..	..	..	..
4600 Other recurrent taxes on property	0	0	0	0	0	0	0	7 345	7 351	7 372
5000 Taxes on goods and services	**38 017**	**128 844**	**273 450**	**468 393**	**650 209**	**646 993**	**611 223**	**686 647**	**712 191**	**740 296**
5100 Taxes on production, sale, transfer, etc	33 300	111 810	235 203	404 065	542 829	538 105	514 619	574 656	596 401	621 287
5110 General taxes	8 016	51 328	125 575	221 358	305 524	300 954	281 577	308 257	319 699	332 944
5111 Value added taxes	0	0	0	0	0	0	0	0	0	0
5112 Sales tax	8 016	51 328	125 575	221 358	305 524	300 954	281 577	308 257	319 699	332 944
General sales - general receipts state and local	7 981	51 328	125 575	221 358	305 524	300 954	281 577	308 257	319 699	332 944
Other state and local	35	0	0	0	0	0	0	0	0	0
5113 Other	0	0	0	0	0	0	0	0	0	0
5120 Taxes on specific goods and services	25 284	60 482	109 628	182 707	237 305	237 151	233 042	266 399	276 702	288 343
5121 Excises	21 209	45 471	64 953	108 600	137 346	133 895	142 125	146 549	153 765	152 877
Alcohol taxes federal govt.	3 689	5 601	5 228	7 281	8 571	8 668	8 645	9 010	9 423	9 025
Tobacco taxes federal govt.	2 142	2 443	4 217	6 741	8 377	7 999	16 309	16 959	16 524	15 781
Airport, airway, highway federal	3 559	6 411	0	0	0	0	0	0	0	0
Manufacturer's excise taxes federal govt.	2 867	6 122	0	0	0	0	0	0	0	0
Sugar tax federal govt.	97	0	0	0	0	0	0	0	0	0
Other taxes excise federal govt.	889	2	0	0	0	0	0	0	0	0
Undistributed tax deposits federal government	-11	152	0	0	0	0	0	0	0	0
Other taxes excise and undist. fed.govt. -	0	0	13 316	32 005	31 747	27 564	28 008	26 779	33 767	33 712
Less special tax liquor occupations federal	-22	-21	0	0	0	0	0	0	0	0
Other federal (refunds)	-7	-32	0	0	0	0	0	0	0	0
Alcohol taxes state and local govt.	949	2 642	3 577	4 485	5 677	5 867	5 941	6 273	6 472	6 606
Tobacco taxes state and local govt.	1 386	3 874	6 009	8 726	16 435	16 992	16 954	17 634	17 506	17 451
Public utilities state and local govt.	871	5 888	11 814	17 989	27 863	28 528	28 501	28 661	28 561	28 578
Motor fuel taxes state and local govt.	4 331	9 822	20 792	31 373	38 676	38 277	37 767	41 233	41 512	41 724
Other state and local taxes	469	2 295	0	0	0	0	0	0	0	0
Coal tonnage tax federal govt.	0	272	0	0	0	0	0	0	0	0
Hazardous substances tax federal	0	0	0	0	0	0	0	0	0	0
Transportation fuels tax federal	0	0	0	0	0	0	0	0	0	0
Boat fuels and equipment tax federal	0	0	0	0	0	0	0	0	0	0
Waste site deposits tax federal	0	0	0	0	0	0	0	0	0	0
Leaking underground storage federal	0	0	0	0	0	0	0	0	0	0
Vaccine injury compens. federal	0	0	0	0	0	0	0	0	0	0
Ozone depletion tax federal	0	0	0	0	0	0	0	0	0	0
Oil spill liability federal	0	0	0	0	0	0	0	0	0	0
Luxury tax federal govt.	0	0	0	0	0	0	0	0	0	0
5122 Profits of fiscal monopolies	275	608	0	0	0	0	0	0	0	0
Liquor store revenue state and local govt.	1 447	3 200	..	..	..	..	..	..	..	..
Liquor store expend. state and local govt.	-1 172	-2 592	..	..	..	..	..	..	..	..
5123 Customs and import duties	1 442	7 436	17 490	21 123	28 773	29 223	23 062	31 870	33 481	35 425
Custom duties federal	1 442	7 436	17 490	21 123	28 773	29 223	23 062	31 870	33 481	35 425
Petroleum import fees federal govt.	0	0	0	0	0	0	0	0	0	0
5124 Taxes on exports	0	0	0	0	0	0	0	0	0	0
5125 Taxes on investment goods	0	0	0	0	0	0	0	0	0	0
5126 Taxes on specific services	2 358	6 967	7 535	9 835	15 472	15 710	15 544	16 436	16 924	17 565
Amusements state and local govt.	23	234	0	0	0	0	0	0	0	0
Parimutuels state and local govt.	386	731	0	0	0	0	0	0	0	0
Transportation of persons federal	126	1 601	0	0	0	0	0	0	0	0
Transport of property	0	92	0	0	0	0	0	0	0	0
General and toll telephone federal	1 079	1 118	0	0	0	0	0	0	0	0
Foreign insurance policies federal	0	75	0	0	0	0	0	0	0	0
Insurance state and local govt.	744	3 113	7 535	9 835	15 472	15 710	15 544	16 436	16 924	17 565
Employee pension plans federal	0	3	0	0	0	0	0	0	0	0
Inland waterway tax federal	0	0	0	0	0	0	0	0	0	0
Ship departure tax federal	0	0	0	0	0	0	0	0	0	0
5127 Other taxes on internat. trade and transactions	0	0	0	0	0	0	0	0	0	0
5128 Other taxes	0	0	19 650	43 149	55 714	58 323	52 311	71 544	72 532	82 476
5130 Unallocable between 5110 and 5120	0	0	0	0	0	0	0	0	0	0
5200 Taxes on use of goods and perform activities	4 717	17 034	38 247	64 328	107 380	108 888	96 604	111 991	115 791	119 009
5210 Recurrent taxes	3 490	9 501	30 655	55 139	86 725	80 111	80 471	87 852	91 324	93 841
5211 Paid by households: motor vehicles	1 211	3 370	8 104	11 408	14 990	14 902	15 391	16 967	17 534	17 776
Motor vehicle regis. license st. and loc.	1 056	2 981	..	..	..	..	..	..	..	..
Motor vehicle oper. license st. and loc.	152	389	..	..	..	..	..	..	..	..
Other motor vehicle	3	0	..	..	..	..	..	..	..	..

Table 74. **United States / État-Unis** *(cont.)*
Details of tax revenue / Recettes fiscales détaillées

Million USD

	1965	1980	1990	2000	2007	2008	2009	2011	2012	2013
5212 Paid by others: motor vehicles	937	2 343	3 564	6 689	8 478	8 423	8 666	9 541	9 920	10 090
Motor vehicle regis. license st. and loc.	937	2 343	..	..	..	..	..	..	..	..
Motor vehicle oper. license st. and loc.	0	0	..	..	..	..	..	..	..	..
5213 Paid in respect of other goods	1 342	3 788	18 987	37 042	63 257	56 786	56 414	61 344	63 870	65 975
Misc. fees permit license federal	19	0	0	0	0	0	0	0	0	0
Special tax liquor occupations federal	22	21	0	0	0	0	0	0	0	0
Use tax of certain vehicles federal	99	277	0	0	0	0	0	0	0	0
Use of internat. travel facilities federal	0	92	0	0	0	0	0	0	0	0
Use tax of aircraft federal	0	21	0	0	0	0	0	0	0	0
Corporation in general license st. and loc.	528	1 388	0	0	0	0	0	0	0	0
Alcoholic beverage license tax st. and loc.	133	179	0	0	0	0	0	0	0	0
Public utilities license tax st. and loc.	30	130	0	0	0	0	0	0	0	0
Amusements license taxes st. and loc.	7	69	0	0	0	0	0	0	0	0
Occupation and business license st. and loc.	349	1 113	0	0	0	0	0	0	0	0
Wagering occupation tax federal	7	12	0	0	0	0	0	0	0	0
Other license taxes st. and loc.	10	69	18 987	37 042	63 257	56 786	56 414	61 344	63 870	65 975
Hunting and fishing license taxes st. and loc.	138	417	0	0	0	0	0	0	0	0
Other	0	0	0	0	0	0	0	0	0	0
5220 Non-recurrent taxes	1 227	7 533	7 592	9 189	20 655	28 777	16 133	24 139	24 467	25 168
Severance state and local govt.	503	4 167	5 224	5 285	12 898	21 275	8 675	16 581	16 559	16 895
Poll taxes state and local govt.	9	0	0	0	0	0	0	0	0	0
Other taxes state and local govt.	715	3 366	2 368	3 904	7 757	7 502	7 458	7 558	7 908	8 273
5300 Unallocable between 5100 and 5200	0	0	0	0	0	0	0	0	0	0
6000 Other taxes	**0**	**15**	**0**	**0**	**0**	**0**	**0**	**0**	**0**	**0**
6100 Paid solely by business	..	0	..	..	..	..	..	..	..	..
6200 Other	..	15	..	..	..	..	..	..	..	..
Non wastable tax credits										
Non-wastable tax credits against 1110	..	..	..	36 511	90 439	113 200	104 064	162 586	124 532	158 160
Tax expenditure component	..	..	..	9 602	35 910	33 800	39 700	65 860	40 392	41 560
Transfer component	..	..	..	26 909	54 529	79 400	64 364	96 726	84 140	116 600
Non-wastable tax credits against 1210	..	..	..	0	0	0	650	6 400	7 720	630
Tax expenditure component	..	..	..	..	..	..	650	6 390	7 700	610
Transfer component	..	..	..	..	..	..	0	10	20	20
Unallocable transfer component	..	..	..	..	..	..	1 070	7 330	4 470	4 280
Total tax revenue on cash basis	**167 022**	**730 672**	**1 518 943**	**2 870 276**	**3 839 516**	**3 827 198**	**3 382 595**	..	..	..
Total tax revenue on accrual basis	..	..	**1 550 453**	**2 896 222**	**3 862 089**	**3 708 617**	**3 311 367**	**3 656 166**	**3 887 222**	**4 260 050**
Conciliation with National Accounts										
Additional taxes included in National Accounts	..	..	0	0	0	0	0	75 424	88 418	79 633
Taxes excluded from National Accounts	..	..	0	0	0	0	0	0	0	0
Difference in treatment of tax credits	..	..	0	0	0	0	0	0	0	0
Capital transfer for uncollected revenue	..	..	0	0	0	0	0	0	0	0
Voluntary social security contributions	..	..	11 719	22 562	51 617	55 369	57 954	63 761	64 680	69 939
Miscellaneous differences	..	..	0	0	0	0	0	0	0	0
National Accounts: Taxes and actual social contributions	..	..	1 585 780	2 944 128	3 948 304	3 795 675	3 416 751	3 719 927	3 951 902	4 329 989
Imputed social contributions	..	..	3 384	3 727	7 077	7 607	8 779	10 148	10 177	9 340
National Accounts: Taxes and all social contributions	..	..	1 589 164	2 947 855	3 955 381	3 803 282	3 425 530	3 730 075	3 962 079	4 339 329

Note:

From 1990, data are on a year ending 31st December basis. For years up to and including 1976 the dated covered fiscal years ending 30th June. Between 1977 and 1989, Federal government data covered fiscal years ending 30th September and State & Local government data covered fiscal years ending 30th June.

From 1990, data are on accrual basis. There are no separate estimates for the State and Local capital gains tax revenues.

Heading 5121: In 1994 through 1996, some Federal excise taxes formerly shown separately were included in 'Other taxes,excises and undistributed, Federal government'.

Source: Federal estimates are derived from the US Budget, the Final Monthly Treasury Statement and the Annual Report of the US Treasury Department. The State and Local estimates are derived from Government Finances, published by the Bureau of the Census.

StatLink http://dx.doi.org/10.1787/888933277365

Revenue Statistics 1965-2014
Statistiques des recettes publiques 1965-2014

PART III/PARTIE III

B. Financing social benefits

B. Le financement des prestations sociales

Table 75. **Financing social benefits / Le financement des prestations sociales**

Memorandum item on the financing of social security benefits
Pour mémoire : le financement des systèmes de sécurité sociale

	1965	1980	1990	2000	2007	2008	2009	2011	2012	2013
Australia, million AUD										
Contribution under 2000 heading	...	...	...	...	...	...	...	...	...	...
Other taxes	...	...	...	...	...	...	...	...	...	...
Voluntary contributions to government	...	...	...	...	...	...	...	...	...	...
Compulsory contributions to private sector	...	...	...	...	...	...	...	...	...	...
Total	**0**	**0**	**0**	**0**	**0**	**0**	**0**	**0**	**0**	**0**
Austria, million EUR										
Contribution under 2000 heading	1 548	9 200	17 763	30 613	38 583	40 300	40 771	43 486	45 058	46 988
Other taxes	0	0	0	0	0	0	0	0	0	0
Voluntary contributions to government	32	135	141	206	256	270	300	343	310	299
Compulsory contributions to private sector	0	0	0	0	0	0	0	0	0	0
Total	**1 580**	**9 335**	**17 904**	**30 820**	**38 839**	**40 570**	**41 070**	**43 828**	**45 368**	**47 286**
Belgique, millions EUR										
Impôts de la série 2000	2 018	10 798	23 386	34 411	45 321	47 940	48 933	52 560	54 633	55 975
Autres impôts	0	171	644	5 375	13 659	15 139	15 344	19 635	18 009	18 319
Contributions volontaires au gouvernement	0	41	52	54	55	62	62	67	71	75
Contributions obligatoires au secteur privé	0	0	0	0	0	0	0	0	0	0
Total	**2 018**	**11 009**	**24 082**	**39 840**	**59 034**	**63 141**	**64 339**	**72 261**	**72 713**	**74 368**
Canada, million CAD										
Contribution under 2000 heading	854	10 649	29 653	53 109	73 722	75 347	76 882	82 508	87 897	92 257
Other taxes	1 199	0	0	0	0	0	0	0	0	0
Voluntary contributions to government	0	0	0	0	0	0	0	0	0	0
Compulsory contributions to private sector	0	0	0	0	0	0	0	0	0	0
Total	**2 053**	**10 649**	**29 653**	**53 109**	**73 722**	**75 347**	**76 882**	**82 508**	**87 897**	**92 257**
Chile, million CLP										
Contribution under 2000 heading	..	..	159 559	576 758	1 148 647	1 289 225	1 371 750	1 623 818	1 802 468	1 968 973
Other taxes	..	..	0	0	0	0	0	0	0	0
Voluntary contributions to government	..	..	0	0	0	0	0	0	0	0
Compulsory contributions to private sector	..	..	328 102	2 021 631	3 808 658	4 357 402	4 832 756	6 103 523	6 843 561	7 583 251
Total	**..**	**..**	**487 661**	**2 598 389**	**4 957 305**	**5 646 627**	**6 204 506**	**7 727 341**	**8 646 029**	**9 552 224**
Czech Republic, million CZK										
Contribution under 2000 heading	...	...	...	341 544	573 417	595 552	557 702	588 996	596 841	603 072
Other taxes	...	...	...	0	0	0	0	0	0	0
Voluntary contributions to government	...	...	...	1 099	974	882	635	423	313	326
Compulsory contributions to private sector	...	...	...	2 837	5 757	6 222	6 140	6 286	6 408	6 424
Total	**..**	**..**	**..**	**345 480**	**580 148**	**602 656**	**564 477**	**595 705**	**603 562**	**609 822**
Denmark, million DKK										
Contribution under 2000 heading	690	710	101	8 453	1 286	1 086	1 018	2 040	1 824	1 618
Other taxes	0	0	0	0	0	0	0	0	0	0
Voluntary contributions to government	0	1 673	8 087	16 633	17 061	17 165	16 816	17 610	16 320	14 655
Compulsory contributions to private sector	145	554	1 278	1 445	4 526	4 887	4 368	3 584	3 458	3 068
Total	**835**	**2 937**	**9 466**	**26 531**	**22 873**	**23 138**	**22 202**	**23 234**	**21 602**	**19 341**
Estonia, million EUR										
Contribution under 2000 heading	...	...	...	674	1 683	1 891	1 819	1 935	2 000	2 077
Other taxes	...	...	...	0	0	0	0	0	0	0
Voluntary contributions to government	...	...	...	0	0	0	0	0	0	0
Compulsory contributions to private sector	...	...	...	1	341	250	119	129	272	280
Total	**..**	**..**	**..**	**674**	**2 024**	**2 141**	**1 939**	**2 064**	**2 273**	**2 358**
Finland, million EUR										
Contribution under 2000 heading	93	2 776	10 012	15 756	21 384	22 335	22 055	23 776	25 261	25 632
Other taxes	47	22	0	404	0	0	0	0	0	0
Voluntary contributions to government	0	262	632	236	228	224	220	261	267	270
Compulsory contributions to private sector	0	123	426	508	631	632	599	626	666	668
Total	**140**	**3 183**	**11 070**	**16 904**	**22 243**	**23 191**	**22 874**	**24 663**	**26 194**	**26 570**

Table 75. **Financing social benefits / Le financement des prestations sociales** *(cont.)*
Memorandum item on the financing of social security benefits
Pour mêmoire : le financement des systèmes de sécurité sociale

	1965	1980	1990	2000	2007	2008	2009	2011	2012	2013
France, millions EUR										
Impôts de la série 2000	8 804	76 235	191 141	231 875	307 663	315 789	317 560	336 595	346 137	356 941
Autres impôts	0	895	2 950	81 001	127 511	137 510	136 019	151 201	158 663	162 838
Contributions volontaires au gouvernement	0	0	0	0	0	0	0	0	0	0
Contributions obligatoires au secteur privé	0	0	0	0	0	0	0	0	0	0
Total	**8 804**	**77 130**	**194 091**	**312 876**	**435 174**	**453 299**	**453 579**	**487 796**	**504 800**	**519 779**
Germany, million EUR										
Contribution under 2000 heading	19 876	98 659	170 449	299 440	320 594	330 453	342 658	372 040	383 487	392 548
Other taxes	0	0	0	0	0	0	0	0	0	0
Voluntary contributions to government	1 946	8 441	13 002	23 329	20 930	20 734	7 763	6 237	6 913	7 353
Compulsory contributions to private sector	107	690	1 462	6 120	8 243	8 520	8 904	9 615	9 564	9 911
Total	**21 929**	**107 791**	**184 914**	**328 889**	**349 767**	**359 707**	**359 325**	**387 892**	**399 964**	**409 812**
Greece, million EUR										
Contribution under 2000 heading	37	485	3 466	14 299	24 941	25 985	24 453	22 410	20 988	19 542
Other taxes	8	0	0	0	0	0	0	0	0	0
Voluntary contributions to government	0	0	0	0	0	0	0	0	0	0
Compulsory contributions to private sector	0	0	0	0	0	0	0	0	0	0
Total	**44**	**485**	**3 466**	**14 299**	**24 941**	**25 985**	**24 453**	**22 410**	**20 988**	**19 542**
Hungary, million HUF										
Contribution under 2000 heading	..	..	..	1 506 755	3 292 206	3 449 129	3 198 477	3 480 809	3 581 998	3 727 979
Other taxes	..	..	..	188 413	158 212	168 574	163 436	122 613	177 266	173 751
Voluntary contributions to government	..	..	..	1 273	1 762	1 792	1 626	1 676	1 590	1 503
Compulsory contributions to private sector	..	..	..	62 836	190 331	366 842	318 563	3 127	0	0
Total	**..**	**..**	**..**	**1 759 277**	**3 642 511**	**3 986 336**	**3 682 102**	**3 608 225**	**3 760 854**	**3 903 233**
Iceland, million ISK										
Contribution under 2000 heading	5	102	3 607	19 680	39 594	41 644	45 912	66 820	64 882	69 899
Other taxes	0	1 047	20 571	26 732	52 444	67 250	98 224	87 142	92 338	90 895
Voluntary contributions to government	0	0	0	0	0	0	0	0	0	0
Compulsory contributions to private sector	0	459	13 454	48 847	118 117	93 193	93 146	103 363	109 865	117 903
Total	**5**	**1 608**	**37 632**	**95 260**	**210 155**	**202 087**	**237 283**	**257 325**	**267 086**	**278 697**
Ireland, million EUR										
Contribution under 2000 heading	21	578	1 729	3 941	8 118	8 325	8 795	9 002	8 474	9 025
Other taxes	0	0	0	0	0	0	0	0	0	0
Voluntary contributions to government	0	0	0	0	0	0	0	0	0	0
Compulsory contributions to private sector	0	0	0	0	0	0	0	0	0	0
Total	**21**	**578**	**1 729**	**3 941**	**8 118**	**8 325**	**8 795**	**9 002**	**8 474**	**9 025**
Israel, million ILS										
Contribution under 2000 heading	..	..	..	27 565	37 909	40 445	41 227	48 759	50 296	53 364
Other taxes	..	..	..	0	0	0	0	0	0	0
Voluntary contributions to government	..	..	..	0	0	0	0	0	0	0
Compulsory contributions to private sector	..	..	..	0	0	2 400	5 300	13 200	17 700	22 500
Total	**..**	**..**	**..**	**27 565**	**37 909**	**42 845**	**46 527**	**61 959**	**67 996**	**75 864**
Italie, millions EUR										
Impôts de la série 2000	1 881	22 976	87 256	143 629	200 772	211 431	207 637	211 647	211 158	210 625
Autres impôts	0	0	0	0	0	0	0	0	0	0
Contributions volontaires au gouvernement	0	0	0	464	567	500	529	569	575	575
Contributions obligatoires au secteur privé	0	0	0	0	0	0	0	0	0	0
Total	**1 881**	**22 976**	**87 256**	**144 093**	**201 339**	**211 931**	**208 166**	**212 216**	**211 733**	**211 200**
Japan, billion JPY										
Contribution under 2000 heading	1 344	18 178	34 593	47 857	53 321	54 227	52 342	56 321	58 068	59 834
Other taxes	0	0	0	0	0	0	0	0	0	0
Voluntary contributions to government	0	0	0	0	0	0	0	0	0	0
Compulsory contributions to private sector	0	0	0	0	0	0	0	0	0	0
Total	**1 344**	**18 178**	**34 593**	**47 857**	**53 321**	**54 227**	**52 342**	**56 321**	**58 068**	**59 834**

Table 75. **Financing social benefits / Le financement des prestations sociales** *(cont.)*
Memorandum item on the financing of social security benefits
Pour mémoire : le financement des systèmes de sécurité sociale

	1965	1980	1990	2000	2007	2008	2009	2011	2012	2013
Korea, billion KRW										
Contribution under 2000 heading	..	73	3 760	22 759	53 588	59 415	63 939	77 234	84 380	91 596
Other taxes	..	0	0	0	0	0	0	0	0	0
Voluntary contributions to government	..	0	0	0	0	0	0	0	0	0
Compulsory contributions to private sector	..	0	0	0	0	0	0	0	0	0
Total	**..**	**73**	**3 760**	**22 759**	**53 588**	**59 415**	**63 939**	**77 234**	**84 380**	**91 596**
Luxembourg, millions EUR										
Impôts de la série 2000	86	443	1 011	2 212	3 696	3 971	4 223	4 654	4 911	5 130
Autres impôts	0	0	0	0	0	0	0	0	0	0
Contributions volontaires au gouvernement	0	0	4	18	18	19	25	31	34	35
Contributions obligatoires au secteur privé	0	0	0	0	0	0	0	0	0	0
Total	**86**	**443**	**1 015**	**2 230**	**3 714**	**3 990**	**4 248**	**4 685**	**4 944**	**5 165**
Mexico, million MXN										
Contribution under 2000 heading	..	109	17 165	167 292	307 026	321 843	346 031	411 289	454 778	490 918
Other taxes	..	0	0	0	0	0	0	0	0	0
Voluntary contributions to government	..	0	0	0	0	0	0	0	0	0
Compulsory contributions to private sector	..	25	3 840	67 352	144 331	134 265	129 207	154 996	160 669	168 111
Total	**..**	**134**	**21 005**	**234 644**	**451 357**	**456 108**	**475 238**	**566 285**	**615 447**	**659 029**
Netherlands, million EUR										
Contribution under 2000 heading	3 342	26 641	39 075	64 464	77 063	86 264	79 188	88 551	94 845	97 512
Other taxes	0	0	0	0	0	0	0	0	0	0
Voluntary contributions to government	168	1 139	163	0	0	0	0	0	0	0
Compulsory contributions to private sector	1 266	7 642	5 727	37 088	..	..	..	..	..	..
Total	**4 776**	**35 422**	**44 965**	**101 552**	**..**	**..**	**..**	**..**	**..**	**..**
New Zealand, million NZD										
Contribution under 2000 heading	..	..	..	..	..	..	..	..	..	..
Other taxes	..	..	..	..	..	..	..	..	..	..
Voluntary contributions to government	..	..	..	..	..	..	..	..	..	..
Compulsory contributions to private sector	..	..	..	..	..	..	..	..	..	..
Total	**0**	**0**	**0**	**0**	**0**	**0**	**0**	**0**	**0**	**0**
Norway, million NOK										
Contribution under 2000 heading	2 009	28 205	79 362	132 170	206 314	224 384	233 083	258 760	276 790	291 781
Other taxes	1 305	4 256	0	0	0	0	0	0	0	0
Voluntary contributions to government	0	0	0	0	0	0	0	0	0	0
Compulsory contributions to private sector	0	242	339	0	0	0	0	0	0	0
Total	**3 314**	**32 703**	**79 701**	**132 170**	**206 314**	**224 384**	**233 083**	**258 760**	**276 790**	**291 781**
Poland, million PLN										
Contribution under 2000 heading	..	..	..	97 411	141 457	145 451	153 386	175 827	196 620	204 634
Other taxes	..	..	..	0	0	0	0	0	0	0
Voluntary contributions to government	..	..	..	0	0	0	0	0	0	0
Compulsory contributions to private sector	..	..	..	0	0	0	0	0	0	0
Total	**..**	**..**	**..**	**97 411**	**141 457**	**145 451**	**153 386**	**175 827**	**196 620**	**204 634**
Portugal, million EUR										
Contribution under 2000 heading	22	531	4 026	10 168	14 274	14 970	14 998	15 671	14 621	15 115
Other taxes	0	1	29	434	658	692	689	715	892	977
Voluntary contributions to government	0	0	0	0	0	0	0	0	0	0
Compulsory contributions to private sector	0	0	0	0	0	0	0	0	0	0
Total	**22**	**532**	**4 055**	**10 602**	**14 932**	**15 661**	**15 687**	**16 386**	**15 513**	**16 092**
Slovak Republic, million EUR										
Contribution under 2000 heading	..	..	..	4 409	7 192	7 909	7 858	8 479	8 907	9 783
Other taxes	..	..	..	0	0	0	0	0	0	0
Voluntary contributions to government	..	..	..	0	22	25	26	34	22	17
Compulsory contributions to private sector	..	..	..	0	701	706	690	756	645	385
Total	**..**	**..**	**..**	**4 409**	**7 915**	**8 640**	**8 574**	**9 270**	**9 574**	**10 186**

Table 75. **Financing social benefits / Le financement des prestations sociales** *(cont.)*
Memorandum item on the financing of social security benefits
Pour mémoire : le financement des systèmes de sécurité sociale

	1965	1980	1990	2000	2007	2008	2009	2011	2012	2013
Slovenia, million EUR										
Contribution under 2000 heading	..	..	..	2 631	4 724	5 221	5 276	5 407	5 365	5 332
Other taxes	..	..	..	0	0	0	0	0	0	0
Voluntary contributions to government	..	..	..	0	0	0	0	0	0	0
Compulsory contributions to private sector	..	..	..	0	0	0	0	0	0	0
Total	**..**	**..**	**..**	**2 631**	**4 724**	**5 221**	**5 276**	**5 407**	**5 365**	**5 332**
Spain, million EUR										
Contribution under 2000 heading	350	10 682	36 722	76 421	129 170	134 372	131 510	129 535	123 967	120 750
Other taxes	0	49	0	0	0	0	0	0	0	0
Voluntary contributions to government	0	0	0	0	0	0	0	0	0	0
Compulsory contributions to private sector	0	0	0	0	0	0	0	0	0	0
Total	**350**	**10 731**	**36 722**	**76 421**	**129 170**	**134 372**	**131 510**	**129 535**	**123 967**	**120 750**
Sweden, million SEK										
Contribution under 2000 heading	4 851	74 647	205 867	306 974	388 505	372 762	357 289	361 987	375 628	376 684
Other taxes	1 407	0	0	0	0	0	0	0	0	0
Voluntary contributions to government	0	0	0	0	0	0	0	0	0	0
Compulsory contributions to private sector	0	0	0	0	0	0	0	0	0	0
Total	**6 258**	**74 647**	**205 867**	**306 974**	**388 505**	**372 762**	**357 289**	**361 987**	**375 628**	**376 684**
Suisse, millions CHF										
Impôts de la série 2000	1 670	10 844	19 961	31 059	35 115	36 860	38 142	40 941	41 840	42 758
Autres impôts	336	778	1 185	1 918	4 919	5 568	5 258	6 450	6 853	6 786
Contributions volontaires au gouvernement	95	431	0	0	0	0	0	0	0	0
Contributions obligatoires au secteur privé	2 505	9 674	17 776	22 928	35 484	35 675	36 810	41 492	41 888	42 807
Total	**4 606**	**21 727**	**38 922**	**55 905**	**75 518**	**78 102**	**80 210**	**88 883**	**90 581**	**92 350**
Turkey, million TRY										
Contribution under 2000 heading	0	0	15	7 543	44 052	57 637	57 595	100 687	106 405	125 871
Other taxes	0	0	0	0	0	0	0	0	0	0
Voluntary contributions to government	0	0	0	0	0	0	0	0	0	0
Compulsory contributions to private sector	0	0	0	0	0	0	0	0	0	0
Total	**0**	**0**	**15**	**7 543**	**44 052**	**57 637**	**57 595**	**100 687**	**106 405**	**125 871**
United Kingdom, million GBP										
Contribution under 2000 heading	1 685	13 531	34 457	60 252	93 210	98 319	94 445	101 441	104 319	106 085
Other taxes	0	0	0	0	0	0	0	0	0	0
Voluntary contributions to government	0	11	3 288	5 907	14 478	15 282	16 089	16 786	19 217	16 759
Compulsory contributions to private sector	1 148	13 350	7 945	8 308	9 969	10 699	9 545	8 928	8 092	6 592
Total	**2 833**	**26 892**	**45 690**	**74 467**	**117 657**	**124 300**	**120 079**	**127 165**	**129 436**	**129 436**
United States, million USD										
Contribution under 2000 heading	22 192	159 763	396 972	683 104	907 433	930 086	902 632	848 299	880 925	1 030 633
Other taxes	0	0	0	0	0	0	0	0	0	0
Voluntary contributions to government	488	3 407	11 719	22 562	51 617	55 369	57 954	63 761	64 680	69 939
Compulsory contributions to private sector	0	0	0	0	0	0	0	0	0	0
Total	**22 680**	**163 170**	**408 691**	**705 666**	**959 050**	**985 455**	**960 586**	**912 060**	**945 605**	**1 100 572**

StatLink http://dx.doi.org/10.1787/888933277370

Revenue Statistics 1965-2014
Statistiques des recettes publiques 1965-2014

PART III/PARTIE III

C. Social security contributions and payroll taxes paid by government

C. Les cotisations de sécurité sociale et impôts sur les salaires payés par les administrations publiques

Social security contributions and payroll taxes paid by government

During the revision of the Interpretative guide in 1984, the question arose of how to treat taxes paid by government. The two most prominent examples of such taxes are social security contributions and payroll taxes paid by government in respect of its employees. After a long discussion it was decided that the data shown in this publication should continue to include taxes paid by government (see §5 of the Interpretative guide in Annex A).

Whilst it was recognised that for certain purposes (e.g. to show the cash flow to the government sector from the private sector) it would be appropriate to eliminate taxes paid by one sector of government to another or tax payments between different units of the same sector of government, the view was taken that to record tax flows in the context of the economy as a whole required that taxes paid by government should be included in the data. This treatment ensures that the different resource flows of an economy, including the calculation of the output of government, are measured consistently in after-tax units. Nevertheless, it was decided that data on identifiable taxes paid by government should be separately identified in a memorandum item and this is the purpose of the country tables which follow.

The data that are reproduced in the following tables refer to actual compulsory payments made by general government in respect of their employees. Fictive, voluntary and imputed contributions are excluded from these data. The definitions of social security contributions, payroll taxes and general government are those set out in §35 to §41, §42 and §3 to §4 of the Interpretative guide. Information on the other taxes paid by government (namely property taxes and consumption taxes) is not available in most countries, although it is believed that in all countries taxes based upon payroll are the most important taxes paid by government. In many cases, the data are estimates and are not always constructed on a basis consistent with that used in the main tables.

Cotisations de sécurité sociale et impôts sur les salaires payés par les administrations publiques

Lors de la révision du Guide d'interprétation en 1984, la question s'est posée de savoir comment il convenait de traiter les impôts acquittés par les administrations. Les deux exemples les plus marquants d'impôts de ce type sont les cotisations de sécurité sociale et les impôts sur les salaires acquittés par les administrations au titre de leurs agents. Après un échange de vues approfondi, il a été décidé que les données présentées dans cette publication continueraient d'inclure les impôts acquittés par les administrations (voir le §5 du Guide d'interprétation dans l'Annexe A).

Alors qu'il a été admis qu'à certaines fins (par exemple, pour mesurer le flux de paiements allant du secteur privé au secteur des administrations), il conviendrait d'exclure les impôts payés par un secteur de l'administration à un autre ou les impôts acquittés entre les différentes unités d'un même secteur de l'administration, il a été décidé que les impôts acquittés par les administrations devaient être inclus dans les données lorsque l'on comptabilise tous les flux d'impôts de l'ensemble de l'économie. Cette prise en compte permet d'être sûr que les différents flux de ressources d'une économie, y compris la valeur de la production des administrations, sont bien mesurés de façon cohérente nette d'impôt.

Il a été toutefois décidé que les données sur les impôts acquittés par les administrations et que l'on pouvait identifier isolément seraient présentées séparément dans un poste pour mémoire et c'est l'objet des tableaux par pays qui suivent.

Les données reproduites dans les tableaux suivants ont trait aux montants effectifs versés par les administrations publiques au titre de leurs agents. Les cotisations fictives, volontaires et imputées sont exclues de ces données. Les définitions des cotisations de sécurité sociale, des impôts sur les salaires et des administrations publiques correspondent aux définitions données aux §35 à § 41, §42 et §3 à § 4 du Guide d'interprétation. Les informations sur les autres impôts payés par les administrations (à savoir impôts sur la propriété et impôts sur la consommation) ne sont pas disponibles pour la plupart des pays, même s'il semble bien que, dans tous les pays, les impôts assis sur les salaires sont les impôts les plus importants qu'acquittent les administrations. Dans beaucoup de cas, les données sont estimées et ne sont pas toujours établies sur une base compatible avec celle utilisée dans les tableaux principaux.

Table 76. **Social security contributions and payroll taxes paid by government / Les cotisations de sécurité sociale et impôts sur les salaires payés par les administrations publiques**

	1965	1980	1990	2000	2007	2008	2009	2011	2012	2013
Australia, million AUD										
2000 Social security contributions										
Federal or Central government	..	..	..	..	..	..	..	..	..	..
State/Regional	..	..	..	..	..	..	..	..	..	..
Local government	..	..	..	..	..	..	..	..	..	..
Social Security Funds	..	..	..	..	..	..	..	..	..	..
Total	**0**	**0**	**0**	**0**	**0**	**0**	**0**	**0**	**0**	**0**
3000 Taxes on payroll and workforce										
Federal or Central government	0	4	0	0	0	0	0	0	0	0
State/Regional	15	302	0	0	0	0	0	0	0	0
Local government	0	0	2	19	41	35	34	30	36	37
Social Security Funds	0	0	0	0	0	0	0	0	0	0
Multi-jurisdictional (University) sector[1]	0	0	90	282	455	485	519	585	634	666
Total	**15**	**306**	**92**	**301**	**496**	**520**	**553**	**615**	**670**	**703**
2000+3000 Total	**15**	**306**	**92**	**301**	**496**	**520**	**553**	**615**	**670**	**703**
Austria, million EUR[2]										
2000 Social security contributions										
Federal or Central government	48	230	337	536	1 161	1 223	1 368	1 414	1 492	1 512
State/Regional	13	166	337	692	988	1 093	1 179	1 221	1 244	1 253
Local government	17	145	292	699	1 036	1 135	1 216	1 290	1 341	1 382
Social Security Funds	11	79	48	176	203	216	224	232	240	250
Total	**88**	**619**	**1 015**	**2 102**	**3 388**	**3 667**	**3 988**	**4 157**	**4 318**	**4 397**
3000 Taxes on payroll and workforce										
Federal or Central government	0	49	134	165	314	434	501	532	549	545
State/Regional	0	48	74	232	351	408	453	470	480	486
Local government	1	29	79	301	262	316	355	364	381	396
Social Security Funds	0	0	39	44	51	54	55	56	59	61
Total	**1**	**125**	**326**	**742**	**977**	**1 211**	**1 365**	**1 423**	**1 470**	**1 488**
2000+3000 Total	**89**	**745**	**1 341**	**2 844**	**4 366**	**4 878**	**5 352**	**5 580**	**5 788**	**5 885**
Belgique, millions EUR										
2000 Cotisations de sécurité sociale										
Administration fédérale ou centrale	..	536	211	255	429	459	480	498	517	532
Administration d'un Etat/Länder	..	0	614	1 186	1 533	1 622	1 714	1 884	1 900	1 988
Administrations locales	..	434	768	1 152	1 816	1 914	2 064	2 343	2 848	3 230
Administrations de sécurite sociale	..	89	176	252	308	333	361	394	417	437
Total	**..**	**1 059**	**1 769**	**2 845**	**4 086**	**4 327**	**4 619**	**5 118**	**5 683**	**6 187**
3000 Impôts sur les salaires										
Administration fédérale ou centrale	..	..	..	..	..	..	..	..	..	..
Administration d'un Etat/Länder	..	..	..	..	..	..	..	..	..	..
Administrations locales	..	..	..	..	..	..	..	..	..	..
Administrations de sécurite sociale	..	..	..	..	..	..	..	..	..	..
Total	**..**	**0**	**0**	**0**	**0**	**0**	**0**	**0**	**0**	**0**
2000+3000 Total	**..**	**1 059**	**1 769**	**2 845**	**4 086**	**4 327**	**4 619**	**5 118**	**5 683**	**6 187**
Canada, million CAD										
2000 Social security contributions										
Federal or Central government	..	..	..	944	1 130	1 212	1 302	1 408	1 452	1 493
State/Regional	..	..	..	3 023	4 269	4 517	4 970	5 348	5 562	5 612
Local government	..	..	..	2 225	2 806	2 888	3 396	3 548	3 742	3 775
Social Security Funds	..	..	..	0	0	0	0	0	0	0
Total	**..**	**..**	**..**	**6 192**	**8 205**	**8 617**	**9 668**	**10 304**	**10 756**	**10 880**
3000 Taxes on payroll and workforce										
Federal or Central government	..	..	..	0	0	0	0	0	0	0
State/Regional	..	..	..	173	234	243	263	259	260	267
Local government	..	..	..	0	0	0	0	0	0	0
Social Security Funds	..	..	..	0	0	0	0	0	0	0
Total	**..**	**..**	**..**	**173**	**234**	**243**	**263**	**259**	**260**	**267**
2000+3000 Total	**..**	**..**	**..**	**6 365**	**8 439**	**8 860**	**9 931**	**10 563**	**11 016**	**11 147**

Table 76. **Social security contributions and payroll taxes paid by government / Les cotisations de sécurité sociale et impôts sur les salaires payés par les administrations publiques** *(cont.)*

	1965	1980	1990	2000	2007	2008	2009	2011	2012	2013
Chile, million CLP										
2000 Social security contributions										
Federal or Central government	..	..	..	43 210	107 911	120 417	125 449	169 141	177 036	186 652
State/Regional	..	..	..	..	..	..	..	..	..	..
Local government	..	..	..	11 317	30 218	34 213	35 262	45 580	48 269	51 114
Social Security Funds	..	..	..	106	263	296	297	467	500	550
Total	**..**	**..**	**..**	**54 633**	**138 392**	**154 927**	**161 008**	**215 188**	**225 805**	**238 315**
3000 Taxes on payroll and workforce										
Federal or Central government	..	..	..	..	..	..	..	..	..	..
State/Regional	..	..	..	..	..	..	..	..	..	..
Local government	..	..	..	..	..	..	..	..	..	..
Social Security Funds	..	..	..	..	..	..	..	..	..	..
Total	**..**	**..**	**..**	**..**	**..**	**..**	**..**	**..**	**..**	**..**
2000+3000 Total	**..**	**..**	**..**	**54 633**	**138 392**	**154 927**	**161 008**	**215 188**	**225 805**	**238 315**
Czech Republic, million CZK										
2000 Social security contributions										
Federal or Central government	..	..	..	28 050	44 437	45 419	46 351	43 857	45 424	46 360
State/Regional	..	..	..	..	..	..	..	..	..	..
Local government	..	..	..	5 660	8 253	8 914	8 917	9 268	9 124	9 448
Social Security Funds	..	..	..	510	791	867	908	935	894	881
Total	**..**	**..**	**..**	**34 220**	**53 481**	**55 200**	**56 177**	**54 060**	**55 442**	**56 689**
3000 Taxes on payroll and workforce										
Federal or Central government	..	..	..	..	..	..	..	..	..	..
State/Regional	..	..	..	..	..	..	..	..	..	..
Local government	..	..	..	..	..	..	..	..	..	..
Social Security Funds	..	..	..	..	..	..	..	..	..	..
Total	**..**	**..**	**..**	**0**	**0**	**0**	**0**	**0**	**0**	**0**
2000+3000 Total	**..**	**..**	**..**	**34 220**	**53 481**	**55 200**	**56 177**	**54 060**	**55 442**	**56 689**
Denmark, million DKK										
2000 Social security contributions										
Federal or Central government	..	179	..	..	..	..	..	..	..	..
State/Regional	..	..	..	..	..	..	..	..	..	..
Local government	..	0	..	..	..	..	..	..	..	..
Social Security Funds	..	0	..	..	..	..	..	..	..	..
Total	**..**	**179**	**0**	**0**	**0**	**0**	**0**	**0**	**0**	**0**
3000 Taxes on payroll and workforce										
Federal or Central government	..	..	..	..	..	..	..	..	..	..
State/Regional	..	..	..	..	..	..	..	..	..	..
Local government	..	..	..	..	..	..	..	..	..	..
Social Security Funds	..	..	..	..	..	..	..	..	..	..
Total	**..**	**0**	**0**	**0**	**0**	**0**	**0**	**0**	**0**	**0**
2000+3000 Total	**..**	**179**	**0**	**0**	**0**	**0**	**0**	**0**	**0**	**0**
Estonia, million EUR										
2000 Social security contributions										
Federal or Central government	..	..	..	127	255	310	319	327	343	365
State/Regional	..	..	..	..	..	..	..	..	..	..
Local government	..	..	..	47	155	186	181	177	181	202
Social Security Funds	..	..	..	0	3	8	38	32	25	24
Total	**..**	**..**	**..**	**175**	**412**	**504**	**538**	**536**	**549**	**591**
3000 Taxes on payroll and workforce										
Federal or Central government	..	..	..	..	..	..	..	..	..	..
State/Regional	..	..	..	..	..	..	..	..	..	..
Local government	..	..	..	..	..	..	..	..	..	..
Social Security Funds	..	..	..	..	..	..	..	..	..	..
Total	**..**	**..**	**..**	**0**	**0**	**0**	**0**	**0**	**0**	**0**
2000+3000 Total	**..**	**..**	**..**	**175**	**412**	**504**	**538**	**536**	**549**	**591**

Table 76. **Social security contributions and payroll taxes paid by government / Les cotisations de sécurité sociale et impôts sur les salaires payés par les administrations publiques** *(cont.)*

	1965	1980	1990	2000	2007	2008	2009	2011	2012	2013
Finland, million EUR										
2000 Social security contributions										
Federal or Central government	..	61	196	908	1 057	1 134	1 140	1 134	1 174	1 226
State/Regional	..	..	..	..	..	..	..	..	..	..
Local government	..	170	1 709	2 786	4 061	4 291	4 318	4 568	4 755	4 881
Social Security Funds	..	9	33	75	88	90	90	93	97	102
Total	**..**	**240**	**1 938**	**3 769**	**5 206**	**5 515**	**5 548**	**5 795**	**6 026**	**6 209**
3000 Taxes on payroll and workforce										
Federal or Central government	..	1	..	..	..	..	..	..	..	..
State/Regional	..	..	..	..	..	..	..	..	..	..
Local government	..	4	..	..	..	..	..	..	..	..
Social Security Funds	..	0	..	..	..	..	..	..	..	..
Total	**..**	**5**	**0**	**0**	**0**	**0**	**0**	**0**	**0**	**0**
2000+3000 Total	**..**	**245**	**1 938**	**3 769**	**5 206**	**5 515**	**5 548**	**5 795**	**6 026**	**6 209**
France, millions EUR										
2000 Cotisations de sécurité sociale										
Administration fédérale ou centrale	..	3 816	8 063	10 474	12 438	12 313	12 608	12 781	12 800	12 839
Administration d'un Etat/Länder	..	..	..	..	..	..	..	..	..	..
Administrations locales	..	2 369	5 542	10 364	15 913	16 915	17 568	18 349	18 935	19 984
Administrations de sécurite sociale	..	2 594	6 940	10 827	14 035	14 519	15 117	15 857	16 131	16 614
Total	**..**	**8 779**	**20 545**	**31 665**	**42 386**	**43 747**	**45 293**	**46 987**	**47 866**	**49 437**
3000 Impôts sur les salaires										
Administration fédérale ou centrale	..	836	494	854	1 558	1 596	1 568	1 639	1 653	1 703
Administration d'un Etat/Länder	..	..	..	..	..	..	..	..	..	..
Administrations locales	..	27	107	324	549	634	675	721	750	791
Administrations de sécurite sociale	..	629	2 234	3 413	4 531	4 696	4 910	5 115	5 156	5 374
Total	**..**	**1 492**	**2 835**	**4 591**	**6 638**	**6 926**	**7 153**	**7 475**	**7 559**	**7 868**
2000+3000 Total	**..**	**10 271**	**23 380**	**36 256**	**49 024**	**50 673**	**52 446**	**54 462**	**55 425**	**57 305**
Germany, million EUR										
2000 Social security contributions										
Federal or Central government	775	1 324	2 376	1 615	1 203	1 252	1 284	1 359	1 398	1 429
State/Regional	293	2 611	4 647	7 645	5 314	5 522	5 652	6 073	6 292	6 419
Local government	325	3 140	5 791	10 561	9 940	10 346	10 594	11 370	11 794	12 035
Social Security Funds	1 495	456	767	1 884	2 283	2 356	2 398	2 574	2 664	2 721
Total	**2 887**	**7 531**	**13 581**	**21 705**	**18 740**	**19 476**	**19 928**	**21 376**	**22 148**	**22 604**
3000 Taxes on payroll and workforce										
Federal or Central government	..	..	..	..	..	..	..	..	..	..
State/Regional	..	..	..	..	..	..	..	..	..	..
Local government	..	..	..	..	..	..	..	..	..	..
Social Security Funds	..	..	..	..	..	..	..	..	..	..
Total	**0**	**0**	**0**	**0**	**0**	**0**	**0**	**0**	**0**	**0**
2000+3000 Total	**2 887**	**7 531**	**13 581**	**21 705**	**18 740**	**19 476**	**19 928**	**21 376**	**22 148**	**22 604**
Greece, million EUR										
2000 Social security contributions										
Federal or Central government	..	..	124	1 542	2 888	3 234	3 403	3 695	3 283	2 990
State/Regional	..	..	..	..	..	..	..	..	..	..
Local government	..	..	0	0	0	0	0	0	0	0
Social Security Funds	..	..	0	200	440	492	502	346	401	347
Total	**..**	**..**	**124**	**1 742**	**3 328**	**3 726**	**3 905**	**4 041**	**3 684**	**3 337**
3000 Taxes on payroll and workforce										
Federal or Central government	..	..	..	..	..	..	..	..	..	..
State/Regional	..	..	..	..	..	..	..	..	..	..
Local government	..	..	..	..	..	..	..	..	..	..
Social Security Funds	..	..	..	..	..	..	..	..	..	..
Total	**0**	**0**	**0**	**0**	**0**	**0**	**0**	**0**	**0**	**0**
2000+3000 Total	**0**	**0**	**124**	**1 742**	**3 328**	**3 726**	**3 905**	**4 041**	**3 684**	**3 337**

Table 76. **Social security contributions and payroll taxes paid by government / Les cotisations de sécurité sociale et impôts sur les salaires payés par les administrations publiques** *(cont.)*

	1965	1980	1990	2000	2007	2008	2009	2011	2012	2013
Hungary, million HUF										
2000 Social security contributions										
Federal or Central government	..	..	..	148 251	293 684	295 793	266 442	243 241	320 040	449 428
State/Regional	..	..	..	..	..	..	..	..	..	..
Local government	..	..	..	173 475	343 306	347 498	307 680	260 764	208 411	124 111
Social Security Funds	..	..	..	4 936	8 052	8 353	7 547	3 016	2 992	2 781
Total	**..**	**..**	**..**	**326 661**	**645 042**	**651 644**	**581 669**	**507 021**	**531 444**	**576 320**
3000 Taxes on payroll and workforce										
Federal or Central government	..	..	..	13 901	7 287	7 195	6 913	7 979	9 140	12 435
State/Regional	..	..	..	..	..	..	..	..	..	..
Local government	..	..	..	25 990	11 928	11 493	11 175	10 656	10 382	4 224
Social Security Funds	..	..	..	406	162	169	171	13	119	101
Total	**..**	**..**	**..**	**40 297**	**19 377**	**18 857**	**18 259**	**18 649**	**19 641**	**16 760**
2000+3000 Total	**..**	**..**	**..**	**366 958**	**664 420**	**670 500**	**599 927**	**525 670**	**551 085**	**593 080**
Iceland, million ISK										
2000 Social security contributions										
Federal or Central government	..	..	..	..	..	..	..	..	..	..
State/Regional	..	..	..	..	..	..	..	..	..	..
Local government	..	..	..	..	..	..	..	..	..	..
Social Security Funds	..	..	..	..	..	..	..	..	..	..
Total	**..**	**..**	**..**	**..**	**..**	**..**	**..**	**..**	**..**	**..**
3000 Taxes on payroll and workforce										
Federal or Central government	..	..	..	..	..	..	..	..	..	..
State/Regional	..	..	..	..	..	..	..	..	..	..
Local government	..	..	..	..	..	..	..	..	..	..
Social Security Funds	..	..	..	..	..	..	..	..	..	..
Total	**..**	**..**	**..**	**..**	**..**	**..**	**..**	**..**	**..**	**..**
2000+3000 Total	**..**	**..**	**..**	**..**	**..**	**..**	**..**	**..**	**..**	**..**
Ireland, million EUR										
2000 Social security contributions										
Federal or Central government	..	21	65	166	460	475	422	429	401	426
State/Regional	..	..	..	..	..	..	..	..	..	..
Local government	..	25	83	277	862	890	792	805	751	799
Social Security Funds	..	0	1	4	6	6	6	6	6	6
Total	**..**	**46**	**149**	**447**	**1 328**	**1 370**	**1 220**	**1 240**	**1 158**	**1 231**
3000 Taxes on payroll and workforce										
Federal or Central government	..	..	..	..	..	..	..	..	..	..
State/Regional	..	..	..	..	..	..	..	..	..	..
Local government	..	..	..	..	..	..	..	..	..	..
Social Security Funds	..	..	..	..	..	..	..	..	..	..
Total	**..**	**0**	**0**	**0**	**0**	**0**	**0**	**0**	**0**	**0**
2000+3000 Total	**..**	**46**	**149**	**447**	**1 328**	**1 370**	**1 220**	**1 240**	**1 158**	**1 231**
Israel, million ILS										
2000 Social security contributions										
Federal or Central government	..	..	..	840	1 030	1 050	1 060	1 320	1 370	1 550
State/Regional	..	..	..	..	..	..	..	..	..	..
Local government	..	..	..	280	340	350	350	440	450	510
Social Security Funds	..	..	..	0	0	0	0	0	0	0
Total	**..**	**..**	**..**	**1 120**	**1 370**	**1 400**	**1 410**	**1 760**	**1 820**	**2 060**
3000 Taxes on payroll and workforce										
Federal or Central government	..	..	..	2 330	3 600	3 830	3 970	4 400	4 680	4 930
State/Regional	..	..	..	..	..	..	..	..	..	..
Local government	..	..	..	780	1 120	920	910	1 010	1 070	1 130
Social Security Funds	..	..	..	0	0	0	0	0	0	0
Total	**..**	**..**	**..**	**3 110**	**4 720**	**4 750**	**4 880**	**5 410**	**5 750**	**6 060**
2000+3000 Total	**..**	**..**	**..**	**4 230**	**6 090**	**6 150**	**6 290**	**7 170**	**7 570**	**8 120**

Table 76. **Social security contributions and payroll taxes paid by government / Les cotisations de sécurité sociale et impôts sur les salaires payés par les administrations publiques** *(cont.)*

	1965	1980	1990	2000	2007	2008	2009	2011	2012	2013
Italie, millions EUR										
2000 Cotisations de sécurité sociale										
Administration fédérale ou centrale	...	...	...	0	0	0	0	0	0	0
Administration d'un Etat/Länder	...	...	...	...	...	...	...	...	...	...
Administrations locales	...	...	...	0	0	0	0	0	0	0
Administrations de sécurite sociale	...	...	...	36 679	47 394	49 002	49 734	50 701	50 129	49 856
Total	..	..	..	**36 679**	**47 394**	**49 002**	**49 734**	**50 701**	**50 129**	**49 856**
3000 Impôts sur les salaires										
Administration fédérale ou centrale	...	...	...	...	...	...	...	...	...	...
Administration d'un Etat/Länder	...	...	...	...	...	...	...	...	...	...
Administrations locales	...	...	...	...	...	...	...	...	...	...
Administrations de sécurite sociale	...	...	...	...	...	...	...	...	...	...
Total	..	..	..	**0**	**0**	**0**	**0**	**0**	**0**	**0**
2000+3000 Total	..	..	..	**36 679**	**47 394**	**49 002**	**49 734**	**50 701**	**50 129**	**49 856**
Japan, billion JPY										
2000 Social security contributions										
Federal or Central government	...	...	507	732	766	791	816	776	778	810
State/Regional	...	...	...	...	...	...	...	...	...	...
Local government	...	...	1 510	2 168	2 216	2 245	2 203	2 387	2 406	2 430
Social Security Funds	...	...	0	0	0	0	0	0	0	0
Total	..	..	**2 017**	**2 900**	**2 982**	**3 036**	**3 019**	**3 163**	**3 184**	**3 240**
3000 Taxes on payroll and workforce										
Federal or Central government	...	...	...	...	...	...	...	...	...	...
State/Regional	...	...	...	...	...	...	...	...	...	...
Local government	...	...	...	...	...	...	...	...	...	...
Social Security Funds	...	...	...	...	...	...	...	...	...	...
Total	..	..	**0**	**0**	**0**	**0**	**0**	**0**	**0**	**0**
2000+3000 Total	..	..	**2 017**	**2 900**	**2 982**	**3 036**	**3 019**	**3 163**	**3 184**	**3 240**
Korea, billion KRW										
2000 Social security contributions										
Federal or Central government	...	...	...	...	...	...	...	...	...	...
State/Regional	...	...	...	...	...	...	...	...	...	...
Local government	...	...	...	...	...	...	...	...	...	...
Social Security Funds	...	...	...	...	...	...	...	...	...	...
Total	..	..	..	..	..	..	..	..	..	..
3000 Taxes on payroll and workforce										
Federal or Central government	...	...	...	...	...	...	...	...	...	...
State/Regional	...	...	...	...	...	...	...	...	...	...
Local government	...	...	...	...	...	...	...	...	...	...
Social Security Funds	...	...	...	...	...	...	...	...	...	...
Total	..	..	..	..	..	..	..	..	..	..
2000+3000 Total	..	..	..	..	..	..	..	..	..	..
Luxembourg, millions EUR										
2000 Cotisations de sécurité sociale										
Administration fédérale ou centrale	...	...	...	...	...	...	...	...	...	...
Administration d'un Etat/Länder	...	...	...	...	...	...	...	...	...	...
Administrations locales	...	...	...	...	...	...	...	...	...	...
Administrations de sécurite sociale	...	...	...	...	...	...	...	...	...	...
Total	..	..	..	..	..	..	..	..	..	..
3000 Impôts sur les salaires										
Administration fédérale ou centrale	...	...	...	...	...	...	...	...	...	...
Administration d'un Etat/Länder	...	...	...	...	...	...	...	...	...	...
Administrations locales	...	...	...	...	...	...	...	...	...	...
Administrations de sécurite sociale	...	...	...	...	...	...	...	...	...	...
Total	..	..	..	..	..	..	..	..	..	..
2000+3000 Total	..	..	**0**	**0**	**0**	**0**	**0**	**0**	**0**	**0**

Table 76. **Social security contributions and payroll taxes paid by government / Les cotisations de sécurité sociale et impôts sur les salaires payés par les administrations publiques** *(cont.)*

	1965	1980	1990	2000	2007	2008	2009	2011	2012	2013
Mexico, million MXN										
2000 Social security contributions										
Federal or Central government	..	25	2 952	73 948	140 647	145 147	167 568	199 488	224 566	243 849
State/Regional	..	0	0	0	0	0	0	0	0	0
Local government	..	0	0	0	0	0	0	0	0	0
Social Security Funds	..	0	0	0	0	0	0	0	0	0
Total	..	**25**	**2 952**	**73 948**	**140 647**	**145 147**	**167 568**	**199 488**	**224 566**	**243 849**
3000 Taxes on payroll and workforce										
Federal or Central government	...	...	...	...	...	...	...	...	...	...
State/Regional	...	...	...	...	...	...	...	...	...	...
Local government	...	...	...	...	...	...	...	...	...	...
Social Security Funds	...	...	...	...	...	...	...	...	...	...
Total	..	**0**	**0**	**0**	**0**	**0**	**0**	**0**	**0**	**0**
2000+3000 Total	..	**25**	**2 952**	**73 948**	**140 647**	**145 147**	**167 568**	**199 488**	**224 566**	**243 849**
Netherlands, million EUR										
2000 Social security contributions										
Federal or Central government	63	1 366	286	..	..	..	..	..	..	..
State/Regional	...	...	...	...	...	...	...	...	...	...
Local government	0	0	0	...	...	...	...	...	...	...
Social Security Funds	7	91	59	...	...	...	...	...	...	...
Total	**70**	**1 457**	**345**	**2 006**	**4 310**	**4 640**	**4 802**	..	..	..
3000 Taxes on payroll and workforce										
Federal or Central government	...	...	...	...	...	...	...	...	...	...
State/Regional	...	...	...	...	...	...	...	...	...	...
Local government	...	...	...	...	...	...	...	...	...	...
Social Security Funds	...	...	...	...	...	...	...	...	...	...
Total	**0**	**0**	**0**	**0**	**0**	**0**	**0**	**0**	**0**	**0**
2000+3000 Total	**70**	**1 457**	**345**	**2 006**	**4 310**	**4 640**	**4 802**	**0**	**0**	**0**
New Zealand, million NZD										
2000 Social security contributions										
Federal or Central government	...	...	...	...	...	...	...	...	...	...
State/Regional	...	...	...	...	...	...	...	...	...	...
Local government	...	...	...	...	...	...	...	...	...	...
Social Security Funds	...	...	...	...	...	...	...	...	...	...
Total	**0**	**0**	**0**	**0**	**0**	**0**	**0**	**0**	**0**	**0**
3000 Taxes on payroll and workforce										
Federal or Central government	...	...	...	...	...	...	...	...	...	...
State/Regional	...	...	...	...	...	...	...	...	...	...
Local government	...	...	...	...	...	...	...	...	...	...
Social Security Funds	...	...	...	...	...	...	...	...	...	...
Total	**0**	**0**	**0**	**0**	**0**	**0**	**0**	**0**	**0**	**0**
2000+3000 Total	**0**	**0**	**0**	**0**	**0**	**0**	**0**	**0**	**0**	**0**
Norway, million NOK										
2000 Social security contributions										
Federal or Central government	..	1 242	2 859	11 895	30 761	34 322	35 295	40 393	43 837	44 214
State/Regional	...	...	...	...	...	...	...	...	...	...
Local government	..	4 538	11 964	24 831	31 862	35 760	39 085	46 292	48 033	52 852
Social Security Funds	..	1 222	3 064	0	0	0	0	0	0	0
Total	..	**7 002**	**17 887**	**36 726**	**62 623**	**70 081**	**74 380**	**86 684**	**91 870**	**97 067**
3000 Taxes on payroll and workforce										
Federal or Central government	...	...	...	...	...	...	...	...	...	...
State/Regional	...	...	...	...	...	...	...	...	...	...
Local government	...	...	...	...	...	...	...	...	...	...
Social Security Funds	...	...	...	...	...	...	...	...	...	...
Total	..	**0**	**0**	**0**	**0**	**0**	**0**	**0**	**0**	**0**
2000+3000 Total	..	**7 002**	**17 887**	**36 726**	**62 623**	**70 081**	**74 380**	**86 684**	**91 870**	**97 067**

Table 76. **Social security contributions and payroll taxes paid by government / Les cotisations de sécurité sociale et impôts sur les salaires payés par les administrations publiques** *(cont.)*

	1965	1980	1990	2000	2007	2008	2009	2011	2012	2013
Poland, million PLN										
2000 Social security contributions										
Federal or Central government	..	..	..	2 834	5 801	5 642	6 403	6 733	7 634	8 172
State/Regional	..	..	..	..	..	..	..	..	..	..
Local government	..	..	..	5 204	9 654	9 994	10 795	11 946	13 152	13 402
Social Security Funds	..	..	..	943	382	393	881	440	498	507
Total	**..**	**..**	**..**	**8 981**	**15 837**	**16 029**	**18 079**	**19 119**	**21 284**	**22 081**
3000 Taxes on payroll and workforce										
Federal or Central government	..	..	..	..	..	..	..	..	..	..
State/Regional	..	..	..	..	..	..	..	..	..	..
Local government	..	..	..	..	..	..	..	..	..	..
Social Security Funds	..	..	..	..	..	..	..	..	..	..
Total	**..**	**..**	**..**	**0**	**0**	**0**	**0**	**0**	**0**	**..**
2000+3000 Total	**..**	**..**	**..**	**8 981**	**15 837**	**16 029**	**18 079**	**19 119**	**21 284**	**22 081**
Portugal, million EUR										
2000 Social security contributions										
Federal or Central government	..	0	0	0	..	..	..	..	..	..
State/Regional	..	..	..	..	..	..	..	..	..	..
Local government	..	0	33	197	..	..	..	..	..	..
Social Security Funds	..	4	0	0	..	..	..	..	..	..
Total	**..**	**4**	**33**	**197**	**0**	**0**	**0**	**0**	**0**	**0**
3000 Taxes on payroll and workforce										
Federal or Central government	..	..	..	..	..	..	..	..	..	..
State/Regional	..	..	..	..	..	..	..	..	..	..
Local government	..	..	..	..	..	..	..	..	..	..
Social Security Funds	..	..	..	..	..	..	..	..	..	..
Total	**..**	**0**	**0**	**0**	**0**	**0**	**0**	**0**	**0**	**0**
2000+3000 Total	**..**	**4**	**33**	**197**	**0**	**0**	**0**	**0**	**0**	**0**
Slovak Republic, million EUR										
2000 Social security contributions										
Federal or Central government	..	..	..	489	592	642	771	870	841	909
State/Regional	..	..	..	..	..	..	..	..	..	..
Local government	..	..	..	130	427	454	489	510	520	561
Social Security Funds	..	..	..	22	26	31	29	30	31	32
Total	**..**	**..**	**..**	**642**	**1 044**	**1 126**	**1 288**	**1 411**	**1 392**	**1 503**
3000 Taxes on payroll and workforce										
Federal or Central government	..	..	..	..	..	..	..	..	..	..
State/Regional	..	..	..	..	..	..	..	..	..	..
Local government	..	..	..	..	..	..	..	..	..	..
Social Security Funds	..	..	..	..	..	..	..	..	..	..
Total	**..**	**..**	**..**	**0**	**0**	**0**	**0**	**0**	**0**	**0**
2000+3000 Total	**..**	**..**	**..**	**642**	**1 044**	**1 126**	**1 288**	**1 411**	**1 392**	**1 503**
Slovenia, million EUR										
2000 Social security contributions										
Federal or Central government	..	..	..	161	333	374	395	421	412	402
State/Regional	..	..	..	..	..	..	..	..	..	..
Local government	..	..	..	86	175	184	188	198	196	197
Social Security Funds	..	..	..	3	7	7	8	8	8	7
Total	**..**	**..**	**..**	**250**	**515**	**565**	**590**	**627**	**616**	**606**
3000 Taxes on payroll and workforce										
Federal or Central government	..	..	..	55	76	48	6	6	7	7
State/Regional	..	..	..	..	..	..	..	..	..	..
Local government	..	..	..	29	36	22	3	3	4	4
Social Security Funds	..	..	..	1	2	1	0	0	0	0
Total	**..**	**..**	**..**	**85**	**114**	**71**	**9**	**9**	**11**	**11**
2000+3000 Total	**..**	**..**	**..**	**335**	**629**	**636**	**600**	**636**	**626**	**617**

Table 76. **Social security contributions and payroll taxes paid by government / Les cotisations de sécurité sociale et impôts sur les salaires payés par les administrations publiques** *(cont.)*

	1965	1980	1990	2000	2007	2008	2009	2011	2012	2013
Spain, million EUR										
2000 Social security contributions										
Federal or Central government	..	387	989	1 401	1 960	2 134	2 150	2 123	1 983	1 961
State/Regional	..	2	0	4 411	9 426	10 534	11 135	11 225	10 553	10 378
Local government	..	252	1 819	2 524	4 098	4 406	4 638	4 819	4 659	4 442
Social Security Funds	..	396	1 202	1 284	484	511	555	515	503	499
Total	**..**	**1 037**	**4 010**	**9 620**	**15 968**	**17 585**	**18 478**	**18 682**	**17 698**	**17 280**
3000 Taxes on payroll and workforce										
Federal or Central government	..	..	..	..	..	..	..	..	..	..
State/Regional	..	..	..	..	..	..	..	..	..	..
Local government	..	..	..	..	..	..	..	..	..	..
Social Security Funds	..	..	..	..	..	..	..	..	..	..
Total	**..**	**0**	**0**	**0**	**0**	**0**	**0**	**0**	**0**	**0**
2000+3000 Total	**..**	**1 037**	**4 010**	**9 620**	**15 968**	**17 585**	**18 478**	**18 682**	**17 698**	**17 280**
Sweden, million SEK										
2000 Social security contributions										
Federal or Central government	..	7 543	12 430	23 215	26 735	25 873	25 589	25 161	26 100	26 420
State/Regional	..	..	..	..	..	..	..	..	..	..
Local government	..	18 149	49 298	63 830	84 331	80 031	75 851	72 979	75 358	75 421
Social Security Funds	..	0	0	0	0	0	0	0	0	0
Total	**..**	**25 692**	**61 728**	**87 045**	**111 066**	**105 905**	**101 439**	**98 140**	**101 458**	**101 841**
3000 Taxes on payroll and workforce										
Federal or Central government	..	..	1 527	3 789	5 731	8 649	8 780	10 797	11 140	12 076
State/Regional	..	..	..	..	..	..	..	..	..	..
Local government	..	..	6 060	10 419	18 077	26 753	26 025	31 318	32 164	34 473
Social Security Funds	..	..	0	0	0	0	0	0	0	0
Total	**..**	**0**	**7 587**	**14 208**	**23 808**	**35 403**	**34 805**	**42 115**	**43 304**	**46 548**
2000+3000 Total	**..**	**25 692**	**69 315**	**101 253**	**134 874**	**141 307**	**136 245**	**140 255**	**144 762**	**148 389**
Suisse, millions CHF										
2000 Cotisations de sécurité sociale										
Administration fédérale ou centrale	13	91	371	407	324	309	344	376	379	398
Administration d'un Etat/Länder	34	380	1 001	1 259	1 703	1 417	1 538	1 649	1 679	1 728
Administrations locales	22	270	636	885	1 131	795	833	873	874	893
Administrations de sécurite sociale	2	21	0	0	0	0	0	0	0	0
Total	**71**	**762**	**2 008**	**2 550**	**3 158**	**2 521**	**2 714**	**2 897**	**2 932**	**3 019**
3000 Impôts sur les salaires										
Administration fédérale ou centrale	..	..	..	..	..	..	..	..	..	..
Administration d'un Etat/Länder	..	..	..	..	..	..	..	..	..	..
Administrations locales	..	..	..	..	..	..	..	..	..	..
Administrations de sécurite sociale	..	..	..	..	..	..	..	..	..	..
Total	**0**	**0**	**0**	**0**	**0**	**0**	**0**	**0**	**0**	**0**
2000+3000 Total	**71**	**762**	**2 008**	**2 550**	**3 158**	**2 521**	**2 714**	**2 897**	**2 932**	**3 019**
Turkey, million TRY										
2000 Social security contributions										
Federal or Central government	..	..	9	3 619	20 442	28 858	31 477	53 162	58 272	71 184
State/Regional	..	..	..	..	..	..	..	..	..	..
Local government	..	..	0	0	0	0	0	0	0	0
Social Security Funds	..	..	0	0	0	0	0	0	0	0
Total	**..**	**..**	**9**	**3 619**	**20 442**	**28 858**	**31 477**	**53 162**	**58 272**	**71 184**
3000 Taxes on payroll and workforce										
Federal or Central government	..	..	..	..	..	..	..	..	..	..
State/Regional	..	..	..	..	..	..	..	..	..	..
Local government	..	..	..	..	..	..	..	..	..	..
Social Security Funds	..	..	..	..	..	..	..	..	..	..
Total	**..**	**..**	**0**	**0**	**0**	**0**	**0**	**0**	**0**	**0**
2000+3000 Total	**..**	**..**	**9**	**3 619**	**20 442**	**28 858**	**31 477**	**53 162**	**58 272**	**71 184**

Table 76. **Social security contributions and payroll taxes paid by government / Les cotisations de sécurité sociale et impôts sur les salaires payés par les administrations publiques** *(cont.)*

	1965	1980	1990	2000	2007	2008	2009	2011	2012	2013
United Kingdom, million GBP										
2000 Social security contributions										
Federal or Central government	87	920	2 134	3 121	5 764	6 095	6 020	6 629	7 019	6 904
State/Regional	..	..	..	..	..	..	..	..	..	..
Local government	83	926	1 957	2 936	5 044	5 431	5 320	5 394	5 157	4 756
Social Security Funds	0	0	0	0	0	0	0	0	0	0
Total	**170**	**1 846**	**4 091**	**6 057**	**10 808**	**11 526**	**11 340**	**12 023**	**12 176**	**11 660**
3000 Taxes on payroll and workforce										
Federal or Central government	..	360	..	..	..	..	..	..	..	..
State/Regional	..	..	..	..	..	..	..	..	..	..
Local government	..	410	..	..	..	..	..	..	..	..
Social Security Funds	..	0	..	..	..	..	..	..	..	..
Total	**0**	**770**	**0**	**0**	**0**	**0**	**0**	**0**	**0**	**0**
2000+3000 Total	**170**	**2 616**	**4 091**	**6 057**	**10 808**	**11 526**	**11 340**	**12 023**	**12 176**	**11 660**
United States, million USD										
2000 Social security contributions										
Federal or Central government	301	2 053	9 055	11 320	19 590	21 239	23 391	26 364	26 512	25 584
State/Regional	699	7 585	19 802	32 815	43 624	44 813	46 367	45 688	45 758	45 687
Local government	0	0	0	0	0	0	0	0	0	0
Social Security Funds	0	0	0	0	0	0	0	0	0	0
Total	**1 000**	**9 638**	**28 857**	**44 135**	**63 214**	**66 052**	**69 758**	**72 052**	**72 270**	**71 271**
3000 Taxes on payroll and workforce										
Federal or Central government	..	..	..	..	..	..	..	..	..	..
State/Regional	..	..	..	..	..	..	..	..	..	..
Local government	..	..	..	..	..	..	..	..	..	..
Social Security Funds	..	..	..	..	..	..	..	..	..	..
Total	**0**	**0**	**0**	**0**	**0**	**0**	**0**	**0**	**0**	**0**
2000+3000 Total	**1 000**	**9 638**	**28 857**	**44 135**	**63 214**	**66 052**	**69 758**	**72 052**	**72 270**	**71 271**

1. The multi-jurisdictional sector contains units where jurisdiction is shared between two or more governments, or classification of a unit to a jurisdiction is otherwise unclear. The main type of units currently falling into this category is public universities.
2. There is a break in the series in 1990. The data are based on ESA 2010 from that year onwards.
1. Le secteur multi-juridictionnel contient des unités où la juridiction est partagée entre deux administrations publiques au moins, ou contient des unités dont le classement dans une juridiction n'est pas clair. Les universités publiques sont le principal type d'unités appartenant actuellement à cette catégorie
2. Il y a une rupture dans les séries en 1990. À partir de cette année, les données se fondent sur le SEC 2010.

StatLink http://dx.doi.org/10.1787/888933277383

PART IV

Tax revenues by subsectors of general government

PARTIE IV

Recettes fiscales par sous-secteur d'administration

Revenue Statistics 1965-2014
Statistiques des recettes publiques 1965-2014

PART IV

Tax revenues by subsectors of general government

The tax data presented in this part of the Report have been attributed to the sub-sectors of general government identified in section J of the Interpretative guide (see Annex A) and the attribution criteria used are those set out in that guide.

The column "supranational" reports the customs duties collected by the twenty-one EU member states on behalf of the European Union.

PARTIE IV

Recettes fiscales par sous-secteur d'administration

Les données présentées dans cette partie ont été réparties entre les sous-secteurs d'administration identifiés dans la section J du Guide d'interprétation (voir annexe A) et les critères d'attribution utilisés sont ceux indiqués dans cette annexe.

La colonne « supranationale » indique les droits de douane collectés par les vingt et un pays membres pour le compte de l'Union européenne.

Chart 5. **The structure of central government tax receipts**
Graphique 5. **Structure des recettes fiscales des administrations centrales 2013**

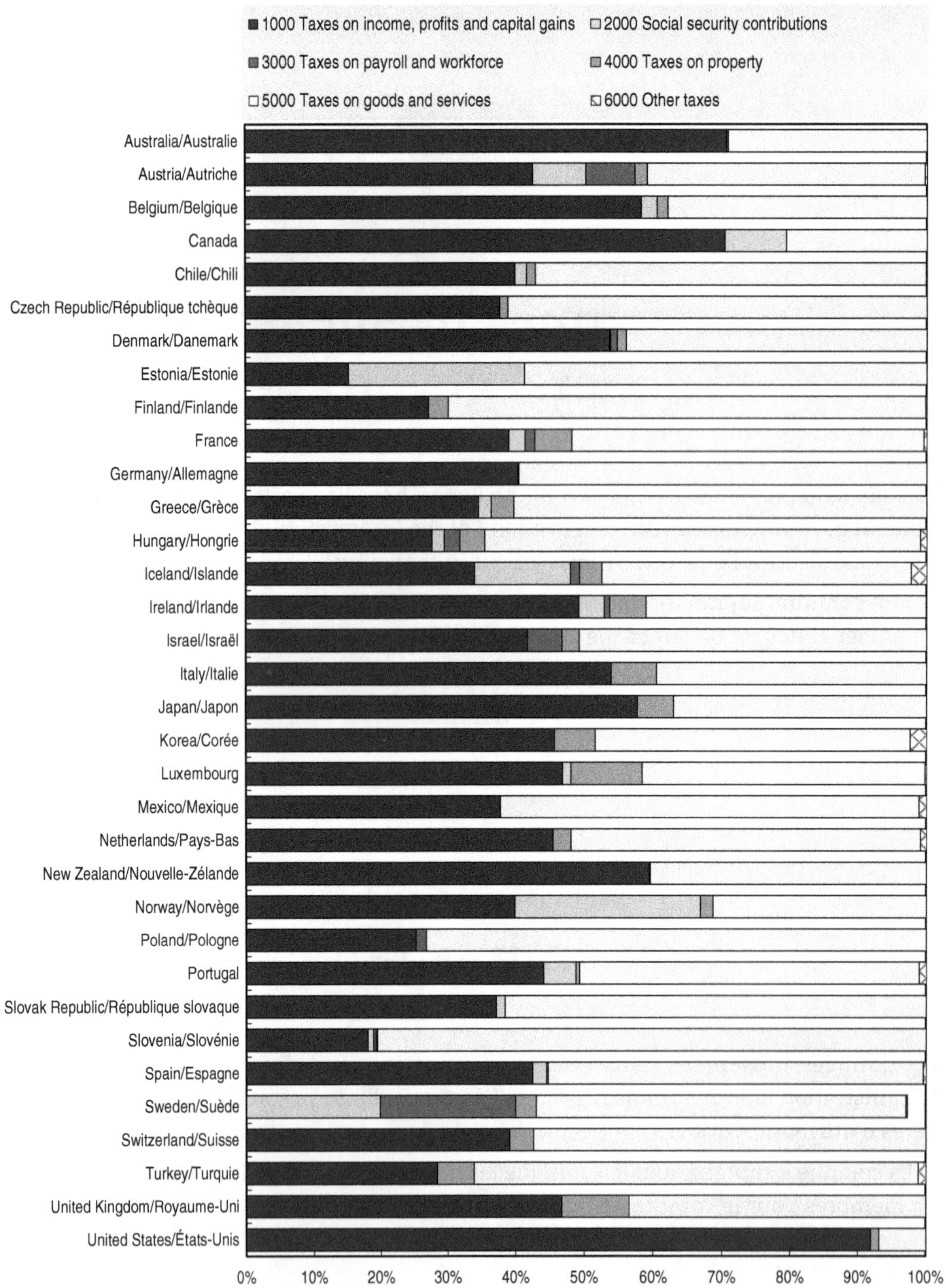

Note : This refers to only those taxes which are classified as central government taxes. Social security contributions paid to social security funds are excluded./Ceci ne tient compte que des impôts des administrations centrales. Les cotisations de sécurité sociale versées au profit des administrations de sécurité sociale sont exclues.

StatLink http://dx.doi.org/10.1787/888933276495

Chart 6. **The structure of State, regional and local government tax receipts**
Graphique 6. **Structure des recettes fiscales des administrations d'État, régionales et locales 2013**

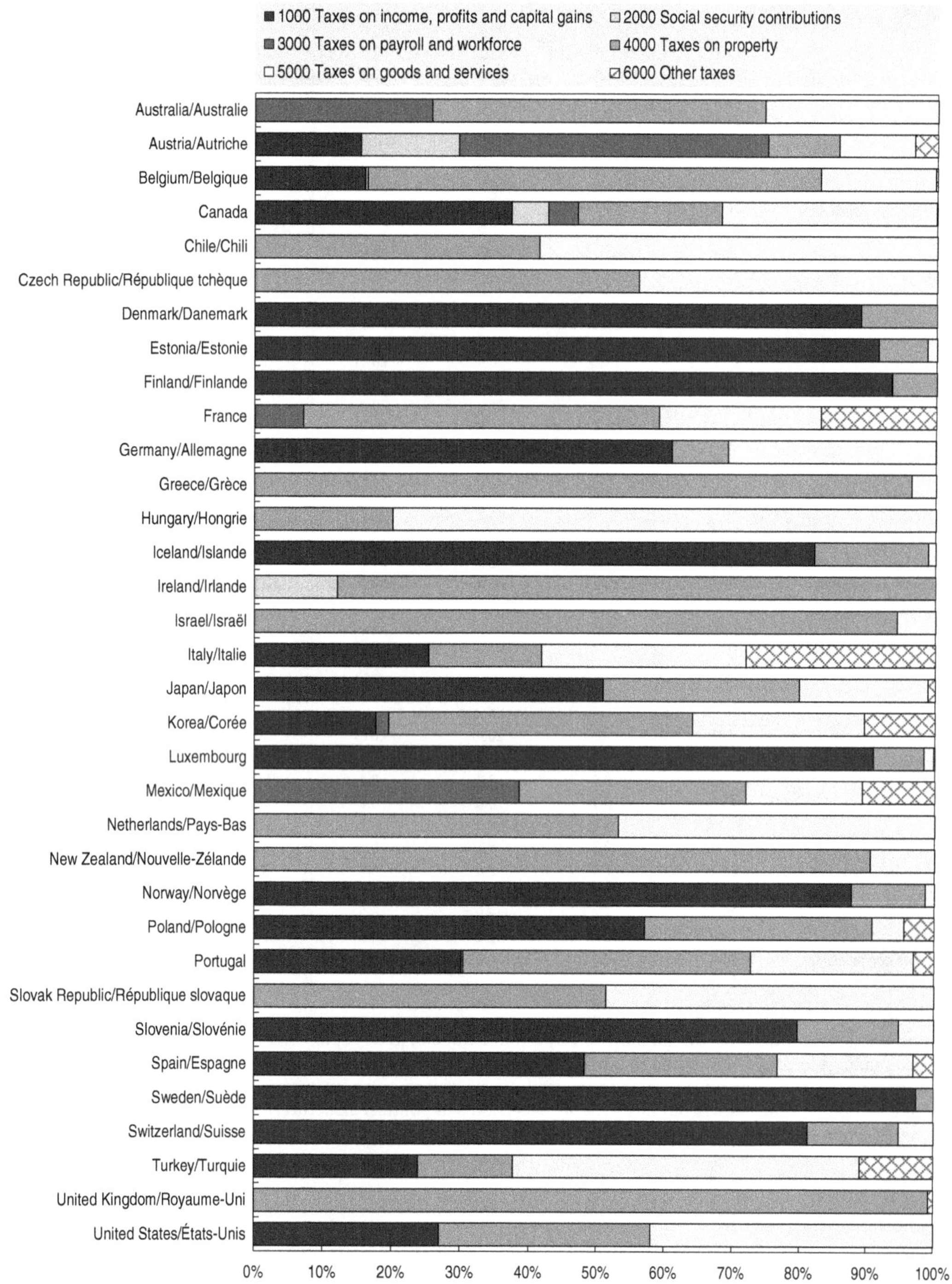

Note : This refers to only those taxes which are classified as sub-central government taxes. Social security contributions paid to social security funds are excluded./Ceci ne tient compte que des impôts des administrations infranationales. Les cotisations de sécurité sociale versées au profit des administrations de sécurité sociale sont exclues.

StatLink http://dx.doi.org/10.1787/888933276507

Table 77. **Tax revenues of sub-sectors of general government as % of total tax revenue (Federal/regional countries)**

Tableau 77. **Recettes fiscales des sous-secteurs de l'administration en % du total des recettes fiscales (Pays fédéraux/régionaux)**

	Total				Supranational / Supranationale			
	1975	1995	2000	2013	1975	1995	2000	2013
Federal countries / Pays fédéraux								
Australia / Australie	100.0	100.0	100.0	100.0	..	..	..	..
Austria / Autriche	100.0	100.0	100.0	100.0	..	0.0	0.5	0.3
Belgium / Belgique	100.0	100.0	100.0	100.0	1.4	1.0	0.9	0.7
Canada	100.0	100.0	100.0	100.0	..	..	..	..
Germany / Allemagne	100.0	100.0	100.0	100.0	1.2	0.6	0.5	0.4
Mexico / Mexique	..	100.0	100.0	100.0	..	..	..	..
Switzerland / Suisse	100.0	100.0	100.0	100.0	..	..	..	..
United States / États-Unis	100.0	100.0	100.0	100.0	..	..	..	..
Unweighted average / Moyenne non pondérée	100.0	100.0	100.0	100.0	1.3	0.6	0.6	0.5
Regional country / Pays régional								
Spain / Espagne[1,2]	100.0	100.0	100.0	100.0	..	0.5	0.4	0.4

	Central government / Administration centrale				State or Regional government / Administration d'un État/Région			
	1975	1995	2000	2013	1975	1995	2000	2013
Federal countries / Pays fédéraux								
Australia / Australie	80.1	77.5	81.8	80.8	15.7	19.0	15.2	15.8
Austria / Autriche	51.7	64.8	66.7	66.5	10.6	1.8	1.6	1.6
Belgium / Belgique	65.3	60.2	61.9	57.1	..	1.8	2.2	5.5
Canada	47.6	39.1	47.3	41.6	32.5	37.1	38.0	39.6
Germany / Allemagne	33.5	31.4	30.6	31.4	22.3	21.6	22.4	21.9
Mexico / Mexique	..	80.1	80.7	80.1	..	2.1	2.0	3.1
Switzerland / Suisse	30.7	31.4	37.3	35.2	27.0	23.8	22.2	24.6
United States / États-Unis	45.4	41.3	45.3	41.2	19.5	20.1	18.9	20.2
Unweighted average / Moyenne non pondérée	50.6	53.2	56.4	54.2	21.3	15.9	15.3	16.5
Regional country / Pays régional								
Spain / Espagne[1,2]	48.2	50.4	49.0	42.1	..	4.8	7.7	13.7

	Local government / Administrations locales				Social Security Funds / Administrations de sécurité sociale			
	1975	1995	2000	2013	1975	1995	2000	2013
Federal countries / Pays fédéraux								
Australia / Australie	4.2	3.4	3.0	3.4	0.0	0.0	0.0	0.0
Austria / Autriche	12.4	4.1	3.6	3.2	25.3	29.3	27.6	28.4
Belgium / Belgique	4.4	4.8	4.1	4.7	28.8	32.1	30.9	32.0
Canada	9.9	9.8	8.1	9.3	10.0	14.0	6.7	9.4
Germany / Allemagne	9.0	7.4	7.4	8.2	34.0	39.0	39.0	38.1
Mexico / Mexique	..	1.1	0.8	1.2	..	16.6	16.5	15.5
Switzerland / Suisse	20.3	17.6	16.0	15.2	22.0	27.3	24.5	25.1
United States / États-Unis	14.7	13.4	12.2	14.5	20.5	25.2	23.6	24.2
Unweighted average / Moyenne non pondérée	10.7	7.7	6.9	7.5	20.1	22.9	21.1	21.6
Regional country / Pays régional								
Spain / Espagne[1,2]	4.3	8.5	9.1	9.9	47.5	35.8	33.8	34.0

1. The total tax revenue has been reduced by the amount of any capital transfer that represents uncollected taxes. The capital transfer has been allocated between tax headings in proportion to the reported tax revenue. / Le total des recettes fiscales a été diminué du montant de tout transfert en capital représentant les impôts non perçus. Le transfert en capital a été réparti entre les différentes rubriques en proportion des recettes fiscales.
2. Spain is constitutionally a non-federal country but has a highly decentralised political structure. / L'Espagne est constitutionnellement un pays non fédéral mais avec une structure politique très décentralisée.

StatLink http://dx.doi.org/10.1787/888933277395

Table 78. **Tax revenues of sub-sectors of general government as % of total tax revenue (Unitary countries)**
Tableau 78. **Recettes fiscales des sous-secteurs de l'administration en % du total des recettes fiscales (Pays unitaires)**

	Supranational / Supranationale				Central government / Administration centrale			
	1975	1995	2000	2013	1975	1995	2000	2013
Chile / Chili	..	..	..	..	..	89.9	87.8	87.0
Czech Republic / République tchèque	..	..	..	0.4	..	57.7	54.9	55.2
Denmark / Danemark[1]	1.1	0.5	0.4	0.3	68.9	68.2	67.6	73.3
Estonia / Estonie	..	..	0.0	0.5	..	72.1	72.2	69.5
Finland / Finlande	..	0.4	0.2	0.2	56.0	46.6	53.0	47.6
France[1]	0.7	0.4	0.3	0.2	51.2	42.3	41.9	33.6
Greece / Grèce[1]	..	0.6	0.5	0.2	67.1	66.8	68.9	63.6
Hungary / Hongrie	..	..	..	0.2	..	63.8	64.5	60.5
Iceland / Islande	..	..	..	..	81.3	79.2	76.7	73.4
Ireland / Irlande	2.3	1.5	0.6	0.5	77.4	83.1	86.2	82.0
Israel / Israël	..	..	..	..	..	80.0	78.9	76.1
Italy / Italie	..	0.4	0.3	0.3	53.2	62.7	55.8	53.8
Japan / Japon	..	..	..	..	45.4	41.2	38.7	35.0
Korea / Corée	..	..	..	..	89.0	69.2	68.2	58.1
Luxembourg	0.8	0.4	0.3	0.1	63.6	67.1	68.8	68.4
Netherlands / Pays-Bas	1.5	1.2	1.0	1.0	58.9	54.1	56.6	54.4
New Zealand / Nouvelle-Zélande	..	..	..	..	92.3	94.7	94.3	93.3
Norway / Norvège	..	..	..	..	50.6	58.4	84.9	86.9
Poland / Pologne	..	..	..	0.3	..	61.9	51.4	48.2
Portugal	..	1.3	0.9	0.7	65.4	71.9	69.4	67.6
Slovak Republic / République slovaque	..	..	..	0.5	..	62.5	58.0	53.6
Slovenia / Slovénie	..	..	..	0.4	..	51.8	55.1	49.1
Sweden / Suède	..	0.4	0.3	0.3	51.3	46.9	60.0	49.9
Turkey / Turquie	..	..	..	..	..	75.1	72.4	63.8
United Kingdom / Royaume-Uni	1.0	1.0	0.6	0.5	70.5	77.5	78.4	75.8
Unweighted average / Moyenne non pondérée	1.2	0.7	0.5	0.4	65.1	65.8	66.6	63.2

	Local government / Administrations locales				Social Security Funds / Administrations de sécurité sociale			
	1975	1995	2000	2013	1975	1995	2000	2013
Chile / Chili	..	6.5	7.9	7.3	..	3.6	4.4	5.7
Czech Republic / République tchèque	..	0.9	0.9	1.3	..	41.4	44.3	43.2
Denmark / Danemark[1]	30.0	31.3	30.8	26.3	0.1	0.0	1.1	0.1
Estonia / Estonie	..	13.1	13.9	13.3	..	14.8	13.9	16.7
Finland / Finlande	23.5	22.3	21.6	23.4	20.4	30.8	25.2	28.9
France[1]	7.6	11.0	10.1	12.9	40.6	46.3	47.7	53.3
Greece / Grèce[1]	3.4	0.9	0.8	5.6	29.5	31.7	29.8	30.5
Hungary / Hongrie	..	2.5	5.2	5.9	..	33.6	30.3	33.3
Iceland / Islande	18.7	20.8	23.3	26.6	0.0	0.0	0.0	0.0
Ireland / Irlande	7.3	2.7	2.0	3.1	13.1	12.7	11.2	14.4
Israel / Israël	..	5.9	6.4	7.3	..	14.1	14.7	16.6
Italy / Italie	0.9	5.4	15.3	16.2	45.9	31.5	28.5	29.8
Japan / Japon	25.6	25.3	26.1	24.2	29.0	33.5	35.2	40.9
Korea / Corée	10.1	18.7	15.1	15.5	0.9	12.1	16.7	26.4
Luxembourg	6.7	6.4	5.8	3.5	29.0	26.1	25.1	28.0
Netherlands / Pays-Bas	1.2	2.7	3.4	3.7	38.4	42.0	39.1	40.8
New Zealand / Nouvelle-Zélande	7.7	5.3	5.7	6.7	0.0	0.0	0.0	0.0
Norway / Norvège	22.4	19.6	15.1	13.1	27.0	22.0	0.0	0.0
Poland / Pologne	..	8.3	9.2	12.9	..	29.8	39.4	38.6
Portugal	0.0	5.4	6.3	7.0	34.6	21.4	23.4	24.7
Slovak Republic / République slovaque	..	1.3	1.4	2.9	..	36.2	40.6	43.1
Slovenia / Slovénie	..	6.3	7.3	10.8	..	41.9	37.6	39.7
Sweden / Suède	29.2	30.9	28.8	36.9	19.5	21.8	10.9	12.8
Turkey / Turquie	..	12.8	8.9	8.8	..	12.1	18.7	27.4
United Kingdom / Royaume-Uni	11.1	3.7	4.0	4.9	17.5	17.8	17.0	18.8
Unweighted average / Moyenne non pondérée	12.8	10.8	11.0	12.0	21.6	23.1	22.2	24.6

1. The total tax revenue has been reduced by the amount of any capital transfer that represents uncollected taxes. The capital transfer has been allocated between tax headings in proportion to the reported tax revenue. / Le total des recettes fiscales a été diminué du montant de tout transfert en capital représentant les impôts non perçus. Le transfert en capital a été réparti entre les différentes rubriques en proportion des recettes fiscales.

StatLink http://dx.doi.org/10.1787/888933277408

Table 79. **Main central government tax revenues as % of GDP at market prices (Federal/regional countries)**
Tableau 79. **Principales recettes fiscales de l'administration centrale en % du PIB aux prix du marché (Pays fédéraux/régionaux)**

	1000 Income & profits / Revenu & bénéfices			2000+3000 Social security & payroll / Sécurité sociale & salaires[3]			4000 Property / Patrimoine		
	1975	1995	2013	1975	1995	2013	1975	1995	2013
Federal countries / Pays fédéraux									
Australia / Australie	14.2	15.6	15.7	0.1	0.6	0.1	0.1	0.0	0.0
Austria / Autriche	6.1	10.5	12.0	3.1	4.3	4.2	0.6	0.4	0.5
Belgium / Belgique	14.2	14.6	14.9	0.5	0.6	0.6	1.0	0.6	0.4
Canada	10.4	9.9	9.0	0.0	0.0	1.1	0.0	0.0	0.0
Germany / Allemagne	4.9	4.8	4.6	0.0	0.0	0.0	0.2	0.0	0.0
Mexico / Mexique	..	3.7	6.0	..	0.0	0.0	..	0.0	0.0
Switzerland / Suisse	2.1	2.5	3.7	0.0	0.0	0.0	0.3	0.5	0.3
United States / États-Unis	9.7	9.7	9.6	0.0	0.0	0.0	0.3	0.2	0.1
Unweighted average / Moyenne non pondérée	8.8	8.9	9.4	0.5	0.7	0.7	0.3	0.2	0.2
Regional country / Pays régional									
Spain / Espagne[1,2]	3.5	8.5	5.8	0.0	0.1	0.3	1.1	0.1	0.0

	5110 General taxes / Impôts généraux			5120 Specific goods and services / Biens et services déterminés			Other taxes / Autres impôts		
	1975	1995	2013	1975	1995	2013	1975	1995	2013
Federal countries / Pays fédéraux									
Australia / Australie	1.7	2.5	3.6	4.2	3.1	2.3	0.0	0.1	0.6
Austria / Autriche	5.0	7.6	7.7	3.9	3.1	3.1	0.1	0.7	0.7
Belgium / Belgique	6.3	6.5	6.9	3.0	2.8	2.8	0.4	0.6	0.0
Canada	1.9	2.3	1.8	2.6	1.4	0.8	0.1	0.0	0.0
Germany / Allemagne	3.4	3.5	3.7	3.1	3.1	2.7	0.0	0.0	0.4
Mexico / Mexique	..	2.5	3.5	..	5.3	6.2	..	0.4	0.2
Switzerland / Suisse	2.0	3.1	3.5	2.6	1.8	1.5	0.0	0.1	0.4
United States / États-Unis	0.0	0.0	0.0	1.2	1.0	0.7	0.0	0.0	0.0
Unweighted average / Moyenne non pondérée	2.9	3.5	3.8	2.9	2.7	2.5	0.1	0.2	0.3
Regional country / Pays régional									
Spain / Espagne[1,2]	2.5	4.4	5.1	1.5	2.6	2.3	0.0	0.0	0.2

Note: Excluding social security contributions accruing to social security funds. / Sont exclues les cotisations de sécurité sociale versées aux administrations de sécurité sociale.

1. The total tax revenue has been reduced by the amount of any capital transfer that represents uncollected taxes. The capital transfer has been allocated between tax headings in proportion to the reported tax revenue. / Le total des recettes fiscales a été diminué du montant de tout transfert en capital représentant les impôts non perçus. Le transfert en capital a été réparti entre les différentes rubriques en proportion des recettes fiscales.
2. Spain is constitutionally a non-federal country but has a highly decentralised political structure. / L'Espagne est constitutionnellement un pays non fédéral mais avec une structure politique très décentralisée.
3. These comprise only social security contributions accruing to central government. / Ne sont incluses que les cotisations de sécurité sociale versées à l'administration centrale.

StatLink http://dx.doi.org/10.1787/888933277412

Table 80. **Main central government tax revenues as % of GDP at market prices (Unitary countries)**
Tableau 80. **Principales recettes fiscales de l'administration centrale en % du PIB aux prix du marché (Pays unitaires)**

	1000 Income & profits / Revenu & bénéfices			2000+3000 Social security & payroll / Sécurité sociale & salaires[2]			4000 Property / Patrimoine		
	1975	1995	2013	1975	1995	2013	1975	1995	2013
Chile / Chili	..	4.6	6.9	..	0.5	0.3	..	0.6	0.2
Czech Republic / République tchèque	..	8.7	7.1	..	0.0	0.0	..	0.2	0.2
Denmark / Danemark[1]	12.3	15.8	18.7	0.1	0.3	0.4	0.8	0.7	0.5
Estonia / Estonie	..	6.4	3.4	..	6.9	5.8	..	0.1	0.0
Finland / Finlande	7.1	6.6	5.6	0.8	0.0	0.0	0.7	0.5	0.6
France[1]	5.5	5.6	5.9	0.7	1.1	0.6	0.6	0.6	0.8
Greece / Grèce	2.4	6.2	7.6	0.0	0.4	0.4	1.8	0.9	0.7
Hungary / Hongrie	..	8.6	6.4	..	1.3	1.0	..	0.2	0.8
Iceland / Islande	3.1	5.8	9.0	2.0	2.5	4.1	0.7	1.5	0.9
Ireland / Irlande	8.4	12.8	11.7	0.2	0.5	1.1	0.7	0.7	1.3
Israel / Israël	..	12.5	9.7	..	1.7	1.2	..	1.3	0.6
Italy / Italie	5.1	13.0	12.7	0.0	0.1	0.0	0.8	1.4	1.6
Japan / Japon	6.2	6.6	6.1	0.0	0.0	0.0	0.6	1.1	0.6
Korea / Corée	3.3	5.4	6.5	0.0	0.0	0.0	0.6	0.6	0.8
Luxembourg	11.9	11.8	12.3	0.1	0.1	0.3	1.4	2.3	2.7
Netherlands / Pays-Bas	13.2	10.3	9.1	0.0	0.0	0.0	0.7	0.9	0.5
New Zealand / Nouvelle-Zélande	18.3	21.8	17.4	0.0	0.0	0.0	0.7	0.2	0.0
Norway / Norvège	3.8	7.0	14.0	0.8	0.6	9.5	0.4	0.4	0.6
Poland / Pologne	..	9.5	3.9	..	0.2	0.2	..	0.0	0.0
Portugal	3.3	7.4	10.3	0.5	1.8	1.1	0.5	0.3	0.1
Slovak Republic / République slovaque	..	10.1	6.0	..	0.4	0.2	..	0.1	0.0
Slovenia / Slovénie	..	4.5	3.3	..	0.5	0.2	..	0.0	0.0
Sweden / Suède	8.3	3.8	-0.6	1.7	3.6	9.0	0.4	1.2	0.7
Turkey / Turquie	..	4.2	5.3	..	0.0	0.0	..	0.5	1.0
United Kingdom / Royaume-Uni	15.3	11.8	11.7	0.0	0.0	0.0	0.6	2.0	2.4
Unweighted average / Moyenne non pondérée	8.0	8.8	8.4	0.4	0.9	1.4	0.7	0.7	0.7

	5110 General taxes / Impôts généraux			5120 Specific goods and services / Biens et services déterminés			Other taxes / Autres impôts		
	1975	1995	2013	1975	1995	2013	1975	1995	2013
Chile / Chili	..	7.5	8.2	..	3.3	1.7	..	-0.1	0.0
Czech Republic / République tchèque	..	5.8	7.5	..	4.5	3.7	..	0.9	0.4
Denmark / Danemark[1]	6.5	9.0	9.6	5.2	5.3	4.5	0.7	0.7	1.2
Estonia / Estonie	..	9.6	8.3	..	2.8	4.4	..	0.3	0.3
Finland / Finlande	5.6	7.7	9.3	5.8	5.4	4.7	0.1	0.4	0.5
France[1]	8.1	7.3	6.3	2.8	3.0	1.4	0.2	0.1	0.1
Greece / Grèce	3.4	6.3	7.1	4.2	4.3	4.3	0.7	0.5	1.8
Hungary / Hongrie	..	7.3	9.7	..	8.5	4.8	..	0.2	0.5
Iceland / Islande	8.3	9.1	8.0	9.4	4.2	3.5	0.2	0.9	1.1
Ireland / Irlande	4.1	6.7	5.9	7.6	5.0	3.0	0.6	0.6	0.9
Israel / Israël	..	10.7	9.3	..	1.6	1.8	..	0.7	0.7
Italy / Italie	3.5	5.3	5.4	3.4	4.0	3.7	0.3	0.4	0.1
Japan / Japon	0.0	1.4	2.2	2.3	1.6	1.5	0.2	0.2	0.1
Korea / Corée	1.9	3.4	3.9	6.9	3.4	2.6	0.6	0.5	0.3
Luxembourg	3.8	4.9	7.4	2.4	4.3	3.3	0.2	0.2	0.2
Netherlands / Pays-Bas	5.5	6.1	6.5	2.5	3.0	3.1	0.6	0.8	0.7
New Zealand / Nouvelle-Zélande	2.5	8.1	9.4	3.7	3.0	1.8	0.3	0.6	0.6
Norway / Norvège	8.0	8.5	7.7	6.2	6.2	2.8	0.5	0.7	0.5
Poland / Pologne	..	6.1	7.0	..	7.3	4.2	..	0.2	0.1
Portugal	2.1	6.2	7.2	5.5	5.3	3.8	0.5	0.3	0.8
Slovak Republic / République slovaque	..	8.2	6.4	..	4.9	3.2	..	0.9	0.4
Slovenia / Slovénie	..	11.3	8.4	..	3.2	5.3	..	0.3	0.8
Sweden / Suède	4.7	8.8	9.1	4.1	3.6	2.7	0.7	0.3	0.5
Turkey / Turquie	..	4.6	5.7	..	0.9	6.0	..	2.6	0.7
United Kingdom / Royaume-Uni	3.2	6.1	6.9	4.6	4.3	3.5	0.4	0.6	0.4
Unweighted average / Moyenne non pondérée	4.4	7.0	7.3	4.8	4.1	3.4	0.4	0.5	0.6

Note: Excluding social security contributions accruing to social security funds. / Sont exclues les cotisations de sécurité sociale versées aux administrations de sécurité sociale.

1. The total tax revenue has been reduced by the amount of any capital transfer that represents uncollected taxes. The capital transfer has been allocated between tax headings in proportion to the reported tax revenue. / Le total des recettes fiscales a été diminué du montant de tout transfert en capital représentant les impôts non perçus. Le transfert en capital a été réparti entre les différentes rubriques en proportion des recettes fiscales.
2. These comprise only social security contributions accruing to central government. / Ne sont incluses que les cotisations de sécurité sociale versées à l'administration centrale.

StatLink http://dx.doi.org/10.1787/888933277427

Table 81. **Main central government taxes as % of total tax revenues of central government (Federal/regional countries)**

Tableau 81. **Principales recettes de l'administration centrale en % du total des recettes fiscales de l'administration centrale (Pays fédéraux/régionaux)**

	1000 Income & profits / Revenu & bénéfices			1100 Individuals / Personnes physiques			1200 Corporate / Sociétés			2000+3000 Social security & payroll / Sécurité sociale & salaires[3]		
	1975	1995	2013	1975	1995	2013	1975	1995	2013	1975	1995	2013
Federal countries / Pays fédéraux												
Australia / Australie	69.9	71.4	70.7	54.5	52.4	48.5	15.5	19.0	22.2	0.3	2.6	0.2
Austria / Autriche	32.2	39.4	42.5	25.0	31.2	33.5	6.9	4.8	7.5	16.5	16.3	14.9
Belgium / Belgique	56.0	57.0	58.3	45.5	47.9	46.1	10.5	9.0	12.1	2.0	2.2	2.3
Canada	69.4	72.5	70.5	46.7	57.7	53.2	20.9	13.0	14.3	0.0	0.0	9.0
Germany / Allemagne	42.3	41.9	40.3	37.0	38.7	36.1	5.2	3.2	4.2	0.0	0.0	0.0
Mexico / Mexique	..	31.1	37.7	..	..	..	..	..	..	..	0.0	0.0
Switzerland / Suisse	30.2	31.3	39.1	24.0	17.6	16.4	6.3	7.3	14.5	0.0	0.0	0.0
United States / États-Unis	86.5	89.2	91.9	64.9	70.5	74.5	21.6	18.6	17.4	0.0	0.0	0.0
Unweighted average / Moyenne non pondérée	55.2	54.2	56.4	42.5	45.1	44.0	12.4	10.7	13.2	2.7	2.6	3.3
Regional country / Pays régional												
Spain / Espagne[1,2]	40.6	53.8	42.5	26.3	43.3	27.5	14.3	10.1	13.5	0.0	0.8	2.0

	4000 Property / Patrimoine			5110 General taxes / Impôts généraux			5120 Specific goods and services / Biens et services déterminés			Other taxes / Autres impôts		
	1975	1995	2013	1975	1995	2013	1975	1995	2013	1975	1995	2013
Federal countries / Pays fédéraux												
Australia / Australie	0.6	0.0	0.0	8.3	11.2	16.2	20.8	14.4	10.1	0.1	0.3	2.8
Austria / Autriche	3.0	1.4	1.8	26.7	28.7	27.4	20.9	11.7	11.1	0.7	2.6	2.4
Belgium / Belgique	3.8	2.5	1.6	24.8	25.3	27.0	11.7	10.8	10.8	1.7	2.2	0.0
Canada	0.0	0.0	0.0	12.8	16.9	14.2	17.0	10.6	6.4	0.7	0.0	0.0
Germany / Allemagne	1.9	0.1	0.2	29.1	31.1	32.6	26.7	26.9	23.7	0.0	0.0	3.2
Mexico / Mexique	..	0.0	0.0	..	21.1	21.9	..	44.5	39.3	..	3.4	1.1
Switzerland / Suisse	4.1	6.3	3.6	28.3	38.4	37.2	37.3	22.7	16.1	0.0	1.3	4.1
United States / États-Unis	2.4	1.8	1.2	0.0	0.0	0.0	10.8	9.0	6.9	0.2	0.0	0.0
Unweighted average / Moyenne non pondérée	2.3	1.5	1.0	18.6	21.6	22.1	20.8	18.8	15.5	0.5	1.2	1.7
Regional country / Pays régional												
Spain / Espagne[1,2]	12.3	0.6	0.2	29.0	28.1	37.2	17.8	16.4	16.8	0.3	0.3	1.3

Note: Excluding social security contributions accruing to social security funds. / Sont exclues les cotisations de sécurité sociale versées aux administrations de sécurité sociale.

1. The total tax revenue has been reduced by the amount of any capital transfer that represents uncollected taxes. The capital transfer has been allocated between tax headings in proportion to the reported tax revenue. / Le total des recettes fiscales a été diminué du montant de tout transfert en capital représentant les impôts non perçus. Le transfert en capital a été réparti entre les différentes rubriques en proportion des recettes fiscales.
2. Spain is constitutionally a non-federal country but has a highly decentralised political structure. / L'Espagne est constitutionnellement un pays non fédéral mais avec une structure politique très décentralisée.
3. These comprise only social security contributions accruing to central government. / Ne sont incluses que les cotisations de sécurité sociale versées à l'administration centrale.

StatLink http://dx.doi.org/10.1787/888933277437

Table 82. **Main central government taxes as % of total tax revenues of central government (Unitary countries)**

Tableau 82. **Principales recettes de l'administration centrale en % du total des recettes fiscales de l'administration centrale (Pays unitaires)**

	1000 Income & profits / Revenu & bénéfices			1100 Individuals / Personnes physiques			1200 Corporate / Sociétés			2000+3000 Social security & payroll / Sécurité sociale & salaires[2]		
	1975	1995	2013	1975	1995	2013	1975	1995	2013	1975	1995	2013
Chile / Chili	..	28.1	40.0	..	..	..	..	..	..	..	3.2	1.7
Czech Republic / République tchèque	..	43.3	37.7	..	22.1	19.4	..	21.2	18.2	..	0.0	0.0
Denmark / Danemark[1]	48.1	49.8	53.7	43.4	37.6	43.1	4.7	7.2	7.6	0.2	0.9	1.1
Estonia / Estonie	..	24.5	15.3	..	15.2	7.4	..	9.3	7.9	..	26.4	26.0
Finland / Finlande	35.3	32.0	27.2	31.0	26.0	19.2	4.3	6.0	7.9	4.1	0.1	0.0
France[1]	31.0	31.6	39.0	20.7	20.1	22.2	10.1	11.5	16.8	3.8	6.4	3.8
Greece / Grèce	18.9	33.3	34.5	12.7	18.0	27.7	5.0	9.5	6.1	0.3	2.2	1.9
Hungary / Hongrie	..	32.8	27.7	..	25.3	21.7	..	7.0	6.0	..	4.9	4.1
Iceland / Islande	13.1	24.2	33.9	10.6	20.4	22.5	2.5	3.8	8.2	8.5	10.2	15.4
Ireland / Irlande	38.8	48.6	49.2	32.5	38.5	39.0	6.2	10.1	10.3	0.9	2.0	4.4
Israel / Israël	..	44.1	41.7	..	33.4	23.6	..	10.0	15.0	..	5.9	5.1
Italy / Italie	39.0	53.9	53.9	27.7	41.4	42.4	11.3	13.8	12.7	0.0	0.5	0.0
Japan / Japon	67.2	60.5	57.7	37.8	35.5	31.0	29.4	25.0	26.7	0.0	0.0	0.0
Korea / Corée	24.7	40.5	45.7	9.6	24.2	23.7	10.0	15.8	22.0	0.0	0.0	0.0
Luxembourg	60.0	49.8	46.9	43.2	32.3	33.4	16.8	17.5	13.5	0.7	0.5	1.2
Netherlands / Pays-Bas	58.7	48.8	45.5	45.6	35.0	35.9	13.1	13.8	9.6	0.0	0.0	0.0
New Zealand / Nouvelle-Zélande	72.1	64.7	59.5	58.8	47.5	40.7	12.8	12.5	15.1	0.0	0.0	0.0
Norway / Norvège	19.2	30.0	39.9	16.1	16.9	14.9	3.2	13.0	24.9	4.0	2.7	27.0
Poland / Pologne	..	40.7	25.2	..	29.7	16.2	..	11.0	9.0	..	1.0	1.6
Portugal	26.7	34.8	44.1	..	24.9	31.2	..	9.9	12.9	3.8	8.3	4.7
Slovak Republic / République slovaque	..	40.9	37.1	..	14.3	17.9	..	23.9	17.7	..	1.7	1.3
Slovenia / Slovénie	..	22.9	18.0	..	19.8	11.3	..	2.6	6.6	..	2.5	1.2
Sweden / Suède	41.7	17.9	-2.9	37.9	5.6	-15.2	3.8	12.4	12.3	8.5	17.0	42.3
Turkey / Turquie	..	32.9	28.4	..	25.1	19.6	..	7.8	8.8	..	0.0	0.0
United Kingdom / Royaume-Uni	63.5	47.7	46.8	56.8	37.2	36.6	8.8	10.4	10.2	0.0	0.0	0.0
Unweighted average / Moyenne non pondérée	41.1	39.1	37.8	32.3	26.9	24.4	9.5	11.9	12.8	2.2	3.9	5.7

	4000 Property / Patrimoine			5110 General taxes / Impôts généraux			5120 Specific goods and services / Biens et services déterminés			Other taxes / Autres impôts		
	1975	1995	2013	1975	1995	2013	1975	1995	2013	1975	1995	2013
Chile / Chili	..	3.7	1.3	..	45.1	46.9	..	20.3	10.0	..	-0.4	0.1
Czech Republic / République tchèque	..	1.2	1.2	..	28.8	39.4	..	22.4	19.4	..	4.2	2.2
Denmark / Danemark[1]	3.0	2.1	1.3	25.4	28.5	27.4	20.5	16.6	13.0	2.8	2.2	3.5
Estonia / Estonie	..	0.4	0.0	..	36.8	37.6	..	10.9	19.7	..	1.0	1.4
Finland / Finlande	3.4	2.6	2.9	27.9	37.3	44.8	28.5	26.0	22.8	0.7	1.9	2.4
France[1]	3.2	3.4	5.4	45.1	41.0	41.9	15.5	16.9	9.0	1.4	0.8	0.9
Greece / Grèce	14.1	4.9	3.3	26.9	33.8	32.5	33.9	23.3	19.6	5.9	2.5	8.2
Hungary / Hongrie	..	0.8	3.7	..	27.9	41.7	..	32.6	20.6	..	0.9	2.2
Iceland / Islande	2.8	6.4	3.2	35.1	37.8	30.2	39.5	17.6	13.2	1.0	3.8	4.1
Ireland / Irlande	3.2	2.6	5.3	19.0	25.4	24.9	35.4	19.1	12.4	2.8	2.4	3.6
Israel / Israël	..	4.5	2.5	..	37.7	39.9	..	5.5	7.8	..	2.4	3.1
Italy / Italie	5.9	5.7	6.6	26.9	22.0	23.1	26.2	16.5	15.8	2.0	1.5	0.6
Japan / Japon	6.0	10.1	5.3	0.0	13.2	21.1	24.7	14.3	14.6	2.1	1.9	1.3
Korea / Corée	4.7	4.4	5.9	14.2	25.8	27.7	51.8	25.6	18.3	4.6	3.7	2.4
Luxembourg	7.1	9.9	10.3	19.1	20.9	28.1	11.9	18.1	12.7	1.2	0.8	0.7
Netherlands / Pays-Bas	3.0	4.2	2.6	24.4	28.9	32.7	11.1	14.3	15.5	2.8	3.8	3.7
New Zealand / Nouvelle-Zélande	2.6	0.7	0.1	9.8	24.0	32.2	14.4	8.9	6.2	1.2	1.7	2.0
Norway / Norvège	2.3	1.6	1.8	40.5	36.3	21.8	31.7	26.5	7.9	2.4	3.0	1.5
Poland / Pologne	..	0.0	0.0	..	26.2	45.6	..	31.2	27.2	..	1.0	0.5
Portugal	3.8	1.2	0.5	17.1	29.1	31.0	44.3	25.0	16.3	4.4	1.6	3.4
Slovak Republic / République slovaque	..	0.5	0.0	..	33.2	39.2	..	19.9	19.7	..	3.7	2.6
Slovenia / Slovénie	..	0.2	0.2	..	57.0	46.7	..	15.9	29.2	..	1.5	4.6
Sweden / Suède	2.2	5.8	3.2	23.4	41.3	42.4	20.7	16.6	12.8	3.6	1.4	2.3
Turkey / Turquie	..	3.7	5.4	..	36.1	30.8	..	7.0	31.9	..	20.3	3.5
United Kingdom / Royaume-Uni	2.4	8.1	9.8	13.4	24.6	27.6	19.0	17.4	14.2	1.8	2.2	1.7
Unweighted average / Moyenne non pondérée	4.4	3.6	3.3	23.0	31.9	34.3	26.8	18.7	16.4	2.5	2.8	2.5

Note: Excluding social security contributions accruing to social security funds. / Sont exclues les cotisations de sécurité sociale versées aux administrations de sécurité sociale.

1. The total tax revenue has been reduced by the amount of any capital transfer that represents uncollected taxes. The capital transfer has been allocated between tax headings in proportion to the reported tax revenue. / Le total des recettes fiscales a été diminué du montant de tout transfert en capital représentant les impôts non perçus. Le transfert en capital a été réparti entre les différentes rubriques en proportion des recettes fiscales.
2. These comprise only social security contributions accruing to central government. / Ne sont incluses que les cotisations de sécurité sociale versées à l'administration centrale.

StatLink http://dx.doi.org/10.1787/888933277440

Table 83. **Main state government tax revenues as % of GDP at market prices (Federal/regional countries)**
Tableau 83. **Principales recettes fiscales des administrations d'états en % du PIB aux prix du marché (Pays fédéraux/régionaux)**

	1000 Income & profits / Revenu & bénéfices			2000 Social security / Sécurité sociale			3000 Payroll / Salaires			4000 Property / Patrimoine		
	1975	1995	2013	1975	1995	2013	1975	1995	2013	1975	1995	2013
Federal countries / Pays fédéraux												
Australia / Australie	0.0	0.0	0.0	0.0	0.0	0.0	1.4	1.3	1.4	1.1	1.5	1.6
Austria / Autriche	1.7	0.3	0.3	0.1	0.2	0.2	0.0	0.1	0.1	0.1	0.0	0.0
Belgium / Belgique[1]	..	0.0	0.0	..	0.0	0.0	..	0.0	0.0	..	0.6	1.8
Canada	4.5	6.3	5.6	0.0	0.0	0.8	0.0	0.8	0.6	0.2	0.8	0.4
Germany / Allemagne[1]	4.8	4.1	4.3	0.0	0.0	0.0	0.0	0.0	0.0	0.5	0.5	0.5
Mexico / Mexique	..	0.0	0.0	..	0.0	0.0	..	0.1	0.3	..	0.1	0.1
Switzerland / Suisse	4.7	4.7	5.2	0.0	0.0	0.0	0.0	0.0	0.0	0.9	0.9	0.9
United States / États-Unis	1.5	2.1	2.2	0.0	0.0	0.0	0.0	0.0	0.0	0.2	0.2	0.1
Unweighted average / Moyenne non pondérée	2.9	2.2	2.2	0.0	0.0	0.1	0.2	0.3	0.3	0.5	0.6	0.7
Regional country / Pays régional												
Spain / Espagne[1,2,3]	..	0.1	3.1	..	0.0	0.0	..	0.0	0.0	..	0.8	0.8

	5110 General taxes / Impôts généraux			5120 Specific goods and services / Biens et services déterminés			5200 Taxes on use of goods / Impôts sur utilisation des biens			6000 Other taxes / Autres impôts		
	1975	1995	2013	1975	1995	2013	1975	1995	2013	1975	1995	2013
Federal countries / Pays fédéraux												
Australia / Australie	0.0	0.0	0.0	0.6	0.9	0.7	0.9	1.6	0.6	0.0	0.0	0.0
Austria / Autriche	1.3	0.0	0.0	0.5	0.1	0.1	0.2	0.0	0.0	0.0	0.0	0.0
Belgium / Belgique[1]	..	0.0	0.0	..	0.0	0.0	..	0.2	0.6	..	0.0	0.0
Canada	2.0	2.6	2.5	1.7	2.0	1.7	1.8	0.5	0.4	0.0	0.0	0.0
Germany / Allemagne[1]	1.7	2.8	3.1	0.2	0.1	0.1	0.5	0.4	0.0	0.0	0.0	0.0
Mexico / Mexique	..	0.0	0.0	..	0.0	0.0	..	0.0	0.1	..	0.0	0.0
Switzerland / Suisse	0.0	0.0	0.0	0.1	0.1	0.2	0.4	0.4	0.3	0.0	0.0	0.0
United States / États-Unis	1.5	1.8	1.5	1.1	0.9	0.8	0.5	0.4	0.5	0.0	0.0	0.0
Unweighted average / Moyenne non pondérée	1.1	0.9	0.9	0.7	0.5	0.5	0.7	0.4	0.3	0.0	0.0	0.0
Regional country / Pays régional												
Spain / Espagne[1,2,3]	..	0.1	0.1	..	0.4	0.3	..	0.0	0.0	..	0.0	0.1

1. Payments to the European Union are excluded from these comparisons. / Les versements à L'Union européenne ne sont pas retenus dans ces comparaisons.
2. The total tax revenue has been reduced by the amount of any capital transfer that represents uncollected taxes. The capital transfer has been allocated between tax headings in proportion to the reported tax revenue. / Le total des recettes fiscales a été diminué du montant de tout transfert en capital représentant les impôts non perçus. Le transfert en capital a été réparti entre les différentes rubriques en proportion des recettes fiscales.
3. Spain is constitutionally a non-federal country but has a highly decentralised political structure. / L'Espagne est constitutionnellement un pays non fédéral mais avec une structure politique très décentralisée.

StatLink http://dx.doi.org/10.1787/888933277452

Table 84. **Main local government tax revenues as % of GDP at market prices (Federal/regional countries)**
Tableau 84. **Principales recettes fiscales des administrations locales en % du PIB aux prix du marché (Pays fédéraux/régionaux)**

	1000 Income & profits / Revenu & bénéfices			2000 Social security / Sécurité sociale			3000 Payroll / Salaires			4000 Property / Patrimoine		
	1975	1995	2013	1975	1995	2013	1975	1995	2013	1975	1995	2013
Federal countries / Pays fédéraux												
Australia / Australie	0.0	0.0	0.0	0.0	0.0	0.0	0.0	0.0	0.0	1.1	1.0	0.9
Austria / Autriche	1.8	0.0	0.0	0.1	0.1	0.1	0.5	0.8	0.9	0.5	0.2	0.2
Belgium / Belgique[1]	1.1	1.4	0.7	0.0	0.0	0.0	0.0	0.0	0.0	0.3	0.4	1.2
Canada	0.0	0.0	0.0	0.0	0.0	0.0	0.0	0.0	0.0	2.7	2.9	2.8
Germany / Allemagne[1]	2.1	2.1	2.4	0.0	0.0	0.0	0.3	0.0	0.0	0.6	0.5	0.4
Mexico / Mexique	..	0.0	0.0	..	0.0	0.0	..	0.0	0.0	..	0.1	0.2
Switzerland / Suisse	3.9	3.8	3.5	0.0	0.0	0.0	0.0	0.0	0.0	0.7	0.6	0.6
United States / États-Unis	0.2	0.2	0.2	0.0	0.0	0.0	0.0	0.0	0.0	3.0	2.6	2.6
Unweighted average / Moyenne non pondérée	1.3	1.0	0.8	0.0	0.0	0.0	0.1	0.1	0.1	1.3	1.0	1.1
Regional country / Pays régional												
Spain / Espagne[1,2,3]	0.4	0.5	0.6	0.0	0.0	0.0	0.0	0.0	0.0	0.1	0.8	1.4

	5110 General taxes / Impôts généraux			5120 Specific goods and services / Biens et services déterminés			5200 Taxes on use of goods / Impôts sur utilisation des biens			6000 Other taxes / Autres impôts		
	1975	1995	2013	1975	1995	2013	1975	1995	2013	1975	1995	2013
Federal countries / Pays fédéraux												
Australia / Australie	0.0	0.0	0.0	0.0	0.0	0.0	0.0	0.0	0.0	0.0	0.0	0.0
Austria / Autriche	0.9	0.0	0.0	0.6	0.3	0.0	0.0	0.1	0.1	0.1	0.0	0.0
Belgium / Belgique[1]	0.0	0.0	0.0	0.3	0.1	0.1	0.0	0.0	0.0	0.0	0.0	0.0
Canada	0.0	0.0	0.0	0.0	0.0	0.0	0.1	0.0	0.1	0.3	0.4	0.0
Germany / Allemagne[1]	0.0	0.0	0.1	0.0	0.0	0.0	0.0	0.0	0.0	0.0	0.0	0.0
Mexico / Mexique	..	0.0	0.0	..	0.0	0.0	..	0.0	0.0	..	0.0	0.1
Switzerland / Suisse	0.0	0.0	0.0	0.0	0.0	0.1	0.0	0.0	0.0	0.0	0.0	0.0
United States / États-Unis	0.3	0.4	0.4	0.1	0.2	0.2	0.1	0.2	0.2	0.0	0.0	0.0
Unweighted average / Moyenne non pondérée	0.2	0.0	0.1	0.2	0.1	0.1	0.0	0.0	0.1	0.1	0.1	0.0
Regional country / Pays régional												
Spain / Espagne[1,2,3]	0.2	0.4	0.5	0.0	0.1	0.2	0.0	0.7	0.4	0.0	0.1	0.2

1. Payments to the European Union are excluded from these comparisons. / Les versements à L'Union européenne ne sont pas retenus dans ces comparaisons.
2. The total tax revenue has been reduced by the amount of any capital transfer that represents uncollected taxes. The capital transfer has been allocated between tax headings in proportion to the reported tax revenue. / Le total des recettes fiscales a été diminué du montant de tout transfert en capital représentant les impôts non perçus. Le transfert en capital a été réparti entre les différentes rubriques en proportion des recettes fiscales.
3. Spain is constitutionally a non-federal country but has a highly decentralised political structure. / L'Espagne est constitutionnellement un pays non fédéral mais avec une structure politique très décentralisée.

StatLink http://dx.doi.org/10.1787/888933277461

Table 85. **Main state government taxes as % of total tax revenues of state government (Federal/regional countries)**

Tableau 85. **Principaux impôts des administrations d'états en % du total des recettes fiscales des administrations d'états (Pays fédéraux/régionaux)**

	1000 Income & profits / Revenu & bénéfices			2000 Social security / Sécurité sociale			3000 Payroll / Salaires			4000 Property / Patrimoine		
	1975	1995	2013	1975	1995	2013	1975	1995	2013	1975	1995	2013
Federal countries / Pays fédéraux												
Australia / Australie	0.0	0.0	0.0	0.0	0.0	0.0	35.3	25.1	31.1	26.6	28.1	37.9
Austria / Autriche	44.2	42.3	45.8	1.8	24.0	23.6	0.0	10.2	8.6	1.8	2.4	1.9
Belgium / Belgique[1]	..	4.7	0.0	..	0.0	0.4	..	0.0	0.0	..	70.4	72.7
Canada	43.6	48.7	45.9	0.0	0.0	6.7	0.0	6.0	5.3	2.3	6.0	3.3
Germany / Allemagne[1]	62.8	51.9	53.9	0.0	0.0	0.0	0.0	0.0	0.0	6.2	6.1	5.8
Mexico / Mexique	..	0.0	0.0	..	0.0	0.0	..	45.3	53.8	..	44.5	16.9
Switzerland / Suisse	77.7	78.3	79.0	0.0	0.0	0.0	0.0	0.0	0.0	14.3	14.7	13.6
United States / États-Unis	31.6	38.8	42.0	0.0	0.0	0.0	0.0	0.0	0.0	4.1	3.6	2.0
Unweighted average / Moyenne non pondérée	43.3	33.1	33.3	0.3	3.0	3.8	5.9	10.8	12.4	9.2	22.0	19.3
Regional country / Pays régional												
Spain / Espagne[1,2,3]	..	8.5	69.7	..	0.0	0.0	..	0.0	0.0	..	55.9	18.9

	5110 General taxes / Impôts généraux			5120 Specific goods and services / Biens et services déterminés			5200 Taxes on use of goods / Impôts sur utilisation des biens			6000 Other taxes / Autres impôts		
	1975	1995	2013	1975	1995	2013	1975	1995	2013	1975	1995	2013
Federal countries / Pays fédéraux												
Australia / Australie	0.0	0.0	0.0	16.0	17.3	16.3	22.0	29.5	14.7	0.0	0.0	0.0
Austria / Autriche	33.9	0.0	0.0	13.5	12.2	8.5	4.4	5.0	6.7	0.4	4.0	4.9
Belgium / Belgique[1]	..	0.0	0.0	..	3.5	1.7	..	21.4	24.7	..	0.0	0.5
Canada	19.6	19.9	20.9	16.8	15.5	14.2	17.8	3.8	3.7	0.0	0.0	0.0
Germany / Allemagne[1]	21.8	35.4	39.0	2.8	1.8	1.2	6.4	4.7	0.0	0.0	0.0	0.0
Mexico / Mexique	..	0.0	0.0	..	0.3	3.3	..	6.4	19.5	..	3.5	6.4
Switzerland / Suisse	0.0	0.0	0.0	1.5	1.0	2.3	6.4	5.9	5.0	0.0	0.0	0.0
United States / États-Unis	30.8	33.2	30.2	23.6	16.1	16.2	10.0	8.3	9.6	0.0	0.0	0.0
Unweighted average / Moyenne non pondérée	17.7	11.1	11.3	12.4	8.5	8.0	11.2	10.6	10.5	0.1	0.9	1.5
Regional country / Pays régional												
Spain / Espagne[1,2,3]	..	9.2	3.3	..	23.6	6.2	..	0.6	0.4	..	2.2	1.5

1. Payments to the European Union are excluded from these comparisons. / Les versements à L'Union européenne ne sont pas retenus dans ces comparaisons.
2. The total tax revenue has been reduced by the amount of any capital transfer that represents uncollected taxes. The capital transfer has been allocated between tax headings in proportion to the reported tax revenue. / Le total des recettes fiscales a été diminué du montant de tout transfert en capital représentant les impôts non perçus. Le transfert en capital a été réparti entre les différentes rubriques en proportion des recettes fiscales.
3. Spain is constitutionally a non-federal country but has a highly decentralised political structure. / L'Espagne est constitutionnellement un pays non fédéral mais avec une structure politique très décentralisée.

StatLink http://dx.doi.org/10.1787/888933277475

Table 86. **Main local government taxes as % of total tax revenues of local governments (Federal/regional countries)**

Tableau 86. **Principaux impôts locaux en % du total des recettes fiscales des administrations locales (Pays fédéraux/régionaux)**

	1000 Income & profits / Revenu & bénéfices			2000 Social security / Sécurité sociale			3000 Payroll / Salaires			4000 Property / Patrimoine		
	1975	1995	2013	1975	1995	2013	1975	1995	2013	1975	1995	2013
Federal countries / Pays fédéraux												
Australia / Australie	0.0	0.0	0.0	0.0	0.0	0.0	0.0	0.0	0.0	100.0	100.0	100.0
Austria / Autriche	38.9	1.5	0.0	1.3	8.6	9.5	11.5	50.0	63.9	11.2	13.2	14.8
Belgium / Belgique[1]	66.3	71.3	34.5	2.6	1.9	0.3	0.0	0.0	0.0	15.0	19.0	58.9
Canada	0.0	0.0	0.0	0.0	0.0	0.0	0.0	0.0	0.0	88.3	85.7	97.4
Germany / Allemagne[1]	69.4	79.5	79.4	0.0	0.0	0.0	9.0	0.0	0.0	20.3	19.3	14.6
Mexico / Mexique	..	0.5	0.0	..	0.0	0.0	..	0.2	0.0	..	77.5	75.3
Switzerland / Suisse	85.5	85.8	84.9	0.0	0.0	0.0	0.0	0.0	0.0	14.3	13.3	13.6
United States / États-Unis	4.3	5.8	6.0	0.0	0.0	0.0	0.0	0.0	0.0	81.9	72.9	71.6
Unweighted average / Moyenne non pondérée	37.8	30.6	25.6	0.5	1.3	1.2	2.9	6.3	8.0	47.3	50.1	55.8
Regional country / Pays régional												
Spain / Espagne[1,2,3]	57.3	19.8	18.4	0.0	0.0	0.0	0.0	0.0	0.0	8.5	29.6	42.0

	5110 General taxes / Impôts généraux			5120 Specific goods and services / Biens et services déterminés			5200 Taxes on use of goods / Impôts sur utilisation des biens			6000 Other taxes / Autres impôts		
	1975	1995	2013	1975	1995	2013	1975	1995	2013	1975	1995	2013
Federal countries / Pays fédéraux												
Australia / Australie	0.0	0.0	0.0	0.0	0.0	0.0	0.0	0.0	0.0	0.0	0.0	0.0
Austria / Autriche	19.7	0.0	0.0	14.1	19.5	3.5	1.0	5.2	5.6	2.4	2.0	2.7
Belgium / Belgique[1]	0.0	0.0	0.0	14.6	6.9	5.1	1.5	0.9	1.2	0.0	0.0	0.0
Canada	0.2	0.1	0.1	0.2	0.0	0.1	2.1	1.2	1.9	9.2	12.9	0.5
Germany / Allemagne[1]	0.0	0.0	4.6	0.5	0.5	0.8	0.4	0.3	0.4	0.4	0.3	0.2
Mexico / Mexique	..	0.0	0.0	..	16.4	3.2	..	0.2	0.0	..	5.1	21.5
Switzerland / Suisse	0.0	0.0	0.0	0.2	0.7	1.3	0.1	0.2	0.2	0.0	0.0	0.0
United States / États-Unis	7.1	10.8	11.9	3.6	4.8	4.6	3.1	5.7	5.9	0.0	0.0	0.0
Unweighted average / Moyenne non pondérée	3.8	1.4	2.1	4.7	6.1	2.3	1.2	1.7	1.9	1.7	2.5	3.1
Regional country / Pays régional												
Spain / Espagne[1,2,3]	31.0	14.8	15.2	3.2	4.1	5.9	0.0	26.9	13.3	0.0	4.7	5.1

1. Payments to the European Union are excluded from these comparisons. / Les versements à L'Union européenne ne sont pas retenus dans ces comparaisons.
2. The total tax revenue has been reduced by the amount of any capital transfer that represents uncollected taxes. The capital transfer has been allocated between tax headings in proportion to the reported tax revenue. / Le total des recettes fiscales a été diminué du montant de tout transfert en capital représentant les impôts non perçus. Le transfert en capital a été réparti entre les différentes rubriques en proportion des recettes fiscales.
3. Spain is constitutionally a non-federal country but has a highly decentralised political structure. / L'Espagne est constitutionnellement un pays non fédéral mais avec une structure politique très décentralisée.

StatLink http://dx.doi.org/10.1787/888933277483

Table 87. Main local government tax revenues as % of GDP at market prices (Unitary countries)
Tableau 87. Principaux impôts locaux en % du PIB aux prix du marché (Pays unitaires)

	1000 Income & profits / Revenu & bénéfices			4000 Property / Patrimoine			5110 General taxes / Impôts généraux		
	1975	1995	2013	1975	1995	2013	1975	1995	2013
Chile / Chili	..	0.0	0.0	..	0.5	0.6	..	0.0	0.0
Czech Republic / République tchèque[1]	..	0.0	0.0	..	0.2	0.2	..	0.0	0.0
Denmark / Danemark[1,2]	9.6	13.6	11.1	1.5	1.0	1.4	0.0	0.0	0.0
Estonia / Estonie[1]	..	4.5	3.9	..	0.3	0.3	..	0.0	0.0
Finland / Finlande[1]	8.5	9.5	9.5	0.0	0.4	0.7	0.0	0.0	0.0
France[1,2]	0.0	0.0	0.0	1.2	2.2	3.0	0.0	0.0	0.0
Greece / Grèce	0.1	0.0	0.0	0.0	0.1	1.9	0.1	0.0	0.0
Hungary / Hongrie[1]	..	0.0	0.0	..	0.3	0.5	..	0.7	1.7
Iceland / Islande	3.5	4.5	7.8	0.8	1.2	1.6	0.0	0.6	0.0
Ireland / Irlande[1]	0.0	0.0	0.0	2.0	0.7	0.8	0.0	0.0	0.0
Israel / Israël	..	0.0	0.0	..	1.9	2.1	..	0.0	0.0
Italy / Italie[1]	0.2	0.6	1.8	0.0	0.8	1.2	0.0	0.0	0.4
Japan / Japon	2.9	3.5	3.7	1.3	2.1	2.1	0.0	0.0	0.5
Korea / Corée	0.3	0.4	0.7	0.8	2.1	1.7	0.0	0.0	0.2
Luxembourg[1]	1.5	2.1	1.2	0.2	0.1	0.1	0.0	0.0	0.0
Netherlands / Pays-Bas[1]	0.1	0.0	0.0	0.2	0.7	0.7	0.0	0.0	0.0
New Zealand / Nouvelle-Zélande	0.0	0.0	0.0	1.9	1.7	1.9	0.0	0.0	0.0
Norway / Norvège	8.0	7.1	4.7	0.4	0.8	0.6	0.0	0.0	0.0
Poland / Pologne[1]	..	1.4	2.3	..	1.3	1.4	..	0.0	0.0
Portugal[1]	0.0	0.3	0.7	0.0	0.7	1.0	0.0	0.4	0.3
Slovak Republic / République slovaque[1]	..	0.0	0.0	..	0.4	0.4	..	0.0	0.0
Slovenia / Slovénie[1]	..	1.8	3.2	..	0.5	0.6	..	0.0	0.0
Sweden / Suède[1]	11.3	14.1	15.4	0.0	0.0	0.4	0.0	0.0	0.0
Turkey / Turquie	..	0.6	0.6	..	0.0	0.4	..	0.7	0.7
United Kingdom / Royaume-Uni[1]	0.0	0.0	0.0	3.8	1.2	1.6	0.0	0.0	0.0
Unweighted average / Moyenne non pondérée	2.9	2.6	2.7	0.9	0.9	1.1	0.0	0.1	0.2

	5120 Specific goods and services / Biens et services déterminés			5200 Taxes on use of goods / Impôts sur utilisation des biens			Other taxes / Autres impôts		
	1975	1995	2013	1975	1995	2013	1975	1995	2013
Chile / Chili	..	0.2	0.2	..	0.5	0.6	..	0.0	0.0
Czech Republic / République tchèque[1]	..	0.0	0.0	..	0.1	0.2	..	0.0	0.0
Denmark / Danemark[1,2]	0.0	0.0	0.0	0.0	0.0	0.0	0.0	0.0	0.0
Estonia / Estonie[1]	..	0.0	0.0	..	0.0	0.0	..	0.0	0.0
Finland / Finlande[1]	0.0	0.0	0.0	0.0	0.0	0.0	0.0	0.0	0.0
France[1,2]	0.1	0.3	1.2	0.1	0.3	0.2	1.2	1.8	1.4
Greece / Grèce	0.2	0.1	0.1	0.1	0.0	0.0	0.1	0.0	0.0
Hungary / Hongrie[1]	..	0.0	0.0	..	0.0	0.1	..	0.0	0.0
Iceland / Islande	0.4	0.0	0.0	0.0	0.0	0.1	0.6	0.0	0.0
Ireland / Irlande[1]	0.0	0.0	0.0	0.0	0.0	0.0	0.0	0.1	0.1
Israel / Israël	..	0.0	0.0	..	0.1	0.1	..	0.0	0.0
Italy / Italie[1]	0.0	0.2	0.5	0.0	0.3	0.5	0.0	0.3	2.6
Japan / Japon	0.8	0.6	0.5	0.3	0.3	0.4	0.0	0.1	0.1
Korea / Corée	0.2	0.6	0.3	0.2	0.4	0.5	0.0	0.1	0.5
Luxembourg[1]	0.0	0.0	0.0	0.0	0.0	0.0	0.3	0.0	0.0
Netherlands / Pays-Bas[1]	0.0	0.0	0.0	0.1	0.3	0.6	0.0	0.0	0.0
New Zealand / Nouvelle-Zélande	0.1	0.0	0.0	0.1	0.2	0.2	0.0	0.0	0.0
Norway / Norvège	0.0	0.0	0.0	0.0	0.0	0.1	0.3	0.0	0.0
Poland / Pologne[1]	..	0.0	0.0	..	0.4	0.2	..	0.0	0.2
Portugal[1]	0.0	0.1	0.1	0.0	0.1	0.2	0.0	0.0	0.1
Slovak Republic / République slovaque[1]	..	0.1	0.0	..	0.0	0.2	..	0.0	0.2
Slovenia / Slovénie[1]	..	0.1	0.1	..	0.0	0.1	..	0.0	0.0
Sweden / Suède[1]	0.0	0.0	0.0	0.0	0.0	0.0	0.0	0.0	0.0
Turkey / Turquie	..	0.1	0.6	..	0.0	0.0	..	0.7	0.3
United Kingdom / Royaume-Uni[1]	0.0	0.0	0.0	0.0	0.0	0.0	0.0	0.0	0.0
Unweighted average / Moyenne non pondérée	0.1	0.1	0.2	0.1	0.1	0.2	0.2	0.1	0.2

1. Payments to the European Union are excluded from these comparisons. / Les versements à l'Union européenne ne sont pas retenus dans ces comparaisons.
2. The total tax revenue has been reduced by the amount of any capital transfer that represents uncollected taxes. The capital transfer has been allocated between tax headings in proportion to the reported tax revenue. / Le total des recettes fiscales a été diminué du montant de tout transfert en capital représentant les impôts non perçus. Le transfert en capital a été réparti entre les différentes rubriques en proportion des recettes fiscales.

StatLink http://dx.doi.org/10.1787/888933277492

Table 88. Main local government taxes as % of total tax revenues of local governments (Unitary countries)
Tableau 88. Principaux impôts locaux en % du total des recettes fiscales des administrations locales (Pays unitaires)

	1000 Income & profits / Revenu & bénéfices			1100 Of individuals / Personnes physiques			1200 Corporate / Sociétés			4000 Property / Patrimoine		
	1975	1995	2013	1975	1995	2013	1975	1995	2013	1975	1995	2013
Chile / Chili	..	0.0	0.0	..	0.0	0.0	..	0.0	0.0	..	45.0	41.2
Czech Republic / République tchèque[1]	..	0.0	0.0	..	0.0	0.0	..	0.0	0.0	..	76.7	55.9
Denmark / Danemark[1,2]	86.3	93.3	88.8	86.3	93.3	88.8	0.0	0.0	0.0	13.7	6.7	11.2
Estonia / Estonie[1]	..	93.9	91.4	..	93.9	91.4	..	0.0	0.0	..	5.5	7.2
Finland / Finlande[1]	99.8	95.4	93.3	89.9	85.2	86.3	9.9	10.2	7.0	0.0	4.5	6.6
France[1,2]	0.0	0.0	0.1	0.0	0.0	0.0	0.0	0.0	0.0	46.0	47.8	51.9
Greece / Grèce	16.5	0.0	0.0	11.0	0.0	0.0	0.0	0.0	0.0	6.6	55.0	96.4
Hungary / Hongrie[1]	..	0.0	0.0	..	0.0	0.0	..	0.0	0.0	..	28.9	20.0
Iceland / Islande	65.1	71.9	81.9	62.0	71.9	81.9	3.1	0.0	0.0	15.3	19.3	17.0
Ireland / Irlande[1]	0.0	0.0	0.0	0.0	0.0	0.0	0.0	0.0	0.0	100.0	87.9	87.9
Israel / Israël	..	0.0	0.0	..	0.0	0.0	..	0.0	0.0	..	93.5	94.3
Italy / Italie[1]	80.0	27.6	25.3	48.0	0.7	23.1	32.0	0.5	2.2	17.5	38.6	16.4
Japan / Japon	54.8	52.7	50.8	26.3	30.5	34.7	28.5	22.2	16.1	24.9	31.6	28.9
Korea / Corée	23.0	11.1	17.7	0.0	7.4	10.0	0.0	3.7	7.7	54.5	58.5	44.6
Luxembourg[1]	74.6	92.8	90.9	0.0	0.0	0.0	74.6	92.8	90.9	9.3	5.9	7.5
Netherlands / Pays-Bas[1]	15.4	0.0	0.0	15.4	0.0	0.0	0.0	0.0	0.0	54.2	69.2	53.1
New Zealand / Nouvelle-Zélande	0.0	0.0	0.0	0.0	0.0	0.0	0.0	0.0	0.0	89.1	89.9	90.5
Norway / Norvège	91.9	89.7	87.7	86.3	81.6	87.7	5.7	8.2	0.0	5.2	9.7	10.9
Poland / Pologne[1]	..	45.5	57.0	..	41.1	47.9	..	4.4	9.2	..	40.6	33.8
Portugal[1]	50.0	21.8	30.2	..	11.1	19.5	..	10.7	10.7	0.0	42.5	42.4
Slovak Republic / République slovaque[1]	..	0.0	0.0	..	0.0	0.0	..	0.0	0.0	..	83.4	51.4
Slovenia / Slovénie[1]	..	75.8	79.7	..	74.9	79.7	..	0.0	0.0	..	20.7	15.1
Sweden / Suède[1]	99.6	99.7	97.4	91.5	99.7	97.4	8.2	0.0	0.0	0.0	0.0	2.6
Turkey / Turquie	..	28.1	23.9	..	21.4	16.1	..	6.7	7.8	..	2.0	13.8
United Kingdom / Royaume-Uni[1]	0.0	0.0	0.0	0.0	0.0	0.0	0.0	0.0	0.0	100.0	100.0	99.3
Unweighted average / Moyenne non pondérée	47.3	36.0	36.6	34.4	28.5	30.6	10.8	6.4	6.1	33.5	42.5	40.0

	5110 General taxes / Impôts généraux			5120 Specific goods and services / Biens et services déterminés			5200 Taxes on use of goods / Impôts sur utilisation des biens			Other taxes / Autres impôts		
	1975	1995	2013	1975	1995	2013	1975	1995	2013	1975	1995	2013
Chile / Chili	..	0.0	0.0	..	15.1	16.0	..	40.0	42.8	..	0.0	0.0
Czech Republic / République tchèque[1]	..	0.0	0.0	..	2.5	1.5	..	20.8	42.6	..	0.0	0.0
Denmark / Danemark[1,2]	0.0	0.0	0.0	0.0	0.0	0.0	0.0	0.0	0.0	0.0	0.0	0.0
Estonia / Estonie[1]	..	0.1	0.0	..	0.1	0.5	..	0.4	0.9	..	0.0	0.0
Finland / Finlande[1]	0.0	0.0	0.0	0.1	0.0	0.0	0.1	0.1	0.0	0.0	0.0	0.1
France[1,2]	0.0	0.0	0.0	4.8	7.4	20.7	3.2	6.9	3.1	46.0	37.9	24.2
Greece / Grèce	9.0	2.9	0.6	32.9	24.4	2.8	18.7	17.6	0.3	16.3	0.0	0.0
Hungary / Hongrie[1]	..	63.5	74.2	..	1.3	1.2	..	4.5	4.5	..	1.8	0.0
Iceland / Islande	0.0	8.8	0.0	7.9	0.0	0.0	0.0	0.0	1.1	11.7	0.0	0.0
Ireland / Irlande[1]	0.0	0.0	0.0	0.0	0.0	0.0	0.0	0.0	0.0	0.0	12.1	12.1
Israel / Israël	..	0.0	0.0	..	0.0	0.0	..	6.5	5.7	..	0.0	0.0
Italy / Italie[1]	0.0	0.0	5.6	0.0	7.3	7.7	2.5	13.8	7.7	0.0	12.7	37.3
Japan / Japon	0.0	0.0	7.5	15.1	9.6	6.7	4.9	5.0	5.0	0.2	1.0	1.1
Korea / Corée	0.0	0.0	5.8	11.7	16.1	7.1	10.8	11.5	12.5	0.0	2.8	12.3
Luxembourg[1]	0.0	0.0	0.0	0.9	0.9	1.3	0.0	0.2	0.2	15.2	0.2	0.2
Netherlands / Pays-Bas[1]	0.0	0.0	0.0	2.7	1.6	2.1	27.7	29.2	44.8	0.0	0.0	0.0
New Zealand / Nouvelle-Zélande	0.0	0.0	0.0	6.7	1.8	0.7	4.2	8.3	8.8	0.0	0.0	0.0
Norway / Norvège	0.0	0.0	0.0	0.0	0.0	0.0	0.0	0.6	1.3	2.9	0.0	0.0
Poland / Pologne[1]	..	0.0	0.0	..	0.0	0.0	..	12.4	4.7	..	1.5	4.5
Portugal[1]	0.0	22.5	12.1	0.0	8.8	5.6	50.0	4.0	6.5	0.0	0.4	3.3
Slovak Republic / République slovaque[1]	..	0.0	0.0	..	10.3	2.2	..	0.9	23.6	..	5.5	22.8
Slovenia / Slovénie[1]	..	0.0	0.0	..	2.8	2.4	..	0.0	2.8	..	0.8	0.0
Sweden / Suède[1]	0.0	0.0	0.0	0.3	0.3	0.0	0.1	0.0	0.0	0.0	0.0	0.0
Turkey / Turquie	..	30.8	26.7	..	6.0	22.9	..	0.5	1.9	..	32.7	10.9
United Kingdom / Royaume-Uni[1]	0.0	0.0	0.0	0.0	0.0	0.0	0.0	0.0	0.0	0.0	0.0	0.7
Unweighted average / Moyenne non pondérée	0.6	5.1	5.3	5.2	4.6	4.1	7.6	7.3	8.8	5.8	4.4	5.2

1. Payments to the European Union are excluded from these comparisons. / Les versements à L'Union européenne ne sont pas retenus dans ces comparaisons.
2. The total tax revenue has been reduced by the amount of any capital transfer that represents uncollected taxes. The capital transfer has been allocated between tax headings in proportion to the reported tax revenue. / Le total des recettes fiscales a été diminué du montant de tout transfert en capital représentant les impôts non perçus. Le transfert en capital a été réparti entre les différentes rubriques en proportion des recettes fiscales.

StatLink http://dx.doi.org/10.1787/888933277508

Table 89. **Australia, tax revenues by sub-sectors of government**

Million AUD

	Federal government					State/Regional				
	1975	1985	1995	2005	2013	1975	1985	1995	2005	2013
1000 Taxes on income, profits and capital gains	**11 831**	**39 435**	**82 615**	**175 929**	**248 448**	**0**	**0**	**0**	**0**	**0**
1100 Of individuals	9 213	32 673	60 602	118 494	170 313	..	..	..	..	..
1200 Corporate	2 618	6 762	22 013	57 435	78 135	..	..	..	..	..
1300 Unallocable between 1100 and 1200	0	0	0	0	0	..	..	..	..	..
2000 Social security contributions	**0**	**0**	**0**	**0**	**0**	**0**	**0**	**0**	**0**	**0**
2100 Employees	..	..	..	..	..	..	..	..	..	..
2200 Employers	..	..	..	..	..	..	..	..	..	..
2300 Self-employed or non-employed	..	..	..	..	..	..	..	..	..	..
2400 Unallocable between 2100, 2200 and 2300	..	..	..	..	..	..	..	..	..	..
3000 Taxes on payroll and workforce	**54**	**56**	**3 065**	**369**	**844**	**1 171**	**3 364**	**7 120**	**13 095**	**21 378**
4000 Taxes on property	**103**	**260**	**8**	**14**	**13**	**883**	**2 770**	**7 988**	**16 923**	**26 044**
4100 Recurrent taxes on immovable property	12	31	0	0	0	217	706	1 840	4 559	8 733
4200 Recurrent taxes on net wealth	0	0	0	0	0	0	0	0	0	0
4300 Estate, inheritance and gift taxes	87	0	0	0	0	227	6	0	0	0
4400 Taxes on financial and capital transactions	4	229	8	14	13	439	2 058	6 148	12 364	17 311
4500 Non-recurrent taxes	0	0	0	0	0	0	0	0	0	0
4600 Other recurrent taxes on property	0	0	0	0	0	0	0	0	0	0
5000 Taxes on goods and services	**4 932**	**19 087**	**30 004**	**68 983**	**102 216**	**1 262**	**4 630**	**13 295**	**14 458**	**21 300**
5100 Taxes on production, sale, transfer, etc	4 919	18 890	29 613	67 822	92 469	532	1 783	4 923	8 166	11 209
5110 General taxes	1 408	5 728	12 970	40 086	56 819	0	0	0	0	0
5120 Taxes on specific goods and services	3 511	13 162	16 643	27 736	35 650	532	1 783	4 923	8 166	11 209
5130 Unallocable between 5110 and 5120	0	0	0	0	0	0	0	0	0	0
5200 Taxes on use of goods and perform activities	13	197	391	1 161	9 747	730	2 847	8 372	6 292	10 091
5300 Unallocable between 5100 and 5200	0	0	0	0	0	0	0	0	0	0
6000 Other taxes	**0**	**0**	**0**	**0**	**0**	**0**	**0**	**0**	**0**	**0**
6100 Paid solely by business	..	..	..	..	..	..	..	..	..	..
6200 Other	..	..	..	..	..	..	..	..	..	..
Total tax revenue	**16 920**	**58 838**	**115 692**	**245 295**	**351 521**	**3 316**	**10 764**	**28 403**	**44 476**	**68 722**

Million AUD

	Local government					Social Security Funds				
	1975	1985	1995	2005	2013	1975	1985	1995	2005	2013
1000 Taxes on income, profits and capital gains	**0**	**0**	**0**	**0**	**0**	**0**	**0**	**0**	**0**	**0**
1100 Of individuals	..	..	..	..	..	..	..	..	..	..
1200 Corporate	..	..	..	..	..	..	..	..	..	..
1300 Unallocable between 1100 and 1200	..	..	..	..	..	..	..	..	..	..
2000 Social security contributions	**0**	**0**	**0**	**0**	**0**	**0**	**0**	**0**	**0**	**0**
2100 Employees	..	..	..	..	..	..	..	..	..	..
2200 Employers	..	..	..	..	..	..	..	..	..	..
2300 Self-employed or non-employed	..	..	..	..	..	..	..	..	..	..
2400 Unallocable between 2100, 2200 and 2300	..	..	..	..	..	..	..	..	..	..
3000 Taxes on payroll and workforce	**0**	**0**	**0**	**0**	**0**	**0**	**0**	**0**	**0**	**0**
4000 Taxes on property	**883**	**2 627**	**5 134**	**8 726**	**14 738**	**0**	**0**	**0**	**0**	**0**
4100 Recurrent taxes on immovable property	883	2 627	5 134	8 726	14 738	..	..	..	..	..
4200 Recurrent taxes on net wealth	0	0	0	0	0	..	..	..	..	..
4300 Estate, inheritance and gift taxes	0	0	0	0	0	..	..	..	..	..
4400 Taxes on financial and capital transactions	0	0	0	0	0	..	..	..	..	..
4500 Non-recurrent taxes	0	0	0	0	0	..	..	..	..	..
4600 Other recurrent taxes on property	0	0	0	0	0	..	..	..	..	..
5000 Taxes on goods and services	**0**	**10**	**0**	**0**	**0**	**0**	**0**	**0**	**0**	**0**
5100 Taxes on production, sale, transfer, etc	0	0	0	0	0	0	0	0	0	0
5110 General taxes	0	0	0	0	0	0	0	0	0	0
5120 Taxes on specific goods and services	0	0	0	0	0	0	0	0	0	0
5130 Unallocable between 5110 and 5120	0	0	0	0	0	0	0	0	0	0
5200 Taxes on use of goods and perform activities	0	10	0	0	0	0	0	0	0	0
5300 Unallocable between 5100 and 5200	0	0	0	0	0	0	0	0	0	0
6000 Other taxes	**0**	**0**	**0**	**0**	**0**	**0**	**0**	**0**	**0**	**0**
6100 Paid solely by business	..	..	..	..	..	..	..	..	..	..
6200 Other	..	..	..	..	..	..	..	..	..	..
Total tax revenue	**883**	**2 637**	**5 134**	**8 726**	**14 738**	**0**	**0**	**0**	**0**	**0**

StatLink http://dx.doi.org/10.1787/888933277510

Table 90. **Austria, tax revenues by sub-sectors of government**

Million EUR

	Federal government					State/Regional				
	1975	1985	1995	2005	2013	1975	1985	1995	2005	2013
1000 Taxes on income, profits and capital gains	**3 064**	**6 436**	**18 452**	**28 781**	**38 777**	**865**	**2 927**	**547**	**742**	**1 015**
1100 Of individuals	2 381	5 389	14 649	22 126	30 594	834	2 738	459	637	880
1200 Corporate	655	1 032	2 267	5 341	6 828	31	189	88	104	135
1300 Unallocable between 1100 and 1200	27	15	1 536	1 313	1 354	0	0	0	0	0
2000 Social security contributions	**352**	**1 687**	**4 243**	**5 720**	**7 071**	**34**	**137**	**311**	**409**	**524**
2100 Employees	225	1 003	2 379	2 978	3 682	34	137	310	395	494
2200 Employers	127	684	1 830	2 498	3 104	0	0	0	0	0
2300 Self-employed or non-employed	0	0	34	243	285	0	0	1	14	30
2400 Unallocable between 2100, 2200 and 2300	0	0	0	0	0	0	0	0	0	0
3000 Taxes on payroll and workforce	**1 217**	**1 654**	**3 394**	**4 384**	**6 489**	**0**	**255**	**132**	**156**	**191**
4000 Taxes on property	**282**	**517**	**655**	**801**	**1 647**	**35**	**57**	**31**	**36**	**43**
4100 Recurrent taxes on immovable property	18	28	32	32	42	15	26	31	36	43
4200 Recurrent taxes on net wealth	226	388	58	0	0	10	9	0	0	0
4300 Estate, inheritance and gift taxes	24	49	82	140	19	10	21	0	0	0
4400 Taxes on financial and capital transactions	14	52	483	629	858	0	0	0	0	0
4500 Non-recurrent taxes	0	0	0	0	728	0	0	0	0	0
4600 Other recurrent taxes on property	0	0	0	0	0	0	0	0	0	0
5000 Taxes on goods and services	**4 554**	**10 021**	**19 830**	**29 148**	**36 976**	**1 013**	**2 142**	**222**	**234**	**337**
5100 Taxes on production, sale, transfer, etc	4 549	9 649	18 974	27 658	35 068	926	1 929	158	139	189
5110 General taxes	2 545	6 186	13 468	19 466	24 978	662	1 644	0	0	0
5120 Taxes on specific goods and services	1 991	3 424	5 462	8 148	10 088	264	285	158	139	189
5130 Unallocable between 5110 and 5120	14	38	44	45	2	0	0	0	0	0
5200 Taxes on use of goods and perform activities	5	372	856	1 489	1 907	87	213	64	95	148
5300 Unallocable between 5100 and 5200	0	0	0	0	0	0	0	0	0	0
6000 Other taxes	**52**	**328**	**305**	**436**	**268**	**8**	**20**	**51**	**64**	**108**
6100 Paid solely by business	..	..	..	..	..	..	..	..	..	..
6200 Other	..	..	..	..	..	..	..	..	..	..
Total tax revenue	**9 521**	**20 644**	**46 879**	**69 270**	**91 226**	**1 955**	**5 538**	**1 295**	**1 640**	**2 217**

Million EUR

	Local government					Social Security Funds[1]				
	1975	1985	1995	2005	2013	1975	1985	1995	2005	2013
1000 Taxes on income, profits and capital gains	**887**	**1 781**	**46**	**0**	**0**	**0**	**0**	**0**	**0**	**0**
1100 Of individuals	771	1 544	19	0	0	..	..	..	..	..
1200 Corporate	115	237	26	0	0	..	..	..	..	..
1300 Unallocable between 1100 and 1200	0	0	0	0	0	..	..	..	..	..
2000 Social security contributions	**29**	**102**	**258**	**393**	**417**	**4 667**	**11 489**	**21 173**	**28 912**	**38 976**
2100 Employees	29	102	207	297	314	1 840	4 315	8 110	10 751	14 507
2200 Employers	0	0	50	95	103	2 375	6 016	10 912	14 037	18 791
2300 Self-employed or non-employed	0	0	0	0	0	453	1 158	2 151	4 125	5 678
2400 Unallocable between 2100, 2200 and 2300	0	0	0	0	0	0	0	0	0	0
3000 Taxes on payroll and workforce	**262**	**495**	**1 492**	**2 035**	**2 809**	**0**	**0**	**0**	**0**	**0**
4000 Taxes on property	**254**	**457**	**395**	**539**	**651**	**0**	**0**	**0**	**0**	**0**
4100 Recurrent taxes on immovable property	139	253	395	539	651	..	..	..	..	..
4200 Recurrent taxes on net wealth	35	21	0	0	0	..	..	..	..	..
4300 Estate, inheritance and gift taxes	0	0	0	0	0	..	..	..	..	..
4400 Taxes on financial and capital transactions	81	183	0	0	0	..	..	..	..	..
4500 Non-recurrent taxes	0	0	0	0	0	..	..	..	..	..
4600 Other recurrent taxes on property	0	0	0	0	0	..	..	..	..	..
5000 Taxes on goods and services	**792**	**1 578**	**738**	**302**	**403**	**0**	**0**	**0**	**0**	**0**
5100 Taxes on production, sale, transfer, etc	769	1 510	582	134	155	..	..	..	..	..
5110 General taxes	448	1 026	0	0	0	..	..	..	..	..
5120 Taxes on specific goods and services	321	484	582	134	155	..	..	..	..	..
5130 Unallocable between 5110 and 5120	0	0	0	0	0	..	..	..	..	..
5200 Taxes on use of goods and perform activities	24	68	155	168	248	..	..	..	..	..
5300 Unallocable between 5100 and 5200	0	0	0	0	0	..	..	..	..	..
6000 Other taxes	**55**	**103**	**59**	**101**	**117**	**0**	**0**	**0**	**0**	**0**
6100 Paid solely by business	..	..	..	..	..	..	..	..	..	..
6200 Other	..	..	..	..	..	..	..	..	..	..
Total tax revenue	**2 279**	**4 516**	**2 986**	**3 369**	**4 398**	**4 667**	**11 489**	**21 173**	**28 912**	**38 976**

Note: Including Vat own resources of the European Union: 2013 = 333.8 and excluding customs duties collected on behalf of the European Union: 2013 = 328.0.

1. These include social security funds whose contributions are controlled by sub-central levels of government. They account for 2.0 percent of contributions in 2013.

StatLink http://dx.doi.org/10.1787/888933277524

Tableau 91. **Belgique, recettes fiscales par sous-secteurs d'administration**

Million EUR

	Administration fédérale					Administration d'État/Régions				
	1975	1985	1995	2005	2013	1975	1985	1995	2005	2013
1000 Impôts sur revenu, bénéfices et gains en capital	**8 534**	**20 536**	**30 899**	**45 809**	**58 796**	**..**	**..**	**79**	**0**	**0**
1100 Des personnes physiques	6 929	17 821	25 973	35 956	46 537	..	..	79	..	..
1200 Des sociétés	1 596	2 706	4 882	9 814	12 222	..	..	0	..	..
1300 Non-ventilables entre 1100 et 1200	10	9	44	39	38	..	..	0	..	..
2000 Cotisations de sécurité sociale	**299**	**866**	**1 181**	**1 904**	**2 336**	**..**	**..**	**0**	**38**	**41**
2100 A la charge des salariés	264	716	854	1 125	1 397	..	..	..	10	11
2200 A la charge des employeurs	36	150	228	608	713	..	..	..	27	29
2300 A charge des travailleurs indép. ou sans emploi	0	0	99	171	226	..	..	..	0	0
2400 Non-ventilables entre 2100, 2200 et 2300	0	0	0	0	0	..	..	..	0	0
3000 Sur salaires ou main d'oeuvre	**0**	**0**	**0**	**0**	**0**	**..**	**..**	**0**	**0**	**0**
4000 Impôts sur le patrimoine	**583**	**1 090**	**1 340**	**873**	**1 574**	**..**	**..**	**1 168**	**4 669**	**7 019**
4100 Impôts périodiques sur la propriété immobilière	12	25	25	41	38	..	..	83	192	245
4200 Impôts périodiques sur l'actif net	0	0	8	189	451	..	..	0	0	0
4300 Impôts sur mut. par décès, succ. et donations	178	326	42	0	0	..	..	647	1 749	3 096
4400 Impôts sur transact. mobilières et immob.	393	739	1 193	521	448	..	..	438	2 728	3 438
4500 Impôts non-périodiques	0	0	73	123	638	..	..	0	0	239
4600 Autres impôts périodiques sur patrimoine	0	0	0	0	0	..	..	0	0	0
5000 Impôts sur les biens et services	**5 813**	**12 732**	**20 795**	**29 816**	**38 158**	**..**	**..**	**412**	**2 044**	**2 543**
5100 Impôts sur production, vente, transfert, etc.	5 562	11 990	19 610	29 574	38 147	..	..	58	76	160
5110 Impôts généraux	3 776	8 735	13 738	21 362	27 259	..	..	0	0	0
5120 Impôts sur biens et services déterminés	1 785	3 255	5 872	8 212	10 888	..	..	58	76	160
5130 Non-ventilables entre 5110 et 5120	0	0	0	0	0	..	..	0	0	0
5200 Impôts sur utilisation des biens et exerc. activites	249	740	1 178	234	1	..	..	355	1 968	2 384
5300 Non-ventilables entre 5100 et 5200	3	2	6	8	10	..	..	0	0	0
6000 Autres impôts	**0**	**0**	**0**	**0**	**0**	**..**	**..**	**0**	**68**	**46**
6100 A la charge exclusive des entreprises	..	..	..	..	..	..	..	..	0	0
6200 A la charge d'autres agents	..	..	..	..	..	..	..	..	68	46
Recettes fiscales totales	**15 230**	**35 224**	**54 215**	**78 402**	**100 864**	**..**	**..**	**1 659**	**6 819**	**9 649**

Million EUR

	Administrations locales					Administrations de sécurité sociale[1]				
	1975	1985	1995	2005	2013	1975	1985	1995	2005	2013
1000 Impôts sur revenu, bénéfices et gains en capital	**683**	**1 868**	**3 058**	**2 249**	**2 871**	**0**	**90**	**335**	**825**	**1 117**
1100 Des personnes physiques	675	1 868	3 058	2 249	2 871	..	90	335	825	1 117
1200 Des sociétés	8	0	0	0	0	..	0	0	0	0
1300 Non-ventilables entre 1100 et 1200	0	0	0	0	0	..	0	0	0	0
2000 Cotisations de sécurité sociale	**27**	**94**	**81**	**23**	**23**	**6 709**	**16 581**	**28 119**	**38 951**	**53 575**
2100 A la charge des salariés	27	94	81	20	19	1 749	4 870	8 268	11 558	15 057
2200 A la charge des employeurs	0	0	0	3	4	4 347	10 121	17 386	24 027	33 681
2300 A charge des travailleurs indép. ou sans emploi	0	0	0	0	0	612	1 590	2 465	3 366	4 837
2400 Non-ventilables entre 2100, 2200 et 2300	0	0	0	0	0	0	0	0	0	0
3000 Sur salaires ou main d'oeuvre	**0**	**0**	**0**	**0**	**0**	**0**	**0**	**0**	**5**	**8**
4000 Impôts sur le patrimoine	**154**	**377**	**815**	**3 599**	**4 904**	**0**	**80**	**121**	**229**	**309**
4100 Impôts périodiques sur la propriété immobilière	154	377	815	3 599	4 904	..	0	0	0	0
4200 Impôts périodiques sur l'actif net	0	0	0	0	0	..	0	0	0	0
4300 Impôts sur mut. par décès, succ. et donations	0	0	0	0	0	..	0	0	0	0
4400 Impôts sur transact. mobilières et immob.	0	0	0	0	0	..	0	0	0	0
4500 Impôts non-périodiques	0	0	0	0	0	..	0	0	0	0
4600 Autres impôts périodiques sur patrimoine	0	0	0	0	0	..	80	121	229	309
5000 Impôts sur les biens et services	**166**	**223**	**332**	**523**	**528**	**14**	**113**	**330**	**1 237**	**1 455**
5100 Impôts sur production, vente, transfert, etc.	150	206	295	437	428	14	113	330	1 237	1 455
5110 Impôts généraux	0	0	0	0	0	0	0	29	373	240
5120 Impôts sur biens et services déterminés	150	206	295	437	428	14	113	301	865	1 214
5130 Non-ventilables entre 5110 et 5120	0	0	0	0	0	0	0	0	0	0
5200 Impôts sur utilisation des biens et exerc. activites	16	17	37	87	100	0	0	0	0	0
5300 Non-ventilables entre 5100 et 5200	0	0	0	0	0	0	0	0	0	0
6000 Autres impôts	**0**	**0**	**0**	**0**	**0**	**0**	**0**	**0**	**0**	**0**
6100 A la charge exclusive des entreprises	..	..	..	..	..	..	..	..	..	..
6200 A la charge d'autres agents	..	..	..	..	..	..	..	..	..	..
Recettes fiscales totales	**1 029**	**2 562**	**4 286**	**6 394**	**8 326**	**6 723**	**16 863**	**28 905**	**41 247**	**56 463**

Note: Y compris les ressources TVA propres à l'Union européenne : 2013 = 507.2 et à l'exclusion des droits de douane collectés pour le compte de l'Union européenne : 2013 = 1 230.0.

1. Y compris les administrations de sécurité sociale dont les cotisations sont contrôlées par les sous-secteurs de l'administration centrale. Leur montant est de 0.1 pour cent des cotisations en 2013.

StatLink http://dx.doi.org/10.1787/888933277533

Table 92. **Canada, tax revenues by sub-sectors of government**

Million CAD

	Federal government					State/Regional				
	1975	1985	1995	2005	2013	1975	1985	1995	2005	2013
1000 Taxes on income, profits and capital gains	**19 047**	**44 908**	**82 237**	**140 013**	**171 401**	**8 165**	**25 979**	**52 373**	**78 331**	**106 201**
1100 Of individuals	12 822	34 676	65 384	102 366	129 452	6 074	21 904	43 428	62 435	84 184
1200 Corporate	5 741	9 176	14 739	32 197	34 665	2 091	4 075	8 944	15 896	22 017
1300 Unallocable between 1100 and 1200	484	1 056	2 114	5 450	7 284	0	0	0	0	0
2000 Social security contributions	**0**	**0**	**0**	**17 936**	**21 822**	**0**	**0**	**0**	**11 759**	**15 433**
2100 Employees	..	..	..	7 429	9 031	..	..	..	1 858	1 966
2200 Employers	..	..	..	10 507	12 791	..	..	..	9 901	13 467
2300 Self-employed or non-employed	..	..	..	0	0	..	..	..	0	0
2400 Unallocable between 2100, 2200 and 2300	..	..	..	0	0	..	..	..	0	0
3000 Taxes on payroll and workforce	**0**	**0**	**0**	**0**	**0**	**0**	**0**	**6 498**	**9 230**	**12 293**
4000 Taxes on property	**13**	**0**	**0**	**0**	**0**	**428**	**2 292**	**6 492**	**9 298**	**7 659**
4100 Recurrent taxes on immovable property	0	..	..	..	..	85	1 112	2 960	2 934	3 977
4200 Recurrent taxes on net wealth	0	..	..	..	..	200	1 139	2 914	3 456	661
4300 Estate, inheritance and gift taxes	13	..	..	..	..	143	41	3	0	0
4400 Taxes on financial and capital transactions	0	..	..	..	..	0	0	0	1 965	2 788
4500 Non-recurrent taxes	0	..	..	..	..	0	0	615	943	233
4600 Other recurrent taxes on property	0	..	..	..	..	0	0	0	0	0
5000 Taxes on goods and services	**8 180**	**21 212**	**31 160**	**48 551**	**50 013**	**10 128**	**29 639**	**42 076**	**67 537**	**89 930**
5100 Taxes on production, sale, transfer, etc	8 180	21 212	31 136	48 506	49 975	6 800	20 727	37 961	61 316	81 402
5110 General taxes	3 504	9 383	19 167	35 069	34 428	3 664	11 741	21 328	33 353	48 497
5120 Taxes on specific goods and services	4 676	11 829	11 969	13 437	15 547	3 136	8 986	16 633	27 963	32 905
5130 Unallocable between 5110 and 5120	0	0	0	0	0	0	0	0	0	0
5200 Taxes on use of goods and perform activities	0	0	24	45	38	3 328	8 912	4 115	6 221	8 528
5300 Unallocable between 5100 and 5200	0	0	0	0	0	0	0	0	0	0
6000 Other taxes	**198**	**-10**	**0**	**0**	**0**	**0**	**0**	**0**	**0**	**0**
6100 Paid solely by business	0	0	..	..	..	..	..	..	..	..
6200 Other	198	-10	..	..	..	..	..	..	..	..
Total tax revenue	**27 438**	**66 110**	**113 397**	**206 500**	**243 236**	**18 721**	**57 910**	**107 439**	**176 156**	**231 516**

Million CAD

	Local government					Social Security Funds[1]				
	1975	1985	1995	2005	2013	1975	1985	1995	2005	2013
1000 Taxes on income, profits and capital gains	**0**	**0**	**0**	**0**	**0**	**0**	**0**	**0**	**0**	**0**
1100 Of individuals	..	..	..	..	..	..	..	..	..	..
1200 Corporate	..	..	..	..	..	..	..	..	..	..
1300 Unallocable between 1100 and 1200	..	..	..	..	..	..	..	..	..	..
2000 Social security contributions	**0**	**0**	**0**	**0**	**0**	**5 787**	**21 648**	**40 559**	**38 834**	**55 002**
2100 Employees	..	..	..	..	..	2 142	7 516	15 028	18 328	25 958
2200 Employers	..	..	..	..	..	3 527	13 858	24 765	18 328	25 958
2300 Self-employed or non-employed	..	..	..	..	..	118	274	766	2 177	3 086
2400 Unallocable between 2100, 2200 and 2300	..	..	..	..	..	0	0	0	0	0
3000 Taxes on payroll and workforce	**0**	**0**	**0**	**0**	**0**	**0**	**0**	**0**	**0**	**0**
4000 Taxes on property	**5 018**	**12 699**	**24 415**	**40 495**	**52 969**	**0**	**0**	**0**	**0**	**0**
4100 Recurrent taxes on immovable property	4 770	11 900	23 150	37 409	48 671	..	..	..	..	..
4200 Recurrent taxes on net wealth	0	0	0	0	0	..	..	..	..	..
4300 Estate, inheritance and gift taxes	0	0	0	0	0	..	..	..	..	..
4400 Taxes on financial and capital transactions	0	0	0	375	868	..	..	..	..	..
4500 Non-recurrent taxes	248	799	1 265	2 711	3 430	..	..	..	..	..
4600 Other recurrent taxes on property	0	0	0	0	0	..	..	..	..	..
5000 Taxes on goods and services	**142**	**247**	**406**	**833**	**1 155**	**0**	**0**	**0**	**0**	**0**
5100 Taxes on production, sale, transfer, etc	22	52	51	104	97	..	..	..	..	..
5110 General taxes	10	25	40	88	53	..	..	..	..	..
5120 Taxes on specific goods and services	12	27	11	16	44	..	..	..	..	..
5130 Unallocable between 5110 and 5120	0	0	0	0	0	..	..	..	..	..
5200 Taxes on use of goods and perform activities	120	195	355	729	1 058	..	..	..	..	..
5300 Unallocable between 5100 and 5200	0	0	0	0	0	..	..	..	..	..
6000 Other taxes	**525**	**2 036**	**3 662**	**1 483**	**286**	**0**	**0**	**0**	**0**	**0**
6100 Paid solely by business	437	1 507	2 946	541	0	..	..	..	..	..
6200 Other	88	529	716	942	286	..	..	..	..	..
Total tax revenue	**5 685**	**14 982**	**28 483**	**42 811**	**54 410**	**5 787**	**21 648**	**40 559**	**38 834**	**55 002**

1. These include social security funds whose contributions are controlled by sub-central levels of government. They account for 16.7 percent of contributions in 2013.

StatLink http://dx.doi.org/10.1787/888933277548

Table 93. **Chile, tax revenues by sub-sectors of government**

Million CLP

	Central government					State/Regional				
	1975	1985	1995	2005	2013					
1000 Taxes on income, profits and capital gains	..	..	**1 359 694**	**5 171 293**	**9 520 709**	..	..	..	..	..
1100 Of individuals	..	..	281 293	738 620	1 964 172	..	..	..	..	..
1200 Corporate	..	..	836 725	3 155 480	6 041 089	..	..	..	..	..
1300 Unallocable between 1100 and 1200	..	..	241 676	1 277 193	1 515 449	..	..	..	..	..
2000 Social security contributions	..	..	**155 855**	**287 422**	**406 360**	..	..	..	..	..
2100 Employees	..	..	142 001	249 526	343 727	..	..	..	..	..
2200 Employers	..	..	13 854	37 896	62 633	..	..	..	..	..
2300 Self-employed or non-employed	..	..	0	0	0	..	..	..	..	..
2400 Unallocable between 2100, 2200 and 2300	..	..	0	0	0	..	..	..	..	..
3000 Taxes on payroll and workforce	..	..	**0**	**0**	**0**	..	..	..	..	..
4000 Taxes on property	..	..	**181 432**	**490 120**	**305 330**	..	..	..	..	..
4100 Recurrent taxes on immovable property	..	..	13 044	4 909	12 407	..	..	..	..	..
4200 Recurrent taxes on net wealth	..	..	0	0	0	..	..	..	..	..
4300 Estate, inheritance and gift taxes	..	..	13 245	23 184	45 550	..	..	..	..	..
4400 Taxes on financial and capital transactions	..	..	155 143	462 027	247 373	..	..	..	..	..
4500 Non-recurrent taxes	..	..	0	0	0	..	..	..	..	..
4600 Other recurrent taxes on property	..	..	0	0	0	..	..	..	..	..
5000 Taxes on goods and services	..	..	**3 179 304**	**6 831 421**	**13 598 329**	..	..	..	..	..
5100 Taxes on production, sale, transfer, etc	..	..	3 169 645	6 811 328	13 548 235	..	..	..	..	..
5110 General taxes	..	..	2 187 602	5 391 285	11 170 794	..	..	..	..	..
5120 Taxes on specific goods and services	..	..	982 043	1 420 043	2 377 441	..	..	..	..	..
5130 Unallocable between 5110 and 5120	..	..	0	0	0	..	..	..	..	..
5200 Taxes on use of goods and perform activities	..	..	9 659	20 094	50 094	..	..	..	..	..
5300 Unallocable between 5100 and 5200	..	..	0	0	0	..	..	..	..	..
6000 Other taxes	..	..	**-29 554**	**-85 954**	**-21 676**	..	..	..	..	..
6100 Paid solely by business	..	..	0	0	0	..	..	..	..	..
6200 Other	..	..	-29 554	-85 954	-21 676	..	..	..	..	..
Total tax revenue	..	..	**4 846 730**	**12 694 301**	**23 809 052**	..	..	..	..	..

Million CLP

	Local government					Social Security Funds				
	1975	1985	1995	2005	2013	1975	1985	1995	2005	2013
1000 Taxes on income, profits and capital gains	..	..	**0**	**0**	**0**	..	..	**0**	**0**	**0**
1100 Of individuals	..	..	0	0	0	..	..	0	0	0
1200 Corporate	..	..	0	0	0	..	..	0	0	0
1300 Unallocable between 1100 and 1200	..	..	0	0	0	..	..	0	0	0
2000 Social security contributions	..	..	**0**	**0**	**0**	..	..	**193 269**	**644 295**	**1 562 613**
2100 Employees	..	..	..	..	..	..	..	193 269	644 295	1 562 613
2200 Employers	..	..	..	..	..	..	..	0	0	0
2300 Self-employed or non-employed	..	..	..	..	..	..	..	0	0	0
2400 Unallocable between 2100, 2200 and 2300	..	..	..	..	..	..	..	0	0	0
3000 Taxes on payroll and workforce	..	..	**0**	**0**	**0**	..	..	**0**	**0**	**0**
4000 Taxes on property	..	..	**157 193**	**411 656**	**828 435**	..	..	**0**	**0**	**0**
4100 Recurrent taxes on immovable property	..	..	157 193	411 656	828 435	..	..	..	..	..
4200 Recurrent taxes on net wealth	..	..	0	0	0	..	..	..	..	..
4300 Estate, inheritance and gift taxes	..	..	0	0	0	..	..	..	..	..
4400 Taxes on financial and capital transactions	..	..	0	0	0	..	..	..	..	..
4500 Non-recurrent taxes	..	..	0	0	0	..	..	..	..	..
4600 Other recurrent taxes on property	..	..	0	0	0	..	..	..	..	..
5000 Taxes on goods and services	..	..	**192 325**	**514 952**	**1 181 586**	..	..	**0**	**0**	**0**
5100 Taxes on production, sale, transfer, etc	..	..	52 690	140 703	321 294	..	..	..	..	..
5110 General taxes	..	..	0	0	0	..	..	..	..	..
5120 Taxes on specific goods and services	..	..	52 690	140 703	321 294	..	..	..	..	..
5130 Unallocable between 5110 and 5120	..	..	0	0	0	..	..	..	..	..
5200 Taxes on use of goods and perform activities	..	..	139 635	374 249	860 292	..	..	..	..	..
5300 Unallocable between 5100 and 5200	..	..	0	0	0	..	..	..	..	..
6000 Other taxes	..	..	**0**	**0**	**0**	..	..	**0**	**0**	**0**
6100 Paid solely by business	..	..	..	..	..	..	..	..	..	..
6200 Other	..	..	..	..	..	..	..	..	..	..
Total tax revenue	..	..	**349 518**	**926 608**	**2 010 021**	..	..	**193 269**	**644 295**	**1 562 613**

StatLink http://dx.doi.org/10.1787/888933277550

Table 94. **Czech Republic, tax revenues by sub-sectors of government**

Million CZK

	Central government[1]					State/Regional				
	1975	1985	1995	2005	2013					
1000 Taxes on income, profits and capital gains	..	..	**137 616**	**273 549**	**290 263**	..	..	..	..	..
1100 Of individuals	..	..	70 361	137 937	149 831	..	..	..	..	..
1200 Corporate	..	..	67 255	135 611	140 432	..	..	..	..	..
1300 Unallocable between 1100 and 1200	..	..	0	0	0	..	..	..	..	..
2000 Social security contributions	..	..	**0**	**0**	**0**	..	..	..	..	..
2100 Employees	..	..	..	..	..	..	..	..	..	..
2200 Employers	..	..	..	..	..	..	..	..	..	..
2300 Self-employed or non-employed	..	..	..	..	..	..	..	..	..	..
2400 Unallocable between 2100, 2200 and 2300	..	..	..	..	..	..	..	..	..	..
3000 Taxes on payroll and workforce	..	..	**0**	**0**	**0**	..	..	..	..	..
4000 Taxes on property	..	..	**3 857**	**8 050**	**9 363**	..	..	..	..	..
4100 Recurrent taxes on immovable property	..	..	0	5	5	..	..	..	..	..
4200 Recurrent taxes on net wealth	..	..	0	0	0	..	..	..	..	..
4300 Estate, inheritance and gift taxes	..	..	393	728	215	..	..	..	..	..
4400 Taxes on financial and capital transactions	..	..	3 464	7 317	9 143	..	..	..	..	..
4500 Non-recurrent taxes	..	..	0	0	0	..	..	..	..	..
4600 Other recurrent taxes on property	..	..	0	0	0	..	..	..	..	..
5000 Taxes on goods and services	..	..	**175 869**	**343 554**	**470 614**	..	..	..	..	..
5100 Taxes on production, sale, transfer, etc	..	..	162 913	325 662	453 594	..	..	..	..	..
5110 General taxes	..	..	91 673	215 118	303 822	..	..	..	..	..
5120 Taxes on specific goods and services	..	..	71 240	110 544	149 772	..	..	..	..	..
5130 Unallocable between 5110 and 5120	..	..	0	0	0	..	..	..	..	..
5200 Taxes on use of goods and perform activities	..	..	12 956	17 892	17 020	..	..	..	..	..
5300 Unallocable between 5100 and 5200	..	..	0	0	0	..	..	..	..	..
6000 Other taxes	..	..	**545**	**55**	**208**	..	..	..	..	..
6100 Paid solely by business	..	..	0	0	0	..	..	..	..	..
6200 Other	..	..	545	55	208	..	..	..	..	..
Total tax revenue	..	..	**317 887**	**625 207**	**770 448**	..	..	..	..	..

Million CZK

	Local government					Social Security Funds				
	1975	1985	1995	2005	2013	1975	1985	1995	2005	2013
1000 Taxes on income, profits and capital gains	..	..	**0**	**0**	**0**	..	..	**0**	**0**	**0**
1100 Of individuals	..	..	0	0	0	..	..	0	0	0
1200 Corporate	..	..	0	0	0	..	..	0	0	0
1300 Unallocable between 1100 and 1200	..	..	0	0	0	..	..	0	0	0
2000 Social security contributions	..	..	**0**	**0**	**0**	..	..	**227 871**	**481 626**	**603 072**
2100 Employees	..	..	..	..	..	..	..	54 536	108 316	123 353
2200 Employers	..	..	..	..	..	..	..	148 342	307 618	382 498
2300 Self-employed or non-employed	..	..	..	..	..	..	..	24 993	65 692	97 221
2400 Unallocable between 2100, 2200 and 2300	..	..	..	..	..	..	..	0	0	0
3000 Taxes on payroll and workforce	..	..	**0**	**0**	**0**	..	..	**0**	**0**	**0**
4000 Taxes on property	..	..	**3 778**	**4 987**	**9 847**	..	..	**0**	**0**	**0**
4100 Recurrent taxes on immovable property	..	..	3 778	4 987	9 847	..	..	..	..	..
4200 Recurrent taxes on net wealth	..	..	0	0	0	..	..	..	..	..
4300 Estate, inheritance and gift taxes	..	..	0	0	0	..	..	..	..	..
4400 Taxes on financial and capital transactions	..	..	0	0	0	..	..	..	..	..
4500 Non-recurrent taxes	..	..	0	0	0	..	..	..	..	..
4600 Other recurrent taxes on property	..	..	0	0	0	..	..	..	..	..
5000 Taxes on goods and services	..	..	**1 150**	**7 395**	**7 773**	..	..	**0**	**0**	**0**
5100 Taxes on production, sale, transfer, etc	..	..	124	199	269	..	..	..	..	..
5110 General taxes	..	..	0	0	0	..	..	..	..	..
5120 Taxes on specific goods and services	..	..	124	199	269	..	..	..	..	..
5130 Unallocable between 5110 and 5120	..	..	0	0	0	..	..	..	..	..
5200 Taxes on use of goods and perform activities	..	..	1 026	7 196	7 504	..	..	..	..	..
5300 Unallocable between 5100 and 5200	..	..	0	0	0	..	..	..	..	..
6000 Other taxes	..	..	**0**	**0**	**0**	..	..	**0**	**0**	**0**
6100 Paid solely by business	..	..	..	..	..	..	..	..	..	..
6200 Other	..	..	..	..	..	..	..	..	..	..
Total tax revenue	..	..	**4 928**	**12 382**	**17 620**	..	..	**227 871**	**481 626**	**603 072**

Note: Including Vat own resources of the European Union: 2013 = 5 134.0 and excluding customs duties collected on behalf of the European Union: 2013 = 5 543.9.

1. Tax revenues of the regions are reported under the heading of central government up to and including 1995 and under local government thereafter.

StatLink http://dx.doi.org/10.1787/888933277564

Table 95. **Denmark, tax revenues by sub-sectors of government**

Million DKK

	Central government					State/Regional				
	1975	1985	1995	2005	2013					
1000 Taxes on income, profits and capital gains	**28 694**	**94 221**	**164 962**	**258 922**	**355 677**	**..**	**..**	**..**	**..**	**..**
1100 Of individuals	25 904	73 303	124 613	167 082	285 308	..	..	..	..	..
1200 Corporate	2 790	14 473	23 803	54 597	50 385	..	..	..	..	..
1300 Unallocable between 1100 and 1200	0	6 445	16 546	37 244	19 984	..	..	..	..	..
2000 Social security contributions	**143**	**3 626**	**562**	**1 180**	**887**	**..**	**..**	**..**	**..**	**..**
2100 Employees	0	1	559	1 177	879	..	..	..	..	..
2200 Employers	142	3 625	3	3	8	..	..	..	..	..
2300 Self-employed or non-employed	0	0	0	0	0	..	..	..	..	..
2400 Unallocable between 2100, 2200 and 2300	0	0	0	0	0	..	..	..	..	..
3000 Taxes on payroll and workforce	**0**	**2 162**	**2 262**	**2 907**	**6 197**	**..**	**..**	**..**	**..**	**..**
4000 Taxes on property	**1 779**	**7 222**	**7 094**	**11 801**	**8 625**	**..**	**..**	**..**	**..**	**..**
4100 Recurrent taxes on immovable property	16	152	170	0	0	..	..	..	..	..
4200 Recurrent taxes on net wealth	414	1 408	930	0	0	..	..	..	..	..
4300 Estate, inheritance and gift taxes	336	1 418	2 372	3 154	3 940	..	..	..	..	..
4400 Taxes on financial and capital transactions	936	4 208	3 584	8 613	4 685	..	..	..	..	..
4500 Non-recurrent taxes	77	36	38	34	0	..	..	..	..	..
4600 Other recurrent taxes on property	0	0	0	0	0	..	..	..	..	..
5000 Taxes on goods and services	**29 014**	**100 038**	**156 578**	**253 352**	**290 970**	**..**	**..**	**..**	**..**	**..**
5100 Taxes on production, sale, transfer, etc	27 338	96 828	149 393	239 951	268 003	..	..	..	..	..
5110 General taxes	15 117	60 462	94 368	154 654	181 759	..	..	..	..	..
5120 Taxes on specific goods and services	12 221	36 365	55 026	85 298	86 244	..	..	..	..	..
5130 Unallocable between 5110 and 5120	0	0	0	0	0	..	..	..	..	..
5200 Taxes on use of goods and perform activities	1 676	3 210	4 739	9 379	16 470	..	..	..	..	..
5300 Unallocable between 5100 and 5200	0	0	2 446	4 021	6 497	..	..	..	..	..
6000 Other taxes	**0**	**0**	**0**	**203**	**152**	**..**	**..**	**..**	**..**	**..**
6100 Paid solely by business	..	..	..	203	152	..	..	..	..	..
6200 Other	..	..	..	0	0	..	..	..	..	..
Total tax revenue	**59 630**	**207 268**	**331 457**	**528 366**	**662 507**	**..**	**..**	**..**	**..**	**..**

Million DKK

	Local government					Social Security Funds				
	1975	1985	1995	2005	2013	1975	1985	1995	2005	2013
1000 Taxes on income, profits and capital gains	**22 171**	**76 364**	**140 762**	**214 581**	**209 343**	**0**	**0**	**0**	**0**	**0**
1100 Of individuals	22 170	76 358	140 758	214 581	209 343	..	..	..	..	..
1200 Corporate	1	5	5	0	0	..	..	..	..	..
1300 Unallocable between 1100 and 1200	0	0	0	0	0	..	..	..	..	..
2000 Social security contributions	**0**	**0**	**0**	**0**	**0**	**58**	**72**	**0**	**529**	**731**
2100 Employees	..	..	..	..	0	0	0	..	0	0
2200 Employers	..	..	..	..	0	58	72	..	529	731
2300 Self-employed or non-employed	..	..	..	..	0	0	0	..	0	0
2400 Unallocable between 2100, 2200 and 2300	..	..	..	..	0	0	0	..	0	0
3000 Taxes on payroll and workforce	**0**	**0**	**0**	**0**	**0**	**0**	**0**	**0**	**0**	**0**
4000 Taxes on property	**3 518**	**5 451**	**10 155**	**17 466**	**26 370**	**0**	**0**	**0**	**0**	**0**
4100 Recurrent taxes on immovable property	3 518	5 451	10 155	17 466	26 370	..	..	..	..	..
4200 Recurrent taxes on net wealth	0	0	0	0	0	..	..	..	..	..
4300 Estate, inheritance and gift taxes	0	0	0	0	0	..	..	..	..	..
4400 Taxes on financial and capital transactions	0	0	0	0	0	..	..	..	..	..
4500 Non-recurrent taxes	0	0	0	0	0	..	..	..	..	..
4600 Other recurrent taxes on property	0	0	0	0	0	..	..	..	..	..
5000 Taxes on goods and services	**0**	**0**	**0**	**0**	**0**	**0**	**0**	**0**	**0**	**0**
5100 Taxes on production, sale, transfer, etc	0	0	0	0	0	..	..	..	..	..
5110 General taxes	0	0	0	0	0	..	..	..	..	..
5120 Taxes on specific goods and services	0	0	0	0	0	..	..	..	..	..
5130 Unallocable between 5110 and 5120	0	0	0	0	0	..	..	..	..	..
5200 Taxes on use of goods and perform activities	0	0	0	0	0	..	..	..	..	..
5300 Unallocable between 5100 and 5200	0	0	0	0	0	..	..	..	..	..
6000 Other taxes	**0**	**0**	**0**	**0**	**0**	**0**	**0**	**0**	**0**	**0**
6100 Paid solely by business	..	..	..	..	..	..	..	..	..	..
6200 Other	..	..	..	..	..	..	..	..	..	..
Total tax revenue	**25 689**	**81 814**	**150 918**	**232 047**	**235 713**	**58**	**72**	**0**	**529**	**731**

Note: Including Vat own resources of the European Union: 2013 = 3 281.0 and excluding customs duties collected on behalf of the European Union: 2013 = 2 926.3.

StatLink http://dx.doi.org/10.1787/888933277576

Table 96. **Estonia, tax revenues by sub-sectors of government**

Million EUR

	Central government					State/Regional				
	1975	1985	1995	2005	2013					
1000 Taxes on income, profits and capital gains	..	..	**177**	**375**	**633**	..	..	..	..	..
1100 Of individuals	..	..	110	215	307	..	..	..	..	..
1200 Corporate	..	..	67	160	327	..	..	..	..	..
1300 Unallocable between 1100 and 1200	..	..	0	0	0	..	..	..	..	..
2000 Social security contributions	..	..	**191**	**636**	**1 079**	..	..	..	..	..
2100 Employees	..	..	0	0	0	..	..	..	..	..
2200 Employers	..	..	191	636	1 068	..	..	..	..	..
2300 Self-employed or non-employed	..	..	0	0	11	..	..	..	..	..
2400 Unallocable between 2100, 2200 and 2300	..	..	0	0	0	..	..	..	..	..
3000 Taxes on payroll and workforce	..	..	**0**	**0**	**0**	..	..	..	..	..
4000 Taxes on property	..	..	**3**	**0**	**0**	..	..	..	..	..
4100 Recurrent taxes on immovable property	..	..	3	..	..	..	..	..	..	..
4200 Recurrent taxes on net wealth	..	..	0	..	..	..	..	..	..	..
4300 Estate, inheritance and gift taxes	..	..	0	..	..	..	..	..	..	..
4400 Taxes on financial and capital transactions	..	..	0	..	..	..	..	..	..	..
4500 Non-recurrent taxes	..	..	0	..	..	..	..	..	..	..
4600 Other recurrent taxes on property	..	..	0	..	..	..	..	..	..	..
5000 Taxes on goods and services	..	..	**352**	**1 374**	**2 434**	..	..	..	..	..
5100 Taxes on production, sale, transfer, etc	..	..	345	1 337	2 376	..	..	..	..	..
5110 General taxes	..	..	266	908	1 558	..	..	..	..	..
5120 Taxes on specific goods and services	..	..	79	429	818	..	..	..	..	..
5130 Unallocable between 5110 and 5120	..	..	0	0	0	..	..	..	..	..
5200 Taxes on use of goods and perform activities	..	..	7	37	58	..	..	..	..	..
5300 Unallocable between 5100 and 5200	..	..	0	0	0	..	..	..	..	..
6000 Other taxes	..	..	**0**	**0**	**0**	..	..	..	..	..
6100 Paid solely by business	..	..	..	..	..	..	..	..	..	..
6200 Other	..	..	..	..	..	..	..	..	..	..
Total tax revenue	..	..	**723**	**2 385**	**4 147**	..	..	..	..	..

Million EUR

	Local government					Social Security Funds				
	1975	1985	1995	2005	2013	1975	1985	1995	2005	2013
1000 Taxes on income, profits and capital gains	..	..	**124**	**407**	**724**	..	..	**0**	**0**	**0**
1100 Of individuals	..	..	124	407	724	..	..	..	..	..
1200 Corporate	..	..	0	0	0	..	..	..	..	..
1300 Unallocable between 1100 and 1200	..	..	0	0	0	..	..	..	..	..
2000 Social security contributions	..	..	**0**	**0**	**0**	..	..	**149**	**511**	**998**
2100 Employees	..	..	..	..	..	..	..	0	31	109
2200 Employers	..	..	..	..	..	..	..	143	466	882
2300 Self-employed or non-employed	..	..	..	..	..	..	..	6	14	7
2400 Unallocable between 2100, 2200 and 2300	..	..	..	..	..	..	..	0	0	0
3000 Taxes on payroll and workforce	..	..	**0**	**0**	**0**	..	..	**0**	**0**	**0**
4000 Taxes on property	..	..	**7**	**32**	**57**	..	..	**0**	**0**	**0**
4100 Recurrent taxes on immovable property	..	..	7	32	57	..	..	..	..	..
4200 Recurrent taxes on net wealth	..	..	0	0	0	..	..	..	..	..
4300 Estate, inheritance and gift taxes	..	..	0	0	0	..	..	..	..	..
4400 Taxes on financial and capital transactions	..	..	0	0	0	..	..	..	..	..
4500 Non-recurrent taxes	..	..	0	0	0	..	..	..	..	..
4600 Other recurrent taxes on property	..	..	0	0	0	..	..	..	..	..
5000 Taxes on goods and services	..	..	**1**	**7**	**11**	..	..	**0**	**0**	**0**
5100 Taxes on production, sale, transfer, etc	..	..	0	2	4	..	..	..	..	..
5110 General taxes	..	..	0	0	0	..	..	..	..	..
5120 Taxes on specific goods and services	..	..	0	2	4	..	..	..	..	..
5130 Unallocable between 5110 and 5120	..	..	0	0	0	..	..	..	..	..
5200 Taxes on use of goods and perform activities	..	..	1	5	7	..	..	..	..	..
5300 Unallocable between 5100 and 5200	..	..	0	0	0	..	..	..	..	..
6000 Other taxes	..	..	**0**	**0**	**0**	..	..	**0**	**0**	**0**
6100 Paid solely by business	..	..	..	..	..	..	..	..	..	..
6200 Other	..	..	..	..	..	..	..	..	..	..
Total tax revenue	..	..	**132**	**446**	**792**	..	..	**149**	**511**	**998**

Note: Including Vat own resources of the European Union: 2013 = 24.9 and excluding customs duties collected on behalf of the European Union: 2013 = 28.7.

StatLink http://dx.doi.org/10.1787/888933277581

Table 97. **Finland, tax revenues by sub-sectors of government**

Million EUR

	Central government					State/Regional				
	1975	1985	1995	2005	2013					
1000 Taxes on income, profits and capital gains	**1 304**	**4 255**	**6 538**	**12 885**	**11 453**	..	..	..	..	..
1100 Of individuals	1 146	3 875	5 320	8 791	8 110	..	..	..	..	..
1200 Corporate	157	380	1 219	4 094	3 343	..	..	..	..	..
1300 Unallocable between 1100 and 1200	0	0	0	0	0	..	..	..	..	..
2000 Social security contributions	**0**	**0**	**25**	**0**	**0**	..	..	..	..	..
2100 Employees	..	..	0	..	..	..	..	..	..	..
2200 Employers	..	..	25	..	..	..	..	..	..	..
2300 Self-employed or non-employed	..	..	0	..	..	..	..	..	..	..
2400 Unallocable between 2100, 2200 and 2300	..	..	0	..	..	..	..	..	..	..
3000 Taxes on payroll and workforce	**153**	**113**	**0**	**0**	**0**	..	..	..	..	..
4000 Taxes on property	**127**	**572**	**534**	**1 169**	**1 236**	..	..	..	..	..
4100 Recurrent taxes on immovable property	0	0	0	0	0	..	..	..	..	..
4200 Recurrent taxes on net wealth	33	47	35	129	0	..	..	..	..	..
4300 Estate, inheritance and gift taxes	14	62	167	486	646	..	..	..	..	..
4400 Taxes on financial and capital transactions	80	463	331	554	590	..	..	..	..	..
4500 Non-recurrent taxes	0	0	0	0	0	..	..	..	..	..
4600 Other recurrent taxes on property	0	0	0	0	0	..	..	..	..	..
5000 Taxes on goods and services	**2 099**	**7 724**	**13 239**	**21 768**	**29 426**	..	..	..	..	..
5100 Taxes on production, sale, transfer, etc	2 082	7 630	12 936	21 178	28 494	..	..	..	..	..
5110 General taxes	1 030	4 173	7 621	13 748	18 888	..	..	..	..	..
5120 Taxes on specific goods and services	1 052	3 457	5 314	7 430	9 606	..	..	..	..	..
5130 Unallocable between 5110 and 5120	0	0	0	0	0	..	..	..	..	..
5200 Taxes on use of goods and perform activities	16	93	304	590	932	..	..	..	..	..
5300 Unallocable between 5100 and 5200	0	0	0	0	0	..	..	..	..	..
6000 Other taxes	**10**	**42**	**91**	**68**	**64**	..	..	..	..	..
6100 Paid solely by business	0	0	0	0	0	..	..	..	..	..
6200 Other	10	42	91	68	64	..	..	..	..	..
Total tax revenue	**3 693**	**12 706**	**20 427**	**35 890**	**42 179**	..	..	..	..	..

Million EUR

	Local government					Social Security Funds				
	1975	1985	1995	2005	2013	1975	1985	1995	2005	2013
1000 Taxes on income, profits and capital gains	**1 547**	**5 049**	**9 313**	**13 574**	**19 344**	**0**	**0**	**0**	**0**	**0**
1100 Of individuals	1 393	4 646	8 320	12 420	17 888	..	..	..	..	..
1200 Corporate	154	403	994	1 154	1 456	..	..	..	..	..
1300 Unallocable between 1100 and 1200	0	0	0	0	0	..	..	..	..	..
2000 Social security contributions	**0**	**0**	**0**	**23**	**16**	**1 347**	**5 005**	**13 492**	**18 856**	**25 616**
2100 Employees	..	..	..	4	4	278	849	2 536	3 460	5 807
2200 Employers	..	..	..	19	12	990	3 787	9 447	14 108	17 876
2300 Self-employed or non-employed	..	..	..	0	0	79	369	1 509	1 288	1 933
2400 Unallocable between 2100, 2200 and 2300	..	..	..	0	0	0	0	0	0	0
3000 Taxes on payroll and workforce	**0**	**0**	**0**	**0**	**0**	**0**	**0**	**0**	**0**	**0**
4000 Taxes on property	**0**	**49**	**441**	**725**	**1 363**	**0**	**0**	**0**	**0**	**0**
4100 Recurrent taxes on immovable property	0	49	441	725	1 363	..	..	..	..	..
4200 Recurrent taxes on net wealth	0	0	0	0	0	..	..	..	..	..
4300 Estate, inheritance and gift taxes	0	0	0	0	0	..	..	..	..	..
4400 Taxes on financial and capital transactions	0	0	0	0	0	..	..	..	..	..
4500 Non-recurrent taxes	0	0	0	0	0	..	..	..	..	..
4600 Other recurrent taxes on property	0	0	0	0	0	..	..	..	..	..
5000 Taxes on goods and services	**3**	**3**	**7**	**8**	**3**	**0**	**0**	**0**	**0**	**0**
5100 Taxes on production, sale, transfer, etc	1	0	1	4	1	..	..	..	..	..
5110 General taxes	0	0	0	0	0	..	..	..	..	..
5120 Taxes on specific goods and services	1	0	1	4	1	..	..	..	..	..
5130 Unallocable between 5110 and 5120	0	0	0	0	0	..	..	..	..	..
5200 Taxes on use of goods and perform activities	2	3	6	4	2	..	..	..	..	..
5300 Unallocable between 5100 and 5200	0	0	0	0	0	..	..	..	..	..
6000 Other taxes	**0**	**0**	**0**	**0**	**0**	**0**	**0**	**0**	**0**	**0**
6100 Paid solely by business	..	..	..	..	..	..	..	..	..	..
6200 Other	..	..	..	..	..	..	..	..	..	..
Total tax revenue	**1 550**	**5 102**	**9 761**	**14 330**	**20 726**	**1 347**	**5 005**	**13 492**	**18 856**	**25 616**

Note: Including Vat own resources of the European Union: 2013 = 285.0 and excluding customs duties collected on behalf of the European Union: 2013 = 166.0.

StatLink http://dx.doi.org/10.1787/888933277598

Tableau 98. **France, recettes fiscales par sous-secteurs d'administration**

Million EUR

	Administration centrale					Administration d'État/Régions				
	1975	1985	1995	2005	2013					
1000 Impôts sur revenu, bénéfices et gains en capital	**13 106**	**50 864**	**69 134**	**98 623**	**126 129**	..	..	..	..	..
1100 Des personnes physiques	8 743	36 441	43 963	56 862	71 830	..	..	..	..	..
1200 Des sociétés	4 282	14 180	25 172	41 761	54 299	..	..	..	..	..
1300 Non-ventilables entre 1100 et 1200	80	244	0	0	0	..	..	..	..	..
2000 Cotisations de sécurité sociale	**419**	**1 984**	**3 733**	**5 796**	**7 685**	..	..	..	..	..
2100 A la charge des salariés	419	1 984	3 733	4 812	5 560	..	..	..	..	..
2200 A la charge des employeurs	0	0	0	984	2 125	..	..	..	..	..
2300 A charge des travailleurs indép. ou sans emploi	0	0	0	0	0	..	..	..	..	..
2400 Non-ventilables entre 2100, 2200 et 2300	0	0	0	0	0	..	..	..	..	..
3000 Sur salaires ou main d'oeuvre	**1 194**	**4 570**	**10 299**	**13 117**	**4 597**	..	..	..	..	..
4000 Impôts sur le patrimoine	**1 372**	**5 315**	**7 356**	**13 945**	**17 436**	..	..	..	..	..
4100 Impôts périodiques sur la propriété immobilière	26	70	9	30	134	..	..	..	..	..
4200 Impôts périodiques sur l'actif net	0	2 021	1 309	3 053	4 372	..	..	..	..	..
4300 Impôts sur mut. par décès, succ. et donations	616	1 932	4 261	9 006	10 456	..	..	..	..	..
4400 Impôts sur transact. mobilières et immob.	731	1 291	1 777	1 856	2 474	..	..	..	..	..
4500 Impôts non-périodiques	0	0	0	0	0	..	..	..	..	..
4600 Autres impôts périodiques sur patrimoine	0	0	0	0	0	..	..	..	..	..
5000 Impôts sur les biens et services	**26 154**	**87 164**	**127 617**	**165 674**	**166 148**	..	..	..	..	..
5100 Impôts sur production, vente, transfert, etc.	25 618	86 328	126 699	163 729	164 489	..	..	..	..	..
5110 Impôts généraux	19 077	62 687	89 768	127 096	135 521	..	..	..	..	..
5120 Impôts sur biens et services déterminés	6 540	23 641	36 931	36 633	28 968	..	..	..	..	..
5130 Non-ventilables entre 5110 et 5120	0	0	0	0	0	..	..	..	..	..
5200 Impôts sur utilisation des biens et exerc. activites	536	836	918	1 945	1 659	..	..	..	..	..
5300 Non-ventilables entre 5100 et 5200	0	0	0	0	0	..	..	..	..	..
6000 Autres impôts	**49**	**595**	**924**	**3 522**	**1 292**	..	..	..	..	..
6100 A la charge exclusive des entreprises	32	595	871	3 502	1 286	..	..	..	..	..
6200 A la charge d'autres agents	17	0	53	21	6	..	..	..	..	..
Recettes fiscales totales	**42 294**	**150 491**	**219 063**	**300 677**	**323 287**	..	..	..	..	..

Million EUR

	Administrations locales					Administrations de sécurité sociale				
	1975	1985	1995	2005	2013	1975	1985	1995	2005	2013
1000 Impôts sur revenu, bénéfices et gains en capital	**0**	**0**	**0**	**0**	**77**	**0**	**33**	**14 997**	**80 173**	**106 424**
1100 Des personnes physiques	0	0	0	0	40	..	33	14 997	80 173	106 424
1200 Des sociétés	0	0	0	0	37	..	0	0	0	0
1300 Non-ventilables entre 1100 et 1200	0	0	0	0	0	..	0	0	0	0
2000 Cotisations de sécurité sociale	**0**	**0**	**0**	**0**	**0**	**33 089**	**136 004**	**217 995**	**275 433**	**349 256**
2100 A la charge des salariés	..	..	..	..	..	6 683	35 579	65 964	65 369	82 405
2200 A la charge des employeurs	..	..	..	..	..	24 236	89 322	135 892	190 090	238 723
2300 A charge des travailleurs indép. ou sans emploi	..	..	..	..	..	2 170	11 103	16 139	19 975	28 128
2400 Non-ventilables entre 2100, 2200 et 2300	..	..	..	..	..	0	0	0	0	0
3000 Sur salaires ou main d'oeuvre	**299**	**1 377**	**2 529**	**5 437**	**8 645**	**107**	**606**	**36**	**1 767**	**20 355**
4000 Impôts sur le patrimoine	**2 876**	**13 078**	**27 105**	**44 534**	**63 663**	**0**	**0**	**0**	**0**	**0**
4100 Impôts périodiques sur la propriété immobilière	2 626	11 085	23 117	35 989	54 123	..	..	..	..	..
4200 Impôts périodiques sur l'actif net	0	0	0	0	0	..	..	..	..	..
4300 Impôts sur mut. par décès, succ. et donations	0	0	0	0	0	..	..	..	..	..
4400 Impôts sur transact. mobilières et immob.	250	1 994	3 988	8 545	9 540	..	..	..	..	..
4500 Impôts non-périodiques	0	0	0	0	0	..	..	..	..	..
4600 Autres impôts périodiques sur patrimoine	0	0	0	0	0	..	..	..	..	..
5000 Impôts sur les biens et services	**496**	**3 625**	**8 056**	**14 708**	**29 242**	**301**	**1 850**	**5 708**	**12 776**	**35 606**
5100 Impôts sur production, vente, transfert, etc.	297	1 417	4 168	12 233	25 437	301	1 810	5 429	12 393	34 423
5110 Impôts généraux	0	0	0	0	0	248	873	1 810	4 271	15 234
5120 Impôts sur biens et services déterminés	297	1 417	4 168	12 233	25 437	53	937	3 620	8 122	19 189
5130 Non-ventilables entre 5110 et 5120	0	0	0	0	0	0	0	0	0	0
5200 Impôts sur utilisation des biens et exerc. activites	198	2 208	3 888	2 475	3 805	0	40	279	383	1 183
5300 Non-ventilables entre 5100 et 5200	0	0	0	0	0	0	0	0	0	0
6000 Autres impôts	**2 577**	**9 612**	**18 971**	**22 334**	**21 084**	**0**	**0**	**0**	**0**	**453**
6100 A la charge exclusive des entreprises	2 577	9 612	18 970	22 334	21 084	..	..	..	..	453
6200 A la charge d'autres agents	0	0	1	0	0	..	..	..	..	0
Recettes fiscales totales	**6 248**	**27 693**	**56 661**	**87 013**	**122 711**	**33 497**	**138 493**	**238 737**	**370 149**	**512 094**

Note: Y compris les ressources TVA propres à l'Union européenne : 2013 = 2 837.0 et à l'exclusion des droits de douane collectés pour le compte de l'Union européenne : 2013 = 1 842.0.

StatLink http://dx.doi.org/10.1787/888933277608

Table 99. **Germany, tax revenues by sub-sectors of government**

Million EUR

	Federal government					State/Regional				
	1975	1985	1995	2005	2013	1975	1985	1995	2005	2013
1000 Taxes on income, profits and capital gains	**26 782**	**49 039**	**90 688**	**89 383**	**130 317**	**26 428**	**49 034**	**77 258**	**83 503**	**121 612**
1100 Of individuals	23 469	40 497	83 710	77 468	116 666	23 267	40 497	71 598	70 916	106 893
1200 Corporate	3 314	8 542	6 978	11 915	13 651	3 160	8 537	5 659	12 587	14 719
1300 Unallocable between 1100 and 1200	0	0	0	0	0	0	0	0	0	0
2000 Social security contributions	**0**	**0**	**0**	**0**	**0**	**0**	**0**	**0**	**0**	**0**
2100 Employees	..	..	..	..	..	..	..	..	..	..
2200 Employers	..	..	..	..	..	..	..	..	..	..
2300 Self-employed or non-employed	..	..	..	..	..	..	..	..	..	..
2400 Unallocable between 2100, 2200 and 2300	..	..	..	..	..	..	..	..	..	..
3000 Taxes on payroll and workforce	**0**	**0**	**0**	**0**	**0**	**0**	**0**	**0**	**0**	**0**
4000 Taxes on property	**1 225**	**836**	**175**	**0**	**521**	**2 606**	**4 192**	**9 080**	**8 985**	**13 027**
4100 Recurrent taxes on immovable property	0	0	0	..	0	0	0	0	0	0
4200 Recurrent taxes on net wealth	920	127	147	..	521	1 993	2 318	4 163	97	0
4300 Estate, inheritance and gift taxes	0	0	0	..	0	271	773	1 815	4 097	4 633
4400 Taxes on financial and capital transactions	305	709	28	..	0	342	1 100	3 102	4 791	8 394
4500 Non-recurrent taxes	0	0	0	..	0	0	0	0	0	0
4600 Other recurrent taxes on property	0	0	0	..	0	0	0	0	0	0
5000 Taxes on goods and services	**35 370**	**62 539**	**125 377**	**147 967**	**192 229**	**13 082**	**24 754**	**62 564**	**75 007**	**90 815**
5100 Taxes on production, sale, transfer, etc	35 370	62 539	125 377	147 967	182 133	10 371	20 996	55 506	66 334	90 815
5110 General taxes	18 458	36 780	67 178	74 361	105 355	9 194	19 373	52 783	62 851	88 032
5120 Taxes on specific goods and services	16 913	25 759	58 200	73 170	76 494	1 177	1 623	2 723	3 483	2 783
5130 Unallocable between 5110 and 5120	0	0	0	436	284	0	0	0	0	0
5200 Taxes on use of goods and perform activities	0	0	0	0	10 096	2 711	3 758	7 058	8 673	0
5300 Unallocable between 5100 and 5200	0	0	0	0	0	0	0	0	0	0
6000 Other taxes	**0**	**0**	**0**	**-1**	**0**	**0**	**0**	**0**	**0**	**0**
6100 Paid solely by business	..	..	..	0	..	..	..	..	..	..
6200 Other	..	..	..	-1	..	..	..	..	..	..
Total tax revenue	**63 378**	**112 414**	**216 240**	**237 349**	**323 067**	**42 116**	**77 980**	**148 902**	**167 495**	**225 454**

Million EUR

	Local government					Social Security Funds				
	1975	1985	1995	2005	2013	1975	1985	1995	2005	2013
1000 Taxes on income, profits and capital gains	**11 819**	**25 467**	**40 295**	**46 725**	**67 460**	**0**	**0**	**0**	**0**	**0**
1100 Of individuals	9 931	20 805	33 761	31 261	45 297	..	..	..	..	..
1200 Corporate	1 888	4 662	6 534	15 464	22 163	..	..	..	..	..
1300 Unallocable between 1100 and 1200	0	0	0	0	0	..	..	..	..	..
2000 Social security contributions	**0**	**0**	**0**	**0**	**0**	**64 290**	**129 761**	**268 052**	**310 301**	**392 548**
2100 Employees	..	..	..	..	..	28 106	56 247	117 916	135 775	174 334
2200 Employers	..	..	..	..	..	34 609	67 255	133 120	149 191	184 429
2300 Self-employed or non-employed	..	..	..	..	..	1 575	6 258	17 016	25 335	33 785
2400 Unallocable between 2100, 2200 and 2300	..	..	..	..	..	0	0	0	0	0
3000 Taxes on payroll and workforce	**1 533**	**0**	**0**	**0**	**0**	**0**	**0**	**0**	**0**	**0**
4000 Taxes on property	**3 461**	**5 705**	**9 794**	**10 247**	**12 377**	**0**	**0**	**0**	**0**	**0**
4100 Recurrent taxes on immovable property	2 122	3 766	7 027	10 247	12 377	..	..	..	..	..
4200 Recurrent taxes on net wealth	911	1 477	2 615	0	0	..	..	..	..	..
4300 Estate, inheritance and gift taxes	0	0	0	0	0	..	..	..	..	..
4400 Taxes on financial and capital transactions	428	462	151	0	0	..	..	..	..	..
4500 Non-recurrent taxes	0	0	0	0	0	..	..	..	..	..
4600 Other recurrent taxes on property	0	0	0	0	0	..	..	..	..	..
5000 Taxes on goods and services	**162**	**238**	**448**	**3 395**	**4 956**	**0**	**0**	**0**	**0**	**0**
5100 Taxes on production, sale, transfer, etc	94	112	271	3 136	4 647	..	..	..	..	..
5110 General taxes	0	0	0	2 909	3 939	..	..	..	..	..
5120 Taxes on specific goods and services	94	112	271	227	708	..	..	..	..	..
5130 Unallocable between 5110 and 5120	0	0	0	0	0	..	..	..	..	..
5200 Taxes on use of goods and perform activities	68	126	176	259	309	..	..	..	..	..
5300 Unallocable between 5100 and 5200	0	0	0	0	0	..	..	..	..	..
6000 Other taxes	**67**	**64**	**130**	**79**	**128**	**0**	**0**	**0**	**0**	**0**
6100 Paid solely by business	0	0	0	0	0	..	..	..	..	..
6200 Other	67	64	130	79	128	..	..	..	..	..
Total tax revenue	**17 042**	**31 475**	**50 666**	**60 446**	**84 921**	**64 290**	**129 761**	**268 052**	**310 301**	**392 548**

Note: Including Vat own resources of the European Union: 2013 = 2 264.9 and excluding customs duties collected on behalf of the European Union: 2013 = 4 250.8.

StatLink http://dx.doi.org/10.1787/888933277612

Table 100. **Greece, tax revenues by sub-sectors of government**

Million EUR

	Central government					State/Regional				
	1975	1985	1995	2005	2013					
1000 Taxes on income, profits and capital gains	**64**	**826**	**5 756**	**15 725**	**13 795**	..	..	..	..	..
1100 Of individuals	43	654	3 112	9 090	11 084	..	..	..	..	..
1200 Corporate	17	130	1 635	6 402	2 429	..	..	..	..	..
1300 Unallocable between 1100 and 1200	4	42	1 010	233	282	..	..	..	..	..
2000 Social security contributions	**0**	**14**	**373**	**1 033**	**755**	..	..	..	..	..
2100 Employees	..	12	354	1 026	754	..	..	..	..	..
2200 Employers	..	1	10	7	1	..	..	..	..	..
2300 Self-employed or non-employed	..	0	9	0	0	..	..	..	..	..
2400 Unallocable between 2100, 2200 and 2300	..	1	0	0	0	..	..	..	..	..
3000 Taxes on payroll and workforce	**1**	**44**	**0**	**0**	**0**	..	..	..	..	..
4000 Taxes on property	**47**	**123**	**854**	**1 975**	**1 336**	..	..	..	..	..
4100 Recurrent taxes on immovable property	1	8	10	0	0	..	..	..	..	..
4200 Recurrent taxes on net wealth	0	0	0	0	0	..	..	..	..	..
4300 Estate, inheritance and gift taxes	5	45	250	258	99	..	..	..	..	..
4400 Taxes on financial and capital transactions	41	69	594	1 469	594	..	..	..	..	..
4500 Non-recurrent taxes	0	1	0	0	0	..	..	..	..	..
4600 Other recurrent taxes on property	0	0	0	248	643	..	..	..	..	..
5000 Taxes on goods and services	**224**	**1 967**	**10 296**	**21 233**	**24 067**	..	..	..	..	..
5100 Taxes on production, sale, transfer, etc	205	1 845	9 865	19 433	21 303	..	..	..	..	..
5110 General taxes	90	815	5 845	13 686	12 967	..	..	..	..	..
5120 Taxes on specific goods and services	114	936	4 020	5 679	7 834	..	..	..	..	..
5130 Unallocable between 5110 and 5120	0	94	95	68	502	..	..	..	..	..
5200 Taxes on use of goods and perform activities	20	122	432	1 725	2 327	..	..	..	..	..
5300 Unallocable between 5100 and 5200	0	0	0	75	437	..	..	..	..	..
6000 Other taxes	**0**	**3**	**0**	**0**	**0**	..	..	..	..	..
6100 Paid solely by business	..	0	..	..	..	..	..	..	..	..
6200 Other	..	3	..	..	..	..	..	..	..	..
Total tax revenue	**337**	**2 976**	**17 280**	**39 966**	**39 953**	..	..	..	..	..

Million EUR

	Local government					Social Security Funds				
	1975	1985	1995	2005	2013	1975	1985	1995	2005	2013
1000 Taxes on income, profits and capital gains	**3**	**6**	**0**	**0**	**0**	**0**	**0**	**0**	**0**	**0**
1100 Of individuals	2	6	0	0	0	0	0	0	0	0
1200 Corporate	0	0	0	0	0	0	0	0	0	0
1300 Unallocable between 1100 and 1200	1	0	0	0	0	0	0	0	0	0
2000 Social security contributions	**0**	**0**	**0**	**0**	**0**	**148**	**1 679**	**8 003**	**20 873**	**18 787**
2100 Employees	..	..	..	..	..	62	742	3 073	7 667	7 188
2200 Employers	..	..	..	..	..	62	709	3 810	9 934	8 472
2300 Self-employed or non-employed	..	..	..	..	..	0	0	1 120	3 272	3 127
2400 Unallocable between 2100, 2200 and 2300	..	..	..	..	..	24	229	0	0	0
3000 Taxes on payroll and workforce	**0**	**26**	**0**	**0**	**0**	**0**	**0**	**0**	**0**	**0**
4000 Taxes on property	**1**	**6**	**131**	**258**	**3 395**	**0**	**0**	**67**	**360**	**28**
4100 Recurrent taxes on immovable property	0	3	109	111	2 314	..	..	33	83	0
4200 Recurrent taxes on net wealth	0	0	14	127	1 081	..	..	0	0	0
4300 Estate, inheritance and gift taxes	0	0	0	0	0	..	..	0	0	0
4400 Taxes on financial and capital transactions	0	2	8	20	0	..	..	34	277	28
4500 Non-recurrent taxes	0	1	0	0	0	..	..	0	0	0
4600 Other recurrent taxes on property	0	1	0	0	0	..	..	0	0	0
5000 Taxes on goods and services	**10**	**26**	**107**	**215**	**128**	**0**	**0**	**124**	**250**	**363**
5100 Taxes on production, sale, transfer, etc	7	18	65	188	117	..	..	101	195	344
5110 General taxes	2	2	7	29	20	..	..	85	85	295
5120 Taxes on specific goods and services	6	17	58	159	97	..	..	16	110	49
5130 Unallocable between 5110 and 5120	0	0	0	0	0	..	..	0	0	0
5200 Taxes on use of goods and perform activities	3	7	42	27	11	..	..	23	55	19
5300 Unallocable between 5100 and 5200	0	0	0	0	0	..	..	0	0	0
6000 Other taxes	**0**	**0**	**0**	**0**	**0**	**0**	**0**	**0**	**0**	**0**
6100 Paid solely by business	..	..	..	..	..	..	..	..	..	..
6200 Other	..	..	..	..	..	..	..	..	..	..
Total tax revenue	**17**	**64**	**238**	**473**	**3 523**	**148**	**1 679**	**8 194**	**21 483**	**19 178**

Note: Including Vat own resources of the European Union: 2013 = 251.1 and excluding customs duties collected on behalf of the European Union: 2013 = 148.0.

StatLink http://dx.doi.org/10.1787/888933277623

Table 101. **Hungary, tax revenues by sub-sectors of government**

Million HUF

	Central government					State/Regional				
	1975	1985	1995	2005	2013					
1000 Taxes on income, profits and capital gains	..	..	**498 608**	**1 915 178**	**1 917 365**	..	..	..	..	..
1100 Of individuals	..	..	383 744	1 449 552	1 501 176	..	..	..	..	..
1200 Corporate	..	..	106 259	465 626	416 189	..	..	..	..	..
1300 Unallocable between 1100 and 1200	..	..	8 605	0	0	..	..	..	..	..
2000 Social security contributions	..	..	**69 554**	**235 148**	**126 400**	..	..	..	..	..
2100 Employees	..	..	18 468	53 611	126 400	..	..	..	..	..
2200 Employers	..	..	51 086	175 013	0	..	..	..	..	..
2300 Self-employed or non-employed	..	..	0	0	0	..	..	..	..	..
2400 Unallocable between 2100, 2200 and 2300	..	..	0	6 524	0	..	..	..	..	..
3000 Taxes on payroll and workforce	..	..	**5 474**	**39 459**	**159 200**	..	..	..	..	..
4000 Taxes on property	..	..	**11 463**	**63 007**	**253 514**	..	..	..	..	..
4100 Recurrent taxes on immovable property	..	..	0	0	54 939	..	..	..	..	..
4200 Recurrent taxes on net wealth	..	..	0	0	128 560	..	..	..	..	..
4300 Estate, inheritance and gift taxes	..	..	1 364	7 678	5 307	..	..	..	..	..
4400 Taxes on financial and capital transactions	..	..	10 099	55 329	64 708	..	..	..	..	..
4500 Non-recurrent taxes	..	..	0	0	0	..	..	..	..	..
4600 Other recurrent taxes on property	..	..	0	0	0	..	..	..	..	..
5000 Taxes on goods and services	..	..	**924 906**	**2 869 329**	**4 414 824**	..	..	..	..	..
5100 Taxes on production, sale, transfer, etc	..	..	919 500	2 853 878	4 322 274	..	..	..	..	..
5110 General taxes	..	..	423 954	1 972 998	2 894 384	..	..	..	..	..
5120 Taxes on specific goods and services	..	..	495 546	880 880	1 427 890	..	..	..	..	..
5130 Unallocable between 5110 and 5120	..	..	0	0	0	..	..	..	..	..
5200 Taxes on use of goods and perform activities	..	..	5 406	15 451	92 550	..	..	..	..	..
5300 Unallocable between 5100 and 5200	..	..	0	0	0	..	..	..	..	..
6000 Other taxes	..	..	**8 901**	**44 873**	**61 542**	..	..	..	..	..
6100 Paid solely by business	..	..	..	..	..	..	..	..	..	..
6200 Other	..	..	..	..	..	..	..	..	..	..
Total tax revenue	..	..	**1 518 905**	**5 166 993**	**6 932 845**	..	..	..	..	..

Million HUF

	Local government					Social Security Funds				
	1975	1985	1995	2005	2013	1975	1985	1995	2005	2013
1000 Taxes on income, profits and capital gains	..	..	**0**	**173**	**68**	..	..	**0**	**26 317**	**109 085**
1100 Of individuals	..	..	0	173	68	..	..	0	26 317	109 085
1200 Corporate	..	..	0	0	0	..	..	0	0	0
1300 Unallocable between 1100 and 1200	..	..	0	0	0	..	..	0	0	0
2000 Social security contributions	..	..	**0**	**0**	**0**	..	..	**778 467**	**2 332 500**	**3 601 579**
2100 Employees	..	..	..	..	..	..	..	116 824	461 793	1 441 922
2200 Employers	..	..	..	..	..	..	..	632 478	1 844 265	2 134 343
2300 Self-employed or non-employed	..	..	..	..	..	..	..	27 466	2 080	0
2400 Unallocable between 2100, 2200 and 2300	..	..	..	..	..	..	..	1 699	24 362	25 314
3000 Taxes on payroll and workforce	..	..	**1 075**	**1 153**	**2**	..	..	**0**	**138 091**	**9 547**
4000 Taxes on property	..	..	**17 531**	**123 929**	**135 310**	..	..	**0**	**0**	**0**
4100 Recurrent taxes on immovable property	..	..	6 068	58 836	135 310	..	..	..	..	..
4200 Recurrent taxes on net wealth	..	..	0	0	0	..	..	..	..	..
4300 Estate, inheritance and gift taxes	..	..	1 364	7 932	0	..	..	..	..	..
4400 Taxes on financial and capital transactions	..	..	10 099	57 162	0	..	..	..	..	..
4500 Non-recurrent taxes	..	..	0	0	0	..	..	..	..	..
4600 Other recurrent taxes on property	..	..	0	0	0	..	..	..	..	..
5000 Taxes on goods and services	..	..	**41 970**	**388 385**	**539 525**	..	..	**0**	**0**	**82 899**
5100 Taxes on production, sale, transfer, etc	..	..	39 240	337 935	509 279	..	..	..	..	82 899
5110 General taxes	..	..	38 472	334 077	500 868	..	..	..	..	19 090
5120 Taxes on specific goods and services	..	..	768	3 858	8 411	..	..	..	..	63 809
5130 Unallocable between 5110 and 5120	..	..	0	0	0	..	..	..	..	0
5200 Taxes on use of goods and perform activities	..	..	2 730	50 450	30 246	..	..	..	..	0
5300 Unallocable between 5100 and 5200	..	..	0	0	0	..	..	..	..	0
6000 Other taxes	..	..	**0**	**0**	**0**	..	..	**21 605**	**9 616**	**14 623**
6100 Paid solely by business	..	..	..	..	..	..	..	..	..	..
6200 Other	..	..	..	..	..	..	..	..	..	..
Total tax revenue	..	..	**60 576**	**513 641**	**674 905**	..	..	**800 072**	**2 506 524**	**3 817 733**

Note: Including Vat own resources of the European Union: 2013 = 32 382.0 and excluding customs duties collected on behalf of the European Union: 2013 = 26 337.3.

StatLink http://dx.doi.org/10.1787/888933277633

Table 102. **Iceland, tax revenues by sub-sectors of government**

Million ISK

	Central government					State/Regional				
	1975	1985	1995	2005	2013					
1000 Taxes on income, profits and capital gains	**68**	**3 741**	**27 156**	**105 705**	**168 441**	..	..	..	..	..
1100 Of individuals	55	3 183	22 914	70 944	111 487	..	..	..	..	..
1200 Corporate	13	558	4 242	20 297	40 479	..	..	..	..	..
1300 Unallocable between 1100 and 1200	0	0	0	14 464	16 475	..	..	..	..	..
2000 Social security contributions	**17**	**841**	**11 452**	**32 777**	**69 899**	..	..	..	..	..
2100 Employees	0	56	460	..	..	..	..	..	..	..
2200 Employers	17	785	10 992	..	..	..	..	..	..	..
2300 Self-employed or non-employed	0	0	0	..	..	..	..	..	..	..
2400 Unallocable between 2100, 2200 and 2300	0	0	0	32 777	69 899	..	..	..	..	..
3000 Taxes on payroll and workforce	**27**	**1 233**	**0**	**324**	**6 534**	..	..	..	..	..
4000 Taxes on property	**15**	**1 534**	**7 198**	**13 340**	**15 996**	..	..	..	..	..
4100 Recurrent taxes on immovable property	0	89	47	0	168	..	..	..	..	..
4200 Recurrent taxes on net wealth	5	588	3 191	2 887	8 886	..	..	..	..	..
4300 Estate, inheritance and gift taxes	0	67	389	866	2 437	..	..	..	..	..
4400 Taxes on financial and capital transactions	9	790	3 571	9 073	3 973	..	..	..	..	..
4500 Non-recurrent taxes	0	0	0	248	233	..	..	..	..	..
4600 Other recurrent taxes on property	0	0	0	266	299	..	..	..	..	..
5000 Taxes on goods and services	**392**	**20 639**	**66 356**	**168 295**	**224 678**	..	..	..	..	..
5100 Taxes on production, sale, transfer, etc	387	20 109	62 140	157 941	215 271	..	..	..	..	..
5110 General taxes	182	11 360	42 358	113 897	149 828	..	..	..	..	..
5120 Taxes on specific goods and services	205	8 749	19 782	44 044	65 444	..	..	..	..	..
5130 Unallocable between 5110 and 5120	0	0	0	0	0	..	..	..	..	..
5200 Taxes on use of goods and perform activities	5	530	4 216	10 354	9 407	..	..	..	..	..
5300 Unallocable between 5100 and 5200	0	0	0	0	0	..	..	..	..	..
6000 Other taxes	**0**	**0**	**0**	**1 504**	**11 020**	..	..	..	..	..
6100 Paid solely by business	..	..	..	565	5 255	..	..	..	..	..
6200 Other	..	..	..	939	5 766	..	..	..	..	..
Total tax revenue	**519**	**27 988**	**112 162**	**321 944**	**496 569**	..	..	..	..	..

Million ISK

	Local government					Social Security Funds				
	1975	1985	1995	2005	2013	1975	1985	1995	2005	2013
1000 Taxes on income, profits and capital gains	**78**	**4 055**	**21 170**	**74 455**	**147 136**	**0**	**0**	**0**	**0**	**0**
1100 Of individuals	74	3 532	21 170	74 455	147 136	..	..	..	..	..
1200 Corporate	4	523	0	0	0	..	..	..	..	..
1300 Unallocable between 1100 and 1200	0	0	0	0	0	..	..	..	..	..
2000 Social security contributions	**0**	**0**	**0**	**0**	**0**	**0**	**0**	**0**	**0**	**0**
2100 Employees	..	..	..	..	..	..	..	..	..	..
2200 Employers	..	..	..	..	..	..	..	..	..	..
2300 Self-employed or non-employed	..	..	..	..	..	..	..	..	..	..
2400 Unallocable between 2100, 2200 and 2300	..	..	..	..	..	..	..	..	..	..
3000 Taxes on payroll and workforce	**0**	**0**	**0**	**0**	**0**	**0**	**0**	**0**	**0**	**0**
4000 Taxes on property	**18**	**979**	**5 674**	**13 931**	**30 496**	**0**	**0**	**0**	**0**	**0**
4100 Recurrent taxes on immovable property	18	979	5 674	13 931	30 496	..	..	..	..	..
4200 Recurrent taxes on net wealth	0	0	0	0	0	..	..	..	..	..
4300 Estate, inheritance and gift taxes	0	0	0	0	0	..	..	..	..	..
4400 Taxes on financial and capital transactions	0	0	0	0	0	..	..	..	..	..
4500 Non-recurrent taxes	0	0	0	0	0	..	..	..	..	..
4600 Other recurrent taxes on property	0	0	0	0	0	..	..	..	..	..
5000 Taxes on goods and services	**9**	**351**	**2 585**	**6 904**	**1 941**	**0**	**0**	**0**	**0**	**0**
5100 Taxes on production, sale, transfer, etc	9	351	2 585	0	0	..	..	..	..	..
5110 General taxes	0	0	2 585	0	0	..	..	..	..	..
5120 Taxes on specific goods and services	9	351	0	0	0	..	..	..	..	..
5130 Unallocable between 5110 and 5120	0	0	0	0	0	..	..	..	..	..
5200 Taxes on use of goods and perform activities	0	0	0	6 904	1 941	..	..	..	..	..
5300 Unallocable between 5100 and 5200	0	0	0	0	0	..	..	..	..	..
6000 Other taxes	**14**	**1 002**	**0**	**93**	**0**	**0**	**0**	**0**	**0**	**0**
6100 Paid solely by business	14	1 002	..	93	..	..	..	..	..	..
6200 Other	0	0	..	0	..	..	..	..	..	..
Total tax revenue	**119**	**6 387**	**29 429**	**95 383**	**179 573**	**0**	**0**	**0**	**0**	**0**

StatLink http://dx.doi.org/10.1787/888933277643

Table 103. **Ireland, tax revenues by sub-sectors of government**

Million EUR

	Central government					State/Regional				
	1975	1985	1995	2005	2013					
1000 Taxes on income, profits and capital gains	**456**	**2 963**	**7 022**	**20 080**	**20 483**	..	..	..	..	..
1100 Of individuals	382	2 686	5 563	14 568	16 205	..	..	..	..	..
1200 Corporate	73	276	1 458	5 511	4 273	..	..	..	..	..
1300 Unallocable between 1100 and 1200	0	0	0	0	4	..	..	..	..	..
2000 Social security contributions	**11**	**96**	**87**	**217**	**1 534**	..	..	..	..	..
2100 Employees	10	89	87	217	1 534	..	..	..	..	..
2200 Employers	0	0	0	0	0	..	..	..	..	..
2300 Self-employed or non-employed	1	7	0	0	0	..	..	..	..	..
2400 Unallocable between 2100, 2200 and 2300	0	0	0	0	0	..	..	..	..	..
3000 Taxes on payroll and workforce	**0**	**201**	**209**	**332**	**314**	..	..	..	..	..
4000 Taxes on property	**37**	**148**	**370**	**2 722**	**2 216**	..	..	..	..	..
4100 Recurrent taxes on immovable property	0	32	15	0	318	..	..	..	..	..
4200 Recurrent taxes on net wealth	5	0	0	0	536	..	..	..	..	..
4300 Estate, inheritance and gift taxes	17	26	76	255	278	..	..	..	..	..
4400 Taxes on financial and capital transactions	15	90	279	2 467	1 084	..	..	..	..	..
4500 Non-recurrent taxes	0	0	0	0	0	..	..	..	..	..
4600 Other recurrent taxes on property	0	0	0	0	0	..	..	..	..	..
5000 Taxes on goods and services	**671**	**3 638**	**6 763**	**18 562**	**17 034**	..	..	..	..	..
5100 Taxes on production, sale, transfer, etc	639	3 481	6 419	17 547	15 546	..	..	..	..	..
5110 General taxes	223	1 768	3 666	12 373	10 372	..	..	..	..	..
5120 Taxes on specific goods and services	416	1 713	2 753	5 174	5 174	..	..	..	..	..
5130 Unallocable between 5110 and 5120	0	0	0	0	0	..	..	..	..	..
5200 Taxes on use of goods and perform activities	33	157	344	1 015	1 488	..	..	..	..	..
5300 Unallocable between 5100 and 5200	0	0	0	0	0	..	..	..	..	..
6000 Other taxes	**0**	**0**	**0**	**0**	**23**	..	..	..	..	..
6100 Paid solely by business	..	..	..	..	0	..	..	..	..	..
6200 Other	..	..	..	..	23	..	..	..	..	..
Total tax revenue	**1 175**	**7 046**	**14 451**	**41 913**	**41 605**	..	..	..	..	..

Million EUR

	Local government					Social Security Funds				
	1975	1985	1995	2005	2013	1975	1985	1995	2005	2013
1000 Taxes on income, profits and capital gains	**0**	**0**	**0**	**0**	**0**	**0**	**0**	**0**	**0**	**0**
1100 Of individuals	0	0	0	0	0	0	0	0	0	0
1200 Corporate	0	0	0	0	0	0	0	0	0	0
1300 Unallocable between 1100 and 1200	0	0	0	0	0	0	0	0	0	0
2000 Social security contributions	**0**	**0**	**56**	**90**	**193**	**198**	**1 170**	**2 215**	**6 205**	**7 299**
2100 Employees	..	..	56	90	193	73	362	576	1 389	1 569
2200 Employers	..	..	0	0	0	125	809	1 528	4 427	5 326
2300 Self-employed or non-employed	..	..	0	0	0	0	0	111	388	403
2400 Unallocable between 2100, 2200 and 2300	..	..	0	0	0	0	0	0	0	0
3000 Taxes on payroll and workforce	**0**	**0**	**0**	**0**	**0**	**0**	**0**	**0**	**0**	**0**
4000 Taxes on property	**110**	**195**	**408**	**1 020**	**1 403**	**0**	**0**	**0**	**0**	**0**
4100 Recurrent taxes on immovable property	110	195	408	1 020	1 403	..	..	..	..	..
4200 Recurrent taxes on net wealth	0	0	0	0	0	..	..	..	..	..
4300 Estate, inheritance and gift taxes	0	0	0	0	0	..	..	..	..	..
4400 Taxes on financial and capital transactions	0	0	0	0	0	..	..	..	..	..
4500 Non-recurrent taxes	0	0	0	0	0	..	..	..	..	..
4600 Other recurrent taxes on property	0	0	0	0	0	..	..	..	..	..
5000 Taxes on goods and services	**0**	**0**	**0**	**0**	**0**	**0**	**0**	**0**	**0**	**0**
5100 Taxes on production, sale, transfer, etc	0	0	0	0	0	0	0	0	0	0
5110 General taxes	0	0	0	0	0	0	0	0	0	0
5120 Taxes on specific goods and services	0	0	0	0	0	0	0	0	0	0
5130 Unallocable between 5110 and 5120	0	0	0	0	0	0	0	0	0	0
5200 Taxes on use of goods and perform activities	0	0	0	0	0	0	0	0	0	0
5300 Unallocable between 5100 and 5200	0	0	0	0	0	0	0	0	0	0
6000 Other taxes	**0**	**0**	**0**	**0**	**0**	**0**	**0**	**0**	**0**	**0**
6100 Paid solely by business	..	..	..	..	..	..	..	..	..	..
6200 Other	..	..	..	..	..	..	..	..	..	..
Total tax revenue	**110**	**195**	**464**	**1 110**	**1 595**	**198**	**1 170**	**2 215**	**6 205**	**7 299**

Note: Including Vat own resources of the European Union: 2013 = 194.3 and excluding customs duties collected on behalf of the European Union: 2013 = 246.9.

The data for personal income tax revenues differs from the ESA2010 presentation as payable tax credits are excluded in accordance with the presentation in earlier editions of the publication.

StatLink http://dx.doi.org/10.1787/888933277656

Table 104. **Israel, tax revenues by sub-sectors of government**

Million ILS

	Central government					State/Regional				
	1975	1985	1995	2005	2013					
1000 Taxes on income, profits and capital gains	..	..	**37 422**	**73 082**	**101 797**	..	..	..	..	..
1100 Of individuals	..	..	28 399	47 062	57 627	..	..	..	..	..
1200 Corporate	..	..	8 514	21 909	36 639	..	..	..	..	..
1300 Unallocable between 1100 and 1200	..	..	509	4 111	7 531	..	..	..	..	..
2000 Social security contributions	..	..	**0**	**0**	**0**	..	..	..	..	..
2100 Employees	..	..	..	..	..	..	..	..	..	..
2200 Employers	..	..	..	..	..	..	..	..	..	..
2300 Self-employed or non-employed	..	..	..	..	..	..	..	..	..	..
2400 Unallocable between 2100, 2200 and 2300	..	..	..	..	..	..	..	..	..	..
3000 Taxes on payroll and workforce	..	..	**5 007**	**9 920**	**12 355**	..	..	..	..	..
4000 Taxes on property	..	..	**3 811**	**5 140**	**6 014**	..	..	..	..	..
4100 Recurrent taxes on immovable property	..	..	786	322	59	..	..	..	..	..
4200 Recurrent taxes on net wealth	..	..	0	0	0	..	..	..	..	..
4300 Estate, inheritance and gift taxes	..	..	0	0	0	..	..	..	..	..
4400 Taxes on financial and capital transactions	..	..	1 738	3 184	3 398	..	..	..	..	..
4500 Non-recurrent taxes	..	..	1 287	1 634	2 557	..	..	..	..	..
4600 Other recurrent taxes on property	..	..	0	0	0	..	..	..	..	..
5000 Taxes on goods and services	..	..	**38 672**	**75 932**	**123 790**	..	..	..	..	..
5100 Taxes on production, sale, transfer, etc	..	..	36 637	70 741	116 335	..	..	..	..	..
5110 General taxes	..	..	31 975	59 374	97 357	..	..	..	..	..
5120 Taxes on specific goods and services	..	..	4 662	11 367	18 978	..	..	..	..	..
5130 Unallocable between 5110 and 5120	..	..	0	0	0	..	..	..	..	..
5200 Taxes on use of goods and perform activities	..	..	2 035	5 192	7 455	..	..	..	..	..
5300 Unallocable between 5100 and 5200	..	..	0	0	0	..	..	..	..	..
6000 Other taxes	..	..	**0**	**0**	**0**	..	..	..	..	..
6100 Paid solely by business	..	..	..	..	..	..	..	..	..	..
6200 Other	..	..	..	..	..	..	..	..	..	..
Total tax revenue	..	..	**84 912**	**164 074**	**243 956**	..	..	..	..	..

Million ILS

	Local government					Social Security Funds				
	1975	1985	1995	2005	2013	1975	1985	1995	2005	2013
1000 Taxes on income, profits and capital gains	..	..	**0**	**0**	**0**	..	..	**0**	**0**	**0**
1100 Of individuals	..	..	0	0	0	..	..	0	0	0
1200 Corporate	..	..	0	0	0	..	..	0	0	0
1300 Unallocable between 1100 and 1200	..	..	0	0	0	..	..	0	0	0
2000 Social security contributions	..	..	**0**	**0**	**0**	..	..	**14 958**	**34 597**	**53 364**
2100 Employees	..	..	..	..	..	..	..	8 905	22 135	35 134
2200 Employers	..	..	..	..	..	..	..	4 672	10 679	15 026
2300 Self-employed or non-employed	..	..	..	..	..	..	..	1 381	1 783	3 204
2400 Unallocable between 2100, 2200 and 2300	..	..	..	..	..	..	..	0	0	0
3000 Taxes on payroll and workforce	..	..	**0**	**0**	**0**	..	..	**0**	**0**	**0**
4000 Taxes on property	..	..	**5 807**	**14 538**	**22 097**	..	..	**0**	**0**	**0**
4100 Recurrent taxes on immovable property	..	..	5 807	14 538	22 097	..	..	..	..	..
4200 Recurrent taxes on net wealth	..	..	0	0	0	..	..	..	..	..
4300 Estate, inheritance and gift taxes	..	..	0	0	0	..	..	..	..	..
4400 Taxes on financial and capital transactions	..	..	0	0	0	..	..	..	..	..
4500 Non-recurrent taxes	..	..	0	0	0	..	..	..	..	..
4600 Other recurrent taxes on property	..	..	0	0	0	..	..	..	..	..
5000 Taxes on goods and services	..	..	**406**	**773**	**1 331**	..	..	**0**	**0**	**0**
5100 Taxes on production, sale, transfer, etc	..	..	0	0	0	..	..	..	..	..
5110 General taxes	..	..	0	0	0	..	..	..	..	..
5120 Taxes on specific goods and services	..	..	0	0	0	..	..	..	..	..
5130 Unallocable between 5110 and 5120	..	..	0	0	0	..	..	..	..	..
5200 Taxes on use of goods and perform activities	..	..	406	773	1 331	..	..	..	..	..
5300 Unallocable between 5100 and 5200	..	..	0	0	0	..	..	..	..	..
6000 Other taxes	..	..	**0**	**0**	**0**	..	..	**0**	**0**	**0**
6100 Paid solely by business	..	..	..	..	..	..	..	..	..	..
6200 Other	..	..	..	..	..	..	..	..	..	..
Total tax revenue	..	..	**6 213**	**15 311**	**23 428**	..	..	**14 958**	**34 597**	**53 364**

Note: The statistical data for Israel are supplied by and under the responsibility of the relevant Israeli authorities. The use of such data by the OECD is without prejudice to the status of the Golan Heights, East Jerusalem and Israeli settlements in the West Bank under the terms of international law.

StatLink http://dx.doi.org/10.1787/888933277665

Tableau 105. **Italie, recettes fiscales par sous-secteurs d'administration**

Million EUR

	Administration centrale					Administration d'État/Régions				
	1975	1985	1995	2005	2013					
1000 Impôts sur revenu, bénéfices et gains en capital	**3 897**	**50 995**	**128 458**	**165 580**	**204 577**	..	..	..	..	..
1100 Des personnes physiques	2 767	38 086	98 695	131 946	161 128	..	..	..	..	..
1200 Des sociétés	1 131	13 011	32 890	38 320	48 311	..	..	..	..	..
1300 Non-ventilables entre 1100 et 1200	0	-101	-3 127	-4 686	-4 862	..	..	..	..	..
2000 Cotisations de sécurité sociale	**0**	**0**	**0**	**0**	**0**	..	..	..	..	..
2100 A la charge des salariés	..	..	..	..	..	..	..	..	..	..
2200 A la charge des employeurs	..	..	..	..	..	..	..	..	..	..
2300 A charge des travailleurs indép. ou sans emploi	..	..	..	..	..	..	..	..	..	..
2400 Non-ventilables entre 2100, 2200 et 2300	..	..	..	..	..	..	..	..	..	..
3000 Sur salaires ou main d'oeuvre	**0**	**815**	**1 136**	**0**	**0**	..	..	..	..	..
4000 Impôts sur le patrimoine	**587**	**3 635**	**13 546**	**15 717**	**25 172**	..	..	..	..	..
4100 Impôts périodiques sur la propriété immobilière	4	0	0	0	4 048	..	..	..	..	..
4200 Impôts périodiques sur l'actif net	0	0	4 494	0	2 547	..	..	..	..	..
4300 Impôts sur mut. par décès, succ. et donations	39	332	587	56	579	..	..	..	..	..
4400 Impôts sur transact. mobilières et immob.	544	3 303	8 464	13 794	16 094	..	..	..	..	..
4500 Impôts non-périodiques	0	0	0	1 322	975	..	..	..	..	..
4600 Autres impôts périodiques sur patrimoine	0	0	0	545	929	..	..	..	..	..
5000 Impôts sur les biens et services	**5 506**	**34 640**	**95 323**	**123 870**	**149 852**	..	..	..	..	..
5100 Impôts sur production, vente, transfert, etc.	5 306	32 897	92 042	121 824	147 513	..	..	..	..	..
5110 Impôts généraux	2 685	20 957	52 531	80 619	87 582	..	..	..	..	..
5120 Impôts sur biens et services déterminés	2 621	11 914	39 245	41 205	59 931	..	..	..	..	..
5130 Non-ventilables entre 5110 et 5120	0	122	323	0	0	..	..	..	..	..
5200 Impôts sur utilisation des biens et exerc. activites	200	1 682	2 802	1 535	2 106	..	..	..	..	..
5300 Non-ventilables entre 5100 et 5200	0	61	479	511	233	..	..	..	..	..
6000 Autres impôts	**1**	**0**	**0**	**0**	**0**	..	..	..	..	..
6100 A la charge exclusive des entreprises	0	..	..	..	..	..	..	..	..	..
6200 A la charge d'autres agents	1	..	..	..	..	..	..	..	..	..
Recettes fiscales totales	**9 991**	**90 086**	**238 462**	**305 167**	**379 601**	..	..	..	..	..

Million EUR

	Administrations locales					Administrations de sécurité sociale				
	1975	1985	1995	2005	2013	1975	1985	1995	2005	2013
1000 Impôts sur revenu, bénéfices et gains en capital	**134**	**2 234**	**5 658**	**18 494**	**28 885**	**0**	**0**	**0**	**0**	**0**
1100 Des personnes physiques	81	535	145	16 870	26 380	..	..	..	..	..
1200 Des sociétés	54	357	97	1 616	2 462	..	..	..	..	..
1300 Non-ventilables entre 1100 et 1200	0	1 342	5 416	8	43	..	..	..	..	..
2000 Cotisations de sécurité sociale	**0**	**0**	**0**	**0**	**0**	**8 607**	**50 156**	**119 612**	**179 362**	**210 625**
2100 A la charge des salariés	..	..	..	..	..	1 692	9 772	23 036	31 998	39 284
2200 A la charge des employeurs	..	..	..	..	..	6 915	35 788	79 716	125 099	141 626
2300 A charge des travailleurs indép. ou sans emploi	..	..	..	..	..	0	4 595	16 860	22 265	29 715
2400 Non-ventilables entre 2100, 2200 et 2300	..	..	..	..	..	0	0	0	0	0
3000 Sur salaires ou main d'oeuvre	**0**	**0**	**0**	**0**	**0**	**0**	**0**	**0**	**0**	**0**
4000 Impôts sur le patrimoine	**29**	**0**	**7 915**	**13 484**	**18 717**	**0**	**0**	**0**	**0**	**0**
4100 Impôts périodiques sur la propriété immobilière	29	..	7 449	11 736	16 681	..	..	..	..	..
4200 Impôts périodiques sur l'actif net	0	..	0	0	0	..	..	..	..	..
4300 Impôts sur mut. par décès, succ. et donations	0	..	0	5	43	..	..	..	..	..
4400 Impôts sur transact. mobilières et immob.	0	..	466	904	997	..	..	..	..	..
4500 Impôts non-périodiques	0	..	0	481	10	..	..	..	..	..
4600 Autres impôts périodiques sur patrimoine	0	..	0	358	986	..	..	..	..	..
5000 Impôts sur les biens et services	**4**	**1 113**	**6 941**	**30 231**	**34 530**	**0**	**0**	**0**	**0**	**0**
5100 Impôts sur production, vente, transfert, etc.	0	341	1 505	17 114	15 181	..	..	..	..	..
5110 Impôts généraux	0	0	0	4 698	6 339	..	..	..	..	..
5120 Impôts sur biens et services déterminés	0	341	1 505	12 416	8 842	..	..	..	..	..
5130 Non-ventilables entre 5110 et 5120	0	0	0	0	0	..	..	..	..	..
5200 Impôts sur utilisation des biens et exerc. activites	4	11	2 838	7 512	8 824	..	..	..	..	..
5300 Non-ventilables entre 5100 et 5200	0	761	2 597	5 605	10 525	..	..	..	..	..
6000 Autres impôts	**0**	**0**	**0**	**34 690**	**31 986**	**0**	**0**	**0**	**0**	**0**
6100 A la charge exclusive des entreprises	..	..	..	34 690	31 986	..	..	..	..	..
6200 A la charge d'autres agents	..	..	..	0	0	..	..	..	..	..
Recettes fiscales totales	**168**	**3 347**	**20 514**	**96 899**	**114 118**	**8 607**	**50 156**	**119 612**	**179 362**	**210 625**

Note: Y compris les ressources TVA propres à l'Union européenne : 2013 = 1 904.0 et à l'exclusion des droits de douane collectés pour le compte de l'Union européenne : 2013 = 1 890.0.

StatLink http://dx.doi.org/10.1787/888933277671

Table 106. **Japan, tax revenues by sub-sectors of government**

Billion JPY

	Central government					State/Regional				
	1975	1985	1995	2005	2013	1975 (assumed)	1985 (assumed)	1995 (assumed)	2005 (assumed)	2013 (assumed)
1000 Taxes on income, profits and capital gains	**9 747**	**27 456**	**33 255**	**29 975**	**29 564**	..	..	..	..	..
1100 Of individuals	5 482	15 435	19 515	16 702	15 865	..	..	..	..	..
1200 Corporate	4 265	12 021	13 740	13 274	13 699	..	..	..	..	..
1300 Unallocable between 1100 and 1200	0	0	0	0	0	..	..	..	..	..
2000 Social security contributions	**0**	**0**	**0**	**0**	**0**	..	..	..	..	..
2100 Employees	..	..	..	..	..	..	..	..	..	..
2200 Employers	..	..	..	..	..	..	..	..	..	..
2300 Self-employed or non-employed	..	..	..	..	..	..	..	..	..	..
2400 Unallocable between 2100, 2200 and 2300	..	..	..	..	..	..	..	..	..	..
3000 Taxes on payroll and workforce	**0**	**0**	**0**	**0**	**0**	..	..	..	..	..
4000 Taxes on property	**871**	**3 156**	**5 561**	**2 735**	**2 701**	..	..	..	..	..
4100 Recurrent taxes on immovable property	0	0	406	0	0	..	..	..	..	..
4200 Recurrent taxes on net wealth	0	0	0	0	0	..	..	..	..	..
4300 Estate, inheritance and gift taxes	310	1 061	2 690	1 566	1 574	..	..	..	..	..
4400 Taxes on financial and capital transactions	561	2 095	2 464	1 169	1 126	..	..	..	..	..
4500 Non-recurrent taxes	0	0	0	0	0	..	..	..	..	..
4600 Other recurrent taxes on property	0	0	0	0	0	..	..	..	..	..
5000 Taxes on goods and services	**3 888**	**8 540**	**16 147**	**19 580**	**18 963**	..	..	..	..	..
5100 Taxes on production, sale, transfer, etc	3 579	7 918	15 083	18 424	18 298	..	..	..	..	..
5110 General taxes	0	0	7 238	10 583	10 829	..	..	..	..	..
5120 Taxes on specific goods and services	3 579	7 918	7 845	7 840	7 468	..	..	..	..	..
5130 Unallocable between 5110 and 5120	0	0	0	0	0	..	..	..	..	..
5200 Taxes on use of goods and perform activities	309	622	1 065	1 157	666	..	..	..	..	..
5300 Unallocable between 5100 and 5200	0	0	0	0	0	..	..	..	..	..
6000 Other taxes	**0**	**0**	**0**	**0**	**0**	..	..	..	..	..
6100 Paid solely by business	..	..	..	..	..	..	..	..	..	..
6200 Other	..	..	..	..	..	..	..	..	..	..
Total tax revenue	**14 504**	**39 150**	**54 963**	**52 291**	**51 227**	..	..	..	..	..

Billion JPY

	Local government					Social Security Funds				
	1975	1985	1995	2005	2013	1975	1985	1995	2005	2013
1000 Taxes on income, profits and capital gains	**4 472**	**13 534**	**17 752**	**16 655**	**17 970**	**0**	**0**	**0**	**0**	**0**
1100 Of individuals	2 147	6 733	10 283	8 520	12 285	..	..	..	..	..
1200 Corporate	2 325	6 801	7 470	8 135	5 685	..	..	..	..	..
1300 Unallocable between 1100 and 1200	0	0	0	0	0	..	..	..	..	..
2000 Social security contributions	**0**	**0**	**0**	**0**	**0**	**9 253**	**27 121**	**44 639**	**50 844**	**59 834**
2100 Employees	..	..	..	..	..	3 436	9 668	18 347	20 980	25 972
2200 Employers	..	..	..	..	..	4 825	13 841	21 333	23 151	27 186
2300 Self-employed or non-employed	..	..	..	..	..	992	3 612	4 958	6 712	6 676
2400 Unallocable between 2100, 2200 and 2300	..	..	..	..	..	0	0	0	0	0
3000 Taxes on payroll and workforce	**0**	**0**	**0**	**0**	**0**	**0**	**0**	**0**	**0**	**0**
4000 Taxes on property	**2 029**	**5 537**	**10 653**	**10 593**	**10 239**	**0**	**0**	**0**	**0**	**0**
4100 Recurrent taxes on immovable property	1 848	5 102	9 865	10 116	9 882	..	..	..	..	..
4200 Recurrent taxes on net wealth	0	0	0	0	0	..	..	..	..	..
4300 Estate, inheritance and gift taxes	0	0	0	0	0	..	..	..	..	..
4400 Taxes on financial and capital transactions	181	435	788	477	357	..	..	..	..	..
4500 Non-recurrent taxes	0	0	0	0	0	..	..	..	..	..
4600 Other recurrent taxes on property	0	0	0	0	0	..	..	..	..	..
5000 Taxes on goods and services	**1 636**	**4 013**	**4 941**	**7 206**	**6 781**	**0**	**0**	**0**	**0**	**0**
5100 Taxes on production, sale, transfer, etc	1 234	2 899	3 245	5 299	5 015	..	..	..	..	..
5110 General taxes	0	0	0	2 551	2 650	..	..	..	..	..
5120 Taxes on specific goods and services	1 234	2 899	3 245	2 747	2 366	..	..	..	..	..
5130 Unallocable between 5110 and 5120	0	0	0	0	0	..	..	..	..	..
5200 Taxes on use of goods and perform activities	402	1 114	1 697	1 907	1 765	..	..	..	..	..
5300 Unallocable between 5100 and 5200	0	0	0	0	0	..	..	..	..	..
6000 Other taxes	**20**	**232**	**329**	**351**	**384**	**0**	**0**	**0**	**0**	**0**
6100 Paid solely by business	15	197	307	297	348	..	..	..	..	..
6200 Other	5	35	22	54	35	..	..	..	..	..
Total tax revenue	**8 155**	**23 317**	**33 675**	**34 804**	**35 374**	**9 253**	**27 121**	**44 639**	**50 844**	**59 834**

StatLink http://dx.doi.org/10.1787/888933277687

Table 107. **Korea, tax revenues by sub-sectors of government**

Billion KRW

	Central government					State/Regional				
	1975	1985	1995	2005	2013					
1000 Taxes on income, profits and capital gains	**344**	..	**23 000**	**55 109**	**92 297**	..	..	..	..	..
1100 Of individuals	134	..	13 713	24 766	47 934	..	..	..	..	..
1200 Corporate	139	..	8 988	30 343	44 363	..	..	..	..	..
1300 Unallocable between 1100 and 1200	71	..	300	0	0	..	..	..	..	..
2000 Social security contributions	**0**	..	**0**	**0**	**0**	..	..	..	..	..
2100 Employees	..	..	..	..	..	..	..	..	..	..
2200 Employers	..	..	..	..	..	..	..	..	..	..
2300 Self-employed or non-employed	..	..	..	..	..	..	..	..	..	..
2400 Unallocable between 2100, 2200 and 2300	..	..	..	..	..	..	..	..	..	..
3000 Taxes on payroll and workforce	**0**	..	**0**	**0**	**0**	..	..	..	..	..
4000 Taxes on property	**65**	..	**2 482**	**6 769**	**11 882**	..	..	..	..	..
4100 Recurrent taxes on immovable property	0	..	106	535	1 474	..	..	..	..	..
4200 Recurrent taxes on net wealth	0	..	0	0	0	..	..	..	..	..
4300 Estate, inheritance and gift taxes	11	..	1 029	1 873	4 290	..	..	..	..	..
4400 Taxes on financial and capital transactions	49	..	1 258	4 363	6 118	..	..	..	..	..
4500 Non-recurrent taxes	5	..	89	-2	0	..	..	..	..	..
4600 Other recurrent taxes on property	0	..	0	0	0	..	..	..	..	..
5000 Taxes on goods and services	**920**	..	**29 170**	**63 480**	**93 004**	..	..	..	..	..
5100 Taxes on production, sale, transfer, etc	920	..	29 170	63 480	93 004	..	..	..	..	..
5110 General taxes	198	..	14 637	36 118	55 963	..	..	..	..	..
5120 Taxes on specific goods and services	722	..	14 533	27 362	37 041	..	..	..	..	..
5130 Unallocable between 5110 and 5120	0	..	0	0	0	..	..	..	..	..
5200 Taxes on use of goods and perform activities	0	..	0	0	0	..	..	..	..	..
5300 Unallocable between 5100 and 5200	0	..	0	0	0	..	..	..	..	..
6000 Other taxes	**64**	..	**2 121**	**2 108**	**4 774**	..	..	..	..	..
6100 Paid solely by business	0	..	0	0	0	..	..	..	..	..
6200 Other	64	..	2 121	2 108	4 774	..	..	..	..	..
Total tax revenue	**1 393**	..	**56 774**	**127 466**	**201 957**	..	..	..	..	..

Billion KRW

	Local government					Social Security Funds				
	1975	1985	1995	2005	2013	1975	1985	1995	2005	2013
1000 Taxes on income, profits and capital gains	**36**	..	**1 704**	**5 500**	**9 495**	**0**	..	**0**	**0**	**0**
1100 Of individuals	0	..	1 137	2 804	5 377	..	..	..	..	..
1200 Corporate	0	..	565	2 696	4 118	..	..	..	..	..
1300 Unallocable between 1100 and 1200	36	..	3	0	0	..	..	..	..	..
2000 Social security contributions	**0**	..	**0**	**0**	**0**	**13**	..	**9 913**	**43 902**	**91 596**
2100 Employees	..	..	..	..	..	0	..	4 539	17 632	38 396
2200 Employers	..	..	..	..	..	13	..	3 918	18 486	41 518
2300 Self-employed or non-employed	..	..	..	..	..	0	..	1 456	7 784	11 682
2400 Unallocable between 2100, 2200 and 2300	..	..	..	..	..	0	..	0	0	0
3000 Taxes on payroll and workforce	**0**	..	**237**	**514**	**981**	**0**	..	**0**	**0**	**0**
4000 Taxes on property	**87**	..	**8 960**	**17 928**	**23 965**	**0**	..	**0**	**0**	**0**
4100 Recurrent taxes on immovable property	45	..	2 636	4 495	9 335	..	..	..	..	..
4200 Recurrent taxes on net wealth	0	..	0	0	0	..	..	..	..	..
4300 Estate, inheritance and gift taxes	0	..	0	0	0	..	..	..	..	..
4400 Taxes on financial and capital transactions	42	..	6 324	13 433	14 630	..	..	..	..	..
4500 Non-recurrent taxes	0	..	0	0	0	..	..	..	..	..
4600 Other recurrent taxes on property	0	..	0	0	0	..	..	..	..	..
5000 Taxes on goods and services	**36**	..	**4 218**	**7 561**	**13 713**	**0**	..	**0**	**0**	**0**
5100 Taxes on production, sale, transfer, etc	19	..	2 464	5 589	6 966	..	..	..	..	..
5110 General taxes	0	..	0	0	3 142	..	..	..	..	..
5120 Taxes on specific goods and services	19	..	2 464	5 589	3 824	..	..	..	..	..
5130 Unallocable between 5110 and 5120	0	..	0	0	0	..	..	..	..	..
5200 Taxes on use of goods and perform activities	17	..	1 754	1 972	6 747	..	..	..	..	..
5300 Unallocable between 5100 and 5200	0	..	0	0	0	..	..	..	..	..
6000 Other taxes	**0**	..	**198**	**4 474**	**5 625**	**0**	..	**0**	**0**	**0**
6100 Paid solely by business	..	..	0	0	0	..	..	..	..	..
6200 Other	..	..	198	4 474	5 625	..	..	..	..	..
Total tax revenue	**159**	..	**15 316**	**35 977**	**53 779**	**13**	..	**9 913**	**43 902**	**91 596**

StatLink http://dx.doi.org/10.1787/888933277692

Tableau 108. **Luxembourg, recettes fiscales par sous-secteurs d'administration**

Million EUR

	Administration centrale					Administration d'État/Régions				
	1975	1985	1995	2005	2013					
1000 Impôts sur revenu, bénéfices et gains en capital	**353**	**992**	**1 873**	**3 454**	**5 706**	..	..	..	..	..
1100 Des personnes physiques	254	672	1 214	2 162	4 062	..	..	..	..	..
1200 Des sociétés	99	320	659	1 293	1 644	..	..	..	..	..
1300 Non-ventilables entre 1100 et 1200	0	0	0	0	0	..	..	..	..	..
2000 Cotisations de sécurité sociale	**4**	**11**	**20**	**77**	**147**	..	..	..	..	..
2100 A la charge des salariés	3	8	15	77	147	..	..	..	..	..
2200 A la charge des employeurs	0	0	0	0	0	..	..	..	..	..
2300 A charge des travailleurs indép. ou sans emploi	1	3	5	0	0	..	..	..	..	..
2400 Non-ventilables entre 2100, 2200 et 2300	0	0	0	0	0	..	..	..	..	..
3000 Sur salaires ou main d'oeuvre	**0**	**0**	**0**	**0**	**0**	..	..	..	..	..
4000 Impôts sur le patrimoine	**42**	**134**	**373**	**934**	**1 258**	..	..	..	..	..
4100 Impôts périodiques sur la propriété immobilière	0	0	0	0	0	..	..	..	..	..
4200 Impôts périodiques sur l'actif net	21	83	268	698	980	..	..	..	..	..
4300 Impôts sur mut. par décès, succ. et donations	3	7	15	44	72	..	..	..	..	..
4400 Impôts sur transact. mobilières et immob.	18	44	89	193	206	..	..	..	..	..
4500 Impôts non-périodiques	0	0	0	0	0	..	..	..	..	..
4600 Autres impôts périodiques sur patrimoine	0	0	0	0	0	..	..	..	..	..
5000 Impôts sur les biens et services	**189**	**632**	**1 488**	**3 287**	**5 041**	..	..	..	..	..
5100 Impôts sur production, vente, transfert, etc.	182	620	1 466	3 255	4 970	..	..	..	..	..
5110 Impôts généraux	112	337	786	1 865	3 425	..	..	..	..	..
5120 Impôts sur biens et services déterminés	70	283	680	1 390	1 545	..	..	..	..	..
5130 Non-ventilables entre 5110 et 5120	0	0	0	0	0	..	..	..	..	..
5200 Impôts sur utilisation des biens et exerc. activites	7	13	22	32	70	..	..	..	..	..
5300 Non-ventilables entre 5100 et 5200	0	0	0	0	0	..	..	..	..	..
6000 Autres impôts	**0**	**0**	**6**	**11**	**21**	..	..	..	..	..
6100 A la charge exclusive des entreprises	..	0	6	10	20	..	..	..	..	..
6200 A la charge d'autres agents	..	0	0	0	0	..	..	..	..	..
Recettes fiscales totales	**588**	**1 769**	**3 760**	**7 763**	**12 172**	..	..	..	..	..

Million EUR

	Administrations locales					Administrations de sécurité sociale				
	1975	1985	1995	2005	2013	1975	1985	1995	2005	2013
1000 Impôts sur revenu, bénéfices et gains en capital	**46**	**145**	**331**	**460**	**569**	**0**	**0**	**0**	**0**	**0**
1100 Des personnes physiques	0	0	0	0	0	..	..	..	..	..
1200 Des sociétés	46	145	331	460	569	..	..	..	..	..
1300 Non-ventilables entre 1100 et 1200	0	0	0	0	0	..	..	..	..	..
2000 Cotisations de sécurité sociale	**0**	**0**	**0**	**0**	**0**	**268**	**679**	**1 464**	**3 091**	**4 983**
2100 A la charge des salariés	..	..	..	..	..	102	247	578	1 321	2 190
2200 A la charge des employeurs	..	..	..	..	..	150	339	685	1 382	2 174
2300 A charge des travailleurs indép. ou sans emploi	..	..	..	..	..	16	94	200	388	619
2400 Non-ventilables entre 2100, 2200 et 2300	..	..	..	..	..	0	0	0	0	0
3000 Sur salaires ou main d'oeuvre	**9**	**14**	**0**	**0**	**0**	**0**	**0**	**0**	**0**	**0**
4000 Impôts sur le patrimoine	**6**	**13**	**21**	**35**	**47**	**0**	**0**	**0**	**0**	**0**
4100 Impôts périodiques sur la propriété immobilière	6	13	17	26	33	..	..	..	..	..
4200 Impôts périodiques sur l'actif net	0	0	0	0	0	..	..	..	..	..
4300 Impôts sur mut. par décès, succ. et donations	0	0	0	0	0	..	..	..	..	..
4400 Impôts sur transact. mobilières et immob.	0	0	4	10	14	..	..	..	..	..
4500 Impôts non-périodiques	0	0	0	0	0	..	..	..	..	..
4600 Autres impôts périodiques sur patrimoine	0	0	0	0	0	..	..	..	..	..
5000 Impôts sur les biens et services	**1**	**2**	**4**	**8**	**9**	**0**	**0**	**0**	**0**	**0**
5100 Impôts sur production, vente, transfert, etc.	1	2	3	7	8	..	..	..	..	..
5110 Impôts généraux	0	0	0	0	0	..	..	..	..	..
5120 Impôts sur biens et services déterminés	1	2	3	7	8	..	..	..	..	..
5130 Non-ventilables entre 5110 et 5120	0	0	0	0	0	..	..	..	..	..
5200 Impôts sur utilisation des biens et exerc. activites	0	0	1	1	1	..	..	..	..	..
5300 Non-ventilables entre 5100 et 5200	0	0	0	0	0	..	..	..	..	..
6000 Autres impôts	**0**	**0**	**1**	**2**	**1**	**0**	**0**	**0**	**0**	**0**
6100 A la charge exclusive des entreprises	..	..	1	2	1	..	..	..	..	..
6200 A la charge d'autres agents	..	..	0	0	0	..	..	..	..	..
Recettes fiscales totales	**62**	**174**	**357**	**505**	**626**	**268**	**679**	**1 464**	**3 091**	**4 983**

Note: Y compris les ressources TVA propres à l'Union européenne : 2013 = 43.0 et à l'exclusion des droits de douane collectés pour le compte de l'Union européenne : 2013 = 15.3.

StatLink http://dx.doi.org/10.1787/888933277709

Table 109. Mexico, tax revenues by sub-sectors of government

Million MXN

	Federal government					State/Regional				
	1975	1985	1995	2005	2013	1975	1985	1995	2005	2013
1000 Taxes on income, profits and capital gains	..	**1 899**	**76 148**	**402 036**	**957 213**	..	**0**	**1**	**0**	**0**
1100 Of individuals	..	..	..	195 869	425 621	..	..	..	..	..
1200 Corporate	..	..	..	135 840	392 199	..	..	..	..	..
1300 Unallocable between 1100 and 1200	..	1 899	76 148	70 327	139 393	..	..	1	..	..
2000 Social security contributions	..	**0**	**0**	**0**	**0**	..	**0**	**0**	**0**	**0**
2100 Employees	..	..	..	..	..	..	..	..	..	..
2200 Employers	..	..	..	..	..	..	..	..	..	..
2300 Self-employed or non-employed	..	..	..	..	..	..	..	..	..	..
2400 Unallocable between 2100, 2200 and 2300	..	..	..	..	..	..	..	..	..	..
3000 Taxes on payroll and workforce	..	**49**	**0**	**0**	**0**	..	**20**	**2 976**	**20 429**	**53 039**
4000 Taxes on property	..	**0**	**0**	**0**	**0**	..	**3**	**2 927**	**10 905**	**16 637**
4100 Recurrent taxes on immovable property	..	..	..	..	..	..	0	2 198	6 544	10 345
4200 Recurrent taxes on net wealth	..	..	..	..	..	..	0	0	0	0
4300 Estate, inheritance and gift taxes	..	..	..	..	..	..	0	2	0	0
4400 Taxes on financial and capital transactions	..	..	..	..	..	..	3	727	4 361	6 292
4500 Non-recurrent taxes	..	..	..	..	..	..	0	0	0	0
4600 Other recurrent taxes on property	..	..	..	..	..	..	0	0	0	0
5000 Taxes on goods and services	..	**5 539**	**163 821**	**942 354**	**1 553 087**	..	**4**	**441**	**2 124**	**22 519**
5100 Taxes on production, sale, transfer, etc	..	5 517	160 741	927 401	1 552 680	..	1	22	1 364	3 280
5110 General taxes	..	1 365	51 785	318 432	556 794	..	1	0	0	0
5120 Taxes on specific goods and services	..	4 152	108 956	608 969	995 886	..	0	22	1 364	3 280
5130 Unallocable between 5110 and 5120	..	0	0	0	0	..	0	0	0	..
5200 Taxes on use of goods and perform activities	..	22	3 080	14 953	408	..	3	419	760	19 239
5300 Unallocable between 5100 and 5200	..	0	0	0	0	..	0	0	0	0
6000 Other taxes	..	**24**	**5 149**	**8 616**	**26 919**	..	**8**	**228**	**1 537**	**6 318**
6100 Paid solely by business	..	0	0	0	0	..	0	0	0	0
6200 Other	..	24	5 149	8 616	26 919	..	8	228	1 537	6 318
Total tax revenue (collecting government)	..	**7 511**	**245 118**	**1 353 007**	**2 537 219**	..	**35**	**6 573**	**34 995**	**98 513**
Adjustment[1]	..	**-1 336**	**-49 115**	**-278 892**	**-532 455**	..	**1 094**	**39 225**	**218 291**	**410 918**
Total tax revenue (beneficiary government)	..	**6 175**	**196 003**	**1 074 114**	**2 004 764**	..	**1 129**	**45 798**	**253 286**	**509 432**

Million MXN

	Local government					Social Security Funds				
	1975	1985	1995	2005	2013	1975	1985	1995	2005	2013
1000 Taxes on income, profits and capital gains	..	**0**	**16**	**0**	**0**	..	**0**	**0**	**0**	**0**
1100 Of individuals	..	..	..	..	..	..	..	..	..	..
1200 Corporate	..	..	..	..	..	..	..	..	..	..
1300 Unallocable between 1100 and 1200	..	..	16	..	..	..	..	..	..	..
2000 Social security contributions	..	**0**	**0**	**0**	**0**	..	**968**	**50 871**	**261 673**	**490 918**
2100 Employees	..	..	..	..	..	..	..	..	..	..
2200 Employers	..	..	..	..	..	..	..	..	..	..
2300 Self-employed or non-employed	..	..	..	..	..	..	..	..	..	..
2400 Unallocable between 2100, 2200 and 2300	..	..	..	..	..	..	968	50 871	261 673	490 918
3000 Taxes on payroll and workforce	..	**0**	**6**	**32**	**3**	..	**0**	**0**	**0**	**0**
4000 Taxes on property	..	**39**	**2 702**	**15 891**	**29 601**	..	**0**	**0**	**0**	**0**
4100 Recurrent taxes on immovable property	..	29	1 854	10 098	20 994	..	..	..	..	..
4200 Recurrent taxes on net wealth	..	0	0	0	0	..	..	..	..	..
4300 Estate, inheritance and gift taxes	..	0	0	0	0	..	..	..	..	..
4400 Taxes on financial and capital transactions	..	10	848	5 793	8 607	..	..	..	..	..
4500 Non-recurrent taxes	..	0	0	0	0	..	..	..	..	..
4600 Other recurrent taxes on property	..	0	0	0	0	..	..	..	..	..
5000 Taxes on goods and services	..	**7**	**582**	**288**	**1 280**	..	**0**	**0**	**0**	**0**
5100 Taxes on production, sale, transfer, etc	..	7	575	214	1 267	..	..	..	..	..
5110 General taxes	..	0	0	0	0	..	..	..	..	..
5120 Taxes on specific goods and services	..	7	572	214	1 267	..	..	..	..	..
5130 Unallocable between 5110 and 5120	..	0	3	0	..	..	..	..	..	..
5200 Taxes on use of goods and perform activities	..	0	7	74	13	..	..	..	..	..
5300 Unallocable between 5100 and 5200	..	0	0	0	0	..	..	..	..	..
6000 Other taxes	..	**5**	**179**	**1 539**	**8 442**	..	**0**	**0**	**0**	**0**
6100 Paid solely by business	..	0	0	0	0	..	..	..	..	..
6200 Other	..	5	179	1 539	8 442	..	..	..	..	..
Total tax revenue (collecting government)	..	**51**	**3 485**	**17 750**	**39 326**	..	**968**	**50 871**	**261 673**	**490 918**
Adjustment[1]	..	**242**	**9 890**	**60 601**	**121 537**	..	**0**	**0**	**0**	**0**
Total tax revenue (beneficiary government)	..	**293**	**13 375**	**78 351**	**160 863**	..	**968**	**50 871**	**261 673**	**490 918**

1. This adjustment is for taxes collected by Federal government in which States and Local governments have a share. Sub-central government's shares cannot be identified by type of tax.

StatLink http://dx.doi.org/10.1787/888933277717

Table 110. **Netherlands, tax revenues by sub-sectors of government**

Million EUR

	Central government					State/Regional				
	1975	1985	1995	2005	2013					
1000 Taxes on income, profits and capital gains	**15 075**	**22 453**	**33 403**	**54 843**	**59 085**	..	..	..	..	..
1100 Of individuals	11 713	16 527	23 941	35 485	46 638	..	..	..	..	..
1200 Corporate	3 361	5 926	9 461	19 358	12 447	..	..	..	..	..
1300 Unallocable between 1100 and 1200	0	0	0	0	0	..	..	..	..	..
2000 Social security contributions	**0**	**0**	**0**	**0**	**0**	..	..	..	..	..
2100 Employees	..	..	..	..	..	..	..	..	..	..
2200 Employers	..	..	..	..	..	..	..	..	..	..
2300 Self-employed or non-employed	..	..	..	..	..	..	..	..	..	..
2400 Unallocable between 2100, 2200 and 2300	..	..	..	..	..	..	..	..	..	..
3000 Taxes on payroll and workforce	**0**	**0**	**0**	**0**	**0**	..	..	..	..	..
4000 Taxes on property	**767**	**1 429**	**2 900**	**6 163**	**3 391**	..	..	..	..	..
4100 Recurrent taxes on immovable property	50	0	0	0	556	..	..	..	..	..
4200 Recurrent taxes on net wealth	231	427	681	32	1	..	..	..	..	..
4300 Estate, inheritance and gift taxes	163	372	771	1 709	1 730	..	..	..	..	..
4400 Taxes on financial and capital transactions	323	631	1 448	4 422	1 104	..	..	..	..	..
4500 Non-recurrent taxes	0	0	0	0	0	..	..	..	..	..
4600 Other recurrent taxes on property	0	0	0	0	0	..	..	..	..	..
5000 Taxes on goods and services	**9 716**	**20 075**	**31 846**	**58 871**	**66 322**	..	..	..	..	..
5100 Taxes on production, sale, transfer, etc	9 113	18 669	29 573	56 347	62 608	..	..	..	..	..
5110 General taxes	6 257	13 790	19 776	38 566	42 424	..	..	..	..	..
5120 Taxes on specific goods and services	2 856	4 878	9 797	17 781	20 184	..	..	..	..	..
5130 Unallocable between 5110 and 5120	0	0	0	0	0	..	..	..	..	..
5200 Taxes on use of goods and perform activities	604	1 407	2 273	2 524	3 714	..	..	..	..	..
5300 Unallocable between 5100 and 5200	0	0	0	0	0	..	..	..	..	..
6000 Other taxes	**109**	**195**	**327**	**436**	**1 123**	..	..	..	..	..
6100 Paid solely by business	109	195	327	389	139	..	..	..	..	..
6200 Other	0	0	0	47	984	..	..	..	..	..
Total tax revenue	**25 667**	**44 153**	**68 475**	**120 313**	**129 921**	..	..	..	..	..

Million EUR

	Local government					Social Security Funds				
	1975	1985	1995	2005	2013	1975	1985	1995	2005	2013
1000 Taxes on income, profits and capital gains	**77**	**0**	**0**	**0**	**0**	**0**	**0**	**0**	**0**	**0**
1100 Of individuals	77	0	0	0	0	0	0	0	0	0
1200 Corporate	0	0	0	0	0	0	0	0	0	0
1300 Unallocable between 1100 and 1200	0	0	0	0	0	0	0	0	0	0
2000 Social security contributions	**0**	**0**	**0**	**0**	**0**	**16 732**	**37 709**	**53 115**	**67 083**	**97 512**
2100 Employees	..	..	..	..	..	7 139	16 835	33 748	32 691	43 258
2200 Employers	..	..	..	..	..	7 687	15 093	8 504	21 179	32 020
2300 Self-employed or non-employed	..	..	..	..	..	1 905	5 781	10 863	13 213	22 234
2400 Unallocable between 2100, 2200 and 2300	..	..	..	..	..	0	0	0	0	0
3000 Taxes on payroll and workforce	**0**	**0**	**0**	**0**	**0**	**0**	**0**	**0**	**0**	**0**
4000 Taxes on property	**272**	**1 529**	**2 355**	**4 280**	**4 692**	**0**	**0**	**0**	**0**	**0**
4100 Recurrent taxes on immovable property	272	1 529	2 355	4 280	4 692	..	..	..	..	..
4200 Recurrent taxes on net wealth	0	0	0	0	0	..	..	..	..	..
4300 Estate, inheritance and gift taxes	0	0	0	0	0	..	..	..	..	..
4400 Taxes on financial and capital transactions	0	0	0	0	0	..	..	..	..	..
4500 Non-recurrent taxes	0	0	0	0	0	..	..	..	..	..
4600 Other recurrent taxes on property	0	0	0	0	0	..	..	..	..	..
5000 Taxes on goods and services	**153**	**508**	**1 048**	**3 424**	**4 146**	**0**	**0**	**0**	**0**	**0**
5100 Taxes on production, sale, transfer, etc	14	23	54	126	186	..	..	..	..	..
5110 General taxes	0	0	0	0	0	..	..	..	..	..
5120 Taxes on specific goods and services	14	23	54	126	186	..	..	..	..	..
5130 Unallocable between 5110 and 5120	0	0	0	0	0	..	..	..	..	..
5200 Taxes on use of goods and perform activities	139	486	994	3 298	3 960	..	..	..	..	..
5300 Unallocable between 5100 and 5200	0	0	0	0	0	..	..	..	..	..
6000 Other taxes	**0**	**0**	**0**	**0**	**0**	**0**	**0**	**0**	**0**	**0**
6100 Paid solely by business	..	..	..	..	..	..	..	..	..	..
6200 Other	..	..	..	..	..	..	..	..	..	..
Total tax revenue	**502**	**2 037**	**3 403**	**7 704**	**8 838**	**16 732**	**37 709**	**53 115**	**67 083**	**97 512**

Note: Including Vat own resources of the European Union: 2013 = 260.0 and excluding customs duties collected on behalf of the European Union: 2013 = 2 210.0.

StatLink http://dx.doi.org/10.1787/888933277723

Table 111. **New Zealand, tax revenues by sub-sectors of government**

Million NZD

	Central government					State/Regional				
	1975	1985	1995	2005	2013					
1000 Taxes on income, profits and capital gains	**2 296**	**10 567**	**21 253**	**37 379**	**40 764**	..	..	..	..	..
1100 Of individuals	1 874	9 212	15 626	24 373	27 904	..	..	..	..	..
1200 Corporate	407	1 270	4 122	9 957	10 344	..	..	..	..	..
1300 Unallocable between 1100 and 1200	16	86	1 505	3 049	2 516	..	..	..	..	..
2000 Social security contributions	**0**	**0**	**0**	**0**	**0**	..	..	..	..	..
2100 Employees	..	..	..	..	..	..	..	..	..	..
2200 Employers	..	..	..	..	..	..	..	..	..	..
2300 Self-employed or non-employed	..	..	..	..	..	..	..	..	..	..
2400 Unallocable between 2100, 2200 and 2300	..	..	..	..	..	..	..	..	..	..
3000 Taxes on payroll and workforce	**0**	**0**	**0**	**0**	**0**	..	..	..	..	..
4000 Taxes on property	**83**	**211**	**218**	**86**	**93**	..	..	..	..	..
4100 Recurrent taxes on immovable property	3	56	-1	0	0	..	..	..	..	..
4200 Recurrent taxes on net wealth	0	0	0	0	0	..	..	..	..	..
4300 Estate, inheritance and gift taxes	54	28	3	3	0	..	..	..	..	..
4400 Taxes on financial and capital transactions	25	127	216	83	93	..	..	..	..	..
4500 Non-recurrent taxes	0	0	0	0	0	..	..	..	..	..
4600 Other recurrent taxes on property	0	0	0	0	0	..	..	..	..	..
5000 Taxes on goods and services	**807**	**3 457**	**11 395**	**18 744**	**27 705**	..	..	..	..	..
5100 Taxes on production, sale, transfer, etc	770	3 336	10 833	17 792	26 313	..	..	..	..	..
5110 General taxes	311	1 577	7 895	14 133	22 063	..	..	..	..	..
5120 Taxes on specific goods and services	459	1 758	2 938	3 659	4 250	..	..	..	..	..
5130 Unallocable between 5110 and 5120	0	0	0	0	0	..	..	..	..	..
5200 Taxes on use of goods and perform activities	37	122	562	952	1 392	..	..	..	..	..
5300 Unallocable between 5100 and 5200	0	0	0	0	0	..	..	..	..	..
6000 Other taxes	**0**	**0**	**0**	**14**	**3**	..	..	..	..	..
6100 Paid solely by business	..	..	..	0	0	..	..	..	..	..
6200 Other	..	..	..	14	3	..	..	..	..	..
Total tax revenue	**3 186**	**14 236**	**32 866**	**56 223**	**68 565**	..	..	..	..	..

Million NZD

	Local government					Social Security Funds				
	1975	1985	1995	2005	2013	1975	1985	1995	2005	2013
1000 Taxes on income, profits and capital gains	**0**	**0**	**0**	**0**	**0**	**0**	**0**	**0**	**0**	**0**
1100 Of individuals	0	0	0	0	0	0	0	0	0	0
1200 Corporate	0	0	0	0	0	0	0	0	0	0
1300 Unallocable between 1100 and 1200	0	0	0	0	0	0	0	0	0	0
2000 Social security contributions	**0**	**0**	**0**	**0**	**0**	**0**	**0**	**0**	**0**	**0**
2100 Employees	..	..	..	..	..	..	..	..	..	..
2200 Employers	..	..	..	..	..	..	..	..	..	..
2300 Self-employed or non-employed	..	..	..	..	..	..	..	..	..	..
2400 Unallocable between 2100, 2200 and 2300	..	..	..	..	..	..	..	..	..	..
3000 Taxes on payroll and workforce	**0**	**0**	**0**	**0**	**0**	**0**	**0**	**0**	**0**	**0**
4000 Taxes on property	**237**	**921**	**1 646**	**2 825**	**4 423**	**0**	**0**	**0**	**0**	**0**
4100 Recurrent taxes on immovable property	237	921	1 646	2 825	4 423	..	..	..	..	..
4200 Recurrent taxes on net wealth	0	0	0	0	0	..	..	..	..	..
4300 Estate, inheritance and gift taxes	0	0	0	0	0	..	..	..	..	..
4400 Taxes on financial and capital transactions	0	0	0	0	0	..	..	..	..	..
4500 Non-recurrent taxes	0	0	0	0	0	..	..	..	..	..
4600 Other recurrent taxes on property	0	0	0	0	0	..	..	..	..	..
5000 Taxes on goods and services	**29**	**66**	**184**	**310**	**465**	**0**	**0**	**0**	**0**	**0**
5100 Taxes on production, sale, transfer, etc	18	18	33	30	33	..	..	..	..	..
5110 General taxes	0	0	0	0	0	..	..	..	..	..
5120 Taxes on specific goods and services	18	18	33	30	33	..	..	..	..	..
5130 Unallocable between 5110 and 5120	0	0	0	0	0	..	..	..	..	..
5200 Taxes on use of goods and perform activities	11	48	151	280	432	..	..	..	..	..
5300 Unallocable between 5100 and 5200	0	0	0	0	0	..	..	..	..	..
6000 Other taxes	**0**	**0**	**0**	**0**	**0**	**0**	**0**	**0**	**0**	**0**
6100 Paid solely by business	..	..	..	..	..	..	..	..	..	..
6200 Other	..	..	..	..	..	..	..	..	..	..
Total tax revenue	**266**	**987**	**1 830**	**3 135**	**4 888**	**0**	**0**	**0**	**0**	**0**

StatLink http://dx.doi.org/10.1787/888933277737

Table 112. **Norway, tax revenues by sub-sectors of government**

Million NOK

	Central government[1]					State/Regional				
	1975	1985	1995	2005	2013					
1000 Taxes on income, profits and capital gains	**6 495**	**47 772**	**67 402**	**315 943**	**430 561**	..	..	..	..	..
1100 Of individuals	5 424	10 115	38 059	87 503	161 395	..	..	..	..	..
1200 Corporate	1 071	37 657	29 343	228 440	269 166	..	..	..	..	..
1300 Unallocable between 1100 and 1200	0	0	0	0	0	..	..	..	..	..
2000 Social security contributions	**1 341**	**2 854**	**6 013**	**173 151**	**291 781**	..	..	..	..	..
2100 Employees	331	569	1 233	58 320	114 994	..	..	..	..	..
2200 Employers	1 010	2 285	4 780	104 794	176 787	..	..	..	..	..
2300 Self-employed or non-employed	0	0	0	10 037	0	..	..	..	..	..
2400 Unallocable between 2100, 2200 and 2300	0	0	0	0	0	..	..	..	..	..
3000 Taxes on payroll and workforce	**0**	**0**	**0**	**0**	**0**	..	..	..	..	..
4000 Taxes on property	**771**	**1 800**	**3 497**	**11 406**	**19 440**	..	..	..	..	..
4100 Recurrent taxes on immovable property	0	0	0	228	1 700	..	..	..	..	..
4200 Recurrent taxes on net wealth	490	940	1 172	4 741	8 185	..	..	..	..	..
4300 Estate, inheritance and gift taxes	146	226	975	1 768	2 246	..	..	..	..	..
4400 Taxes on financial and capital transactions	135	634	1 350	4 669	7 309	..	..	..	..	..
4500 Non-recurrent taxes	0	0	0	0	0	..	..	..	..	..
4600 Other recurrent taxes on property	0	0	0	0	0	..	..	..	..	..
5000 Taxes on goods and services	**25 056**	**87 964**	**148 088**	**232 759**	**337 991**	..	..	..	..	..
5100 Taxes on production, sale, transfer, etc	24 367	85 468	141 408	220 835	321 353	..	..	..	..	..
5110 General taxes	13 670	42 889	81 772	153 820	235 610	..	..	..	..	..
5120 Taxes on specific goods and services	10 697	42 579	59 636	67 015	85 743	..	..	..	..	..
5130 Unallocable between 5110 and 5120	0	0	0	0	0	..	..	..	..	..
5200 Taxes on use of goods and perform activities	689	2 496	6 680	11 924	16 638	..	..	..	..	..
5300 Unallocable between 5100 and 5200	0	0	0	0	0	..	..	..	..	..
6000 Other taxes	**130**	**24**	**15**	**0**	**0**	..	..	..	..	..
6100 Paid solely by business	124	15	1	..	..	..	..	..	..	..
6200 Other	6	9	14	..	..	..	..	..	..	..
Total tax revenue	**33 793**	**140 414**	**225 015**	**733 259**	**1 079 773**	..	..	..	..	..

Million NOK

	Local government					Social Security Funds				
	1975	1985	1995	2005	2013	1975	1985	1995	2005	2013
1000 Taxes on income, profits and capital gains	**13 725**	**38 655**	**67 978**	**100 512**	**142 969**	**2 728**	**7 163**	**0**	**0**	**0**
1100 Of individuals	12 877	35 739	61 784	100 512	142 969	2 728	7 163	..	..	..
1200 Corporate	848	2 916	6 194	0	0	0	0	..	..	..
1300 Unallocable between 1100 and 1200	0	0	0	0	0	0	0	..	..	..
2000 Social security contributions	**0**	**0**	**0**	**0**	**0**	**15 224**	**46 106**	**84 563**	**0**	**0**
2100 Employees	..	..	..	..	..	2 949	12 623	30 417	..	..
2200 Employers	..	..	..	..	..	11 315	31 628	48 396	..	..
2300 Self-employed or non-employed	..	..	..	..	..	960	1 855	5 750	..	..
2400 Unallocable between 2100, 2200 and 2300	..	..	..	..	..	0	0	0	..	..
3000 Taxes on payroll and workforce	**0**	**0**	**0**	**0**	**0**	**0**	**0**	**0**	**0**	**0**
4000 Taxes on property	**772**	**2 755**	**7 352**	**10 283**	**17 822**	**0**	**0**	**0**	**0**	**0**
4100 Recurrent taxes on immovable property	278	1 072	2 792	4 324	8 873	..	..	..	..	..
4200 Recurrent taxes on net wealth	494	1 683	4 560	5 959	8 949	..	..	..	..	..
4300 Estate, inheritance and gift taxes	0	0	0	0	0	..	..	..	..	..
4400 Taxes on financial and capital transactions	0	0	0	0	0	..	..	..	..	..
4500 Non-recurrent taxes	0	0	0	0	0	..	..	..	..	..
4600 Other recurrent taxes on property	0	0	0	0	0	..	..	..	..	..
5000 Taxes on goods and services	**0**	**211**	**431**	**2 281**	**2 170**	**51**	**157**	**267**	**0**	**0**
5100 Taxes on production, sale, transfer, etc	0	0	0	0	0	51	157	267	..	..
5110 General taxes	0	0	0	0	0	0	0	0	..	..
5120 Taxes on specific goods and services	0	0	0	0	0	51	157	267	..	..
5130 Unallocable between 5110 and 5120	0	0	0	0	0	0	0	0	..	..
5200 Taxes on use of goods and perform activities	0	211	431	2 281	2 170	0	0	0	..	..
5300 Unallocable between 5100 and 5200	0	0	0	0	0	0	0	0	..	..
6000 Other taxes	**432**	**0**	**0**	**0**	**0**	**0**	**0**	**0**	**0**	**0**
6100 Paid solely by business	0	..	..	..	..	..	..	..	..	..
6200 Other	432	..	..	..	..	..	..	..	..	..
Total tax revenue	**14 929**	**41 621**	**75 761**	**113 076**	**162 961**	**18 003**	**53 426**	**84 830**	**0**	**0**

1. The Norwegian National Insurance has been integrated into the Central government sector from the year 2000 and onwards.

StatLink http://dx.doi.org/10.1787/888933277740

Table 113. **Poland, tax revenues by sub-sectors of government**

Million PLN

	Central government					State/Regional				
	1975	1985	1995	2005	2013					
1000 Taxes on income, profits and capital gains	..	..	**32 774**	**40 398**	**64 522**	..	..	..	..	..
1100 Of individuals	..	..	23 937	24 518	41 437	..	..	..	..	..
1200 Corporate	..	..	8 837	15 880	23 085	..	..	..	..	..
1300 Unallocable between 1100 and 1200	..	..	0	0	0	..	..	..	..	..
2000 Social security contributions	..	..	**0**	**0**	**0**	..	..	..	..	..
2100 Employees	..	..	..	..	..	..	..	..	..	..
2200 Employers	..	..	..	..	..	..	..	..	..	..
2300 Self-employed or non-employed	..	..	..	..	..	..	..	..	..	..
2400 Unallocable between 2100, 2200 and 2300	..	..	..	..	..	..	..	..	..	..
3000 Taxes on payroll and workforce	..	..	**831**	**2 555**	**3 998**	..	..	..	..	..
4000 Taxes on property	..	..	**0**	**0**	**0**	..	..	..	..	..
4100 Recurrent taxes on immovable property	..	..	..	..	..	..	..	..	..	..
4200 Recurrent taxes on net wealth	..	..	..	..	..	..	..	..	..	..
4300 Estate, inheritance and gift taxes	..	..	..	..	..	..	..	..	..	..
4400 Taxes on financial and capital transactions	..	..	..	..	..	..	..	..	..	..
4500 Non-recurrent taxes	..	..	..	..	..	..	..	..	..	..
4600 Other recurrent taxes on property	..	..	..	..	..	..	..	..	..	..
5000 Taxes on goods and services	..	..	**46 749**	**120 625**	**187 373**	..	..	..	..	..
5100 Taxes on production, sale, transfer, etc	..	..	46 129	120 223	186 112	..	..	..	..	..
5110 General taxes	..	..	21 051	75 783	116 607	..	..	..	..	..
5120 Taxes on specific goods and services	..	..	25 078	44 440	69 505	..	..	..	..	..
5130 Unallocable between 5110 and 5120	..	..	0	0	0	..	..	..	..	..
5200 Taxes on use of goods and perform activities	..	..	620	402	1 261	..	..	..	..	..
5300 Unallocable between 5100 and 5200	..	..	0	0	0	..	..	..	..	..
6000 Other taxes	..	..	**145**	**18**	**0**	..	..	..	..	..
6100 Paid solely by business	..	..	0	0	..	..	..	..	..	..
6200 Other	..	..	145	18	..	..	..	..	..	..
Total tax revenue	..	..	**80 499**	**163 596**	**255 893**	..	..	..	..	..

Million PLN

	Local government					Social Security Funds				
	1975	1985	1995	2005	2013	1975	1985	1995	2005	2013
1000 Taxes on income, profits and capital gains	..	..	**4 896**	**23 093**	**39 045**	..	..	**0**	**0**	**0**
1100 Of individuals	..	..	4 427	17 916	32 779	..	..	..	..	..
1200 Corporate	..	..	469	5 177	6 266	..	..	..	..	..
1300 Unallocable between 1100 and 1200	..	..	0	0	0	..	..	..	..	..
2000 Social security contributions	..	..	**0**	**0**	**0**	..	..	**38 808**	**121 522**	**204 634**
2100 Employees	..	..	..	..	..	..	..	15 801	47 656	81 128
2200 Employers	..	..	..	..	..	..	..	20 416	48 706	86 300
2300 Self-employed or non-employed	..	..	..	..	..	..	..	2 591	25 160	37 206
2400 Unallocable between 2100, 2200 and 2300	..	..	..	..	..	..	..	0	0	0
3000 Taxes on payroll and workforce	..	..	**0**	**0**	**0**	..	..	**0**	**0**	**0**
4000 Taxes on property	..	..	**4 370**	**14 723**	**23 120**	..	..	**0**	**0**	**0**
4100 Recurrent taxes on immovable property	..	..	3 579	12 718	20 747	..	..	..	..	..
4200 Recurrent taxes on net wealth	..	..	0	0	0	..	..	..	..	..
4300 Estate, inheritance and gift taxes	..	..	44	242	252	..	..	..	..	..
4400 Taxes on financial and capital transactions	..	..	747	1 763	2 121	..	..	..	..	..
4500 Non-recurrent taxes	..	..	0	0	0	..	..	..	..	..
4600 Other recurrent taxes on property	..	..	0	0	0	..	..	..	..	..
5000 Taxes on goods and services	..	..	**1 332**	**3 329**	**3 245**	..	..	**0**	**0**	**0**
5100 Taxes on production, sale, transfer, etc	..	..	0	0	0	..	..	..	..	..
5110 General taxes	..	..	0	0	0	..	..	..	..	..
5120 Taxes on specific goods and services	..	..	0	0	0	..	..	..	..	..
5130 Unallocable between 5110 and 5120	..	..	0	0	0	..	..	..	..	..
5200 Taxes on use of goods and perform activities	..	..	1 332	3 329	3 245	..	..	..	..	0
5300 Unallocable between 5100 and 5200	..	..	0	0	0	..	..	..	..	..
6000 Other taxes	..	..	**166**	**317**	**3 068**	..	..	**0**	**0**	**0**
6100 Paid solely by business	..	..	0	0	0	..	..	..	..	..
6200 Other	..	..	166	317	3 068	..	..	..	..	..
Total tax revenue	..	..	**10 764**	**41 462**	**68 478**	..	..	**38 808**	**121 522**	**204 634**

Note: Including Vat own resources of the European Union: 2013 = 2 239.0 and excluding customs duties collected on behalf of the European Union: 2013 = 1 613.0.

StatLink http://dx.doi.org/10.1787/888933277753

Table 114. **Portugal, tax revenues by sub-sectors of government**

Million EUR

	Central government					State/Regional				
	1975	1985	1995	2005	2013					
1000 Taxes on income, profits and capital gains	**81**	**1 306**	**6 557**	**11 506**	**17 426**	..	..	..	..	..
1100 Of individuals	..	..	4 691	7 757	12 325	..	..	..	..	..
1200 Corporate	..	..	1 866	3 705	5 101	..	..	..	..	..
1300 Unallocable between 1100 and 1200	81	1 306	0	43	0	..	..	..	..	..
2000 Social security contributions	**0**	**0**	**1 560**	**1 887**	**1 852**	..	..	..	..	..
2100 Employees	..	..	941	1 629	1 657	..	..	..	..	..
2200 Employers	..	..	619	259	195	..	..	..	..	..
2300 Self-employed or non-employed	..	..	0	0	0	..	..	..	..	..
2400 Unallocable between 2100, 2200 and 2300	..	..	0	0	0	..	..	..	..	..
3000 Taxes on payroll and workforce	**12**	**137**	**0**	**0**	**0**	..	..	..	..	..
4000 Taxes on property	**12**	**103**	**226**	**261**	**207**	..	..	..	..	..
4100 Recurrent taxes on immovable property	0	0	0	0	0	..	..	..	..	..
4200 Recurrent taxes on net wealth	0	0	0	0	0	..	..	..	..	..
4300 Estate, inheritance and gift taxes	4	45	57	25	2	..	..	..	..	..
4400 Taxes on financial and capital transactions	7	58	169	236	205	..	..	..	..	..
4500 Non-recurrent taxes	0	0	0	0	0	..	..	..	..	..
4600 Other recurrent taxes on property	0	0	0	0	0	..	..	..	..	..
5000 Taxes on goods and services	**198**	**2 362**	**10 402**	**19 661**	**19 638**	..	..	..	..	..
5100 Taxes on production, sale, transfer, etc	187	2 290	10 194	19 243	18 692	..	..	..	..	..
5110 General taxes	52	681	5 481	11 846	12 240	..	..	..	..	..
5120 Taxes on specific goods and services	135	1 609	4 713	7 397	6 451	..	..	..	..	..
5130 Unallocable between 5110 and 5120	0	0	0	0	0	..	..	..	..	..
5200 Taxes on use of goods and perform activities	12	72	179	375	741	..	..	..	..	..
5300 Unallocable between 5100 and 5200	0	0	30	43	205	..	..	..	..	..
6000 Other taxes	**2**	**15**	**98**	**229**	**395**	..	..	..	..	..
6100 Paid solely by business	1	11	18	137	193	..	..	..	..	..
6200 Other	0	4	81	92	202	..	..	..	..	..
Total tax revenue	**304**	**3 922**	**18 844**	**33 544**	**39 518**	..	..	..	..	..

Million EUR

	Local government					Social Security Funds				
	1975	1985	1995	2005	2013	1975	1985	1995	2005	2013
1000 Taxes on income, profits and capital gains	**0**	**126**	**307**	**725**	**1 230**	**0**	**0**	**0**	**0**	**0**
1100 Of individuals	..	..	156	298	794	..	..	..	..	..
1200 Corporate	..	..	151	427	435	..	..	..	..	..
1300 Unallocable between 1100 and 1200	0	126	0	0	0	..	..	..	..	..
2000 Social security contributions	**0**	**0**	**2**	**7**	**10**	**161**	**1 440**	**5 267**	**11 100**	**13 253**
2100 Employees	..	..	2	7	10	62	563	2 100	4 053	4 737
2200 Employers	..	..	0	0	0	97	827	3 167	7 047	8 517
2300 Self-employed or non-employed	..	..	0	0	0	2	32	0	0	0
2400 Unallocable between 2100, 2200 and 2300	..	..	0	0	0	0	18	0	0	0
3000 Taxes on payroll and workforce	**0**	**0**	**0**	**0**	**0**	**0**	**0**	**0**	**0**	**0**
4000 Taxes on property	**0**	**3**	**599**	**1 532**	**1 730**	**0**	**0**	**0**	**0**	**0**
4100 Recurrent taxes on immovable property	..	0	310	827	1 269	..	..	..	..	..
4200 Recurrent taxes on net wealth	..	0	0	0	0	..	..	..	..	..
4300 Estate, inheritance and gift taxes	..	1	0	1	0	..	..	..	..	..
4400 Taxes on financial and capital transactions	..	2	289	704	461	..	..	..	..	..
4500 Non-recurrent taxes	..	0	0	0	0	..	..	..	..	..
4600 Other recurrent taxes on property	..	0	0	0	0	..	..	..	..	..
5000 Taxes on goods and services	**0**	**68**	**499**	**971**	**984**	**0**	**0**	**335**	**823**	**1 154**
5100 Taxes on production, sale, transfer, etc	0	59	442	837	720	..	..	335	823	1 154
5110 General taxes	0	18	318	563	493	..	..	276	592	977
5120 Taxes on specific goods and services	0	41	124	273	228	..	..	59	231	177
5130 Unallocable between 5110 and 5120	0	0	0	0	0	..	..	0	0	0
5200 Taxes on use of goods and perform activities	0	8	57	133	263	..	..	0	0	0
5300 Unallocable between 5100 and 5200	0	0	0	1	0	..	..	0	0	0
6000 Other taxes	**0**	**0**	**3**	**28**	**124**	**0**	**0**	**1**	**3**	**9**
6100 Paid solely by business	..	0	0	25	18	..	..	0	0	0
6200 Other	..	0	3	3	107	..	..	1	3	9
Total tax revenue	**0**	**197**	**1 410**	**3 262**	**4 078**	**161**	**1 440**	**5 603**	**11 926**	**14 417**

Note: Including Vat own resources of the European Union: 2013 = 230.8 and excluding customs duties collected on behalf of the European Union: 2013 = 143.8.

StatLink http://dx.doi.org/10.1787/888933277769

Table 115. **Slovak Republic, tax revenues by sub-sectors of government**

Million EUR

	Central government					State/Regional				
	1975	1985	1995	2005	2013					
1000 Taxes on income, profits and capital gains	..	..	**1 993**	**2 968**	**4 440**	..	..	..	..	..
1100 Of individuals	..	..	695	1 496	2 144	..	..	..	..	..
1200 Corporate	..	..	1 166	1 345	2 118	..	..	..	..	..
1300 Unallocable between 1100 and 1200	..	..	132	128	178	..	..	..	..	..
2000 Social security contributions	..	..	**85**	**200**	**158**	..	..	..	..	..
2100 Employees	..	..	10	104	49	..	..	..	..	..
2200 Employers	..	..	75	95	108	..	..	..	..	..
2300 Self-employed or non-employed	..	..	0	0	0	..	..	..	..	..
2400 Unallocable between 2100, 2200 and 2300	..	..	0	0	0	..	..	..	..	..
3000 Taxes on payroll and workforce	..	..	**0**	**0**	**0**	..	..	..	..	..
4000 Taxes on property	..	..	**27**	**28**	**0**	..	..	..	..	..
4100 Recurrent taxes on immovable property	..	..	8	9	0	..	..	..	..	..
4200 Recurrent taxes on net wealth	..	..	0	0	0	..	..	..	..	..
4300 Estate, inheritance and gift taxes	..	..	2	1	0	..	..	..	..	..
4400 Taxes on financial and capital transactions	..	..	16	18	0	..	..	..	..	..
4500 Non-recurrent taxes	..	..	0	0	0	..	..	..	..	..
4600 Other recurrent taxes on property	..	..	0	0	0	..	..	..	..	..
5000 Taxes on goods and services	..	..	**2 766**	**5 994**	**7 373**	..	..	..	..	..
5100 Taxes on production, sale, transfer, etc	..	..	2 588	5 781	7 058	..	..	..	..	..
5110 General taxes	..	..	1 616	3 880	4 696	..	..	..	..	..
5120 Taxes on specific goods and services	..	..	971	1 901	2 362	..	..	..	..	..
5130 Unallocable between 5110 and 5120	..	..	0	0	0	..	..	..	..	..
5200 Taxes on use of goods and perform activities	..	..	177	212	316	..	..	..	..	..
5300 Unallocable between 5100 and 5200	..	..	2	2	0	..	..	..	..	..
6000 Other taxes	..	..	**0**	**0**	**0**	..	..	..	..	..
6100 Paid solely by business	..	..	..	..	..	..	..	..	..	..
6200 Other	..	..	..	..	..	..	..	..	..	..
Total tax revenue	..	..	**4 870**	**9 190**	**11 971**	..	..	..	..	..

Million EUR

	Local government					Social Security Funds				
	1975	1985	1995	2005	2013	1975	1985	1995	2005	2013
1000 Taxes on income, profits and capital gains	..	..	**0**	**0**	**0**	..	..	**0**	**0**	**0**
1100 Of individuals	..	..	0	0	0	..	..	0	0	0
1200 Corporate	..	..	0	0	0	..	..	0	0	0
1300 Unallocable between 1100 and 1200	..	..	0	0	0	..	..	0	0	0
2000 Social security contributions	..	..	**0**	**0**	**0**	..	..	**2 817**	**6 037**	**9 625**
2100 Employees	..	..	..	..	..	..	..	540	1 377	2 189
2200 Employers	..	..	..	..	..	..	..	1 774	3 356	5 383
2300 Self-employed or non-employed	..	..	..	..	..	..	..	503	1 304	2 054
2400 Unallocable between 2100, 2200 and 2300	..	..	..	..	..	..	..	0	0	0
3000 Taxes on payroll and workforce	..	..	**0**	**0**	**0**	..	..	**0**	**0**	**0**
4000 Taxes on property	..	..	**84**	**220**	**327**	..	..	**0**	**0**	**0**
4100 Recurrent taxes on immovable property	..	..	72	220	327	..	..	..	..	..
4200 Recurrent taxes on net wealth	..	..	0	0	0	..	..	..	..	..
4300 Estate, inheritance and gift taxes	..	..	0	0	0	..	..	..	..	..
4400 Taxes on financial and capital transactions	..	..	12	0	0	..	..	..	..	..
4500 Non-recurrent taxes	..	..	0	0	0	..	..	..	..	..
4600 Other recurrent taxes on property	..	..	0	0	0	..	..	..	..	..
5000 Taxes on goods and services	..	..	**17**	**198**	**310**	..	..	**0**	**0**	**0**
5100 Taxes on production, sale, transfer, etc	..	..	10	10	14	..	..	..	..	..
5110 General taxes	..	..	0	0	0	..	..	..	..	..
5120 Taxes on specific goods and services	..	..	10	10	14	..	..	..	..	..
5130 Unallocable between 5110 and 5120	..	..	0	0	0	..	..	..	..	..
5200 Taxes on use of goods and perform activities	..	..	1	94	151	..	..	..	..	..
5300 Unallocable between 5100 and 5200	..	..	6	95	145	..	..	..	..	..
6000 Other taxes	..	..	**0**	**0**	**0**	..	..	**0**	**0**	**0**
6100 Paid solely by business	..	..	..	..	..	..	..	..	..	..
6200 Other	..	..	..	..	..	..	..	..	..	..
Total tax revenue	..	..	**101**	**418**	**637**	..	..	**2 817**	**6 037**	**9 625**

Note: Including Vat own resources of the European Union: 2013 = 67.9 and excluding customs duties collected on behalf of the European Union: 2013 = 114.6.

StatLink http://dx.doi.org/10.1787/888933277775

Table 116. **Slovenia, tax revenues by sub-sectors of government**

Million EUR

	Central government					State/Regional				
	1975	1985	1995	2005	2013					
1000 Taxes on income, profits and capital gains	..	..	**479**	**1 828**	**1 176**	..	..	..	..	..
1100 Of individuals	..	..	413	1 029	740	..	..	..	..	..
1200 Corporate	..	..	54	795	433	..	..	..	..	..
1300 Unallocable between 1100 and 1200	..	..	12	5	3	..	..	..	..	..
2000 Social security contributions	..	..	**38**	**42**	**53**	..	..	..	..	..
2100 Employees	..	..	20	24	26	..	..	..	..	..
2200 Employers	..	..	17	15	21	..	..	..	..	..
2300 Self-employed or non-employed	..	..	1	3	6	..	..	..	..	..
2400 Unallocable between 2100, 2200 and 2300	..	..	0	0	0	..	..	..	..	..
3000 Taxes on payroll and workforce	..	..	**14**	**521**	**23**	..	..	..	..	..
4000 Taxes on property	..	..	**5**	**3**	**14**	..	..	..	..	..
4100 Recurrent taxes on immovable property	..	..	0	0	13	..	..	..	..	..
4200 Recurrent taxes on net wealth	..	..	0	3	0	..	..	..	..	..
4300 Estate, inheritance and gift taxes	..	..	0	0	0	..	..	..	..	..
4400 Taxes on financial and capital transactions	..	..	0	0	0	..	..	..	..	..
4500 Non-recurrent taxes	..	..	5	0	1	..	..	..	..	..
4600 Other recurrent taxes on property	..	..	0	0	0	..	..	..	..	..
5000 Taxes on goods and services	..	..	**1 554**	**3 805**	**5 256**	..	..	..	..	..
5100 Taxes on production, sale, transfer, etc	..	..	1 524	3 624	4 955	..	..	..	..	..
5110 General taxes	..	..	1 192	2 467	3 048	..	..	..	..	..
5120 Taxes on specific goods and services	..	..	332	1 156	1 907	..	..	..	..	..
5130 Unallocable between 5110 and 5120	..	..	0	0	0	..	..	..	..	..
5200 Taxes on use of goods and perform activities	..	..	31	181	301	..	..	..	..	..
5300 Unallocable between 5100 and 5200	..	..	0	0	0	..	..	..	..	..
6000 Other taxes	..	..	**0**	**0**	**0**	..	..	..	..	..
6100 Paid solely by business	..	..	..	..	..	..	..	..	..	..
6200 Other	..	..	..	..	..	..	..	..	..	..
Total tax revenue	..	..	**2 090**	**6 199**	**6 522**	..	..	..	..	..

Million EUR

	Local government					Social Security Funds				
	1975	1985	1995	2005	2013	1975	1985	1995	2005	2013
1000 Taxes on income, profits and capital gains	..	..	**194**	**559**	**1 149**	..	..	**0**	**0**	**0**
1100 Of individuals	..	..	192	556	1 149	..	..	..	..	..
1200 Corporate	..	..	0	0	0	..	..	..	..	..
1300 Unallocable between 1100 and 1200	..	..	2	2	0	..	..	..	..	..
2000 Social security contributions	..	..	**0**	**0**	**0**	..	..	**1 690**	**4 042**	**5 279**
2100 Employees	..	..	..	..	..	..	..	810	2 122	2 648
2200 Employers	..	..	..	..	..	..	..	802	1 572	2 028
2300 Self-employed or non-employed	..	..	..	..	..	..	..	78	348	604
2400 Unallocable between 2100, 2200 and 2300	..	..	..	..	..	..	..	0	0	0
3000 Taxes on payroll and workforce	..	..	**2**	**0**	**0**	..	..	**0**	**0**	**0**
4000 Taxes on property	..	..	**53**	**167**	**218**	..	..	**0**	**0**	**0**
4100 Recurrent taxes on immovable property	..	..	37	122	186	..	..	..	..	..
4200 Recurrent taxes on net wealth	..	..	0	0	0	..	..	..	..	..
4300 Estate, inheritance and gift taxes	..	..	1	5	8	..	..	..	..	..
4400 Taxes on financial and capital transactions	..	..	12	40	23	..	..	..	..	..
4500 Non-recurrent taxes	..	..	3	0	1	..	..	..	..	..
4600 Other recurrent taxes on property	..	..	0	0	0	..	..	..	..	..
5000 Taxes on goods and services	..	..	**7**	**91**	**75**	..	..	**0**	**0**	**0**
5100 Taxes on production, sale, transfer, etc	..	..	7	43	35	..	..	..	..	..
5110 General taxes	..	..	0	0	0	..	..	..	..	..
5120 Taxes on specific goods and services	..	..	7	43	35	..	..	..	..	..
5130 Unallocable between 5110 and 5120	..	..	0	0	0	..	..	..	..	..
5200 Taxes on use of goods and perform activities	..	..	0	48	40	..	..	..	..	..
5300 Unallocable between 5100 and 5200	..	..	0	0	0	..	..	..	..	..
6000 Other taxes	..	..	**0**	**0**	**0**	..	..	**0**	**0**	**0**
6100 Paid solely by business	..	..	..	..	..	..	..	..	..	..
6200 Other	..	..	..	..	..	..	..	..	..	..
Total tax revenue	..	..	**256**	**817**	**1 442**	..	..	**1 690**	**4 042**	**5 279**

Note: Including Vat own resources of the European Union: 2013 = 52.2 and excluding customs duties collected on behalf of the European Union: 2013 = 52.1.

StatLink http://dx.doi.org/10.1787/888933277780

Table 117. Spain, tax revenues by sub-sectors of government

Million EUR

	Federal government					State/Regional[1]				
	1975	1985	1995	2005	2013	1975	1985	1995	2005	2013
1000 Taxes on income, profits and capital gains	**1 388**	**11 321**	**38 969**	**73 405**	**63 373**	..	**126**	**584**	**19 504**	**33 168**
1100 Of individuals	897	8 800	31 410	37 806	41 066	..	112	459	19 102	32 990
1200 Corporate	490	2 410	7 338	33 713	20 132	..	14	125	396	171
1300 Unallocable between 1100 and 1200	1	111	221	1 886	2 175	..	0	0	6	7
2000 Social security contributions	**0**	**183**	**583**	**3 027**	**3 021**	..	**0**	**1**	**0**	**0**
2100 Employees	..	183	583	1 369	1 514	..	..	1	..	..
2200 Employers	..	0	0	1 658	1 507	..	..	0	..	..
2300 Self-employed or non-employed	..	0	0	0	0	..	..	0	..	..
2400 Unallocable between 2100, 2200 and 2300	..	0	0	0	0	..	..	0	..	..
3000 Taxes on payroll and workforce	**0**	**0**	**0**	**0**	**0**	..	**0**	**0**	**0**	**0**
4000 Taxes on property	**421**	**795**	**451**	**140**	**330**	..	**568**	**3 851**	**19 246**	**9 002**
4100 Recurrent taxes on immovable property	1	0	0	6	8	..	0	0	0	0
4200 Recurrent taxes on net wealth	0	58	166	37	23	..	88	417	1 251	1 209
4300 Estate, inheritance and gift taxes	56	60	1	25	165	..	131	713	2 315	2 247
4400 Taxes on financial and capital transactions	364	674	235	10	3	..	348	2 721	15 680	5 544
4500 Non-recurrent taxes	0	0	0	0	0	..	0	0	0	2
4600 Other recurrent taxes on property	0	3	48	62	131	..	0	0	0	0
5000 Taxes on goods and services	**1 609**	**11 013**	**32 482**	**72 684**	**81 839**	..	**1 050**	**2 304**	**7 355**	**4 718**
5100 Taxes on production, sale, transfer, etc	1 599	10 904	32 262	72 297	80 532	..	1 050	2 261	7 159	4 510
5110 General taxes	990	5 416	20 360	52 627	55 441	..	581	637	1 455	1 577
5120 Taxes on specific goods and services	608	5 488	11 902	19 670	25 091	..	469	1 624	5 704	2 933
5130 Unallocable between 5110 and 5120	0	0	0	0	0	..	0	0	0	0
5200 Taxes on use of goods and perform activities	10	3	2	50	196	..	0	43	196	208
5300 Unallocable between 5100 and 5200	0	106	218	337	1 111	..	0	0	0	0
6000 Other taxes	**0**	**0**	**-11**	**52**	**582**	..	**16**	**155**	**116**	**715**
6100 Paid solely by business	..	..	0	52	49	..	0	0	0	0
6200 Other	..	..	-11	0	533	..	16	155	116	715
Total tax revenue	**3 418**	**23 313**	**72 474**	**149 307**	**149 146**	..	**1 760**	**6 895**	**46 221**	**47 603**

Million EUR

	Local government					Social Security Funds				
	1975	1985	1995	2005	2013	1975	1985	1995	2005	2013
1000 Taxes on income, profits and capital gains	**175**	**825**	**2 431**	**5 216**	**6 236**	**0**	**0**	**0**	**0**	**0**
1100 Of individuals	131	703	2 051	3 406	4 265	..	..	..	..	..
1200 Corporate	0	122	349	1 440	1 206	..	..	..	..	..
1300 Unallocable between 1100 and 1200	44	0	31	370	765	..	..	..	..	..
2000 Social security contributions	**0**	**0**	**0**	**0**	**0**	**3 367**	**19 976**	**51 393**	**108 048**	**117 729**
2100 Employees	..	..	..	..	..	645	3 393	7 781	16 164	17 305
2200 Employers	..	..	..	..	..	2 722	15 152	35 929	78 925	81 981
2300 Self-employed or non-employed	..	..	..	..	..	0	1 432	7 684	12 959	18 443
2400 Unallocable between 2100, 2200 and 2300	..	..	..	..	..	0	0	0	0	0
3000 Taxes on payroll and workforce	**0**	**0**	**0**	**0**	**0**	**0**	**0**	**0**	**0**	**0**
4000 Taxes on property	**26**	**1 574**	**3 625**	**8 545**	**14 234**	**0**	**0**	**0**	**0**	**0**
4100 Recurrent taxes on immovable property	26	1 102	2 825	6 038	11 936	..	..	..	..	..
4200 Recurrent taxes on net wealth	0	10	42	107	138	..	..	..	..	..
4300 Estate, inheritance and gift taxes	0	12	18	79	106	..	..	..	..	..
4400 Taxes on financial and capital transactions	0	82	162	423	110	..	..	..	..	..
4500 Non-recurrent taxes	0	367	579	1 898	1 944	..	..	..	..	..
4600 Other recurrent taxes on property	0	1	0	0	0	..	..	..	..	..
5000 Taxes on goods and services	**104**	**1 989**	**5 619**	**12 749**	**11 676**	**0**	**0**	**0**	**0**	**0**
5100 Taxes on production, sale, transfer, etc	104	1 679	2 326	6 800	7 143	..	..	..	..	..
5110 General taxes	95	1 288	1 818	4 718	5 161	..	..	..	..	..
5120 Taxes on specific goods and services	10	391	508	2 082	1 982	..	..	..	..	..
5130 Unallocable between 5110 and 5120	0	0	0	0	0	..	..	..	..	..
5200 Taxes on use of goods and perform activities	0	301	3 294	5 937	4 513	..	..	..	..	..
5300 Unallocable between 5100 and 5200	0	9	0	12	20	..	..	..	..	..
6000 Other taxes	**0**	**16**	**576**	**866**	**1 725**	**0**	**0**	**0**	**0**	**0**
6100 Paid solely by business	..	6	457	691	1 195	..	..	..	..	..
6200 Other	..	10	118	175	530	..	..	..	..	..
Total tax revenue	**305**	**4 404**	**12 251**	**27 376**	**33 871**	**3 367**	**19 976**	**51 393**	**108 048**	**117 729**

Note: Including Vat own resources of the European Union: 2013 = 1 292.0 and excluding customs duties collected on behalf of the European Union: 2013 = 1 316.0.

1. Spain is constitutionally a non-federal country but has a highly decentralised political structure.

StatLink http://dx.doi.org/10.1787/888933277798

Table 118. **Sweden, tax revenues by sub-sectors of government**

Million SEK

	Central government					State/Regional				
	1975	1985	1995	2005	2013					
1000 Taxes on income, profits and capital gains	**28 216**	**51 824**	**72 342**	**94 015**	**-23 250**	..	..	..	..	..
1100 Of individuals	25 626	38 521	22 541	-7 974	-122 856	..	..	..	..	..
1200 Corporate	2 590	13 303	49 801	101 989	99 605	..	..	..	..	..
1300 Unallocable between 1100 and 1200	0	0	0	0	0	..	..	..	..	..
2000 Social security contributions[1]	**0**	**40 675**	**50 560**	**212 964**	**169 166**	..	..	..	..	..
2100 Employees	..	551	0	0	0	..	..	..	..	..
2200 Employers	..	38 386	49 222	209 370	167 850	..	..	..	..	..
2300 Self-employed or non-employed	..	1 738	1 338	4 639	2 549	..	..	..	..	..
2400 Unallocable between 2100, 2200 and 2300	..	0	0	-1 044	-1 233	..	..	..	..	..
3000 Taxes on payroll and workforce	**5 723**	**16 107**	**17 800**	**62 432**	**172 170**	..	..	..	..	..
4000 Taxes on property	**1 469**	**10 157**	**23 260**	**40 116**	**25 776**	..	..	..	..	..
4100 Recurrent taxes on immovable property	11	3 861	15 263	25 139	16 190	..	..	..	..	..
4200 Recurrent taxes on net wealth	647	1 871	3 583	4 998	0	..	..	..	..	..
4300 Estate, inheritance and gift taxes	335	1 114	1 388	1 092	-4	..	..	..	..	..
4400 Taxes on financial and capital transactions	476	3 311	3 026	8 887	9 590	..	..	..	..	..
4500 Non-recurrent taxes	0	0	0	0	0	..	..	..	..	..
4600 Other recurrent taxes on property	0	0	0	0	0	..	..	..	..	..
5000 Taxes on goods and services	**31 985**	**114 957**	**237 720**	**353 031**	**461 710**	..	..	..	..	..
5100 Taxes on production, sale, transfer, etc	29 820	110 367	233 671	342 011	445 208	..	..	..	..	..
5110 General taxes	15 806	60 523	166 557	250 470	341 952	..	..	..	..	..
5120 Taxes on specific goods and services	14 014	49 844	67 114	91 541	103 256	..	..	..	..	..
5130 Unallocable between 5110 and 5120	0	0	0	0	0	..	..	..	..	..
5200 Taxes on use of goods and perform activities	2 165	4 590	4 049	11 019	16 502	..	..	..	..	..
5300 Unallocable between 5100 and 5200	0	0	0	0	0	..	..	..	..	..
6000 Other taxes	**260**	**623**	**1 438**	**1 347**	**1 806**	..	..	..	..	..
6100 Paid solely by business	0	0	0	0	0	..	..	..	..	..
6200 Other	260	623	1 438	1 347	1 806	..	..	..	..	..
Total tax revenue	**67 653**	**234 343**	**403 120**	**763 906**	**807 378**	..	..	..	..	..

Million SEK

	Local government					Social Security Funds				
	1975	1985	1995	2005	2013	1975	1985	1995	2005	2013
1000 Taxes on income, profits and capital gains	**38 415**	**131 242**	**265 068**	**435 577**	**581 934**	**0**	**0**	**0**	**0**	**0**
1100 Of individuals	35 269	129 401	265 068	435 577	581 934	..	..	..	..	..
1200 Corporate	3 146	1 841	0	0	0	..	..	..	..	..
1300 Unallocable between 1100 and 1200	0	0	0	0	0	..	..	..	..	..
2000 Social security contributions[1]	**0**	**0**	**0**	**0**	**0**	**25 756**	**67 531**	**186 992**	**151 019**	**207 518**
2100 Employees	..	..	..	..	..	0	2	28 989	74 178	100 861
2200 Employers	..	..	..	..	..	24 203	64 916	154 154	74 377	103 599
2300 Self-employed or non-employed	..	..	..	..	..	1 553	2 613	3 849	2 464	3 058
2400 Unallocable between 2100, 2200 and 2300	..	..	..	..	..	0	0	0	0	0
3000 Taxes on payroll and workforce	**0**	**0**	**0**	**0**	**0**	**0**	**0**	**0**	**0**	**0**
4000 Taxes on property	**0**	**0**	**0**	**0**	**15 406**	**0**	**0**	**0**	**0**	**0**
4100 Recurrent taxes on immovable property	..	..	..	..	15 406	..	..	..	..	..
4200 Recurrent taxes on net wealth	..	..	..	..	0	..	..	..	..	..
4300 Estate, inheritance and gift taxes	..	..	..	..	0	..	..	..	..	..
4400 Taxes on financial and capital transactions	..	..	..	..	0	..	..	..	..	..
4500 Non-recurrent taxes	..	..	..	..	0	..	..	..	..	..
4600 Other recurrent taxes on property	..	..	..	..	0	..	..	..	..	..
5000 Taxes on goods and services	**149**	**358**	**786**	**0**	**0**	**0**	**0**	**0**	**0**	**0**
5100 Taxes on production, sale, transfer, etc	119	290	732	0	0	0	0	0	0	0
5110 General taxes	0	0	0	0	0	0	0	0	0	0
5120 Taxes on specific goods and services	119	290	732	0	0	0	0	0	0	0
5130 Unallocable between 5110 and 5120	0	0	0	0	0	0	0	0	0	0
5200 Taxes on use of goods and perform activities	30	68	54	0	0	0	0	0	0	0
5300 Unallocable between 5100 and 5200	0	0	0	0	0	0	0	0	0	0
6000 Other taxes	**0**	**0**	**0**	**0**	**0**	**0**	**0**	**0**	**0**	**0**
6100 Paid solely by business	..	..	..	..	..	..	..	..	..	..
6200 Other	..	..	..	..	..	..	..	..	..	..
Total tax revenue	**38 564**	**131 600**	**265 854**	**435 577**	**597 340**	**25 756**	**67 531**	**186 992**	**151 019**	**207 518**

Note: Including VAT own resources of the European Union: 2013 = 1 714.2 and excluding customs duties collected on behalf of the European Union: 2013 = 4 976.4.

1. From 1985, social security contributions are classified using the SNA definition of Social security Funds which means that a proportion of these payments are shown under the heading of Central Government. Prior to that year, all such payments were classified under the heading of Social Security Funds.

StatLink http://dx.doi.org/10.1787/888933277802

Tableau 119. **Suisse, recettes fiscales par sous-secteurs d'administration**

Million CHF

	Administration fédérale					État/Régions				
	1975	1985	1995	2005	2013	1975	1985	1995	2005	2013
1000 Impôts sur revenu, bénéfices et gains en capital	**3 422**	**6 523**	**10 145**	**16 341**	**23 453**	**7 756**	**12 652**	**19 183**	**26 233**	**33 166**
1100 Des personnes physiques	2 712	5 330	5 699	7 823	9 818	6 342	10 770	15 987	21 034	26 055
1200 Des sociétés	710	1 193	2 355	4 519	8 698	1 414	1 882	2 598	4 571	5 944
1300 Non-ventilables entre 1100 et 1200	0	0	2 092	4 000	4 938	0	0	598	628	1 166
2000 Cotisations de sécurité sociale	**0**	**0**	**0**	**0**	**0**	**0**	**0**	**0**	**0**	**0**
2100 A la charge des salariés	..	..	..	..	..	..	..	..	..	..
2200 A la charge des employeurs	..	..	..	..	..	..	..	..	..	..
2300 A charge des travailleurs indép. ou sans emploi	..	..	..	..	..	..	..	..	..	..
2400 Non-ventilables entre 2100, 2200 et 2300	..	..	..	..	..	..	..	..	..	..
3000 Sur salaires ou main d'oeuvre	**0**	**0**	**0**	**0**	**0**	**0**	**0**	**0**	**0**	**0**
4000 Impôts sur le patrimoine	**463**	**1 877**	**2 026**	**2 703**	**2 133**	**1 428**	**2 543**	**3 605**	**4 739**	**5 722**
4100 Impôts périodiques sur la propriété immobilière	0	0	0	0	0	60	95	162	230	303
4200 Impôts périodiques sur l'actif net	89	175	323	0	0	988	1 442	2 438	3 639	4 511
4300 Impôts sur mut. par décès, succ. et donations	0	0	0	0	0	270	552	974	824	853
4400 Impôts sur transact. mobilières et immob.	374	1 702	1 703	2 703	2 133	110	454	31	47	55
4500 Impôts non-périodiques	0	0	0	0	0	0	0	0	0	0
4600 Autres impôts périodiques sur patrimoine	0	0	0	0	0	0	0	0	0	0
5000 Impôts sur les biens et services	**7 431**	**12 521**	**20 208**	**28 581**	**34 438**	**795**	**1 258**	**1 706**	**2 390**	**3 104**
5100 Impôts sur production, vente, transfert, etc.	7 431	12 521	19 772	26 899	31 996	154	213	249	462	985
5110 Impôts généraux	3 205	6 777	12 428	18 119	22 336	0	0	0	0	0
5120 Impôts sur biens et services déterminés	4 226	5 744	7 345	8 780	9 660	154	213	249	462	985
5130 Non-ventilables entre 5110 et 5120	0	0	0	0	0	0	0	0	0	0
5200 Impôts sur utilisation des biens et exerc. activites	0	0	436	1 681	2 442	641	1 045	1 457	1 929	2 119
5300 Non-ventilables entre 5100 et 5200	0	0	0	0	0	0	0	0	0	0
6000 Autres impôts	**0**	**0**	**0**	**0**	**0**	**0**	**0**	**0**	**0**	**0**
6100 A la charge exclusive des entreprises	..	..	..	..	..	..	..	..	..	..
6200 A la charge d'autres agents	..	..	..	..	..	..	..	..	..	..
Recettes fiscales totales	**11 316**	**20 921**	**32 379**	**47 625**	**60 024**	**9 979**	**16 453**	**24 493**	**33 363**	**41 992**

Million CHF

	Administrations locales					Administrations de sécurité sociale				
	1975	1985	1995	2005	2013	1975	1985	1995	2005	2013
1000 Impôts sur revenu, bénéfices et gains en capital	**6 403**	**9 842**	**15 540**	**18 023**	**21 951**	**0**	**0**	**0**	**0**	**0**
1100 Des personnes physiques	5 398	8 644	13 326	15 300	17 817	..	..	..	..	..
1200 Des sociétés	1 005	1 198	1 602	2 273	3 323	..	..	..	..	..
1300 Non-ventilables entre 1100 et 1200	0	0	611	450	810	..	..	..	..	..
2000 Cotisations de sécurité sociale	**0**	**0**	**0**	**0**	**0**	**8 111**	**14 344**	**28 099**	**32 426**	**42 758**
2100 A la charge des salariés	..	..	..	..	..	3 589	6 469	12 938	14 916	19 989
2200 A la charge des employeurs	..	..	..	..	..	3 618	6 503	12 938	14 916	20 007
2300 A charge des travailleurs indép. ou sans emploi	..	..	..	..	..	840	1 372	2 223	2 593	2 762
2400 Non-ventilables entre 2100, 2200 et 2300	..	..	..	..	..	64	0	0	0	0
3000 Sur salaires ou main d'oeuvre	**0**	**0**	**0**	**0**	**0**	**0**	**0**	**0**	**0**	**0**
4000 Impôts sur le patrimoine	**1 068**	**1 462**	**2 409**	**3 061**	**3 508**	**0**	**0**	**0**	**0**	**0**
4100 Impôts périodiques sur la propriété immobilière	182	240	443	588	721	..	..	..	..	..
4200 Impôts périodiques sur l'actif net	809	1 040	1 865	2 383	2 655	..	..	..	..	..
4300 Impôts sur mut. par décès, succ. et donations	27	44	89	79	117	..	..	..	..	..
4400 Impôts sur transact. mobilières et immob.	50	138	13	11	15	..	..	..	..	..
4500 Impôts non-périodiques	0	0	0	0	0	..	..	..	..	..
4600 Autres impôts périodiques sur patrimoine	0	0	0	0	0	..	..	..	..	..
5000 Impôts sur les biens et services	**22**	**39**	**170**	**176**	**401**	**0**	**0**	**0**	**0**	**0**
5100 Impôts sur production, vente, transfert, etc.	17	30	128	146	344	..	..	..	..	..
5110 Impôts généraux	0	0	0	0	0	..	..	..	..	..
5120 Impôts sur biens et services déterminés	17	30	128	146	344	..	..	..	..	..
5130 Non-ventilables entre 5110 et 5120	0	0	0	0	0	..	..	..	..	..
5200 Impôts sur utilisation des biens et exerc. activites	5	9	42	30	57	..	..	..	..	..
5300 Non-ventilables entre 5100 et 5200	0	0	0	0	0	..	..	..	..	..
6000 Autres impôts	**0**	**0**	**0**	**0**	**0**	**0**	**0**	**0**	**0**	**0**
6100 A la charge exclusive des entreprises	..	..	..	..	..	..	..	..	..	..
6200 A la charge d'autres agents	..	..	..	..	..	..	..	..	..	..
Recettes fiscales totales	**7 493**	**11 343**	**18 119**	**21 260**	**25 860**	**8 111**	**14 344**	**28 099**	**32 426**	**42 758**

StatLink http://dx.doi.org/10.1787/888933277812

Table 120. **Turkey, tax revenues by sub-sectors of government**

Million TRY

	Central government					State/Regional				
	1975	1985	1995	2005	2013					
1000 Taxes on income, profits and capital gains	..	**2**	**433**	**30 324**	**83 159**	..	..	..	..	..
1100 Of individuals	..	1	330	20 458	57 289	..	..	..	..	..
1200 Corporate	..	0	103	9 866	25 870	..	..	..	..	..
1300 Unallocable between 1100 and 1200	..	0	0	0	0	..	..	..	..	..
2000 Social security contributions	..	**0**	**0**	**0**	**0**	..	..	..	..	..
2100 Employees	..	..	..	..	..	..	..	..	..	..
2200 Employers	..	..	..	..	..	..	..	..	..	..
2300 Self-employed or non-employed	..	..	..	..	..	..	..	..	..	..
2400 Unallocable between 2100, 2200 and 2300	..	..	..	..	..	..	..	..	..	..
3000 Taxes on payroll and workforce	..	**0**	**0**	**0**	**0**	..	..	..	..	..
4000 Taxes on property	..	**0**	**49**	**3 626**	**15 742**	..	..	..	..	..
4100 Recurrent taxes on immovable property	..	0	0	0	0	..	..	..	..	..
4200 Recurrent taxes on net wealth	..	0	0	0	0	..	..	..	..	..
4300 Estate, inheritance and gift taxes	..	0	1	78	306	..	..	..	..	..
4400 Taxes on financial and capital transactions	..	0	29	3 548	15 436	..	..	..	..	..
4500 Non-recurrent taxes	..	0	19	0	0	..	..	..	..	..
4600 Other recurrent taxes on property	..	0	0	0	0	..	..	..	..	..
5000 Taxes on goods and services	..	**2**	**574**	**71 956**	**190 607**	..	..	..	..	..
5100 Taxes on production, sale, transfer, etc	..	2	567	69 266	183 463	..	..	..	..	..
5110 General taxes	..	1	475	30 343	90 022	..	..	..	..	..
5120 Taxes on specific goods and services	..	1	92	38 923	93 441	..	..	..	..	..
5130 Unallocable between 5110 and 5120	..	0	0	0	0	..	..	..	..	..
5200 Taxes on use of goods and perform activities	..	0	8	2 691	7 144	..	..	..	..	..
5300 Unallocable between 5100 and 5200	..	0	0	0	0	..	..	..	..	..
6000 Other taxes	..	**0**	**259**	**4 181**	**3 175**	..	..	..	..	..
6100 Paid solely by business	..	0	0	0	0	..	..	..	..	..
6200 Other	..	0	259	4 181	3 175	..	..	..	..	..
Total tax revenue	..	**4**	**1 316**	**110 088**	**292 683**	..	..	..	..	..

Million TRY

	Local government					Social Security Funds				
	1975	1985	1995	2005	2013	1975	1985	1995	2005	2013
1000 Taxes on income, profits and capital gains	..	**0**	**63**	**4 011**	**9 590**	..	**0**	**0**	**0**	**0**
1100 Of individuals	..	0	48	2 706	6 472	..	..	..	..	..
1200 Corporate	..	0	15	1 305	3 118	..	..	..	..	..
1300 Unallocable between 1100 and 1200	..	0	0	0	0	..	..	..	..	..
2000 Social security contributions	..	**0**	**0**	**0**	**0**	..	**1**	**212**	**35 321**	**125 871**
2100 Employees	..	..	..	..	..	..	0	82	12 128	49 831
2200 Employers	..	..	..	..	..	..	0	110	16 132	71 184
2300 Self-employed or non-employed	..	..	..	..	..	..	0	19	7 061	4 856
2400 Unallocable between 2100, 2200 and 2300	..	..	..	..	..	..	0	0	0	0
3000 Taxes on payroll and workforce	..	**0**	**0**	**0**	**0**	..	**0**	**0**	**0**	**0**
4000 Taxes on property	..	**0**	**4**	**1 627**	**5 538**	..	**0**	**0**	**0**	**0**
4100 Recurrent taxes on immovable property	..	0	0	1 148	3 847	..	..	..	..	..
4200 Recurrent taxes on net wealth	..	0	0	0	0	..	..	..	..	..
4300 Estate, inheritance and gift taxes	..	0	0	10	34	..	..	..	..	..
4400 Taxes on financial and capital transactions	..	0	4	469	1 657	..	..	..	..	..
4500 Non-recurrent taxes	..	0	0	0	0	..	..	..	..	..
4600 Other recurrent taxes on property	..	0	0	0	0	..	..	..	..	..
5000 Taxes on goods and services	..	**0**	**84**	**5 649**	**20 650**	..	**0**	**0**	**0**	**0**
5100 Taxes on production, sale, transfer, etc	..	0	82	5 295	19 901	..	..	..	..	..
5110 General taxes	..	0	69	4 014	10 700	..	..	..	..	..
5120 Taxes on specific goods and services	..	0	13	1 281	9 200	..	..	..	..	..
5130 Unallocable between 5110 and 5120	..	0	0	0	0	..	..	..	..	..
5200 Taxes on use of goods and perform activities	..	0	1	354	750	..	..	..	..	..
5300 Unallocable between 5100 and 5200	..	0	0	0	0	..	..	..	..	..
6000 Other taxes	..	**0**	**73**	**721**	**4 366**	..	**0**	**0**	**0**	**0**
6100 Paid solely by business	..	0	0	0	0	..	..	..	..	..
6200 Other	..	0	73	721	4 366	..	..	..	..	..
Total tax revenue	..	**1**	**224**	**12 008**	**40 145**	..	**1**	**212**	**35 321**	**125 871**

StatLink http://dx.doi.org/10.1787/888933277828

Table 121. **United Kingdom, tax revenues by sub-sectors of government**

Million GBP

	Central government					State/Regional				
	1975	1985	1995	2005	2013					
1000 Taxes on income, profits and capital gains	**16 716**	**51 674**	**92 147**	**171 995**	**199 816**	..	..	..	..	..
1100 Of individuals	14 936	34 820	71 973	130 216	156 299	..	..	..	..	..
1200 Corporate	2 310	16 854	20 174	41 779	43 517	..	..	..	..	..
1300 Unallocable between 1100 and 1200	-530	0	0	0	0	..	..	..	..	..
2000 Social security contributions	**0**	**0**	**0**	**0**	**0**	..	..	..	..	..
2100 Employees	..	..	..	..	..	..	..	..	..	..
2200 Employers	..	..	..	..	..	..	..	..	..	..
2300 Self-employed or non-employed	..	..	..	..	..	..	..	..	..	..
2400 Unallocable between 2100, 2200 and 2300	..	..	..	..	..	..	..	..	..	..
3000 Taxes on payroll and workforce	**-1**	**96**	**0**	**0**	**0**	..	..	..	..	..
4000 Taxes on property	**619**	**2 425**	**15 730**	**32 583**	**41 777**	..	..	..	..	..
4100 Recurrent taxes on immovable property	44	343	12 369	19 523	26 858	..	..	..	..	..
4200 Recurrent taxes on net wealth	0	0	0	0	0	..	..	..	..	..
4300 Estate, inheritance and gift taxes	307	923	1 441	3 150	3 379	..	..	..	..	..
4400 Taxes on financial and capital transactions	266	1 159	1 920	9 910	11 540	..	..	..	..	..
4500 Non-recurrent taxes	2	0	0	0	0	..	..	..	..	..
4600 Other recurrent taxes on property	0	0	0	0	0	..	..	..	..	..
5000 Taxes on goods and services	**8 982**	**40 673**	**85 507**	**135 205**	**185 787**	..	..	..	..	..
5100 Taxes on production, sale, transfer, etc	8 502	38 260	81 175	129 969	178 585	..	..	..	..	..
5110 General taxes	3 515	21 228	47 539	83 425	118 106	..	..	..	..	..
5120 Taxes on specific goods and services	4 987	17 032	33 636	46 544	60 479	..	..	..	..	..
5130 Unallocable between 5110 and 5120	0	0	0	0	0	..	..	..	..	..
5200 Taxes on use of goods and perform activities	698	2 413	4 332	5 236	7 202	..	..	..	..	..
5300 Unallocable between 5100 and 5200	-218	0	0	0	0	..	..	..	..	..
6000 Other taxes	**0**	**0**	**0**	**0**	**0**	..	..	..	..	..
6100 Paid solely by business	..	..	..	..	..	..	..	..	..	..
6200 Other	..	..	..	..	..	..	..	..	..	..
Total tax revenue	**26 316**	**94 868**	**193 384**	**339 783**	**427 380**	..	..	..	..	..

Million GBP

	Local government					Social Security Funds				
	1975	1985	1995	2005	2013	1975	1985	1995	2005	2013
1000 Taxes on income, profits and capital gains	**0**	**0**	**0**	**0**	**0**	**0**	**0**	**0**	**0**	**0**
1100 Of individuals	0	0	0	0	0	0	0	0	0	0
1200 Corporate	0	0	0	0	0	0	0	0	0	0
1300 Unallocable between 1100 and 1200	0	0	0	0	0	0	0	0	0	0
2000 Social security contributions	**0**	**0**	**0**	**0**	**0**	**6 540**	**23 769**	**44 397**	**84 459**	**106 085**
2100 Employees	..	..	..	..	..	2 562	11 220	18 646	35 159	41 587
2200 Employers	..	..	..	..	..	4 068	12 245	24 210	46 475	61 912
2300 Self-employed or non-employed	..	..	..	..	..	195	745	1 541	2 825	2 586
2400 Unallocable between 2100, 2200 and 2300	..	..	..	..	..	-285	-441	0	0	0
3000 Taxes on payroll and workforce	**0**	**0**	**0**	**0**	**0**	**0**	**0**	**0**	**0**	**0**
4000 Taxes on property	**4 127**	**13 582**	**9 303**	**21 255**	**27 581**	**0**	**0**	**0**	**0**	**0**
4100 Recurrent taxes on immovable property	3 978	13 582	9 303	21 255	27 581	..	..	..	..	..
4200 Recurrent taxes on net wealth	0	0	0	0	0	..	..	..	..	..
4300 Estate, inheritance and gift taxes	0	0	0	0	0	..	..	..	..	..
4400 Taxes on financial and capital transactions	0	0	0	0	0	..	..	..	..	..
4500 Non-recurrent taxes	0	0	0	0	0	..	..	..	..	..
4600 Other recurrent taxes on property	149	0	0	0	0	..	..	..	..	..
5000 Taxes on goods and services	**0**	**0**	**0**	**0**	**0**	**0**	**0**	**0**	**0**	**0**
5100 Taxes on production, sale, transfer, etc	0	0	0	0	0	0	0	0	0	0
5110 General taxes	0	0	0	0	0	0	0	0	0	0
5120 Taxes on specific goods and services	0	0	0	0	0	0	0	0	0	0
5130 Unallocable between 5110 and 5120	0	0	0	0	0	0	0	0	0	0
5200 Taxes on use of goods and perform activities	0	0	0	0	0	0	0	0	0	0
5300 Unallocable between 5100 and 5200	0	0	0	0	0	0	0	0	0	0
6000 Other taxes	**0**	**0**	**0**	**0**	**204**	**0**	**0**	**0**	**0**	**0**
6100 Paid solely by business	..	..	..	..	0	..	..	..	..	..
6200 Other	..	..	..	..	204	..	..	..	..	..
Total tax revenue	**4 127**	**13 582**	**9 303**	**21 255**	**27 785**	**6 540**	**23 769**	**44 397**	**84 459**	**106 085**

Note: Including Vat own resources of the European Union: 2013 = 2 154.0 and excluding customs duties collected on behalf of the European Union: 2013 = 2 914.0.

StatLink http://dx.doi.org/10.1787/888933277832

Table 122. **United States, tax revenues by sub-sectors of government**

Million USD

	Federal government					State/Regional				
	1975	1985	1995	2005	2013	1975	1985	1995	2005	2013
1000 Taxes on income, profits and capital gains	**163 072**	**396 098**	**745 636**	**1 263 687**	**1 611 264**	**25 509**	**81 281**	**157 598**	**278 072**	**360 932**
1100 Of individuals	122 386	334 625	589 705	944 197	1 305 971	..	63 644	128 429	228 997	314 231
1200 Corporate	40 686	61 473	155 931	319 490	305 293	..	17 637	29 169	49 075	46 701
1300 Unallocable between 1100 and 1200	0	0	0	0	0	..	0	0	0	0
2000 Social security contributions	**0**	**0**	**0**	**0**	**0**	**0**	**0**	**0**	**0**	**0**
2100 Employees	..	..	..	..	..	..	..	..	..	..
2200 Employers	..	..	..	..	..	..	..	..	..	..
2300 Self-employed or non-employed	..	..	..	..	..	..	..	..	..	..
2400 Unallocable between 2100, 2200 and 2300	..	..	..	..	..	..	..	..	..	..
3000 Taxes on payroll and workforce	**0**	**0**	**0**	**0**	**0**	**0**	**0**	**0**	**0**	**0**
4000 Taxes on property	**4 613**	**6 422**	**14 948**	**24 989**	**20 880**	**3 284**	**7 902**	**14 494**	**16 993**	**17 616**
4100 Recurrent taxes on immovable property	0	0	0	0	0	1 451	3 984	9 433	11 793	9 779
4200 Recurrent taxes on net wealth	0	0	0	0	0	0	0	0	0	0
4300 Estate, inheritance and gift taxes	4 611	6 422	14 948	24 989	20 880	1 418	2 328	5 061	5 200	4 875
4400 Taxes on financial and capital transactions	2	0	0	0	0	415	1 590	0	0	0
4500 Non-recurrent taxes	0	0	0	0	0	0	0	0	0	0
4600 Other recurrent taxes on property	0	0	0	0	0	0	0	0	0	2 962
5000 Taxes on goods and services	**20 773**	**48 027**	**75 553**	**99 393**	**120 884**	**52 032**	**126 501**	**234 419**	**390 979**	**481 037**
5100 Taxes on production, sale, transfer, etc	20 442	47 512	75 553	99 393	120 884	43 960	105 687	200 495	325 649	398 723
5110 General taxes	0	0	0	0	0	24 916	69 629	135 132	221 461	259 426
5120 Taxes on specific goods and services	20 442	47 512	75 553	99 393	120 884	19 044	36 058	65 363	104 188	139 297
5130 Unallocable between 5110 and 5120	0	0	0	0	0	0	0	0	0	0
5200 Taxes on use of goods and perform activities	331	515	0	0	0	8 072	20 814	33 924	65 330	82 314
5300 Unallocable between 5100 and 5200	0	0	0	0	0	0	0	0	0	0
6000 Other taxes	**0**	**16**	**0**	**0**	**0**	**0**	**0**	**0**	**0**	**0**
6100 Paid solely by business	..	0	..	..	..	..	..	..	..	..
6200 Other	..	16	..	..	..	..	..	..	..	..
Total tax revenue	**188 458**	**450 563**	**836 137**	**1 388 069**	**1 753 028**	**80 825**	**215 684**	**406 511**	**686 044**	**859 585**

Million USD

	Local government					Social Security Funds				
	1975	1985	1995	2005	2013	1975	1985	1995	2005	2013
1000 Taxes on income, profits and capital gains	**2 635**	**7 974**	**15 795**	**28 382**	**37 045**	**0**	**0**	**0**	**0**	**0**
1100 Of individuals	..	6 496	13 308	22 514	28 472	..	..	..	..	..
1200 Corporate	..	1 478	2 487	5 868	8 573	..	..	..	..	..
1300 Unallocable between 1100 and 1200	..	0	0	0	0	..	..	..	..	..
2000 Social security contributions	**0**	**0**	**0**	**0**	**0**	**85 039**	**269 144**	**510 476**	**831 410**	**1 030 633**
2100 Employees	..	..	..	..	..	36 382	112 114	221 800	362 834	456 902
2200 Employers	..	..	..	..	..	45 241	146 562	261 805	423 933	519 074
2300 Self-employed or non-employed	..	..	..	..	..	3 416	10 468	26 871	44 643	54 657
2400 Unallocable between 2100, 2200 and 2300	..	..	..	..	..	0	0	0	0	0
3000 Taxes on payroll and workforce	**0**	**0**	**0**	**0**	**0**	**0**	**0**	**0**	**0**	**0**
4000 Taxes on property	**50 040**	**99 772**	**197 342**	**345 840**	**441 384**	**0**	**0**	**0**	**0**	**0**
4100 Recurrent taxes on immovable property	50 040	99 772	197 312	345 724	436 579	..	..	..	..	..
4200 Recurrent taxes on net wealth	0	0	0	0	0	..	..	..	..	..
4300 Estate, inheritance and gift taxes	0	0	30	116	395	..	..	..	..	..
4400 Taxes on financial and capital transactions	0	0	0	0	0	..	..	..	..	..
4500 Non-recurrent taxes	0	0	0	0	0	..	..	..	..	..
4600 Other recurrent taxes on property	0	0	0	0	4 410	..	..	..	..	..
5000 Taxes on goods and services	**8 389**	**26 777**	**57 558**	**111 114**	**138 375**	**0**	**0**	**0**	**0**	**0**
5100 Taxes on production, sale, transfer, etc	6 518	21 007	42 240	76 369	101 680	..	..	..	..	..
5110 General taxes	4 322	14 663	29 316	53 838	73 518	..	..	..	..	..
5120 Taxes on specific goods and services	2 196	6 344	12 924	22 531	28 162	..	..	..	..	..
5130 Unallocable between 5110 and 5120	0	0	0	0	0	..	..	..	..	..
5200 Taxes on use of goods and perform activities	1 871	5 770	15 318	34 745	36 695	..	..	..	..	..
5300 Unallocable between 5100 and 5200	0	0	0	0	0	..	..	..	..	..
6000 Other taxes	**0**	**0**	**0**	**0**	**0**	**0**	**0**	**0**	**0**	**0**
6100 Paid solely by business	..	..	..	..	..	..	..	..	..	..
6200 Other	..	..	..	..	..	..	..	..	..	..
Total tax revenue	**61 064**	**134 523**	**270 695**	**485 336**	**616 804**	**85 039**	**269 144**	**510 476**	**831 410**	**1 030 633**

StatLink http://dx.doi.org/10.1787/888933277845

Revenue Statistics 1965-2014
Statistiques des recettes publiques 1965-2014

ANNEX A

The OECD classification of taxes and Interpretative Guide

Table of contents

The OECD classification of taxes

1. 1000 *Taxes on income, profits and capital gains*
    - 1100 Taxes on income, profits and capital gains of individuals
        - 1110 On income and profits
        - 1120 On capital gains
    - 1200 Corporate taxes on income, profits and capital gains
        - 1210 On income and profits
        - 1220 On capital gains
    - 1300 Unallocable as between 1100 and 1200
2. 2000 *Social security contributions*
    - 2100 Employees
        - 2110 On a payroll basis
        - 2120 On an income tax basis
    - 2200 Employers
        - 2210 On a payroll basis
        - 2220 On an income tax basis
    - 2300 Self-employed or non-employed
        - 2310 On a payroll basis
        - 2320 On an income tax basis
    - 2400 Unallocable as between 2100, 2200 and 2300
        - 2410 On a payroll basis
        - 2420 On an income tax basis
3. 3000 *Taxes on payroll and workforce*
4. 4000 *Taxes on property*
    - 4100 Recurrent taxes on immovable property
        - 4110 Households
        - 4120 Other
    - 4200 Recurrent taxes on net wealth
        - 4210 Individual
        - 4220 Corporate
    - 4300 Estate, inheritance and gift taxes
        - 4310 Estate and inheritance taxes
        - 4320 Gift taxes
    - 4400 Taxes on financial and capital transactions
    - 4500 Other non-recurrent taxes on property
        - 4510 On net wealth
        - 4520 Other non-recurrent taxes
    - 4600 Other recurrent taxes on property
5. 5000 *Taxes on goods and services*
    - 5100 Taxes on production, sale, transfer, leasing and delivery of goods and rendering of services
        - 5110 General taxes

		5111	Value added taxes
		5112	Sales taxes
		5113	Other general taxes on goods and services
	5120	Taxes on specific goods and services	
		5121	Excises
		5122	Profits of fiscal monopolies
		5123	Customs and import duties
		5124	Taxes on exports
		5125	Taxes on investment goods
		5126	Taxes on specific services
		5127	Other taxes on international trade and transactions
		5128	Other taxes on specific goods and services
	5130	Unallocable as between 5110 and 5120	
5200	Taxes on use of goods, or on permission to use goods or perform activities		
	5210	Recurrent taxes	
		5211	Paid by households in respect of motor vehicles
		5212	Paid by others in respect of motor vehicles
		5213	Other recurrent taxes
	5220	Non-recurrent taxes	
5300	Unallocable as between 5100 and 5200		
6. 6000 *Other taxes*			
6100	Paid solely by business		
6200	Paid by other than business or unidentifiable		

The OECD Interpretative Guide

A. Coverage

General criteria

1. In the OECD classification the term "taxes" is confined to compulsory unrequited payments to general government. Taxes are unrequited in the sense that benefits provided by government to taxpayers are not normally in proportion to their payments.

2. The term 'tax' does not include fines unrelated to tax offences and compulsory loans paid to government. Borderline cases between tax and non-tax revenues in relation to certain fees and charges are discussed in §9-13.

3. General government consists of the central administration, agencies whose operations are under its effective control, state and local governments and their administrations, certain social security schemes and autonomous governmental entities, excluding public enterprises. This definition of government follows that of the 2008 *System of National Accounts* (SNA).[1] In that publication, the general government sector and its sub-sectors are defined in chapter 4, section F, pages 80-84.

4. Compulsory payments to supra-national bodies and their agencies are no longer included as taxes as from 1998, with some exceptions. However, custom duties collected by EU member states on behalf of the European Union are still identified as memorandum items and included in overall tax revenue amounts in the country tables (Part III) of the country in which they are collected. (See §95). In countries where the church forms part of general government church taxes are included, provided they meet the criteria set out in §1 above. As the data refer to receipts of general government, levies paid to non-government bodies, welfare agencies or social insurance schemes outside general government, trade unions or trade associations, even where such levies are compulsory, are excluded. Compulsory payments to general government earmarked for such bodies are, however, included, provided that the government is not simply acting in an agency capacity.[2] Profits from fiscal monopolies are distinguished from those of other public enterprises and are treated as taxes because they reflect the exercise of the taxing power of the state by the use of monopoly powers (see §62-64), as are profits received by the government from the purchase and sale of foreign exchange at different rates (see §70).

5. Taxes paid by governments (e.g., social security contributions and payroll taxes paid by governments in their capacity as an employer, consumption taxes on their purchases or taxes on their property) are not excluded from the data provided. However, where it is possible to identify the amounts of revenue involved,[3] they are shown in section III.C of this Report.

6. The relationship between this classification and that of the System of National Accounts (SNA) is set out in Sections H and J below. Because of the differences between the

two classifications, the data shown in national accounts are sometimes calculated or classified differently from the practice set out in this guide. These and other differences are mentioned where appropriate (e.g., in §13 and §26 below) but it is not possible to refer to all of them. There may also be some differences between this classification and that employed domestically by certain national administrations (e.g., see §10 below), so that OECD and national statistics data may not always be consistent: any such differences, however, are likely to be very slight in terms of amounts of revenues involved.

Social security contributions

7. Compulsory social security contributions, as defined in §35 below, paid to general government, are treated here as tax revenues. Being compulsory payments to general government they clearly resemble taxes. They may, however, differ from other taxes in that the receipt of social security benefits depends, in most countries, upon appropriate contributions having been made, although the size of the benefits is not necessarily related to the amount of the contributions. Better comparability between countries is obtained by treating social security contributions as taxes, but they are listed under a separate heading so that they can be distinguished in any analysis.

8. Social security contributions which are either voluntary or not payable to general government (see §1) are not treated as taxes, though in some countries, as indicated in the country footnotes, there are difficulties in eliminating voluntary contributions and certain compulsory payments to the private sector.

Fees, user charges and licence fees

9. Apart from vehicle licence fees, which are universally regarded as taxes, it is not easy to distinguish between those fees and user charges which are to be treated as taxes and those which are not, since, whilst a fee or charge is levied in connection with a specific service or activity, the strength of the link between the fee and the service provided may vary considerably, as may the relation between the amount of the fee and the cost of providing the service. Where the recipient of a service pays a fee clearly related to the cost of providing the service, the levy may be regarded as requited and under the definition of §1 would not be considered as a tax. In the following cases, however, a levy could be considered as "unrequited":

a) where the charge greatly exceeds the cost of providing the service;

b) where the payer of the levy is not the receiver of the benefit (e.g., a fee collected from slaughterhouses to finance a service which is provided to farmers);

c) where government is not providing a specific service in return for the levy which it receives even though a licence may be issued to the payer (e.g., where the government grants a hunting, fishing or shooting licence which is not accompanied by the right to use a specific area of government land);

d) where benefits are received only by those paying the levy but the benefits received by each individual are not necessarily in proportion to his payments (e.g., a milk marketing levy paid by dairy farmers and used to promote the consumption of milk).

10. In marginal cases, however, the application of the criteria set out in §1 can be particularly difficult. The solution adopted – given the desirability of international uniformity and the relatively small amounts of revenue usually involved – is to follow the predominant practice among tax administrations rather than to allow each country to

adopt its own view as to whether such levies are regarded as taxes or as non-tax revenue.[4]

11. A list of the main fees and charges in question and their normal[5] treatment in this publication is as follows:

Non-tax revenues:	court fees; driving licence fees; harbour fees; passport fees; radio and television licence fees where public authorities provide the service.
Taxes within heading 5200:	permission to perform such activities as distributing films; hunting, fishing and shooting; providing entertainment or gambling facilities; selling alcohol or tobacco; permission to own dogs or to use or own motor vehicles or guns; severance taxes.

12. In practice it may not always be possible to isolate tax receipts from non-tax revenue receipts when they are recorded together. If it is estimated that the bulk of the receipts derive from non-tax revenues, the whole amount involved is treated as a non-tax revenue; otherwise, such government receipts are included and classified according to the rules provided in §28 below.

13. Two differences between the OECD classification and SNA regarding the borderline between tax and non-tax revenues are:

a) SNA classifies a number of levies as indirect taxes if paid by enterprises, but as non-tax revenues if paid by households, a distinction which is regarded as irrelevant in this classification for distinguishing between tax and non-tax revenues.[6]

b) Predominant practice among most OECD tax administrations, which is occasionally used in this classification for distinguishing between tax and non-tax revenues, is not a relevant criterion for SNA purposes.

Royalties

14. Royalty payments for the right to extract oil and gas or to exploit other mineral resources are normally regarded as non-tax revenues since they are property income from government-owned land or resources.

Fines and penalties

15. Receipts from fines and penalties paid for infringement of regulations identified as relating to a particular tax and interest on payments overdue in respect of a particular tax are recorded together with receipts from that tax. Other kinds of fines identifiable as relating to tax offences are classified in the residual heading 6000. Fines not relating to tax offences (e.g., for parking offences), or not identifiable as relating to tax offences, are not treated as taxes.

B. Basis of reporting

Accrual reporting

16. The data reported in this publication for recent years are predominantly recorded on an accrual basis, i.e. recorded at the time that the tax liability was created. Further information is provided in the footnotes to the country table in Part III of the Report.

17. However, data for earlier years are still predominantly recorded on a cash basis, i.e. at the time at which the payment was received by government. Thus, for example, taxes

withheld by employers in one year but paid to the government in the following year and taxes due in one year but actually paid in the following year are both included in the receipts of the second year. Corrective transactions, such as refunds, repayments and drawbacks, are deducted from gross revenues of the period in which they are made.

18. Data on tax revenues are recorded without offsets for the administrative expenses connected with tax collection. Similarly, where the proceeds of tax are used to subsidise particular members of the community, the subsidy is not deducted from the yield of the tax, though the tax may be shown net of subsidies in the national records of some countries.

19. As regards fiscal monopolies (heading 5122), only the amount actually transferred to the government is included in government revenues. However, if any expenditures of fiscal monopolies are considered to be government expenditures (e.g., social expenditures undertaken by fiscal monopolies at the direction of the government) they are added back for the purpose of arriving at tax revenue figures (see §62 below).

The distinction between tax and expenditure provisions[7]

20. Because this publication is concerned only with the revenue side of government operations, no account being taken of the expenditure side, a distinction has to be made between tax and expenditure provisions. Normally there is no difficulty in making this distinction as expenditures are made outside the tax system and the tax accounts and under legislation separate from the tax legislation. In borderline cases, cash flow is used to distinguish between tax provisions and expenditure provisions. Insofar as a provision affects the flow of tax payments from the taxpayer to the government, it is regarded as a tax provision and is taken into account in the data shown in this publication. A provision which does not affect this flow is seen as an expenditure provision and is disregarded in the data recorded in this publication.

21. Tax allowances, exemptions and deductions against the tax base clearly affect the amount of tax paid to the government and are therefore considered as tax provisions. At the other extreme, those subsidies which cannot be offset against tax liability and which are clearly not connected with the assessment process, do not reduce tax revenues as recorded in this publication. Tax credits are amounts deductible from tax payable (as distinct from deductions from the tax base). Two types of tax credits are distinguished, those (referred to here as wastable tax credits) which are limited to the amount of the tax liability and therefore cannot give rise to a payment by the authorities to the taxpayer, and those (referred to as non-wastable tax credits) which are not so limited, so that the excess of the credit over the tax liability can be paid to the taxpayer.[8] A wastable tax credit, like a tax allowance, clearly affects the amount of tax paid to the government, and is therefore considered as a tax provision. The practice followed for non-wastable tax credits[9] is to distinguish between the "tax expenditure component",[10] which is that portion of the credit that is used to reduce or eliminate a taxpayer's liability, and the "transfer component", which is the portion that exceeds the taxpayer's liability and is paid to that taxpayer. Reported tax revenues should be reduced by the amount of the tax expenditure component but not by the amount of the transfer component. In addition, the amounts of the tax expenditure and transfer components should be reported as memorandum items in the country tables. Countries that are unable to distinguish between the tax expenditure and transfer components should indicate whether or not the tax revenues have been reduced by the total of these components, and provide any available estimates of the amounts of

the two components. Further information is given in section C of Part I of the Report, which illustrates the effect of alternative treatments of non-wastable tax credits on Tax to GDP.

Calendar and fiscal years

22. National authorities whose fiscal years do not correspond to the calendar year show data, where possible, on a calendar year basis to permit maximum comparability with the data of other countries. There remain a few countries where data refer to fiscal years. For these the GDP data used in the comparative tables also correspond to the fiscal years.

C. General classification criteria

The main classification criteria

23. The classification of receipts among the main headings (1000, 2000, 3000, 4000, 5000 and 6000) is generally governed by the base on which the tax is levied: 1000 income, profits and capital gains; 2000 and 3000 earnings, payroll or number of employees; 4000 property; 5000 goods and services; 6000 multiple bases, other bases or unidentifiable bases. Where a tax is calculated on more than one base, the receipts are, where possible, split among the various headings (see §28 and §78). The headings 4000 and 5000 cover not only taxes where the tax base is the property, goods or services themselves but also certain related taxes. Thus, taxes on the transfer of property are included in 4400[11] and taxes on the use of goods or on permission to perform activities in 5200. In headings 4000 and 5000 a distinction is made in certain sub-headings between recurrent and non-recurrent taxes: recurrent taxes are defined as those levied at regular intervals (usually annually) and non-recurrent taxes are levied once and for all (see also §43 to §46, §49, §50 and §76 for particular applications of this distinction).

24. Earmarking of a tax for specific purposes does not affect the classification of tax receipts. However, as explained in §35 on the classification of social security contributions, the conferment of an entitlement to social benefits is crucial to the definition of the 2000 main heading.

25. The way that a tax is levied or collected (e.g., by use of stamps) does not affect classification.

Classification of taxpayers

26. In certain sub-headings distinctions are made between different categories of taxpayers. These distinctions vary from tax to tax:

a) Between individuals and corporations in relation to income and net wealth taxes

The basic distinction is that corporation income taxes, as distinct from individual income taxes, are levied on the corporation as an entity, not on the individuals who own it, and without regard to the personal circumstances of these individuals. The same distinction applies to net wealth taxes on corporations and those on individuals. Taxes paid on the profits of partnerships and the income of institutions, such as life insurance or pension funds, are classified according to the same rule. They are classified as corporate taxes (1200) if they are charged on the partnership or institution as an entity without regard to the personal circumstances of the owners. Otherwise, they are treated as individual taxes (1100). Usually, there is different legislation for the corporation taxes and for the individual taxes.[12] The distinction made here between individuals and corporations does not follow the sector classification between households, enterprises, and so on of the System of National Accounts for income and outlay accounts. The SNA classification requires certain unincorporated businesses[13] to be excluded from the household sector and included with non-financial enterprises and financial institutions. The tax on the profits of these businesses, however, cannot always be separated from the tax on the other income of their owners, or can be separated only on an arbitrary basis. No attempt at this separation is made here and the whole of the individual income tax is shown together without regard to the nature of the income chargeable.

b) Between households and others in relation to taxes on immovable property

Here the distinction is that adopted by the SNA for the production and consumption expenditure accounts. The distinction is between households as consumers (i.e. excluding non-incorporated business) on the one hand and producers on the other hand. However, taxes on dwellings occupied by households, whether paid by owner-occupiers, tenants or landlords, are classified under households. This follows the common distinction made between taxes on domestic property versus taxes on business property. Some countries are not, however, in a position to make this distinction.

c) Between households and others in relation to motor vehicle licences

Here the distinction is between households as consumers on the one hand and producers on the other, as in the production and consumption expenditure accounts of the SNA.

d) Between business and others in relation to the residual taxes (6000)

The distinction is the same as in c) above between producers on the one hand and households as consumers on the other hand. Taxes which are included under the heading 6000 because they involve more than one tax base or because the tax base does not fall within any of the previous categories but which are identifiable as levyable only on producers and not on households are included under "business". The rest of the taxes which are included under the heading 6000 are shown as "other" or non-identified.

Surcharges

27. Receipts from surcharges in respect of particular taxes are usually classified with the receipts from the relevant tax whether or not the surcharge is temporary. If, however, the surcharge has a characteristic which would render it classifiable in a different heading of the OECD list, receipts from the surcharge are classified under that heading separately from the relevant tax.

Unidentifiable tax receipts and residual sub-headings

28. A number of cases arise where taxes cannot be identified as belonging entirely to a heading or sub-heading of the OECD classification and the following practices are applied in such cases:

a) The heading is known, but it is not known how receipts should be allocated between sub-headings: receipts are classified in the appropriate residual sub-heading (1300, 2400, 4520, 4600, 5130, 5300 or 6200).

b) It is known that the bulk of receipts from a group of taxes (usually local taxes) is derived from taxes within a particular heading or sub-heading, but some of the taxes in the group whose amount cannot be precisely ascertained may be classifiable in other headings or sub-headings: receipts are shown in the heading or sub-heading under which most of the receipts fall.

c) Neither the heading nor sub-heading of a tax (usually local) can be identified: the tax is classified in 6200 unless it is known that it is a tax on business in which case it is classified in 6100.

D. Commentaries on items of the list

1000 – Taxes on income, profits and capital gains

29. This heading covers taxes levied on the net income or profits (i.e. gross income minus allowable tax reliefs) of individuals and enterprises. Also covered are taxes levied on the capital gains of individuals and enterprises, and gains from gambling.

30. Included in the heading are:

a) taxes levied predominantly on income or profits, though partially on other bases. Taxes on various bases which are not predominantly income or profits are classified according to the principles laid down in §28 and §78;

b) taxes on property, which are levied on a presumed or estimated income as part of an income tax (see also §43(a), (c) and (d));

c) compulsory payments to social security fund contributions that are levied on income but do not confer an entitlement to social benefits. When such contributions do confer an entitlement to social benefits, they are included in heading 2000 (see §35);

d) receipts from integrated scheduler income tax systems are classified as a whole in this heading, even though certain of the scheduler taxes may be based upon gross income and may not take into account the personal circumstances of the taxpayer.

31. The main subdivision of this heading is between levies on individuals (1100) and those on corporate enterprises (1200). Under each subdivision a distinction is made between taxes on income and profits (1110 and 1210), and taxes on capital gains (1120 and 1220). If certain receipts cannot be identified as appropriate to either 1100 or 1200, or if in practice this distinction cannot be made (e.g., because there are no reliable data on the recipients of payments from which withholding taxes are deducted) they are classified in 1300 as not-allocable.

Treatment of credits under imputation systems

32. Under imputation systems of corporate income tax, a company's shareholders are wholly or partly relieved of their liability to income tax on dividends paid by the company out of income or profits liable to corporate income tax. In countries with such systems,[14] part of the tax on the company's profits is available to provide relief against the shareholders' own tax liability. The relief to the shareholder takes the form of a tax credit, the amount of which may be less than, equal to, or more than the shareholder's overall tax liability. If the tax credit exceeds this tax liability the excess may be payable to the shareholder. As this type of tax credit is an integral part of the imputation system of corporate income tax, any payment to the shareholders is treated as a repayment of tax and not as expenditure (compare the treatment of other tax credits described in §21).

33. As the tax credit under imputation systems (even when exceeding tax liability) is to be regarded as a tax provision, the question arises whether it should be deducted from individual income tax receipts (1110) or corporate income tax receipts (1210). In this Report, the full amount of corporate income tax paid is shown under 1210 and no imputed tax is included under 1110. Thus, the full amount of the credit reduces the amount of 1110

whether the credit results in a reduction of personal income tax liability or whether an actual refund is made because the credit exceeds the income tax liability. (Where, however, such tax credits are deducted from corporation tax in respect of dividends paid to corporations the amounts are deducted from the receipts of 1210).

1120 and 1220 – Taxes on capital gains

34. These sub-headings comprise taxes imposed on capital gains, 1120 covering those levied on the gains of individuals and 1220 those levied on the gains of corporate enterprises, where receipts from such taxes can be separately identified. In many countries this is not the case and the receipts from such taxes are then classified with those from the income tax. Heading 1120 also includes taxes on gains from gambling.

2000 – Social security contributions

35. Classified here are all compulsory payments that confer an entitlement to receive a (contingent) future social benefit. Such payments are usually earmarked to finance social benefits and are often paid to institutions of general government that provide such benefits. However, such earmarking is not part of the definition of social security contributions and is not required for a tax to be classified here. However, conferment of an entitlement is required for a tax to be classified under this heading. So, levies on income or payroll that are earmarked for social security funds but do not confer an entitlement to benefit are excluded from this heading and shown under personal income taxes (1100) or taxes on payroll and workforce (3000). Taxes on other bases, such as goods and services, which are earmarked for social security benefits are not shown here but are classified according to their respective bases because they generally confer no entitlement to social security benefits.

36. Contributions for the following types of social security benefits would, *inter alia*, be included: unemployment insurance benefits and supplements, accident, injury and sickness benefits, old-age, disability and survivors' pensions, family allowances, reimbursements for medical and hospital expenses or provision of hospital or medical services. Contributions may be levied on both employees and employers.

37. Contributions may be based on earnings or payroll ("on a payroll basis") or on net income after deductions and exemptions for personal circumstances ("on an income tax basis"), and the revenues from the two bases should be separately identified if possible. However, where contributions to a general social security scheme are on a payroll basis, but the contributions of particular groups (such as the self-employed) cannot be assessed on this basis and net income is used as a proxy for gross earnings, the receipts may still be classified as being on a payroll basis. In principle, this heading excludes voluntary contributions paid to social security schemes. When separately identifiable these are shown in the memorandum item on the financing of social security benefits. In practice, however, they cannot always be separately identified from compulsory contributions, in which case they are included in this heading.

38. Contributions to social insurance schemes which are not institutions of general government and to other types of insurance schemes, provident funds, pension funds, friendly societies or other saving schemes are not considered as social security contributions. Provident funds are arrangements under which the contributions of each employee and of the corresponding employer on his/her behalf are kept in a separate account earning interest and withdrawable under specific circumstances. Pension funds are separately organised schemes negotiated between employees and employers and carry provisions for different

contributions and benefits, sometimes more directly tied to salary levels and length of service than under social security schemes. When contributions to these schemes are compulsory or quasi-compulsory (e.g., by virtue of agreement with professional and union organisations) they are shown in the memorandum item (refer to Section III.B of the Report).

39. Contributions by government employees and by governments in respect of their employees, to social security schemes classified within general government are included in this heading. Contributions to separate schemes for government employees, which can be regarded as replacing general social security schemes, are also regarded as taxes.[15] Where, however, a separate scheme is not seen as replacing a general scheme and has been negotiated between the government, in its role as an employer, and its employees, it is not regarded as social security and contributions to it are not regarded as taxes, even though the scheme may have been established by legislation.

40. This heading excludes 'imputed' contributions, which correspond to social benefits paid directly by employers to their employees or former employees or to their representatives (e.g., when employers are legally obliged to pay sickness benefits for a certain period).

41. Contributions are divided into those of employees (2100), employers (2200), and self-employed or non-employed (2300), and then further sub-divided according to the basis on which they are levied. Employees are defined for this purpose as all persons engaged in activities of business units, government bodies, private non-profit institutions, or other paid employment, except the proprietors and their unpaid family members in the case of unincorporated businesses. Members of the armed forces are included, irrespective of the duration and type of their service, if they contribute to social security schemes. The contributions of employers are defined as their payments on account of their employees to social security schemes. Where employees or employers are required to continue the payment of social security contributions when the employee becomes unemployed these contributions, data permitting, are shown in 2100 and 2200 respectively. Accordingly, the sub-heading 2300 is confined to contributions paid by the self-employed and by those outside of the labour force (e.g., disabled or retired individuals).

3000 – Taxes on payroll and workforce

42. This heading covers taxes paid by employers, employees or the self-employed either as a proportion of payroll or as a fixed amount per person, and which do not confer entitlement to social benefits. Examples of taxes classified here are the United Kingdom national insurance surcharge (introduced in 1977), the Swedish payroll tax (1969-79), and the Austrian Contribution to the Family Burden Equalisation Fund and Community Tax.

4000 – Taxes on property

43. This heading covers recurrent and non-recurrent taxes on the use, ownership or transfer of property. These include taxes on immovable property or net wealth, taxes on the change of ownership of property through inheritance or gift and taxes on financial and capital transactions. The following kinds of tax are excluded from this heading:

a) taxes on capital gains resulting from the sale of a property (1120 or 1220);

b) taxes on the use of goods or on permission to use goods or perform activities (5200); see §73;

c) taxes on immovable property levied on the basis of a presumed net income which take into account the personal circumstances of the taxpayer. They are classified as income taxes along with taxes on income and capital gains derived from property (1100);

d) taxes on the use of property for residence, where the tax is payable by either proprietor or tenant and the amount payable is a function of the user's personal circumstances (pay, dependants, and so on). They are classified as taxes on income (1100);

e) taxes on building in excess of permitted maximum density, taxes on the enlargement, construction or alteration of certain buildings beyond a permitted value and taxes on building construction. They are classified as taxes on permission to perform activities (5200);

f) taxes on the use of one's own property for special trading purposes like selling alcohol, tobacco, meat or for exploitation of land resources (e.g., United States severance taxes). They are classified as taxes on permission to perform activities (5200).

4100 – *Recurrent taxes on immovable property*

44. This sub-heading covers taxes levied regularly in respect of the use or ownership of immovable property.

- these taxes are levied on land and buildings;
- they can be in the form of a percentage of an assessed property value based on a national rental income, sales price, or capitalised yield; or in terms of other characteristics of real property, (for example size or location) from which a presumed rent or capital value can be derived.
- such taxes can be levied on proprietors, tenants, or both. They can also be paid by one level of government to another level of government in respect of property under the jurisdiction of the latter.
- debts are not taken into account in the assessment of these taxes, and they differ from taxes on net wealth in this respect.

45. Taxes on immovable property are further sub-divided into those paid by households (4110) and those paid by other entities (4120), according to the criteria set out in §26(*b*) above.

4200 – *Recurrent taxes on net wealth*

46. This sub-heading covers taxes levied regularly (in most cases annually) on net wealth, i.e. taxes on a wide range of movable and immovable property, net of debt. It is sub-divided into taxes paid by individuals (4210) and taxes paid by corporate enterprises (4220) according to the criteria set out in §26(*a*) above. If separate figures exist for receipts paid by institutions, the tax payments involved are added to those paid by corporations.

4300 – *Estate, inheritance and gift taxes*

47. This sub-heading is divided into taxes on estates and inheritances (4310) and taxes on gifts (4320).[16] Estate taxes are charged on the amount of the total estate whereas inheritance taxes are charged on the shares of the individual recipients; in addition the latter may take into account the relationship of the individual recipients to the deceased.

4400 – *Taxes on financial and capital transactions*

48. This sub-heading comprises, *inter alia*, taxes on the issue, transfer, purchase and sale of securities, taxes on cheques, and taxes levied on specific legal transactions such as validation of contracts and the sale of immovable property. The heading does not include:

a) taxes on the use of goods or property or permission to perform certain activities (5200);

b) fees paid to cover court charges, charges for birth, marriage or death certificates, which are normally regarded as non-tax revenues (see §9);

c) taxes on capital gains (1000);

d) recurrent taxes on immovable property (4100);

e) recurrent taxes on net wealth (4200);

f) once-and-for-all levies on property or wealth (4500).

4500 – *Other non-recurrent taxes on property*[16]

49. This sub-heading covers once-and-for-all, as distinct from recurrent, levies on property. It is divided into taxes on net wealth (4510) and other non-recurrent taxes on property (4520). Heading 4510 would include taxes levied to meet emergency expenditures, or for redistribution purposes. Heading 4520 would cover taxes levied to take account of increases in land value due to permission given to develop or provision of additional local facilities by general government, any taxes on the revaluation of capital and once-and-for-all taxes on particular items of property.

4600 – *Other recurrent taxes on property*

50. These rarely exist in OECD member countries, but the heading would include taxes on goods such as cattle, jewellery, windows, and other external signs of wealth.

5000 – *Taxes on goods and services*

51. All taxes and duties levied on the production, extraction, sale, transfer, leasing or delivery of goods, and the rendering of services (5100), or in respect of the use of goods or permission to use goods or to perform activities (5200) are included here. The heading thus covers:

a) multi-stage cumulative taxes;

b) general sales taxes – whether levied at manufacture/production, wholesale or retail level;

c) value-added taxes;

d) excises;

e) taxes levied on the import and export of goods;

f) taxes levied in respect of the use of goods and taxes on permission to use goods, or perform certain activities;

g) taxes on the extraction, processing or production of minerals and other products.

52. Borderline cases between this heading and heading 4000 (taxes on property) and 6100 (other taxes on business) are referred to in §43, §48 and §75. Residual sub-headings (5300) and (5130) cover tax receipts which cannot be allocated between 5100 and 5200 and between 5110 and 5120, respectively; see §28.

5100 – *Taxes on the production, sale, transfer, leasing and delivery of goods and rendering of services*

53. This sub-heading consists of all taxes, levied on transactions in goods and services on the basis of their intrinsic characteristics (e.g., value, weight of tobacco, strength of alcohol, and so on) as distinct from taxes imposed on the use of goods, or permission to use goods or perform activities, which fall under 5200.

5110 – *General taxes on goods and services*

54. This sub-heading includes all taxes, other than import and export duties (5123 and 5124), levied on the production, leasing, transfer, delivery or sales of a wide range of goods and/or the rendering of a wide range of services, irrespective of whether they are domestically produced or imported and irrespective of the stage of production or distribution at which they are levied. It thus covers value-added taxes, sales taxes and multi-stage cumulative taxes. Receipts from border adjustments in respect of such taxes when goods are imported are added to gross receipts for this category, and repayments of such taxes when goods are exported are deducted. These taxes are subdivided into 5111 value-added taxes, 5112 sales taxes, 5113 other general taxes on goods and services.

55. Borderline cases arise between this heading and taxes on specific goods (5120) when taxes are levied on a large number of goods, for example, the United Kingdom purchase tax (repealed in 1973) and the Japanese commodity tax (repealed in 1988). In conformity with national views, the former United Kingdom purchase tax is classified as a general tax (5112) and the former Japanese commodity tax as excises (5121).

5111 – *Value-added taxes*

56. All general consumption taxes charged on value-added are classified in this sub-heading, irrespective of the method of deduction and the stages at which the taxes are levied. In practice, all OECD countries with value-added taxes normally allow immediate deduction of taxes on purchases by all but the final consumer and impose tax at all stages. In some countries the heading may include certain taxes, such as those on financial and insurance activities, either because receipts from them cannot be identified separately from those from the value-added tax, or because they are regarded as an integral part of the value-added tax, even though similar taxes in other countries might be classified elsewhere (e.g., 5126 as taxes on services or 4400 as taxes on financial and capital transactions).

5112 – *Sales taxes*

57. All general taxes levied at one stage only, whether at manufacturing or production, wholesale or retail stage are classified here.

5113 – *Other general taxes on goods and services*

58. This sub-heading covers multi-stage cumulative taxes (also know as "cascade taxes") where tax is levied each time a transaction takes place without deduction for tax paid on inputs, and also those general consumption taxes where elements of value-added, sales or cascade taxes are combined.

5120 – *Taxes on specific goods and services*

59. Excises, profits generated and transferred from fiscal monopolies, and customs and imports duties as well as taxes on exports, foreign exchange transactions, investment goods and betting stakes and special taxes on services, which do not form part of a general tax of 5110, are included in this category.

5121 – *Excises*

60. Excises are taxes levied on particular products, or on a limited range of products, which are not classifiable under 5110 (general taxes), 5123 (import duties) and 5124 (export duties). They may be imposed at any stage of production or distribution and are usually assessed by reference to the weight or strength or quantity of the product, but sometimes by reference to value. Thus, special taxes on, for example, sugar, beetroot, matches, chocolates, and taxes at varying rates on a certain range of goods, as well as those levied in most countries on tobacco goods, alcoholic drinks and hydrocarbon oils and other energy sources, are included in this sub-heading.

61. Excises are distinguished from:

a) 5110 (general taxes). This is discussed in §54-55;

b) 5123 (import duties). If a tax collected principally on imported goods also applies, or would apply, under the law by which the tax is imposed to comparable home-produced goods, the receipts there from would be classified as excises (5121). This principle applies even if there is no comparable home production or no possibility of it (see also §65);

c) 5126 (taxes on services). The problem here arises in respect of taxes on electricity, gas and energy. All of these are regarded as taxes on goods and are included under 5121.

5122 – *Profits of fiscal monopolies*

62. This sub-heading covers that part of the profits of fiscal monopolies which is transferred to general government or which is used to finance any expenditures considered to be government expenditures (see §19). Amounts are shown when they are transferred to general government or used to make expenditures considered to be government expenditures.

63. Fiscal monopolies reflect the exercise of the taxing power of government by the use of monopoly powers. Fiscal monopolies are non-financial public enterprises exercising a monopoly in most cases over the production or distribution of tobacco, alcoholic beverages, salt, matches, playing cards and petroleum or agricultural products (i.e. on the kind of products which are likely to be, alternatively or additionally, subject to the excises of 5121), to raise the government revenues which in other countries are gathered through taxes on dealings in such commodities by private business units. The government monopoly may be at the production stage or, as in the case of government-owned and controlled liquor stores, at the distribution stage.

64. Fiscal monopolies are distinguished from public utilities such as rail transport, electricity, post offices, and other communications, which may enjoy a monopoly or quasi-monopoly position but where the primary purpose is normally to provide basic services rather than to raise revenue for government. Transfers from such other public enterprises to the government are considered as non-tax revenues. The traditional concept of fiscal monopoly has not been extended to include state lotteries, the profits of which are accordingly regarded as non-tax revenues. Fiscal monopoly profits are distinguished from export and import monopoly profits (5127) transferred from marketing boards or other enterprises dealing with international trade.

5123 – *Customs and other import duties*

65. Taxes, stamp duties and surcharges restricted by law to imported products are included here. Also included are levies on imported agricultural products which are imposed in

member countries of the European Union and amounts paid by certain of these countries under the Monetary Compensation Accounts (MCA) system.[17] Starting from 1998, customs duties collected by European Union member states on behalf of the European Union are no longer reported under this heading in the country tables (in Part III of the Report). Excluded here are taxes collected on imports as part of a general tax on goods and services, or an excise applicable to both imported and domestically produced goods.

5124 – *Taxes on exports*

66. In the 1970s, export duties were levied in Australia, Canada and Portugal as a regular measure and they have been used in Finland for counter-cyclical purposes. Some member countries of the European Union pay, as part of the MCA system, a levy on exports (see note 18 to §65). Where these amounts are identifiable, they are shown in this heading. This heading does not include repayments of general consumption taxes or excises or customs duties on exported goods, which should be deducted from the gross receipts under 5110, 5121 or 5123, as appropriate.

5125 – *Taxes on investment goods*

67. This sub-heading covers taxes on investment goods, such as machinery. These taxes may be imposed for a number of years or temporarily for counter-cyclical purposes. Taxes on industrial inputs which are also levied on consumers [e.g., the Swedish energy tax which is classified under (5121)] are not included here.

5126 – *Taxes on specific services*

68. All taxes assessed on the payment for specific services, such as taxes on insurance premiums, banking services, gambling and betting stakes (e.g., from horse races, football pools, lottery tickets), transport, entertainment, restaurant and advertising charges, fall into this category. Taxes levied on the gross income of companies providing the service (e.g., gross insurance premiums or gambling stakes received by the company) are also classified under this heading. Tax revenues from bank levies and payments to deposit insurance and financial stability schemes are provisionally included here for the 2012 edition. The detailed classification is set out in paragraph 105.

69. Excluded from this sub-heading are:

a) taxes on services forming part of a general tax on goods and services (5110);

b) taxes on electricity, gas and energy (5121 as excises);

c) taxes on individual gains from gambling (1120 as taxes on capital gains of individuals and non-corporate enterprises) and lump-sum taxes on the transfer of private lotteries or on the permission to set up lotteries (5200);[18]

d) taxes on cheques and on the issue, transfer or redemption of securities (4400 as taxes on financial and capital transactions).

5127 – *Other taxes on international trade and transactions*

70. This sub-heading covers revenue received by the government from the purchase and sale of foreign exchange at different rates. When the government exercises monopoly powers to extract a margin between the purchase and sales price of foreign exchange, other than to cover administrative costs, the revenue derived constitutes a compulsory levy exacted in indeterminate proportions from both purchaser and seller of foreign

exchange. It is the common equivalent of an import duty and export duty levied in a single exchange rate system or of a tax on the sale or purchase of foreign exchange. Like the profits of fiscal monopolies and import or export monopolies transferred to government, it represents the exercise of monopoly powers for tax purposes and is included in tax revenues.

71. The sub-heading covers also the profits of export or import monopolies, which do not however exist in OECD countries, taxes on purchase or sale of foreign exchange, and any other taxes levied specifically on international trade or transactions.

5128 – *Other taxes on specific goods and services*

72. This item includes taxes on the extraction of minerals, fossil fuels and other exhaustible resources from deposits owned privately or by another government together with any other unidentifiable receipts from taxes on specific goods and services. Taxes on the extraction of exhaustible resources are usually a fixed amount per unit of quality or weight, but can be a percentage of value. The taxes are recorded when the resources are extracted. Payments from the extraction of exhaustible resources from deposits owned by the government unit receiving the payment are classified as rent.

5200 – *Taxes on use of goods or on permission to use goods or perform activities*

73. This sub-heading covers taxes which are levied in respect of the use of goods as distinct from taxes on the goods themselves. Unlike the latter taxes – reported under 5100 –, they are not assessed on the value of the goods but usually as fixed amounts. Taxes on permission to use goods or to perform activities are also included here, as are pollution taxes not based upon the value of particular goods. It is sometimes difficult to distinguish between compulsory user charges and licence fees which are regarded as taxes and those which are excluded as non-tax revenues. The criteria which are employed are noted in §9-10.

74. Although the sub-heading refers to the "use" of goods, registration of ownership rather than use may be what generates liability to tax, so that the taxes of this heading may apply to the ownership of animals or goods rather than their use (e.g., race horses, dogs and motor vehicles) and may apply even to unusable goods (e.g., unusable motor vehicles or guns).

75. Borderline cases arise with:

a) taxes on the permission to perform business activities which are levied on a combined income, payroll or turnover base and, accordingly, are classified following the rules in §78;

b) taxes on the ownership or use of property of headings 4100, 4200 and 4600. The heading 4100 is confined to taxes on the ownership or tenancy of immovable property and – unlike the taxes of 5200 – they are related to the value of the property. The net wealth taxes and taxes on chattels of 4200 and 4600 respectively are confined to the ownership rather than the use of assets, apply to groups of assets rather than particular goods and again are related to the value of the assets,

5210 – *Recurrent taxes on use of goods and on permission to use goods or perform activities*

76. The principal characteristic of taxes classified here is that they are levied at regular intervals and that they are usually fixed amounts. The most important item in terms of revenue receipts is vehicle licence taxes. This sub-heading also covers taxes on permission to hunt, shoot, fish or to sell certain products and taxes on the ownership of dogs and on

the performance of certain services, provided that they meet the criteria set out in §9-10. The sub-divisions of 5210 are user taxes on motor vehicles paid by households (5211) and those paid by others (5212).[19] Sub-heading 5213 covers dog licences and user charges for permission to perform activities such as selling meat or liquor when the levies are on a recurring basis. It also covers recurrent general licences for hunting, shooting and fishing where the right to carry out these activities is not granted as part of a normal commercial transaction (e.g., the granting of the licence is not accompanied by the right to use a specific area which is owned by government).

5220 – Non-recurrent taxes on use of goods and on permission to use goods or perform activities

77. This section covers non-recurrent taxes levied on the use of goods or on permission to use goods or perform activities and taxes levied each time goods are used. It includes taxes levied on the emission or discharge into the environment of noxious gases, liquids or other harmful substances.

- Payments for tradable emission permits issued by governments under cap and trade schemes should be recorded here at the time the emissions occur. No revenue should be recorded for permits that governments issue free of charge. The accrual basis of recording means that there can be a timing difference between the cash being received by government for the permits and the time the emission occurs. In the national accounts, this timing gives rise to a financial liability for government during the period.
- Payments made for the collection and disposal of waste or noxious substances by public authorities should be excluded as they constitute a sale of services to enterprises.

78. Other taxes falling under heading 5200 that are not levied recurrently are also included here. Thus, once-and-for-all payments for permission to sell liquor or tobacco or to set up betting shops are included provided they meet the criteria set out in §9-10.

6000 – Other taxes

79. Taxes levied on a base, or bases, other than those described under headings 1000, 3000, 4000 and 5000, or on bases of which none could be regarded as being predominantly the same as that of any one of these headings, are covered here. As regards taxes levied on a multiple base, if it is possible to estimate receipts related to each base (e.g., the Austrian and German 'Gewerbesteuer') this is done and the separate amounts included under the appropriate headings. If the separate amounts cannot be estimated, but it is known that most of the receipts are derived from one base, the whole of the receipts are classified according to that base. If neither of these procedures can be followed, they are classified here. The sub-headings may also include receipts from taxes which governments are unable to identify or isolate (see §28). Included here also are fines and penalties paid for infringement of regulations relating to taxes but not identifiable as relating to a particular category of taxes (see §15). A subdivision is made between taxes levied wholly or predominantly on business (6100) and those levied on others (6200).

E. Conciliation with National Accounts

80. This section of the tables provides a re-conciliation between the OECD calculation of total tax revenues and the total of all taxes and social contributions paid to general government as recorded in the country's National Accounts. Where the country is a member of the European Union (EU), the comparison is between the OECD calculation of

total tax revenues and the sum of tax revenues and social contributions recorded in the combination of the general government and the institutions of the EU sectors of the National Accounts.

F. Memorandum item on the financing of social security benefits

81. In view of the varying relationship between taxation and social security contributions and the cases referred to in §35 to §41, a memorandum item collects together all payments earmarked for social security-type benefits, other than voluntary payments to the private sector. Data are presented as follows (refer section III.B of the Report):

a) Taxes of 2000 series.

b) Taxes earmarked for social security benefits.

c) Voluntary contributions to the government.

d) Compulsory contributions to the private sector.

Guidance on the breakdown of (a) to (d) above is provided in §35 to §41.

G. Memorandum item on identifiable taxes paid by government

82. Identifiable taxes actually paid by government are presented in a memorandum item classified by the main headings of the OECD classification of taxes. In the vast majority of countries, only social security contributions and payroll taxes paid by government can be identified. These are, however, usually the most important taxes paid by governments (refer section III.C of the Report).

H. Relation of OECD classification of taxes to national accounting systems

83. A system of national accounts (SNA) seeks to provide a coherent framework for recording and presenting the main flows relating respectively to production, consumption, accumulation and external transactions of a given economic area, usually a country or a major region within a country. Government revenues are an important part of the transactions recorded in SNA. The final version of the 2008 SNA was jointly published by five international organisations: the United Nations, the International Monetary Fund, the European Union, the Organisation for Economic Co-operation and Development, and the World Bank in August 2009. The *System* is a comprehensive, consistent and flexible set of macroeconomic accounts. It is designed for use in countries with market economies, whatever their stage of economic development, and also in countries in transition to market economies. The important parts of the SNA's conceptual framework and its definitions of the various sectors of the economy have been reflected in the OECD's classification of taxes.

84. There are, however, some differences between the OECD classification of taxes and SNA concepts that are listed below. They arise because the aim of the former is to provide the maximum disaggregation of statistical data on what are generally regarded as taxes by tax administrations.

a) OECD includes social security contributions in total tax revenues (§7 and §8 above);

b) there are different points of view on whether or not some levies and fees are classified as taxes (§9 and §10 above);

c) OECD excludes imputed taxes or subsidies resulting from the operation of official multiple exchange rates;

d) there are differences in the treatment of non-wastable tax credits

85. As noted in §1 and §2, headings 1000 to 6000 of the OECD list of taxes cover all unrequited payments to general government, other than compulsory loans and fines. Such unrequited payments including fines, but excluding compulsory loans can be obtained from adding together the following figures in the 2008 SNA

- value-added type taxes (D.211);
- taxes and duties on imports, excluding VAT (D.212);
- export taxes (D.213);
- taxes on products, excluding VAT, import and export taxes (D.214);
- other taxes on production (D.29);
- taxes on income (D.51);
- other current taxes (D.59);
- social contributions (D.61), excluding voluntary contributions;
- capital taxes (D.91).

I. The OECD classification of taxes and the International Monetary Fund (GFS) system

86. The coverage and valuation of tax revenues in the GFS system and the 2008 SNA are very similar. Therefore, the differences between the OECD classification and that of the 2008 SNA (see §84 above) also apply to the GFS. In addition the International Monetary Fund subdivides the OECD 5000 heading into section IV (Domestic Taxes on Goods and Services) and section V (Taxes on International Trade and Transactions). This reflects the fact that while the latter usually yield insignificant amounts of revenue in OECD countries, this is not the case in many non-OECD countries.

J. Comparison of the OECD classification of taxes with other international classifications

87. The table below describes an item by item comparison of the OECD classification of taxes and the classifications used in the following:

i) System of National Accounts (2008 SNA);

ii) European System of Accounts (2010 ESA);

iii) IMF *Government Finance Statistics Manual* (GFSM2014).

88. These comparisons represent those that would be expected to apply in the majority of cases. However in practice some flexibility should be used in their application. This is because in particular cases, countries can adopt varying approaches to the classification of revenues in National Accounts.

OECD Classification	2008 SNA	2010 ESA	GFSM2014
1000 Taxes on income, profits and capital gains			
1100 Individuals			
1110 Income and profits	D51-8.61a	D51A	1111
1120 Capital gains	D51-8.61c, d	D51C, D	1111
1200 Corporations			
1210 Income and profits	D51-8.61b	D51B	1112
1220 Capital gains	D51-8.61c	D51C	1112
1300 Unallocable as between 1100 and 1200			1113
2000 Social security contributions			
2100 Employees	D613-8.85	D613	1211
2200 Employers	D611-8.83	D612	1212
2300 Self-employed, non-employed	D613-8.85	D613	1213
2400 Unallocable as between 2100, 2200 and 2300			1214
3000 Taxes on payroll and workforce	D29-7.97a	D29C	112
4000 Taxes on property			
4100 Recurrent taxes on immovable property			
4110 Households	D59-8.63a	D59A	1131
4120 Other	D29-7.97b	D29A	1131
4200 Recurrent net wealth taxes			
4210 Individual	D59-8.63b	D59A	1132
4220 Corporations	D59-8.63b	D59A	1132
4300 Estate, inheritance and gift taxes			
4310 Estate and inheritance taxes	D91-10.207b	D91A	1133
4320 Gift taxes	D91-10.207b	D91A	1133
4400 Taxes on financial and capital transactions	D59-7.96d; D29-7.97e	D214B, C	114114; 1161
4500 Other non-recurrent taxes on property	D91-10.207a	D91B	1135
4600 Other recurrent taxes on property	D59-8.63c	D59A	1136
5000 Taxes on goods and services			
5100 Taxes on production, sale and transfer of goods and services			
5110 General taxes on goods and services			
5111 Value-added taxes	D211-7.89	D211; D29G	11411
5112 Sales taxes	D2122-7.94a; D214-7.96a	D21224; D214I	11412
5113 Other general taxes on goods and services	D214-7.96a	D214I	11413
5120 Taxes on specific goods and services			
5121 Excises	D2122-7.94b; D214-7.96b	D21223; D214A, B, D	1142
5122 Profits of fiscal monopolies	D214-7.96e	D214J	1143
5123 Customs and other import duties	D2121-7.93	D2121; D21221, 2	1151
5124 On exports	D213-7.95a	D214K	1152-4
5125 On investment goods			
5126 On specific services	D2122-7.94c; D214-7.96c	D21225; D214E, F, G; D29F	1144; 1156
5127 Other taxes on international trade and transactions	D2122-7.94d D29-7.95b D29-7.97g D59-8.64d	D21226; D29D; D59E	1153; 1155-6
5128 Other taxes on specific goods and services			1146
5130 Unallocable between 5110 and 5120			
5200 Taxes on use of goods and on permission to use goods or perform activities			
5210 Recurrent taxes on use of goods and on permission to use goods or perform activities			
5211 Motor vehicle taxes households	D59-8.64c	D59D	11451
5212 Motor vehicles taxes others	D29-7.97d	D214D; D29B	11451
5213 Other recurrent taxes on use of goods and on permission to use goods or perform activities	D29-7.97c, d, f D59-8.64c	D29B, E, F; D59D	11452
5220 Non-recurrent taxes on permission to use goods or perform activities			11452
5300 Unallocable as between 5100 and 5200			
6000 Other taxes			
6100 Payable solely by business			1161
6200 Payable by other than business, or unidentifiable	D59-8.64a, b	D59B, C	1162

K. Attribution of tax revenues by sub-sectors of general government

89. The OECD classification requires a breakdown of tax revenues by sub-sectors of government. The definition of each sub-sector and the criteria to be used to attribute tax revenues between these sub-sectors are set out below. They follow the guidance of the 2008 SNA and GFSM2014.

Sub-sectors of general government to be identified

a) Central government

90. The central government sub-sector includes all governmental departments, offices, establishments and other bodies which are agencies or instruments of the central authority whose competence extends over the whole territory, with the exception of the administration of social security funds. Central government therefore has the authority to impose taxes on all resident and non-resident units engaged in economic activities within the country.

b) State, provincial or regional government

91. This sub-sector consists of intermediate units of government exercising a competence at a level below that of central government. It includes all such units operating independently of central government in a part of a country's territory encompassing a number of smaller localities, with the exception of the administration of social security funds. In unitary countries, regional governments may be considered to have a separate existence where they have substantial autonomy to raise a significant proportion of their revenues from sources within their control and their officers are independent of external administrative control in the actual operation of the unit's activities.

92. At present, federal countries comprise the majority of cases where revenues attributed to intermediate units of government are identified separately. Spain is the only unitary country in this position. In the remaining unitary countries, regional revenues are included with those of local governments.

c) Local government

93. This sub-sector includes all other units of government exercising an independent competence in part of the territory of a country, with the exception of the administration of social security funds. It encompasses various urban and/or rural jurisdictions (e.g., local authorities, municipalities, cities, boroughs, districts).

d) Social security funds

94. Social security funds form a separate sub-sector of general government. The social security sub-sector is defined in the 2008 SNA by the following extracts from paragraphs 4.124 to 4.126 and 4.147:

> "Social security schemes are social insurance schemes covering the community as a whole or large section of the community that are imposed and controlled by government units. The schemes cover a wide variety of programmes, providing benefits in cash or in kind for old age, invalidity or death, survivors, sickness and maternity, work injury, unemployment, family allowance, health care, etc. There is not necessarily a direct link between the amount of the contribution paid by an individual and the benefits he or she may receive." (Paragraph 4.124).
>
> "When social security schemes are separately organised from the other activities of government units and hold their assets and liabilities separately from the latter and

engage in financial transactions on their own account they qualify as institutional units that are described as social security funds." (Paragraph 4.125).

"The amounts raised, and paid out, in social security contributions and benefits may be deliberately varied in order to achieve objectives of government policy that have no direct connection with the concept of social security as a scheme to provide social benefits to members of the community. They may be raised or lowered in order to influence the level of aggregate demand in the economy, for example. Nevertheless, so long as they remain separately constituted funds, they must be treated as separate institutional units in the SNA. (Paragraph 4.126).

"The social security funds sub-sector (of general government) consists of the social security funds operating at all levels of government. Such funds are social insurance schemes covering the community as a whole or large section of the community that are imposed by government units." (Paragraph 4.147).

95. This definition of social security funds is followed in the OECD classification with the two following exceptions which are excluded

- Schemes imposed by government and operated by bodies outside the general government sector, as defined in §3 of this manual; and
- Schemes to which all contributions are voluntary.

Supra-national Authorities

96. This sub-sector covers the revenue-raising operations of supra-national authorities within a country. In practice, the only relevant supra-national authority in the OECD area is that of the institutions of the European Union (EU). As from 1998, supra-national authorities are no longer included in the *Revenue Statistics*, to achieve consistency with the SNA definition of general government which excludes them. For example, income taxes and social security contributions collected by European Institutions and paid by European civil servants who are resident of EU member countries should not be included. However the specific levies paid by the member states of the EU continue to be included in total tax revenues and they are shown under this heading.

Criteria to be used for the attribution of tax revenues

97. When a government collects taxes and pays them over in whole or in part to other governments, it is necessary to determine whether the revenues should be considered to be those of the collecting government which it distributes to others as grants, or those of the beneficiary governments which the collecting government receives and passes on only as their agent. The criteria to be used in the attribution of revenues are set out in §98 to §101 which replicate paragraphs 3.70 to 3.73 from the 2008 SNA.

98. In general, a tax is attributed to the government unit that

a) exercises the authority to impose the tax (either as a principal or through the delegated authority of the principal),

b) has final discretion to set and vary the rate of the tax

99. Where an amount is collected by one government for and on behalf of another government, and the latter government has the authority to impose the tax, and set and vary its rate, then the former is acting as an agent for the latter and the tax is reassigned. Any amount retained by the collecting government as a collection charge should be treated

as a payment for a service. Any other amount retained by the collecting government, such as under a tax-sharing arrangement, should be treated as a current grant. If the collecting government was delegated the authority to set and vary the rate, then the amount collected should be treated as tax revenue of this government.

100. Where different governments jointly and equally set the rate of a tax and jointly and equally decide on the distribution of the proceeds, with no individual government having ultimate overriding authority, then the tax revenues are attributed to each government according to its respective share of the proceeds. If an arrangement allows one government unit to exercise ultimate overriding authority, then all of the tax revenue is attributed to that unit.

101. There may also be the circumstance where a tax is imposed under the constitutional or other authority of one government, but other governments individually set the tax rate in their jurisdictions. The proceeds of the tax generated in each respective government's jurisdiction are attributed as tax revenues of that government.

Levies paid by member states of the European Union

102. The levies paid by the member states of the EU take the form

- VAT own resources; and
- Specific levies which include
  - *a)* custom duties and levies on agricultural goods (5123),
  - *b)* gross monetary compensation accounts (5123 if relating to imports and 5124 if relating to exports); and
  - *c)* Steel, coal, sugar and milk levies (5128).

103. The custom duties collected by member states on behalf of the EU are recorded

- on a gross of collection fee basis;
- using figures adjusted so that duties are shown on a "final destination" as opposed to a "country of first entry" basis where such adjustments can be made. These adjustments concern in particular duties collected at important (sea) ports. Although the EU duties are collected by the authorities of the country of first entry, when possible these duties should be excluded from the revenue of the collecting country and be included in the revenue of the country of final destination.

104. This is the specific EU levy that most clearly conforms to the attribution criterion described in §96 above. Consequently as from 1998, these amounts are footnoted as a memorandum item to the EU member state country tables (in Part III) and no longer shown under heading 5123. However the figures are included in the total tax revenue figures on the top line for all the relevant years shown in the tables.

105. The VAT own resources, which are determined by applying a rate not exceeding 1 per cent to an assessment basis specified in the Sixth Directive,[20] are more of a borderline case. They have some of the characteristics of a transfer (they are not derived from a clearly identifiable source of funds that are actually collected) and some of a tax (the amount of the transfer is determined by the receiving sub-sector of government). In this publication they are *not* shown as a tax of the European Union (but as a tax of the EU member states), though the amounts involved are footnoted in the tables contained in Part IV.

L. Provisional classification of revenues from bank levies and payments to deposit insurance and financial stability schemes

106. The OECD have adopted the following interim approach to reporting revenue from bank levies plus deposit insurance and stability fees for the 2012 and subsequent editions of OECD *Revenue Statistics*. It is recommended that the amounts should be recorded under category 5126.

- Compulsory payments of stability fees, bank levies and deposit insurance should generally be treated as tax revenues where the payments are made to General Government and allocated to the governments' consolidated or general funds so that the Government is free to make immediate use of the money for the purposes that it chooses. This principle would apply regardless of whether the Government is promising to make payments to guarantee the banks' customer deposits in some future contingency.
- If the compulsory payments are made to general government and placed in funds that are earmarked to be entirely channelled back to the sector of the economy that comprises the companies that are subject to the payment, they would still generally be treated as tax revenues on the grounds that the funds would be available for the government and would reduce its budget deficit, the fee is unrequited for an individual entity and the amounts raised could be unrelated to any eventual pay out to depositors or expenditure on wider support for the financial sector.
- Payments to made to the smaller long-standing schemes for insuring 'retail' deposits, where the payment levels are consistent with the costs of insurance should be classified as fee for service.
- Any payments which involve governments realising the assets of a failed institution or receiving a priority claim on its assets in liquidation in order to fund payments of compensation to customers for their lost deposits would be treated as a fee for a service as opposed to tax revenues.
- Compulsory payments that are made to funds operated outside the government sector and non-state institutions backed by the deposit takers and all payments to voluntary schemes should not be treated as tax revenues.

Notes

1. All references to SNA are to the 2008 edition.
2. See section K of this guide for a discussion of the concept of agency capacity.
3. It is usually possible to identify amounts of social security contributions and payroll taxes, but not other taxes paid by government.
4. If, however, a levy which is considered as non-tax revenue by most countries is regarded as a tax – or raises substantial revenue – in one or more countries, the amounts collected are footnoted at the end of the relevant country tables, even though the amounts are not included in total tax revenues.
5. Names, however, can frequently be misleading. For example, though a passport fee would normally be considered a non-tax revenue, if a supplementary levy on passports (as is the case in Portugal) were imposed in order to raise substantial amounts of revenue relative to the cost of providing the passport, the levy would be regarded as a tax under 5200.
6. There are practical difficulties in operating the distinction made by 1993 SNA.
7. A more detailed explanation of this distinction can be found in the special feature, "Current issues in reporting tax revenues", in the 2001 edition of the *Revenue Statistics*.
8. Sometimes the terms "non-refundable" and "refundable" are used, but it may be considered illogical to talk of "refundable" when nothing has been paid.

9. A different treatment, however, is accorded to non-wastable tax credits under imputation systems of corporate income tax (§32-34).
10. This is not strictly a true tax expenditure in the formal sense. Such tax expenditures require identification of a benchmark tax system for each country or, preferably, a common international benchmark. In practice it has not been possible to reach agreement on a common international benchmark.
11. Unless based on the profit made on a sale, in which case they would be classified as capital gains taxes under 1120 or 1220.
12. In some countries the same legislation applies to both individual and corporate enterprises for particular taxes on income. However, the receipts from such taxes are usually allocable between individuals and enterprises and can therefore be shown in the appropriate sub-heading.
13. For example, "...sufficiently self-contained and independent that they behave in the same way as corporations... (including) keeping a complete set of accounts" (2008 SNA, section 4.44).
14. In Canada – a country also referred to as having an imputation system – the (wastable) tax credit for the shareholder is in respect of domestic corporation tax deemed to have been paid whether or not a corporation tax liability has arisen. As there is no integral connection between the corporation tax liability and the credit given against income tax under such systems, these credits for dividends are treated, along with other tax credits, on the lines described in §21.
15. This may also apply where a scheme for government employees existed prior to the introduction of a general social security scheme.
16. In the 2008 SNA these are regarded as capital transfers and not as taxes (see section G).
17. This is the system by which the European Union adjusts for differences between the exchange rates used to determine prices under the Common Market Agricultural Policy and actual exchange rates. Payments under the system may relate to imports or exports and where these amounts are separately identifiable they are shown under the appropriate heading (5123 or 5124). In this Report, these amounts are shown gross (i.e. without deducting any subsidies paid out under the MCA system).
18. Transfers of profits of State lotteries are regarded as non-tax revenues (see also §64).
19. See §26(c) as regards this distinction.
20. At the Edinburgh Summit (1992) EU Member countries have decided to gradually reduce this percentage from 1.4 to 1, and to effectuate this reduction between years 1995 and 1999. During the period 1970-83 this percentage also amounted to 1.

Revenue Statistics 1965-2014
Statistiques des recettes publiques 1965-2014

ANNEXE A

Classification des impôts de l'OCDE et Guide d'interprétation

Table des matières

Classification d'impôts de l'OCDE

1. 1000 *Impôts sur le revenu, les bénéfices et les gains en capital*
   - 1100 Impôts sur le revenu, les bénéfices et les gains en capital des personnes physiques
     - 1110 Sur le revenu et les bénéfices
     - 1120 Sur les gains en capital
   - 1200 Impôts sur le revenu, les bénéfices et les gains en capital des sociétés
     - 1210 Sur le revenu et les bénéfices
     - 1220 Sur les gains en capital
   - 1300 Non ventilables entres les rubriques 110 et 1200
2. 2000 *Cotisations de sécurité sociale*
   - 2100 À la charge des salariés
     - 2110 Sur la base du salaire
     - 2120 Sur la base de l'impôt sur le revenu
   - 2200 À la charge des employeurs
     - 2210 Sur la base du salaire
     - 2220 Sur la base de l'impôt sur le revenu
   - 2300 À la charge des travailleurs indépendants ou des personnes n'occupant pas d'emploi
     - 2310 Sur la base du salaire
     - 2320 Sur la base de l'impôt sur le revenu
   - 2400 Non ventilables entre les rubriques 2100, 2200 et 2300
     - 2410 Sur la base du salaire
     - 2420 Sur la base de l'impôt sur le revenu
3. 3000 *Impôts sur les salaires et la main-d'œuvre*
4. 4000 *Impôts sur le patrimoine*
   - 4100 Impôts périodiques sur la propriété immobilière
     - 4110 Ménages
     - 4120 Autres agents
   - 4200 Impôts périodiques sur l'actif net
     - 4210 Personnes physiques
     - 4220 Sociétés
   - 4300 Impôts sur les mutations par décès, les successions et les donations
     - 4310 Impôts sur les mutations par décès et les successions
     - 4320 Impôts sur les donations
   - 4400 Impôts sur les transactions mobilières et immobilières
   - 4500 Autres impôts non périodiques sur le patrimoine
     - 4510 Impôts sur l'actif net
     - 4520 Autres impôts non périodiques
   - 4600 Autres impôts périodiques sur le patrimoine
5. 5000 *Impôts sur les biens et services*
   - 5100 Impôts sur la production, la vente, le transfert, la location et la livraison des biens et la prestation de services
     - 5110 Impôts généraux
       - 5111 Taxes sur la valeur ajoutée
       - 5112 Impôts sur les ventes
       - 5113 Autres impôts généraux sur les biens et services
     - 5120 Impôts sur des biens et des services déterminés
       - 5121 Accises

			5122	Bénéfices des monopoles fiscaux
			5123	Droits de douane et droits à l'importation
			5124	Taxes à l'exportation
			5125	Impôts sur les biens d'équipement
			5126	Impôts sur des services déterminés
			5127	Autres impôts sur les transactions et les échanges internationaux
			5128	Autres impôts sur des biens et services déterminés
		5130	Non ventilables entre les rubriques 5110 et 5120	
	5200	Impôts sur l'utilisation des biens ou l'autorisation d'utiliser des biens ou d'exercer des activités		
		5210	Impôts périodiques	
			5211	À la charge des ménages au titre de véhicules à moteur
			5212	À la charge d'autres agents au titre de véhicules à moteur
			5213	Autres impôts périodiques
		5220	Impôts non périodiques	
	5300	Non ventilables entre les rubriques 5100 et 5200		
6. 6000	*Autres impôts*			
	6100	À la charge exclusive des entreprises		
	6200	À la charge d'autre agents que les entreprises ou non identifiables		

Le Guide d'interprétation de l'OCDE

A. Champ couvert

Principes généraux

1. Dans la classification de l'OCDE, le terme « impôts » désigne uniquement les versements obligatoires effectués sans contrepartie au profit des administrations publiques. Les impôts n'ont pas de contrepartie en ce sens que, normalement, les prestations fournies par les administrations au contribuable ne sont pas proportionnelles à ses versements.

2. Le terme « impôts » ne couvre pas les amendes sans lien avec une infraction fiscale ni les prêts obligatoires aux administrations. Les cas dans lesquels la délimitation entre recettes fiscales et non fiscales est délicate à tracer, pour certains droits et taxes d'utilisation, sont examinés dans les § 9 à § 13.

3. Les administrations publiques comprennent l'administration centrale et les organismes dont les opérations sont sous son contrôle effectif, les administrations régionales et locales et leurs services, les organismes de sécurité sociale et les entités publiques autonomes, à l'exception des entreprises publiques. Cette définition des administrations est calquée sur celle du *Système de comptabilité nationale* 2008 (SCN)[1]. Dans cette publication, les administrations publiques et leurs sous-secteurs sont décrits dans le chapitre 4, section F, pages 80-84.

4. Les paiements obligatoires à des organismes supranationaux et aux organismes qui en dépendent ne sont plus compris depuis 1998 parmi les impôts sauf quelques exceptions. En effet, les droits de douane collectés par les États membres de l'Union européenne pour le compte de celle-ci sont toujours présentés à titre de rubrique « Pour mémoire » et compris dans le total des recettes fiscales, à la Partie III, tableaux par pays. (Voir § 95.) Dans les pays où les églises font partie des administrations publiques, les impôts sur les cultes sont inclus dans ces paiements, à condition qu'ils répondent aux critères énoncés au § 1 ci-dessus. Comme les données se réfèrent aux montants encaissés par les administrations publiques, les contributions versées à des organismes privés, aux organismes sociaux ou régimes de sécurité sociale extérieurs aux administrations publiques, aux syndicats ou aux associations professionnelles sont exclues, même si elles sont obligatoires. Sont toutefois inclus les versements obligatoires aux administrations publiques dont le montant est affecté à ces organismes, à condition que l'administration ne fasse pas simplement office d'agent collecteur[2]. On a distingué les bénéfices des monopoles fiscaux de ceux d'autres entreprises publiques et on les a considérés comme des impôts parce qu'ils reflètent l'exercice du pouvoir d'imposition de l'État par l'intermédiaire du monopole (voir § 62 à § 64), comme le sont les bénéfices de l'État provenant de l'achat et de la vente de monnaies étrangères à des taux différents (voir § 70).

5. Les impôts payés par les administrations elles-mêmes (tels que les cotisations de sécurité sociale et les impôts sur les salaires payés par les administrations en tant qu'employeurs (2200 et 3000), les impôts sur la consommation qu'elles acquittent à l'occasion de leurs achats ou les impôts sur leur patrimoine) sont inclus dans les données présentées. Toutefois, lorsqu'il est possible de les isoler, les montants provenant de ces impôts[3] sont indiqués dans section III.C de cette publication.

6. Les rapports entre cette classification et celle du Système de comptabilité nationale (SCN) sont indiquées dans les sections H et J. À cause des différences qui existent entre les deux classifications, les statistiques de la comptabilité nationale ne sont pas toujours établies ou classées suivant la pratique adoptée dans le présent guide. Ces différences et d'autres encore sont mentionnées dans les cas appropriés (voir par exemple § 13 et § 26), mais il est impossible de toutes les signaler. Il peut y avoir aussi certaines différences entre cette classification et celle utilisée par certaines administrations nationales (voir par exemple § 10), aussi les statistiques nationales et celles de l'OCDE ne peuvent pas toujours être compatibles ; ces différences, cependant, sont vraisemblablement très insignifiantes dans les montants des recettes en cause.

Cotisations de sécurité sociale

7. Les cotisations de sécurité sociale, définies au § 35, qui sont versées aux administrations publiques, font partie des recettes fiscales. Elles sont évidemment assimilables à des impôts puisqu'il s'agit de versements obligatoires à des administrations publiques. Mais elles peuvent différer toutefois des autres impôts du fait que le paiement des prestations de sécurité sociale dépend dans la plupart des pays du versement des cotisations appropriées, encore qu'il n'y ait pas forcément un lien entre l'importance des prestations et le montant des cotisations. La comparabilité entre les pays sera meilleure si on considère les cotisations de sécurité sociale comme des impôts ; elles figurent cependant sous une rubrique distincte de façon à permettre un traitement séparé pour n'importe quelle analyse.

8. Les cotisations de sécurité sociale qui sont volontaires ou qui ne sont pas versées à des administrations publiques (voir § 1) ne sont pas considérées comme des impôts, bien que dans certains pays (comme il est indiqué dans les notes correspondantes) il soit difficile d'éliminer les cotisations volontaires et certains versements obligatoires au secteur privé.

Droits, taxes d'utilisation et droits de licence

9. Si l'on excepte les droits perçus sur les permis de circulation des véhicules à moteur, qui sont universellement considérés comme des impôts, il n'est pas facile de distinguer les droits et taxes d'utilisation qui doivent être traitées comme des impôts de celles qui ne doivent pas l'être. Si, en effet, un droit ou une taxe est perçu au titre d'un service ou d'une activité déterminée, le lien entre ce prélèvement et la prestation fournie peut être plus ou moins important, de même que la relation entre le montant du prélèvement et le coût de la prestation. Lorsque le bénéficiaire d'une prestation acquitte un droit dont le montant est clairement lié au coût de la prestation fournie, on peut considérer que le prélèvement comporte une contrepartie, et d'après la définition donnée au § 1, il ne sera pas traité comme un impôt. Toutefois, dans les cas suivants, les prélèvements seraient « sans contrepartie »:

a) lorsque le prélèvement est très supérieur au coût de la prestation fournie ;

b) lorsque le redevable de la contribution n'est pas le bénéficiaire de la prestation correspondante (par exemple, un droit perçu sur l'abattage du bétail pour financer un service qui est fourni aux agriculteurs) ;

c) lorsque l'État ne fournit pas un service déterminé en contrepartie du droit qu'il perçoit, même si un permis est délivré à celui qui acquitte le droit (par exemple, lorsque l'État délivre des permis de chasse, de pêche ou de port d'armes qui ne sont pas assortis du droit d'utiliser une parcelle déterminée de terres appartenant à l'État) ;

d) lorsque les bénéficiaires de la prestation sont les personnes qui ont acquitté le droit, mais que la prestation dont chacun bénéficie n'est pas nécessairement en rapport avec le montant de ses propres versements (par exemple, le droit de commercialisation du lait acquitté par les fermiers qui sert à promouvoir la consommation de lait.

10. Dans des cas limites, cependant, l'application des critères énoncés au § 1 peut être particulièrement difficile. La solution adoptée, dans un souci d'uniformité entre les pays et eu égard aux montants relativement faibles des recettes en cause, consiste à s'en tenir à la pratique prépondérante des administrations fiscales plutôt que de laisser chaque pays décider si ces prélèvements sont des impôts ou des recettes non fiscales[4].

11. On trouvera ci-après la liste des principaux droits et taxes en question et leur traitement normal[5] dans la présente publication :

Recettes non fiscales :	frais de justice ; droits de délivrance de permis de conduire ; droits portuaires ; redevances de passeport ; redevances de radio et de télévision lorsque le service est assuré par les pouvoirs publics.
Impôts du sous-groupe 5200 :	autorisation d'exercer certaines activités telles que : distribution de films ; chasse, pêche et utilisation d'armes à feu ; organisation de spectacles ou de jeux et paris ; vente de boissons alcoolisées ou de tabacs ; autorisation de posséder des chiens et d'utiliser ou posséder des véhicules à moteur ou des armes à feu ; droit de lotissement.

12. Dans la pratique, il se peut qu'il ne soit pas toujours possible d'isoler les recettes fiscales des recettes non fiscales quant elles sont enregistrées ensemble. Si l'on estime qu'il s'agit surtout de recettes non fiscales, l'ensemble sera traité comme tel ; dans le cas contraire, les recettes seront comptabilisées et classées conformément aux règles énoncées au § 28.

13. La classification de l'OCDE et celle du SCN présentent deux différences concernant la définition entre recettes fiscales et non fiscales :

a) Le SCN traite un certain nombre de prélèvements comme des impôts indirects quand ils sont à la charge des entreprises et comme des recettes non fiscales quand ils sont à la charge des ménages, distinction dont il n'est pas tenu compte dans la présente classification pour séparer les recettes fiscales des recettes non fiscales[6].

b) La solution qui consiste à s'en tenir à la pratique la plus courante des administrations fiscales dans la zone de l'OCDE et qui est parfois utilisée dans la présente classification pour distinguer les recettes fiscales des recettes non fiscales n'est pas un critère retenu aux fins du SCN.

Redevances

14. Les redevances versées pour obtenir le droit d'extraire du pétrole et du gaz ou de mettre en valeur d'autres ressources minérales sont considérées normalement comme des recettes non fiscales, car il s'agit de revenus immobiliers procurés par des terres ou des ressources appartenant à l'État.

Amendes et pénalités

15. Les recettes provenant d'amendes et pénalités acquittées pour infraction aux réglementations relatives à un impôt particulier et les intérêts de retard afférents au dit impôt sont enregistrés avec les recettes procurées par cet impôt. Mais les autres catégories d'amendes identifiables comme se rapportant à des infractions fiscales sont classées au poste résiduel 6000. Les amendes qui ne concernent pas des infractions fiscales (comme les infractions au stationnement), ou qui ne sont pas identifiables en tant que telles, ne sont pas considérées comme des impôts.

B. Bases de comptabilisation

Droits constatés

16. Les données enregistrées dans cette publication pour les années récentes sont essentiellement indiquées en droits constatés, c'est-à-dire qu'elles sont enregistrées au moment du fait générateur de l'impôt. D'autres informations sont fournies dans les notes des tableaux par pays de la Partie III de ce rapport.

17. Toutefois, les données des années antérieures sont encore principalement comptabilisées sur la base des décaissements, c'est-à-dire au moment où l'administration reçoit le versement. Ainsi, les impôts retenus à la source par les employeurs au cours d'un exercice, mais versés à l'administration au cours de l'exercice suivant, et les impôts dus au titre d'une année mais effectivement versés l'année suivante, figurent les uns et les autres dans les recettes du second exercice. Les restitutions, remboursements et retraits résultant d'opérations rectificatives sont déduits des recettes brutes de la période au cours de laquelle ces opérations sont effectuées.

18. Les données relatives aux recettes fiscales sont comptabilisées, sans déduction compensatoire des dépenses administratives liées au recouvrement de l'impôt. De même, lorsque le produit d'un impôt sert à subventionner certains membres de la collectivité, la subvention n'est pas déduite du rendement de l'impôt, encore que certains pays fassent figurer dans leurs données l'impôt après déduction des subventions.

19. Pour les monopoles fiscaux (sous-groupe 5122), seul le montant effectivement transféré à l'État est inclus dans les recettes publiques. Toutefois, les dépenses des monopoles fiscaux qui sont considérées comme des dépenses publiques (par exemple, des dépenses de caractère social engagées par les monopoles fiscaux à l'instigation de l'État) sont ajoutées après coup pour calculer le montant des recettes fiscales (voir § 62).

La distinction entre dispositions fiscales et dépenses directes[7]

20. Étant donné que la présente publication ne vise que les recettes publiques en faisant abstraction des dépenses, il convient de distinguer entre les dispositions fiscales et les dépenses directes. Normalement, cette distinction ne soulève aucune difficulté, car les dépenses directes sont effectuées en dehors du système fiscal et des comptes fiscaux et en vertu de dispositions législatives distinctes. Dans les cas limites, on recourt, pour établir la distinction, au principe de la comptabilisation sur la base des paiements. Dans la mesure où une disposition affecte le montant des paiements du contribuable à l'État, elle est considérée comme une disposition fiscale dont il est tenu compte dans les données figurant dans cette publication. Une disposition qui n'affecte pas ce montant est considérée comme une dépense directe dont il n'est pas tenu compte dans les données reproduites dans cette publication.

21. Il est clair que les abattements fiscaux, exonérations et déductions de l'assiette de l'impôt modifient le montant de l'impôt acquitté à l'État ; il s'agit donc de dispositions fiscales. Inversement, les formes d'aides qui ne sont pas imputables sur l'impôt et n'ont donc aucun lien avec le processus d'imposition, ne réduisent pas les recettes publiques qui sont consignées dans ce volume. Les crédits d'impôt sont des montants déductibles de l'impôt à acquitter (par opposition aux déductions, qui sont opérées sur l'assiette de l'impôt). On distingue deux catégories de crédits d'impôt : ceux (que l'on qualifiera ici de 'non récupérables') qui sont limités au montant de l'impôt à acquitter et ne peuvent donc donner lieu à un versement de l'administration au contribuable, et ceux (qualifiés ici de « récupérables ») qui n'ont pas cette limite, de sorte que l'excédent du crédit sur l'impôt peut être versé au contribuable[8]. Le crédit d'impôt non récupérable, comme un abattement fiscal, affecte évidemment le montant de l'impôt acquitté à l'État ; aussi est-il considéré comme une disposition fiscale. La solution adoptée pour les crédits d'impôts récupérables[9] consiste à distinguer l'élément de « dépense fiscale »[10], qui est la part du crédit utilisée pour réduire ou supprimer l'impôt dû par le contribuable, et l'« élément de transfert », qui correspond à la part excédant l'impôt dû par le contribuable et qui lui est reversée. Les recettes fiscales rapportées doivent être diminuées du montant de l'élément de dépense, mais non de l'élément de transfert. En outre, les montants de l'élément de dépense fiscale et de l'élément de transfert doivent être indiqués pour mémoire dans les tableaux par pays. Les pays qui ne sont pas en mesure de faire la distinction entre l'élément de dépense fiscale et l'élément de transfert doivent indiquer si leurs recettes fiscales ont été ou non diminuées du montant total de ces éléments, et fournir toutes les estimations dont ils disposent concernant les montants de ces deux éléments. Des informations complémentaires figurent à la section C de la Partie I de ce Rapport, qui fait apparaître les effets des différents traitements possibles des crédits d'impôts récupérables sur les ratios impôt rapportant les impôts au PIB.

Année civile et année fiscale (exercice budgétaire)

22. Les autorités nationales dont l'exercice budgétaire ne correspond pas à l'année civile fournissent, autant que possible, leurs données sur la base de l'année civile afin de faciliter au maximum la comparaison avec les données des autres pays. Les données d'un petit nombre de pays se réfèrent à l'exercice budgétaire. Pour ceux-ci, les statistiques de PIB utilisées dans les tableaux comparatifs portent aussi sur les exercices budgétaires.

C. Principes généraux de classification

Les fondements essentiels de la classification

23. Les recettes sont classées par groupes principaux (1000, 2000, 3000, 4000, 5000, 6000) suivant l'assiette de l'impôt : 1000 revenus, bénéfices et gains en capital ; 2000 et 3000 salaires et nombre d'employés ; 4000 patrimoine ; 5000 biens et services ; 6000 assiettes diverses, autres ou non identifiables. Lorsqu'un impôt est calculé en fonction de plusieurs assiettes, les recettes sont, chaque fois que c'est possible, réparties entre les divers groupes (voir § 28 et § 78). Les groupes 4000 et 5000 ne comprennent pas seulement les impôts ayant pour assiette le patrimoine, les biens ou les services eux-mêmes, mais aussi certains impôts connexes. Ainsi, les impôts sur les mutations du patrimoine sont classés dans le groupe 4400[11] et les impôts sur l'utilisation des biens, ou l'autorisation d'exercer une activité, dans le groupe 5200. Dans les groupes 4000 et 5000, une distinction est faite dans certains sous-groupes entre impôts périodiques et impôts non périodiques : on entend par

impôts périodiques ceux qui sont perçus à intervalles réguliers (ordinairement tous les ans) et par impôts non périodiques ceux qui ne sont perçus qu'une seule fois (voir aussi les § 43 à § 46, § 49, § 50, § 76 et § 77 pour une application particulière de cette distinction).

24. L'affectation spéciale de certaines recettes fiscales n'influe pas sur leur classification. Toutefois comme explicité au § 35 sur la classification des cotisations de sécurité sociale, l'octroi d'un droit aux prestations sociales est crucial dans la définition de la rubrique principale 2000.

25. La manière selon laquelle un impôt est perçu ou recouvré (par exemple, au moyen de timbres) n'affecte pas sa classification.

Classification des contribuables

26. Dans certains sous-groupes, des distinctions sont faites entre les différentes catégories de contribuables. Ces distinctions varient d'un impôt à l'autre :

a) *Ventilation des impôts sur le revenu et sur l'actif net entre personnes physiques et sociétés*

La distinction fondamentale entre les impôts sur le revenu des sociétés et les impôts sur le revenu des personnes physiques est que les premiers sont perçus sur la société en tant qu'entité et non sur les personnes physiques qui en sont propriétaires, donc sans tenir compte de la situation personnelle de celles-ci. La même distinction est applicable aux impôts sur l'actif net des sociétés et des personnes physiques. Les impôts perçus sur les bénéfices des sociétés de personnes et sur le revenu de certaines institutions comme les caisses d'assurance-vie ou de retraite, sont classés selon le même principe. Ils sont compris dans les impôts sur les sociétés (1200) lorsqu'ils sont perçus sur la société de personnes ou l'institution en tant qu'entité sans que la situation personnelle des propriétaires entre en ligne de compte ; dans les autres cas, ils sont considérés comme des impôts sur les personnes physiques (1100). Ordinairement, les impôts sur les sociétés et les impôts sur les personnes physiques sont régis par des dispositions législatives différentes[12]. La distinction qui est faite ici entre personnes physiques et sociétés ne reprend pas la classification par secteur (ménages, entreprises, etc.) adoptée dans les comptes de revenus et de dépenses du SCN. Cette dernière classification exclut du secteur des ménages certaines entreprises non constituées en sociétés[13] et les fait figurer parmi les entreprises non financières et les institutions financières. Toutefois, l'impôt sur les bénéfices de ces entreprises ne peut pas toujours être isolé de l'impôt sur les autres revenus des propriétaires de ces entreprises, ou ne peut l'être que d'une façon arbitraire. On n'a pas cherché ici à faire la distinction et l'impôt sur le revenu des personnes physiques figure globalement, quelle que soit la nature du revenu imposable.

b) *Ventilation des impôts sur les biens immobiliers entre ménages et autres agents*

En l'occurrence, la distinction est celle qui a été adoptée par le SCN dans les comptes de production et de consommation. On distingue, en effet, les ménages en tant que consommateurs d'une part (c'est-à-dire à l'exclusion des entreprises individuelles), et les producteurs d'autre part. Cependant, les impôts sur les logements occupés par les ménages, qu'ils soient à la charge des propriétaires qui les occupent, du locataire ou du propriétaire, sont classés comme étant à la charge des ménages. C'est la distinction faite habituellement entre les impôts sur les biens des personnes et les impôts sur les biens des entreprises. Toutefois, certains pays ne sont pas en mesure d'établir cette distinction.

c) Ventilation des permis de circuler des véhicules à moteur entre taxes à la charge des ménages et à la charge d'autres agents

On distingue ici les ménages en tant que consommateurs d'une part, et producteurs d'autre part, comme dans les comptes de production et de consommation du SCN.

d) Ventilation des autres impôts (6000) entre les entreprises et les autres agents

Il est fait la même distinction qu'au point (c) ci-dessus entre les producteurs, d'une part, et les ménages consommateurs d'autre part. Les impôts qui figurent dans le groupe 6000 parce qu'ils ne comportent pas une assiette unique ou parce que leur assiette ne relève d'aucune des catégories précédentes, mais qui ne sont manifestement perçus que sur les producteurs et non sur les ménages, sont classés comme étant « à la charge des entreprises ». Les autres impôts du groupe 6000 figurent sous la rubrique « à la charge d'autres agents » ou « non identifiés ».

Surtaxes

27. Les recettes des surtaxes relatives à des impôts particuliers sont classées ordinairement avec les recettes de l'impôt correspondant, que la surtaxe ait ou non un caractère temporaire. Toutefois, si l'une des caractéristiques de la surtaxe permet de la classer sous une rubrique différente de la classification de l'OCDE, les recettes de cette surtaxe sont classées sous cette rubrique et non pas avec les recettes de l'impôt correspondant.

Recettes fiscales non identifiables et sous-groupes résiduels

28. Il arrive parfois qu'on ne puisse déterminer si des impôts relèvent entièrement d'un groupe ou d'un sous-groupe de la classification de l'OCDE ; dans ces cas on applique les méthodes suivantes :

a) le groupe est connu, mais on ne sait pas comment répartir les recettes entre les sous-groupes ; les recettes sont alors classées dans le sous-groupe résiduel approprié (1300, 2400, 4520, 4600, 5130, 5300 ou 6200) ;

b) on sait que l'ensemble des recettes d'un groupe d'impôts (ordinairement des impôts locaux) provient d'impôts relevant d'un groupe ou sous-groupe particulier, mais certains impôts du groupe, dont le montant ne peut être déterminé avec précision, peuvent être classés dans d'autres groupes ou sous-groupes ; dans ce cas les recettes sont comptabilisées dans le groupe ou sous-groupe dont relève l'essentiel des recettes ;

c) il est impossible d'identifier le groupe ou le sous-groupe d'un impôt (ordinairement un impôt local) ; l'impôt est alors classé dans le groupe 6200, à moins qu'il ne s'agisse d'un impôt manifestement à la charge des entreprises, auquel cas il est classé dans le sous-groupe 6100.

D. Commentaires sur les postes de la liste

1000 – Impôts sur le revenu, les bénéfices et les gains en capital

29. Ce groupe couvre les impôts prélevés sur le revenu ou le bénéfice net (c'est-à-dire le revenu brut déduction faite des abattements autorisés) des personnes physiques et des entreprises. Sont aussi couverts les impôts prélevés sur les gains en capital des personnes physiques et des entreprises et sur les gains provenant de jeux.

30. Ce groupe comprend :

a) les impôts perçus principalement sur les revenus ou les bénéfices, bien qu'ils puissent l'être partiellement sur d'autres bases. Les impôts qui ont une autre assiette principale que le revenu ou les bénéfices sont classés selon les principes énoncés au § 28 et § 78 ;

b) les impôts sur la propriété immobilière, qui sont perçus sur la base d'un revenu présumé ou estimé faisant partie de l'assiette de l'impôt sur le revenu (voir aussi § 43 (a), (c) et (d)) ;

c) les versements obligatoires aux caisses de sécurité sociale qui sont prélevés sur les revenus mais ne donnent pas droit à des prestations sociales. Lorsque ces contributions donnent droit à des prestations sociales, elles figurent à la rubrique 2000 (voir § 35) ;

d) les recettes provenant d'impôts cédulaires sur le revenu intégrés dans le régime général qui sont globalement classés dans ce groupe, bien que certains de ces impôts soient sur le revenu brut et ne tiennent pas toujours compte de la situation personnelle du contribuable.

31. Les impôts figurant dans ce groupe sont subdivisés en deux grands sous-groupes, les impôts sur le revenu des personnes physiques (1100) et les impôts sur le revenu des sociétés (1200), une ventilation étant faite dans chacun d'eux entre les impôts sur le revenu et les bénéfices (1110 et 1210) et les impôts sur les gains en capital (1120 et 1220). Si certaines recettes ne peuvent être identifiées comme relevant soit du sous-groupe 1100, soit du sous-groupe 1200, ou si cette distinction ne peut être faite dans la pratique (parce qu'il n'y a pas de données fiables sur les bénéficiaires des paiements sur lesquels la retenue à la source est faite), elles sont classées dans le sous-groupe 1300 (non ventilables).

Traitement des crédits d'impôt dans les systèmes d'imputation

32. Dans les régimes d'imputation de l'impôt sur les bénéfices des sociétés, les actionnaires bénéficient d'une compensation totale ou partielle d'imposition sur les dividendes que la société leur a versés et pour lesquels elle a acquitté l'impôt sur le revenu des sociétés. Dans les pays[14] qui appliquent un tel régime, une fraction de l'impôt sur les bénéfices des sociétés sert à alléger l'impôt dû par l'actionnaire. Cet allégement prend la forme d'un crédit d'impôt, dont le montant peut être inférieur, égal ou supérieur au montant total de l'impôt dont il est redevable. Si le crédit d'impôt dépasse ce montant, l'excédent peut être versé à l'actionnaire. Comme ce type de crédit d'impôt fait partie intégrante des systèmes d'imputation de l'impôt sur le revenu des sociétés, tout paiement à l'actionnaire est considéré comme un remboursement d'impôt et non comme une dépense (se référer au traitement des autres crédits d'impôt exposé au § 21).

33. Puisque, dans les systèmes d'imputation, le crédit d'impôt (même lorsqu'il dépasse l'impôt dû) est censé être une disposition fiscale, on peut se demander s'il doit être déduit des recettes de l'impôt sur le revenu des personnes physiques (1110) ou de celles de l'impôt sur les bénéfices de sociétés (1210). Dans ce Rapport le montant intégral de l'impôt acquitté sur les bénéfices des sociétés figure sous le poste 1210 et aucun impôt imputé n'est inclus dans le poste 1110. Le montant total du crédit d'impôt réduit donc le montant des recettes du poste 1110, que ce crédit se traduise par une réduction de l'impôt dû sur le revenu des personnes physiques ou par un remboursement réel du fait que le crédit dépasse le montant de l'impôt. (Cependant, lorsque ces crédits sont déduits de l'impôt sur les sociétés au titre de dividendes versés à des sociétés, le montant est déduit des recettes du poste 1210).

1120 et 1220 – Impôts sur les gains en capital

34. Ces postes comprennent les impôts perçus sur les gains en capital, le sous-groupe 1120 comptabilisant les impôts prélevés sur les gains des personnes physiques et le sous-groupe 1220 ceux qui sont perçus sur les gains des entreprises constituées sous forme de sociétés, lorsque ces recettes peuvent être ventilées. Ce n'est pas le cas dans de nombreux pays et les recettes de ces impôts sont alors classées avec celles de l'impôt sur le revenu. Les impôts sur les gains provenant de jeux sont aussi classés sous le poste 1120.

2000 – Cotisations de sécurité sociale

35. Figurent dans ce groupe tous les versements obligatoires qui donnent le droit de bénéficier d'une prestation sociale future (éventuelle). Ces versements sont généralement affectés au financement de prestations sociales et souvent effectués au profit d'institutions ou d'administrations publiques qui fournissent de telles prestations. Cependant, cette affectation n'entre pas dans la définition des cotisations de sécurité sociale et n'est pas nécessaire pour qu'un impôt soit classé dans cette rubrique. Cependant, il faut qu'un impôt confère un droit pour être classé dans cette rubrique. Par conséquent, les prélèvements sur les revenus ou la masse salariale qui sont affectés aux caisses de sécurité sociale mais ne donnent aucun droit à des prestations sont exclus de cette rubrique et figurent à celle des impôts sur le revenu des personnes physiques (1100) ou des impôts sur les salaires et la main-d'œuvre (3000). Les impôts assis sur d'autres bases, telles que les biens et services, qui sont affectés à des prestations de sécurité sociale, ne sont pas indiqués ici, mais sont classés en fonction de leurs bases respectives parce qu'en général ils ne donnent pas droit à des prestations de sécurité sociale.

36. Seraient entre autres incluses les cotisations au titre des catégories suivantes de prestations de sécurité sociale : les allocations d'assurance-chômage et les compléments, les allocations pour accidents, blessures et maladie, les pensions de retraite, d'invalidité et de survivant, les allocations familiales, les remboursements de dépenses médicales et d'hospitalisation ou la fourniture de services médicaux ou hospitaliers. Les cotisations peuvent être collectées à la fois auprès des employés et des employeurs.

37. Les cotisations peuvent être assises sur les gains ou la masse salariale (« sur la base du salaire ») ou sur le revenu net après déductions et exemptions en fonction de la situation personnelle (« sur la base de l'impôt sur le revenu ») et les recettes correspondant à ces deux bases doivent être identifiées séparément si possible. Cependant, lorsque les cotisations à un régime général de sécurité sociale sont assises sur la masse salariale, mais que les cotisations de groupes particuliers (tels que les travailleurs indépendants) ne peuvent être évaluées sur cette base et que le revenu net est utilisé comme valeur rapprochée des gains bruts, les recettes peuvent encore être considérées comme assises sur la masse salariale. En principe, cette rubrique exclut les contributions volontaires à des régimes de sécurité sociale. Lorsqu'elles peuvent être identifiées séparément, elles figurent pour mémoire dans le tableau indiquant le financement des prestations de sécurité sociale. Toutefois, en pratique, elles ne peuvent pas toujours être distinguées des cotisations volontaires, et dans ce cas elles figurent à cette rubrique.

38. Les cotisations à des régimes d'assurance sociale qui ne relèvent pas des pouvoirs publics et à d'autres régimes d'assurance ou de prévoyance, aux caisses de retraite, sociétés de secours mutuel ou autres systèmes d'épargne, ne sont pas considérées comme

des cotisations de sécurité sociale. Les caisses de prévoyance résultant d'arrangements aux termes desquels les cotisations de chaque salarié et celles que l'employeur verse en son nom sont comptabilisées séparément dans un compte productif d'intérêts d'où elles peuvent être retirées dans des conditions biens déterminées. Les caisses de retraite sont des régimes autonomes organisés par négociations entre salariés et employeurs, qui comportent diverses contributions et prestations, parfois liées plus directement au salaire et à la durée d'activité que dans les régimes de sécurité sociale. Lorsque les cotisations à ces régimes sont obligatoires ou quasi obligatoires (par exemple en vertu d'un accord entre organisations professionnelles et syndicales), elles sont comptabilisées dans le poste pour mémoire (voir Section B dans la partie III du rapport).

39. Les cotisations versées par les agents des administrations et par les administrations au titre de leurs agents à des régimes de sécurité sociale relevant des pouvoirs publics sont incluses dans ce groupe. Sont aussi assimilées à des impôts les cotisations à des régimes particuliers réservés aux agents des administrations qui sont censés remplacer un régime général de la sécurité sociale[15]. Par contre, lorsqu'un régime distinct n'est pas censé remplacer un régime général et résulte de négociations entre l'administration, agissant en qualité d'employeur, et ses agents, il n'est pas considéré comme un régime de sécurité sociale et les cotisations à ce titre ne sont pas assimilées à des impôts, même si le régime a été institué par des dispositions législatives.

40. Cette rubrique ne comprend pas les cotisations « imputées », qui correspondent aux prestations sociales versées directement par les employeurs à leurs salariés, ou anciens salariés, ou à leurs représentants (par exemple, lorsque des employeurs sont légalement tenus de verser des prestations maladies pendant une certaine période).

41. Le groupe comprend les cotisations à la charge des salariés (2100), à la charge des employeurs (2200), et à la charge des travailleurs indépendants ou des personnes n'occupant pas d'emploi (2300). À cet effet, on entend par salariés toutes les personnes qui exercent une activité dans des entreprises, des administrations, des institutions privées sans but lucratif, ou qui occupent d'autres emplois rémunérés, à l'exception des propriétaires et des membres de leur famille non rémunérés dans le cas d'entreprises individuelles. Sont également compris les membres des forces armées, quelle que soit la durée et la nature de leurs services, s'ils cotisent à un régime de sécurité sociale. Par cotisations à la charge des employeurs, on entend les versements qu'ils effectuent au régime de sécurité sociale pour le compte de leurs salariés. Si, en cas de chômage, les salariés ou employeurs sont tenus de continuer à effectuer ces versements, ces derniers doivent figurer respectivement dans les sous-groupes 2100 et 2200. En conséquence, le sous-groupe 2300 est réservé aux cotisations versées par les travailleurs indépendants et par ceux qui n'appartiennent pas à la population active (comme les handicapés ou les retraités).

3000 – Impôts sur les salaires et la main-d'œuvre

42. Ce groupe couvre les impôts acquittés par les employeurs, les salariés et les travailleurs indépendants, en pourcentage du salaire ou d'après un montant forfaitaire par personne, qui ne sont pas affectés aux dépenses de sécurité sociale. Parmi les impôts classés ici, on peut citer l'impôt complémentaire d'assurance nationale sans affectation (institué en 1977) au Royaume-Uni, l'impôt sur la masse salariale en Suède (1969-79), la fraction du « Gewerbesteuer » autrichien et allemand qui reposait sur la masse salariale (1965-78).

4000 – Impôts sur le patrimoine

43. Ce groupe couvre les impôts périodiques et non périodiques sur l'utilisation, la propriété ou la mutation des biens. Sont comptabilisés ici les impôts sur la propriété immobilière et sur l'actif net, les impôts sur les mutations par décès, les successions et les donations, et les impôts sur les transactions mobilières et immobilières. Sont exclus de ce groupe :

a) les impôts sur les gains en capital provenant de la vente d'un bien (1120 ou 1220) ;

b) les impôts sur l'utilisation des biens ou l'autorisation d'utiliser des biens ou d'exercer des activités (5200) [voir § 73] ;

c) les impôts immobiliers perçus sur la base d'un revenu net présumé qui tiennent compte de la situation personnelle du contribuable. Ces impôts sont classés dans le groupe 1100 en tant qu'impôts sur le revenu, avec les impôts sur le revenu et les gains en capital provenant des biens immobiliers ;

d) les impôts sur l'utilisation de biens immobiliers aux fins d'habitation qui sont à la charge du propriétaire ou du locataire et dont le montant est fonction de la situation personnelle de l'utilisateur (salaire, personnes à charge, etc.). Ils sont classés dans le groupe 1100 en tant qu'impôts sur le revenu ;

e) les impôts sur les constructions dépassant la densité autorisée, les impôts sur l'extension, la construction ou la modification de certains immeubles au-delà d'une valeur autorisée et les impôts sur la construction d'immeubles. Ces impôts sont classés dans le poste 5200 en tant qu'impôts sur l'autorisation d'exercer certaines activités ;

f) les impôts sur l'utilisation de biens immobiliers par le propriétaire à des fins commerciales particulières, comme la vente de boissons alcoolisées, de tabac, de viande, ou pour l'exploitation de sols ou terrains (par exemple aux États-Unis, les taxes de lotissement). Ils sont classés dans le poste 5200 en tant qu'impôts sur l'autorisation d'exercer certaines activités.

4100 – Impôts périodiques sur la propriété immobilière

44. Ce sous-groupe comprend les impôts prélevés régulièrement au titre de l'utilisation ou de la propriété de biens immobiliers.

- ces impôts sont prélevés sur les terrains et les bâtiments ;
- ces impôts sont calculés en pourcentage de la valeur du bien évalué d'après un revenu locatif fictif, le prix de vente ou le rendement capitalisé, ou en fonction d'autres caractéristiques du bien, comme sa dimension ou son emplacement, d'où l'on peut déduire une valeur locative présumée ou la valeur du capital.
- ces impôts sont à la charge du propriétaire, du locataire ou des deux. Ils peuvent également être payés par une administration à une autre administration au titre d'un bien relevant de la compétence de cette dernière.
- il n'est pas tenu compte des dettes pour la détermination de l'assiette de ces impôts, contrairement aux impôts sur l'actif net.

45. Les impôts sur la propriété immobilière sont en outre subdivisés en impôts acquittés par les ménages (4110) et impôts acquittés par d'autres agents (4120), suivant les critères exposés au § 26(*b*) ci-dessus.

4200 – Impôts périodiques sur l'actif net

46. Ce sous-groupe comprend les impôts prélevés régulièrement (dans la plupart des cas annuellement) sur l'actif net, c'est-à-dire les impôts perçus sur un large éventail de biens mobiliers et immobiliers, endettement déduit. Il est subdivisé en impôts acquittés par des personnes physiques (4210), et en impôts acquittés par des sociétés (4220) selon les critères exposés plus haut au § 26(*a*). Si les recettes provenant des institutions sont comptabilisées à part, elles doivent être ajoutées aux impôts des entreprises.

4300 – Impôts sur les mutations par décès, les successions et les donations

47. Ce sous-groupe comprend les impôts sur les mutations par décès et les successions (4310) et les impôts sur les donations (4320)[16]. Les impôts sur les mutations par décès sont calculés soit sur l'ensemble de la masse successorale, soit en fonction de la part de chacun des bénéficiaires (« part héréditaire ») ; en outre, ces derniers impôts peuvent tenir compte du degré de parenté entre chacun des bénéficiaires et le défunt.

4400 – Impôts sur les transactions mobilières et immobilières

48. Sont compris, entre autres, dans ce sous-groupe les impôts sur l'émission, le transfert, l'achat et la vente de valeurs mobilières, les impôts sur les chèques, ainsi que les droits perçus à l'occasion d'actes juridiques déterminés, comme la validation de contrats et la vente de biens immobiliers. Sont exclus :

a) les impôts sur l'utilisation de biens, mobiliers ou immobiliers, ou l'autorisation d'exercer certaines activités (5200) ;

b) les droits acquittés au titre de frais de justice, ou pour la délivrance de certificats de naissance, de mariage ou de décès, car ces droits sont considérés comme des recettes non fiscales (voir § 9) ;

c) les impôts sur les gains en capital (1000) ;

d) les impôts périodiques sur la propriété immobilière (4100) ;

e) les impôts périodiques sur l'actif net (4200) ;

f) les prélèvements sur le patrimoine ou sur l'actif net effectués une fois pour toutes (4500) ;

4500 – Autres impôts non périodiques sur le patrimoine[16]

49. Ce sous-groupe comprend les prélèvements sur le patrimoine effectués une fois pour toutes (par opposition aux prélèvements périodiques). Il est subdivisé en impôts sur l'actif net (4510) et en autres impôts non périodiques sur le patrimoine (4520). Le poste 4510 inclurait les impôts perçus pour couvrir des dépenses exceptionnelles ou à des fins de redistribution. Le poste 4520 comprendrait les impôts prélevés pour tenir compte d'une plus-value prise par les terrains du fait que les administrations publiques ont autorisé l'extension ou l'aménagement d'installations locales, ainsi que les impôts sur la réévaluation du capital ou les impôts perçus une seule fois sur certains biens déterminés.

4600 – Autres impôts périodiques sur le patrimoine

50. Ils sont rares dans des pays Membres de l'OCDE ; ce sous-groupe comprendrait les impôts sur des biens tels que le cheptel, les bijoux, les fenêtres et les signes extérieurs de richesse.

5000 – *Impôts sur les biens et services*

51. Ce poste couvre tous les impôts et droits perçus sur la production, l'extraction, la vente, le transfert, la location ou la livraison de biens et la prestation de services (5100), ou sur l'utilisation ou l'autorisation d'utiliser des biens ou d'exercer des activités (5200). Ce groupe comprend donc :

a) les taxes cumulatives en cascade ;

b) les taxes générales sur les ventes – perçues au stade de la production ou de la fabrication, du gros ou du détail ;

c) les taxes sur la valeur ajoutée ;

d) les accises ;

e) les taxes perçues à l'importation et à l'exportation de biens ;

f) les impôts perçus sur l'utilisation de biens et sur l'autorisation d'utiliser des biens ou d'exercer certaines activités ;

g) les impôts sur l'extraction, le traitement ou la production de minéraux et autres produits.

52. Les cas douteux de délimitation entre ce groupe et le groupe 4000 (impôts sur le patrimoine) et le sous-groupe 6100 (autres impôts à la charge des entreprises) sont examinés au § 43, § 48 et § 75. Des postes résiduels (5300 et 5130) ont été prévus pour comptabiliser les recettes fiscales qui ne peuvent être ventilées respectivement entre les postes 5100 et 5200 et entre les postes 5110 et 5120 (voir § 28).

5100 – *Impôts sur la production, la vente, le transfert, la location et la livraison de biens et la prestation de services*

53. Ce sous-groupe comprend tous les impôts perçus sur les transactions afférentes à des biens ou services, en fonction de leurs caractéristiques propres (comme la valeur, le poids du tabac, le degré d'alcool, etc.), à la différence des impôts perçus au titre de l'utilisation ou de l'autorisation d'utiliser des biens ou d'exercer des activités, qui entrent dans le sous-groupe 5200.

5110 – *Impôts généraux sur les biens et services*

54. Ce sous-groupe comprend tous les impôts, autres que les droits à l'importation et à l'exportation (5123 et 5124), perçus sur la production, la location, le transfert, la livraison ou la vente d'une gamme de biens ou la prestation d'une gamme de services, qu'ils soient produits dans le pays ou importés, et quel que soit le stade de la production ou de la distribution aux quel ils sont perçus. Il couvre ainsi les taxes sur la valeur ajoutée, les taxes sur les ventes et les taxes de caractère cumulatif en cascade. On a ajouté aux recettes brutes de cette catégorie les recettes provenant de la compensation à la frontière de ces impôts lorsque les biens sont importés, et déduit les remboursements d'impôts effectués lorsque les marchandises sont exportées. Ces impôts sont ventilés en : taxes sur la valeur ajoutée (5111), impôts sur les ventes (5112), autres impôts généraux sur les biens et services (5113).

55. Certains cas se trouvent à la limite entre ce sous-groupe et celui des impôts sur des biens et services déterminés (5120) lorsque ces impôts sont perçus sur un grand nombre de biens, comme dans le cas de la « purchase tax » au Royaume-Uni (abrogée en 1973) et l'impôt japonais sur les biens marchands (abrogé en 1988). Conformément aux options nationales, la « purchase tax » britannique est classée impôt général (5112) et l'impôt japonais dans les accises (5121).

5111 – *Taxes sur la valeur ajoutée*

56. Sont classés dans ce sous-groupe tous les impôts généraux sur la consommation prélevés sur la valeur ajoutée, quels que soient le mode de déduction et les stades auxquels ils sont perçus. En pratique, tous les pays de l'OCDE où existe une taxe sur la valeur ajoutée autorisent normalement la déduction immédiate des taxes sur les achats par tous les redevables, à l'exception du consommateur final, et imposent la taxe à tous les stades. Dans certains pays, le poste peut inclure aussi certains impôts, comme les taxes sur les activités financières et les assurances, soit parce que les recettes correspondantes ne peuvent être dissociées de celles de la taxe sur la valeur ajoutée, soit parce qu'elles sont considérées comme faisant partie intégrante de la taxe sur la valeur ajoutée, même si les taxes similaires qui existent dans d'autres pays peuvent être classées autrement (par exemple, sous le poste 5126 comme impôts sur les services ou sous le poste 4400 comme impôts sur les transactions mobilières et immobilières).

5112 – *Impôts sur les ventes*

57. Sont classés ici tous les impôts perçus à un stade unique, que ce soit celui de la fabrication, de la production, du gros ou du détail.

5113 – *Autres impôts généraux sur les biens et services*

58. Ce sous-groupe comprend les impôts cumulatifs, connus également sous le nom d'impôt en cascade, qui sont perçus sans déduction de l'impôt sur les moyens de production chaque fois qu'une opération a lieu, ainsi que les impôts généraux sur la consommation lorsqu'il s'y ajoute des éléments qui les font assimiler à la taxe sur la valeur ajoutée, à la taxe sur les ventes ou à des taxes en cascade.

5120 – *Impôts sur des biens et des services déterminés*

59. Ce sous-groupe couvre les accises, les bénéfices engendrés et transférés par les monopoles fiscaux, et les droits de douane et à l'importation, ainsi que les taxes à l'exportation, les opérations de change, les biens d'équipement et les paris, et aussi les impôts spéciaux sur les services qui ne font pas partie d'un impôt général du sous-groupe 5110.

5121 – Accises

60. Les accises sont perçues sur des produits particuliers, ou sur une gamme limitée de produits, qui ne peuvent être classés sous le poste 5110 (impôts généraux), 5123 (droits à l'importation) ou 5124 (droits à l'exportation). Elles peuvent être perçues à un stade quelconque de la production ou de la distribution et sont calculées ordinairement par référence au poids, au degré ou au volume du produit, mais parfois aussi à sa valeur. Cette subdivision couvre ainsi les impôts spéciaux, qui frappent notamment le sucre, la betterave, les allumettes, les chocolats, et les impôts auxquels sont soumis à des taux divers certains produits, comme ceux perçus dans la plupart des pays sur les tabacs, boissons alcoolisées, hydrocarbures et autres sources d'énergie.

61. Les accises sont à distinguer de :

a) 5110 (impôts généraux) ; ce cas est examiné aux § 54 et § 55 ;

b) 5123 (droits à l'importation) ; lorsqu'un impôt perçu principalement sur des biens importés s'applique, ou s'appliquerait, aussi légalement à un bien comparable produit dans le pays, les recettes procurées par cet impôt seront classées avec les accises (5121) ;

ce principe s'applique même lorsqu'il n'y a pas de production locale, réelle ou potentielle, comparable (voir aussi § 65) ;

c) 5126 (impôts sur les services) ; le problème ici concerne les impôts sur l'électricité, le gaz et l'énergie ; ils sont tous considérés comme des impôts sur les biens et inclus dans le poste 5121.

5122 – *Bénéfices des monopoles fiscaux*

62. Ce sous-groupe couvre la fraction des bénéfices des monopoles fiscaux qui est transférée aux administrations publiques ou qui sert à financer des dépenses considérées comme dépenses publiques (voir § 19). Les montants sont comptabilisés lorsqu'ils sont transférés aux administrations publiques ou utilisés pour effectuer des dépenses considérées comme des dépenses publiques.

63. Les monopoles fiscaux reflètent l'exercice du pouvoir d'imposition de l'État par l'intermédiaire du monopole. Les monopoles fiscaux sont des entreprises publiques non financières, qui exercent dans la plupart des cas un monopole sur la production ou la distribution du tabac, des boissons alcoolisées, du sel, des allumettes, des cartes à jouer et des produits pétroliers ou agricoles (c'est-à-dire, sur le genre de produits qui peuvent être soumis, principalement ou accessoirement, aux accises du poste 5121), pour procurer des recettes publiques qui, dans d'autres pays, sont obtenues par le biais d'impôts frappant les transactions sur ces produits d'entreprises privées. Le monopole d'État peut être exercé au stade de la production, ou au stade de la distribution comme dans le cas des magasins de vente de boissons alcoolisées qui appartiennent à l'État et sont contrôlés par lui.

64. Les monopoles fiscaux sont différents des services publics, comme les chemins de fer, l'électricité, les postes et autres moyens de communication, qui peuvent avoir une position de monopole ou de quasi-monopole, mais dont l'objet principal est, normalement, de fournir des services essentiels et non pas de procurer des recettes à l'État. Les transferts à l'administration de ces autres entreprises publiques sont considérés comme des recettes non fiscales. La notion traditionnelle de monopole fiscal n'a pas été élargie pour inclure les loteries nationales, dont les bénéfices sont donc considérés comme des recettes non fiscales. On distingue les bénéfices des monopoles fiscaux des bénéfices des monopoles d'exportation et d'importation (5127), qui sont transférés des offices de commercialisation ou d'autres entreprises s'occupant du commerce international.

5123 – *Droits de douane et autres droits à l'importation*

65. Figurent ici les taxes, droits de timbre et surtaxes qui, selon la loi sont perçus exclusivement sur des produits importés. Sont aussi inclus dans ce poste les droits perçus sur l'importation de denrées agricoles dans les pays Membres de l'Union Européenne et les montants acquittés par certains de ces pays en vertu du Système de Montants Compensatoires[17]. À partir de 1998 les droits de douane collectés par les États membres de l'Union européenne pour le compte de l'Union européenne ne sont plus reportés sous cette rubrique dans les tableaux par pays (Partie III de ce rapport). Sont exclues ici les taxes perçues sur les importations au titre d'un impôt général sur les biens et les services ou d'une accise applicable aussi bien aux produits importés qu'aux produits fabriqués dans le pays.

5124 – *Taxes à l'exportation*

66. Pendant les années 70, les droits à l'exportation étaient perçus normalement en Australie, au Canada et au Portugal, et ils étaient utilisés en Finlande à des fins conjoncturelles. Certains pays Membres de l'Union Européenne acquittent, dans le cadre du système des montants compensatoires, une taxe sur les exportations (voir la note 18 du § 65). Lorsque ces montants sont identifiables, ils sont inclus dans ce poste. Ce dernier ne comprend pas les remboursements effectués au titre d'impôts généraux sur la consommation d'accises ou de droits de douane sur des biens exportés, qui doivent être déduits des recettes brutes comptabilisées, selon le cas, sous le poste 5110, 5121 ou 5123.

5125 – *Impôts sur les biens d'équipement*

67. Ce sous-groupe comprend les impôts perçus sur les biens d'équipement, comme les machines. Ils peuvent exister depuis un certain nombre d'années ou avoir un caractère temporaire et être prélevés à des fins conjoncturelles. Ne sont pas inclus les impôts sur les « inputs » industriels qui frappent aussi les consommateurs (comme l'impôt suédois sur l'énergie qui est classé sous le poste 5121).

5126 – *Impôts sur des services déterminés*

68. Sous ce poste figurent tous les impôts calculés sur la rémunération de services spécifiques, comme les taxes sur les primes d'assurance, les taxes sur les services bancaires, sur les jeux et paris (par exemple : courses de chevaux, pronostics de football, billets de loterie nationale), les transports, les spectacles, les restaurants et la publicité. Les impôts prélevés sur le revenu brut des sociétés prestataires d'un service (exemple : primes d'assurance brutes, mises de jeux encaissées par les sociétés) sont classés sous ce poste. Les recettes fiscales provenant des prélèvements sur les banques et des contributions aux mécanismes de garantie des dépôts et de stabilité financière sont provisoirement classés ici pour l'édition 2012. La classification détaillée est présentée dans le paragraphe 105.

69. Ne figurent pas sous ce poste :

a) les impôts sur les services qui font partie d'un impôt général sur les biens et services et sont classés sous le poste 5110 ;

b) les taxes sur l'électricité, le gaz et l'énergie (classées sous le poste 5121 en tant qu'accises) ;

c) les taxes sur les gains personnels tirés de jeux et paris (qui sont classées sous le poste 1120, en tant qu'impôts sur les gains en capital des personnes physiques et entreprises individuelles) et les montants forfaitaires perçus sur le transfert de loteries privées ou sur l'autorisation de créer des loteries (5200)[18] ;

d) les impôts sur les chèques et sur l'émission, le transfert ou le remboursement de valeurs mobilières, (qui sont classés sous le poste 4400, en tant qu'impôts sur les transactions mobilières et immobilières).

5127 – *Autres impôts sur les transactions et les échanges internationaux*

70. Ce sous-groupe couvre les recettes perçues par l'État sur l'achat et la vente de monnaies étrangères à des taux différents. Lorsque l'État exerce le privilège exclusif dont il dispose pour s'assurer une marge entre le prix d'achat et le prix de vente de devises qui ne se réduit pas à la simple couverture des frais administratifs, ce bénéfice représente un prélèvement obligatoire imposé dans des proportions indéterminées à l'acheteur et au vendeur des monnaies étrangères. Il équivaut normalement au droit à l'importation et au

droit à l'exportation perçus dans un système de taux de change unique, ou à une taxe sur la vente ou l'achat de monnaies étrangères. Comme les bénéfices des monopoles fiscaux et des monopoles d'importation ou d'exportation transférés à l'État, il représente l'exercice d'un monopole aux fins d'imposition et est inclus dans les recettes fiscales.

71. Ce sous-groupe comprend aussi les bénéfices des monopoles d'exportation ou d'importation, bien qu'il n'en existe pas dans les pays de l'OCDE, les impôts sur l'achat ou la vente de devises et tous les autres impôts perçus spécifiquement sur les opérations ou les échanges internationaux.

5128 – *Autres impôts sur des biens et services déterminés*

72. Cette rubrique comprend les impôts sur l'extraction de minéraux, combustibles fossiles et autres ressources non renouvelables provenant de gisements privés ou détenus par une autre administration, ainsi que toute autre recette non ventilable provenant des impôts sur des biens et services déterminés. Les impôts sur l'extraction de ressources non renouvelables correspondent généralement à un montant forfaitaire par unité de qualité ou de poids, mais peuvent être calculés ad valorem. Les impôts sont comptabilisés à la date d'extraction des ressources. Les versements tirés de l'extraction de ressources non renouvelables issues de gisements appartenant à l'administration publique qui perçoit ces versements sont classés en tant que loyers.

5200 – *Impôts sur l'utilisation des biens ou l'autorisation d'utiliser des biens ou d'exercer des activités*

73. Ce sous-groupe comprend les taxes prélevées en raison de l'utilisation de biens, indépendamment des impôts frappant les biens eux-mêmes. Contrairement à ceux-ci (5100), les impôts du sous-groupe 5200 ne sont pas calculés d'après la valeur des biens, mais ordinairement d'après un montant forfaitaire. Sont aussi couverts les impôts perçus au titre du droit d'utiliser des biens ou d'exercer des activités, comme les taxes sur la pollution qui ne reposent pas sur la valeur de biens déterminés. Il est parfois difficile de distinguer les taxes d'utilisation et droits de licence obligatoires, qui sont considérés comme des impôts, de ceux qui ne le sont pas parce qu'ils sont assimilés à des recettes non fiscales ; les critères appliqués sont ceux indiqués aux § 9 et § 10.

74. Bien que le sous-groupe se réfère à l'utilisation des biens, le fait générateur de l'impôt peut être aussi bien l'enregistrement de la propriété, de sorte que les impôts relevant de ce sous-groupe peuvent viser la possession d'animaux ou de biens plutôt que leur utilisation (par exemple, les chevaux de course, les chiens, les véhicules à moteur) et même s'appliquer à des biens inutilisables (comme les véhicules à moteur ou les fusils inutilisables).

75. Les cas limites concernent :

a) les impôts sur l'autorisation d'exercer des activités commerciales, qui sont classés selon les règles exposées au § 78 lorsqu'ils ont une assiette mixte associant le revenu, les salaires versés ou le chiffre d'affaires ;

b) les impôts sur la propriété ou l'utilisation de la propriété de biens visés par les postes 4100, 4200 et 4600. Le poste 4100 ne vise que les impôts sur la propriété ou la location de biens immobiliers et, contrairement aux impôts du sous-groupe 5200, ils sont fonction de la valeur du bien. Les impôts sur l'actif net et les impôts sur les biens meubles des sous-groupes 4200 et 4600 visent la propriété et non pas l'utilisation des biens, couvrent un groupe d'actifs et non pas de biens particuliers et sont aussi fonction de la valeur du bien.

5210 – Impôts périodiques sur l'utilisation de biens ou sur l'autorisation d'utiliser des biens ou d'exercer certaines activités

76. Ces impôts ont pour principale caractéristique d'être perçus à intervalles réguliers et de représenter ordinairement des montants forfaitaires. Le poste le plus important, du point de vue du volume des recettes, est constitué par les permis de circulation des véhicules. Ce sous-groupe inclut aussi les taxes perçues lors de la délivrance de permis de chasse, de tir ou de pêche, ou l'autorisation de vendre certains produits, ainsi que les taxes sur la possession de chiens et sur la prestation de certains services à condition qu'elles répondent aux critères définis aux § 9 et § 10. Les subdivisions du poste 5210 comprennent les taxes d'utilisation de véhicules à moteur à la charge des ménages (5211) et à la charge d'autres agents (5212)[19]. Le poste 5213 couvre les plaques de chiens et les taxes perçues pour l'autorisation d'exercer certaines activités, comme la vente de viande et d'alcool, lorsque les prélèvements ont un caractère périodique. Il couvre aussi les permis généraux de chasse, de port d'armes et de pêche, lorsque le droit d'exercer ces activités n'est pas accordé au titre d'une opération commerciale normale (par exemple, la délivrance du permis ne comporte pas le droit d'utiliser une parcelle déterminée de terrain appartenant à l'État).

5220 – Impôts non périodiques sur l'utilisation de biens ou sur l'autorisation d'utiliser des biens ou d'exercer certaines activités

77. Cette rubrique recouvre les taxes non périodiques perçues sur l'utilisation de biens ou sur l'autorisation d'utiliser des biens ou d'exercer certaines activités et celles qui sont prélevées chaque fois que des biens sont utilisés.

- Les impôts prélevés sur l'émission ou le rejet dans l'environnement de gaz toxiques, liquides nocifs ou autres substances dangereuses figurent ici. Les paiements au titre des permis d'émission négociables délivrés par les administrations publiques dans le cadre des dispositifs de plafonnement et d'échange doivent également être comptabilisés sous cette rubrique au moment où les émissions sont produites. Les permis délivrés gratuitement par les administrations ne donnent lieu à aucun enregistrement comptable de recettes.
- La comptabilisation en droits constatés implique un éventuel délai entre la date à laquelle l'administration perçoit le règlement des permis et la date à laquelle les émissions sont produites. Dans les comptes nationaux, ce délai se traduit pour l'administration par un engagement financier sur la période.
- Il convient d'exclure les paiements effectués au titre de la collecte et de l'élimination de déchets ou de substances nocives par les autorités publiques, étant donné qu'il s'agit là de vente de services aux entreprises.

78. D'autres impôts non périodiques qui relèvent du poste 5200 sont aussi classés dans cette rubrique. Ainsi figurent les paiements uniques effectués au titre de l'autorisation de vendre des boissons alcoolisées ou des tabacs ou d'ouvrir des guichets de « paris mutuels », à condition qu'ils répondent aux critères définis aux § 9 et § 10.

6000 – Autres impôts

79. Ce groupe couvre les impôts prélevés sur une ou plusieurs bases différentes de celles qui sont indiquées pour les groupes 1000, 3000, 4000 et 5000, ou sur des bases dont aucune ne pourrait être considérée comme étant essentiellement la même que l'une de celles

afférentes à ces groupes. Quant aux impôts perçus sur plusieurs bases différentes, il convient si possible d'évaluer les recettes liées à chaque base de perception (par exemple, pour l'impôt allemand 'Gewerbesteuer') et d'inclure les montants séparés dans le groupe approprié. S'il est impossible d'évaluer les montants séparés, mais si l'on sait que la plus grande partie des recettes provient de l'impôt perçu sur une même base, la totalité des recettes sont classées en fonction de cette base. Si aucune de ces procédures ne peut être appliquée, les impôts sont classés dans le présent groupe. Les sous-groupes peuvent comprendre également les recettes provenant d'impôts que les administrations ne sont pas en mesure d'identifier ou d'isoler (voir § 28). Figurent aussi dans ce groupe les recettes provenant d'amendes et de pénalités acquittées pour infraction aux réglementations fiscales, mais qui ne peuvent être identifiées comme se rapportant à une catégorie particulière d'impôts (voir § 15). Ce poste est divisé en impôts exclusivement ou principalement à la charge des entreprises (6100) et en impôts à la charge d'autres contribuables (6200).

E. Conciliation avec les comptes nationaux

80. Cette section des tableaux permet de concilier les calculs des recettes fiscales totales de l'OCDE et l'ensemble des impôts et cotisations sociales versés aux administrations publiques qui sont enregistrés dans les comptes nationaux par pays. Lorsque le pays en question est membre de l'Union européenne (UE) la comparaison est effectuée entre les calculs des recettes fiscales totales des pays de l'OCDE et la somme des recettes fiscales et cotisations de sécurité sociale perçues par les administrations publiques et les institutions des secteurs de l'Union européenne des comptes nationaux.

F. Poste pour mémoire relatif au financement des prestations de sécurité sociale

81. Le rapport entre les impôts et les cotisations de sécurité sociale étant variable, et en raison des problèmes évoqués aux § 35 et § 41, on a réuni dans un poste pour mémoire l'ensemble des versements affectés à des prestations du type sécurité sociale, en dehors des versements volontaires au secteur privé. Les données sont présentées de la façon suivante (voir Partie III.B)

a) impôts du groupe 2000 ;

b) impôts affectés aux prestations de sécurité sociale ;

c) cotisations volontaires à l'administration ;

d) cotisations obligatoires au secteur privé.

Les § 35 et § 41 ci-dessus contiennent des directives pour la ventilation entre ces quatre catégories

G. Poste pour mémoire relatif aux impôts identifiables payés par les administrations

82. Les impôts effectivement payés par les administrations elles-mêmes et que l'on peut identifier sont indiqués dans un poste pour mémoire et classés suivant les grandes rubriques de la classification des impôts de l'OCDE. Dans la très grande majorité des pays, seuls peuvent être identifiées en l'occurrence les cotisations de sécurité sociale et les impôts sur les salaires, mais il s'agit là en général des impôts les plus importants acquittés par les administrations (voir Partie III.C de cette publication).

H. Rapport de la classification des impôts de l'OCDE avec les systèmes nationaux de comptabilité nationale

83. Un système de comptabilité nationale (SCN) tend à fournir un cadre cohérent pour enregistrer et présenter les principaux flux relatifs à la production, à la consommation, à l'accumulation et aux transactions extérieures d'une zone économique donnée, d'ordinaire un pays ou une grande région d'un pays. Les recettes publiques sont une partie importante des transactions enregistrées dans le SCN. La version finale du SCN 2008 a été diffusée conjointement par cinq organisations internationales : les Nations Unies, le Fonds Monétaire International, l'Union européenne, l'Organisation de Coopération et de Développement Économiques et la Banque Mondiale, en août 2009. Le *Système* est un ensemble complet, cohérent et souple de comptes macro-économiques. Il est élaboré pour être utilisé dans les pays à économie de marché quel que soit leur niveau de développement économique ainsi que dans les pays en transition vers l'économie de marché. De larges extraits du cadre théorique ainsi que les définitions des divers secteurs de l'économie du SCN figurent dans la classification des impôts de l'OCDE.

84. Il existe cependant un certain nombre de différences entre la classification des impôts de l'OCDE et les concepts du SCN qui sont indiqués ci-dessous. Ils proviennent du fait que l'objectif de cette classification est de permettre une ventilation aussi large que possible des données statistiques pour ce que les administrations fiscales conviennent de considérer de manière générale comme des impôts.

a) l'OCDE inclut les cotisations de sécurité sociale dans les recettes fiscales totales (§ 7 et § 8 ci-dessus) ;

b) les avis diffèrent sur la question de savoir s'il y a lieu de classer certains prélèvements et redevances dans les impôts (§ 9 et §10 ci-dessus) ;

c) l'OCDE exclut les impôts imputés ou les subventions résultant d'opérations de taux de change officiels multiples ;

d) il existe des différences dans le traitement des crédits d'impôt récupérables.

85. Comme on l'a noté aux § 1 et § 2, les groupes 1000 à 6000 de la classification de l'OCDE comprennent tous les versements sans contrepartie aux administrations publiques, à l'exclusion des prêts obligatoires et des amendes. On peut obtenir le total de ces versements sans contrepartie, amendes incluses, mais prêts obligatoires exclus, en additionnant les postes suivants du SCN 2008 :

- impôts du type valeur ajoutée (D.211) ;
- droits et taxes sur les importations à l'exclusion de la TVA (D.212) ;
- droits sur les exportations (D.213) ;
- taxes sur les produits, à l'exclusion de la TVA, des droits sur les importations et les exportations (D.214) ;
- autres impôts sur la production (D.29) ;
- impôts sur le revenu (D.51) ;
- autres impôts périodiques (D.59) ;
- cotisations de sécurité sociale (D.61) à l'exclusion des cotisations volontaires ;
- impôts sur le capital (D.91).

I. La classification des impôts de l'OCDE et le système du Fonds monétaire international (GFS)

86. Le champ d'application et l'évaluation des recettes fiscales dans le système GFS et dans le système SCN 2008 sont très proches. Par conséquent, les différences entre la classification de l'OCDE et celle du SCN 2008 (voir § 84 ci-dessus) sont également valables pour le GFS. En outre, le Fonds monétaire international subdivise le groupe 5000 de la classification de l'OCDE en une section iv (Taxes intérieures sur les biens et services) et une section v (Taxes sur les transactions et les échanges internationaux). Cela tient à ce que le rendement de ces dernières taxes représente généralement des sommes infimes dans les pays de l'OCDE ce qui n'est pas le cas dans beaucoup de pays non membres.

J. Comparaison de la classification des impôts de l'OCDE et des autres classifications internationales des recettes publiques

87. Le tableau ci-dessous décrit point par point la comparaison entre la classification des impôts de l'OCDE et les classifications suivantes :

i) Système des comptes nationaux (SCN 2008) ;

ii) Système européen des comptes (SEC 2010) ;

iii) Manuel de statistiques des finances publiques du Fonds monétaire international (MSFP 2014).

88. Ces comparaisons correspondent à celles qui devraient s'appliquer dans la majorité des cas. Toutefois, en pratique il faut faire preuve d'une certaine souplesse dans leur application. En effet, dans certains cas, les pays peuvent adopter des méthodes diverses de classification des recettes dans les comptes nationaux.

K. Répartition des recettes fiscales par sous-secteurs d'administration publique

89. La classification de l'OCDE appelle une ventilation des recettes fiscales par sous-secteurs d'administration. On trouvera ci-après la définition de chaque sous-secteur et les critères à utiliser pour répartir entre eux les recettes fiscales. Ces définitions et critères suivent les orientations qui figurent dans le SCN 2008 et le MSFP 2014.

Sous-secteurs des administrations publiques à identifier

a) Administration centrale

90. Le sous-secteur des administrations centrales groupe tous les ministères, bureaux, établissements et autres organismes qui sont des services ou des moyens d'action du pouvoir central et dont la compétence s'étend à la totalité du territoire, à l'exception de l'administration des caisses de sécurité sociale. L'administration centrale a donc le pouvoir de prélever des impôts sur toutes les unités résidentes et non résidentes exerçant des activités économiques à l'intérieur du pays.

b) Administration d'un État fédéré, d'une province ou d'une région

91. Ce sous-secteur comprend les unités administratives intermédiaires et inclut toutes les unités administratives dont la compétence s'exerce indépendamment de l'Administration centrale sur une partie du territoire englobant un certain nombre de petites localités, à l'exception des caisses de sécurité sociale. Dans les pays unitaires, les

	Classification de l'OCDE	SCN 2008	SEC 2010	MSFP 2014
1000	Impôts sur le revenu, les bénéfices et les gains en capital			
	1100 Personnes physiques			
	1110 Sur le revenu et les bénéfices	D51-8.61a	D51A	1111
	1120 Sur les gains en capital	D51-8.61c, d	D51C, D	1111
	1200 Sociétés			
	1210 Sur le revenu et les bénéfices	D51-8.61b	D51B	1112
	1220 Sur les gains en capital	D51-8.61c	D51C	1112
	1300 Non ventilables entre les rubriques 1100 et 1200			1113
2000	Cotisations de sécurité sociale			
	2100 Salariés	D613-8.85	D613	1211
	2200 Employeurs	D611-8.83	D612	1212
	2300 À la charge des travailleurs indépendants ou des personnes sans occupation	D613-8.85	D613	1213
	2400 Non ventilables entre les rubriques 2100, 2200 et 2300			1214
3000	Impôts sur les salaires et la main-d'œuvre	D29-7.97a	D29C	112
4000	Impôts sur le patrimoine			
	4100 Impôts périodiques sur la propriété immobilière			
	4110 Ménages	D59-8.63a	D59A	1131
	4120 Autres agents	D29-7.97b	D29A	1131
	4200 Impôts périodiques sur l'actif net			
	4210 Personnes physiques	D59-8.63b	D59A	1132
	4220 Sociétés	D59-8.63b	D59A	1132
	4300 Impôts sur les mutations par décès, les successions et les donations			
	4310 Impôts sur les mutations par décès et les successions	D91-10.207b	D91A	1133
	4320 Impôts sur les donations	D91-10.207b	D91A	1133
	4400 Impôts sur les transactions mobilières et immobilières	D59-7.96d ; D29-7.97e	D214B, C	114114 ; 1161
	4500 Autres impôts non périodiques sur le patrimoine	D91-10.207a	D91B	1135
	4600 Autres impôts périodiques sur le patrimoine	D59-8.63c	D59A	1136
5000	Impôts sur les biens et services			
	5100 Impôts sur les biens et services			
	5110 Impôts généraux sur les biens et services			
	5111 Taxes sur la valeur ajoutée	D211-7.89	D211 ; D29G	11411
	5112 Impôts sur les ventes	D2122-7.94a ; D214-7.96a	D21224 ; D214I	11412
	5113 Autres impôts généraux sur les biens et services	D214-7.96a	D214I	11413
	5120 Impôts sur des biens et services déterminés			
	5121 Accises	D2122-7.94b ; D214-7.96b	D21223 ; D214A, B, D	1142
	5122 Bénéfices des monopoles fiscaux	D214-7.96e	D214J	1143
	5123 Droits de douane et autres droits à l'importation	D2121-7.93	D2121 ; D21221, 2	1151
	5124 Taxes à l'exportation	D213-7.95a	D214K	1152-4
	5125 Impôts sur les biens d'équipements			
	5126 Impôts sur les services déterminés	D2122-7.94c ; D214-7.96c	D21225 ; D214E, F, G ; D29F	1144 ; 1156
	5127 Autres impôts sur les transactions et les échanges internationaux	D2122-7.94d D29-7.95b D29-7.97g D59-8.64d	D21226 ; D29D ; D59E	1153 ; 1155-6
	5128 Autres impôts sur des et services déterminés			1146
	5130 Non ventilable entre les rubriques 5110 et 5120			
	5200 Impôts sur l'utilisation des biens ou l'autorisation d'utiliser des biens ou d'exercer des activités			
	5210 Impôts périodiques sur l'utilisation des biens ou l'autorisation d'utiliser des biens ou d'exercer des activités			
	5211 À la charge des ménages au titre de véhicules à moteurs	D59-8.64c	D59D	11451
	5212 À la charge d'autres agents au titre de véhicules à moteurs	D29-7.97d	D214D ; D29B	11451
	5213 Autres impôts périodiques sur l'utilisation des biens ou l'autorisation d'utiliser des biens ou d'exercer des activités	D29-7.97c, d, f D59-8.64c	D29B, E, F ; D59D	11452
	5220 Impôts non périodiques			11452
	5300 Non ventilable entre les rubriques 5100 et 5200			
6000	Autres impôts			
	6100 À la charge exclusive des entreprises			1161
	6200 À la charge d'autres agents que les entreprises ou non identifiables	D59-8.64a, b	D59B, C	1162

administrations régionales peuvent être considérées comme dotées d'une existence distincte lorsqu'elles disposent d'une autonomie substantielle pour percevoir une part importante de leurs recettes de sources placées sous leur contrôle et lorsque leurs agents ne sont pas soumis à un contrôle administratif externe dans l'exercice des activités de l'unité.

92. Actuellement, les pays à structure fédérale représentent la majorité des cas dans lesquels les recettes attribuées aux unités administratives intermédiaires sont identifiées séparément. L'Espagne est le seul pays à structure unitaire qui se trouve dans cette situation. Dans les autres pays unitaires, les recettes des administrations régionales sont incluses dans celles des administrations locales.

c) Collectivités locales

93. Ce sous-secteur comprend toutes les autres unités administratives exerçant une compétence indépendante sur une partie du territoire d'un pays, à l'exception des administrations des caisses de sécurité sociale. Il englobe les diverses circonscriptions urbaines et/ou rurales (par exemple les collectivités locales, les municipalités, les villes, les bourgs ou les districts).

d) Caisses de sécurité sociale

94. Les caisses de sécurité sociale constituent un sous-secteur distinct des administrations publiques. Le sous-secteur de la sécurité sociale est défini dans le SCN de 2008 par les extraits suivants des paragraphes 4.124 à 4.126 et 4.147 :

> « Les systèmes de sécurité sociale sont des systèmes d'assurance sociale qui couvrent l'ensemble de la collectivité ou d'importants sous-ensembles de la collectivité : ces systèmes sont imposés et contrôlés par les administrations publiques. Ces systèmes couvrent une grande variété de programmes qui consistent à fournir des prestations, en espèces ou en nature, au titre des circonstances suivantes : vieillesse, invalidité ou décès, survie, maladie et maternité, accident du travail, chômage, allocations familiales, soins de santé etc. Il n'existe pas nécessairement de lien direct entre le montant de la cotisation versée par un particulier et les prestations qu'il est susceptible de recevoir » (paragraphe 4.124).
>
> « Lorsque les systèmes de sécurité sociale ont une organisation distincte des autres activités des administrations publiques et détiennent des actifs et des engagements indépendamment de ces dernières et effectuent des opérations financières pour leur propre compte, ils peuvent être considérés comme des unités institutionnelles désignées sous le nom de caisses de sécurité sociale » (paragraphe 4.125).
>
> « Il est possible de faire varier de façon discrétionnaire les montants prélevés et versés sous forme de cotisations de sécurité sociale et de prestations afin d'atteindre des objectifs de politique publique qui n'ont pas de lien direct avec la notion de sécurité sociale en tant que système visant à fournir des prestations à des membres de la collectivité. Ainsi, ces cotisations ou prestations peuvent être augmentées ou diminuées afin d'influer sur le niveau de la demande globale au sein de l'économie. Néanmoins, tant que ces caisses restent indépendantes, elles doivent être traitées comme des unités institutionnelles distinctes dans le SCN ». (paragraphe 4.126).
>
> « Le sous-secteur des administrations de sécurité sociale comprend les administrations de sécurité sociale opérant à tous les niveaux des administrations publiques. Les administrations de sécurité sociale sont des systèmes couvrant l'ensemble de la

collectivité ou d'importants sous-ensembles de la collectivité qui sont rendus obligatoires et contrôlés par des administrations publiques » (paragraphe 4.147).

95. Cette définition des administrations de sécurité sociale est suivie dans la classification de l'OCDE à l'exception des régimes suivants :

- Les régimes imposés par l'administration et exploités par des organismes extérieurs au secteur des administrations publiques, tel qu'il est défini au § 3 de ce manuel et
- Les régimes qui perçoivent des cotisations volontaires.

Autorités supranationales

96. Ce sous-secteur s'applique aux activités de collecte de recettes publiques des autorités supranationales sur le territoire d'un pays. En pratique, le seul cas d'autorité supranationale de la zone de l'OCDE est celui des institutions de l'Union européenne (UE). Depuis 1998, les autorités supranationales ne figurent plus dans les Statistiques des recettes publiques dans un souci de cohérence avec la définition du SCN des administrations publiques qui les exclut. Par exemple, les impôts sur le revenu et des contributions de sécurité sociale rassemblées par des Institutions européennes et payé par les fonctionnaires européens qui sont résidents de pays membres de l'Union européenne ne devraient pas être inclus. Toutefois, les prélèvements spécifiques versés par les États membres à l'Union européenne continuent à être inclus dans les recettes fiscales totales et ils sont indiqués sous cette rubrique.

Critères à utiliser pour l'attribution des recettes fiscales

97. Lorsqu'une administration collecte l'impôt et le reverse, en totalité ou en partie, à d'autres administrations, il est nécessaire de déterminer si ces recettes doivent être considérées comme étant celles de l'administration qui les perçoit et les répartit entre d'autres administrations ou celles des administrations bénéficiaires auxquelles l'administration qui les a perçues les a transférées en simple qualité d'agent. Les critères à utiliser dans l'attribution des recettes sont indiqués aux paragraphes 98 à 101, qui reprennent les paragraphes 3.70 à 3.73 du SCN 2008.

98. En général, un impôt est attribué à l'Unité administrative qui

a) exerce le pouvoir de percevoir l'impôt (soit en tant que détenteur de ce pouvoir soit par délégation de l'autorité qui le détient),

b) dispose du pouvoir discrétionnaire final de fixer et de faire varier le taux de l'impôt.

99. Lorsqu'une somme est collectée par une administration au profit d'une autre administration et en son nom, et que cette dernière a le pouvoir de percevoir l'impôt et de fixer et de faire varier son taux, la première intervient comme agent pour le compte de la dernière et l'impôt est réaffecté. Toute somme retenue par l'administration collectrice au titre des frais de recouvrement doit être considérée comme la rémunération d'un service rendu. Toute autre somme conservée par l'administration collectrice, notamment dans le cadre d'un accord de partage d'impôt, doit être considérée comme une subvention courante. Si l'administration collectrice s'est vu déléguer le pouvoir de fixer et de faire varier le taux, le montant recouvré doit être considéré comme une recette fiscale de cette administration.

100. Lorsque des administrations différentes fixent conjointement et sur un pied d'égalité la répartition du produit de cet impôt, aucune administration ne disposant d'un pouvoir

prépondérant en dernier ressort, les recettes fiscales sont attribuées à chaque administration en fonction de sa part respective du produit de l'impôt. Si un accord permet à une unité administrative d'exercer un pouvoir prépondérant en dernier ressort, la totalité des recettes fiscales est attribuée à cette unité.

101. Dans certains cas aussi, un impôt est perçu dans le cadre des compétences d'une administration qui résulte de la constitution ou d'autres dispositions mais d'autres administrations fixent individuellement le taux d'imposition sur leurs territoires. Le produit de l'impôt généré sur les territoires respectifs de chaque administration est attribué à l'administration en question comme constituant ses recettes fiscales.

Versements effectués par les États membres de l'Union européenne

102. Les versements effectués par les États membres de l'Union européenne prennent la forme :

- Ressources TVA, et
- Prélèvements spécifiques qui comprennent :
  - *a)* les droits de douane et les prélèvements agricoles (5123),
  - *b)* les montants compensatoires monétaires bruts (5123 si relatifs aux importations et 5124 si relatifs aux exportations), et
  - *c)* les prélèvements de la CECA, les cotisations sucre et les taxes de co-responsabilité sur le lait (5128).

103. Les droits de douane collectés par les États membres pour le compte de l'Union européenne sont comptabilisés :

- sur une base qui ne tient pas compte des droits d'encaissement,
- en utilisant des chiffres corrigés de manière à exprimer les droits sur la base de la « destination finale » et non du « pays de première entrée » lorsque de telles corrections sont possibles. Ces corrections concernent en particulier les droits prélevés dans des ports (maritimes) importants. Bien que les droits de l'UE soient prélevés par les autorités du pays de première entrée, ces droits doivent être dans la mesure du possible déduits des recettes du pays qui les recouvre et inclus dans les recettes du pays de destination finale.

104. Ces droits de l'UE sont le plus clairement conformes au critère d'attribution décrit au § 96 ci-dessus. En conséquence, à partir de 1998, ces montants sont mentionnés dans une note de bas de page à titre de rubrique « Pour mémoire » dans les tableaux des États membres de l'UE (partie III du Rapport) et ne figurent plus sous la rubrique 5123. Toutefois, ces montants sont inclus dans les grands totaux des recettes fiscales à la ligne supérieure pour toutes les années indiquées dans les tableaux.

105. Les ressources TVA qui sont déterminées par l'application d'un taux ne pouvant dépasser 1 % d'une assiette précisée dans la 6e Directive des Communautés, constituent un cas particulier[20]. Elles ont en effet certaines caractéristiques d'une subvention (elles ne proviennent pas d'une source clairement identifiable de fonds effectivement collectés à cet effet) et certaines autres d'un impôt (le montant de la subvention est fixé par le sous-secteur d'administration bénéficiaire). Dans cette publication, ces ressources ne figurent pas comme un impôt de l'Union européenne (mais comme un impôt des États membres de l'Union) bien que les montants en question soient indiqués en note de bas de page dans la partie IV.

L. Classification provisoire des recettes provenant des prélèvements sur les banques et des contributions aux mécanismes de garantie des dépôts et de stabilité financière

106. L'OCDE a provisoirement adopté, depuis l'édition 2012 de ses *Statistiques des recettes publiques*, le principe suivant concernant l'enregistrement comptable des recettes issues des prélèvements sur les banques ainsi que des redevances acquittées au titre de la garantie des dépôts et de la stabilité financière. Il est recommandé que les montants concernés soient comptabilisés à la rubrique 5126.

- Les redevances de stabilité, les prélèvements sur les banques et les contributions à la garantie des dépôts, qu'il est obligatoire d'acquitter, doivent généralement être traitées comme des recettes fiscales lorsque les versements sont effectués au profit de l'administration publique et affectés au budget consolidé ou général des administrations de sorte que les pouvoirs publics soient libres d'utiliser les fonds sans délai aux fins qu'ils jugent opportunes. Ce principe s'appliquerait indépendamment du fait que l'administration promette ou non d'effectuer des versements pour garantir les dépôts des clients des établissements bancaires si la situation l'exigeait à l'avenir.
- Si les paiements obligatoires sont effectués au profit de l'administration publique et imputés à des budgets dont les ressources doivent être entièrement réaffectées au secteur de l'économie qui englobe les entreprises assujetties à ces paiements, ceux-ci seront toujours traités, en règle générale, comme des recettes fiscales étant donné que les fonds seraient disponibles pour l'administration et réduiraient son déficit budgétaire, que la redevance est sans contrepartie pour les entités individuelles et que les montants collectés pourraient être dissociés de tout versement en faveur des déposants ou de toute dépense visant à soutenir plus largement le secteur financier.
- Les contributions aux mécanismes traditionnels de moindre envergure destinés à garantir les dépôts de détail, contributions dont le montant est aligné sur le coût de la garantie, doivent être classées en tant que redevances pour services rendus.
- Tout versement au titre de la réalisation par une administration des actifs d'un établissement en faillite ou du recouvrement par cette administration d'une créance prioritaire sur les actifs de l'établissement en cours de liquidation, effectué en vue de financer l'indemnisation des clients ayant perdu leurs dépôts, serait traité comme une redevance par opposition aux recettes fiscales.
- Les contributions obligatoires aux fonds administrés en-dehors du secteur public et aux organismes non étatiques bénéficiant du soutien des institutions collectrices de dépôts ainsi que toutes les contributions aux mécanismes volontaires ne doivent pas être traitées comme des recettes fiscales.

Notes

1. Toutes les références au SCN concernent l'édition de 2008.
2. Se reporter à la section J de ce manuel pour l'examen de cette notion.
3. Il est en général possible d'identifier les montants des cotisations de sécurité sociale et les impôts sur les salaires, mais pas les autres impôts payés par les administrations.
4. En revanche si un ou plusieurs pays considèrent comme un impôt un droit que la plupart des pays font entrer dans les recettes non fiscales ou qui procure des recettes substantielles, les montants ainsi perçus figureront dans une note de renvoi à la fin des tableaux par pays correspondants, même s'ils ne sont pas inclus dans le total des recettes fiscales.

5. Les appellations peuvent cependant être souvent trompeuses. Ainsi, une redevance de passeport sera normalement considérée comme une recette non fiscale, alors qu'un prélèvement additionnel sur les passeports (comme c'est le cas au Portugal), qui a pour but de procurer un montant substantiel de recettes eu égard au coût de délivrance du passeport, sera considéré comme un impôt du sous-groupe 5200.
6. La distinction prévue par le SCN 1993 est difficile à opérer dans la pratique.
7. On trouvera des précisions sur cette distinction dans l'étude spéciale intitulée « L'information sur les recettes fiscales : problèmes actuels », de l'édition de 2001 des *Statistiques des recettes publiques*.
8. On utilise parfois les expressions « non remboursable » et « remboursable » mais il peut paraître illogique de parler de « remboursement » lorsque rien n'a été versé.
9. Toutefois, dans les systèmes d'imputation de l'impôt sur les sociétés, les crédits d'impôts récupérables sont traités différemment (§ 32-34).
10. Il ne s'agit pas d'une véritable dépense fiscale au sens strict. De telles dépenses fiscales supposent que l'on identifie un système fiscal de référence pour chaque pays ou, de préférence, une norme internationale commune. En pratique, il n'a pas été possible de parvenir à un accord sur une norme internationale commune.
11. Sauf s'ils sont calculés sur le bénéfice résultant de la vente, auquel cas ils seraient classés parmi les impôts sur les gains en capital dans le sous-groupe 1120 ou 1220.
12. Dans certains pays, la même législation est applicable aux personnes physiques et aux entreprises dans le cas d'impôts sur le revenu particuliers. Cependant, les recettes procurées par ces impôts peuvent, en général, être ventilées et figurent donc dans les deux sous-groupes appropriés.
13. Ainsi, « celles qui sont suffisamment autonomes et indépendantes pour que leur fonctionnement soit comparable à celui d'une société… (y compris) la tenue de comptes complets » (2008 SCN section 4.44).
14. Au Canada – pays généralement considéré comme appliquant un système d'imputation – le crédit d'impôt (non récupérable) offert à l'actionnaire concerne l'impôt national sur les sociétés censé avoir été acquitté, qu'un impôt sur les sociétés soit ou ne soit pas dû. Comme, dans ces systèmes, il n'y a aucun lien complet entre le montant de l'impôt sur le revenu, ces crédits pour les dividendes sont traités, comme les autres crédits d'impôt, selon les principes exposés au § 21.
15. Il peut en être ainsi lorsqu'un régime en faveur des administrations existait avant l'instauration d'un régime général de sécurité sociale.
16. Dans le SCN 2008, ils sont considérés comme des transferts en capital et non pas comme des impôts (voir section G).
17. Système selon lequel l'Union Européenne ajuste les effets des différences entre les taux de change utilisés pour fixer les prix des produits agricoles dans le cadre de la politique agricole commune, et le taux de change réel. Les paiements effectués selon ce système portent sur les importations ou les exportations; lorsqu'ils sont identifiables, ces montants figurent dans la rubrique appropriée (5123 ou 5124). Dans ce guide, sont inclus les montants bruts, c'est-à-dire sans déduction d'aucune prime payée par le SMC.
18. Les transferts de bénéfices de loteries d'État sont considérés comme des recettes non fiscales (voir aussi § 64).
19. Voir à ce sujet le § 26(c).
20. Au sommet d'Édimbourg (1992) les membres de l'Union européenne ont décidé de réduire le pourcentage de 1.4 à 1, et d'effectuer cette réduction entre les années 1995 et 1999. Pendant la période 1970-83 ce pourcentage était également de 1.

ORGANISATION FOR ECONOMIC CO-OPERATION AND DEVELOPMENT

The OECD is a unique forum where governments work together to address the economic, social and environmental challenges of globalisation. The OECD is also at the forefront of efforts to understand and to help governments respond to new developments and concerns, such as corporate governance, the information economy and the challenges of an ageing population. The Organisation provides a setting where governments can compare policy experiences, seek answers to common problems, identify good practice and work to co-ordinate domestic and international policies.

The OECD member countries are: Australia, Austria, Belgium, Canada, Chile, the Czech Republic, Denmark, Estonia, Finland, France, Germany, Greece, Hungary, Iceland, Ireland, Israel, Italy, Japan, Korea, Luxembourg, Mexico, the Netherlands, New Zealand, Norway, Poland, Portugal, the Slovak Republic, Slovenia, Spain, Sweden, Switzerland, Turkey, the United Kingdom and the United States. The European Union takes part in the work of the OECD.

OECD Publishing disseminates widely the results of the Organisation's statistics gathering and research on economic, social and environmental issues, as well as the conventions, guidelines and standards agreed by its members.

ORGANISATION DE COOPÉRATION ET DE DÉVELOPPEMENT ÉCONOMIQUES

L'OCDE est un forum unique en son genre où les gouvernements œuvrent ensemble pour relever les défis économiques, sociaux et environnementaux que pose la mondialisation. L'OCDE est aussi à l'avant-garde des efforts entrepris pour comprendre les évolutions du monde actuel et les préoccupations qu'elles font naître. Elle aide les gouvernements à faire face à des situations nouvelles en examinant des thèmes tels que le gouvernement d'entreprise, l'économie de l'information et les défis posés par le vieillissement de la population. L'Organisation offre aux gouvernements un cadre leur permettant de comparer leurs expériences en matière de politiques, de chercher des réponses à des problèmes communs, d'identifier les bonnes pratiques et de travailler à la coordination des politiques nationales et internationales.

Les pays membres de l'OCDE sont : l'Allemagne, l'Australie, l'Autriche, la Belgique, le Canada, le Chili, la Corée, le Danemark, l'Espagne, l'Estonie, les États-Unis, la Finlande, la France, la Grèce, la Hongrie, l'Irlande, l'Islande, Israël, l'Italie, le Japon, le Luxembourg, le Mexique, la Norvège, la Nouvelle-Zélande, les Pays-Bas, la Pologne, le Portugal, la République slovaque, la République tchèque, le Royaume-Uni, la Slovénie, la Suède, la Suisse et la Turquie. L'Union européenne participe aux travaux de l'OCDE.

Les Éditions OCDE assurent une large diffusion aux travaux de l'Organisation. Ces derniers comprennent les résultats de l'activité de collecte de statistiques, les travaux de recherche menés sur des questions économiques, sociales et environnementales, ainsi que les conventions, les principes directeurs et les modèles développés par les pays membres.

OECD PUBLISHING, 2, rue André-Pascal, 75775 PARIS CEDEX 16
(23 2015 52 3 P) ISBN 978-92-64-24518-1 – 2015

www.ingramcontent.com/pod-product-compliance
Lightning Source LLC
Chambersburg PA
CBHW061157240926
51846CB00006B/1037